USING AUTOCAD
Release 12

"Draw from Experience" to build your AutoCAD® library

COMPREHENSIVE AUTOCAD

- Stellman/HARNESSING AUTOCAD
  (Release 12 with Simulator® Tutorial Disk Package)   ISBN 0-8273-5917-9
  (Release 12 with Project Exercise Disk)   ISBN 0-8273-5930-6
  (Release 11)   ISBN 0-8273-4685-9

- Fuller/Using AUTOCAD
  (Release 12)   ISBN 0-8273-5838-5
  (Release 11)   ISBN 0-8273-5344-8

- Kalameja/THE AUTOCAD TUTOR FOR ENGINEERING GRAPHICS
  (Release 12)   ISBN 0-8273-5914-4
  (Release 11)   ISBN 0-8273-5081-3

- Rubenstein/AUTOCAD THE DRAWING TOOL
  (Release 11)   ISBN 0-8273-4885-1

- McGrew EXPLORING THE POWER OF AUTOCAD
  (Release 10)   ISBN 0-8273-3694-2

AUTOLISP & CUSTOMIZING

- Kramer/AUTOLISP PROGRAMMING FOR PRODUCTIVITY   ISBN 0-8273-5832-6

- Tickoo/CUSTOMIING AUTOCAD
  (Release 12)   ISBN 0-8273-58954
  (Release 11)   ISBN 0-8273-50414

ADVANCED AUTOCAD

- Grabowski/AUTOCAD FOR WINDOWS   ISBN 0-8273-5581-5

- Grabowski/THE SUCCESSFUL CAD MANAGER'S HANDBOOK   ISBN 0-8273-5233-6

AUTOCAD APPLICATIONS

- Miller/AUTOCAD FOR THE APPAREL INDUSTRY   ISBN 0-8273-5224-7

GENERIC CADD

- White USING GENERIC CADD 6.0   ISBN 0-8273-5571-8

CAD REFERENCE

- Grabowski/THE ILLUSTRATED AUTOCAD QUICK REFERENCE
  (Release 12)   ISBN 0-8273-5839-3
  (Release 11)   ISBN 0-8273-4820-7

To purchase, contact your local bookseller or write directly to: Delmar Publishers Inc, 3 Columbia Circle Drive, P. O. Box 15015, Albany, NY 12212

USING AUTOCAD
Release 12
with AME, AutoLISP, and Customizing

JAMES E. FULLER

Delmar Publishers Inc.

NOTICE TO THE READER

Cover design by Nancy Gworek
All chapter opening art Courtesy of Autodesk

Delmar Staff
Executive Editor: Michael McDermott
Project Editor: Mary Beth Ray
Senior Production Supervisor: Karen Leet
Production Coordinator: Sandra Woods
Art Supervisor: Judi Orozco
Art Coordinator: Cheri Plasse

For information, address
Delmar Publishers Inc.
3 Columbia Circle, Box 15-015
Albany, New York 12212

Printed in the United States of America
Published simultaneously in Canada
by Nelson Canada,
A division of The Thomson Corporation

3   4   5   6   7   8   9   10   xxx   99   98   97   96   95   94   93

Library of Congress Cataloging-in-Publication Data
Fuller, James Edward.
    Using AutoCAD: release 12 with AME, AutoSHAPE, AutoLISP, and
customizing/James E. Fuller.—6th ed.
        p. cm.
    Includes index.
    ISBN 0-8273-5838-5
    1. Computer graphics.   2. AutoCAD (Computer file)   I. Title.
T385.F852 1993
620'.0042'02855369—dc20   92-43585
                                                     CIP

CONTENTS

SECTION III

Intermediate AutoCAD

SECTION IV

Advanced AutoCAD

SECTION V

AutoCAD 3-D

SECTION VI

Professional AutoCAD

SECTION VII

Appendices

PREFACE

AutoCAD is the industry standard drafting and design software with more than 600,000 users around the world. It offers the engineer, architect, or draftsperson a fast, accurate, and extremely versatile drawing tool. AutoCAD has enabled even schools and small businesses the ability to use advanced AutoCAD techniques in drawing and design.

Using AutoCAD has been successful through six editions because it has presented the end user with an accessible, easy-to-master, step-by-step tutorial through all the commands of AutoCAD. This textbook introduced the method of using menus and sub-menus in side blocks (margins) to illustrate the steps the user must take to execute a command. The book was designed to lead the AutoCAd novice from the basics of AutoCAD to more advanced features to customizing, 3-D, and shading.

Section I Computer Aided Design

This section provides a brief overview of CAD, hardware components, and DOS. It may be passed over for those users who wish to get right into the AutoCAD program. A new chapter, The AutoCAD Quick Start, gets the user up and running in AutoCAD drawing immediately.

Section II Introduction to AutoCAD

This section was designed to provide the basic introductory information on AutoCAD. It begins with a short tutorial, and then leads the user through basic drawing commands. It teaches the student how to edit, add text, and set up a drawing. It ends with several modules that explain dimensioning and plotting your work. New chapters are added on multiview drawings, constructing sections, and patterns.

This section would, ideally, cover most topics in an introductory AutoCAD course. It can also be combined with Section III to take the first-time user to intermediate functions.

Section III Intermediate AutoCAD

Intermediate Autocad drawing techniques are discussed in this section. Isometrics, editing, and layering are explained to the end user. This section is modular and can either be combined for a first-term course on AutoCAD or serve as an excellent starting point for the second-term course. The self-paced learner will find it an easy-to-use section.

Section IV Advanced AutoCAD

Advanced AutoCAD discusses advanced operations–arcs, polylines, external reference drawings, attributes, and customizing. The course instructor will find this a complete section appropriate for the second term or more advanced students in the first course.

Section V AutoCAD 3-D

AutoCAD 3-D–Completely rewritten and dramatically improved, this section leads the end user through the commands on drawing in 3-D.

Section VI Professional AutoCAD

Professional AutoCAD–AutoSOLID and AutoLISP are contained in this section.

Section VII

Appendices–This section offers the most complete appendices available in a textbook.

Learning Features

Side Menus

Side menus throughout the text offer an easy way for users to follow their progress through the menu tree for each branch of the main menu.

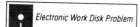
Electronic Work Disk Problem

TIPS and Professional Tips

These boxes highlight helpful programming and end user hints on working with the AutoCAD commands. They serve as a help function for the first-time user.

AutoCAD In the Real World

Case studies from the industry offer a glimpse into the profes-sional work environment and highlight interesting and innova-tive uses of AutoCAD. These actual stories help reinforce learn-ing by demonstrating the varied ways this exciting design tool can be utilized.

Disk Exercises

Through the text, there are references to exercises on the work disk that help expedite the learning process. The book is written in a modular format, so these sections can be easily skipped over if the user decides not to use the disk. The disk is available as a separate, for-sale item. Instructors can obtain a review copy by contacting their Delmar field representative.

Tutorials

This revision has many more tutorials than any other edition, ranging from easy-to-accomplish, brief tutorials to chapter-long tutorials.

Review Questions and Exercises

Chapter-ending reviews provide self-tests. Additional drawing exercises reinforce student learning.

What's New?

Release 12 of AutoCAD has added many features to streamline tasks for the professional draftsperson. These latest release fea-tures combine to form a set of new tools never available in a single desktop CAD software product. We have revised our book for Release 12 by addressing those features of Release 12 that enhance the end-user's ability to produce professional CAD drawings. We've enhanced our text with coverage of all new commands and capabilities. All command coverage was rewrit-ten to reflect usage under the new interface. In addition, the number of professional tips, exercises, and chapter-end exercis-es have been greatly increased.

ACKNOWLEDGMENTS

A book cannot be successfully completed without assistance from other people. I am very grateful to many people for their support during the production of this publication. Special thanks to Mike McDermott, Mary Beth Ray, Gwen Ceruti-Vincent, and Ralph Grabowski of Delmar Publishers. The author and publisher especially wish to thank Lionel Johnston of Autodesk for his professional and helpful cooperation in development and production. We are also indebted to Wayne Hodgins at Autodesk. To the staff of J.E. Fuller & Associates and Microvision, in which I have professional interest, and to an understanding family.

James E. Fuller

SECTION I

COMPUTER AIDED DESIGN

- AutoCAD Quick Start
- Computer Aided Design
- Components of a CAD System
- Your Computer
- The Disk Operating System

CHAPTER 1

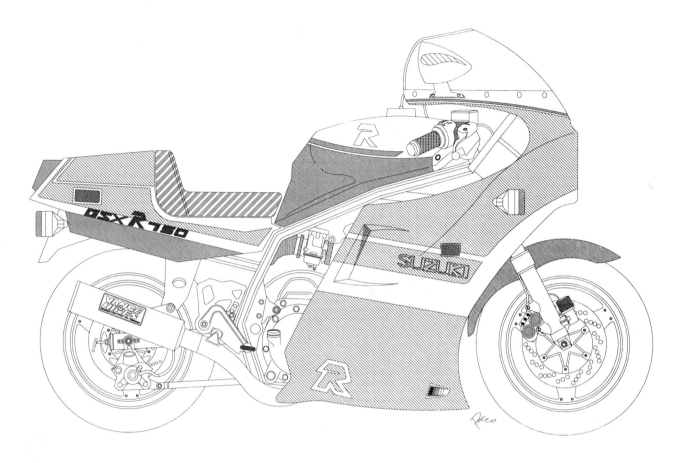

AutoCAD Quick Start

OBJECTIVES:

The new user needs an opportunity to experience the "feel" of the AutoCAD program. The concept and operation of graphic design software can be unique to a first time user. Chapter 1 objectives are:

● To obtain an initial "hands on" feel for the AutoCAD program.

● To become accustomed to the AutoCAD menuing system.

● To observe the methodology of placing entities into a drawing.

● To examine the basic 3-D capabilities of AutoCAD.

INTRODUCTION TO USING AUTOCAD

Welcome to USING AUTOCAD! This chapter is specifically designed to acquaint you with the AutoCAD drawing program from the start. Subsequent chapters will cover the subject more thoroughly. Let's get started!

STARTING AUTOCAD

In order to start AutoCAD, you must type a start command from the keyboard. This is a word such as ACAD, ACAD386, or ACADR12. The word to start the program depends on the response given for the start word when the program was installed. If you know the correct response, enter it at the keyboard and press the Enter key.

Your computer will now load the AutoCAD program. After an opening screen is displayed, you will see a drawing screen. This screen is referred to as the drawing editor and should be similar to the following illustration.

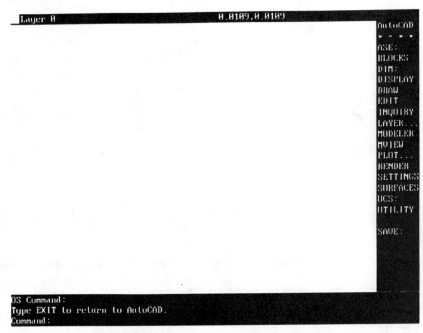

FIGURE 1-1 AutoCAD Drawing Screen

DRAWING IN AUTOCAD

The intersection of the crosshair is used to specify points on your drawing.

AutoCAD is used with a pointing device. This device is usually a digitizing tablet or mouse. Move the pointing device and notice how a *"crosshair"* moves around the screen. The intersection of the crosshair is used to specify points on your drawing. From this point forward, we will refer to the pointing device as the "mouse".

AutoCAD draws or edits objects by using "commands".

AutoCAD draws or edits objects by using "commands". Commands are words such as line, circle, arc, and erase that describe the object to be drawn or operation that you wish to perform.

At the bottom of the drawing editor is an area known as the "command prompt area" (refer to Figure 1-1). This area lists the commands you have entered. You should see the word "Command:" on that line now. You can specify commands from menus or by typing them from the keyboard.

STARTING A NEW DRAWING

Let's continue by typing a command to start a new drawing. Type NEW from the keyboard. Notice how the command is listed on the command line. It doesn't matter whether the commands are typed in upper case or lower case letters. If you make a mistake, just use the backspace key to back up and retype. After you have typed NEW, press the enter key. Pressing the Enter key "sends" the command to AutoCAD. You should now see a *"dialogue box"* similar to the one in the following illustration.

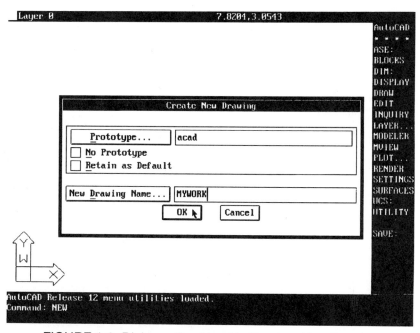

FIGURE 1-2 Dialogue Box Used to Create a New Drawing

Type "MYWORK" from the keyboard. The text will appear at the blinking bar next to the "New Drawing Name..." box. Now move the mouse and notice how the crosshairs have turned into an arrow pointer. Move the pointer to the OK box and press the mouse button. AutoCAD will initialize a new drawing screen.

If you wish to type any command from the keyboard, you must first have a "clear" command line.

If you wish to type any command from the keyboard, you must first have a "clear" command line. The line must have the "Command:" prompt, without anything after it. If there is other text, just clear it by entering CTRL-C from the keyboard before typing in the new command. To do this, hold down the control key on the keyboard (usually marked "Ctrl") and type the C key once.

USING PULL DOWN MENUS

Let's enter a command. Move the crosshairs above the top of the screen. A menu bar that extends the width of the drawing area appears. Refer to Figure 1-3.

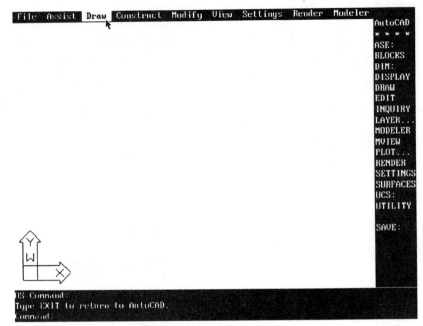

FIGURE 1-3 Accessing Pull-Down Menus

As you move the arrow across each word in the menu bar, it is "high-lighted". Highlight the word Draw and press the left hand mouse button. A *pull down menu* extends downward into the drawing area.

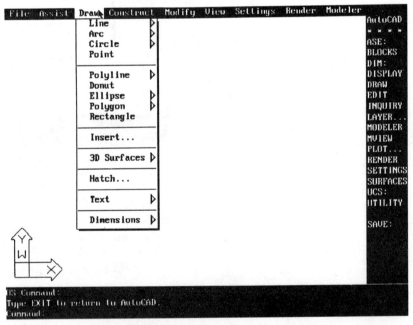

FIGURE 1-4 The Draw Pull-Down Menu

Pull down menus contain commands that can be selected with the pointing device.

Pull down menus contain commands that can be selected with the pointing device. Let's pick the Line command from the Draw menu. Move the pointer down and highlight the word Line, then press the mouse button. A second menu will appear. The arrow head next to the word Line in the initial menu indicates that an additional menu of options will be displayed. Select "Segments" from this menu. Notice that the word "line" appears on the command line at the bottom of the screen. After the line command is displayed, the words "line From point" appear. This is called a prompt. AutoCAD always tells you what it expects on the command line. AutoCAD is now asking for the point the line starts <u>from</u> (the From point). Move the crosshairs into the screen area and enter a point at approximately the location shown in Figure 1-5.

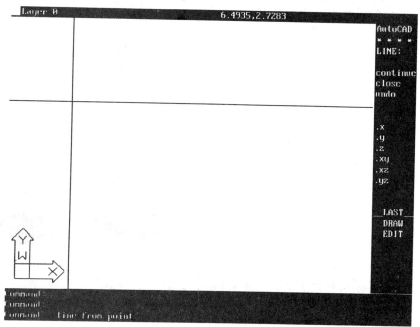

FIGURE 1-5 Drawing a Line

You are now prompted for a "To point". Notice how the line "sticks" to the intersection of the crosshairs. As you move the crosshairs around the screen, the line will stretch and follow. This is called "rubberbanding". Move the crosshairs and enter a point at approximately the point shown in the following illustration.

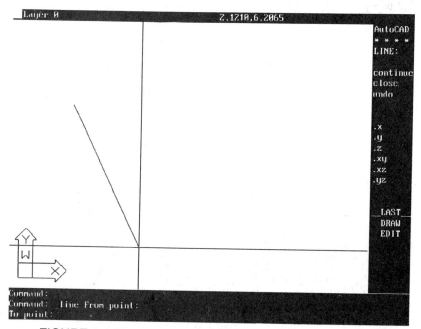

FIGURE 1-6 Designating the Endpoint of the Line Segment

Continue and enter lines as shown in the following illustrative sequence.

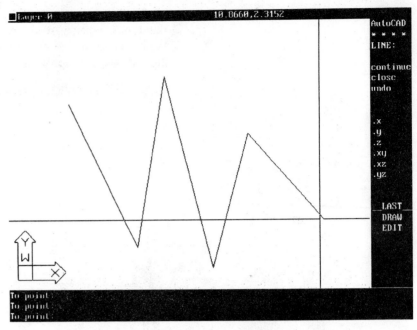

FIGURE 1-7 Drawing Multiple Line Segments

After you have entered the last point, click the right mouse button to end the line command. Alternately you may enter Ctrl-C from the keyboard to terminate any command. To do this, hold down the control key, then press the letter C key once. Some commands terminate automatically, while others must be terminated when you are finished. The Line command remains active so you can draw as many line segments as you desire without having to reselect the command repeatedly.

BLIP MARKS

If you look closely at the endpoints of the lines, you will see some small crosses. These are called *blip marks*. These temporary blips are <u>not</u> part of your drawing. They are displayed for reference purposes at points you have entered. Let's remove the blips from our drawing. Highlight the menu bar and pull down the View menu. Select the Redraw command. AutoCAD will "redraw" the screen and remove any blip marks.

USING THE SCREEN MENU

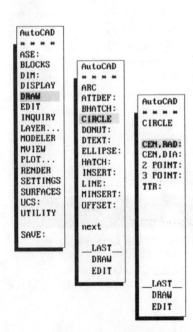

Let's continue and select a command from the *screen menu*. This menu is located at the right of the drawing area. You may have already noticed that it automatically changed when you selected the Line and Redraw commands. Move the crosshairs into the screen menu area. Notice how the words in the menu highlight when they are passed over. Move toward the bottom of the menu and highlight the word "DRAW". The screen menu will change and list commands used to draw objects. Highlight "CIRCLE:" and press the left mouse button. Highlight and select "CEN,RAD:". Notice how the Circle command is displayed on the command line. AutoCAD also prompts you for the next move as shown in the following "command sequence".

> Command: <u>CIRCLE</u>
> 3P/2P/TTR/<Center point>:

Don't worry about what all this means right now. The <Center point> entry is the one we will use. Since it is in the brackets, it is what

AutoCAD expects us to do. This is called the *default response*. Let's enter the center point for the circle. Move the crosshairs to a point approximately at the location shown in the first screen of the following illustrative sequence and press the left mouse key. Next, move the crosshairs until the circle rubberbands to about the size shown and press the mouse key again.

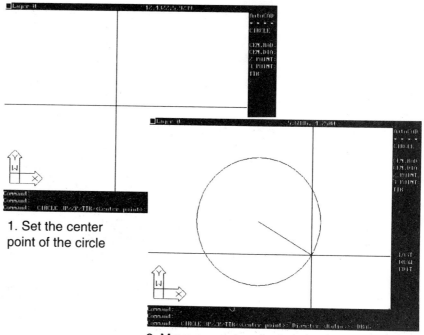

1. Set the center point of the circle

2. Move cursor to adjust circle size

FIGURE 1-8 Drawing a Circle

Now move the crosshairs back to the screen menu and pick the "AutoCAD" entry at the top of the menu. You should now see the original menu (referred to as the root menu). This is the starting point for the screen menu. You can return to this menu from any other menu by selecting the "AutoCAD" entry at the top.

Let's erase an object. Move to the screen menu at the side of the drawing area. Select the EDIT menu. A new menu replaces the root menu. This menu contains edit commands. Select ERASE. Move back into the drawing screen. Notice how the crosshairs change to a small square. This is called a *"pickbox"*. Move the pickbox on the top of one of the lines and select. The line will be *"highlighted"*. On some displays, this means that it will change color; on others it will become a broken line.

Now press the Enter key to tell AutoCAD that you are finished picking items to be erased. The line will be erased. Now type OOPS from the keyboard and Enter. Notice how the line is placed back into the drawing. You can use the Oops command to undo an erase.

Now it is time for you to get used to using AutoCAD. Read the following summations, then draw as much as you want. When you are finished, read the following section for instructions on how to save or discard your work. After that, we have furnished a full step-by-step tutorial so you can draw your first real drawing in 3-D!

SUMMATION

- AutoCAD drawings are constructed by using commands.

- Commands can be entered from the keyboard, pull down menus, screen menus, and from a digitizer template (you will learn about this later).

- The command line shows your command activities and displays prompts that tell you what input AutoCAD expects from you.

- The command line must be "clear" before typing a new command from the keyboard. You can use either upper or lower case when entering a command from the keyboard.

- The Line command is used to draw lines. The Circle command is used to draw circles. Erase objects with the Erase command and restore them with the Oops command. Use the Redraw command to clear the temporary blip marks from your drawing.

EXITING A DRAWING

How you exit your drawing will depend on the command you use. The following four sections outline the possibilities. Choose the one you want and follow the instructions. If you intend to continue with the tutorial, select one the last two choices.

DISCARD THE DRAWING AND QUIT AUTOCAD

If you don't want to keep your drawing and you wish to stop work now, enter the QUIT command (you can do this from the keyboard). AutoCAD will display a dialogue box (see Figure 1-9) that asks you to confirm your choice. Move the pointer to and select the "Discard Changes" box. AutoCAD will not record your work to disk and will return you to the DOS prompt.

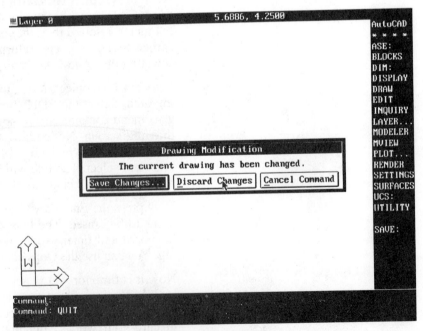

FIGURE 1-9 Drawing Modification Dialogue Box

SAVE THE DRAWING AND QUIT AUTOCAD

If you want to save your work to disk and quit AutoCAD, enter the END command. AutoCAD will save your work under the name MYWORK and return you to the DOS prompt.

DISCARD THE DRAWING AND REMAIN IN AUTOCAD

If you do not want your drawing saved, but would like a new AutoCAD screen, use the New command.

We used the New command to start this drawing. You will need to specify a name for the new drawing. If you will be constructing the following tutorial drawing, enter TUTOR as the drawing name.

SAVE YOUR WORK AND REMAIN IN AUTOCAD

If you want to keep your work and remain in AutoCAD, enter the SAVE command. A dialogue box will be displayed on the screen. Verify that the drawing name MYWORK is listed in the File box, then select OK. Next, use the New command to start the new drawing name. If you will be constructing the following tutorial, enter TUTOR as the drawing name.

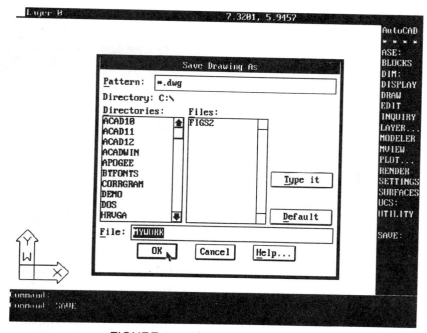

FIGURE 1-10 Saving Your Drawing

TUTORIAL

Type NEW from the keyboard. AutoCAD will display the Create New Drawing dialogue box. Respond to the "New Drawing Name..." box with the drawing name "TUTOR". The following illustration shows the drawing you will construct.

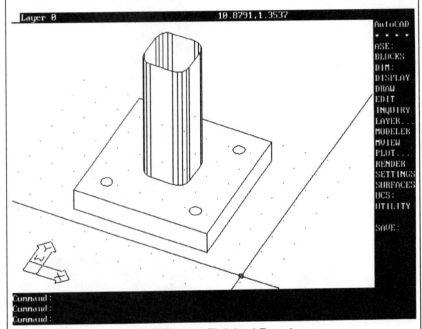

FIGURE 1-11 Finished Drawing

GETTING STARTED

The following is a listing of items to be typed and "entered" to complete the drawing. The items you type will appear at the bottom of the screen on the "command line". The word Command: appears at this location now. Your response is shown underlined in this tutorial. You may type the items in either upper or lower case. Be sure to press the Return (sometimes referred to as Enter) key after each response. Items enclosed in parentheses are to be done and not typed. For example, if (ENTER) is shown, press the Enter key on the keyboard.

If you mess up, just press "U".

If you mess up, just press "U" and then press the Return key. This will "undo" the previous step. You may use it several times to undo each step in reverse order. In order to enter a new "command", the prompt on the command line must say "Command:". If it does not, hold down the control key (Ctrl), then press the letter "C" key. This cancels the current command, and places AutoCAD ready for the next command.

Let's first set up the size of the drawing area.

```
Command: LIMITS
Reset Model space limits:
ON/OFF <Lower left corner> <0.0000,0.0000>: (ENTER)
Upper right corner <12.0000,9.0000>: 12,10
```

Let's continue by zooming out to display the entire screen. "Zooms" are the way your drawing is enlarged or reduced. Since we changed the size of the work area with the Limits command, we need to zoom out to show the entire work space.

Command: ZOOM
All/Center/Dynamic/Extents/Left/Previous/Window/ <Scale
(X/XP)>: A
Regenerating drawing.

This will not have a visible effect on the drawing screen.

We will now display a grid with a spacing of 1.

Command: GRID
Grid spacing (X) or ON/OFF/Snap/Aspect <0.0000>: 1

Let's set the snap so that our crosshair cursor moves at increments
of 1. The crosshair cursor is moved by the input device (mouse, digitizer pad, or cursor keys) and is the way you show AutoCAD where
you want to place points when drawing.

The crosshair cursor is moved by the input device.

Command: SNAP
Snap spacing (X) or ON/OFF/Aspect/Style/<1.0000>: 1

DRAWING THE BASEPLATE

Now we will set the thickness for the baseplate part of the object.

Command: ELEV
New current elevation <0.0000>: (ENTER)
New current thickness <0.0000>: 1

Let's draw the baseplate. We are looking down in plan and in two
dimensional view. We will change into a 3-D view later.

Command: PLINE
From point: 3,2
Current line-width is 0.0000
Arc/Close/Halfwidth/Length/Undo/Width/<Endpoint of line>: @6,0
Arc/Close/Halfwidth/Length/Undo/Width/<Endpoint of line>: @0,6
Arc/Close/Halfwidth/Length/Undo/Width/<Endpoint of line>: @-6,0
Arc/Close/Halfwidth/Length/Undo/Width/<Endpoint of line>:
CLOSE

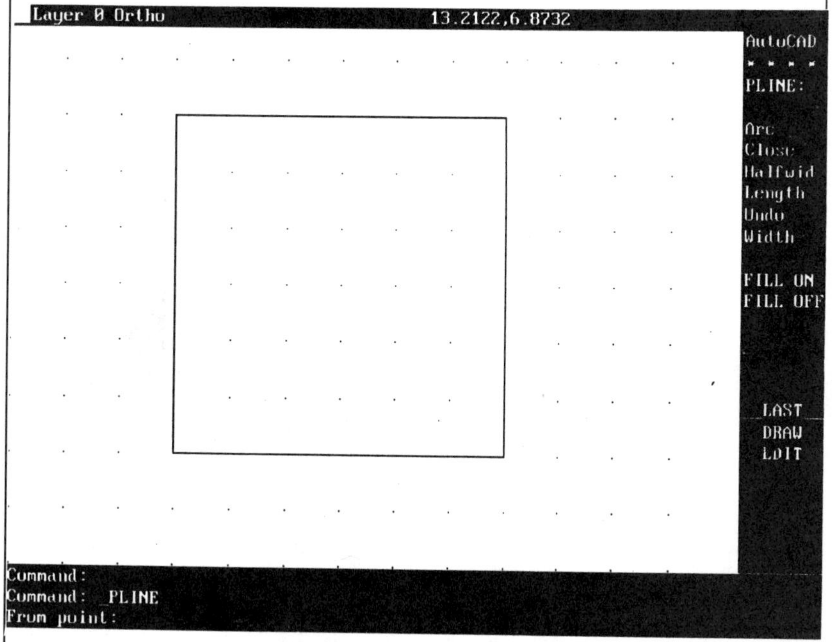

FIGURE 1-12 Baseplate

Your drawing should look similar to Figure 1-12.

```
Command: ELEV
New current elevation <0.0000>: 1
New current thickness <1.0000>: 0
```

CONSTRUCTING THE 3-D FACE

We will now place a "3DFACE" on the top of the baseplate. This will cause it to view as a "solid" in 3-D views.

In the following sequence, place the cursor over each of the four corners and press the "pick" button on the input device in response to points one through four. When you are prompted again for point three, press the Enter key.

```
Command: 3DFACE
First point: (PICK)
Second point: (PICK)
Third point: (PICK)
Fourth point: (PICK)
Third point: (ENTER)
```

DRAWING THE SHAFT

Let's now draw the shaft.

Change the elevation and thickness again.

```
Command: ELEV
New current elevation <1.0000>: 1
New current thickness <0.0000>: 6
```

Now draw the shaft.

```
Command: LINE
From point: 5,4
To point: @6,0
To point: @0,6
To point: @-6,0
To point: CLOSE
```

Your drawing should look similar to Figure 1-13.

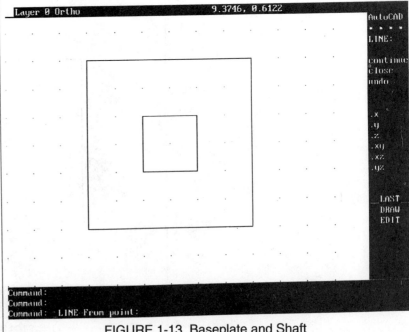

FIGURE 1-13 Baseplate and Shaft

FILLETING THE CORNERS

Let's use the Fillet command to round the corners.

    Command: FILLET
    Polyline/Radius/ <Select two objects>: R
    Enter fillet radius <0.0000>: .5

Continue with the FILLET command again (refer to Figure 1-14).

    Command: FILLET
    Polyline/Radius/ <Select first object>: (SELECT ONE OF THE
    LINES JUST DRAWN)
    Select second object: (SELECT AN ADJACENT LINE)

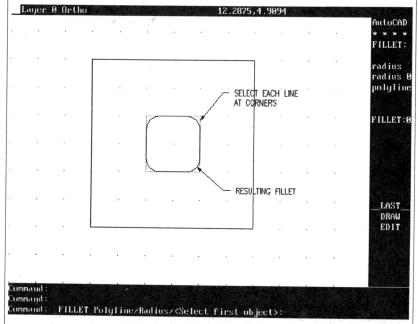

FIGURE 1-14 Filleting the Shaft

Continue and select each of the lines that fall on either side of the corners to place a rounded fillet at each intersection.

Reset the elevation and thickness.

    Command: ELEV
    New current elevation <1.0000>: 0
    New current thickness <3.0000>: 1

DRAWING THE CIRCLES

Let's now draw a circle.

    Command: CIRCLE
    3P/2P/TTR/ <Center point>: 4,3
    Diameter/ <Radius>: .25

We will now copy the circle to the other parts of the baseplate. Let's use a copy option called Multiple. This will allow us to make multiple copies easier.

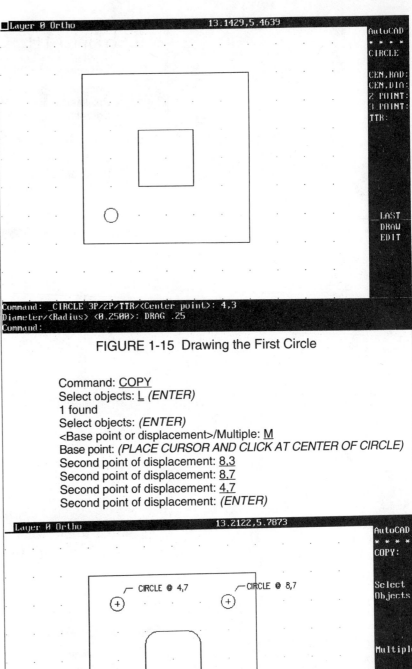

FIGURE 1-15 Drawing the First Circle

Command: <u>COPY</u>
Select objects: <u>L</u> *(ENTER)*
1 found
Select objects: *(ENTER)*
<Base point or displacement>/Multiple: <u>M</u>
Base point: *(PLACE CURSOR AND CLICK AT CENTER OF CIRCLE)*
Second point of displacement: <u>8,3</u>
Second point of displacement: <u>8,7</u>
Second point of displacement: <u>4,7</u>
Second point of displacement: *(ENTER)*

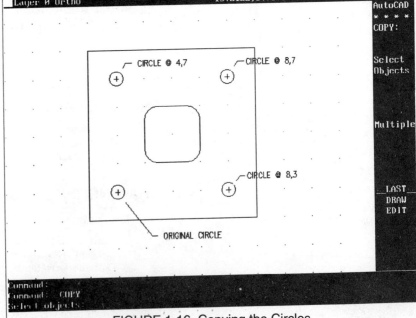

FIGURE 1-16 Copying the Circles

VIEWING THE DRAWING IN 3-D

Congratulations, you have just finished the drawing! Let's have some fun and view the drawing in 3-D.

Command: VPOINT
Rotate/<View point> <0.0000,0.0000,1.0000>: .5,- 1,1
Regenerating drawing.

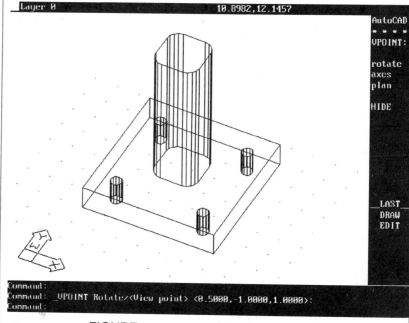

FIGURE 1-17 Viewing the Object in 3-D

This is a wireframe view. Let's remove the hidden lines. Removing
the hidden lines takes a small amount of time.

Command: HIDE
Regenerating drawing.

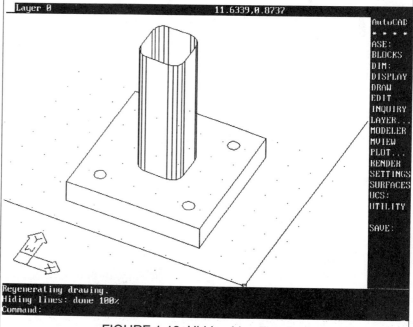

FIGURE 1-18 Hidden Line Drawing

Save or discard your drawing in the manner you learned earlier in
this chapter.

EXERCISES

The following drawings are exercises that you can use to practice with the AutoCAD program.

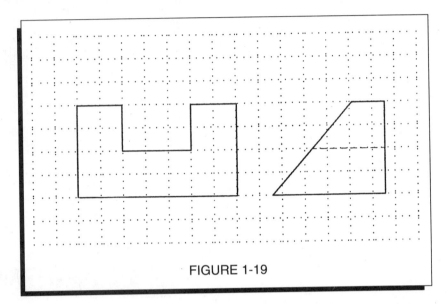

FIGURE 1-19

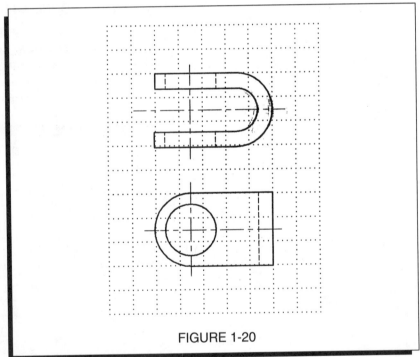

FIGURE 1-20

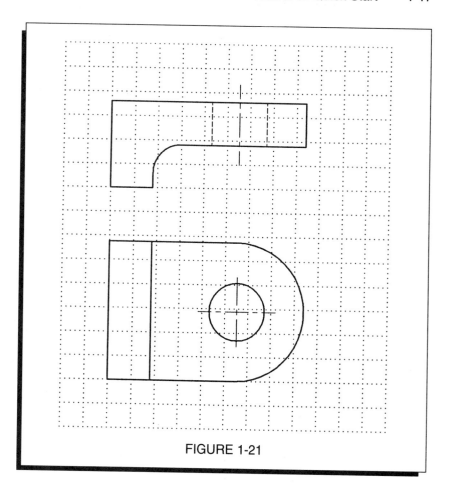

FIGURE 1-21

CHAPTER 2

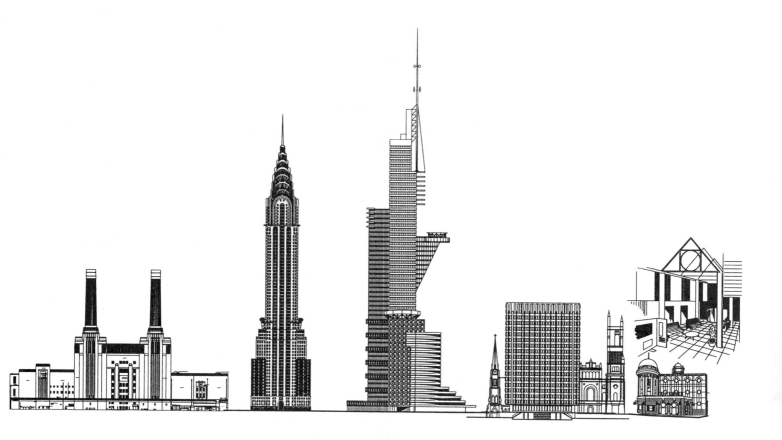

Computer Aided Design

OBJECTIVES:

Computer aided design can be used to do many jobs more effectively. This chapter reviews the benefits and applications of CAD. Chapter 2 objectives are:

● To acquaint the new user with the benefits of using computer aided design.

● To obtain a review of the standard applications of computer aided design and the benefits of using CAD for these disciplines.

TRADITIONAL DRAFTING TECHNIQUES

The necessity to perform drawings as a means of communication has been present throughout history. While other types of work have benefited from technology, traditional drafting techniques have remained relatively unchanged.

The introduction of Computer Aided Drafting (CAD) has had an impact on the industry that is greater than all the previous changes combined. The acceptance of the graphics world of CAD and its capabilities has been phenomenal. CAD presents advantages that are undeniably superior to traditional techniques.

BENEFITS OF CAD

Computer Aided Drafting is a more efficient and versatile drafting method than traditional techniques. Some of the advantages are:

ACCURACY

Computer generated drawings can be drawn and plotted to an accuracy of up to fourteen decimal places of the units used. The numerical entry of critical dimensions and tolerances is more reliable than the traditional methods of manual scaling.

SPEED

The ability of the CAD operator to copy, array items, and to edit his work on the screen speeds up the drawing process. If the operator customizes his system to a specific task, the work speed can be greatly increased.

NEATNESS AND LEGIBILITY

The ability of the plotter to produce exact and legible drawings is an obvious advantage over the traditional methods of "hand-drawn" work. The uniformity of CAD drawings, which produce lines of constant thickness, print quality lettering, and no smudges or other editing marks, is preferred.

CONSISTENCY

Since the system is constant in its methodology, the problem of individual style is eliminated. A company can have a number of draftspersons working on the same project and produce a consistent set of graphics.

EFFICIENCY

The CAD operator must approach a drafting task in a different manner than he would when using traditional techniques. Since the CAD program is capable of performing much of the work for the operator, the job should be preplanned to utilize all the benefits of the system.

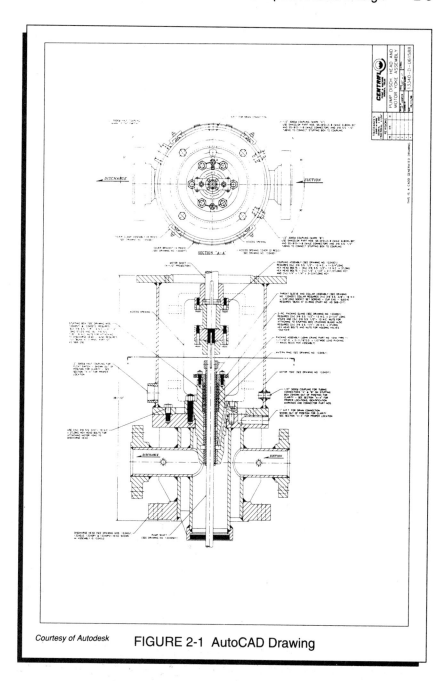

FIGURE 2-1 AutoCAD Drawing

APPLICATIONS OF CAD

Applications of CAD are now present in many industries. The flexibility of the many programs now available has had a major impact in the manner in which various tasks are performed. Some applications of CAD which are now being used are:

ARCHITECTURAL

Architects have found CAD to be one of the most useful tools that has ever been available to them. Designs can be formulated for presentation to a client in a shorter period of time than is possible by traditional techniques. The work is neater and more uniform. The designer can use 3-D modeling capabilities to assist him and his client to better visualize the finished design. Changes can be performed and resubmitted in a very short time.

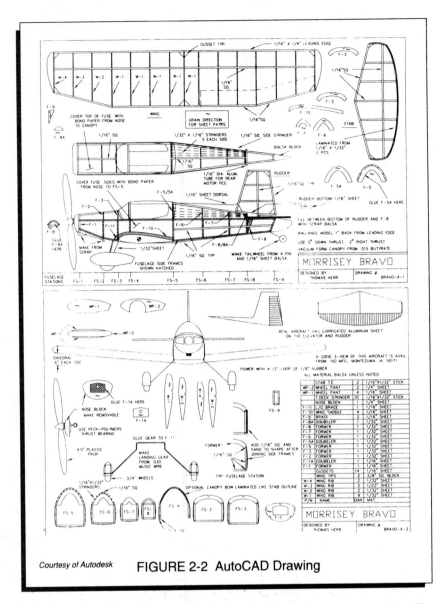

Courtesy of Autodesk   **FIGURE 2-2 AutoCAD Drawing**

The architect can assemble construction drawings using stored details. Data base capabilities can be used to extract information from the drawings and perform cost estimates and bills of materials.

ENGINEERING

Engineers use CAD in many ways. They may also use programs which interact with CAD and perform calculations that would take more time using traditional techniques.

Among the many engineering uses are:

Electronics engineering   Mechanical engineering
Chemical engineering   Automotive engineering
Civil engineering   Aerospace engineering

INTERIOR DESIGN

AutoCAD is a valuable tool for interior designers. The 3-D capabilities can be used to model interiors for their clients. Floor plan layouts can

FIGURE 2-3 AutoCAD Drawing (Architectural)

be drawn and modified very quickly. Many third party programs are available that make 3-D layouts of areas such as kitchens and baths relatively simple.

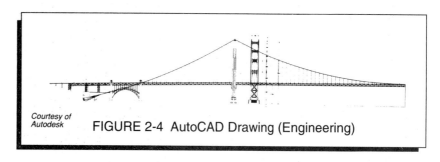

FIGURE 2-4 AutoCAD Drawing (Engineering)

MANUFACTURING

Manufacturing uses for CAD are many. One of the main advantages is integrating the program with a database for record keeping and tracking purposes. The ability to maintain information in a central data base simplifies much of the work required in the manufacturing process.

Technical drawings used in manufacturing can be constructed quickly and legible.

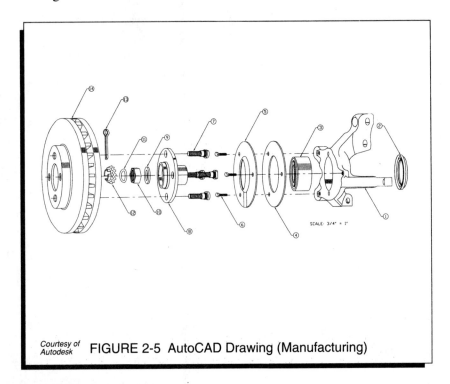

Courtesy of Autodesk   FIGURE 2-5 AutoCAD Drawing (Manufacturing)

YACHT DESIGN

Yacht and ship designers use AutoCAD to create the complex drawings for their unique designs.

BUSINESS

The business use of CAD has been increasing. Visual aids of all types are being used on an increasing basis. Advertising agencies are finding CAD to be an invaluable aid in many types of graphic work.

Other business of CAD are for workflow charts, organizational charts, and all types of graphs.

ENTERTAINMENT

Since the entertainment field is largely based in the electronic media, the use of CAD graphics is a perfect match. Television stations and networks use electronic graphics in place of the traditional artwork that must be photographed and converted. The weather graphics you view daily are a form of CAD graphics. Movie makers are turning to forms of electronic graphics for manipulations and additions to their work.

The introduction of AutoCAD related programs such as Animator and 3-D Studio has brought life-like realism and animation to many entertainment applications.

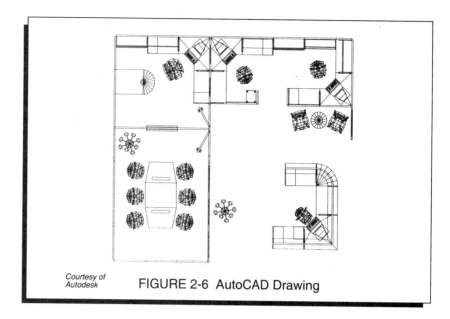

Courtesy of Autodesk   FIGURE 2-6 AutoCAD Drawing

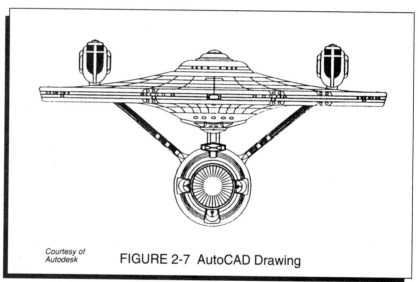

Courtesy of Autodesk   FIGURE 2-7 AutoCAD Drawing

CHAPTER REVIEW

1. If drawings are a means of communication, how has CAD helped in this process?

_____

_____

_____

2. Name some applications of CAD.

_____

_____

_____

_____

3. Why is CAD a more flexible method of drafting than traditional drafting techniques?

_____

_____

_____

4. Why would an office using several CAD stations produce more consistent work than a traditional office?

_____

_____

_____

5. Why is CAD more accurate than traditional methods of scaling?

_____

_____

_____

6. How has the entertainment industry been helped by CAD?

_____

_____

_____

7. How can programs that interact with CAD be useful for engineering purposes?

_____

_____

_____

8. What benefits does CAD provide for the user over traditional drafting techniques?

_____

_____

_____

9. Does the construction or editing capabilities of CAD provide the greater increase in production speed?

_____

_____

10. Has CAD altered the traditional drafting industry significantly?

_____

_____

_____

CHAPTER 3

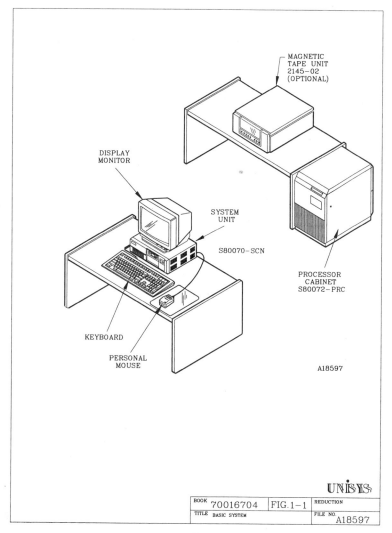

MAGNETIC
TAPE UNIT
2145-02
(OPTIONAL)

DISPLAY
MONITOR

SYSTEM
UNIT

S80070-SCN

PROCESSOR
CABINET
S80072-PRC

KEYBOARD

PERSONAL
MOUSE

A18597

UNISYS

| BOOK 70016704 | FIG.1-1 | REDUCTION |
| TITLE BASIC SYSTEM | | FILE NO. A18597 |

Components of a CAD System

OBJECTIVES:

The many parts of the CAD computer system can be confusing to the uninitiated user. Chapter 3 reviews the hardware components used in CAD drawing. The objectives of Chapter 3 are:

● To learn the categories of computers used in computer aided design.

● To obtain a review of the peripheral equipment unique to CAD systems.

● To review the advantages and disadvantages of the various types of peripheral equipment.

COMPONENTS OF A CAD SYSTEM

CAD systems are comprised of several pieces of equipment that perform various functions. Equipment that is added to the basic computer is called peripheral equipment. The following is a description of each of the items that could be used with a CAD system.

THE COMPUTER

The computer is the central part of the CAD system.

The computer is the central part of the CAD system. The peripheral equipment is connected to the computer. There are several types of computers that can be used with a CAD system. Let's look at the categories of computers.

CATEGORIES OF COMPUTERS

Computer systems are divided into three main categories. These are:

> Microcomputers
> Minicomputers
> Mainframe Computers

MICROCOMPUTERS

The microcomputer is the type you often see on a desktop. These small, versatile machines are often referred to as personal computers, since they are mostly designed for use by one person at a time (although more powerful microcomputers can be "networked", allowing use by more than one operator at a time). Microcomputers usually consist of a case which contains the central processing unit and one or more disk drives, a display device, and a keyboard.

Courtesy of Autodesk   FIGURE 3-1 Microcomputer

MINICOMPUTERS

Minicomputers are larger, faster and more expensive than micro-computers. They allow many users to work on a single computer at one time. This class of computer can run larger and more sophisticated programs than microcomputers.

MAINFRAME COMPUTERS

This is the largest type of computer. Mainframes are capable of processing a large amount of data. Mainframes are used by government and companies which handle large amounts of data.

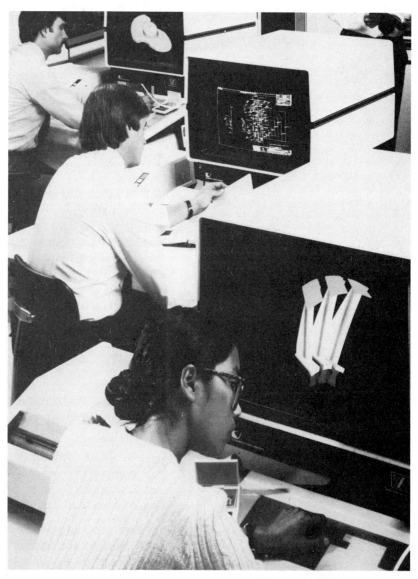

Courtesy of Computervision Corporation   FIGURE 3-2 Mainframe Computer

COMPONENTS OF A COMPUTER

A computer is made up of several parts that are essential to its operation. In addition, components can be added that speed up and/or enhance the operation of the computer. Let's look at some of the components that make up a computer.

SYSTEM BOARD

The system board (sometimes referred to as the "motherboard") is an electronics board that holds many of the computer's chips and boards. The central processing unit, memory chips, ROM chips and others are mounted on this board. In addition, the board contains what is referred to as "bus slots". These are slots in which you can mount add-on boards such as display and disk drive adapters.

CENTRAL PROCESSING UNIT

The central processing unit (or "CPU") is the center of activity of the computer. It is here that the software program you are using is processed. After processing, instructions are sent out to the display, printer, plotter, or other peripheral. With few exceptions, all information passes through the central processing unit.

Physically, the central processor is a computer chip mounted on the system board. There are several types of processing chips. In a microcomputer, the type of CPU used determines what is known as the "class" of computer. For most purposes, the most basic class of microcomputer is the "XT" class, named for the IBM PC/XT computer. The most common CPU used in XT class machines is the "8088" processor by Intel, although other chips are manufactured under different references.

The "AT" class of machine is the next step up in microcomputers. They are named after the IBM PC/AT and known as "advanced technology" computers. These computers use faster processors (measured in Mhz) and use 16-bit bus slots in addition to the XT class 8-bit bus slots. The CPU for AT class machines are the 80286, 80386, and 80486. Each CPU is designed with more capacity than the previous. The 80386 (referred to as a '386) and the 80486 (referred to as a '486) are 32-bit processors, which process software much faster than 8- and 16-bit processors.

MEMORY

Computer memory can be divided into two categories; ROM (read-only memory) and RAM (random access memory). ROM memory is contained on preprogrammed chips on the system and is used to store basic command sets for the computer.

Random access memory is used to temporarily store information in your computer.

Random access memory (RAM) is the memory that is mostly referred to when computer memory is being discussed. Random access memory is used to temporarily store information in your computer. It is temporary storage because all data in RAM is lost when the computer is turned off.

Software programs (such as AutoCAD and others) have a minimum requirement for the amount of RAM necessary to run the program. This amount is given in kilobytes. A common reference might be "640K", meaning 640 kilobytes. You may see a reference to "megabytes". A megabyte is 1,000 kilobytes. In reality, these numbers are rounded, since a megabyte actually contains 1024 kilobytes.

MATH COPROCESSOR

A math coprocessor works in tandem with the CPU. The CPU is very good at processing text-based instructions sets that are the heart of many programs, but it is not as efficient when asked to calculate numeric information. When a math coprocessor is installed, it allows the CPU to "hand off" math calculations to the coprocessor, resulting in faster operation of programs that are essentially math based. CAD programs, and other graphics oriented programs are heavily math based and benefit greatly from math coprocessors. Note that in order to benefit from the coprocessor, the software program must be written to use it.

Coprocessors are named according to the class of computer they are designed for. They are named the Intel 8087, 80287, and 80387. The 80486 CPU contains an integral coprocessor. In addition to Intel, other companies such as Weitek manufacture coprocessors.

PERIPHERAL HARDWARE

Peripheral hardware consists of add-on devices which perform specific functions.

Peripheral hardware consists of add-on devices which perform specific functions. A properly equipped CAD station consists of several peripheral devices. Among these are:

| Plotters | Displays |
| Printers | Input devices |

PLOTTERS

Plotters are used to produce a "hard copy" of your work. The three main types of plotters used most often are pen plotters, printer plotters, and electrostatic plotters.

PEN PLOTTERS

Pen plotters can produce the most pleasing type of plot. The pen plotter uses technical ink pens to draw on vellum, mylar, or other suitable surfaces.

Some pen plotters can use other types of pens such as ballpoint, pencil, and marker-type pens.

The plotter is controlled by signals sent by the computer to the plotter. The pen movement results from the response to the signals by servo motors. These motors control both the pen movement and the up and down motion of the pen. The accuracy (resolution) of the plotter is determined by the interval which the servo motors are capable of moving.

Pen plotters are produced in two major types: the flatbed and the drum plotter.

FLATBED PLOTTERS

A flatbed plotter moves the pen over a stationary sheet of paper. The pen carriage moves in both the X and Y direction. Since a flatbed plotter must have a surface large enough to contain the paper sheet, large sheet capacity flatbed plotters can take up a large amount of space.

DRUM PLOTTERS

A drum plotter moves both the paper and the pen. The paper is placed over a drum, or roller. The paper is then "rolled" back and forth over the roller while the pen is moved along the other direction. The combination of the two motions, along with the up and down pen movements,

Courtesy of Houston Instruments   FIGURE 3-3 Flatbed Plotter

create the drawing. While most drum plotters use standard paper sizes, some are capable of using roll paper.

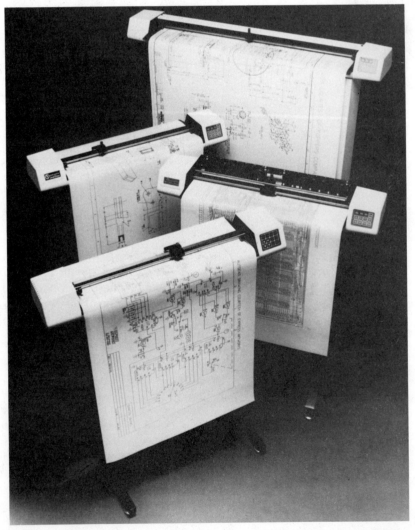

Courtesy of Houston Instruments   FIGURE 3-4 Drum Plotter

PRINTER PLOTTERS

Many CAD programs now allow the use of a dot-matrix printer to produce a plot. Although a dot matrix print doesn't contain the same fine resolution and line quality as a pen plot, it provides an easy, inexpensive manner to produce check plots, or plots in which a high degree of quality is not necessary.

ELECTROSTATIC PLOTTERS

Electrostatic plotters produce plots very quickly. The advantages of electrostatic plotters are a short plotting time and a relatively high resolution plot. The disadvantage is the high initial equipment cost. Electrostatic plotters are very useful for companies that plot large volumes of drawings.

PRINTERS

Printers provide a means of producing a hardcopy of text information. There are four main types of printers: dot matrix, letter quality, laser, and ink jet.

DOT MATRIX PRINTERS

Dot matrix printers produce letters and graphics by impacting a ribbon with tiny striker pins. These pins are contained in a head which thrusts

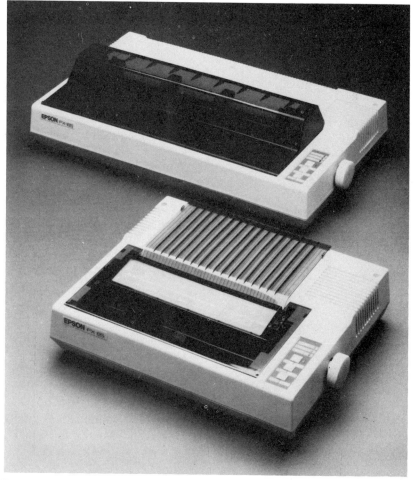

Courtesy of Epson America, Inc.   FIGURE 3-5 Dot Matrix Printer

the pins outward in the designated pattern. Dot matrix printers are fast and relatively inexpensive to operate.

Dot matrix printers can be used as printer plotters if they are equipped with graphics capabilities. The advantage is the relatively low cost of equipment and operation. The disadvantage is the low quality of plot for most dot matrix printers. Some specialized dot matrix printers, however, can plot relatively high resolution drawings up to C-size (18" × 24").

LASER PRINTERS

Laser printers create prints similar to a pen plot. They use a laser-copy process that produces sharp, clear prints. Although some laser printers have excellent graphics capabilities, they are relatively expensive to purchase when compared with other types of printers. Another disadvantage is the restriction to small paper size.

Courtesy of Hewlett-Packard Company   FIGURE 3-6 Laser Printer

INK JET PRINTERS

Ink jet printers create letters and graphics by spraying a fine jet of ink onto the media. Ink jet printers can produce graphic plots of good quality. Advantages are the ability to create good quality plots in a reasonable time and the capability of some ink jet printers to use color. One disadvantage is the less than optimum quality.

DISPLAY SYSTEMS

Displays are used to view the work while in progress. Displays are often referred to as monitors or CRT's (cathode ray tubes). The quality of the image on the display is determined by its resolution. The resolution is controlled by the number of dots (pixels) contained on the screen. It is these pixels that make up the image. A 320 × 200 resolution display contains 320 pixels horizontal and 200 pixels vertical on the screen. Many professional CAD users prefer higher resolution displays such as 1024 × 768 or 1280 × 1024.

In order to display higher resolution, both the software program and the graphics board contained in the computer, must be capable of displaying the higher resolution. The monitor must also be matched to the graphics board.

CAD drafters use both monochrome and color display systems. The advantages of monochrome displays are the lower cost, and in many cases, a clearer display. The advantages of color systems are the ability to color code drawing layers and entities and the ability to produce more realistic rendered models.

Courtesy of Autodesk   FIGURE 3-7 CAD System With Display

INPUT DEVICES

Just as a word processing program requires a keyboard to input the individual letters, numbers, and symbols, a CAD program requires an input device to create and manipulate drawing elements. Although many programs allow input from the keyboard arrow keys, an input device speeds up the drawing process. The most common input devices used for CAD drawing are:

Digitizers	Track balls
Mice	Light pens

DIGITIZERS

A digitizer is an electronic input device that transmits the X and Y location of a cursor which is resting on a sensitized pad. Digitizers may be used as a pointing device to move a point around the screen, or as a tracing device for copying drawings into the computer in scale and proper proportion.

The points are located on the pad by means of a stylus (similar in appearance to a pencil), or a puck (alternately referred to as a cursor).

Digitizers use a fine grid of wires sandwiched between glass layers. The cursor is then moved across the pad and the relative location is read and transmitted to the computer.

In "tablet" mode, the digitizing pad is calibrated to the actual absolute coordinates of the drawing. When used as a pointing device, the tablet is not calibrated.

Courtesy of Houston Instruments   FIGURE 3-8 Digitizer

Digitizers are available in several sizes. Small pads may be used to digitize drawings larger than the pad surface. This is accomplished by moving the drawing on the pad and recalibrating. However, this can be very annoying if you frequently work with large scale drawings to be digitized.

MICE

A mouse is an input device that is used for pointing only. The name comes from its appearance. There are primarily two types of mice: mechanical mice and optical mice.

Mechanical mice have a ball under the housing. The rolling ball transmits its relative movement to the computer through a wire connecting the mouse to the computer.

An optical mouse uses optical technology to read lines from a special pad to sense relative movement. Although an optical mouse uses a pad, it is not capable of digitizing.

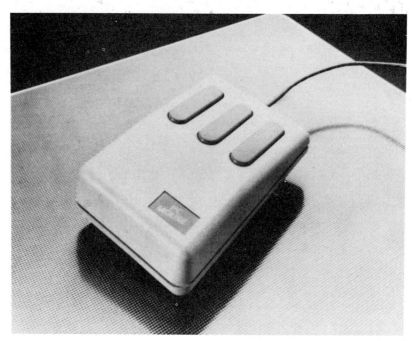

Courtesy of Mouse Systems   FIGURE 3-9 Optical Mouse

TRACK BALLS

A track ball can be thought of as an inverted roller ball mouse. A ball is moved by rolling it with the palm of the hand. In the same way as a roller ball mouse, relative movement of the ball is translated to the screen.

LIGHT PENS

A light pen has the size and appearance of an average pen with a wire leading from it to the computer. The pen is used to enter points directly on the CRT. A special monitor must be used with a light pen.

SUMMARY

A large number of peripheral devices are available for use by the CAD operator. The reason for choosing each peripheral is as diverse as the number of devices and users. In choosing the proper peripherals for you, the following criteria should be considered:

1. What will the primary use for the device be?

2. Does the software you plan to use support the device?

3. How much money are you willing to spend? (Large digitizing pads can cost several thousand dollars).

CHAPTER REVIEW

1. What are the three main categories of computers?

   _____

   _____

   _____

2. What is peripheral hardware?

   _____

   _____

   _____

3. What are the advantages of pen plotters over dot-matrix plots? Of dot-matrix plots over pen plotter plots?

   _____

   _____

   _____

   _____

   _____

4. What does the term resolution mean?

   _____

   _____

   _____

5. How does a mouse differ from a digitizing pad as an input device?

   _____

   _____

   _____

   _____

6. Can the performance and/or speed of a computer be altered or enhanced?

   _____

   _____

   _____

7. What is the center of activity of the computer?

   _____

   _____

8. Explain the difference in RAM and ROM memory.

_____

_____

_____

_____

_____

9. How are coprocessors categorized?

_____

_____

_____

10. Discuss the advantages and disadvantages of electrostatic plotters.

_____

_____

_____

_____

11. Compare laser and ink jet printers.

_____

_____

_____

_____

_____

12. How do an optical mouse and a mechanical mouse differ?

_____

_____

_____

_____

_____

13. How is a light pen operated?

_____

_____

_____

14. What is a track ball?

_____

_____

_____

_____

15. How is a stylus used with a digitizing pad?

_____

_____

_____

16. Would a complete CAD system with necessary peripherals be appropriate for architectural as well as manufacturing applications? Why?

_____

_____

_____

_____

_____

CHAPTER 4

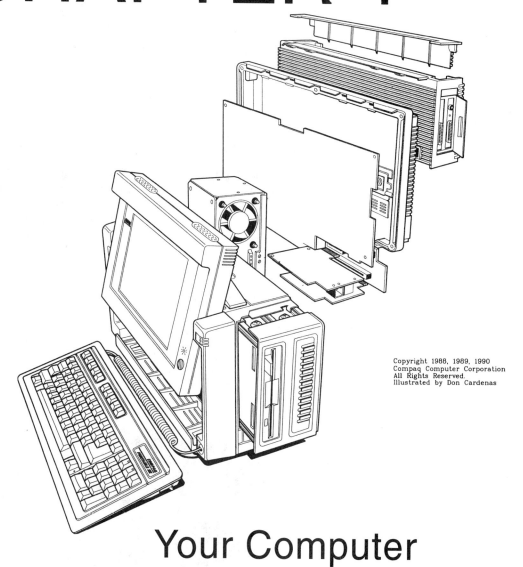

Your Computer

OBJECTIVES:

In order to use a CAD program effectively, knowledge of basic computer principles is essential. This chapter introduces the new computer user to the various principles of computer use. The objectives of Chapter 4 are:

● To introduce the new user to the basic parts of the computer.

● To achieve an understanding of the proper care of data storage disks and diskettes.

● To understand how data is stored in directories and subdirectories.

INTRODUCTION

In order to operate your AutoCAD program best, it is helpful to understand your computer. There are several aspects of computer use to become familiar with. This chapter is an overview of computer operation. The next chapter discusses the disk operating system, covering the basic operations you need to compute effectively. Let's start by looking at an important part of your computer: disks and disk drives.

DISK DRIVES

Disk drives are identified either as hard drives or floppy drives.

Disk drives are identified either as hard drives or floppy drives. Floppy drives use disks that are referred to as floppy disks. They are called floppy disks because the original disks are bendable (although they might damage if bent). Some new floppy disks now have hard shells instead of the vinyl shell. There are also removable drives available, such as SyQuest and Bernouli.

FLOPPY DISKS

Floppy disks used with personal computers are found in two predominate sizes: 5¼" and 3½". The 5¼" disks have the vinyl "floppy" shell. They typically hold either 360 kilobytes or 1.2 megabytes or 1.44 megabytes of data files. The 1.2 megabyte disk is referred to as a high capacity disk.

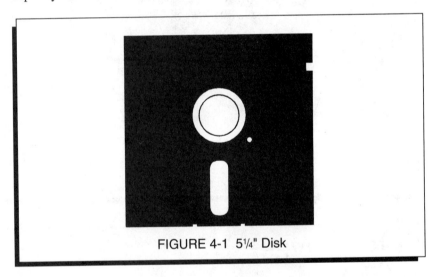

FIGURE 4-1 5¼" Disk

The second size is the 3½" disk. These disks use the plastic shells and are made in two capacities. They hold 720 kilobytes in the standard format, or 1.44 megabytes in the high capacity format.

HARD DRIVES

Hard disks are usually non-removable drives. These drives are typically installed inside the computer case. Hard disks (alternately referred to as hard drives) are manufactured in different capacities. The smallest capacity is usually 20 megabytes, although these have mostly been replaced by 40 megabyte capacity disks at the lower end. The size can range up to a thousand megabytes (a gigabyte).

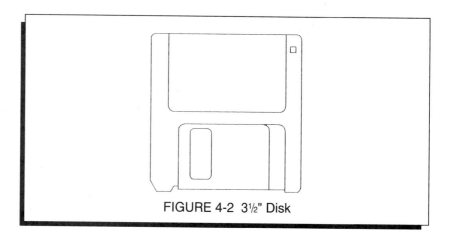

FIGURE 4-2 3½" Disk

DISK CARE

Since all your work is recorded to disk, care of the computer disk is very important. If a disk is damaged, you may lose your files! Frequent back-ups (copying files to a second diskette or computer tape) and proper handling of your disks can minimize the possibility of file loss.

Hard disks are installed inside the computer and are not handled. This may eliminate the danger of improper handling, but does not prevent damage. A hard drive can be damaged by shock. If you move the computer, be sure the power is off and move it gently. If the hard drive does not have self parking heads, use the included software to park them before moving the machine. This moves the heads to a sector that does not have data stored on it. If the hard drive is on, do not move or tilt the computer.

Floppy disks are especially subject to damage from handling. A 5¼" disk has an open area in its jacket where the writing head is positioned when the disk is in the drive. Touching the disk surface through this opening leaves oil from the skin on the disk, possibly leaving it unreadable.

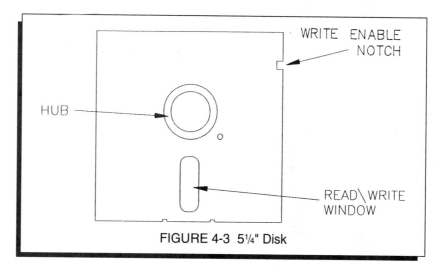

FIGURE 4-3 5¼" Disk

Dust and smoke can also leave particles on the disk surface that can prevent the drive from reading the disk properly. Heat and cold can cause the disk material to expand or contract, causing problems. Magnets scramble the data on the disk's tracks. Spilling a liquid onto a disk leaves a residue. If the liquid is hot or cold, it can cause temperature damage.

The smaller hard shelled 3½" disks are less prone to handling damage. The read/write surface is protected by a sliding door. The purpose of this door, of course, is defeated if you open it to look or touch. Otherwise, all the perils of a 5¼" disk also apply to the 3½" disk.

WRITE-PROTECTING DATA

If you do not want to be able to write to a disk, you can "write-protect" the disk.

Normally, a disk can be read from or written to. If you do not want to be able to write to a disk, you can "write-protect" the disk. This allows the disk to be read, but not written to.

The method of doing this depends on the type of disk you are write-protecting. The 5¼" disk usually comes with a set of write-protect tabs. These are small stickers that are placed over the write-enable notch on the disk. This notch can be found on the upper right side of the disk. Place the sticker over the notch, wrapping it around to the back of the diskette. To allow disk writing, simply remove the sticker.

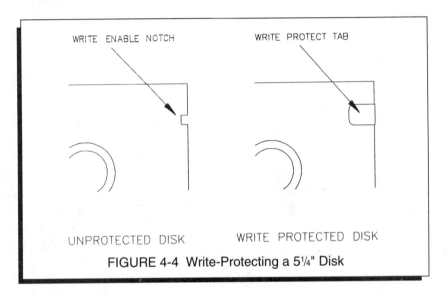

FIGURE 4-4 Write-Protecting a 5¼" Disk

The 3½" hard shell disk has a small slide switch in one corner of the disk. Sliding the switch alternates between write-protecting and write-enabling.

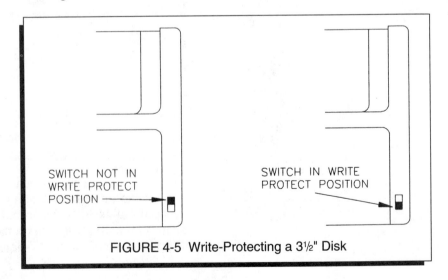

FIGURE 4-5 Write-Protecting a 3½" Disk

FILE DIRECTORIES & PATHS

As you add files to your disk, file management becomes an increasing problem. Imagine trying to find a single file out of hundreds on your disk! Computer files are usually able to be categorized, either by files generated by a single program (such as AutoCAD), or by jobs (such as drawing files for the Smith Widget Company). This is similar to standard office files. If you file work, you place it in a file that is designated for that type of information. You wouldn't throw it into a pile. Placing files indiscriminately on a disk is like throwing it into a pile.

You can make "file drawers" for your work. They are called "directories". You can also make files for the drawers. They are called "subdirectories". This electronic equivalent of a filing system is used to organize files on disks.

To properly plan your filing system, you should outline an overview of your programs and data files. Let's look at an example. We have several software programs we wish to use. They are AutoCAD, Lotus, WordPerfect, and dBase. We also would like to keep work files in a separate place.

The following outline shows the software programs in separate directories (file drawers) and work files in separate subdirectories (file folders).

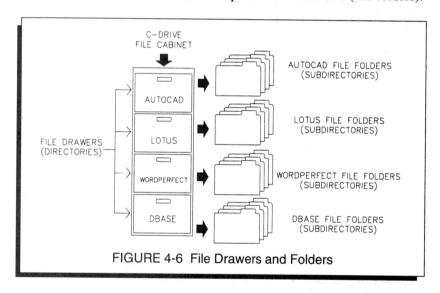

FIGURE 4-6 File Drawers and Folders

Note also that subdirectories can be created several "layers" deep. This is convenient when your outline breakdown of files requires subcategories.

This type of file management is standard for hard drives that can record large amounts of data. The methodology for doing this is found within the disk operating system. We will study this in the next chapter.

BATCH FILES

Batch files are files that contain text that is executed when the file name is entered.

Batch files are files that contain text that is executed when the file name is entered. Batch files always end with a ".BAT" file extension. Let's look at an example of a batch file. The following instructions are found in a file named "START.BAT".

```
C:
CD \ACAD12
ACAD
```

If you type the file name "START", the active drive will be changed to the C-drive (see line 1), the ACAD12 directory will be made current (see line 2), and the AutoCAD program will be started (see line 3).

Note that the contents of the batch file are executed as if they were typed from the keyboard. DOS adds an "Enter" at the end of each line. The START.BAT file would be executed as if you entered the following from the keyboard:

C: (ENTER) CD \ACAD12 (ENTER) ACAD (ENTER)

AUTOMATIC BATCH FILE EXECUTION

There may be items that we want to type in every time the computer is started. We can create a batch file that is executed automatically each time the computer is started.

Each time the computer is turned on or reset, DOS looks for a batch file named "AUTOEXEC.BAT". This stands for "automatically execute batch". If this file is present, it is automatically executed. The file must reside in the root directory of the "boot" (startup) drive.

CREATING BATCH FILES

Batch files can be created in different ways. You can use a word processor in "non-document" mode. This is a mode that does not include embedded characters. This creates a text file that is referred to as ASCII text. ASCII text is pure text without other special code characters. Another method is to use the DOS Edlin utility which is a rudimentary text processor.

The easiest way to create simple ASCII text files is to use the DOS Copy Con method. Copy Con instructs DOS to copy from console (keyboard). The following shows the keystrokes to create the previous START.BAT file using this method.

COPY CON START.BAT (ENTER)
CD \ACAD12
ACAD
(F6) (ENTER)

Note that the file is ended by pressing the F6 function key and then Enter. This records the file to the current drive and directory. You may also enter Ctrl-Z (control key + Z) to record the file. This is the same as pressing the F6 function key.

CREATING PROMPTS

The prompt, by default, is the drive designation. You can change the default prompt to one of your choice. Let's change our prompt. From DOS, type the following, putting a space after the last letter in "HELLO":

PROMPT HELLO

Now Enter and look at the prompt. The space was placed so the cursor would not start against the last letter in the new prompt.

To return to the default prompt, just type "PROMPT".

We can use the prompt options to create a very convenient prompt. Enter the following:

PROMPT PG

Use the CD command to change to a directory and look at the prompt. The directory name is listed as the prompt! Many computer operators place this line in the Autoexec.Bat file to automatically create this type of prompt.

CHAPTER REVIEW

1. List two ways of creating batch files.

   _____

   _____

2. What sizes floppy disks are available? What space capacities are they usually available in?

   _____

   _____

   _____

3. How might you avoid complete loss of a file, other than proper disk maintenance?

   _____

   _____

   _____

4. What does the term "write protect" mean? How is this accomplished?

   _____

   _____

   _____

5. What is entered at the DOS prompt to change from one directory to another?

   _____

   _____

   _____

6. What are batch files?

   _____

   _____

   _____

7. Why is file management important?

   _____

   _____

   _____

8. What makes a hard shell floppy disk less prone to damage?

_____

_____

_____

9. What may happen to the information on a disk if it passes through a magnetic field?

_____

_____

10. Is write protection of a disk permanent?

_____

_____

11. What would be a good initial approach to file management?

_____

_____

_____

12. What does the Copy Con DOS command do?

_____

_____

_____

13. What is a directory within a directory called?

_____

14. List 5 improper care procedures when handling floppy disks.

_____

_____

_____

_____

_____

CHAPTER 5

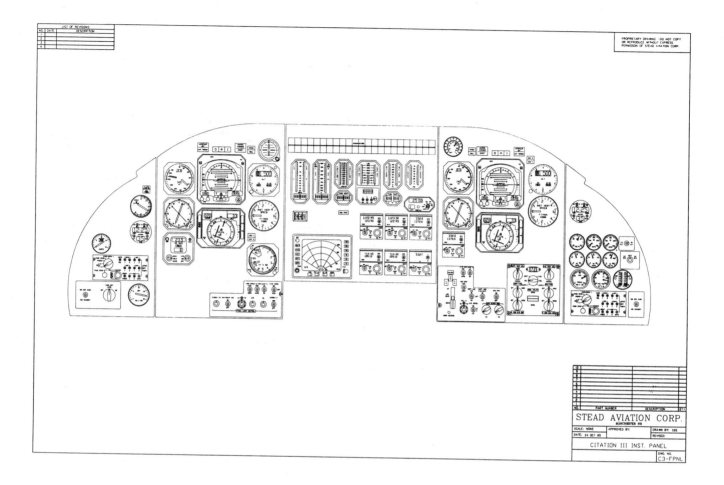

STEAD AVIATION CORP.
MANCHESTER NH

| SCALE: NONE | APPROVED BY: | DRAWN BY: SBS |
| DATE: 24 OCT 85 | | REVISED: |

CITATION III INST. PANEL

DWG. NO.
C3-FPNL

The Disk Operating System

OBJECTIVES:

The disk operating system is the most basic level of computing. The new user must achieve a basic level of understanding of the DOS system in order to perform fundamental computing operations. The objectives of Chapter 5 are:

● To acquaint the user with the disk operating system.

● To achieve a basic level of proficiency of the DOS system.

● To obtain a reference of DOS operations the user may need to perform in the future.

THE DISK OPERATING SYSTEM

To use AutoCAD and other software, your computer must have a program which translates between it and the computer. This program is called the Disk Operating System, or "DOS" for short.

DOS can be thought of as an umbrella program under which all other programs can be run.

DOS can be thought of as an umbrella program under which all other programs can be run. You must first start DOS before beginning other programs. If DOS is installed on your hard drive, it will be loaded automatically when you start your computer.

When you start your computer, it looks for certain DOS files. If they are present, they are loaded. You may notice a disk operating system message and/or DOS version number when you start your computer.

The disk operating system is originally supplied on floppy disk and is often included in the purchase price of your computer.

The DOS designates which disk drive is currently being worked on (or "active") by showing a "drive specifier".

DOS designates which disk drive is currently being worked on (or "active") by showing a "drive specifier". Disk drives are identified by a letter, such as "A", "B", or "C". The active, or current drive is shown by a letter, followed by a "greater than" symbol. For example, if the A-drive is active, it is designated on the computer screen by:

    A>

The letters designating the drives have a significance. Your computer first looks in the A-drive for the DOS files, then in the first hard drive.

In all computers, drives "A" and "B" are floppy drives, while drives "C" and above are hard drives.

The position of the drives in the computer can differ, according to the computer cabinet design. The following illustrations show the typical setup for different cabinet designs.

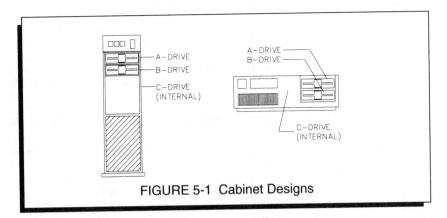

FIGURE 5-1 Cabinet Designs

CHANGING ACTIVE DRIVES

The active drive can be easily changed. If you are in DOS (that is, not currently in a program), you will notice that the active drive is shown on the screen. For example, if the active drive is now the C-drive, the bottom line on the screen shows:

    C>

To change to another drive, simple enter the drive letter, followed by a colon (:). For example, if the C-drive is current, enter the "A:", followed by pressing the Enter key.

C>A:

The last line of the screen will now display:

A>

The A-drive is now the active drive!

DISPLAYING FILES

The Directory (Dir) command is used to display a listing of files on the disk. If you wish to display a list of files on the active drive, simply enter:

DIR

You can show the files on any drive by adding the drive specifier after the Dir command. For example, if you want to display the files on the disk in the B-drive, enter:

DIR B:

You can do this from any active drive.

If you have a lot of files on the disk, they will "scroll" by before you have a chance to read them. You can place a "pause" in the directory by entering:

DIR /P

This will cause the directory of files to scroll up on the screen until the screen is filled, then pause. Press any key once to continue the scrolling until the screen is filled again. You can remember this by thinking of the "P" option as the "Pause" option.

You can pause the scrolling of the listing at any time by pressing the Control key, then striking the "S" letter key. You can remember this by thinking of the "S" key as the "Stop" key.

If you noticed the screen when you displayed the files with the Dir command, you observed that the listing is one file per line. You can display a "wide" directory with the "W" option. It is used in the same manner as the pause option. To display a file listing in wide format, enter:

DIR/W

You can remember this by thinking of the "W" option as the "Wide" option.

You may mix the options and obtain a wide listing with a pause by entering:

DIR/W/P

FILE NAMES AND DIRECTORY LISTINGS

The following is an example of a directory listing. Notice the difference between files and directory listings.

File names can have up to eight letters and/or characters.

Also notice the file names. The names are listed, then a three letter code is listed after them. These are called "file extensions". File names can

```
C:\> DIR
    Volume in drive C has no label
    Directory of C:\
COMMAND      COM          23456      1-23-88
DOS                       <DIR>      1-23-88
AUTOEXEC     BAT            128      2-13-88
ACAD         BAT             28      3-21-88
ACAD                      <DIR>      3-21-88
PIPESTAR                  <DIR>      4-12-88
SIDEKICK                  <DIR>      4-30-88
MENU                      <DIR>      (the current date)
```

FIGURE 5-2 Directory Listing

have up to eight letters and characters (some characters are exempted). The file extension can be up to three letters or characters long. The file extensions usually denote the type of file it is. For example, an AutoCAD drawing file has a "DWG" extension. If you refer to the file name in DOS, the correct notation is the file name, followed by a period (.), then the file extension. For example, an AutoCAD drawing named "WIDGET1" would be written "WIDGET1.DWG". Some programs create their own file extensions, while you must create file names in other programs. Note that a file extension is not required if you have the option of creating the extension.

WILDCARD CHARACTERS

When using the directory and other DOS commands, you can use "wildcard" characters to specify files. The two wildcard characters are the question mark (?) and the asterisk (*).

The question mark can fill in for any single character. For example, you may want to display a directory of all the files that are listed as "CAR_.DWG", where the underlined space can be any letter. If you enter:

    DIR CAR?.DWG

you could display a listing of files such as:

    CAR1.DWG
    CAR2.DWG
    CART.DWG
    CARD.DWG

The question mark wildcard can be used in either the file name or extension and can be used to represent as many letters as desired.

The asterisk is used to represent all the characters on either side of the period in a file name. For example, if you enter:

    DIR *.DWG

you will display all the files with the ".dwg" file extension. Alternately, if you enter:

    DIR FLPLAN.*

you will display all the drawings named "FLPLAN", regardless of their file extension (or even if no file extension exists).

DISPLAYING FILES IN DIRECTORIES

If you use directories, you must specify the directory under which you wish to list the files. For example, if you wish to see the files under the "ACAD12" directory, enter:

    DIR \ACAD12

The backslash used before the name indicates that the file name is a directory.

Notice the use of the backslash (\). The backslash used before the name indicates that the file name is a directory. If you had a subdirectory named "DWGS" under the ACAD12 directory and wished to see the contents of that subdirectory, you would enter:

    DIR \ACAD12\DWGS

If you are in a directory (we will learn how to make a directory active later), and wish to see the contents of any other directory, the process is the same. If, however, you are in a directory and wish to the see the contents of the root directory, you simply place a backsplash after the DIR command. For example, the \ACAD11\DWGS directory is current and you wish to see the contents of the root directory. Enter the following:

    DIR \

MAKING A DIRECTORY CURRENT

There may be times that you wish to make the current directory active. This might be necessary to run a program that is copied in that directory. For example, you may want to change to a directory named WRITER to start a word processing program. To change to the directory, type:

    CD \WRITER

To return to the root directory, enter the change directory (CD) command, followed by a space and backslash.

    CD \

Since directories and subdirectories can be created several levels deep, there may be times that you want to "back up" one level. To do this, enter:

    CD..

CREATING AND DELETING DIRECTORIES

Now that you know how to navigate through directories and subdirectories, it is time to learn how to create and delete them.

To create a directory, use the make directory (MD) command, followed by a space and the directory name you wish to create. For example, to create a directory named "DWGS", enter:

    MD DWGS

To create a subdirectory, first enter the directory you want the subdirectory to be created under (using the CD command discussed earlier) and use the MD command to create the subdirectory while in the directory.

To remove a directory, use the Remove Directory (RD) command. For example, to remove a directory named "OLDFILES", enter:

RD OLDFILES

Note that you can not remove a directory if it contains files or a subdirectory. You must first delete (we will learn how to do this later) files and/or remove subdirectories if you wish to remove the directory. If you attempt to remove a directory that contains files or subdirectories, DOS will display an error message.

If you wish to remove a subdirectory, change (CD) to the level "above" the subdirectory and use the RD command. Like directories, if files or sub-sub directories exist, you must first delete them before removing the subdirectory.

DELETING FILES

As you work, you will create files that you no longer wish to have on your disks. You can use the Delete (Del) command to remove files. The Delete command is the same as the Erase command. Delete is typically used since the command can be accessed by typing the shorter Del entry.

If you wish to delete files that are in a directory or subdirectory, it is recommended that you first change to that directory or subdirectory before deleting the file. This eliminates the possibility of a fatal error.

WARNING: Unless you are familiar with utility programs that can "unerase" files, your deleted files will not be recoverable. Be sure before you proceed! "Undelete" is now a standard utility with DOS 5.

Let's look at how we would erase a file. The file we wish to erase is named PLAN.DWG. To delete the file, enter:

DEL PLAN.DWG

Note that you could delete all the drawing files in a directory or subdirectory (if, of course, you were really sure you wanted to) by using the asterisk wildcard character and entering:

DEL *.DWG

COPYING FILES

The Copy function is used to copy files from disk to disk or to different locations on the same disk.

There are some rules to be aware of. You can not have two files of identical names in the same directory. You must include the file extension when referring to files to be copied. If you are copying a file from a directory or subdirectory, you must include the path to the file.

Let's look at some examples of file copying.

COPY DISK TO DISK

To copy a file from one disk to another, use the following format:

COPY A:FILENAME.EXT B:

This would copy a file from drive A to drive B.

COPYING FROM DIRECTORY TO DIRECTORY

To copy from or to directories, you must specify the directory paths.

COPY C:\ACAD\PLAN.DWG D:\DWGS

This would copy a file named PLAN.DWG in a directory named ACAD11 on the C-drive to a directory named DWGS on the D-drive.

COPY FILES AND RENAMING

You can copy a file and rename the file in a single step.

COPY A:PLAN.DWG B:SCHEME1.DWG

This would copy the drawing named PLAN.DWG from the A-drive to the B-drive and rename the file SCHEME1.DWG. The original file name from the A-drive would remain unchanged.

This is a good method for copying a file to the same directory. As mentioned earlier, you can not have two files by the same name. You can, however, have two identical files, each with a different name. The following is an example of copying a file to the same directory with a new name.

COPY PLAN.DWG PLAN2.DWG

Note that we did not have to list a drive specifier, since we were both copying from and to the default drive.

NOTE: If you copy a file to a disk that already has a file by the same name, that file will be replaced by the new file of the same name!

COPYING DISKS

It is often desirable to copy (or back up) an entire disk. The Diskcopy command is used to do this. Diskcopy is somewhat different than the Copy command. You could use the following format to copy all the files from the A-drive to the B-drive:

COPY A:*.* B:

This would copy all the files from the A-drive to the B-drive one by one. If the disk in the B-drive had existing files, the new files would simply be added in addition to the existing files.

Diskcopy makes an exact copy of the original disk.

Diskcopy, however, makes an exact copy of the original disk. If there are files on the target disk, the files will be removed before the new ones are copied.

Diskcopy is a DOS program. Because of this, you must be in the directory where the DOS files reside before you can use Diskcopy. The following format is used for Diskcopy.

    DISKCOPY A: B:

This would duplicate the disk in the A-drive with the disk in the B-drive.

Not everyone, however, has two floppy drives. If you only have one floppy (it will be an A-drive), the following format can be used:

    DISKCOPY A: A:

DOS will prompt you to place either the Target disk (the disk to copy to or the Source disk (the disk to copy from) in the disk drive. You will have to swap disks as DOS prompts you to do on the screen.

Note that you can not use diskcopy between two drives and/or disks that are not the same capacity.

RENAMING FILES

You can rename a file by using the Rename (Ren) command. Use the following format:

    REN FILE1.EXT FILE2.EXT

For example, to rename the file SPROCKET.DWG to COG.DWG, enter:

    REN SPROCKET.DWG COG.DWG

FORMATTING DISKS

Before you can use a disk, it must be formatted.

Before you can use a disk, it must be formatted. Formatting installs the tracks, sectors, and other items needed to make your disk usable. This is achieved by using the Format command. Format, like Diskcopy, is a DOS program. You must be in the directory where the DOS files are located before you can use it.

A simple format can be started by using the following format:

    FORMAT A:

This will format the disk in the A-drive.

Note: The format command is destructive to any existing files.

You can create a "bootable" disk (one that has the necessary DOS files to start your computer) by using the "/s" (system) option. Note the following format:

    FORMAT A:/S

This option copies files (both visible and hidden) to the formatted disk, making it a "bootable" disk. You do not need to use this option for a disk that is not used to start the computer.

Hard drives are also formatted. The procedure for doing this, however, is more complicated and potentially damaging unless performed by a knowledgeable operator.

Some types of drives use special options for formatting. The product information with the drive gives any special instructions you may need.

DISPLAYING FILE CONTENTS

If a file is written with ASCII text, its contents can be displayed in DOS by using the Type command. To display a file, use the following format:

    TYPE FILENAME.EXT

If the file is not ASCII, you will get some very unusual looking characters. If the file you display is more than one screen in length, you can use Ctrl-S to stop the screen. Use Ctrl-S again to continue the scrolling.

CHAPTER REVIEW

1. What function does DOS perform?

_____

_____

_____

2. What are wildcard characters? List them.

_____

_____

_____

_____

3. When can you not remove a subdirectory?

_____

_____

_____

4. What would you type at the prompt to rename a drawing file named FLPLAN as FLOORPL?

_____

_____

5. What do the following DOS commands stand for: MD, CD, DEL, REN, RD?

_____

_____

_____

_____

6. How would you return to the root directory from a subdirectory?

_____

_____

7. What would you type to make the current directory active?

_____

8. How does a /P affect the DIR command?

_____

_____

9. How can you stop the scrolling of file listings?

_____

_____

10. How does DOS indicate the active drive?

_____

_____

11. How can you display a listing of files?

_____

_____

12. Why is it necessary to format a disk before using it?

_____

_____

13. What is a "bootable" disk?

_____

_____

14. What would the effect be of formatting a disk containing files?

_____

_____

_____

15. Is the procedure for formatting a hard disk different from that of a floppy disk?

_____

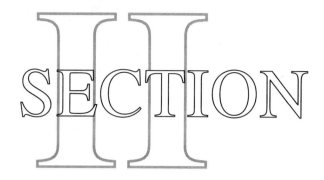

SECTION II

INTRODUCTION TO AUTOCAD

- Using AutoCAD
- Drawing With AutoCAD
- Setting Up a Drawing
- Getting Started
- Editing a Drawing
- Constructing Multiview Drawings
- Constructing Sectional and Patterned Drawings
- Text, Fonts, and Styles
- Layering Your Drawings
- Introduction to Dimensioning
- Dimension Styles and Variables
- Dimensioning Practices
- Plotting Your Work
- Inquiry and Utility Commands

CHAPTER 6

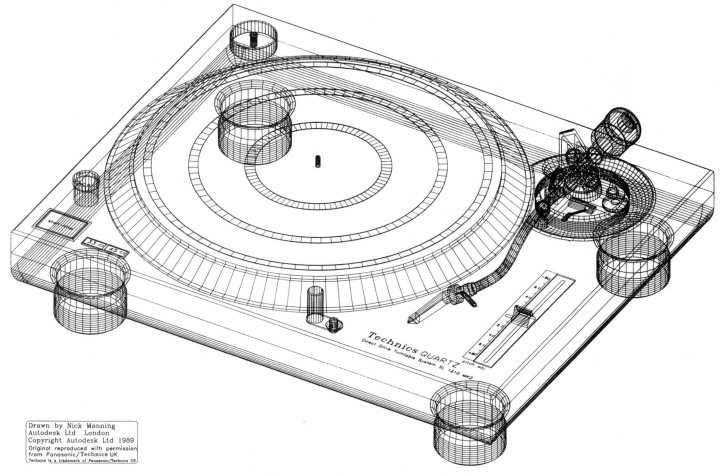

Drawn by Nick Manning
Autodesk Ltd   London
Copyright Autodesk Ltd 1989
Original reproduced with permission
from Panasonic/Technics UK
Technics is a trademark of Panasonic/Technics UK

Using AutoCAD

OBJECTIVES:

The operation of a computer aided design system is unique among other types of software programs. This chapter introduces the user to the principles of the AutoCAD program. Chapter 6 objectives are:

● To introduce the concepts of a computer aided design program.

● To understand the AutoCAD screen layouts.

● To introduce the terms used in this text and in AutoCAD.

● To learn the functions of special keyboard keys.

AutoCAD
In The
Real
World

Smithsonian Institution Project
Modern Study of a Venerable Museum

The National Museum of Natural History at the Smithsonian Institution is one of nine museums located on the Capital Mall in Washington, D.C. Among its many treasures are the Hope Diamond, moon rocks, and fossilized dinosaurs resurrected from the earth's distant past. Since the completion of its construction in 1911, the museum has served the Nation as a repository of its natural historical wealth and as a center for a wide range of research into the Nation's natural heritage. On any day of the year you will find thousands of visitors to the Museum, virtually suspended in time, attentively surveying its vast collection of artifacts and specimens.

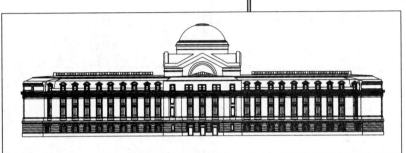

Developing a computer-based model of the 957,000 square foot National Museum of Natural History at the Smithsonian Institution in Washington, D.C., was a fitting challenge for the university of Maryland's design students.

Besides documenting the main structure with greater accuracy and consistency than originally drawn by the architects, and producing a comprehensive set of ACAD drawings of the research wings for future remodeling and renovation, the students developed AutoCAD drawings of an addition that included a three-story movie theater, a new naturalist center, restaurant, film archive, museum shop, and educational facility in the West Court. In addition, the students used AutoCAD to generate a model of an in-progress design of an exhibit for comparison and analysis.

North elevation of main structure drawing, exterior facade.

While AutoCAD exhibition design was the guiding theme and principal aspect of the project, other uses for the computer model became apparent to Museum personnel. Their interests currently revolve around use of the model, or parts thereof, for facilities management, architectural renovation and preservation, and, perhaps most importantly, inventory control—the Museum of Natural History houses a staggering 80,000,000 artifacts and specimens.

The curators at the Smithsonian weren't the only beneficiaries of this project. The students at the University of Maryland were able to add a complex project to their portfolios. They were also motivated to learn more about CAD and to seek opportunities to further develop their expertise.

Adapted with permission from an article by Michael Eckersley. Excerpted from *CADENCE*, January 1989, copyright © 1989, Ariel Communications, Inc.

OVERVIEW

A computer aided drafting system is to drafting what a word processor is to words and writing.

AutoCAD is a powerful computer aided drafting package. A computer aided drafting system is to drafting what a word processor is to words and writing.

Your drawings are displayed on a graphics monitor screen. This monitor takes the place of the paper in traditional drafting techniques. All the additions and changes to your work are shown on the monitor screen as you perform them.

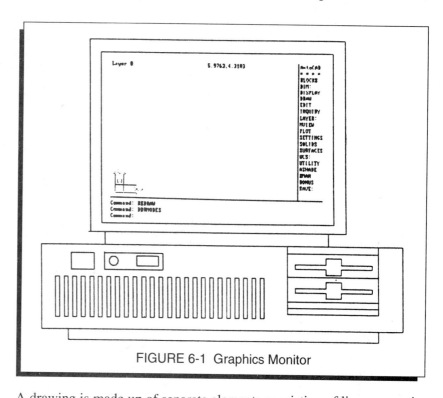

FIGURE 6-1 Graphics Monitor

A drawing is made up of separate elements.

A drawing is made up of separate elements consisting of lines, arcs, circles, strings of text, and other elements supplied for your use. These elements are called *entities.*

The commands are selected from a screen menu or from the keyboard. A menu is a list of items from which you may choose what you want. AutoCAD provides for menu selections to be placed on the screen and on a digitizing pad. The next chapter illustrates the parts of the AutoCAD drawing screen.

Entities are placed in the drawing by means of commands.

Entities are placed in the drawing by means of commands. Each command is performed by choosing an entity or function from the menu. You are then asked to identify the parameters of the command. After identifying all the information which AutoCAD requests, the entities or changes are shown on the screen.

TERMINOLOGY

This manual contains terms and concepts that you need to understand in order to use AutoCAD properly. Some of the terms you need to know now are briefly listed in this chapter. If you need other help, refer to the Glossary and special Command Summary, in the Appendix. In addition, the index contains all the terms used and the pages on which they are explained.

COORDINATES

The *Cartesian coordinate system* is used in AutoCAD. The diagram shown below illustrates the system. The *X-axis* is represented by the horizontal line. The *Y-axis* is represented by the vertical line. Any point on the graph can be represented by an X and Y value shown in the form of (X,Y). The normal position of the AutoCAD screen is overlaid on the axis.

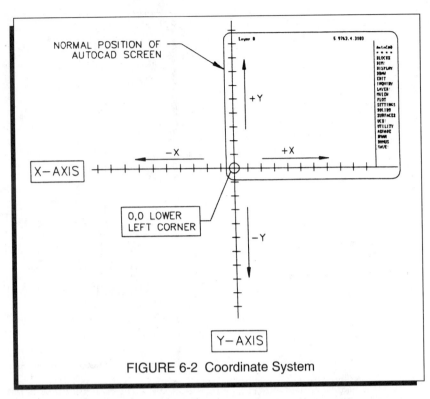

FIGURE 6-2 Coordinate System

The intersection of the X and Y axis is the (0,0) point. This point is normally the lower left corner of the drawing editor. (You may, however specify a different lower left corner).

The AutoCAD 3-D system uses a third axis called the *Z axis*.

DISPLAY

In this manual, the term display refers to the part of the drawing that is currently visible on the monitor screen.

DRAWING FILES

The drawing file *is the file which contains the information used to describe the drawn graphics image.*

The *drawing file* is the file which contains the information used to describe the drawn graphics image. A drawing file automatically has a file extension of .DWG added to it. A file extension is a three character suffix that is sometimes placed after the period which follows the file name.

LIMITS

When using AutoCAD, you draw in a rectangular area. The borders of this area are called the *Limits*. You may draw anywhere in these limits, but not outside them. You may set the limits to whatever size you wish. You may also change them at any time. The limits are described by (X,Y) coordinates for the lower left corner and the upper right corner. Your drawing limits may be thought of as the "sheet size" that you are drawing on.

UNITS

The distance between two points is described in units.

The distance between two points is described in *units*. The units for AutoCAD may be set to any of the following:

1. Scientific
2. Decimal
3. Engineering
4. Architectural
5. Fractional

With the exception of Architectural units, one unit may be equal to whatever form of measurement (for example, feet or meters) you wish.

ZOOMING/PANNING

You will often want to enlarge a portion of the drawing to see the work in greater detail, or to reduce it to see the entire drawing. The *Zoom* command facilitates this. AutoCAD's zoom ratio is about one trillion to one!

The *Pan* command allows you to move around the drawing while at the same zoom level.

USE OF THE MANUAL

Each chapter contained in this manual is designed to build on the previous chapters. Many sections contain tutorials which you should follow. The problems found at the end of a chapter are specifically designed to use the commands covered in the manual to that point.

This method allows your learning to be self paced. Remember, not everyone will grasp each command in the same amount of time.

KEYS

Several references are made to different keyboard keys in this manual. The following keys will be referred to in this manual. Note that the keys may be located in a different location on some keyboards.

The Control key is used in conjunction with another key.

Control key: Some commands are executed by a multiple keystroke. The Control key is used in conjunction with another key.

Flip Screen: On single screen configurations, the text and graphics screens may be alternately displayed by using the Flip Screen key. On most models using ten function keys, the "F1" key is used for this.

Fast Cursor: When using the arrow keys to move the screen cursor, the movement interval may be adjusted using the fast and slow cursor keys. On IBM compatible models, the "Pg Up" and "Pg Dn" keys perform this function.

COMMAND NOMENCLATURE

When a command sequence is shown, the following notations are used:

> **UNDERLINED:** An underlined response designates user input. This is what you enter. Entry may be made from either the screen menu or the keyboard.

> **<DEFAULT>:** Entries enclosed in brackets are the default values for the current command. The default value will be executed if you press the Enter key.

> **ENTER POINT:** When prompted to "enter point", you should enter a point on the screen at the designated place. You will usually be shown a point on a drawing. The points will be designated, such as "point A".

> **RETURN or ENTER:** Means to press the "Enter" key after the entry. (You will need to do this after each input).

> **CHOOSE** or **SELECT:** Make the desired choice.

You may use either the upper or lower case in response to any command inquiry.

When a response option has one letter capitalized, the capital letter for that response is all that is required to be entered. For example, if an option is "eXit", simply entering "X" is sufficient for choosing that option.

The menus shown with tutorials serve to guide you through the complex menu structure. The boxed part of the menu represents the correct choice to make from the screen menu.

USING AUTOCAD NOTE SHEETS

Note sheets are provided throughout the text. These note sheets contain helpful hints in using AutoCAD.

Be sure to read the note sheets in each chapter for helpful hints for using AutoCAD.

Tip

Be sure to read the note sheets in each chapter for helpful hints for using AutoCAD.

FIGURE 6-3 Note Box

CHAPTER REVIEW

1. The area on the screen in which you draw is surrounded by borders called what?

   _____

2. Some commands prompt for additional information in order to continue execution of the command, and in some instances a default setting can be chosen. If a default setting is present, how can it be identified and what must be done to select it?

   _____

   _____

   _____

   _____

3. What are the drawing elements used in computer aided drafting called? Give three examples of drawing elements.

   _____

   _____

   _____

   _____

4. For each of the following options, list the required response you would enter at the prompt:

   Close: _____

   eXit: _____

   circle: _____

   LAyer:_____

   Edit vertex: _____

5. Where can the commands used to draw and edit be selected from?

   _____

   _____

6. When using the F1 key to facilitate to flip screen function, in what way will the display be altered and what information is presented by using this option?

   _____

   _____

   _____

7. Using the figure below, label each portion of the axis indicated. Next, draw a rectangle on the figure to represent the drawing screen orientation relative to the coordinate axis.

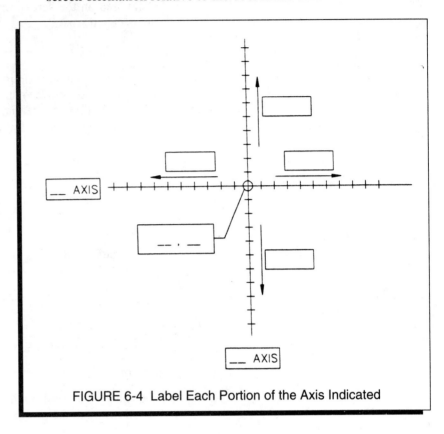

FIGURE 6-4 Label Each Portion of the Axis Indicated

8. To enlarge or reduce all or a portion of your drawing on the screen, what command would you use?

_____

9. What term is used to refer to the portion of the drawing that is currently visible on the screen?

_____

10. What can be done to increase or decrease the increment of movement in the screen cursor when the arrow keys are used?

_____

_____

11. What is the increment of length in which a drawing is constructed?

_____

12. When using this manual, where would you look for extra help or information about commands listed?

_____

13. What happens when you press the Control key?

_____

14. If you have zoomed in to a portion of the drawing for close examination, how can you move to another part of the drawing while staying in the same zoom?

_____

15. What is used to place entities into a drawing?

_____

16. What is the only option that designates the units a drawing is constructed in?

_____

CHAPTER 7

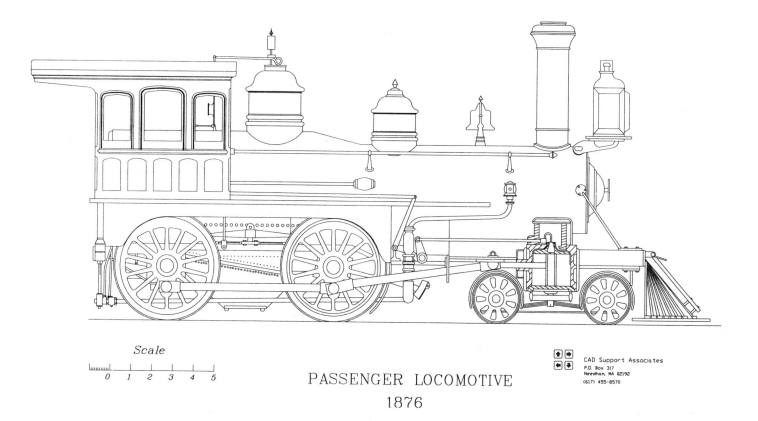

Scale

```
|mummul_____|_____|_____|_____|
     0    1    2    3    4    5
```

PASSENGER LOCOMOTIVE
1876

CAD Support Associates
P.O. Box 317
Needham, MA 02192
(617) 455-8570

Drawing With AutoCAD

OBJECTIVES:

In order to use the AutoCAD program, you must learn how to start the program and manage the files. The objectives of this chapter are:

● To learn how to start the AutoCAD program.

● Learning the commands used to save and discard your work.

● Differentiating the differences between the different file management commands.

BEGINNING A DRAWING SESSION

Your drawing sessions with AutoCAD will begin by starting the AutoCAD program. The program is started by entering the start command from the keyboard. The command is determined by your response for a start command when the AutoCAD program is installed. This will be commands such as ACAD, ACAD386, ACADR12, etc.

Depending on the response about "logging in" during the installation of the AutoCAD program, you may be prompted to *"login"* to the program. If a default login name was listed, AutoCAD will display a line similar to the following:

Login was successful as JOHN DOE.

If you entered a period (.) in response to the login name during the installation, a login dialogue box will be displayed. Enter your name from the keyboard, then click on the OK button.

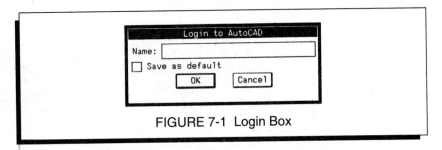

FIGURE 7-1 Login Box

After you have started AutoCAD, you will see the drawing editor. The drawing editor is the screen where your drawing activities will take place.

THE DRAWING EDITOR

Once in the Drawing Editor, you are presented with a drawing area in which to perform your work. You will notice that the top, bottom and right sides of the screen contain information. Let's look at these areas.

SCREEN COORDINATES

The top center of the screen contains two sets of numbers which represent the X and Y coordinates of the crosshair. The type of numerical read-out is controlled by the Units command. The constantly updating coordinates may be switched between absolute coordinate display, polar coordinate display, and off by using Control-D or function key F6. If the coordinates do not update as you move the cursor, they are toggled off.

LAYER-ORTHO-SNAP-TABLET INDICATORS

The upper left corner of the screen displays the mode indicators.

The upper left corner of the screen displays the mode indicators. This includes the following:

Layer name: Lists the name of the current layer.

Ortho mode: Indicates whether the orthogonal mode is on or off.

Snap mode: Indicates whether the snap mode is on or off.

Tablet mode: Indicates whether tablet mode is on or off. Tablet mode is used to digitize (trace) paper drawings.

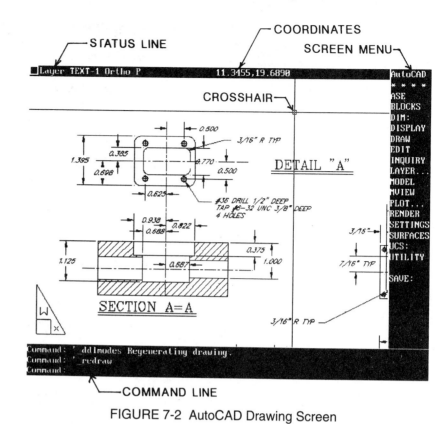

FIGURE 7-2 AutoCAD Drawing Screen

If the mode is listed, it is currently active or "on". If you do not wish a status line, it can be eliminated at the time of configuration.

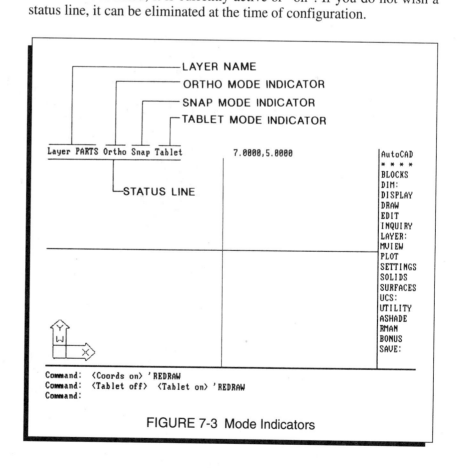

FIGURE 7-3 Mode Indicators

The bottom of the screen contains the prompt area.

THE SCREEN PROMPT AREA

The bottom of the screen contains the prompt area. This area is where your commands are listed and the resulting prompts are displayed. If you become confused as to the present status of AutoCAD, the prompt line is the place to look for the answer. On a dual-screen system, the text monitor also displays prompts.

ENTERING COMMANDS

Commands may be entered in AutoCAD in several different ways. Let's look at the methods you can use to enter commands in AutoCAD.

KEYBOARD

The most basic method of input is the keyboard. You may type the command directly from the keyboard. Your input will be displayed on the prompt line. If you make a mistake, simply backspace to correct. After typing, you must press Enter or the spacebar to activate the command. AutoCAD doesn't care if you use upper case, lower case, or a combination of each.

In order to type a command from the keyboard, the command line must be "clear". That is, another command must not be in progress. If the command line is not clear, you can clear it by using Ctrl-C.

SCREEN MENUS

The most basic method of command entry is from the screen menu. Selecting items from the menu will have the same effect as typing them from the keyboard, except you don't have to press Enter.

PULL-DOWN MENUS

Selecting items from a pull-down has the same effect as selecting from the screen menu.

TABLET MENUS

AutoCAD allows the use of tablet menus. These are printed templates that are placed on a digitizing tablet. The user may customize the tablet menu for a particular application. Items chosen from a tablet menu respond in the same manner as those chosen from the screen menu.

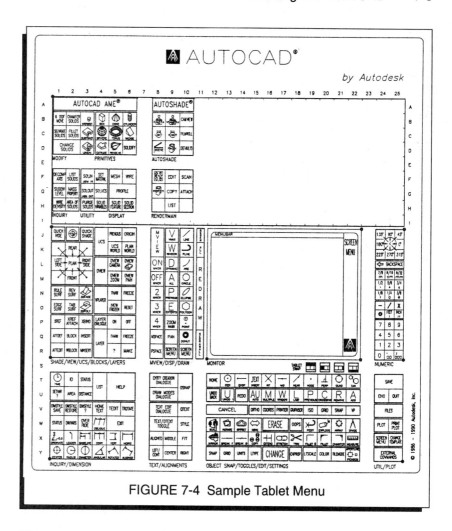

FIGURE 7-4 Sample Tablet Menu

SCREEN MENUS

On the right side of the screen, you will see an on-screen menu. This menu and its associated submenus contain all the AutoCAD commands. Using commands is the way you draw objects in AutoCAD.

Items are "entered" from the menu in different ways, depending on the input device which you are using.

> **Mouse or digitizer:** Move the cursor to the far right of the screen to "light up" the menu items. Move up or down to select the desired command and press the pick button.

> **Keyboard:** Press the Menu Cursor key (some computers such as IBM and most IBM compatibles use other keys such as Ins) to light up the menu items and move up and down the menu using the arrow keys on the keypad. Select the desired item by pressing Enter.

ROOT MENU AND SUBMENUS

The menu which is initially displayed on the screen is the ROOT MENU. This menu is made up of several items which represent Submenus. Each sub menu, in turn, contains several commands that are associated with it. When you enter each sub menu, a new menu will appear which lists the options associated with the previous menu. The commands listed

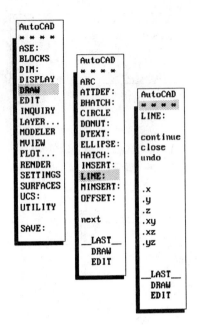

in the menus are capitalized and have colons (:) after them. Commands that are followed by three periods (such as PLOT...) prompt a dialogue box. This means that selecting this command will cause a dialogue box to be displayed on the screen. You will use this dialogue box to enter information. Use of dialogue boxes is covered later in this chapter.

Each submenu contains options which allow you to "jump" between other submenus. In most cases, you will have the choice to move either to the Last (previous) menu or the Root menu.

The illustration to the side shows the menu path taken from the Root Menu to the Line command (contained in the Draw submenu) and back to the Root Menu. Notice that the commands are followed by a colon and command "modifiers" are not.

The commands are arranged in a logical manner under headings in the root menu. For example, the Line, Circle, and Arc commands are located under the DRAW heading. The Erase command is located under the EDIT menu. After some practice, the location of each command within the screen menu system will become familiar. It takes a bit of practice to become proficient in the use of nested menus, but once mastered, it speeds up the drawing process.

PULL-DOWN MENUS

If you move the cursor to the area of the status line at the top of the screen, a listing of pull-down menus is displayed. Clicking on one of the listings will cause a pull-down menu to appear on the screen. You may select a command or function from the pull-down menu in the same manner as a screen menu.

FIGURE 7-5 Pull-Down Menu

If you pull down a menu and do not want to select an item, you can exit the menu by clicking outside of the menu area.

Pull-down menus are also arranged in a logical manner. In many cases, however, they do not parallel the screen menus. Figure 7-6 shows the sequence used to pull down and select an item from a pull-down menu.

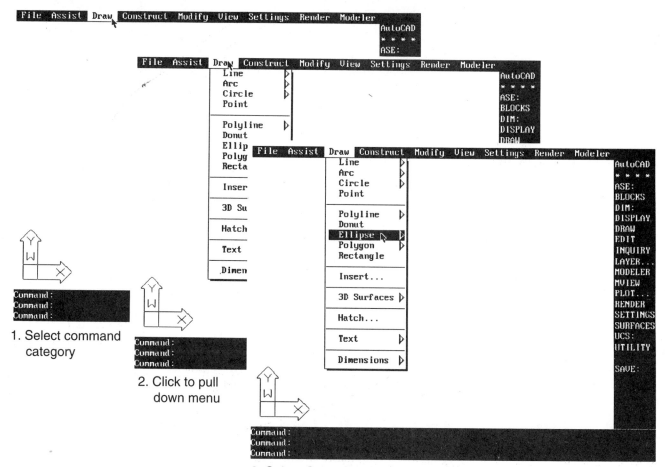

1. Select command category

2. Click to pull down menu

3. Select Command from menu and click

FIGURE 7-6 Selecting a Command From a Pull-Down Menu

KEYBOARD KEYS USED IN AUTOCAD

Modes may be toggled on and off even if you are currently in a command.

AutoCAD provides special keys to aid in toggling modes on and off and for correcting errors in command entry. Modes may be toggled on and off even if you are currently in a command.

COMMAND LINE ENTRY KEYS

The following keys can be used to edit your keyboard input at the command line.

Backspace: The backspace key removes one character at a time from the command line. You may use the backspace at any time before you Enter the contents of the command line.

CTRL-H: Used the same as the backspace key.

CTRL-X: Cancels all the characters on the command line.

CTRL-C: Cancels the current command and returns the command line.

CTRL-C: Cancels the current command and returns the command line. You may enter Ctrl-C at any time. If entered while an operation is in progress, it will terminate the command at its present point.

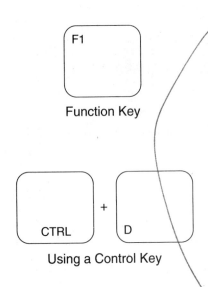

F1

Function Key

CTRL + D

Using a Control Key

TOGGLE KEYS

Computer keyboards use function keys that are interchangeable with the normal toggle keys. The function keys are designated as "F" keys. For example, "F9" refers to the function nine key.

F1: Toggles between the graphics and text screens on single screen systems.

CTRL-D or F6: Toggles the screen coordinate display on and off.

CTRL-E: Toggles to the next isometric plane when in ISO mode. The planes are activated in a rotating fashion (left, top, right, and then repeated).

CTRL-G or F7: Toggles Grid on and off.

CTRL-O or F8: Toggles Ortho mode on and off.

CTRL-B or F9: Toggles Snap mode on and off.

CTRL-T or F10: Toggles tablet mode on and off. You must first calibrate the pad before you can toggle the Tablet mode on.

OTHER KEYS

CTRL-Q: Turns the printer echo on and off. The printer echo is used to send all text from the text screen (prompt area) to a printer. To turn off the printer echo, issue Ctrl-Q again.

INS: Turns on the menu cursor. You only need to use this key if you are using the keyboard arrow keys to move the cursor. This is the light bar that is used to highlight screen menu items.

HOME: Turns the crosshairs on. After some types of command entries, the crosshairs are not visible on the screen. The crosshairs will also be redisplayed if you use an arrow key from the key pad to move the crosshair.

UP ARROW: Moves the crosshairs up.

DOWN ARROW: Moves the crosshairs down.

LEFT ARROW: Moves the crosshairs left.

RIGHT ARROW: Moves the crosshairs right.

PgUp: "Speeds up" crosshair movement by increasing the interval which it moves with each press of an arrow key.

PgDn: "Slows down" crosshair movement by decreasing the interval which it moves with each press of an arrow key.

REPEATING COMMANDS

If you would like to repeat the previous command given to AutoCAD, press the Enter (or Return) key or press the spacebar.

If you would like to repeat the previous command given to AutoCAD, press the Enter (or Return) key when the "Command" prompt appears. The last command entered will repeat. The space bar can also be used for the same purpose.

Some commands require that you enter additional information. The Zoom command, for example, prompts you for the type of zoom you desire. In most case, the first letter of your choice will be adequate (such as responding with a "W" for "window" when prompted by the Zoom command).

SCREEN POINTING

Points, distances and angles may also be entered simply by "showing" AutoCAD the information on the screen. Entering two points could indicate the distance and angle requested.

On some commands (such as Line) the absolute coordinate display converts to a relative distance and angle display. Using this as a method of measurement is quite suitable in most circumstances, although actual numerical entry using coordinates is more accurate.

SHOWING POINTS BY WINDOW CORNERS

Some commands require input which specifies both a horizontal and a vertical displacement. Both points may be shown at one time by requesting a "window" and using the X and Y distances from the lower left corner and the upper right corner as the displacement.

For example, the window in Figure 7-7 displaces a value of (5,3) from the lower left corner of the window.

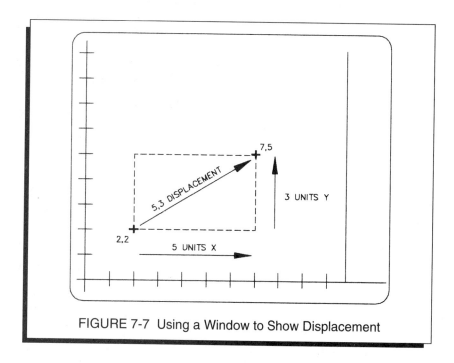

FIGURE 7-7 Using a Window to Show Displacement

DIALOGUE BOXES

Certain commands allow you to enter or select information from a dialogue box. Note that not all display systems are capable of showing dialogue boxes.

Figure 7-8 shows the dialogue for controlling layer settings.

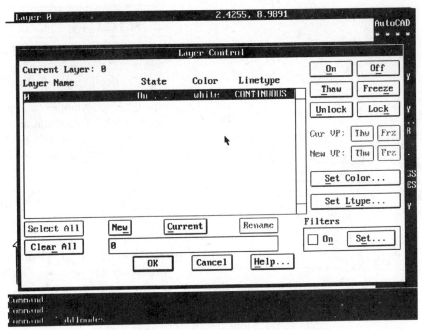

FIGURE 7-8 Layer Control Dialogue Box

DISPLAYING DIALOGUE BOXES BY COMMAND

Many commands automatically display dialogue boxes. Others are invoked by command. The following is a list of commands used to display a dialogue box. Each command starts with DD (Dynamic Dialogue).

DDEMODES: Used for setting entity properties of linetypes, colors, etc.

DDLMODES: Controls layer settings.

DDRMODES: Drawing modes and aids such as snap, grid, etc.

DDATE: Attribute editing.

DDUCS: Dialogue control for the User Coordinate System.

DDEDIT: Dialogue control for attribute definitions.

DDIM: Controls dimension settings.

DDGRIPS: Controls Autoedit grips and settings.

DDSELECT: Determines entity selection modes (pickbox size, etc.).

DDOSNAP: Sets object snap modes and aperture size.

DDINSERT: Used for block insertion.

DDRENAME: Renames various named items.

DDATTEXT: Used to extract information from a drawing file for use with another program.

DDATTDEF: Used to create attribute definitions.

DDUNITS: Sets drawing units, coordinates, and angles.

DDLIST: Used to display database information about selected objects in a drawing.

DDCHPROP: Controls the layer, color, linetype, and thickness of selected objects.

DDSV: Displays system variables and settings.

The display of dialogue boxes can either be on or off. The Filedia system variable is used to turn the display of dialogue boxes on or off. If the Filedia system variable is set to 0 (off), you will be prompted for input on the command line.

If the Filedia is off, you can override by placing a tilde (~) in response to a command request if a dialogue would normally be available.

USING A DIALOGUE BOX

The arrow pointer is used to select items from the dialogue box.

When a dialogue box is displayed, the crosshairs are replaced by an arrow pointer. The arrow pointer is used to select items from the dialogue box.

You can also choose an item by pressing the letter key on the keyboard that corresponds with an underlined letter in the dialogue box. The arrow pointer must be outside the box to do this.

Some dialogue boxes contain sub-dialogue boxes.

Some dialogue boxes contain sub-dialogue boxes. If a sub box is displayed, you must reply to the prompt or select Cancel to continue.

Many dialogue boxes contain a Help button. Selecting the help button will display a help box that explains the purpose and use of the dialogue box.

You can move a dialogue box by moving the pointer over its title box and holding down the key while moving the box. Moving dialogue boxes is useful if you need to pick a screen object that is under the box.

Figure 7-9 shows a typical dialogue box, with the parts labeled.

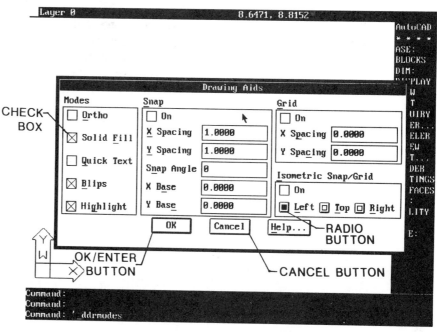

FIGURE 7-9 Typical Dialogue Box

Let's look at the parts of a dialogue box.

SCROLL BARS

A list box can contain more entries than can be displayed at one time. Scroll bars are present on some list boxes that are used to move (scroll) the items up or down.

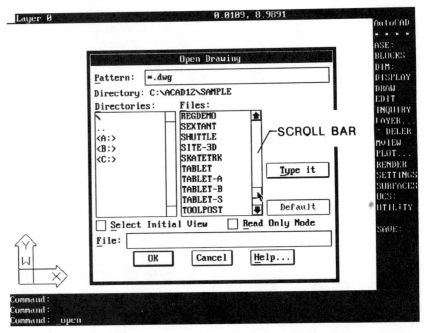

FIGURE 7-10 List Box Scroll Bars

To move the displayed entries up or down one item, move the arrow to either the up or down arrow and click.

If you move the arrow on the slider box and click, you can move the box up or down with the arrow. When you click again, the entries will be redisplayed at the new location. Note that the position of the slider box is relative to the position of the displayed items. Thus, if there are a lot of items in the list, a relatively small movement of the slider box will scroll several items. If you click the slider bar and then wish to cancel before clicking the second time, entering Ctrl-C or Esc will cancel, returning the list to the original location.

BUTTONS IN DIALOGUE BOXES

Buttons are used to select items. The buttons can be selected with the pointer.

Buttons that have a heavy border are the default. Selecting OK from the dialogue box will automatically select the default buttons.

Three periods (...) after a button prompt a sub-dialogue box.

Buttons with three arrow pointers (<<<) refer to an action that is required in the graphics screen, such as selecting an object.

If a button is "grayed out" it is not available at that time.

The following is a summary of the buttons used in dialogue boxes.

> **Check button:** Boxes following items that show a check mark if selected. These are mostly used to "turn on" a function. If a check mark is present, the function is "on".

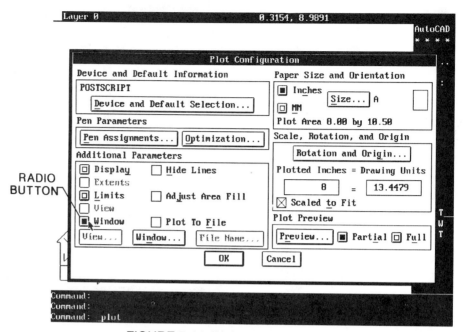

FIGURE 7-11 Dialogue Box Check Button

Radio button: A radio button selects between a series of items, only one of which can be "active" at a time.

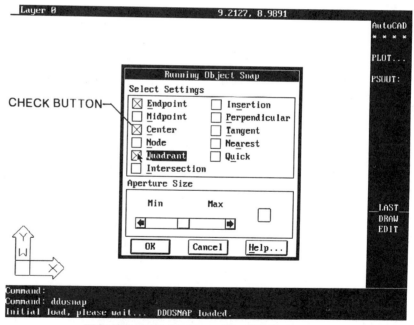

FIGURE 7-12 Dialogue Box Radio Button

List box: A list box contains a list of items that you can choose. List boxes contain scroll bars that allow you to scroll among the available choices.

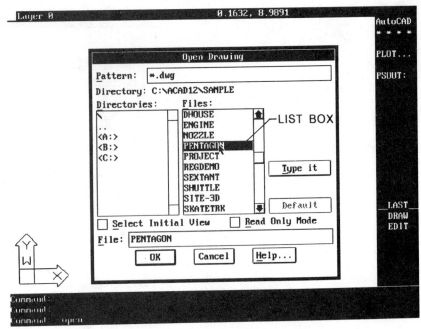

FIGURE 7-13 Dialogue Box List Box

Popup List Box: A popup list box is a type of list box, except it "pops up" when an item with an arrow follows it. An example of a popup list box is shown in Figure 7-14.

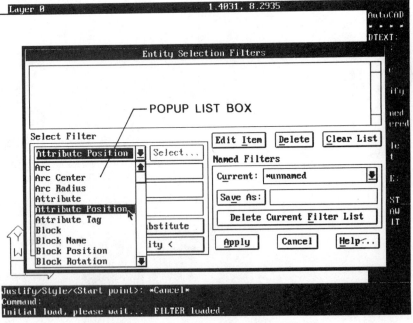

FIGURE 7-14 Dialogue Box Popup List Box

Edit box: Edit boxes contain a single line of text that can be edited. To edit the text in the box, click in the box. A cursor bar will appear at the text. You can move the cursor bar with the arrow keys on the keyboard.

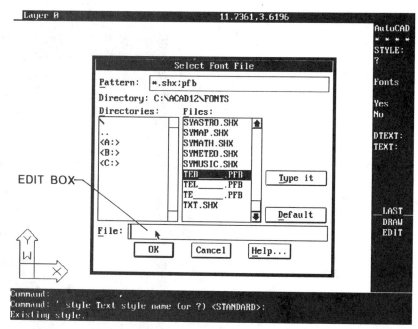

FIGURE 7-15 Dialogue Box List Box

Image tile: Some dialogue boxes contain an image tile. This is a small window that displays a selected item such as a drawing file or line type.

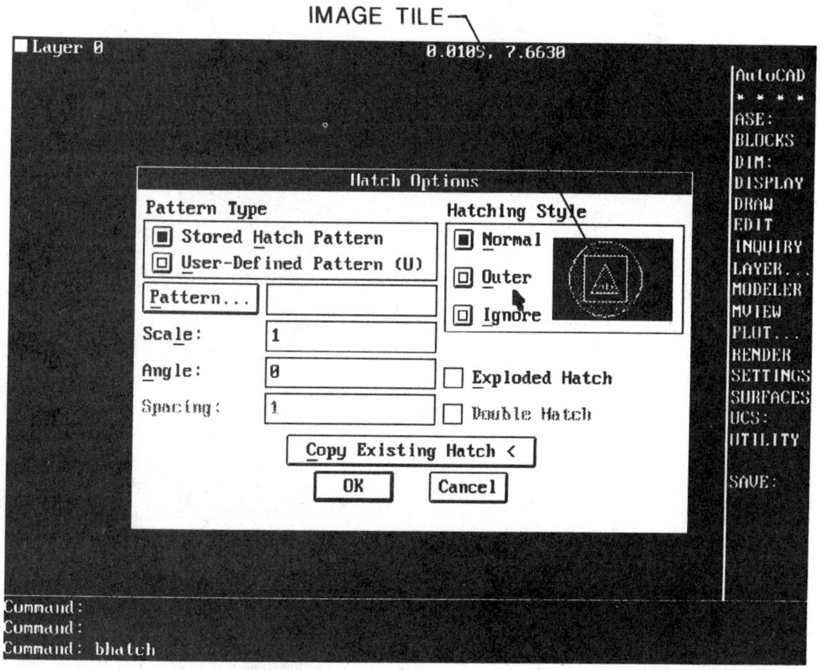

IMAGE TILE

FIGURE 7-16 Dialogue Box Image Tile

ICON MENUS

Icon menus are displayed on the page as graphic images instead of words. You can select the image you wish with the screen pointer. Figure 7-17 shows a sample icon menu.

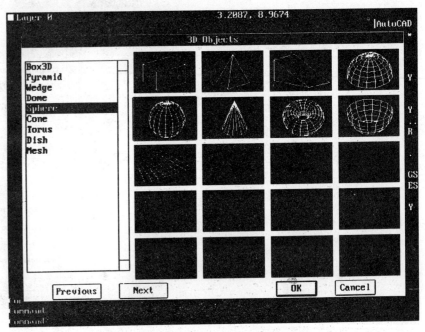

FIGURE 7-17 Icon Menu

Icon menus are prompted by certain command selections. For example, if you select Hatch from the Draw pull-down menu, then the appropriate items, an icon box displaying hatch patterns will be displayed.

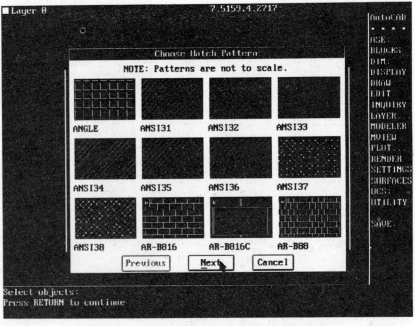

FIGURE 7-18 Icon Menu for Hatch Selection

SELECTING FROM AN ICON MENU

When an icon box appears, the crosshairs change to an arrow pointer. Each selection has a box next to it. If you move the pointer to the box, an outline appears around the selection. Clicking on the selection box will select the item.

An icon box is cleared from the screen by selecting an item, pressing Ctrl-C or the Escape (Esc) key. Any other keyboard activity is suppressed.

STARTING A NEW OR EXISTING DRAWING

When you start AutoCAD, you will either begin a new drawing, or call up an existing drawing you have previously saved. Let's look at how to perform these functions.

STARTING A NEW DRAWING

The NEW command is used to start a new drawing.

The New command is used to start a new drawing. Type New from the keyboard and press the Enter key. AutoCAD will display a *dialogue box.* Enter the new drawing name from the keyboard. The drawing name will be displayed in the dialogue box (see Figure 7-19).

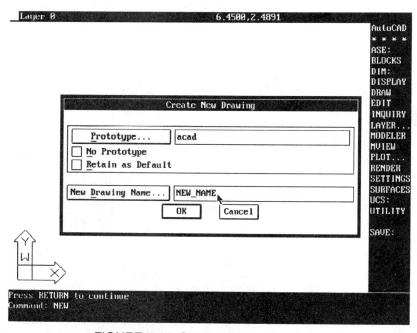

FIGURE 7-19 Starting a New Drawing

Place the pointer over the OK button and click. The drawing editor will return and you will be ready to start your drawing session!

PROTOTYPE DRAWINGS

Your new drawing will be exactly equal to the prototype drawing.

When you begin a new drawing, AutoCAD uses a standard list of settings for the drawing. These settings are taken from a *prototype drawing* named "ACAD". A prototype drawing is a separate drawing containing settings and, optionally, drawing elements, that your new drawing can use as a template. Your new drawing will be exactly equal to the prototype drawing.

Although the default prototype drawing is ACAD, you can use any drawing as a prototype drawing. For example, you may want to create a drawing that contains all the settings you normally use and has a title block already drawn. You could then use this prototype drawing to create a starting point for all your new drawings. Each new drawing that used this prototype would have the same settings and the title block at the moment it was created. It is not necessary, however, to use a named prototype drawing. If you do not select a prototype drawing, AutoCAD will assume the standard settings. Note that you can change any of the settings, regardless of the prototype drawing. The following sections explain how to use prototype drawings with AutoCAD.

Selecting a Prototype Drawing

You select a prototype drawing when a new drawing is started. When you enter New, the **Create New Drawing** dialogue box is displayed. Enter the new drawing name, then click on the "Prototype..." box. A new dialogue box will paste over the top of the existing box.

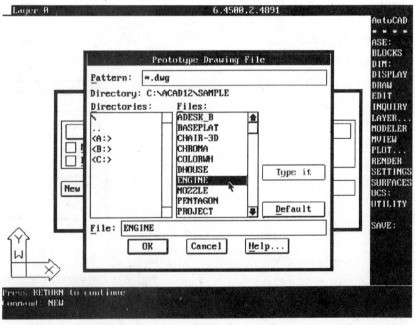

FIGURE 7-20 Selecting a Prototype Drawing

This is the **Prototype Drawing File** dialogue box. Select a prototype drawing from the files list and click on the OK button. You will now be returned to the Create New Drawing dialogue box. Click on OK to start the new drawing.

An alternate method of creating a new drawing with a prototype is to specify the new drawing to be "equal" to another drawing. To do this, simply enter the new drawing name in the **Create New Drawing** dialogue box, then place an equals sign (=) followed by the prototype drawing name.

For example, if you wish to start a new drawing named WIDGET and use a drawing named PROTO1 as the prototype drawing, enter;

WIDGET=PROTO1

as the drawing name in the dialogue box as shown in Figure 7-21.

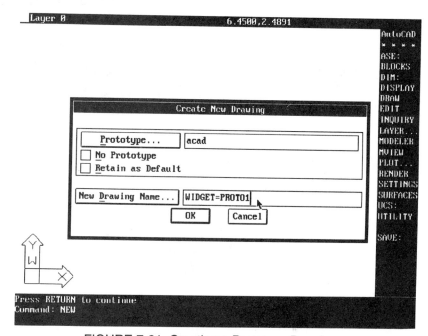

FIGURE 7-21 Creating a Prototype Drawing

Configuring a Default Prototype Drawing

You may wish to retain a drawing as the default prototype. This would allow you to use the default prototype drawing as the template for all new drawings without having to select it each time you start a new drawing. To retain a drawing as the default prototype, click on the **Prototype...** box in the **Create New Drawing** dialogue box and select the drawing you want to use as the prototype from the **Prototype Drawing File** dialogue box that is displayed. Next select OK, then click on the **Retain As Default** box. The following figure shows the sequence.

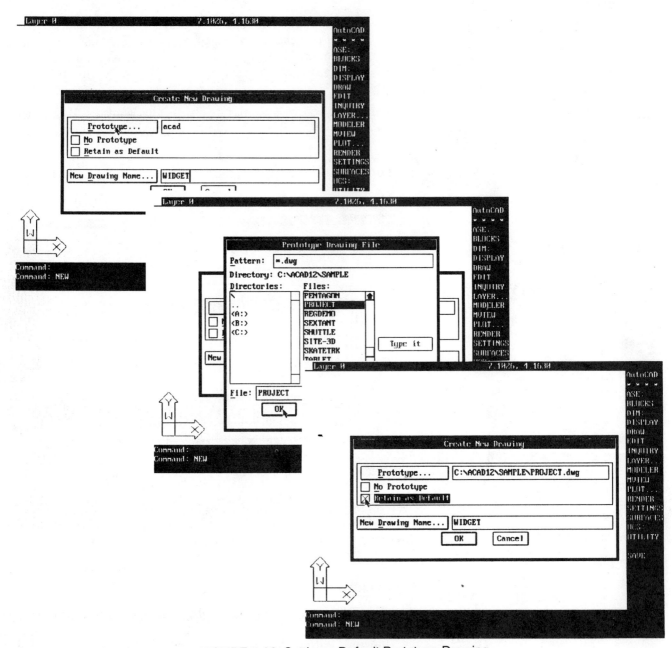

FIGURE 7-22 Setting a Default Prototype Drawing

Starting a New Drawing With No Prototype

If you do not want to use a prototype drawing, click on the **No Prototype** box in the **Create New Drawing** dialogue box. This sets the drawing values to the default settings.

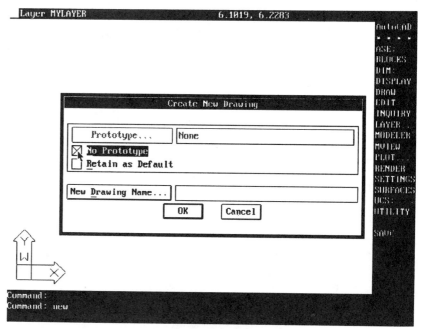

FIGURE 7-23 Starting a New Drawing Without a Prototype

EDITING AN EXISTING DRAWING

To open an existing drawing, use the OPEN command.

Many times a drawing that was previously saved must be edited. In order to edit an existing drawing, you must first "open" it. To open an existing drawing, use the Open command.

When you enter Open from the keyboard, an **Open Drawing** dialogue box is displayed.

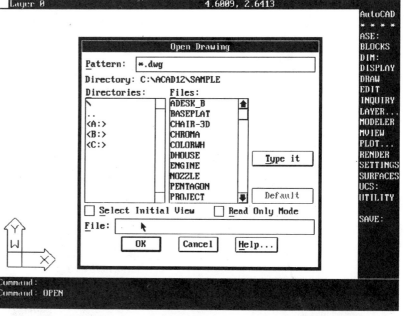

FIGURE 7-24 "Open Drawing" Dialogue Box

Figure 7-25 shows the Open Drawing dialogue box.

To open a drawing, select the drawing from the files listing. When you select the drawing, it will be entered for you on the file line. Click on the OK button to open the drawing. The following figure illustrates the sequence to open an existing drawing file.

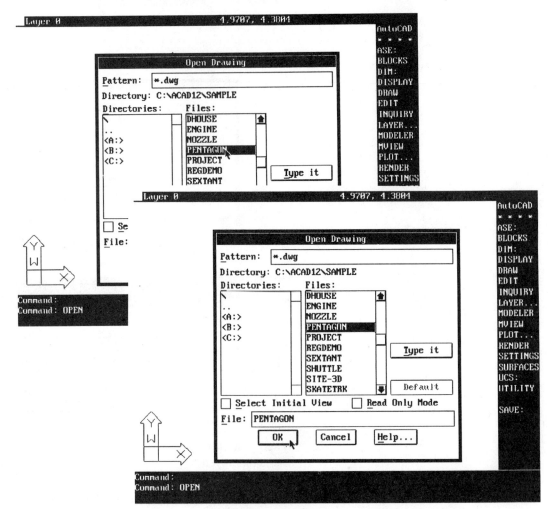

FIGURE 7-25 Opening an Existing Drawing

If you wish to choose a different directory, *"double click"* on the desired directory in the directories listing. Double clicking means to rapidly click the mouse button twice on the entry you desire.

SAVING AND DISCARDING DRAWINGS

Either during a drawing session or when you have completed a session, you will want to either save or discard the work you have just completed. If you save your work, it will be recorded to the hard drive on your computer. A saved file is recorded with the name you specified when the drawing was originated as new.

You may also save your work and remain in the drawing file. It is good practice to save your work to disk periodically. If you experience a power outage or your computer hangs up, you will lose the work completed since you last saved to disk.

If you choose to discard your work, only the part of the drawing performed since the last save will be discarded. If you have not saved any of the work since the drawing was created, discarding the work will delete all instances of the drawing.

SAVING DRAWINGS

There are four commands you can use to save drawings

There are four commands you can use to save drawings. The following listings explains how each method works.

> **SAVE:** Use the Save command if you wish to save your work and remain in AutoCAD. This is useful if you want to save your work at periodic intervals and continue to work. When you use Save, a dialogue box is displayed. You may select the current file name, or a new file name to save the drawing under. Selecting a new file name functions the same as the Saveas commands that follows.

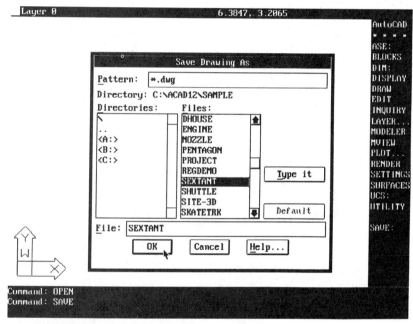

FIGURE 7-26 Dialogue Box Used to Save a Drawing

> **SAVEAS:** The Saveas command is used in the same manner as the Save command, except the drawing is saved in its current state under a new drawing name. When you use Saveas, the **Save Drawing As** dialogue box is displayed.
>
> If AutoCAD is set to suppress dialogue boxes (using the Filedia system variable), a prompt will appear on the command line:
>
> > Save current changes as <default>:
>
> Using the Saveas command creates a new file that contains the drawing in its current state. Note, however, that the original drawing has not been saved. If you wish to save the original drawing you working in, use the Save command.
>
> If you enter the name of a drawing that already exists, Auto-CAD displays the following message box:

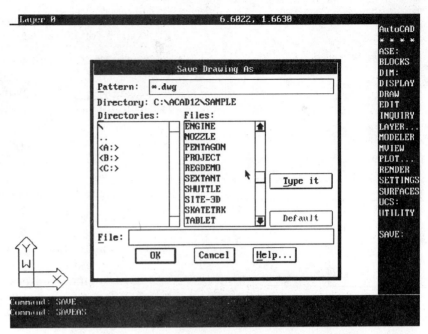

FIGURE 7-27 "Save Drawing As" Dialogue Box

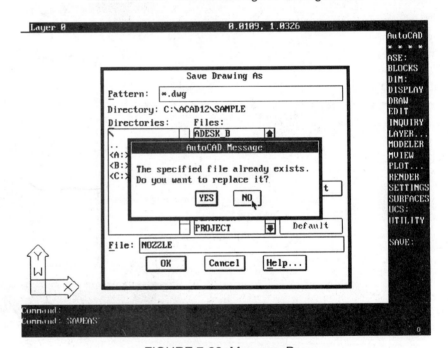

FIGURE 7-28 Message Box

If you want to replace the existing drawing with the new one, click on YES. If you do not, click on the NO button.

WARNING: Selecting YES will write over and delete the existing file.

QSAVE: The Qsave command is functionally the same as the Save command, except the dialogue box is not displayed. The drawing is automatically saved to disk under the name specified when the drawing was created.

END: The End command is used to record the work to disk and exit the AutoCAD program. This is one way to exit the AutoCAD program (see Quit for the other way).

NOTE: Although there are four methods of recording your work to disk, they do not function in the same manner. The Save, Saveas, and Qsave commands "clean up" the drawing file by omitting items marked for deletion (previously erased, etc.). This results in a file size that is smaller. The End command does not perform a cleanup. If you wish to compact your drawing file size and exit AutoCAD, use the Save or Qsave command, then use End or Quit (the Quit command is covered later in this chapter) to terminate your drawing session.

SAVING YOUR DRAWING AUTOMATICALLY

If you wish, you can set a time interval for AutoCAD to save your work automatically. The Savetime system variable is used to set the time interval.

DISCARDING YOUR WORK

Occasionally you will create a drawing that you do not wish to keep. If you want to exit the current drawing, discard the changes, and start a new drawing, use the New command. AutoCAD will display a message box that the drawing has been changed and ask you what you want to do.

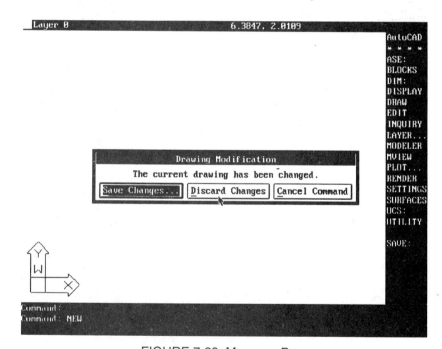

FIGURE 7-29 Message Box

Click on the box you want. The **Create New Drawing** dialogue box will be displayed next.

If you want to exit the drawing, discard the changes, and exit the AutoCAD program, use the Quit command. A message box is displayed asking you whether you wish to save the changes, discard the changes, or cancel the Quit command and reenter the command. The message box is shown in Figure 7-29.

CHAPTER EXERCISES

1. Move the cursor around with your input device (mouse, digitizer, etc.). Do the coordinates at the top of the screen move? Press the F6 function key. Move the cursor again and watch the coordinates.

2. Press the F8 function key. Watch the status line to see the display show the ORTHO mode turn on and off. Press the F9 function key for SNAP mode. Look at the left of the status line. What layer is current?

3. Press Ctrl-C. The command prompt line should clear and display:

    Command:

    Let's select a command. Move the cursor to the right of the screen, and into the screen menu area. Move the input device up and down. Watch the menu highlight bar move along the menu items.

    Stop the menu highlight bar over the entry "DRAW" and click. Notice how the menu changes to a new listing. This is a submenu. From this new menu, select "LINE".

    Move the cursor into the drawing area. Move to any point and click. Now move the cursor and notice the line "rubber banding" from the point you entered to the cursor location. Pick another position and click. Pick a third point and click.

    Cancel the command by entering Ctrl-C. You could also cancel the command by selecting another command.

    Check the command line to verify the prompt says:

    Command:

    If it does not, use Ctrl-C to "clear" it. Type the word "LINE" from the keyboard (it doesn't matter if it is upper or lower case). It will appear on the command line. Return and notice how AutoCAD prompts for the "From point". You can type a command from the keyboard, or choose it from the menu.

4. Move the crosshairs to the top of the drawing area and into the status line. If your display is capable of displaying pull-down menus, a menu bar will appear at the top of the screen.

    A highlight bar will appear over one of the entries. Move the bar from left to right over the entries. Position the bar over the name "DRAW". A pull-down menu will extend down into the drawing area. Move the highlight bar up and down the menu items. You select items the same way as you do from the side screen menu. Move the cursor outside of the pull-down menu and click in an open spot in the screen. The pull-down menu will disappear.

    Select the "DRAW" pull-down menu again and select "LINE". Draw some more lines.

5. Clear the command line with Ctrl-C. Type "FILEDIA" and Enter. Enter a "1" in response to the prompt. This turns on the dialogue boxes.

    From the screen menu, select "LAYER...". Do you see the **Modify Layer** dialogue box?

Let's enter a new layer. Move the cursor. Notice the arrow pointer. Click in the text entry box. Type "MYLAYER". Move the arrow to the New box and click. Notice how the new layer name is now listed in the layer names listing. Make your layer current by clicking on the layer name, then in the "Current" box. Now select the OK box at the bottom of the dialogue box. Look at the layer name on the status line at the top of the screen. Is the layer "MYLAYER" current?

8. If you have a single screen system, press the F1 function key. Do you see the text screen? Press F1 again to return to the drawing screen.

9. Select LINE again. Draw some lines and use Ctrl-C to cancel. Press the enter key. Did the Line command repeat? Clear the command line with Ctrl-C again. Press the spacebar. The Line command will repeat again. Either Enter or the spacebar can be used to repeat a command.

10. Clear the command line again. Enter a question mark from the keyboard and press Enter. You should see the Help dialogue box. Type "LINE" in the text entry box and Enter. Read the help screen.

CHAPTER REVIEW

1. Is it necessary to add a .DWG extension to the drawing name when you create a drawing file from the main menu?

2. When you are ready to plot a drawing, how is the distinction made to let AutoCAD know that you desire a printer plot instead of a pen plot, or vice versa?

3. What is the difference in command functions selected from the screen menu and those selected from pull-down menus?

4. What would be some of the benefits of using prototype drawings?

5. What are mode indicators? Where are they located when turned on?

_____

_____

_____

_____

6. A linkage of menus and submenus progressing from one to another is referred to as what?

_____

_____

_____

7. Must you exit AutoCAD to copy or delete a file?

_____

_____

_____

8. List the control and\or function key associated with the following definitions.

turns Ortho mode on and off _____

turns the printer echo on and off _____

used to turn on or redisplay the crosshairs_____

removes characters from the prompt line one at a time_____

allows you to toggle between graphic and text screens_____

toggles Tablet mode on and off _____

turns on the menu cursor _____

cancels all the characters on the command line_____

toggles to the next isometric plane in iso mode_____

used the same as the backspace key_____

cancels the current command
and returns to the command line _____

toggles the screen coordinate display on and off_____

toggles the grid on and off_____

toggles snap on and off _____

9. After executing a command, and you have returned to the command prompt, what happens when you press the Enter key?

_____

_____

_____

10. How is the Help facility invoked?

_____

_____

_____

11. What is the purpose of the prompt area?

_____

_____

_____

CHAPTER 8

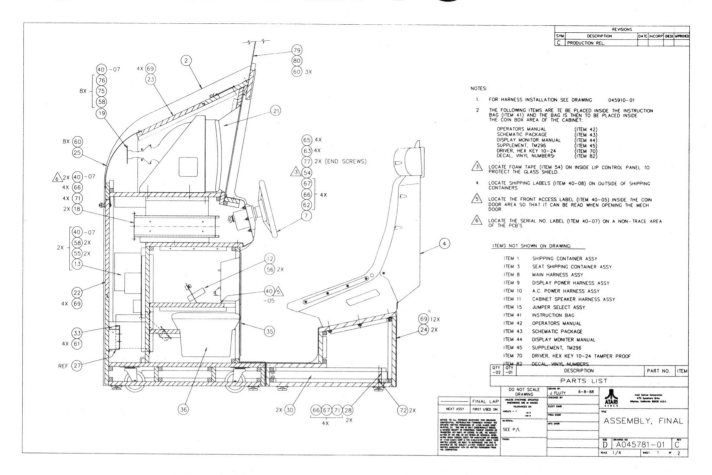

Setting Up a Drawing

OBJECTIVES:

Before starting any drawing, you should set the type of measurement units to be used, and the size of the workspace. In this chapter you will learn the following.

● To understand the difference between the available methods of measurement in AutoCAD.

● To set the type of measurement used in your drawing.

● Set the size of the workspace in the current units.

● To set units and limits that will match the size of plot media and scale.

● Display the status of the current drawing.

Handwritten margin notes:
Units
Linear   Angular
Scientific
decimal
engineering
Architectural
Fractional

SETTING UP A DRAWING

If you begin a drawing on a traditional drawing board, you start by determining the scale and size of the drawing. You would not draw the first line before choosing the paper size, or before selecting the scale at which you would construct the drawing.

AutoCAD uses settings that somewhat parallel these decisions. You could, as you have seen, just start drawing with AutoCAD's default settings. The problem is that these settings are not suitable for every type of drawing. Consider the difference between architectural and engineering (decimal) scales, or the differences between drawing on 8½" × 11" and 36" × 48" media.

To properly use AutoCAD, you must learn to perform some basic settings. In this chapter, we will learn the following concepts and commands:

* **Units:** Setting AutoCAD to draw in specified units such as architectural, engineering, decimal, or scientific. *Fractional*
* **Limits:** Setting the actual "real world" drawing area.
* **Scaling:** Setting units and limits to match a desired plot scale.
* **Status:** Displaying the settings in the drawing.

SETTING THE DRAWING UNITS

Since CAD programs are utilized in many different types of work, the units in which distances are measured can be many. An engineer, scientist or architect may require different notations for coordinates, distances and angles. AutoCAD provides the capabilities for each through the *Units* command. Setting the units is the first step in setting up a new drawing.

To set the units format for your drawing, select "Units Control." from the Settings pull-down menu. AutoCAD will display a dialogue box that you will use to set the type of units. Figure 8-1 shows the dialogue box.

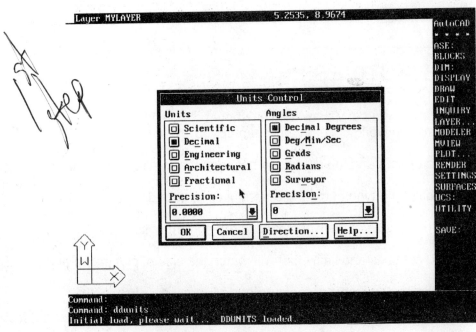

FIGURE 8-1 Units Control Dialogue Box

The first "section" of the dialogue box is titled "Units". Let's look at the available choices.

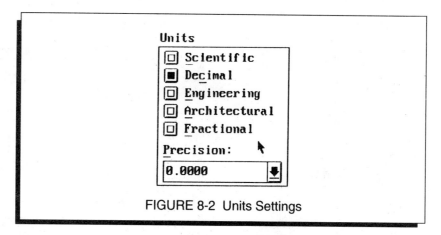

FIGURE 8-2 Units Settings

There are five selections:

Scientific: AutoCAD provides scientific units for use in projects that deal with very large dimensions. An example of scientific units represents 21.75 units as 2.175E+01.

Decimal: Decimal units are common in engineering drawings. An example of decimal units would be 21.75.

Engineering: Engineering units are used for applications such as civil engineering such as highway construction. In engineering units, 1' 9¾" would be shown as 1'-9.75".

Architectural: Architectural drawings use the feet, inches, and fractions style of showing measurements. For example, 1' 9¾" is an example of architectural units.

NOTE: The Architectural format designates that one unit equals one inch.

Fractional: AutoCAD can also be set to display fractional units. An example of fractional units would be 21¾.

To set the desired units, simply click on the corresponding radio button next to listing.

SETTING THE PRECISION FOR THE UNITS

After you have selected the format, you should set the precision for the coordinates and distances. For example, if you choose architectural format, you will need to determine the smallest fractional denominator. To do this, use the popup list box to change the number in the precision box.

SETTING THE ANGLE MEASUREMENT

After selecting the format and the precision for the units, set the method of angle measurement. The angle measurement setting determines the type of coordinate listing (at the top of the drawing editor screen), and the type of input you enter from the keyboard.

The type of angle measurement is set in the right box of the **Units Control** dialogue box.

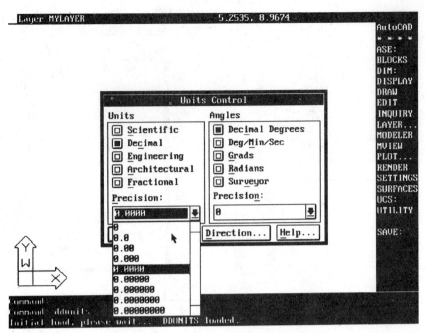

FIGURE 8-3 Setting Units Precision

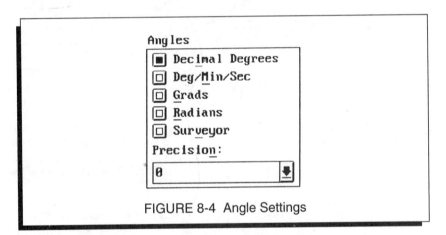

FIGURE 8-4 Angle Settings

Settings
Pull down
Gets Units Controls
· Units   Angles

Angular

AutoCAD can display five types of angle measurement. The following is a listing of the different types of measurement and an example of each.

Decimal degrees: Using decimal degrees will instruct AutoCAD to display whole degrees as whole numbers and partial degrees as decimals (45.0000).

Degrees/minutes/seconds: Degrees can be represented as whole degrees, with partial degrees represented as "minutes", and partial minutes as "seconds". One degree contains 60 minutes and one minute contains 60 seconds. AutoCAD uses a "d" to represent degrees, a (') to designate minutes and a (") to represent seconds. For example, 22 degrees, 14 minutes, 45 seconds is listed as 22d14'45".

Grads: AutoCAD can also specify angles in grads. An example is 35.0000g.

Radians: For mathematical work, you can use radians to display angle. An example is 0.678r.

Surveyor's units: Surveyor's units are used to designate property lines. They are a form of the degrees/minutes/seconds type of

Surveyor's units are degrees/minutes/seconds format.

format, except that they are relative to compass points. An example is N22d15'32"W, with "N" and "W" representing North and West, respectively.

To set the angle measurement for your drawing, select the radio button next the type of angle measurement you wish to use.

SETTING THE PRECISION FOR THE ANGLE MEASUREMENT

After you have specified the angle format, set the precision of the angle format. You may select up to eight decimal places. The angle precision is set at the angle precision box and in the same manner as explained before.

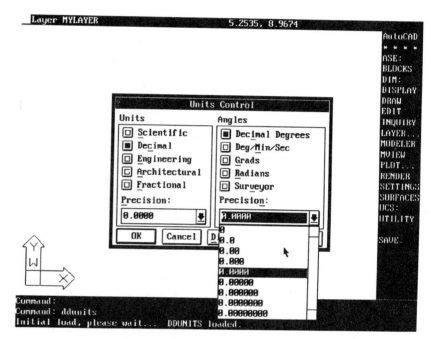

FIGURE 8-5 Setting Angle Precision

SETTING THE ZERO-ANGLE DIRECTION

The zero-angle direction is set by first selecting the "Direction..." button. The resulting dialogue box appears as follows.

AutoCAD, by default, sets the angle zero to the right (east). This setting makes all angles that have a direction of zero read to the right. You may set the zero angle to display in any direction you wish (this will not affect text in the drawing, since you set the text angle relative to this setting).

For example, you may want the zero angle to be straight up on the screen. Selecting "North 90.0" would achieve this. To set the desired zero angle direction, select the radio button next to the desired listing.

After have you selected the zero angle direction, you can designate whether AutoCAD measures angles in a clockwise or counter-clockwise direction. As you become familiar with the operation of some commands, you will better understand the effect of this setting. The default setting is counterclockwise.

Once you have set the type of unit measurement and the method of angle definition, the settings will remain in effect throughout the

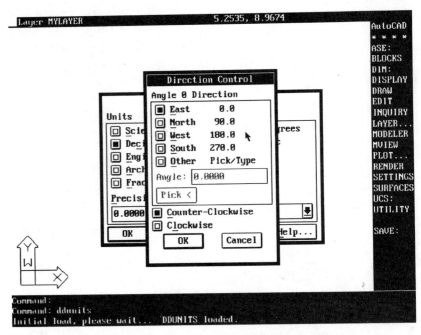

FIGURE 8-6 Setting Zero-Angle Direction

PROFESSIONAL TIP

You may, if you wish, "show" AutoCAD the new angle for "0". To do this, you must use the Units command instead of the dialogue prompted by the pull-down menu. When you enter the Units command, you will be prompted for the settings on the text screen. If you are working with a dual screen system, you will see both the drawing and the text screen. If you are using a single screen system, you will have to use the F1 (flip screen) key to toggle back to the drawing, as described below

To show AutoCAD the zero direction, when you are prompted for the "Direction for angle 0:", press the F1 key to display the drawing screen, then select any point on the screen. Next, move the cursor in the direction of the desired angle and enter a second point.

This can be especially useful if you must work in reference to a certain angle.

remainder of the drawing. If you save your drawing and return, the settings will remain intact. It is only necessary to set the units when you are beginning a new drawing.

You can alternately use a prototype drawing to preset the drawing units.

SETTING DRAWING LIMITS

Setting the *Limits* of your drawing allows you to determine the size of working area which you need to draw in. This can be important, since the area needed to construct different types of drawings can be dramatically different. For example, a grid map showing an area of a city or a detailed section of a watch would obviously require different limits.

learn 37

Setting Limits

Limits = working Area

In order to better understand how drawing limits work, you should also read the following section on "scaling your drawings".

Limits are set in the <u>current drawing units</u>. For this reason, you should set the units <u>before</u> specifying the limits. <u>To set the limits, select the "Drawing Limits" from the Settings pull-down menu, or the Limits command from the Settings screen menu.</u> The following sequence is shown at the command line.

```
Command: LIMITS
Reset Model space limits:
ON/OFF/<Lower left corner> <default>:
```

Let's look at each of the command line options.

ON: Turns the limits "on". When limits are on, you may only draw within the area of the limits.

OFF: Turns the limits "off". When limits are off, you may draw either inside or outside the area defined by the limits.

LOWER LEFT CORNER: The default, allows setting of the lower left corner (by coordinates) for the drawing area. If you enter a coordinate for the lower left corner, you will be prompted for the coordinate of the upper right corner.

```
Command: Limits
Reset Model space Limits:
On/Off/Lower left corner <current>:
Upper right corner <current>:
```

ENTER: Retains the current (default) value for the lower left corner and prompts you for the coordinates for the upper right corner.

The initial setting of the drawing limits is determined by the prototype drawing. You may, however, change the drawing limits at any time with the Limits command. The following exercise will help you better understand the use of the limits command.

LIMITS EXERCISE

Let's suppose that you would like to set limits that have 180.00 units horizontal (X value) and 120.00 units vertical (Y value). First, verify that the units are set to decimal units. Next, from the Root menu, select the Settings menu and choose Limits.

```
Command: Limits
Reset Model space limits:
On/Off/Lower left corner <current value>: 0,0
Upper right corner <current value>: 180,120
```

This will set limits that have a lower left corner origin at 0,0 and an upper right corner at the coordinates at 180,120.

You do not have to retain 0,0 for the lower left corner; however this should be maintained unless you have special circumstances which require it.

NOTES ABOUT LIMITS:

1. *The screen does not display the new limits after setting. Make a habit of executing a "zoom all" after setting new limits. This displays the actual "drawing page size" on the screen.*

2. *To see the size of your "drawing page", turn on a grid pattern. This will allow you to visualize the "edges" of your paper.*

1.125
.250
1.375

SCALING YOUR DRAWINGS

One of the hardest concepts for a new CAD user to grasp is that of scale. Some of the most-asked questions are:

How do the drawing limits and the plot size relate?

Does the plot scale affect the size of my limits?

How do I know where the edges of the paper are? I need to see the paper size on the drawing to compose the work.

All you need to answer these questions is just some simple arithmetic.

First of all, with the exception of architectural units, you draw in generic units. Not in feet, inches, miles or anything else. A unit may equal one centimeter or it may equal one mile. AutoCAD really doesn't care what your units equal. Until you plot.

At the time of the plot, you must specify what one unit is equal to. You do this by telling AutoCAD that one inch, (or one centimeter if you are working in centimeters) is equal to x number of units on the paper. For example, if 1" = 10 units and you have determined that one unit would equal a foot when you began drawing, then the scale of the plot would be 1" = 10' (remember, you determined that one unit equals one foot).

Let's suppose that you were planning to plot on paper that was 36" × 24". How would you set limits that were in true relation to the page size?

First, since you intend to plot at 1" = 10', and one inch on the paper will contain ten units, we can multiply the dimensions of the paper by the units per inch and determine the number of units contained in both dimensions of the paper.

$$10 \text{ units/inch} \times 36" = 360 \text{ (X limit)}$$
$$10 \text{ units/inch} \times 24" = 240 \text{ (Y limit)}$$

If you now set limits of 0,0 (lower left) and 360,240 (upper right) the limits will match the page size (assuming again that you intend to plot at one inch equals ten units and you have assigned one unit to equal one foot).

You may, of course, change plotting scale at a later time. If you do, you will have to change the limits if you desire to "match" the limits to the paper size.

Knowing the methodology of calculating the sheet size to the intended plotting scale allows you to set up your drawing to see the available "drawing page" size.

Table 8-A shows the relationship between drawing scale and plot sheet size. You can use this table to set up the limits for your drawings.

CHECKING THE DRAWING STATUS

AutoCAD has a multitude of modes, defaults, limits, and other parameters that you will occasionally require knowledge of. The Status command displays the current state or value of each of these. The status command may be used any time you are in the drawing editor. To enter it, choose Inquiry from the Root menu, and then Status.

Command: <u>Status</u>

You will be presented with a text page layout as shown in the following illustration.

SHEET SIZE

FINAL PLOT SCALE	A 11 x 8½	B 17 x 11	C 24 x 18	D 36 x 24	E 48 x 36
1/16	176', 136'	272', 176'	384', 288'	576', 384'	768', 576'
3/32	132', 102'	204', 132'	288', 216'	432', 288'	576', 432'
1/8	88', 68'	136', 88'	192', 144'	288', 192'	384', 288'
3/16	66', 51'	102', 66'	144', 108'	216', 144'	288', 216'
1/4	44', 34'	68', 44'	96', 72'	144', 96'	192', 144'
3/8	29'-4", 22'-8"	45'-4", 29'-4"	64', 48'	96', 64'	128', 96'
1/2	22', 17'	34', 22'	48', 36'	72', 48'	96', 72'
3/4	14'-8", 11'-4"	22'-8", 14'-8"	32', 24'	48', 32'	64', 48'
1	11', 8'-6"	17', 11'	24', 18'	36', 24'	48', 36'
1½	7'-4", 5'-8"	11'-4", 7'-4"	16', 12'	24', 16'	32', 24'
3	3'-8", 2'-10"	5'-8", 3'-8"	8', 6"	12', 8'	16,' 12'

SHEET SIZE

FINAL PLOT SCALE	A 11 x 8½	B 17 x 11	C 24 x 18	D 36 x 24	E 48 x 36
10	110, 85	170, 110	240, 180	360, 240	480, 360
20	220, 170	340, 220	480, 360	720, 480	960, 720
30	330, 255	510, 330	720, 540	1080, 720	1440, 1080
40	440, 340	680, 440	960, 720	1440, 960	1920, 1440
50	550, 425	850, 550	1200, 900	1800, 1200	2400, 1800
60	660, 510	1020, 660	1440, 1080	2160, 1440	2880, 2160
100	1100, 850	1700, 1100	2400, 1800	3600, 2400	4800, 3600
Full Size	11, 8.5	17, 11	24, 18	36, 24	48, 36

Table 8-A

```
5458 entities in C:\ACAD12\SAMPLE\HOUSEPLN
Model space limits are X:      0'-0"    Y:      0'-0"   (World)
                        X:    128'-3"   Y:     91'-3"
Model space uses        X:   -128'-3"   Y:    -91'-3"
                        X:      0'-0"    Y:      0'-0"
Display shows           X:   -128'-3"   Y:    -91'-3"
                        X: 0'-7 7/16"   Y: 1'-7 5/8"
Insertion base is       X: -64'-1 1/2"  Y: -44'-9 11/16"  Z:      0'-0"
Snap resolution is      X:      0'-6"   Y:      0'-6"
Grid spacing is         X:      1'-0"   Y:      1'-0"

Current space:      Model space
Current layer:      0
Current color:      BYLAYER -- 7 (white)
Current linetype:   BYLAYER -- CONTINUOUS
Current elevation:      0'-0"  thickness:      0'-0"
Fill on  Grid off  Ortho on  Qtext off  Snap on  Tablet off
Object snap modes:   None
Free disk: 19058688 bytes
Virtual memory allocated to program: 5196 KB
Amount of program in physical memory/Total (virtual) program size: 55%
-- Press RETURN for more --
Total conventional memory: 16 KB     Total extended memory: 3072 KB
Swap file size: 1104 KB
Command:
```

FIGURE 8-7 Drawing Status Screen

CHAPTER EXERCISES

1. Calculate drawing limits for a drawing that will be plotted on a 24" × 18" sheet of paper at ¼"=1'-0" scale.

2. Calculate drawing limits for a drawing that will be plotted on a 36" × 24" sheet of paper at 1"=50.00'.

3. Use the Status command to check the limits of your current drawing.

CHAPTER REVIEW

1. How might you obtain a listing of your drawing parameters?

_____

_____

2. How are angles measured in surveyor's units?

_____

_____

3. What choices of units systems are available under the units option?

_____

_____

_____

4. What might you do to visualize the drawing limits you have set?

_____

_____

5. Can the zero angle position be altered? How?

_____

_____

_____

6. Why should the units of a drawing be set before the limits?

_____

_____

_____

7. What restrictions apply to your drawing when the Limits are turned on?

_____

_____

8. Why would you want to change the zero angle setting from the default position?

_____

_____

_____

9. What is the only exception to drawing in generic units?

_____

_____

10. At what point does AutoCAD need to know the units you have used to construct your drawing?

_____

_____

CHAPTER 9

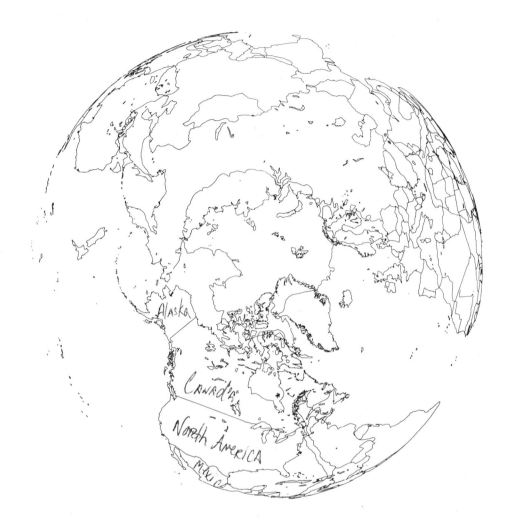

Getting Started

OBJECTIVES:

Most CAD drawing activities involve the most basic drawing commands. Objectives for Chapter 9 are:

● To learn the most basic drawing commands.

● To use display commands to magnify and maneuver around the drawing.

● To learn the commands used to save and record work to disks.

AutoCAD
In The
Real
World

U.S. Coast Guard Uses AutoCAD to Design and Upgrade Fleet
AutoCAD Increases Productivity

Phillip Stevens' daily office routine isn't so routine anymore. The 41-year-old U.S. Coast Guard ship designer taps a few keys on his PC in the morning and, faster than you can say "ship ahoy," a 17,000-ton polar icebreaker appears on his screen.

Stevens has recently become proficient at using AutoCAD for his drafting work. His previous tools were little more than pencil and paper.

Now, with a quick flick of the mouse in his right hand, he spins the ice breaker design at will and instantly zooms in on any compartment of the ship.

He scans the vessel fore and aft to make corrections to the electrical system. He could just as easily examine any of more than 60 systems in the ship, ranging from plumbing to armaments. All are readily visible to him in layered, multi-colored lines featuring a near 3-D appearance.

The Coast Guard's new design tool, AutoCAD on a PC, replaces an obsolete and more expensive minicomputer system. It is expected to increase the drafting staff's productivity at least 30%, by placing more automation into the hands of more people.

AutoCAD is used to prepare conceptual and preliminary designs of new vessels and to make periodic alterations to the 245 ships and patrol boats in the Coast Guard fleet.

The use of AutoCAD on a PC has worked out better than the Coast Guard expected. Some of the pluses are:

• **Improved Productivity.** The Coast Guard estimates that using AutoCAD saves about thirty-nine hours of every completed drawing.

• **Better Quality and Uniformity.** With standardized symbols and lettering, the Coast Guard's drawings now have a neater, more professional look.

• **Expanded Capabilities.** The Coast Guard sees growing uses for its new system in design-related areas. For example, updating the ship drawings will now take a few hours, where it used to take weeks.

Adapted with permission from an article by Peter Heyne, in *CADENCE*, copyright © 1989, Ariel Communications, Inc.

GETTING STARTED

Now that we know how to set up a drawing, let's jump in and start drawing right now. We will be using some basic drawing commands, modes, and assistance. They are:

LINE: Drawing basic line entities.

POINT: Constructing point entities.

CIRCLE: Drawing circle by different methods.

ARC: Constructing multiple types of arcs.

OBJECT SNAP: Connecting precisely to points on an entity.

REDRAW: Clearing the drawing screen of clutter.

REGEN: Regenerating the drawing display from the database.

ZOOM: Enlarging and reducing the view of the drawing.

PAN: Moving the screen around the drawing.

GRID: Placing "grid paper" dots on the screen.

SNAP: Setting a drawing increment.

ORTHO: Forcing cursor movements to be either perfectly horizontal or vertical.

DRAGMODE: Determining whether items are moved "real time" on the screen.

U (single undo): Undoing a single drawing operation.

REDO: Negating an undo operation.

DRAWING LINES

To draw a line, you must first select the Line command.

Lines are drawn with the Line command. The line command is the most basic part of a CAD program. To draw a line, you must first select the Line command.

DRAWING A LINE

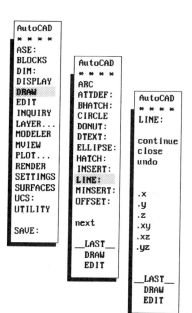

In the Main Menu select DRAW. You will then be presented with the draw submenu. From the submenu, select LINE.

You will notice that two things happen. First, the command line prompts you for a "From point". Second, you are presented with a special "Line menu." Before we proceed to draw, let's first talk about "from points" and "to points."

You must first show AutoCAD which point you wish to start drawing from. Think of this as the place which you put your pencil to the paper. This is the "from point." Now you must determine the point at which the line will end. This is the "to point." Since many drawings contain lines that connect, (such as a box consisting of four consecutive and connecting lines) the "to point" prompt is repeated until you terminate the command by choosing CANCEL from the menu, entering Ctrl-C, or pressing the Enter key a second time. This allows you to enter a series of lines without the inconvenience of invoking the Line command each time.

LINE EXERCISE

Let's draw a box using the Line command.

        Command: <u>LINE</u>
        From point: (*enter point 1*)
        To Point: (*enter point 2*)
        To Point: (*enter point 3*)
        To Point: (*enter point 4*)
        To Point: (*enter point 1*)

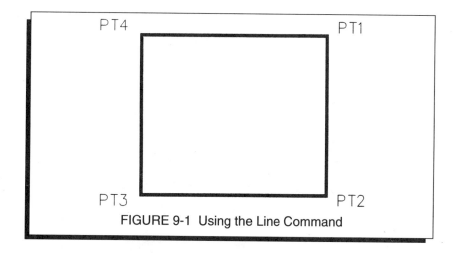

FIGURE 9-1 Using the Line Command

You may have noticed that the line "stretched" behind the crosshair. This is called *rubberbanding*.

DRAWING LINES FROM THE PULL-DOWN MENU

Select the Line command from the Draw pull-down menu. You will notice that a submenu appears that contains several options. Let's look at the options.

Segments: Lines are drawn in the same manner you use when selecting the Line command from the screen menu. The command will repeat until canceled, allowing you to draw several line "segments" without the necessity of reentering the Line command.

1 Segment: After a single line segment is drawn, the Line command is terminated.

Double Lines: Allows you to draw two parallel lines at one time.

Sketch: Sketching is "free hand" drawing.

LINE OPTIONS

There are some drawing aids which are associated with the Line command. These aids provide assistance that is unique to a CAD drawing system. These are found on the Line submenu (screen menu).

They are:

1. Continue
2. Close
3. Undo

Let's continue and look at each option.

CONTINUE

If you terminate the line command, you are free to begin a new line elsewhere. However, if you wish to go back and begin at the last endpoint, you may "reconnect" by using the Continue option. This option is found in the line submenu.

CLOSE

When you constructed the box, the last line you drew was connected to the beginning point. Aligning the end of the line with the beginning of the first line was a tedious process, wasn't it? The Close option will automatically perform this for you. Let's construct the box again. This time we will connect the lines at the final intersection with the Close option.

```
Command: LINE
From point: (enter Point 1)
To point: (enter Point 2)
To point: (enter Point 3)
To point: (enter Point 4)
To point: CLOSE
```

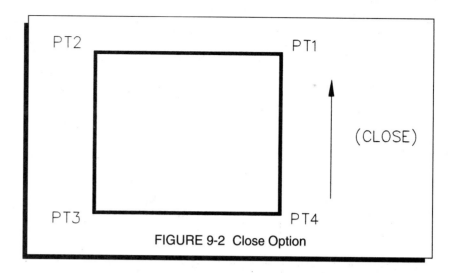

PT2   PT1

                                     (CLOSE)

PT3   PT4

FIGURE 9-2 Close Option

The Close option may be used to return to the start (from point) of any consecutive string of lines. Using Close will terminate the string.

UNDO

Sometimes you may draw a line in the series that you wish to erase. Instead of the time-consuming task of erasing and then reconnecting with the continue option, you can "step back" through the series. This is accomplished with the Undo option. Undo takes you back, one line segment at a time. Undo is used while you are still active in the Line command. Since the Undo option does not repeat, you do not have to terminate the command. When you have backed up to the desired point, simply continue the line entries. Notice that the Undo option in the Line command is similar to the U command, except that it can be used on a single line segment while the Line command is active. Using the U command after the Line command undoes all lines drawn by that Line command.

CANCELING THE LINE COMMAND

Unless you are using the Segment option in the pull-down menu, you can cancel the command by pressing the Enter key, using Ctrl-C, or by selecting another command from the menu.

DRAWING LINES BY USING COORDINATES

Accurate drawing construction requires that lines and other entities in a drawing be placed in a precise manner.

One method of placing lines and other entities precisely is the use of coordinates. There are three types of two dimensional coordinates: absolute, relative, and polar. Let's look at each type and learn how to use them.

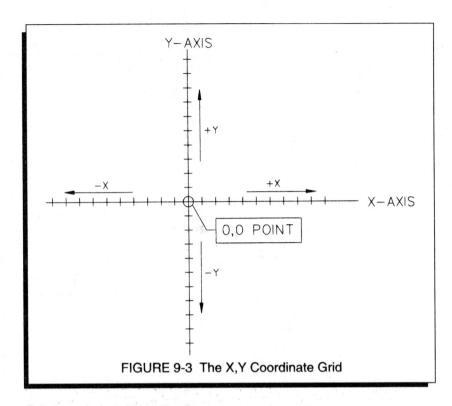

FIGURE 9-3 The X,Y Coordinate Grid

ABSOLUTE COORDINATES

Absolute coordinates specify a point on an X,Y grid, with the 0,0 point as a reference. Let's look at how the X,Y coordinate grid works. Figure 9-3 shows a coordinate grid. The 0,0 point is at the center of the grid.

Notice that the grid has two lines, known as axes. There is an X-axis that runs horizontally and a Y-axis that runs vertically. The intersection of the X and Y axis is located at the 0,0 point. The increments increase in positive numbers as you move to the right on the X-axis and up on the Y-axis. Likewise, they decrease to the left in the X-axis and down along the Y-axis.

The AutoCAD drawing screen can be overlaid on the grid as shown in Figure 9-4. Notice that the 0,0 point is in the lower left corner of the screen. This is the "normal" work screen in AutoCAD. If you remember, when we learned how to set the drawing limits in Chapter 8, we set the lower left drawing corner to 0,0. This places the AutoCAD screen in the upper right quadrant of the grid where all the X and Y values are positive.

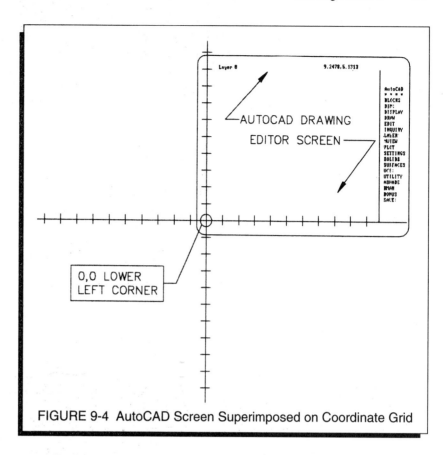

FIGURE 9-4 AutoCAD Screen Superimposed on Coordinate Grid

A single point on the grid can be identified by a coordinate.

A single point on the grid can be identified by a coordinate. This coordinate is called an absolute coordinate and is specified by the numeric value of the location where it lines up with the X and Y axes, in respect to the 0,0 point. That designation is listed in an "X,Y" format. Let's look at an example.

Figure 9-5 shows a coordinate grid with the AutoCAD screen placed in the normal location. The point 6,4 is shown on the grid. Notice that it is six units to the right along the X-axis and four units up on the Y-axis.

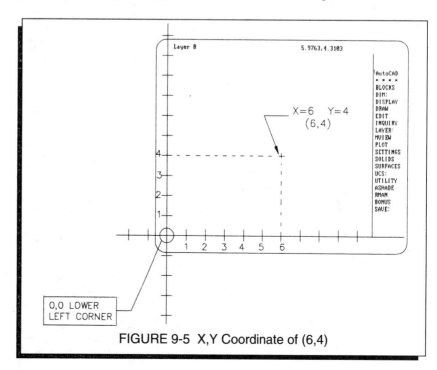

FIGURE 9-5 X,Y Coordinate of (6,4)

We can use absolute coordinates to specify points for our commands. Consider the example of a line command. If we select the line command, we are first prompted for the beginning point, then the end point of the line segment. If we enter 2,2 for the beginning point and 5,4 for the end point, we will draw a line as shown in Figure 9-6.

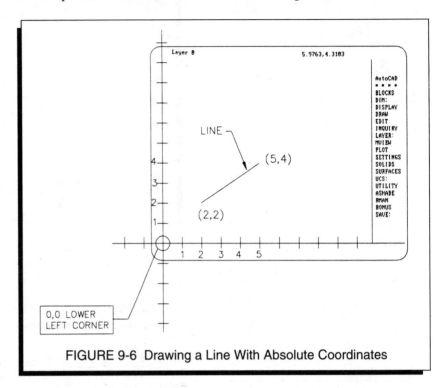

FIGURE 9-6 Drawing a Line With Absolute Coordinates

Let's practice our knowledge of absolute coordinates in the following exercises.

ABSOLUTE COORDINATE EXERCISES

1. Draw lines on grid paper, connecting the points designated by the following absolute coordinates.

   x y

   Point 1: 1,1
   Point 2: 5,1
   Point 3: 5,5
   Point 4: 1,5
   Point 5: 1,1

2. Use the following illustration to fill in the missing absolute coordinates. Each side of the shape is dimensioned. Place the answers in the boxes provided.

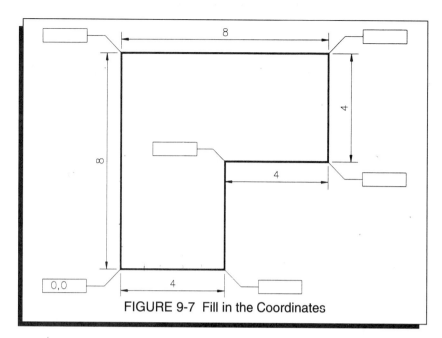

FIGURE 9-7 Fill in the Coordinates

3. List the length of each side of the object in Figure 9-8. (Calculate from the absolute coordinates given).

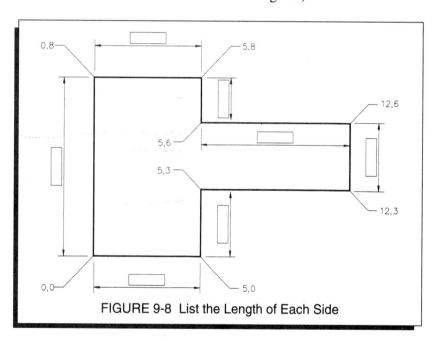

FIGURE 9-8 List the Length of Each Side

RELATIVE COORDINATES

Relative coordinates are not specified from the 0,0 point, but from any *given point*. Relative coordinates are typically specified from the last point entered. By their nature, relative coordinates can not be the first point entered.

Relative coordinates are specified in the same X,Y format as absolute coordinates. The difference is that absolute coordinates describe the X,Y distance from the *0,0 point* and relative coordinates describe the distance from the *last point entered*. Let's look at an example.

always
use
@
has A comma
don't use degrees

We can draw the same line we constructed in Figure 9-8 with relative coordinates. Refer to Figure 9-9.

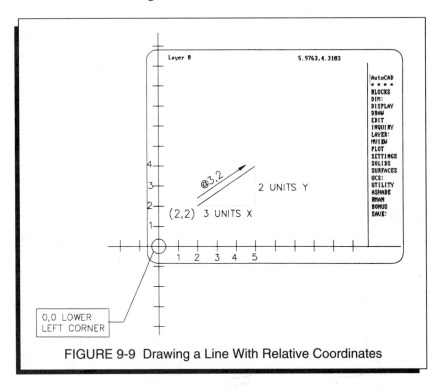

FIGURE 9-9 Drawing a Line With Relative Coordinates

If we choose the line command, we can specify the first point with the absolute coordinate of 2,2. When prompted for the end point of the line segment, we can enter:

@3,2

Notice the format used. The "@" symbol is used to specify a relative coordinate. You can think of this as "at the last point, go 3 units in the X-direction and two units in the Y-direction." The "@X,Y" format is always used in this manner.

Our line will be drawn three units X and two units Y from the first point (2,2) as shown in Figure 9-9. Note also that you could have entered the first end point of the line by simply moving the cursor on the screen and entering the beginning point wherever you wished.

Let's use the following exercises to test our knowledge of relative coordinates.

RELATIVE COORDINATE EXERCISES

1. Use the following coordinates to draw the object.

   Point 1: 0,0
   Point 2: @3,0
   Point 3: @0,1
   Point 4: @-2,0
   Point 5: @0,2
   Point 6: @0,-1
   Point 7: 0,0

2. List the coordinates used to draw the following object. Use relative coordinates.

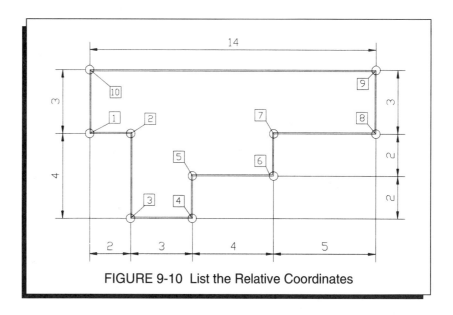

FIGURE 9-10 List the Relative Coordinates

POLAR COORDINATES

Polar coordinates are a type of relative coordinates. Polar coordinates, however, specify a point by defining a distance and angle from the last point. The format is:

@distance<angle

Before we can properly specify an angle, we need to look at the default AutoCAD angle specification. Figure 9-11 shows the angles used by AutoCAD. The default direction for angle zero is to the right (east). The default angle rotation is counter-clockwise. The direction for angle zero and the angle rotation direction can be changed with the Units command.

Now that we know AutoCAD's angle specifications, let's look at an example using polar coordinates. We could specify the endpoints of a line by entering the first endpoint, then entering;

@10<30

for the endpoint of the segment. This would draw a line segment that is 10 units and 30 degrees from the first point as shown on the graph in Figure 9-12.

As you proceed through each of AutoCAD's commands you will acquire a perception of the best method of point entry to be used for the task.

always us @

uses < sign in degrees

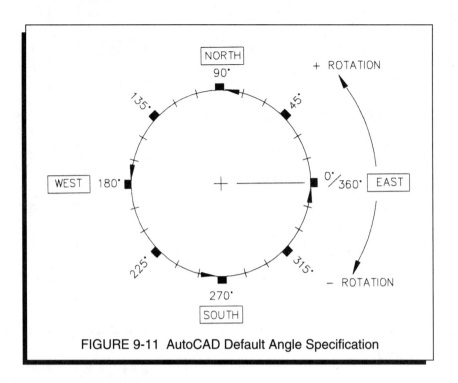

FIGURE 9-11 AutoCAD Default Angle Specification

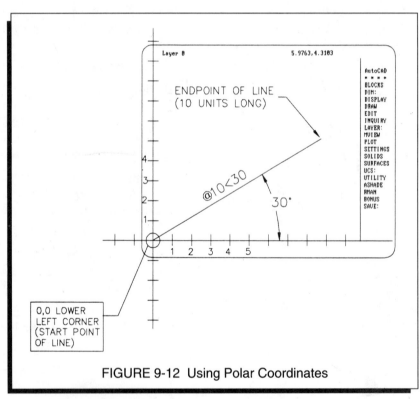

FIGURE 9-12 Using Polar Coordinates

POLAR COORDINATE EXERCISES

1. Use the following coordinates to draw the object.

> Point 1: 0,0
> Point 2: @4<0
> Point 3: @4<120
> Point 4: @4<240

2. List the coordinates used to construct the following object. Use polar coordinates whenever possible.

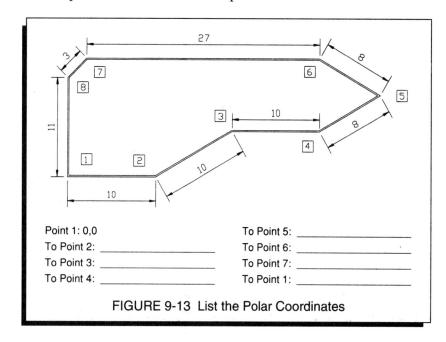

Point 1: 0,0

To Point 2: _____   To Point 5: _____

To Point 3: _____   To Point 6: _____

To Point 4: _____   To Point 7: _____

                             To Point 1: _____

FIGURE 9-13 List the Polar Coordinates

COORDINATE EXERCISES

Write a list of the coordinates used to construct the following objects. You may use any combination of absolute, relative, or polar coordinates.

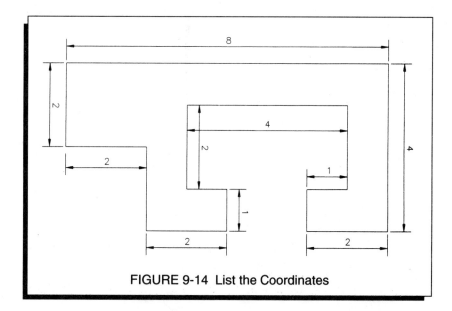

FIGURE 9-14 List the Coordinates

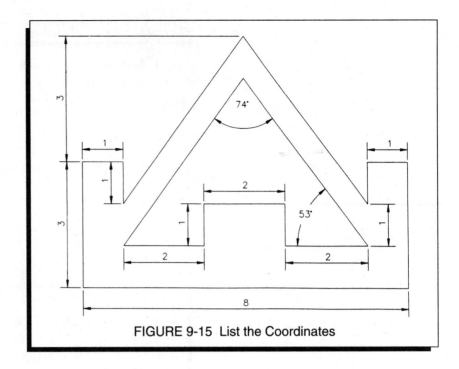

FIGURE 9-15 List the Coordinates

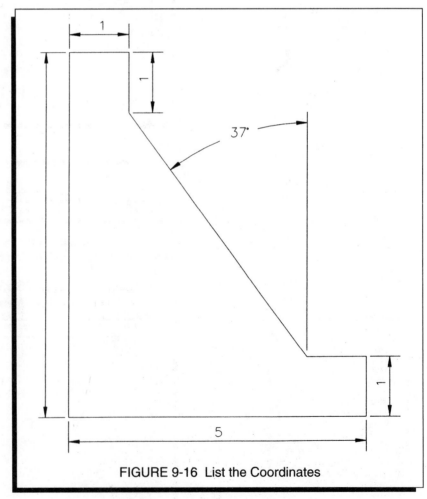

FIGURE 9-16 List the Coordinates

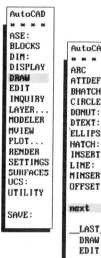

You can specify the type and size of point you want by using the Pdmode and Pdsize; system variables.

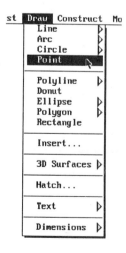

DRAWING POINTS

A point, by default, is a dot (like a single touch of a pen point) that is placed on the drawing. To place the point, enter the DRAW menu and select POINT.

> Command: Point
> Point: (enter)

POINT TYPE AND SIZES

Points can also be different designs. You can specify the type and size of point you want by using the Pdmode and Pdsize system variables. These variables are accessed through the Setvar command or by selecting Pdmode or Pdsize from the POINT submenu. You may also use Pdmode and Pdsize as commands, typing them directly on the command line. Pdmode designates the type of point drawn and Pdsize controls the size of the point entry.

Let's look at how to specify a particular point type using Pdmode. You may set a Pdmode value of 1 to 4 to select a figure to be drawn at the point. The following table shows each setting and its corresponding figure:

VALUE	POINT TYPE DRAWN
0	·A DOT ON THE POINT (DEFAULT)
1	NOTHING
2	+ A CROSS THROUGH THE POINT
3	× AN "X" THROUGH THE POINT
4	ǀ VERTICAL LINE (UPWARD FROM THE POINT)

FIGURE 9-17 Point Types

You may also add a circle, square, or both to the point. Each of these figures also has a numerical value. To add one of these to the point entity, simply add the numerical value to the point figure in the preceding table. The following table shows the values of the circle, box, and both:

VALUE	POINT TYPE DRAWN
32	◯ CIRCLE AROUND POINT
64	☐ SQUARE AROUND POINT
96	◲ BOTH CIRCLE AND SQUARE

FIGURE 9-18 Adding Point Figures

Adding the values allows several point types.

Adding the values allows several point types. The following illustration shows the possible combinations and their corresponding point entities:

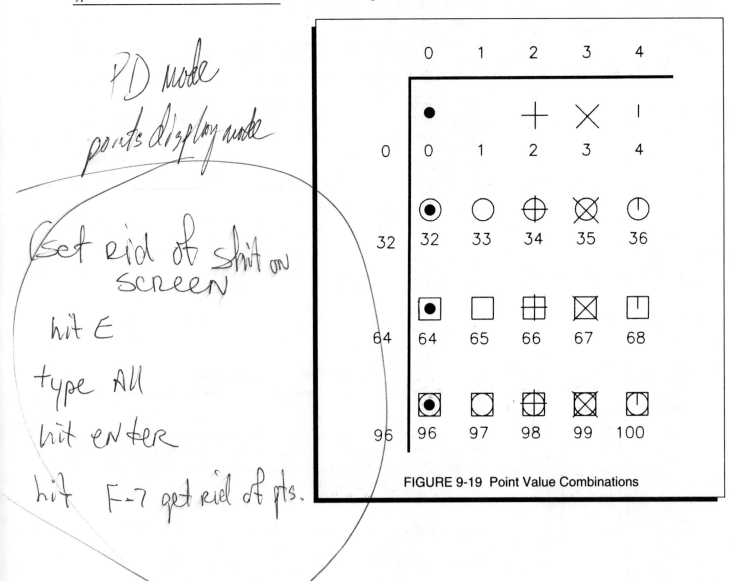

FIGURE 9-19 Point Value Combinations

PD mode

points display mode

Get rid of shit on
screen

hit E

type All

hit enter

hit F-7 get rid of pts.

POINT COMMAND EXERCISE

Let's set up a point type of 66 and place it in our drawing. First, execute the Setvar command:

> Command: <u>SETVAR</u>
> Variable name or ?: <u>PDMODE</u>
> New value for PDMODE <*default*>: <u>66</u>

Each point entered after setting a new Pdmode will be the type specified. Point entities entered before changing to the new setting will be updated at the next command that causes a regeneration. To place the point we defined in the drawing, enter:

> Command: <u>POINT</u>
> Point: (*enter location on screen*)

Pdsize controls the size of the point entities. Pdmode values of 0 and 1 are not affected by Pdsize. If a positive number is entered, an absolute size for the point entity is specified. If the number is negative, AutoCAD uses the number as a percentage of the screen size. Thus, if you zoom in or out, the size is approximately the same in relation to screen size.

> **WARNING: Pdmode and Pdsize are retroactive. Setting new Pdmode or Pdsize values will change all existing points to reflect the new size and style.**

DRAWING CIRCLES

AutoCAD provides six methods of constructing circles. These are:

1. Center and radius
2. Center and diameter
3. Two point circles
4. Three point circles
5. Tangent circles
6. Tangent three-point circles

Let's look at each type of circle construction. It is helpful to read each brief section, then follow the short exercise that follows.

DRAWING A CIRCLE WITH CENTER AND RADIUS

AutoCAD allows you to enter the center point of the circle and stipulate the radius. The radius may be designated by either entering a numerical value or showing AutoCAD the distance on the screen by entering a point on the circumference of the circle.

EXERCISE

Let's construct a circle with a radius of 5. From the main menu, select DRAW. From the DRAW menu, select CIRCLE. You will be presented a special Circle menu on the screen. You may then select the type of entry desired. Select "CEN,RAD".

> Command: <u>CIRCLE</u>
> 3P/2P/TTR/<Center point>: (*select a point on the screen*)
> Diameter/<Radius>: <u>5</u>

AutoCAD provides six methods of constructing circles.

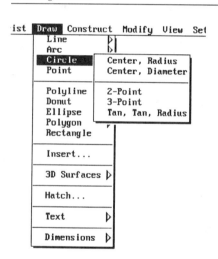

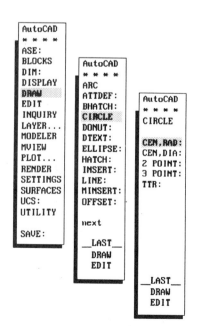

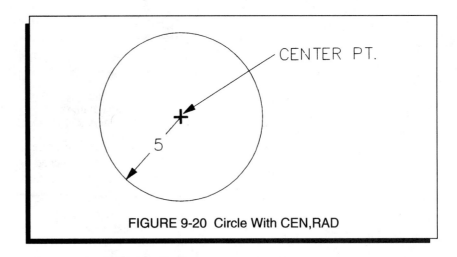

FIGURE 9-20 Circle With CEN,RAD

```
AutoCAD
* * * *
CIRCLE

CEN,RAD:
CEN,DIA:
2 POINT:
3 POINT:
TTR:




__LAST__
DRAW
EDIT
```

DRAWING A CIRCLE WITH CENTER AND DIAMETER

A circle may be constructed by stipulating the center point and a diameter. Either pick CEN,DIA from the circle menu or enter "D" when prompted for the diameter or radius. You will then be prompted for the diameter.

EXERCISE

Let's suppose you want to construct a circle using a center point and a diameter of 3.

Command: <u>CIRCLE</u>
3P/2P/TTR/<Center point>: (*enter point 1*)
Diameter/<Radius>: <u>D</u>
Diameter: <u>3</u>

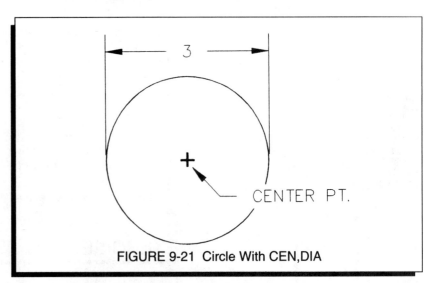

FIGURE 9-21 Circle With CEN,DIA

DRAWING A CIRCLE BY DESIGNATING TWO-POINTS

Responding to the "3P/2P/<Center point> prompt with "2P" allows you to construct the circle by showing AutoCAD two points on the circumference.

```
Command: CIRCLE
3P/2P/TTR/<Center point>: 2P
First point on diameter: (select first point)
Second point on diameter: (select second point)
```

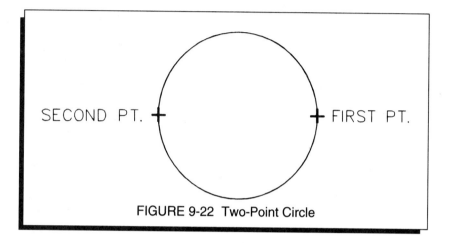

FIGURE 9-22 Two-Point Circle

DRAWING A CIRCLE BY DESIGNATING THREE POINTS

A circle may also be drawn by simply entering three points on the circumference.

```
Command: CIRCLE
3P/2P/TTR/<Center point>: 3P
First point: (select first point)
Second point: (select second point)
Third point: (select third point)
```

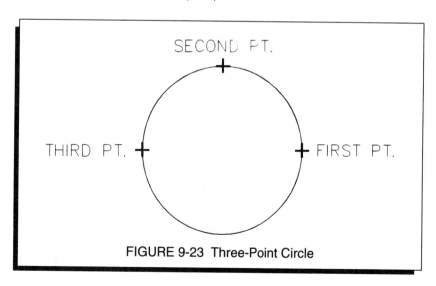

FIGURE 9-23 Three-Point Circle

DRAWING CIRCLES TANGENT TO OBJECTS

AutoCAD allows you to construct circles tangent to lines or circles. You can do this by identifying two lines, two circles, or one line and one circle to construct a tangent circle to, and the tangent circle's radius. To construct tangents, choose the "TTR" (tangent, tangent, radius) option from the Circle submenu.

> Command: CIRCLE 3P/2P/TTR/<Center point>: TTR
> Enter Tangent spec: (*select first circle/line-point "A"*)
> Enter second Tangent spec: (*select second line/circle-point "B"*)
> Radius: (*enter value*)

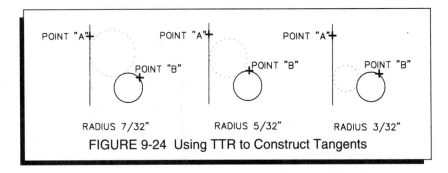

FIGURE 9-24 Using TTR to Construct Tangents

The following illustrations show the different effects of the TTR command in constructing circles tangent to lines and/or circles.

DRAWING TANGENT THREE-POINT CIRCLES

Three-Point circles may be constructed to any combination of lines and circles by specifying each point using the TANgent snap mode option. Let's look at an example of this. Construct a square box of two units on each side as shown in the following illustration. Enter the Circle submenu and choose "3 POINT".

> Command: CIRCLE 3P/2P/TTR/<Center point>: 3P
> First point: TANGENT to (*choose point "A"*)
> Second point: TANGENT to (*choose point "B"*)
> Third point: TANGENT to (*choose point "C"*)

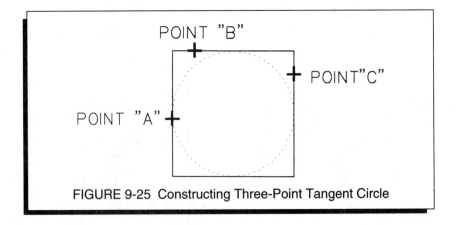

FIGURE 9-25 Constructing Three-Point Tangent Circle

Arcs are segments of a circle.

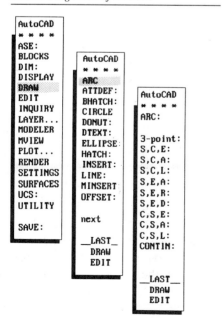

Choose the TANgent option from the override mode OSNAP submenu by picking the "* * * *" from the screen menu, or set up the TANgent option in continuous from the OSNAP submenu under the SETTINGS menu.

The following illustrations show 3-point circles constructed using the TANgent object snap method.

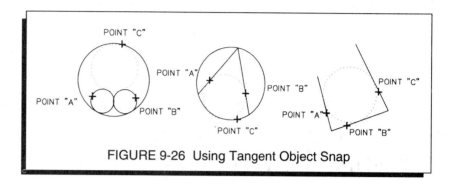

FIGURE 9-26 Using Tangent Object Snap

DRAWING ARCS

Arcs are segments of a circle. There are eleven different methods of constructing an arc in AutoCAD. To properly utilize the Arc command, you must have a thorough understanding of the different ways in which it can be used. You may specify an arc in the following ways:

1. Three points on an arc
2. Start, center and end point
3. Start, center and included angle
4. Start, center and length of chord
5. Start, end and included angle
6. Start, end and radius
7. Start, end and starting direction
8. Center, start and end point
9. Center, start and included angle
10. Center, start and length of chord
11. Continuation of a previous line or arc

References to "center" mean the radius point of the arc.

If you do not specifically choose any of the above combinations of arc construction, method one (three points on an arc) is used as the default.

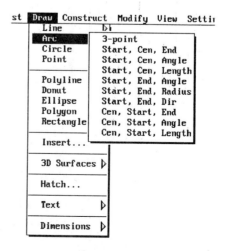

Although eleven methods might seem like a lot to learn, you really only have to understand a few principles to able to use them all.

The arc menu uses letters which designate particular methods of arc construction. The arc command options are designated by the following:

A — included Angle
C — Center
D — starting Direction
E — End point
L — Length of chord
R — Radius
S — Start point

By using combinations of the abbreviations, you can specify any type of arc construction you wish. For example, to construct an arc using the start, center and end points, the correct choice from the arc menu would be S,C,E.

Let's review each of the methods of arc construction and look at some examples.

DRAWING THREE-POINT ARCS (3-POINT)

The "three points on an arc" is the default method of constructing an arc. The first and third points are the endpoints of the arc, while the second point is any point on the arc which occurs between the beginning and end points.

Command: ARC
Center/<Start point>: (enter point "1")
Center/End/<Second point>: (enter point "2")
End point: (enter point "3")

Three point arcs may be constructed from either direction (clockwise or counterclockwise). The arc will run from the first point toward the second and third points.

The arc will run from the first point toward the second and third points.

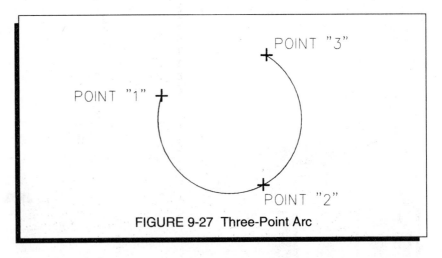

FIGURE 9-27 Three-Point Arc

START, CENTER, AND END (S,C,E)

This method constructs an arc counterclockwise from the start to the specified end point. The arc will be constructed from a radius using the specified center point. The radius will be equal to the actual distance from the center point to the start point. For this reason, the arc will not pass through the specified end point if it is not the same distance from the center.

Relative coordinates and specified angles from the center point may be used if desired.

Some examples of angles constructed with this method are shown in the following illustration.

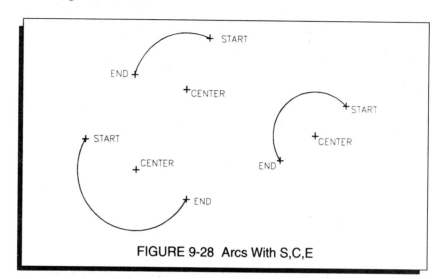

FIGURE 9-28 Arcs With S,C,E

AutoCAD
* * * *
ARC:

3-point:
S,C,E:
S,C,A:
S,C,L:
S,E,A:
S,E,R:
S,E,D:
C,S,E:
C,S,A:
C,S,L:
CONTIN:

__LAST__
DRAW
EDIT

START, CENTER, INCLUDED ANGLE (S,C,A)

This method draws an arc with a specified start and center point and of an indicated angle. The arc is drawn in a counterclockwise direction if the indicated angle is positive and clockwise if the indicated angle is negative. Examples of arcs constructed by this method are shown in Figure 9-29.

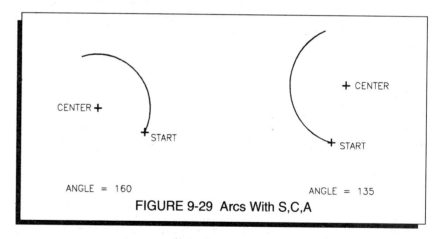

FIGURE 9-29 Arcs With S,C,A

START, CENTER, LENGTH OF CHORD (S,C,L)

A chord is a straight line connecting an arc's start and end point.

A chord is a straight line connecting an arc's start and end point. (See Figure 9-30).

In some applications, an arc of a specified chord length is required. AutoCAD allows construction of such an arc and allows the user to specify the chord length.

For construction of this type of arc, the chord length is used to determine the ending angle. The arc is drawn in a counterclockwise direction. An example of an arc with a specified chord length is shown in the following illustration.

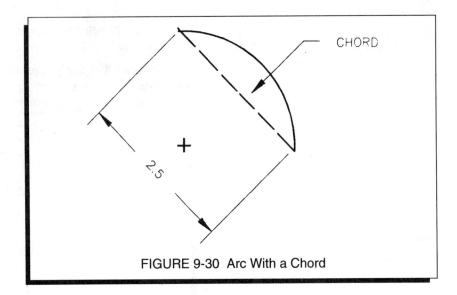

FIGURE 9-30 Arc With a Chord

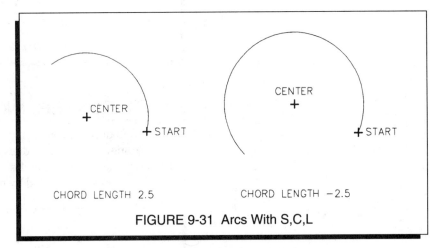

FIGURE 9-31 Arcs With S,C,L

START, END, INCLUDED ANGLE (S,E,A)

This type of arc is drawn counterclockwise if the specified angle is positive, and clockwise if the specified angle is negative.

Two examples, one using a positive angle, and one using a negative angle are shown in Figure 9-32.

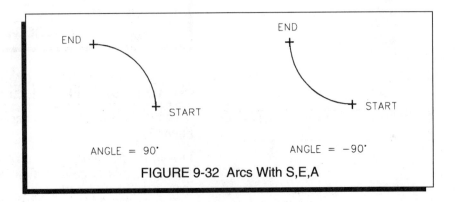

FIGURE 9-32 Arcs With S,E,A

```
AutoCAD
* * * *
ARC:

3-point:
S,C,E:
S,C,A:
S,C,L:
S,E,A:
S,E,R:
S,E,D:
C,S,E:
C,S,A:
C,S,L:
CONTIN:


__LAST__
DRAW
EDIT
```

START, END, RADIUS (S,E,R)

This type of arc is always drawn counterclockwise from the start point and normally will draw the minor arc. However a negative value for the radius will cause the major arc to be drawn. Two examples of this type of arc are shown in the following illustration.

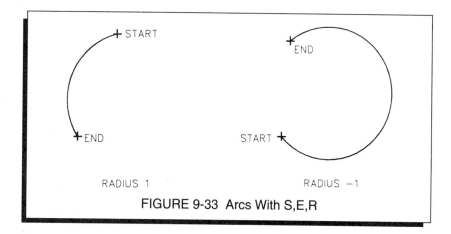

FIGURE 9-33 Arcs With S,E,R

```
AutoCAD
* * * *
ARC:

3-point:
S,C,E:
S,C,A:
S,C,L:
S,E,A:
S,E,R:
S,E,D:
C,S,E:
C,S,A:
C,S,L:
CONTIN:


__LAST__
DRAW
EDIT
```

START, END, STARTING DIRECTION (S,E,D)

This method allows you to draw an arc in a specified direction. It will create an arc in any direction, clockwise or counterclockwise, major or minor. The type of arc depends strictly on the relation of direction specified from the starting point. You may specify the direction by using a single point.

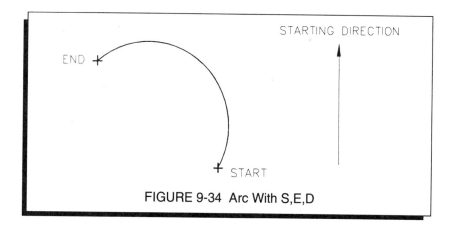

FIGURE 9-34 Arc With S,E,D

```
AutoCAD
* * * *
ARC:

3-point:
S,C,E:
S,C,A:
S,C,L:
S,E,A:
S,E,R:
S,E,D:
C,S,E:
C,S,A:
C,S,L:
CONTIN:


__LAST__
DRAW
EDIT
```

```
AutoCAD
* * * *
ARC:

3-point:
S,C,E:
S,C,A:
S,C,L:
S,E,A:
S,E,R:
S,E,D:
C,S,E:
C,S,A:
C,S,L:
CONTIN:


__LAST__
DRAW
EDIT
```

CENTER, START AND END POINT (C,S,E)

The construction method is similar to the SCE option, except the order of entry is different.

CENTER, START AND INCLUDED ANGLE (C,S,A)

Constructs an arc from a specified center point, using a start point and an included angle that describes the length of the arc. The construction method is similar to the SCA method, except for the order or entry.

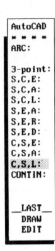

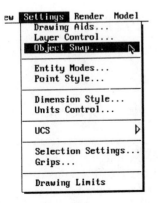

CENTER, START AND LENGTH OF CHORD (C,S,L)

This method of construction draws an arc that is described from a center point, then a point that designates the start of one end of the arc. The other end is specified by the length of a chord from the first endpoint to a second endpoint. This is similar to the SCL method, except for the order of entry.

LINE/ARC CONTINUATION (CONTIN)

This method allows you to attach an arc to a line or arc previously drawn. To invoke this method, simply respond with a space or RETURN when prompted for the first point. The start point and direction are taken from the end point and starting direction of the previous line or arc drawn.

This method is very useful for smooth connection of arcs to lines and other arcs.

An example of this method is shown in Figure 9-35.

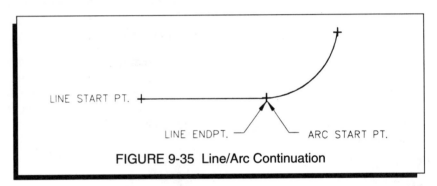

FIGURE 9-35 Line/Arc Continuation

MANUAL ENTRY METHOD OF CONSTRUCTING AN ARC

In addition to the arc menu's choices for arcs, you may choose your own combination and order of input to construct an arc.

After entering the arc command, simply type one of the letters which designates a particular option (for example, "C" for Center) and press Enter. AutoCAD will then prompt you for the designated information.

You may also use this method even if you have already entered one of the sequences of the arc menu. Doing so will allow you to change the order or even the method of entry.

USING OBJECT SNAP

You have probably noticed in your drawings, that you spend a great deal of time lining up points on the screen. Connecting to desired points on lines, circles, arcs, and other entities can be a very tedious procedure.

AutoCAD has provided a drawing aid that makes this process much easier. It is called "object snap".

Object snap provides a "window" that is attached to the intersection of the crosshairs. This window is called an "Aperture." You may stipulate parts

You may stipulate parts of an entity, such as an endpoint or intersection, that can be "captured" if they are within the aperture .

Object Snaps only work on objects *(handwritten note)*

of an entity, such as an endpoint or intersection, that can be "captured" if they are within the aperture (sort of like target practice). These points are then treated as though you entered them precisely from the screen.

Object snap can be used "in the middle" of commands that request the entry of a point. We can refer to this use of object snap as "temporary mode" because the object snap will only be effective for one operation. For example, if you are using the Line command and wish to place the endpoint of the currently drawn line segment in the middle of a circle, you would choose object snap mode CENter before placing the point.

Let's look at an example. The following command sequence illustrates how you would connect a line to the center point of a circle as shown in Figure 9-36.

Command: <u>LINE</u>
From point: (*point "1"*)
To point: <u>CEN</u>
of (*point "2"*)
To point:

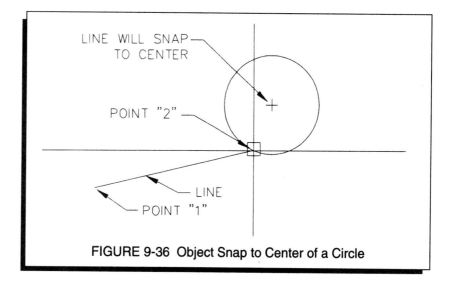

FIGURE 9-36 Object Snap to Center of a Circle

OBJECT SNAP MODES

The following modes describe the different object snap capture methods, with an illustration of each application.

CENter: Captures the center point (radius point) of a circle or arc. The aperture must contain a part of the circle or arc in order to identify the entity.

ENDpoint: Causes the nearest endpoint of a line or arc to be captured.

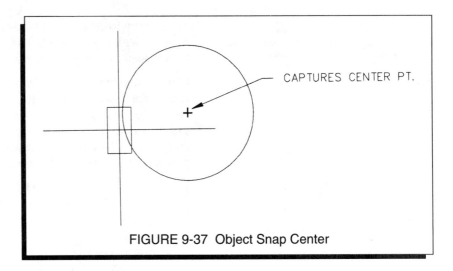

FIGURE 9-37 Object Snap Center

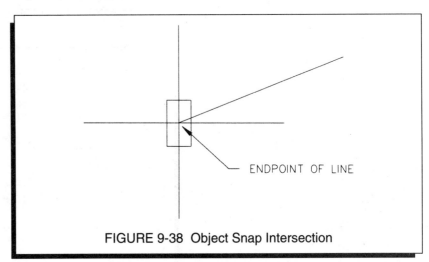

FIGURE 9-38 Object Snap Intersection

INSert: Captures the insert point of a block.

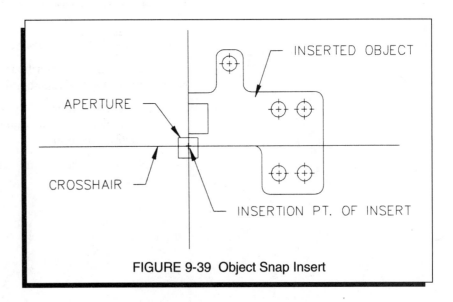

FIGURE 9-39 Object Snap Insert

INTersection: Captures the intersection of two lines, of a line and either a circle or an arc, or the intersection of two circles and/or arcs.

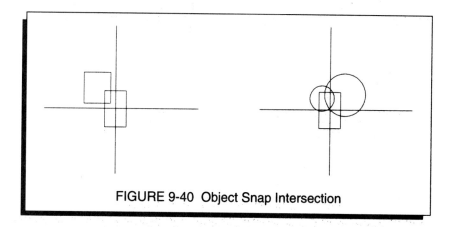

FIGURE 9-40 Object Snap Intersection

MIDpoint: Captures the midpoint of a line or arc.

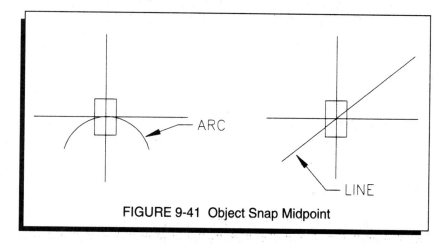

FIGURE 9-41 Object Snap Midpoint

NEArest: This causes the nearest point on a line, circle or arc to be captured. Circles and arcs that are part of a block are not captured.

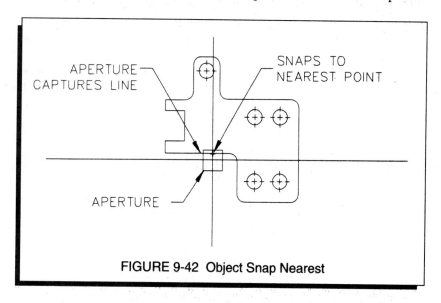

FIGURE 9-42 Object Snap Nearest

NODe: Snaps to a point.

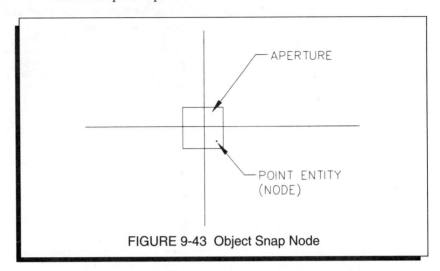

FIGURE 9-43 Object Snap Node

QUAdrant: Snaps to the nearest quadrant point of a circle or arc. The quadrants are the parts of a circle or arc that occur at 0, 90, 180, and 270 degrees. Only the parts of an arc that are visible will be captured. If the circle or arc is part of a rotated block, the quadrant points are rotated with it.

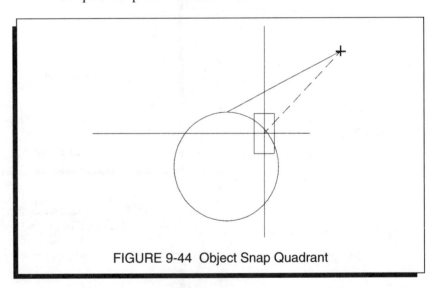

FIGURE 9-44 Object Snap Quadrant

PERpendicular: Snaps to a point on the entity that forms a perpendicular from the last point.

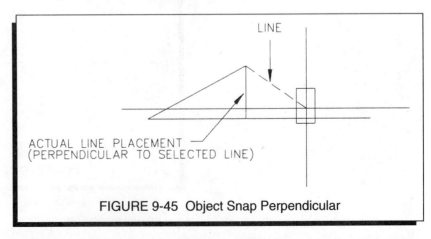

FIGURE 9-45 Object Snap Perpendicular

TANgent: Snaps to a point on a circle or arc that will construct a tangent to the last point entered.

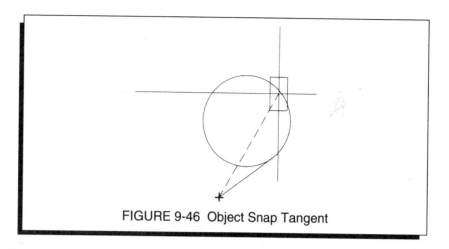

FIGURE 9-46 Object Snap Tangent

QUIck: Quick is a modifier that is entered before choosing each snap function. Choosing Quick will cause the object snap routine to choose the first point that it finds instead of choosing the one that is closest to the intersection of the crosshairs. This may cause problems if there are several entities in the aperture. Quick is used to save "search time" when there are several entities to choose from. If you encounter problems using Quick, cancel the point captured and try again without using Quick. Quick is a modifier that you should use only after you are proficient with the use of the object snap feature.

A menu of object snap modes can be found by selecting "∗ ∗ ∗ ∗" line in most screen menus or pressing the middle button of a three-button mouse.

METHODS OF USING OBJECT SNAP

Object snap may be used in two different ways. The first is what we will call *running mode*. When used in this way, you may set the points which will be captured in the aperture whenever AutoCAD prompts for a situation that may require a captured point. At these times, the aperture will appear on the screen, then disappear when it is not required. (The aperture does not affect normal drawing activities.)

The second way to use object snap is what we will refer to as *temporary mode*. In temporary mode, object snap is only used after selecting the mode for a single operation.

Let's look at how to use each mode.

RUNNING MODE OBJECT SNAP

To set the object snap modes, select "Object Snap..." from the Settings pull-down menu. AutoCAD will display a special object snap dialogue for setting running mode object snap.

Always use Temp Overrides

Blue button Bring up overrides

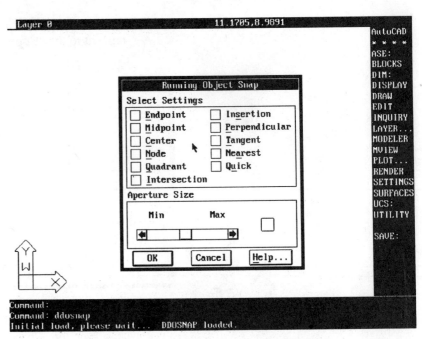

FIGURE 9-47 Object Snap Dialogue Box

Select each object snap mode that you want to be in effect in continuous mode. You may choose more than one. Selecting the same mode a second time will "deselect" it. The selected modes will be highlighted and contain a check in the check box next to them.

You may also set the size of the aperture. The slide bar at the bottom of the dialogue box is used to set the size. The window to the right of the slide bar shows the actual size of the aperture box.

To clear object snap running mode, deselect the modes from the dialogue box.

TEMPORARY MODE OBJECT SNAP

Object snap may also be invoked in what we previously referred to as "temporary" mode. This is for those special times when you need an object snap for just one capture.

Tip

The temporary mode may be used in the middle of other commands without disturbing the current status.

The object snap (temporary mode) submenu is accessible from most screen menus. Choose the "∗ ∗ ∗ ∗" line from the screen menu.

You may also override the running object snap functions by invoking the temporary method. For example, if you are using running mode object snap and want to enter a point without using object snap, access any "∗ ∗ ∗ ∗" screen menu and select NONE. After you enter the point, the running mode will return.

The Status command displays the current object snap features selected.

OBJECT SNAP EXERCISES

1. Start a new drawing named "SNAP". Draw a line, circle, and arc of any size on the screen. From the screen menu, select the "* * * *". You should now see an object snap menu.

   Select ENDpoint from the submenu. Now select the Line command from the DRAW submenu. Move the crosshairs into the screen area and notice the aperture at the intersection of the crosshairs. Place the aperture over one end of the line and click. The new line should "snap" precisely to the endpoint of the existing line.

   Before placing the endpoint of the line, select CENter from the object snap menu (remember to display the object snap menu by select the "* * * *" from the screen menu). Place the aperture over any part of the circle circumference and click. Notice how the line snapped to the center of the circle. Repeat the same procedure, except select a part of the arc. The line will snap to the center point of the arc.

2. Draw several more lines, circles, and arcs. Use each of the object snap modes to capture the parts of the entities. Be sure to use TANgent object to construct tangent lines with circles.

Redraw clears the screen and redraws the entities.

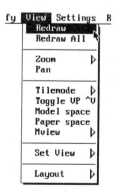

CLEARING THE SCREEN WITH THE REDRAW COMMAND

After you have been drawing for a while, you begin to build up a number of "markers". While these markers are often helpful in locating points on a drawing, too many of them can be distracting.

AutoCAD provides a method of "cleaning up" a drawing called Redraw. Redraw clears the screen and redraws the entities.

Redraw is also useful when an erase command causes a partial loss of some entity which is to remain. This is common when an erased entity overlaid an entity that remained.

   Command: Redraw

Some commands, such as zooms, automatically execute a redraw, so it is not necessary to perform the redraw before executing these commands.

REDRAWING "TRANSPARENTLY"

A redraw may be executed while another command is active.

A redraw may be executed while another command is active. This is called a "transparent" redraw. To perform a transparent redraw, enter an apostrophe (') before the command. For example, to perform a transparent redraw, enter 'Redraw at a non-text prompt. When the transparent redraw is completed, the previously active command will be resumed. The Redraw command contained in the screen menu will always redraw transparently. This means you can select Redraw from the menu while you are currently in a command without exiting that command.

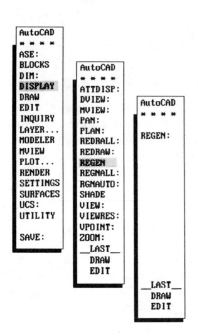

REGENERATING A DRAWING

The Regen command causes AutoCAD to regenerate the drawing display from the data base. This differs from the Redraw command that just redraws the screen, in that AutoCAD actually recalculates line end points, hatched areas, etc., as well as "cleaning up" erased entities by removing them from the data base. To invoke the Regen command, enter:

Command: REGEN

Several commands may cause an automatic regeneration. Among these are the zoom, pan and view restore. The regeneration will occur if the new display contains areas that are not within the currently generated area. The Regenauto command controls the automatic regeneration in AutoCAD. See Chapter 30 for an explanation of Regenauto.

You may cancel the regeneration by pressing Ctrl-C. If the regen is terminated, however, some of the drawing may not be redisplayed. To redisplay the drawing, you must reissue the Regen command. Normally, a redraw is used to "clean up" the screen since a regen takes longer to perform.

Tip
REGEN a drawing after extensive editing to see the "actual" state of the modified drawing.

ZOOMING YOUR DRAWINGS

The Zoom command allows you to enlarge or reduce the view of your drawing. You can think of zoom as a magnifier.

Most drawings would be too small and detailed to work with on a small drawing screen. CAD operators zoom into small areas to show greater detail. Let's consider an analogy to zooming.

The Zoom command allows you to enlarge or reduce the view of your drawing.

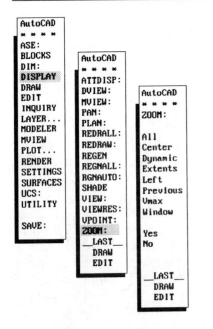

Imagine that your drawing is the size of a wall in a room. The closer you walk to the wall, the more detail you can see. But you can only see a portion of the wall. If you move a great distance from the wall, you may see the entire drawing, but not much detail. Note that the wall does not change size; you just change your viewing distance.

The Zoom command works much in the same way. You may enlarge or reduce the drawing size on the screen, but the drawing does not actually change size. If you zoom closer, you can see more detail, but not all of the drawing. If you zoom out (further away), you can see more of the drawing, but less detail.

USING THE ZOOM COMMAND

A zoom is performed by the zoom command:

Command: ZOOM
All/Center/Dynamic/Extents/Left/Previous/Vmax/Window/<Scale(X)>:

Let's look at the options for the Zoom command.

ZOOM SCALE

A zoom scale allows you to enlarge or reduce the entire drawing (original size) by a numerical factor. This is the default option. For example, entering a "5" will result in a zoom that shows the drawing five times its normal size. The entire drawing, of course, can not be displayed on the screen in this instance. The zoom will be centered on the previous screen center point.

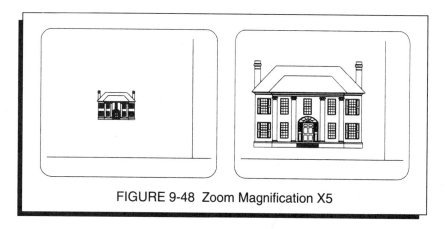

FIGURE 9-48 Zoom Magnification X5

If the zoom factor is followed by a "X", the zoom is computed relative to the *current* display.

Only positive values can be used in zooms. If you desire a zoom that is smaller than current, use a decimal value. For example, .5 results in a zoom that is one-half normal size.

ZOOM ALL

A "zoom all" causes the entire drawing to be displayed on the screen.

A "zoom all" causes the entire drawing to be displayed on the screen. This typically results in the entire area of the limits to be shown. If, however, the drawing extends outside of the current limits, the zoom all will show all the drawing, including the area of the drawing that is outside of the limits.

Occasionally, the zoom all has to generate the drawing twice. If this is necessary, the following will display on the prompt line:

* * Second regeneration caused by change in drawing extents.

If the limits are changed, the entire drawing area will not be shown until a zoom all is performed.

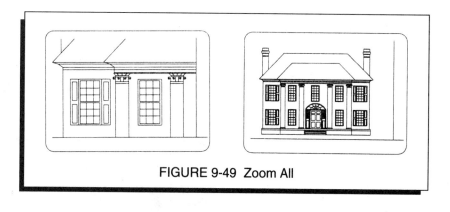

FIGURE 9-49 Zoom All

ZOOM CENTER

The zoom center option allows you to determine the center for the zoom. You are then given the choice for a magnification or a height for the display screen in units.

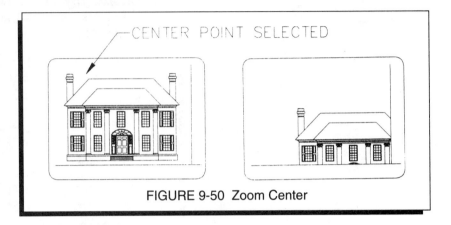

FIGURE 9-50 Zoom Center

Command: <u>ZOOM</u>
All/ Center/ Dynamic/ Extents/ Left/ Previous/Vmax/ Window/
<Scale(X)>: <u>C</u>
Center point: (*SELECT*)
Magnification or Height <default>: (*SELECT*)

If the magnification value is followed by a "X", the zoom factor will be relative to the current display.

ZOOM DYNAMIC

Allows dynamic zoom placement. To use this option, enter the ZOOM command and choose "Dynamic" from the screen menu, or enter "D" from the keyboard.

Command: <u>ZOOM</u>
All/ Center/ Dynamic/ Extents/ Left/ Previous/Vmax/ Window/
<Scale(X)>: <u>D</u>

When you choose dynamic zoom, you are presented with a special view selection screen containing information about current and possible view screen selections. The screen shown in the following illustration is representative of a typical display for dynamic zoom.

When you choose dynamic zoom, you are presented with a special view selection screen containing information about current and possible view screen selections.

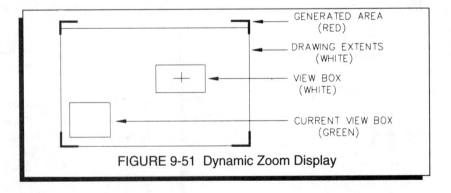

FIGURE 9-51 Dynamic Zoom Display

Each of the viewing windows are labeled and noted as to their respective colors. (Monochrome displays will not, of course, show these colors.)

Let's look at the meaning of each of these "windows".

DRAWING EXTENTS The drawing extents window is the white, solid line box. The drawing extents can be thought of as the actual "sheet of paper" on which the drawing resides.

CURRENT VIEW WINDOW The current view window is the highlighted (usually dotted and green in color) box. This box defines the screen when you invoked the dynamic zoom command. This box will contain the elements of the drawing that were shown on the screen at that time.

Drawings outside of this area will be regenerated, and thus require more time to zoom.

GENERATED AREA The four corner brackets in red define the area of the drawing that AutoCAD has currently generated. Zooms that fall into this area will be zoomed at about half-redraw speed (which is faster than Regen speed). Drawings outside of this area will be regenerated, and thus require more time to zoom. If the generated area is the same size as the drawing extents, the red brackets will be located at the corners of the monochrome display, this may make the brackets invisible; if it is the same size as the current view window, the brackets will overlay its dotted lines.

VIEW BOX The white, solid line view box defines the size and location of the desired view. You may manipulate this box to achieve the view you want. The view box is initially the same size as the current view window.

The view box can be enlarged or reduced, and moved to the desired location. A large X is initially placed in the center of the box. This denotes panning mode. When the X is present, moving the cursor will cause the box to move around the screen.

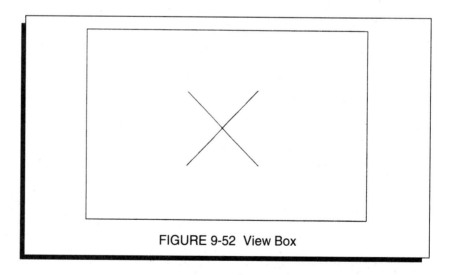

FIGURE 9-52 View Box

Pressing the pick button will cause the X to change to an arrow at the right side of the box. The arrow denotes the zoom mode. Moving the cursor right or left will increase or decrease the size of the view box. The view box will increase and decrease in proportion to your screen dimensions, resulting in a "what you see is what you get" definition of the zoomed area. This differs from the standard "Window" zoom, which works from a stationary window corner and may show more of the screen depending on the proportions of the defined zoom window.

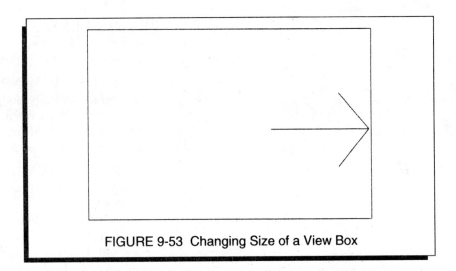

FIGURE 9-53 Changing Size of a View Box

You may toggle between zoom and pan modes as many times as you wish to set the size and location of the view box. When you have "windowed" the desired area, press the Enter key and zoom will be performed. The area defined by the zoom box is now the current screen view.

Redrawing and Regenerating Dynamic Zooms

Choosing a view box within the current generated area results in the zoom being performed at redraw speed. If you choose a view box outside of this area, the zoom will be performed at the slower regen speed. AutoCAD displays an hourglass at the lower left of the dynamic zoom screen to alert you of the necessity to perform the zoom at regen speed if you move the view box outside of the current generated area.

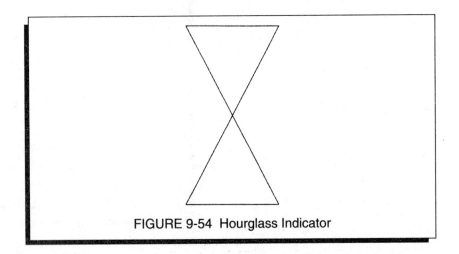

FIGURE 9-54 Hourglass Indicator

In 3-D mode, AutoCAD does not generate any area outside the present view. Because of this, if you use the dynamic zoom while in 3-D mode, you only choose view windows within the current screen view area. In addition, all zooms in 3-D are performed at regen speed, regardless of the location of the view box. When you execute the dynamic zoom command while in 3-D, AutoCAD displays a three-dimensional cube at the lower left corner of the screen. This cube has no other purpose than to remind you that you are in 3-D.

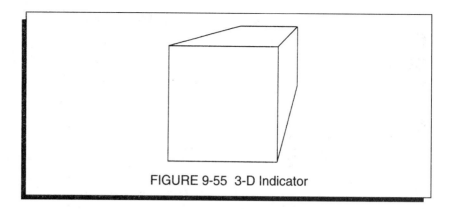

FIGURE 9-55 3-D Indicator

Using Dynamic Zoom Without a Pointing Device

Although recommended, it is not necessary to have a pointing device installed to use the dynamic zoom. Simply use the arrow keys to move the view box. If you have used the arrow keys, the Enter key will toggle between pan mode and zoom mode. If you have not used the arrow keys since last toggling with the Enter key, pressing it will perform the zoom at the current location of the view box.

The easy way to perform this is to manipulate the view box to the desired location and size, and press the Enter key twice.

ZOOM EXTENTS

Zoom Extents will display the drawing at its maximum size on the display screen. This results in the largest possible display, while showing the entire drawing. Note that areas within the limits that do not contain drawing entities will not be displayed.

FIGURE 9-56 Zoom Extents

ZOOM LOWER LEFT CORNER

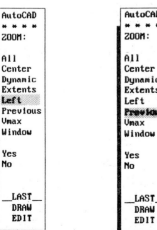

The zoom left corner is the same as a center zoom, except that you may choose the lower left corner instead of the center. You may use the "X" option in the same manner.

ZOOM PREVIOUS

The zoom previous option allows you to return to the last zoom you used. This option is often useful if you need to interact between two areas frequently. AutoCAD remembers the last zoom for you. Up to ten previous zooms are stored. Since the zooms are stored automatically, you are not required to use any special procedure to use them.

ZOOM VMAX (Maximum virtual screen)

Zoom Vmax zooms to the maximum virtual screen size. The virtual screen size is the pre-generated area of the display. Using the "V" option will allow you to zoom out to the maximum zoom that does not force a regeneration.

ZOOM WINDOW

The zoom window command will allow you to determine the area you wish to see in the zoom. The zoom window uses a "window" to specify this area. To use a zoom window, enter:

    Command: ZOOM
    All/ Center/ Dynamic/ Extents/ Left/ Previous/ Window/ <Scale(X)>: W
    First corner: SELECT
    Other corner: SELECT

A box will be displayed around the area to be zoomed.

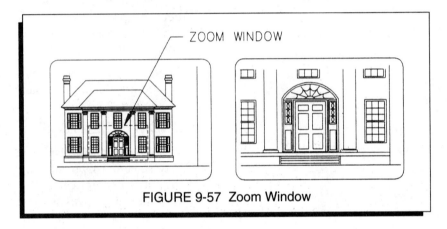

FIGURE 9-57 Zoom Window

TRANSPARENT ZOOMS

A transparent zoom may be executed while another command is active.

A transparent zoom may be executed while another command is active. Enter 'Zoom at any non-text prompt. The Zoom command found in the screen menu performs a transparent zoom. The following notes apply to using transparent zooms.

The fast zoom mode must be on. This is set with the Viewres command.

You may not perform a transparent zoom if a regeneration is required (zoom outside of the generated area—see "Zoom Dynamic").

You may not perform transparent zooms with the zoom all or zoom extents options. These options always force a regeneration.

Transparent zooms cannot be performed when certain commands are in progress. These include the Vpoint command, Pan, View, or another Zoom.

PANNING AROUND YOUR DRAWING

The Pan command is used in conjunction with the Zoom commands.

Many times a CAD operator will zoom into an area of the drawing in order to see more detail. He may want to "move" the screen a short distance to continue work while still in the same zoom magnification. You can think of a pan as similar to placing your eyes at a certain distance from a paper drawing, then moving your head about the drawing. This

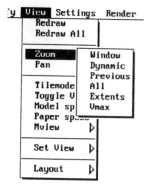

would allow you to see all parts of the drawing at the same distance from your eyes.

Panning is performed with the Pan command. To use the Pan command, enter:

Command: <u>PAN</u>
Displacement: (*select*)
Second point: (*select*)

You may show a point on the screen for the "displacement" prompt and another point for the "second point" prompt. This has the effect of "dragging" the drawing the specified distance and angle.

This distance and angle is called the "displacement". AutoCAD computes the distance and angle automatically and performs the pan.

The following illustration shows a pan using this method:

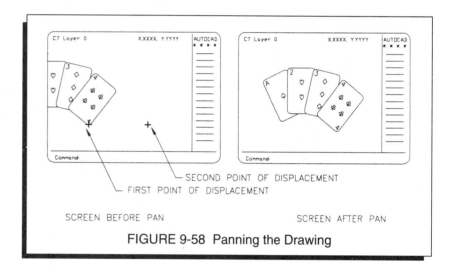

FIGURE 9-58 Panning the Drawing

You may also use relative coordinates to tell AutoCAD how far to move the drawing relative to the screen. For example, using the following coordinates would move the drawing 5 units X and 3 units Y:

Command: <u>PAN</u>
Displacement: (*select a point on the screen*)
Second point: <u>@5,3</u>

TRANSPARENT PANNING

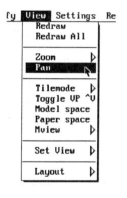

A pan may be performed transparently while another command is in progress.

A pan may be performed transparently while another command is in progress. To do this, enter 'Pan at any non-text prompt. The same restrictions for transparent pans apply as for transparent zooms. Note that the Pan command in the screen menu performs transparent pans.

DRAWING AIDS AND MODES

AutoCAD contains many commands that make drawing more accurate, efficient, and easy. In this chapter, we will learn to use the following commands and modes:

GRID COMMAND
SNAP COMMAND
OBJECT SNAP MODES
ORTHO MODE
DRAGMODE COMMAND

PLACING A GRID ON THE DRAWING SCREEN

The Grid command is used to display a grid of dots with a specified spacing. You may determine the spacing of the dots. You may additionally specify the X and Y spacing separately.

The grid dot is for reference purposes and is not part of the drawing. You can not erase the grid markers. The grid will not print or plot.

To display a grid, enter the command:

The grid will not print or plot.

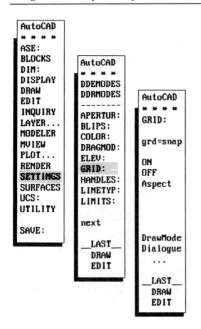

    Command: GRID
    Grid spacing (X) or ON/OFF/Snap/Aspect <default>:

The options are as follows:

Grid Spacing: The grid spacing is the default. If you enter a numerical value, that value becomes the grid spacing. It is not necessary to first enter a letter to designate the grid spacing option.

The grid spacing may be set to a multiple of the snap setting by placing an "X" after the value. For example, if the snap spacing is 1, entering a value of 10X will display a grid dot at every 10th snap point. A grid spacing of zero will set the grid to exactly match the snap value.

On The On option activates the grid. The previously set grid value is used.

Off The Off option turns off the grid. The current value is stored for later use.

Snap Sets the grid spacing equal to the current snap setting. If the snap resolution is changed, the grid value will be automatically changed to match.

Aspect The aspect option allows you to specify a different X and Y value. For example, you may choose a value of 10 units of spacing for the X value and a value of 5 units of spacing for the Y value.

    Command: GRID
    On/Off/Value(X)/Aspect: A
    Horizontal Spacing(X): 10
    Vertical Spacing(Y): 5

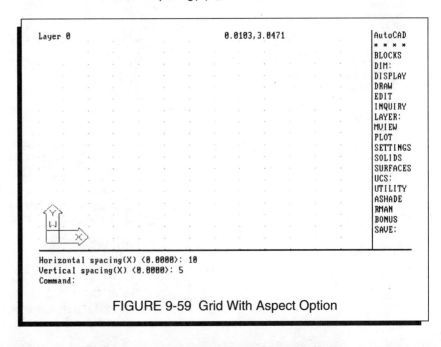

FIGURE 9-59 Grid With Aspect Option

If the grid spacing is too close to display properly, the message;

> Grid too dense to display

will appear. This may also happen when you zoom the drawing.

PROFESSIONAL TIP

Many designers use a grid when laying out or "sketching" design ideas. Setting the grid spacing to a convenient interval allows better visualization of scale.

GRID EXERCISES

1. Type in the Grid command. In response to AutoCAD's prompt, enter a value of 1. The grid should be visible on the screen.

2. Press the F7 function key. This key toggles the grid on and off.

3. Enter the Grid command again. In response to the prompt, enter "A" for aspect. Set the horizontal grid to a value of 1, and the vertical grid to a value of .5. The grid should line up with the axis marks you set previously.

SNAPPING TO A GRID

Points which are entered on the screen may be aligned to an imaginary grid.

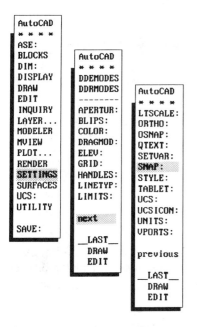

Points which are entered on the screen may be aligned to an imaginary grid. This grid is known as the "snap grid". The spacing of this grid is the "snap resolution". If a point is entered that is not exactly aligned with a snap point, the point is forced to the nearest snap point.

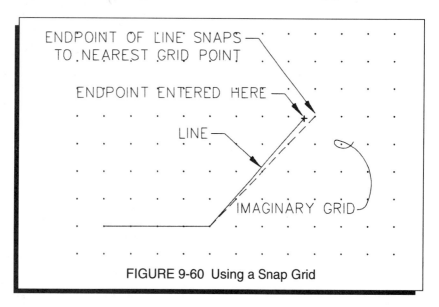

FIGURE 9-60 Using a Snap Grid

You may specify different X and Y spacing for the snap grid. The snap spacing may also be set to coincide with the grid spacing. Unless the snap spacing is set with the grid spacing and the grid is currently displayed, the snap settings are invisible.

To set a snap grid, select SNAP from the Settings/Next menu.

Command: <u>SNAP</u>
Snap spacing or ON/OFF/ Aspect/ Rotate/ Style <default>:

SNAP OPTIONS

The options for the snap command are as follows.

Snap Spacing: The snap spacing is the default. If you enter a numerical value, that value becomes the snap spacing. It is not necessary to first enter a letter to designate the snap spacing option. The value must be non-zero and positive.

ON: Causes the Snap mode to turn on. The default snap value is determined by the prototype drawing.

OFF: Turns off the snap. The last value is remembered for use if you turn the snap back on.

Aspect: Used to set different X and Y snap spacings. If you enter the "A" (Aspect) option, AutoCAD will prompt you for the different X and Y values.

Rotate: Entering the "R" (Rotate) option, will allow you to set a rotation angle for the snap grid and the base point at which the grid will be positioned from. This also has the effect of rotating the crosshairs.

Command: <u>SNAP</u>
Snap spacing or On/Off/Aspect/ Rotate/Style <default>: <u>R</u>
Base point <0,0>: (*select*)
Rotation angle <default>: (*select*)

Style: The Style option is used to choose the format of the snap grid. You may choose either the "standard" or "isometric" format.

SNAP EXERCISES

1. Let's set up an ordinary snap grid, with a snap resolution of .25. Start a new drawing named "SNAP". Select the Snap command from the Settings/Next menu.

   Command: <u>SNAP</u>
   Snap spacing or ON/OFF/Aspect/Rotate/Style <default>: <u>.25</u>

   Next, select the Line command and enter the line endpoints on the screen. Did you notice the crosshairs "snapping" to a point?

2. Use the Grid command to set a grid with .25 spacing. Use the Line command to set some endpoints. Notice how the crosshairs line up with the grid points.

3. Use the F9 function key to turn the snap mode on and off. Draw two boxes; one with snap mode on, and one with snap mode off. Notice how the points are easier to line up with snap mode on.

4. Use the Zoom Window command to zoom in on one of the boxes. Move the crosshairs around the area of the box with the snap mode on (use F9 to turn the mode on and off). Notice how the movement of the crosshairs is more exaggerated with the closer zoom. This is because the "screen distance" between the snap points is larger when zoomed in. The actual snap distance (resolution), however, remains unchanged.

5. Select the Snap command again and enter values as shown in the following command sequence.

> Command: <u>SNAP</u>
> Snap spacing or ON/OFF/Aspect/Rotate/Style <*default*>: <u>A</u>
> Horizontal spacing <*default*>: <u>.25</u>
> Vertical spacing <*default*>: <u>.50</u>

Next, select the Grid command. Choose the grid option of Aspect and enter the same values. Notice how the spacing for the vertical and horizontal snap resolution is different. It is not necessary for the vertical and horizontal values to be the same. Try drawing another box with the snap on.

6. Let's try rotating the snap points and the crosshairs. Select the Snap command again.

> Command: <u>SNAP</u>
> Snap spacing or ON/OFF/Aspect/Rotate/Style <*default*>: <u>R</u>
> Base point <0.0000,0.0000>: (*Return*)
> Rotation angle <0>: <u>45</u>

Your display should look like the following illustration.

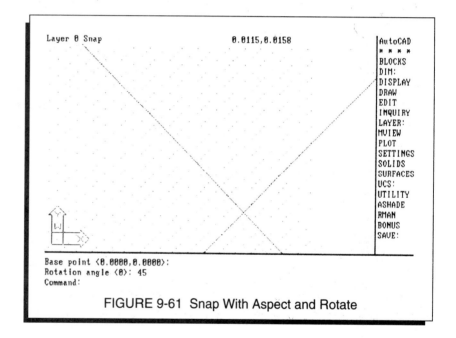

FIGURE 9-61 Snap With Aspect and Rotate

Notice how the snap resolution and aspect are maintained. The entire snap grid and crosshairs are rotated. Draw a box with the rotated snap grid and crosshairs. This is an excellent method of drawing objects that have many angular lines.

7. The base point can be placed at a particular position, relative to a drawing. Select the Snap command again and choose the Rotate option. When prompted for the base point, select a corner of one of your boxes. Maintain the rotation angle of 45 degrees. Notice how a point falls on the corner of the box. Use the base point position to locate the snap grid where you want it.

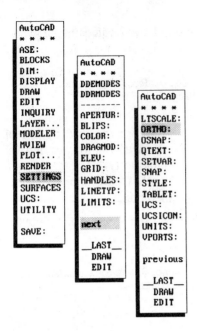

DRAWING WITH ORTHOGONAL CONTROL

When you use an input device, such as a mouse or digitizer, drawing lines at true horizontal and vertical angles requires extra effort. The Ortho mode assures that all lines will be orthogonal (either horizontal or vertical).

You can turn on the Ortho mode either by pressing the F8 function key, or by entering the Ortho command:

    Command: ORTHO
    On/Off: ON

Ortho mode is turned off by reentering the command and responding to the prompt with "off", or by pressing the F8 function key again. If ortho is on, the status line at the top of the screen will display the word ORTHO.

When the ortho mode is on, all the lines will be forced either horizontal or vertical. If a point is entered that is not true to either, the point will be forced to the nearest true point. That is, if the point is more nearly vertical, the line will be forced vertical.

ORTHO EXERCISES

1. Start a new drawing named "ORTHO". Select the Line command and draw a 4 sided box with horizontal and vertical lines. Do not use the Ortho mode. Now press function key F8 to turn on Ortho mode and draw another box. Notice how much easier it is to create straight lines with the Ortho mode.

2. Select line again and enter the first endpoint. Now move the crosshairs around the first endpoint and notice how AutoCAD forces the line to be horizontal or vertical, depending on the location relative to the first endpoint.

3. Use the Snap command to set a snap increment of .25. Be sure Ortho is on and draw another box. Notice how the combination of Snap and Ortho makes drawing the box very easy.

AutoCAD allows you to draw many entities by "dragging" them dynamically.

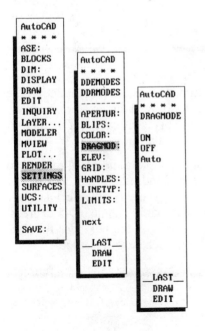

SETTING THE DRAGMODE

AutoCAD allows you to draw many entities by "dragging" them dynamically. For example, a circle radius may be dynamically set by dragging the circle from its center point. The advantage of dragging, for example, is that you can see the circle "grow" as you move the crosshairs away from the center. Many edit and other commands also use dragging in their operations. In addition, "drag" may be selected from some menus to aid in visual placement of points and objects.

The Dragmode command is used to enable or disable dragging. The command sequence is:

    Command: DRAGMODE
    ON/OFF/Auto <current>:

Setting the mode to OFF disables all drag requests, whether selected from the menu or built into a command macro.

Selecting "Auto" will enable the dragmode for each command that supports it.

Setting Dragmode to ON permits selecting dragmode manually by entering "DRAG" transparently from the command line.

Using Drag on some computers and display systems can be time consuming. Disabling dragmode in these situations can speed up the drawing process.

> **TIP**
>
> Disabling the dragmode is useful when complex objects that slow down AutoCAD are being drawn or manipulated.

DRAGMODE EXERCISE

1. Start a new drawing named "DRAG". Draw a circle on the screen. Select the Dragmode command and turn the mode OFF. Select the Move command and move the circle. Notice how the circle does not move.

2. Enter the Dragmode command again and set it to Auto. Move the circle again. Notice how the circle "drags" with the crosshairs.

3. Select the Dragmode command again and set it to ON. Select the Move command and select the circle with a pickbox and Return. Move the circle. The circle will not drag. Repeat the same procedure, except when AutoCAD prompts;

   Base point or displacement:

   enter "DRAG" on the command line. Continue the sequence and move the circle. The circle will drag to the new position. Setting the dragmode to ON allows you to select the times you wish to drag an object.

UNDOING AND REDOING OPERATIONS

AutoCAD allows you to undo your work, then to redo it! This is very useful if you have just performed an operation that you wish to "undo". After you undo an operation, you use the Redo command to reverse the undo. Let's take a look at how to do these interesting operations.

UNDOING DRAWING OPERATIONS

The U command will undo the most recent command. You may execute a series of "Undo's" to back up through a string of changes. The U command should not be confused with the more complex Undo command, although it functions the same as Undo 1.

Undoing a command will restore the drawing to the state it was in before the command was executed.

Undoing a command will restore the drawing to the state it was in before the command was executed. For example, if you erase an object, then execute the U command, the object will be restored. If you scale an object, then undo it, the object will be rescaled to its original size. The

U command will list the command that is undone to alert you of the type of command that was affected. For example, executing the U command after the Scale command would result in the following:

Command: <u>U</u>
SCALE

Several commands cannot be undone. Some Plot, Prplot, and Wblock, for example are not affected. If you attempt to use the U command after these commands, they will be displayed, but not undone.

Undoing a just completed block command will restore the block and delete the block definition that was created, leaving the drawing exactly as it was before the block was performed.

UNDO EXERCISES

1. Start a new drawing named "TEST". Select the Line command and draw a line segment. Use Ctrl-C to clear the command line. Enter "U" from the keyboard and Return. Did the line segment disappear?

2. Use the Line command to draw several line segments. Select the Line command and draw more line segments. Use the U command to undo the lines drawn with the last line command. Which segments were undone? Press the space bar to repeat the U command. What happened?

3. Use the line command to draw two line segments. Before entering the last point, use the F8 function key to turn on Ortho mode. Notice the ORTHO listing on the status line. Now use the U command to undo the sequence. Is the ortho mode on now?

4. Use F8 to turn on Ortho. Notice the listing on the status line. Now use the Line command to draw a line segment. Next, use the U command to undo the sequence. Is Ortho mode still turned on? What is the difference between this and the last sequence you performed?

REDOING A DRAWING OPERATION

The Redo command is the antidote of the U command.

Redo "undoes" the undo. The Redo command must be used immediately after undo commands.

The Redo command must be used immediately after undo commands.

To use Redo, enter:

Command: <u>REDO</u>

REDO EXERCISES

1. Use the Line command to draw several line segments. Use the U command to undo the lines. Now use the Redo command. Did the lines reappear?

2. Enter the Redo command again. What does the prompt line say? Why?

CHAPTER EXERCISES

Use the commands you have learned to draw the following objects.

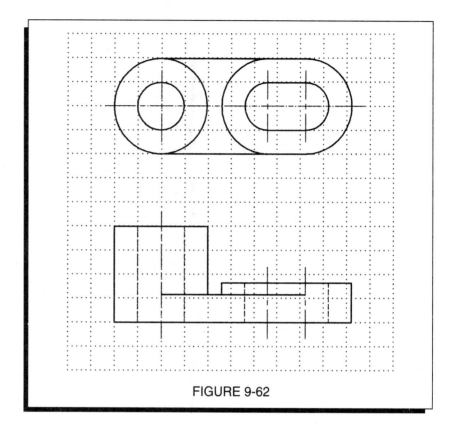

FIGURE 9-62

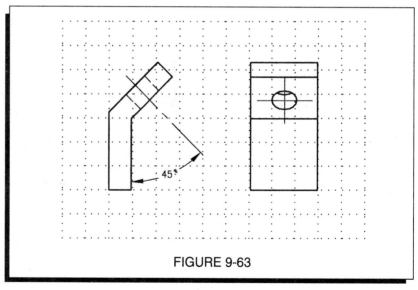

FIGURE 9-63

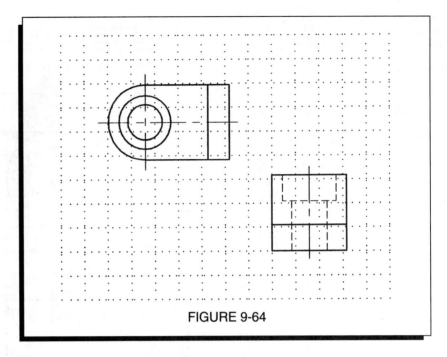

FIGURE 9-64

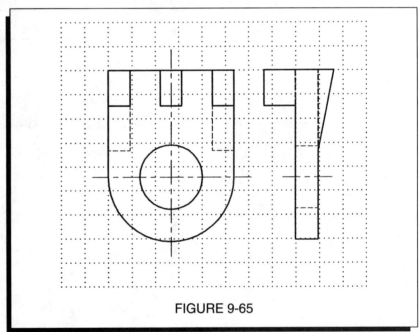

FIGURE 9-65

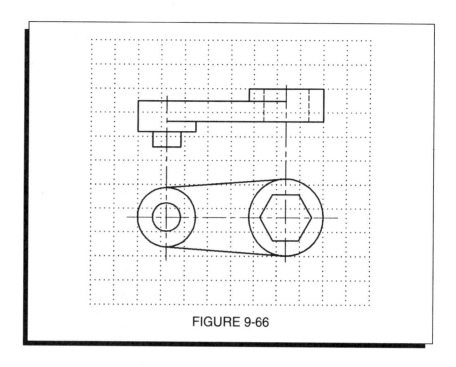

FIGURE 9-66

CHAPTER REVIEW

1. What command allows you to enlarge and reduce the display size of your drawing?

   zoom

2. When drawing a circle and you are prompted for a diameter or radius, a numerical value can be given, but can the distance be shown by screen pointing as well?

3. Explain the function of the close option under the Line command.

4. Why does AutoCAD offer so many methods of arc construction?

5. What is the purpose of the Pan command?

6. What is the default method of arc construction?

7. What two variables can by altered to change the design and size of points?

   _____

   _____

8. Why is the close option of the Line command a more accurate method of closing lines than attempting to line up the endpoints manually?

   _____

   _____

9. Can the U command be used to undo a sequence of commands?

   _____

10. Pdmode and Pdsize are retroactive. What does this mean?

   _____

   _____

   _____

11. What is the Vmax option under the Zoom command used for?

   _____

   _____

   _____

12. When an arc sequence is in progress, can you override the preset selections? How?

   _____

   _____

   _____

13. How might you make a backup file of the drawing in progress without ending the drawing?

   _____

   _____

   _____

14. How is the line command terminated?

   _____

   _____

   _____

15. There are six methods of constructing circles. What four circle properties are used in various combinations to comprise these methods?

   _____

   _____

   _____

16. What is the chord of an arc?

_____

_____

_____

17. Can the U command be entered from the screen menus as well as from the keyboard?

_____

18. How do Pan and Zoom commands differ?

_____

_____

_____

19. When a dynamic Zoom is invoked, what information appears on the screen in reference to your drawing?

_____

_____

_____

20. What is a transparent command? How is this option invoked?

_____

_____

_____

21. If the Undo command is used while in a line sequence, does the entire sequence disappear or is each endpoint stepped through backwards?

_____

_____

_____

22. How do redraw and regen differ?

_____

_____

_____

23. What option allows you to enlarge or reduce the original drawing size by a numerical factor for viewing?

_____

_____

24. Relative and polar coordinates use the last point entered as a reference point. What reference point are absolute coordinate entries relative to?

_____

_____

25. In what type of coordinate entry is the @ symbol required?

_____

26. Using the figure shown, list the coordinate entry necessary to enter the second point, first using absolute coordinates and then relative coordinates.

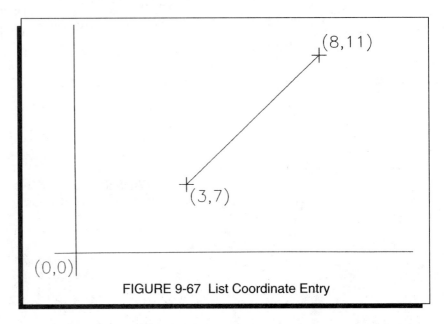

FIGURE 9-67 List Coordinate Entry

27. AutoCAD uses a default angle setting that may be altered if the user desires. Where would these setting changes be made?

_____

_____

_____

28. When using polar coordinates, from what point is the distance and angle measured?

_____

_____

29. What method of point entry is entered in the X,Y format?

_____

30. What type of coordinate identifies a single point on the coordinate axis?

_____

31. What direction is negative in AutoCAD's default angle specification?

_____

32. List the differences in the three types of coordinate entry, using illustrative examples of each.

_____

_____

_____

_____

_____

_____

33. The coordinate readout at the top of the AutoCAD drawing screen is in absolute coordinates (X,Y), so how could the length of a line resting at an angle be determined if the point entry were from screen pointing rather than through the keyboard?

_____

_____

_____

34. At what point on the coordinate axis is the lower left corner of the AutoCAD drawing screen normally located?

_____

35. Where is the zero angle located in AutoCAD's default angle specification?

_____

_____

36. Given the first point of a line at 12,37, what coordinate entry would you use to locate an endpoint 15 units and 79 degrees from the first point?

_____

_____

37. Using AutoCAD's default angle settings, in which direction does the angle measurement increase?

_____

_____

38. How is the format different for absolute coordinate entry and relative coordinate entry?

_____

_____

39. What is the aperture?

_____

_____

_____

40. What object snap mode would you choose to snap on to a point entity?

_____

41. Can you snap on the midpoint of an arc?

_____

42. Define the Dragmode command.

_____

_____

_____

43. May different X and Y spacing be given to the snap grid? Can it coincide with the grid spacing?

_____

_____

44. What term is given to the dynamic insertion of an object?

_____

45. What mode can provide great accuracy in creating true horizontal and vertical lines?

_____

46. When must the quick modifier be entered? What purpose does it serve?

_____

_____

_____

47. Can you overrun the running object snap mode?

_____

48. When does the Redo command have to be used?

_____

49. How can the results of the last command executed be removed?

_____

_____

50. Although the grid is not a part of the drawing, can it be plotted?

_____

51. Will the U command undo any command just executed?

_____

_____

CHAPTER 10

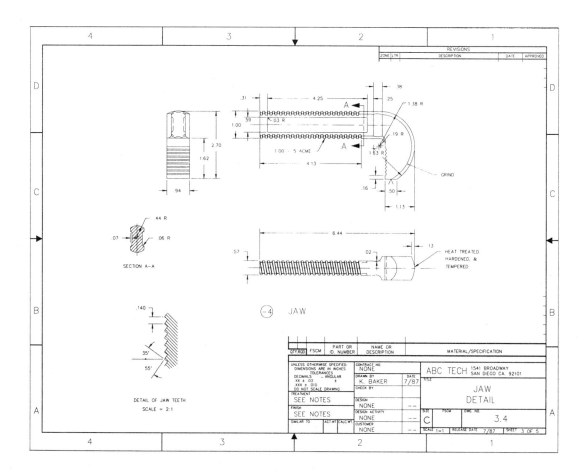

Editing a Drawing

OBJECTIVES:

Editing drawings is one of the strengths of computer aided drawing. AutoCAD provides an exceptional toolbox of editing functions. The objectives of Chapter 10 are:

● To provide the user with an overview of AutoCAD's basic editing commands.

● To introduce the methodology of selecting the part(s) of the drawing to be edited with the object selection process.

● To learn how to use AutoCAD's edit commands by using the functions with work problems.

INTRODUCTION

So far you have learned how to use AutoCAD to create a simple drawing with lines, circles, arcs and points.

From time to time you will have reason to change parts of your work. AutoCAD supplies edit commands to achieve this. In this chapter you will learn about:

Object selection—Selecting the entities to be edited.

Select—Preselects objects to be edited.

Erase—deleting one or more entities from the drawing.

Oops—restoring to the drawing what you just erased.

Move—moving entities around the screen.

Copy—copying entities already drawn.

Break—removing portions of entities.

Fillet—making smooth and perfect corners with lines and arcs.

These commands are found in the screen menu under "EDIT", and under the "MODIFY" pull-down menu.

The ability to electronically edit your work is a very powerful feature of CAD drafting.

The ability to electronically edit your work is a very powerful feature of CAD drafting. Last minute changes, correction of mistakes or any other reason for change can be accomplished quickly and accurately.

In order to edit a drawing, you must first determine the following:

Which entity (or entities) would you like to edit?

How would you like to edit them?

After determining which entities you would like to edit, you use the object selection process to isolate them.

USING OBJECT SELECTION

In order to identify which entities are to be edited, you will use the method of identification called object selection.

In order to identify which entities are to be edited, you will use the method of identification called "object selection". Object selection is the standard method of entity identification in AutoCAD and is used with most edit commands.

In order to efficiently edit objects, it is essential that you understand the object selection options. As you will see, the edit commands are very easy to use. Efficiency will result from innovative use of the methods used to select objects to be edited. This is especially true of intricate drawings. You may use any combination of selection methods or a single method several times to build the selected set of objects.

METHODS OF SELECTING OBJECTS FOR EDITING

You may select objects for editing by many methods. Let's look at each method.

SELECTING BY OBJECT POINTING

When you first select an edit command, the cursor is replaced with a small box that we will refer to as a "pick box". If you place the "pick-box" over the object and press the Enter key, the drawing is scanned and the entity that the pickbox covers will be selected.

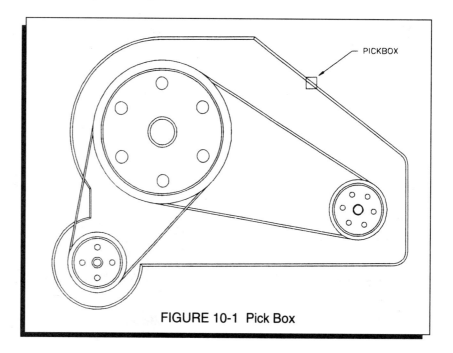

FIGURE 10-1 Pick Box

The pickbox can be changed in size to assist in working in drawings of differing complexities. The Ddselect dialogue box is used to change the pickbox size and is covered later in this chapter.

Tip

Don't place the pickbox at an intersection of two objects. This will give unpredictable results, since AutoCAD won't know which entity you desire to choose.

After you select the item(s) to be edited, you will notice that AutoCAD highlights the items which were isolated. Each selected item will become dotted instead of solid. On color monitors they will change color. This helps you to see which items were selected. (The method of highlighting may be different or not present at all on some display systems.)

USING THE MULTIPLE OPTION

Each time you select an entity, AutoCAD will scan the drawing to find that entity. If you are selecting an entity in a drawing that contains a large number of objects, there can be a noticeable delay. The "M" option causes AutoCAD to scan the drawing only once. This can result in a shorter selection time if the drawing is complex. Press Enter when you finish object selection to begin the scan.

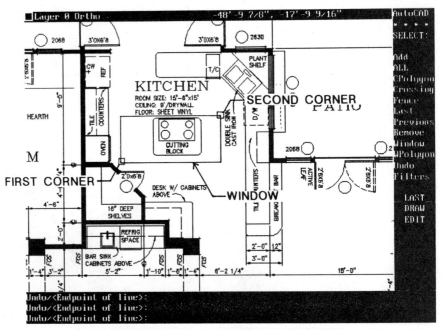

FIGURE 10-2 Selecting With a Window

SELECTING OBJECTS WITH A WINDOW

A window may be placed around a group of objects that you wish to select for editing. A window is a box that you define by its opposite corners. You may choose the window option by entering a "W" in response to the "Select objects:" prompt.

Any entity that is entirely in the window box will be selected.

Only objects that are currently visible on the screen may be selected. Any entity that is entirely in the window box will be selected. If all of an entity is not currently on the screen, it will only be chosen if all parts that are visible are inside the box.

> ### Tip
>
> Selection of certain objects may be made by placing the box so that all parts of those you want to choose are contained in the box and those which you don't want chosen are not entirely contained. With this method, you may make certain selections in areas of your drawing where objects overlap.

SELECTING THE LAST OBJECT DRAWN

The "Last" option selects the last object drawn. If the command is repeated and Last is used again as the object selection technique, the selection will choose the current "last" entity drawn.

RESELECTING THE PREVIOUSLY DESIGNATED SELECTION SET

The "Previous" option uses the previously selected group of entities for the edit set. This option is useful for performing several edit functions on the same group without the necessity of redefining them.

SELECTING OBJECTS BY DEFINING A CROSSING WINDOW

The "Crossing" option is similar to the Window option. When you use Window, entities which are entirely contained within the window are selected. Using the Crossing option allows you to place a window that will select any entities that are either within or cross through the window. On many display systems, the Crossing window box will be dashed (or highlighted in some other fashion). This distinguishes the crossing box from a standard "window" box

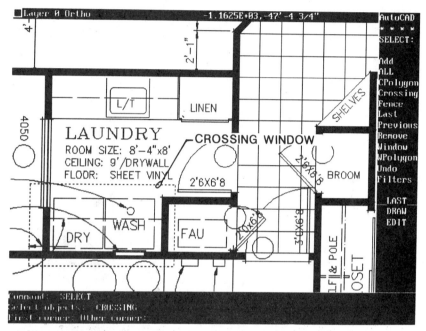

FIGURE 10-3 Selecting With a Crossing Window

SELECTING OBJECTS WITH A BOX

Entering "Box" in response to the "select objects" prompt allows you to place either a Crossing or Window box to select objects.

Entering "Box" in response to the "select objects" prompt allows you to place either a Crossing or Window box to select objects. If you set the first corner of the box, then move to the right, the resulting box is a Window box and will select objects in accordance with the standard window box method of object selection. Placing the first point of the box, then moving left will designate a crossing box.

SELECTING OBJECTS WITH THE AUTOMATIC OPTION

If "AU" is entered in response to the "select objects" a pick box is used for selection. If you select a point with the pick box and an object is found, a selection is made. If an object is not found, the selection point becomes the first corner of a "Box" method of object selection. Move the box to right for Window or the left for Crossing. The automatic method of object selection is excellent for advanced users who wish to reduce the number of modifier selections that must be input.

SELECTING ENTITIES BY USING A POLYGON WINDOW

The Wpolygon (WP) option is used to select entities by placing a polygon window around the desired objects. The polygon window functions

the same as the Window option, except that you build a multi-sided window that surrounds the desired entities. Let's look at a sample command sequence using the Erase edit command.

    Command: ERASE
    Select objects: WP
    First polygon point:
    Undo/<Endpoint of line>:

After you enter the first polygon point, you can proceed to build a window by placing endpoints. The window lines rubberband to the cursor intersection, always creating a closed polygon window.

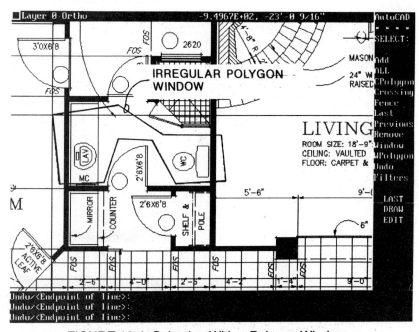

FIGURE 10-4 Selection With a Polygon Window

You can undo the last point entered by entering a "U" in response to the prompt. Pressing the Enter key will complete the polygon window and complete the process.

The polygon window must not cross itself or be placed directly on a polygon entity.

SELECTING OBJECTS BY PLACING A CROSSING POLYGON WINDOW

The crossing polygon window (CP) option works in the same manner as the WP option, except the window functions in the same manner as a crossing window.

The crossing polygon is displayed as a dashed line similar to a crossing window. Any entity crossing (touching) the crossing polygon window is selected for editing.

USING A FENCE TO SELECT ENTITIES

The Fence (F) option is similar to the crossing and polygon crossing methods, except that AutoCAD uses a crossing "fence line" to select objects.

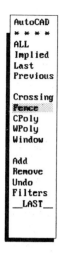

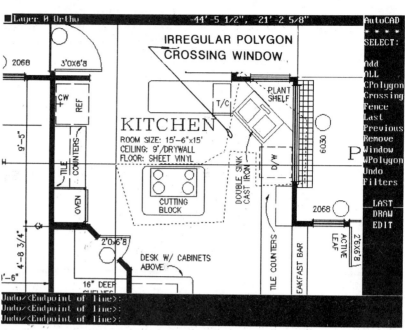

FIGURE 10-5 Selecting With a Crossing Polygon Window

The fence line is displayed as a dashed line in the same way that a crossing window is displayed. The fence lines are constructed the same as line entities, except that all objects that are crossed or touch the fence line(s) are selected.

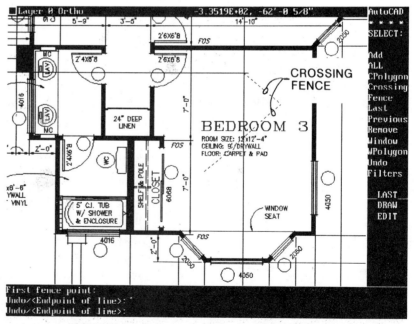

FIGURE 10-6 Selecting With a Crossing Fence

You may consecutively construct as many fence lines as you wish, and may use the "U" option to undo a fence line segment.

SINGLE ENTITY OBJECT SELECTION

Selecting "SI" (Single) causes AutoCAD to allow only a single "select objects" prompt, suppressing subsequent "select objects" prompts. The

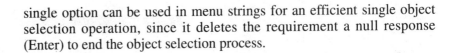

single option can be used in menu strings for an efficient single object selection operation, since it deletes the requirement a null response (Enter) to end the object selection process.

SELECTING ALL THE OBJECTS IN THE DRAWING

Selecting All picks all the entities in the drawing except those contained on frozen or locked layers.

Professional Tip

If most of the entities in a drawing are to be selected for edit, first designate all the drawing entities with the All option, then use the Remove (explanation follows) option to "deselect" the items to remain.

CANCELING THE SELECTION PROCESS

Entering Ctrl-C at any time during selection will cancel the selection process and restore all previously selected objects to normal. The prompt line will return to "Command:".

CHANGING THE ITEMS SELECTED

You may also add or remove objects to be edited from the group of selected objects by using "modifier" commands. Modifier commands are entered after you have selected objects with the object selection process, but before you press the Enter key to accept the designated objects.

UNDOING THE LAST SELECTED ENTITY

U (undo) removes the most recent addition to the set of selections. If the undo is repeated, you will step back through the selection set.

REMOVING DESIGNATED OBJECTS FROM THE SELECTION SET

Entering a "R" will cause the object selection process to begin to remove the next selected objects from the set.

When you start the selection process, you may add objects until you identify every object you wish to edit. "Remove" allows you to begin to remove objects from the selection set that you do not wish to edit. The prompt line will show "Remove objects:" when you are in the Remove mode. You may remove objects from the selection set by any object selection method.

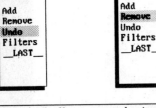

"Remove" allows you to begin to remove objects from the selection set that you do not wish to edit.

Professional Tip

Many new CAD operators only think of object selection in terms of adding entities to a selection set. It is often the case that you wish to choose a large number of entities, with the exception of one or two entities that are located within the area of the other entities.

Each of the edit commands require the object selection process to identify the entities to be edited.

ADDING DESIGNATED OBJECTS TO THE SELECTION SET

Entering a "A" will cause the object selection process to add objects to the set. The Add option is usually used to toggle back to the Add mode after the Remove option has set the process to the Remove mode. Add changes the prompt line back to "Select objects:" so you may add objects to be edited to the selection set with the select objects options.

Each of the edit commands require the object selection process to identify the entities to be edited. Let's examine each command to see how to edit your work.

DESIGNATING ENTITY SELECTION SETTINGS

AutoCAD allows you to set different modes of entity selection. The previous sections covered the basic entity selection methods. As you gain more proficiency, you will want to use other modes of selection.

USING DDSELECT TO SET SELECTION MODE

The Ddselect dialogue box is used to set selection modes. This dialogue box is accessed through the Settings pull-down menu. From the Settings menu, select "Selection Settings...". You may alternately type "DDSELECT" at the command line.

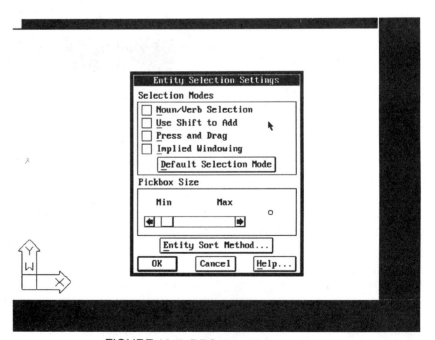

FIGURE 10-7 DDSelect Dialogue Box

The dialogue contains four selection modes. They are "turned on" by clicking in the check box next to the selection. Let's look at how each mode functions.

NOUN/VERB SELECTION

So far you have learned to edit entities by first selecting the edit command, then the objects to modify with that command. An analogy of this method would be choosing the verb (action represented by the edit command), then the noun (object of the action represented by the selection set). AutoCAD also allows you to reverse this procedure by first picking the object(s) you wish to modify, then the edit command to use. This is called "noun/verb selection".

The DDSELECT dialogue box is used to set this type of selection. When you set the noun/verb selection to on, AutoCAD places a box at the intersection of the crosshairs. This box is used to select entities in the same way as a pickbox.

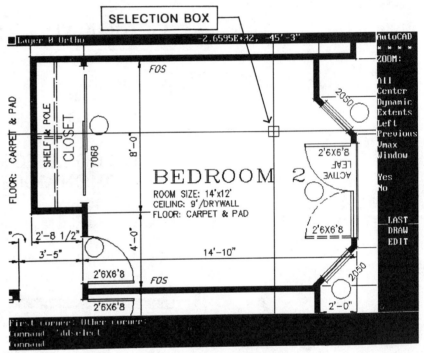

FIGURE 10-8 Selection Box

To edit objects, first select the object(s) to be edited, then choose the edit command. The desired edit command can be either typed at the command line, or selected from the menus. Let's look at how the command sequence would look if we used this method to erase a single entity.

Command: *SELECT THE OBJECT*
Command: <u>ERASE</u>
1 found

The following edit commands can be used with the noun/verb selection method.

Array	List
Block	Mirror
Change	Move
Chprop	Rotate
Copy	Scale
Ddchprop	Stretch
Dview	Wblock
Erase	Explode
Hatch	

USE SHIFT TO ADD

When using the selection process, you have learned to select the objects, then press the Enter key when you are finished. As you choose each entity, it is automatically added to the selection set.

If you check the "Use Shift to Add" box, each selection will only choose that entity, canceling the choice of the one previously selected. To add entities, you must hold down the shift key on the keyboard. This is similar to the method used by many computer "draw" programs.

CLICK AND DRAG

The traditional method of using a window to select entities is to click on one corner, then moving the cursor to the other corner and clicking again.

If you check "Click and Drag", a window is built by clicking on one corner, then moving to the other corner *while holding down the mouse button*. Like the "shift to add" option, this is also similar to the windowing method used by many "draw" programs.

IMPLIED WINDOWING

You have already learned how to use a selection window or a crossing window to select objects. All you have to do is enter either a "W" or a "C" to invoke the window mode. Checking "Implied Windowing" allows you do this automatically.

A window can be "implied" by clicking on an empty area of the drawing when building a selection set. If AutoCAD does not find an entity within the area of the pickbox, then it assumes that you want to use a window. If you move the crosshair away from the area of the first click, a window will be built. If the movement is to the right, a *selection window* will be made. If you move to the left, a *crossing window* will occur.

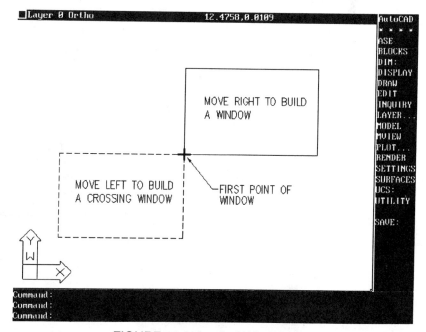

FIGURE 10-9 Implied Windowing

Since the first point entered describes the first corner of the window, be sure to select a position that is desirable.

RESETTING TO THE DEFAULT MODES

Selecting the "Default Selection Mode" button resets the selection modes to the original settings. By default, "Use Shift to Add" and "Implied Windowing" are selected.

SETTING THE PICKBOX SIZE

The pickbox size is set from the Ddselect dialogue box. To change the size, use the slidebar by clicking and holding the button in the slidebar and moving to left to decrease the size and to the right to increase the size. The window to the right of the slidebar shows the actual size of the pickbox as you change it.

Tip

The pickbox size can aid in building the selection set. A larger pickbox makes selection less tedious, while a smaller pickbox allows you to select entities in a crowded without the necessity of enlarging the drawing area with the zoom command. Change the pickbox size as the conditions warrant.

PRESELECTING OBJECTS FOR EDITING

The Select command is used to preselect entities for editing. To execute the Select command, enter:

```
Command: SELECT
Select objects: (select objects to be edited)
```

When next using an edit command, you may simply enter the "previous" option to choose the preselected entities.

Tip

The select command is especially helpful when edits of several types must be performed on the same group of entities. The target group of entities may be reselected by executing the Previous option when using each successive edit command.

ERASING OBJECTS FROM YOUR DRAWING

The Erase command is used to remove entities from the drawing.

The Erase command is used to remove entities from the drawing. The command sequence for an erase is as follows:

```
Command: ERASE
Select objects:
```

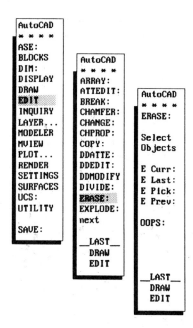

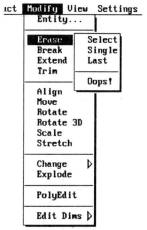

Electronic Work Disk Problem

You will notice that the screen crosshair is now a pickbox. The pickbox can be used to select an object (point method). If you wish to use one of the other object selection options (such as Window), enter the letter for the option after the "Select objects:" prompt.

ERASE TUTORIAL

Let's use the erase command to delete some objects from a drawing. We will use a drawing from the work disk named "EDIT1". Start the drawing. You should see the following on your screen.

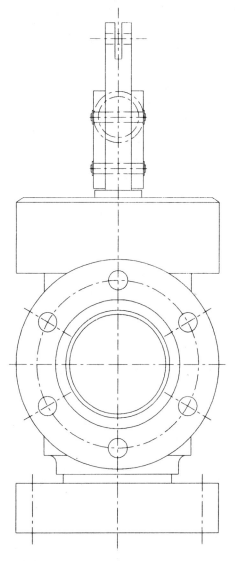

FIGURE 10-10 EDIT1 Exercise

USING A PICKBOX

Let's use the Erase command to delete some of the entities. From the Edit menu, select Erase. You should now see a pickbox on the screen. Place the pickbox over the bottom line of the part as shown in Figure 10-11 and click. The line should now be highlighted. Now select the remainder of the lines as shown in the figure in the same manner. Finally, press the Enter key.

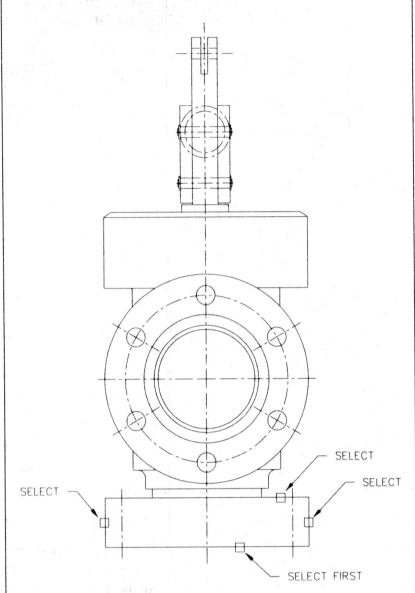

SELECT

SELECT

SELECT

SELECT FIRST

FIGURE 10-11 Selecting Entries to Erase

USING A WINDOW

Let's continue. First, use the U command to undo the erase. Let's now use some of the object selection options.

Select Erase again and enter a "W" in response to the prompt. Refer to Figure 10-12 for the points referenced in the command following sequence.

```
Command: ERASE
Select objects: W
First corner: (select point "1")
Other corner: (select point "2")
58 found
Select objects: (Enter)
```

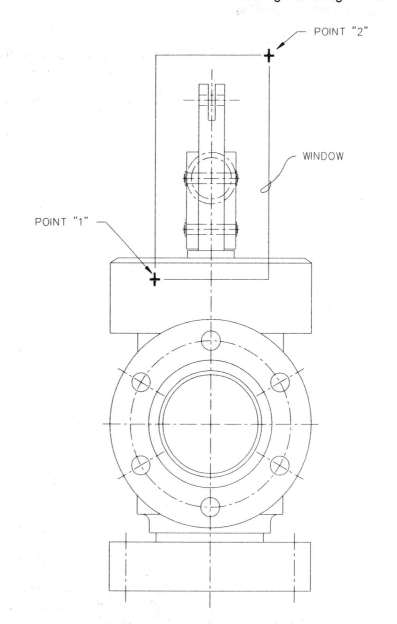

FIGURE 10-12 Erasing With a Window

All the items that were contained in the window were selected. The selected items are highlighted. Notice that entities that extended into the window area, but were not wholly contained within the window, were not selected. Press Enter and the selected objects will be deleted.

USING A CROSSING WINDOW

Use the U command to undo the erase. Select Erase again, entering "C" (for Crossing) as the option. Refer to the following command sequence and Figure 10-13.

```
Command: ERASE
Select objects: C
First corner: (select point "1")
Other corner: (select point "2")
61 found
Select objects:
```

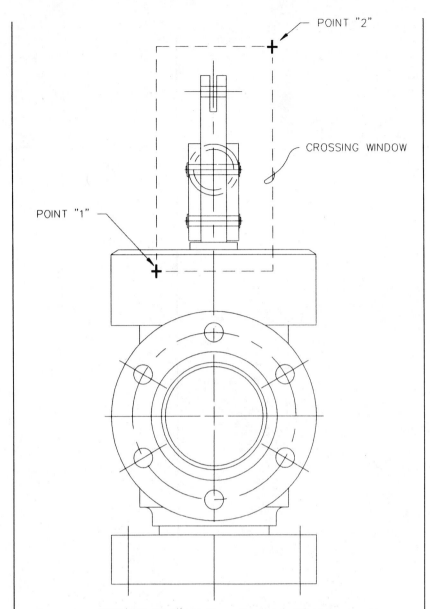

FIGURE 10-13 Using a Crossing Window

REMOVING OBJECTS FROM THE SELECTION SET

Notice that <u>all</u> the objects that were touched by the window were selected (as noted by the highlighting). Let's remove some of the objects. After you placed the crossing window, AutoCAD again asked you to "Select objects:" (see the previous command sequence). Enter "R" for Remove. The command sequence will continue:

    Remove objects: (*select one of the horizontal lines*)
    1 selected, 1 found, 1 removed
    Remove objects: (*select the other horizontal line*)
    1 selected, 1 found, 1 removed
    Remove objects: (*Enter*)

The objects you removed from the object selection set were not erased.

We will use this drawing for some additional exercises in this chapter. If you exit the drawing, discard the changes so any edits are not recorded. If you want to practice with some of the edit commands, you can restore the drawing by using the U command to undo the edits.

RESTORING ERASED OBJECTS

The Oops command restores the entities that were last erased from the drawing.

The Oops command restores the entities that were last erased from the drawing.

     Command: <u>OOPS</u>

You cannot always Oops backward through a drawing to return objects erased several commands back. Most of the time you will be required to Oops back objects immediately after you erased them. Don't press your luck by executing any commands between the two!

If you find yourself unable to Oops back erased entities, remember that you can undo the erase with the U command.

EXERCISE

Use the work disk drawing named "EDIT1". Use the Erase command to delete some of the entities. Next, issue the Oops command. Did the objects return?

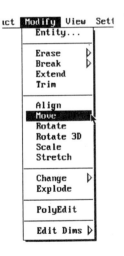

Electronic Work Disk Problem

MOVING OBJECTS IN THE DRAWING

The Move command allows you to move one or more objects to another location.

The Move command allows you to move one or more objects to another location.

Objects are moved by showing a point to start from and a point to move to. The selected object(s) will then move relative to the specified displacement.

     Command: <u>MOVE</u>
     Select objects:
     Base point or displacement:
     Second point of displacement:

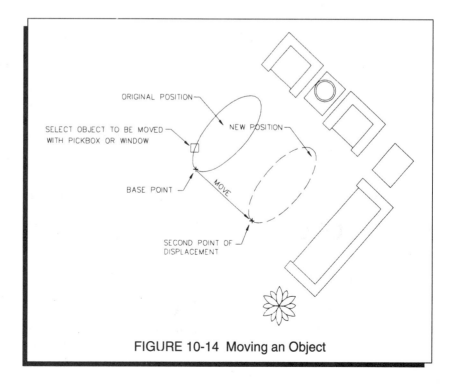

FIGURE 10-14 Moving an Object

Tip

Your first point need not be on the object to be moved; however, using a corner point or other convenient point of reference on the object makes the displacement easier to visualize.

EXERCISE

Start the drawing named "EDIT2" from the work disk. This exercise is a jig-saw puzzle. The drawing is the same as Figure 10-10. When you start the drawing, it will appear as in Figure 10-15. Use the Move command to move the pieces into position, leaving a small space between them. The most effective method is to move the pieces roughly into position while the drawing is in a zoom-all, then zoom in and fine position the pieces.

Electronic Work Disk Problem

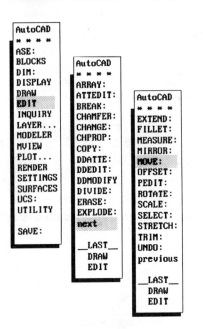

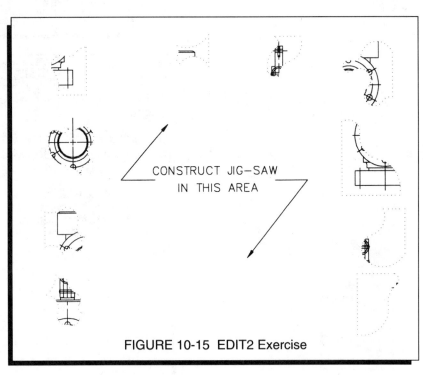

FIGURE 10-15 EDIT2 Exercise

MAKING COPIES OF DRAWING ENTITIES

The Copy command is used to make copies of existing objects in the drawing.

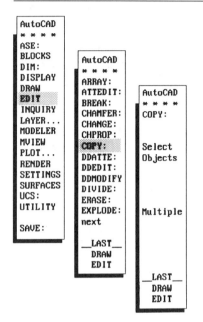

Electronic Work Disk Problem

The Copy command is used to make copies of existing objects in the drawing.

Use the object selection process to choose the object to be copied. The prompt line will then ask for the displacement from the original object to the location of the new object.

Command: COPY
Select objects:
<Base point or displacement>/Multiple:
Second point of displacement:

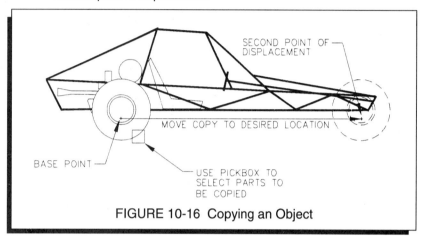

FIGURE 10-16 Copying an Object

Tip

Use the Copy command freely to repeat items "on the go" as you draw.

EXERCISE

From the work disk, start the drawing named "EDIT3". Figure 10-17 shows the drawing. Use the copy command to copy the windows from the left side to the right side. Then copy all the windows on the lower level (including those you just copied) to the upper level.

FIGURE 10-17 EDIT3 Exercise

When you copy, use the object selection options you think will work best.

MAKING MULTIPLE COPIES

The Multiple option allows placement of multiple copies.

The Multiple option allows placement of multiple copies.

> Command: <u>COPY</u>
> Select objects:
> <Base point or displacement>/Multiple: <u>M</u>
> Base point:
> Second point of displacement:
> Second point of displacement:

The "Second point of displacement:" prompt will repeat until you cancel the command. The copy will originate from the originally selected object, using the base point you first selected.

EXERCISE

Electronic Work Disk Problem

From the workdisk, start the drawing named "EDIT4". The drawing is a site plan as shown in Figure 10-18.

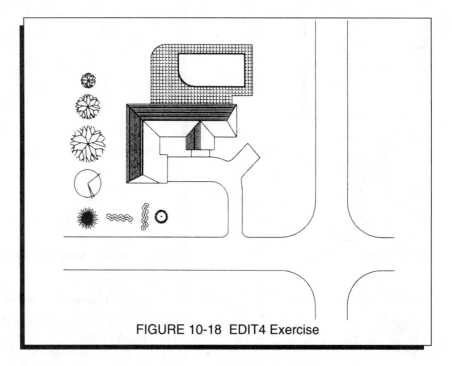

FIGURE 10-18 EDIT4 Exercise

Use the Copy command, with the Multiple option, to copy the landscaping items (trees, shrubbery) and create your own landscape scheme.

PARTIALLY ERASING WITH THE BREAK COMMAND

The Break command is used to erase parts of a line, circle, arc, trace or 2-D polyline.

The Break command is used to erase parts of a line, circle, arc, trace or 2-D polyline.

> Command: <u>BREAK</u>
> Select object:
> Enter first point:
> Enter second point (or F for first point):

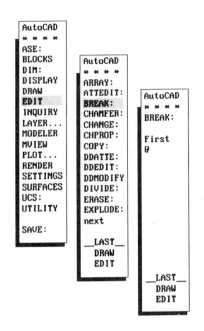

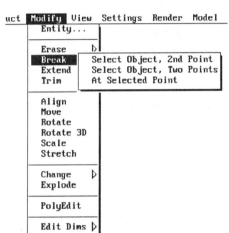

To Break an object, select the two points on the object between which the Break is to take place. The object selection process may be used to select the desired object to be broken.

If object pointing is used to select the entity, AutoCAD assumes that point is also the first Break point. If you wish to redefine the first break point, enter F in response to the prompt line's request for the second point and you will be prompted again for a first point.

Command: <u>BREAK</u>
Select object: (*SELECT*)
Enter second point (or F for first point): <u>F</u>
Enter first point:
Enter second point:

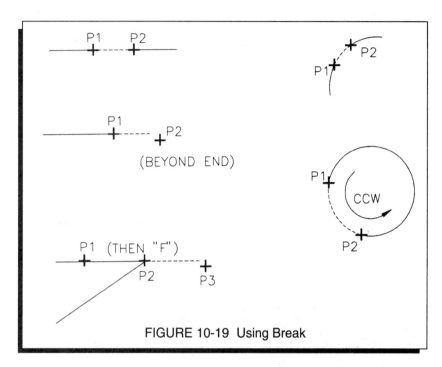

FIGURE 10-19 Using Break

NOTE: The ability to redefine the first point is useful if the drawing is crowded or the break occurs at an intersection where pointing to the object at the first break point might result in the wrong object being selected.

The Break command affects entities in different ways:

Line: The portion of line between the points is removed. If one point is on the line and the other point is off the end of the line, the line is "trimmed off" at the first break point.

Trace: Traces are broken in the exact manner as lines. The new endpoints of the trace are trimmed square.

Circle: A circle is changed into an arc by removing the unwanted piece going <u>counterclockwise</u> from the first point to the second point.

Arc: An arc breaks the same as a line.

Polyline: Polylines of non-zero length are cut square (similar to breads on traces). Breaking a closed polyline creates an open polyline.

Viewport entities: Viewport entity borders can not be broken.

Electronic Work Disk Problem

BREAK EXERCISE

From the work disk, start the drawing named "EDIT5". The following figure shows the drawing.

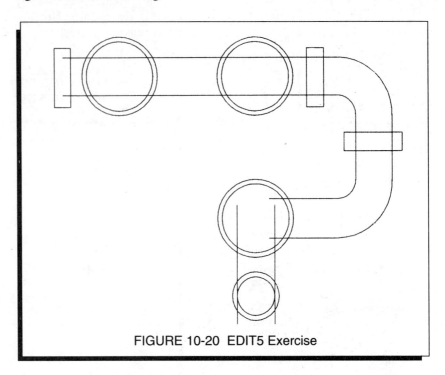

FIGURE 10-20 EDIT5 Exercise

Use the Break command as shown in Figure 10-21 to break each of the objects in the drawing, achieving the results shown.

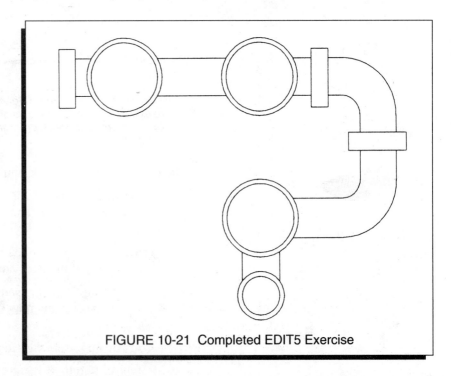

FIGURE 10-21 Completed EDIT5 Exercise

CONNECTING OBJECTS WITH A FILLET

The Fillet command is used to connect two lines or polylines with a perfect intersection or with an arc of a specified radius.

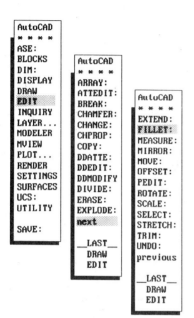

The Fillet command is used to connect two lines or polylines with a perfect intersection or with an arc of a specified radius. Fillet can also be used to connect two circles, two arcs, a line and a circle, a line and an arc, or a circle and an arc.

The two objects do not have to touch in order to perform a fillet, but must be capable of intersecting.

Fillet expects you to choose two lines or polylines. After you have chosen the second line, you do not have to press Enter.

FILLETING TWO LINES

The fillet radius is a default setting which you specify. A zero radius fillet will connect two lines with a perfect intersection.

FILLET EXERCISE

Let's look at an example of connecting two lines with a "zero" radius intersection. Refer to the following command sequences and Figure 10-16. First, draw lines similar to those in the illustration. Now let's set the fillet radius to zero.

> Command: <u>FILLET</u>
> Polyline/Radius/<Select two objects>: <u>R</u>
> Enter fillet radius: <u>0</u>

Now, issue the Fillet command again and select the two lines.

> Command: <u>FILLET</u>
> Polyline/Radius/<Select two objects>: (*select the two lines*)

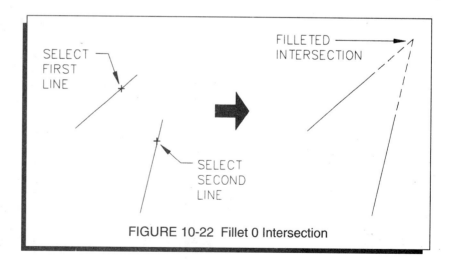

FIGURE 10-22 Fillet 0 Intersection

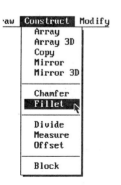

Notice how the two lines are now connected in a perfect intersection.

Let's continue and connect the same two lines with a radiused fillet. We will connect the lines with an arc with a radius of .15. Let's first set the fillet radius to .15.

```
Command: FILLET
Polyline/Radius/<Select two objects>: R
Enter fillet radius <default>: .15
```

The default radius is now set to .15 and will remain until it is changed to another value.

Now, select the Fillet command again. Refer to the following command sequence and Figure 10-23.

```
Command: FILLET
Polyline/Radius/<select two objects>: (select the two lines)
```

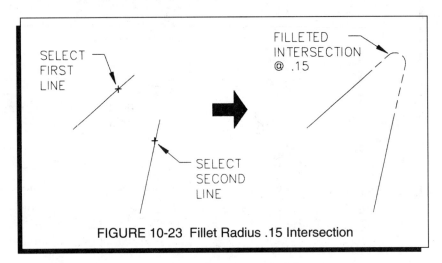

FIGURE 10-23 Fillet Radius .15 Intersection

FILLETING POLYLINES

You may fillet an entire polyline in one operations. If you select the "P" (Polyline) option, the fillet radius is constructed at all intersections of the polyline. If arcs exist at any intersections, they will be changed to the new fillet radius. Note that the fillet is applied to one continuous polyline only.

The following figure illustrates a fillet on a polyline.

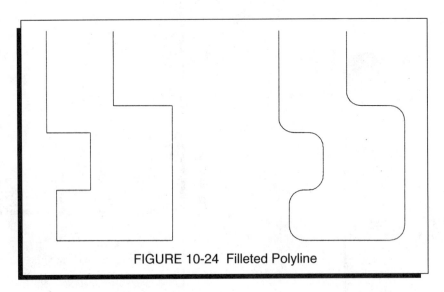

FIGURE 10-24 Filleted Polyline

FILLETING ARCS, CIRCLES, AND LINES TOGETHER

Lines, arcs, and circles can be filleted together. When filleting such entities, there are often several possible fillet combinations. You can specify which type of fillet you desire by the placement of points when you select the objects. AutoCAD will attempt to fillet the endpoint that the selection point is closest to.

Figure 10-25 shows several combinations between a line and arc. Observe the placement of the points used to pick the objects in the middle row, and the resulting fillet shown in the top row.

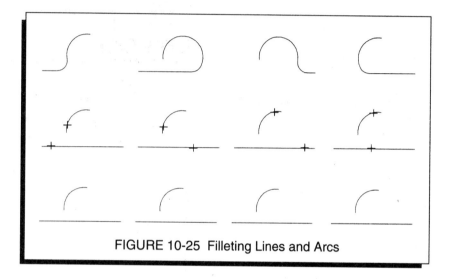

FIGURE 10-25 Filleting Lines and Arcs

If you select two objects for filleting and get undesirable results, use the U command to undo the fillet and try respecifying the points closer to the endpoints you desire to fillet.

FILLETING CIRCLES

As with lines and arcs, the result of filleting two circles depend on the location of the two points you use to select the circles. Figure 10-26 shows three possible combinations, each using different selection points.

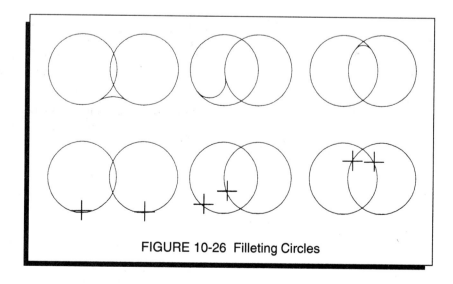

FIGURE 10-26 Filleting Circles

Professional Tips

If you have several filleted corners to draw, construct your intersections at right angles, then fillet each one later. This allows you to continue your line command, without interruptions, and results in fewer commands to be executed.

Your line intersections can be "cleaned up" by setting your fillet radius to zero and filleting the intersections.

Changing an arc radius by fillet is cleaner and easier than erasing the old arc and cutting in a new one. Let AutoCAD do the work for you!

EXERCISE

Electronic Work Disk Problem

Start the drawing named "EDIT6" from the work disk. Perform fillets on the objects to achieve the results shown in Figure 10-27.

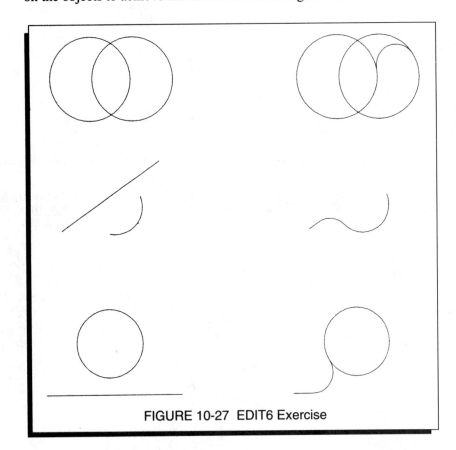

FIGURE 10-27 EDIT6 Exercise

Electronic Work Disk Problem

TUTORIAL

Let's try some edit commands with a drawing on the work disk project named "EDIT7". Figure 10-28 shows the drawing.

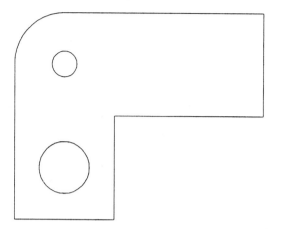

FIGURE 10-28 EDIT7 Exercise

REMOVING THE LOWER CIRCLES

Suppose that a design change has been initiated and you have been instructed to remove the lower circle from the drawing.

>   Go to the ROOT MENU
>   Select EDIT
>   In the edit menu, select ERASE

The prompt line should now say "Select objects".

Move the pickbox until it intersects on the lower circle. Click on the circle.

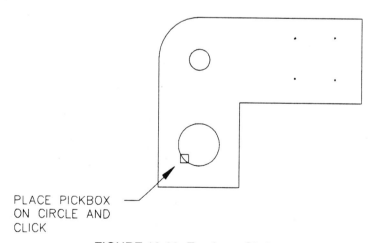

PLACE PICKBOX
ON CIRCLE AND
CLICK

FIGURE 10-29 Erasing a Circle

The circle is now highlighted! The prompt line shows that AutoCAD is ready to add more entities, but let's stop with this one now.

Press the Enter key to tell AutoCAD to execute the Erase command on the highlighted object, and watch the object disappear!

REMOVING THE POINTS

Now, remove the four "Points" on the object by using a window selection:

    Command: ERASE
    Select objects: W
    First corner: (select point "1")
    Other corner: (select point "2")

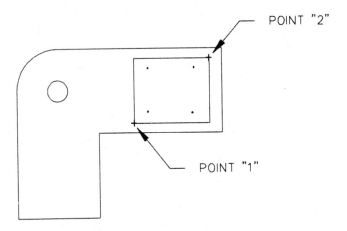

FIGURE 10-30 Erasing the Points

Notice how the window stretched out and followed the crosshair! You may "stretch" the window to any size you wish. It is only "set" when you enter the second corner location.

RESTORING THE POINTS

Let's put back the four points you just erased. You could redraw them. Or you could say "Oops! I made a mistake!" Over in the erase menu, you will find the Oops command. Execute it and watch the points return.

MOVING A CIRCLE

Now that you have erased the lower circle on your drawing, move the remaining circle to the middle of the object. Refer to Figure 10-31.

    Command: MOVE
    Select objects: (select the circle)
    Base point or displacement: (select point "1")
    Second point of displacement: (select point "2")

COPYING A CIRCLE

Let's suppose that you have now been directed to add another circle to your drawing which is identical to the remaining circle. (Remember erasing the larger circle earlier?)

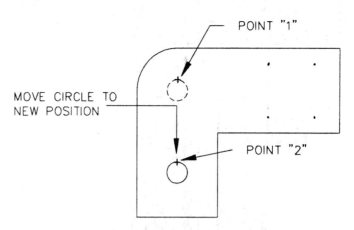

FIGURE 10-31 Moving a Circle

Command: <u>COPY</u>
Select objects: *(select the circle)*
<Base point or displacement>/Multiple: *(select point "1")*
Second point of displacement: *(select point "2")*

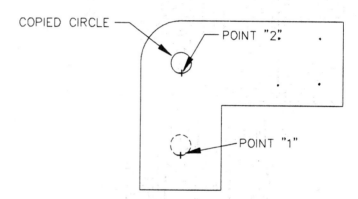

FIGURE 10-32 Copying a Circle

You now have an exact copy of the first circle.

ADDING A NOTCH

Let's add a notch to the object by breaking a line to receive the notched-in area. Refer to Figure 10-33.

Command: <u>(BREAK)</u>
Select objects: *(select the bottom line)*
Enter second point (or F for first point): <u>F</u>
First point: *(select point "1")*
Second point: *(select point "2")*

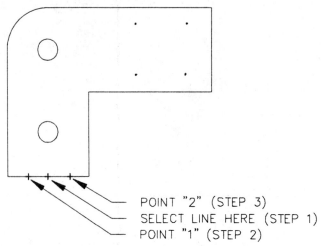

POINT "2" (STEP 3)
SELECT LINE HERE (STEP 1)
POINT "1" (STEP 2)

FIGURE 10-33 Breaking a Line

Now, using the Line command, draw in the notch.

RADIUSING THE CORNERS

Let's add a radius to each of the two right corners of the object. We will set the radius to .5.

> Command: <u>FILLET</u>
> Polyline/Radius/<Select first object>: <u>R</u>
> Enter fillet radius <*default*>: <u>.5</u>

Now repeat the Fillet command again.

> Command: <u>FILLET</u> *(or Return to repeat the command)*
> Polyline/Radius/<Select first object>: *(select point "1")*
> Select second object: *(select point "2")*

The corner now has an arc with a radius of 5. Now repeat the fillet on the lower corner.

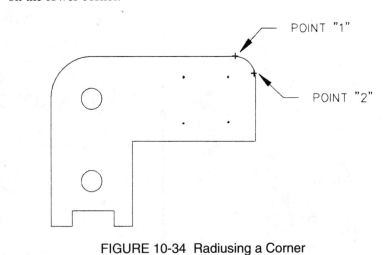

POINT "1"

POINT "2"

FIGURE 10-34 Radiusing a Corner

CHAPTER EXERCISES

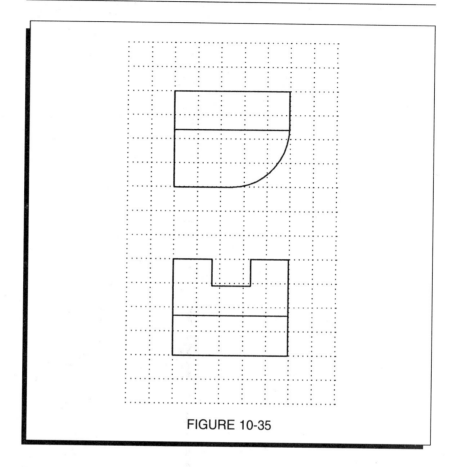

FIGURE 10-35

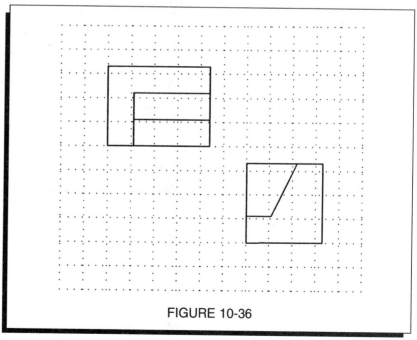

FIGURE 10-36

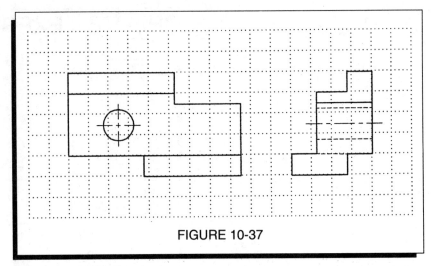

FIGURE 10-37

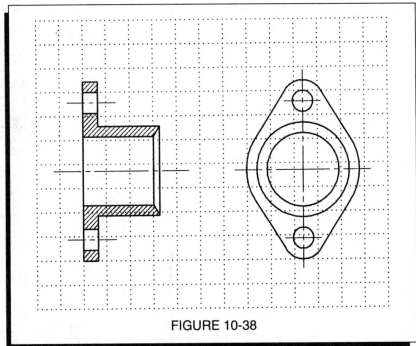

FIGURE 10-38

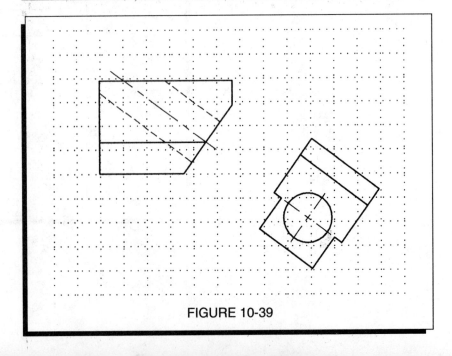

FIGURE 10-39

CHAPTER REVIEW

1. When an edit command is invoked, must a selection option, such as single or window, be entered before an entity is selected?

2. What two changes can a fillet make to an intersection?

3. When choosing a set of objects to edit, other than using the U command, how can you alter an incorrect selection without starting over?

4. If you wish to edit an item that was not drawn last, but was the last item selected, would the "Last" selection option allow you to select the desired item?

5. How do you increase or decrease the size of the pickbox?

6. When moving an object, must the base point of displacement be on the selected object?

7. What five entities are affected by the Break command?

8. When using the Multiple option of the Copy command, is each copy relative to the point of the last copy made, or the first base point entered?

9. In breaking an object, what happens if you do not enter an F, for selection of the first point?

_____

_____

_____

10. Can elements of different types be filleted (such as a line and an arc), or must they be alike?

_____

_____

11. When entering 'box' in response to the select object prompt, how are you then allowed to choose entities?

_____

_____

_____

_____

12. What command will restore entities just erased?

_____

13. What makes it evident that an item has been selected?

_____

_____

14. How can entities be completely removed from the drawing?

_____

_____

15. Once you have begun selecting objects during a command sequence, can you alter your method of selection?

_____

_____

_____

16. When a group of items are selected by using the window option, will an item become a part of the selection set as long as it is partially inside of the window?

_____

_____

17. What happens when you enter the U option during a selection process? Can you use this option more than one time in a row?

_____

_____

_____

18. In the object selection process, how is the box option different from the automatic option?

_____

_____

_____

CHAPTER 11

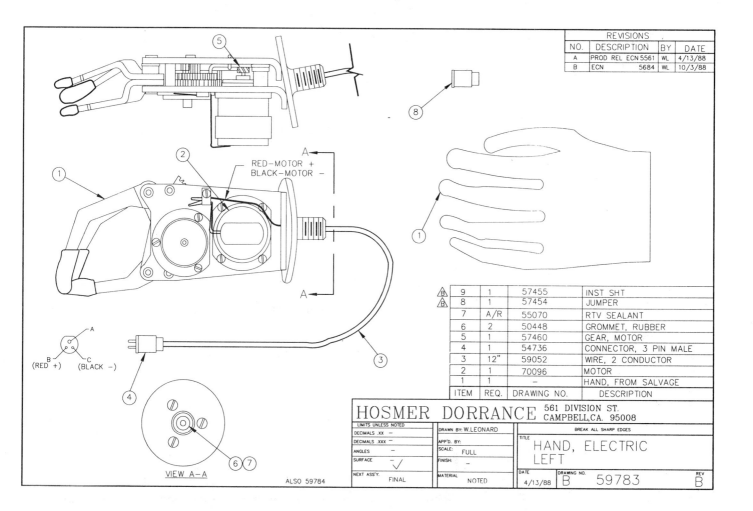

RED—MOTOR +
BLACK—MOTOR —

A

A

A
B   C
(RED +)   (BLACK —)

VIEW A—A

ALSO 59784

	9	1	57455	INST SHT
	8	1	57454	JUMPER
	7	A/R	55070	RTV SEALANT
	6	2	50448	GROMMET, RUBBER
	5	1	57460	GEAR, MOTOR
	4	1	54736	CONNECTOR, 3 PIN MALE
	3	12"	59052	WIRE, 2 CONDUCTOR
	2	1	70096	MOTOR
	1	1	—	HAND, FROM SALVAGE
	ITEM	REQ.	DRAWING NO.	DESCRIPTION

HOSMER DORRANCE 561 DIVISION ST.
CAMPBELL,CA. 95008

LIMITS UNLESS NOTED			
DECIMALS .XX —	DRAWN BY: W.LEONARD	BREAK ALL SHARP EDGES	
DECIMALS .XXX —	APP'D. BY:	TITLE	
ANGLES —	SCALE: FULL	HAND, ELECTRIC LEFT	
SURFACE —	FINISH: —		
NEXT ASS'Y. FINAL	MATERIAL NOTED	DATE 4/13/88	DRAWING NO. B 59783	REV B

Constructing Multiview Drawings

OBJECTIVES:

Three dimensional objects are commonly described by multiview drawings. Chapter 11 covers the use of AutoCAD for constructing multiview drawings. The objectives of this chapter are:

● To acquaint the user with the fundamentals of multiview drawings.

● Learning the commands that draw multiview drawings.

● To explore the methodologies of using AutoCAD to construct multiview drawings.

MULTIVIEW DRAWINGS

The description of three dimensional objects by use of flat, two dimensional drawings is a common drafting practice. An accurate 2-D description can be accomplished by drawing the object from several directions, thus *multiple views*.

ORTHOGRAPHIC PROJECTION

An orthographic projection *is a view of an object that is created by projecting a single view onto an imaginary projection plane.*

An *orthographic projection* is a view of an object that is created by projecting a single view onto an imaginary projection plane. Let's look at an example. The face of an object in Figure 11-1 is projected onto the viewing plane.

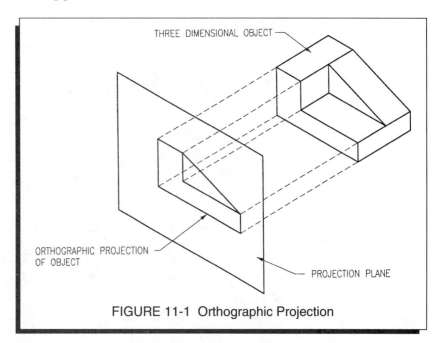

FIGURE 11-1 Orthographic Projection

The image that is projected onto the projection plane represents the true lengths of the edges on the object. The projection plane in this example is parallel to a viewing face on the object. This is referred to as a *normal* view of the object. Normal views are a more accurate method of viewing an object in orthographic projection.

ONE VIEW ORTHOGRAPHIC PROJECTIONS

Many thin, simple objects can be described by a single orthographic projection, such as the one in Figure 11-2.

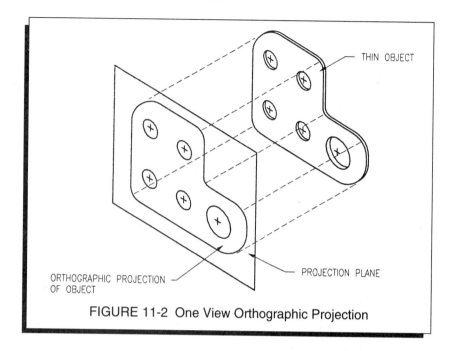

FIGURE 11-2 One View Orthographic Projection

TWO VIEW ORTHOGRAPHIC PROJECTIONS

More often, a single view can not adequately describe a three dimensional object. Faces that do not lie in the same plane can be projected onto the projection plane. The viewer may see the edge lines, but can not determine the location of the different planes.

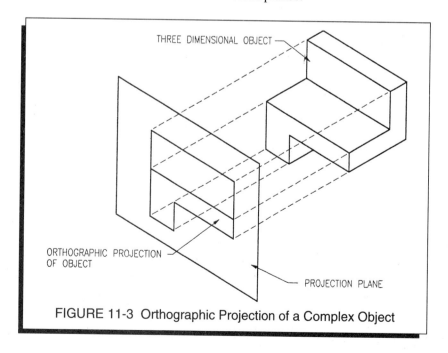

FIGURE 11-3 Orthographic Projection of a Complex Object

Two orthographic views can be used to accurately describe such an object. To do this, two projection planes must be used.

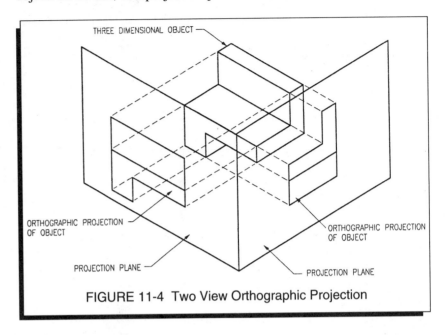

FIGURE 11-4 Two View Orthographic Projection

The views should show the length, height, and width of the object.

MULTIPLE VIEW ORTHOGRAPHIC PROJECTIONS

The term "multiview" *describes several views of an object.*

More complex objects may require multiple views to adequately describe them. These views can be projected from several sides of the object. The term *"multiview"* describes several views of an object.

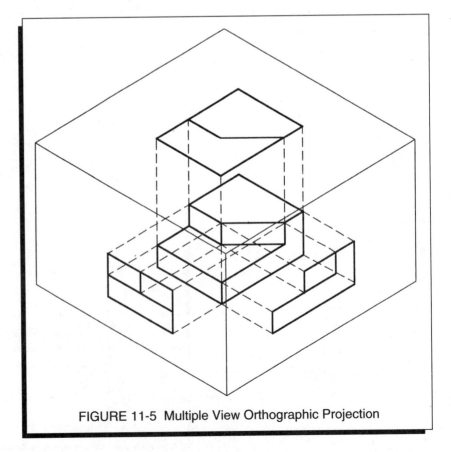

FIGURE 11-5 Multiple View Orthographic Projection

POSITIONING VIEWS

In most situations, three views of an object will adequately describe an object. The views are usually labeled as the front, top, and side. The front view is considered the primary view, with the top view positioned above it and the side view to one side of the front view.

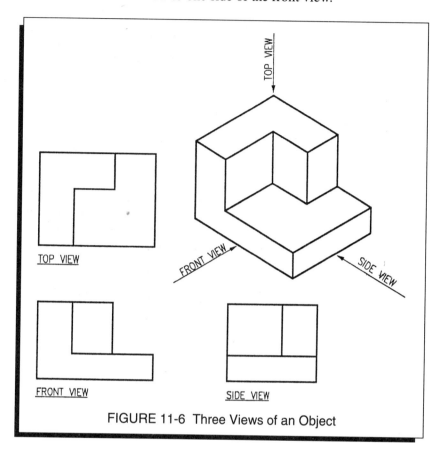

FIGURE 11-6 Three Views of an Object

With this arrangement, the dimensions for the side view can be transferred from the top and front views. Figure 11-7 shows the previous

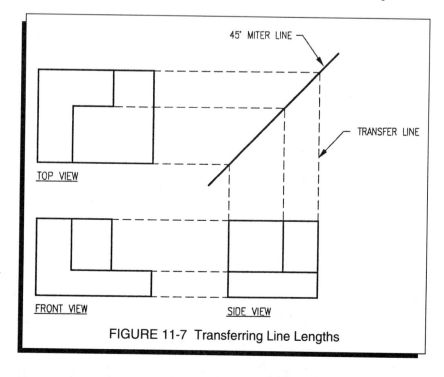

FIGURE 11-7 Transferring Line Lengths

example with imaginary transfer lines shown. Note how the transfer lines from the top view are reflected off a 45 degree miter line.

This method can be used as an alternate technique to constructing each line length.

DRAWING MULTIVIEWS WITH AUTOCAD

AutoCAD is an excellent tool for constructing multiview drawings. The method of construction closely follows that used on the drawing board.

MULTIVIEW TUTORIAL

Let's construct a simple three view drawing with AutoCAD. The following figure shows the object we will use.

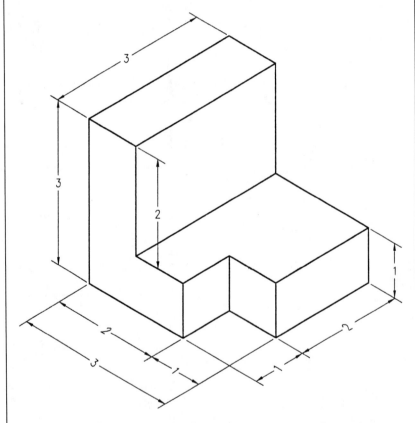

FIGURE 11-8 3-D Object (With Dimensions Shown)

Let's begin a new drawing. Enter New from the command line. Specify the drawing name 3VIEW. Let's set a snap increment so our crosshairs will only move one unit at a time.

```
Command: SNAP
Snap spacing or ON/OFF/Aspect/Rotate/Style <default>: 1
```

Now use the Line command to draw the front view of the object. Figure 11-9A shows the dimensions of the front view. Figure 11-9B shows how your drawing should look after you have drawn the front view.

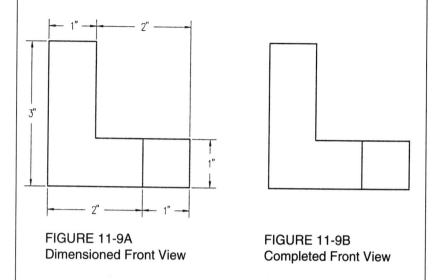

FIGURE 11-9A
Dimensioned Front View

FIGURE 11-9B
Completed Front View

Now we will draw the top view. Use the Line command to draw transfer lines to transfer the widths of the object, then draw a line that will serve as the upper edge of the top view as shown in the following illustration.

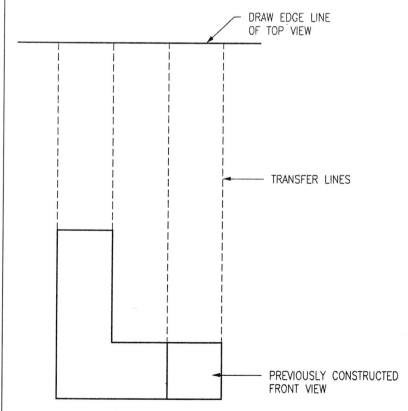

FIGURE 11-10 Transferring Object Widths

Next, we will use a command called Offset to offset the 3" width of the object. Following this, we will again use the Offset command to create the "notch". Use the following illustrated sequence.

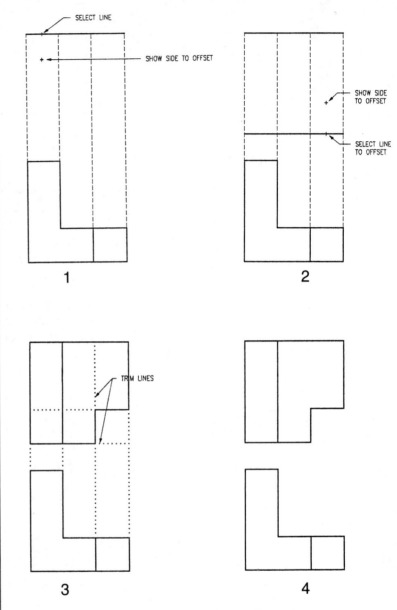

FIGURE 11-11 Illustrated Sequence

Now we will draw the side view. Let's start by placing a miter line so we can transfer the top view dimensions to the side view.

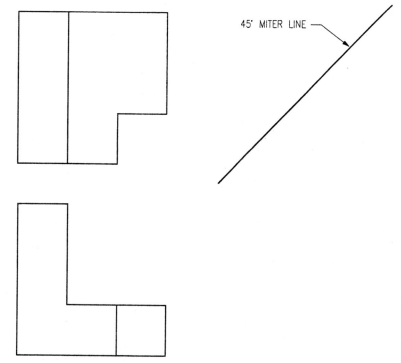

FIGURE 11-12 Placement of Miter Line

Now use the line command to transfer the object's edges from the top and front views as shown in Figure 11-12. Using Ortho mode and object snap will aid you in constructing accurate transfer lines.

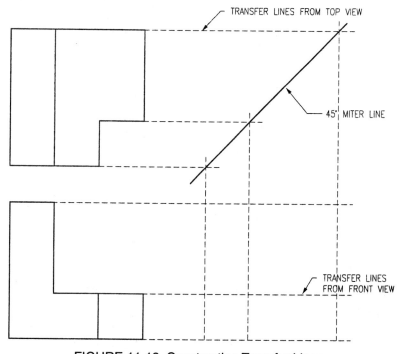

FIGURE 11-13 Constructing Transfer Lines

Now use the Trim command to trim away lines so your drawing looks like the one in Figure 11-14. Be sure to erase any remaining transfer lines.

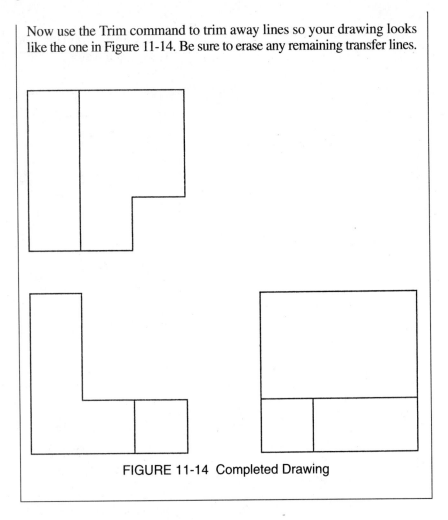

FIGURE 11-14 Completed Drawing

AUXILIARY VIEWS

Objects sometimes have angular faces that are not parallel to the projection plane. The object shown in Figure 11-15 contains an angular face that is not truly represented in the top or side view.

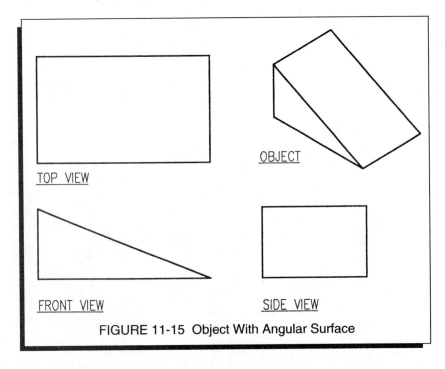

FIGURE 11-15 Object With Angular Surface

An auxiliary view is one that is projected onto a projection plane that is parallel to the angular surface.

We can show the true size of the angular face by adding a projection from the object called an *auxiliary view.* An auxiliary view is one that is projected onto a projection plane that is parallel to the angular surface. You can also think of this as the view you would see if you looked at the object from a point perpendicular to the angular face. Figure 11-16 shows the previous object with an auxiliary view added.

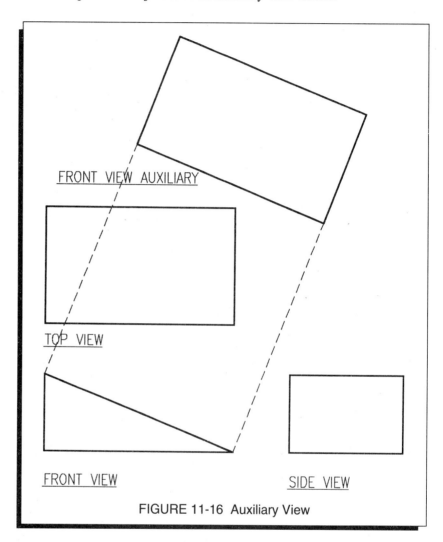

FRONT VIEW AUXILIARY

TOP VIEW

FRONT VIEW

SIDE VIEW

FIGURE 11-16 Auxiliary View

Auxiliary views serve three purposes that can not be achieved by the normal three views.

- To show the true size of the angular surface.

- To illustrate the true shape of the surface.

- To aid in the projection of other views.

Auxiliary views can be projected from any other view. The name of the view is determined from the view from which it is projected. For example, if you project the auxiliary view from the front view, it is named the *front view auxiliary.*

CONSTRUCTING AUXILIARY VIEWS WITH AUTOCAD

Constructing an auxiliary view with AutoCAD involves drawing the view at an angle parallel to the angular face. There are some tricks that make this process easier. Let's look at how we would draw an auxiliary view.

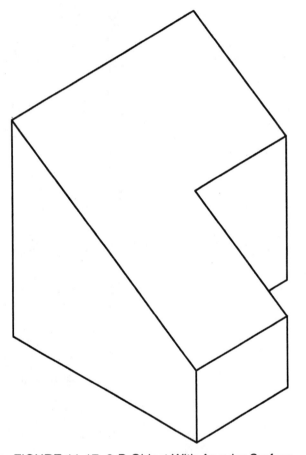

▪ Electronic Work Disk Problem

AUXILIARY VIEW TUTORIAL

We will construct an auxiliary view for the following object. The *electronic work disk* contains a drawing named "AUX_VIEW" that can be used if you wish to follow along.

FIGURE 11-17 3-D Object With Angular Surface

A simple trick to get started is to copy the angle line from a projected view into the position where the auxiliary view will be positioned. Figure 11-18 illustrates this procedure.

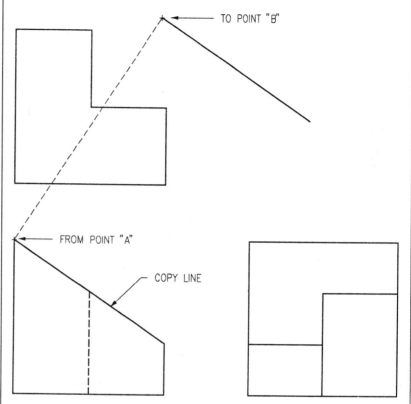

FIGURE 11-18 Copying the Angle Line

Next, use the Snap command to rotate the snap grid. This will not only rotate the snap grid, but will also rotate the crosshairs so we can draw at the proper angle. The following command sequence and Figure 11-19 snow how to do this.

Command: SNAP
Snap spacing or ON/OFF/Aspect/Rotate/Style <default>: R
Base point <0.0000,0.0000>: INT
of select point "1"
Rotation angle <0>: INT
of select point "2"
Angle adjusted to (angle of rotation)

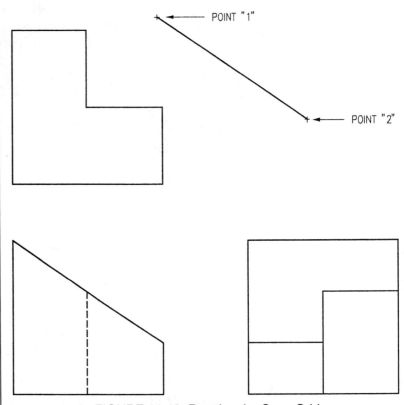

FIGURE 11-19 Rotating the Snap Grid

Notice how using object snap assists in obtaining greater accuracy. If you move the crosshair around the screen, you will notice that it is rotated to the same angle as the line you copied.

Next, use the Line command to complete the drawing. Be sure to use the Ortho mode and the snap increment setting to assist in drawing the object. You may also want to construct some temporary transfer lines to assist in determining the intersections. Figure 11-20 shows the completed view with transfer lines shown dashed.

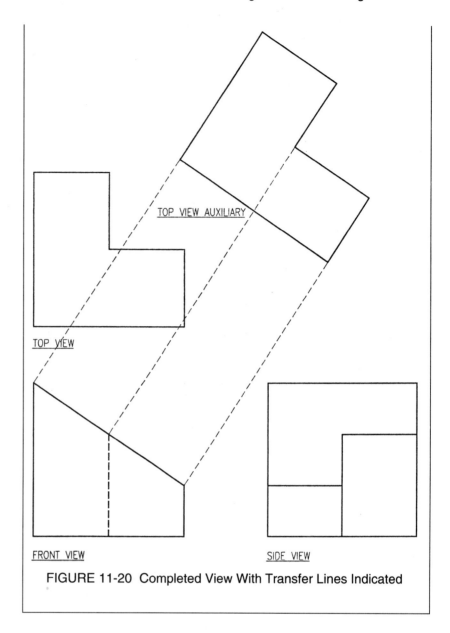

TOP VIEW AUXILIARY

TOP VIEW

FRONT VIEW

SIDE VIEW

FIGURE 11-20 Completed View With Transfer Lines Indicated

SHOWING HIDDEN LINES IN MULTIVIEW DRAWINGS

Auxiliary views are line drawings. Solid lines are used to represent the edges of the object. In AutoCAD, solidly drawn lines are referred to as *continuous* lines. Edges that are hidden from view are shown in a linetype referred to as *hidden*.

This is a line that is constructed from a series of short line segments. Let's look at an example. Figure 11-21 shows an object containing edges that are hidden in some views. These edges are defined with the hidden linetype.

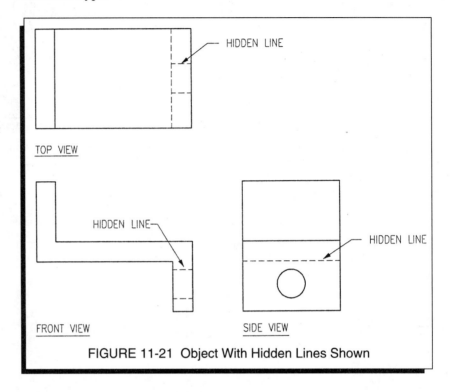

TOP VIEW

FRONT VIEW   SIDE VIEW

FIGURE 11-21 Object With Hidden Lines Shown

AutoCAD provides several linetypes for your use. Let's look at how to draw different types of lines.

USING THE LINETYPE COMMAND

Different linetypes are used frequently in drawings. The following figure shows the linetypes provided in AutoCAD.

BORDER		DIVIDE	
BORDER2		DIVIDE2	
BORDERX2		DIVIDEX2	
CENTER		DOT	
CENTER2		DOT2	
CENTERX2		DOTX2	
DASHDOT		HIDDEN	
DASHDOT2		HIDDEN2	
DASHDOTX2		HIDDENX2	
DASHED		PHANTOM	
DASHED2		PHANTOM2	
DASHEDX2		PHANTOMX2	

FIGURE 11-22 AutoCAD Linetypes

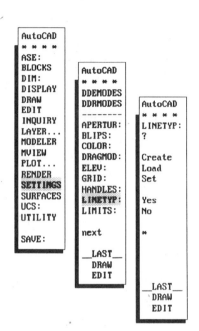

These linetypes can be added to your drawing by using the LINETYPE command. Before you can use a linetype, you must first load that linetype. Let's look at how to use the LINETYPE command to load a linetype.

LOADING LINETYPES

You must load a linetype before using it. When you use the Layer Ltype command, the linetype is automatically loaded from ACAD.LIN when it is needed.

If you explicitly want to load a linetype into your drawing, issue the Linetype command:

> Command: <u>LINETYPE</u>
> ?/ Create /Load /Set: <u>L</u>
> Linetype(s) to load: (*NAME*)
> File to search: (*NAME*)

You should reply to the prompt for the linetype to load with the linetype name. The file to search is the file in which the linetype is located. Initially, you will use the ACAD file. It is not necessary to enter the .LIN file extension. If the linetype was previously loaded, the following prompt is displayed:

> Linetype was loaded before. Reload it <Y>

You may use this process to reload current linetypes. If a regeneration is performed, the effect of the new linetype is immediately seen on the screen.

? (LISTING THE LINETYPES)

If you wish to see the linetypes that are available, enter "?" at the prompt. AutoCAD will display a dialogue box that prompts for the linetype file. 11-23

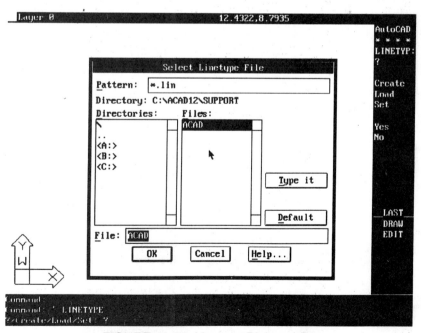

FIGURE 11-23 Linetype Dialogue Box

After the linetype file is selected, a text screen(s) displays the linetypes available in that file.

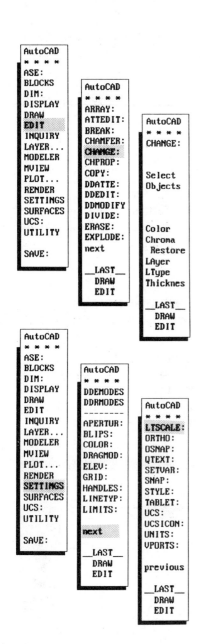

Linetypes are constructed of line segments and dots.

SPECIFYING LINETYPES IN OTHER WAYS

Linetypes can be designated in many ways.

1. The Linetype command can be used to designate the current linetype.

2. The linetype can be specified as the default type of line for a layer.

3. The linetype can be assigned during the plotting setup to a specified entity color.

USING THE CHANGE COMMAND TO DESIGNATE LINETYPES

You can use the Change command to designate linetypes for existing entities. Let's look at the command sequence used to change a linetype.

Command: CHANGE
Select objects: *select the entities you want to change*
Properties/<Change point>: P
Change what property (Color/Elev/LAyer/LType/Thickness) ? LT
New linetype <*default*>:

LINETYPE SCALES

Linetypes are constructed of line segments and dots. The line segments are of a specified length of one. The scale of these segments may be adjusted by use of the Ltscale (linetype scale) command:

Command: LTSCALE
New scale factor <*default*>:

Entering larger numbers results in longer line segments, while smaller numbers create shorter line segments.

To properly display the new linetype scale, a regeneration must be performed. In certain conditions, AutoCAD will automatically regenerate. If a regeneration does not occur after changing the linetype scale, you can force a regeneration with the Regen command.

If you change linetypes and the line still appears as a continuous line, change the Ltscale to a different setting. It is possible for the linetype scale to be too large or small to display.

WRITING LINETYPES

The Create option of the Linetype command is used to create a linetype. In order to do this, we must understand how linetype files work.

Linetype descriptions are held in linetype files. The linetype descriptions you received are held in a file named ACAD.LIN. Each linetype description is described by two lines. The first is a visual description of the line. This description is not actually a part of the description, but is used to display if you enter a question mark (?) in response to the Linetype prompt. Do this now and look at the linetype descriptions in the ACAD linetype file.

The second line is the actual description AutoCAD uses to build the line from. This line uses a numerical description to create the line. This line always begins with "A,", then continues with the description. The numerical description can be thought of as simple pen-up and pen-down commands, with the numbers as segment lengths. A positive number is a pen-down length, and negative numbers are pen-up lengths.

EXERCISE

Let's write a new linetype definition. We will construct a new linetype that could be used for property line definitions. This line will have a long length, followed by two short dashes, then repeat. Let's enter the Linetype command.

```
Command: LINETYPE
?/Create/Load/Set: C
File name for storage of linetype <ACAD>: ACAD2
Creating new file
```

We have just designated a new linetype file to hold our linetype and named it ACAD2. We could have just used the file named ACAD and appended the linetype description. The command sequence continues with:

```
Descriptive text: --------- -- -- --------
```

Enter a series of dashes and spaces as shown. It doesn't matter how many. Remember, this is just a visual representation of the line you are about to write a description for. Let's continue with the command sequence.

```
Enter pattern (on next line):
A,1,-.1,.1,-.1,.1-.1
```

Press Enter when you are finished. The command sequence will continue:

```
New definition written to file.
?/Create/Load/Set: L
Linetype to load: PROP
File to search <ACAD@>: ACAD2

Linetype PROP loaded.

?/Create/Load/Set: (cancel the command with Ctrl-C)
```

Now use the Line command to draw several lines with your new linetype. If the linetype appears as a solid line, use the Ltscale command to change the linetype scale.

CHAPTER EXERCISES

Use AutoCAD to draw three views of the following 3-D objects.

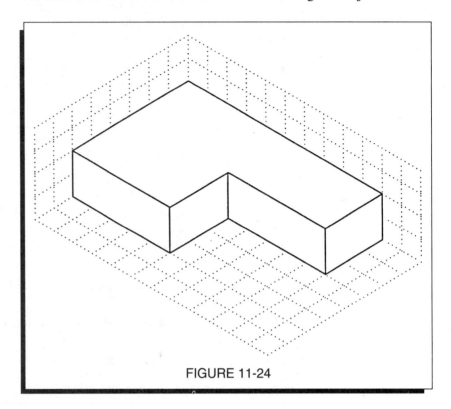

FIGURE 11-24

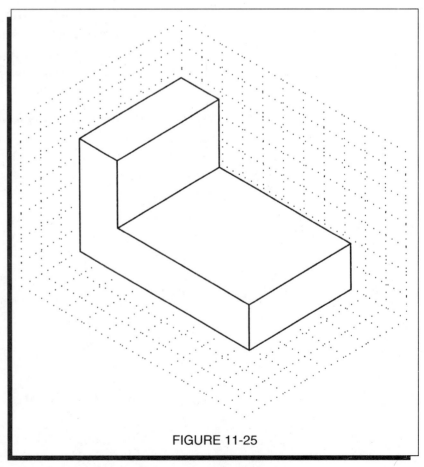

FIGURE 11-25

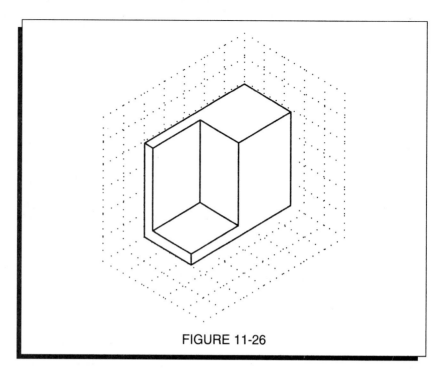

FIGURE 11-26

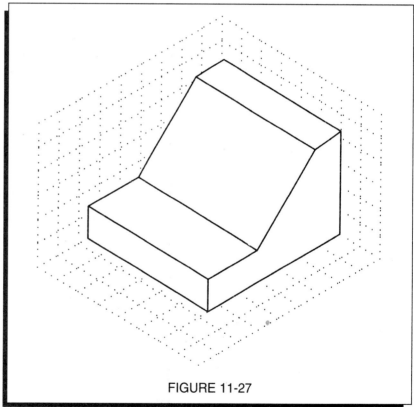

FIGURE 11-27

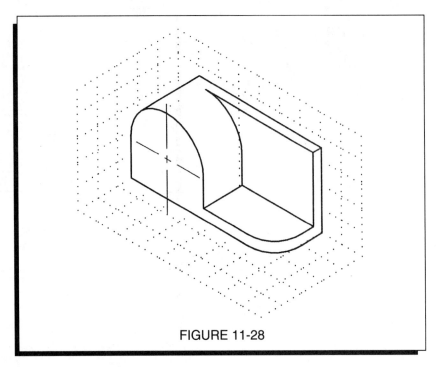

FIGURE 11-28

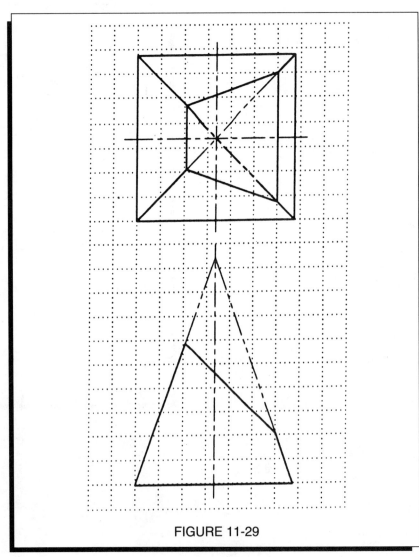

FIGURE 11-29

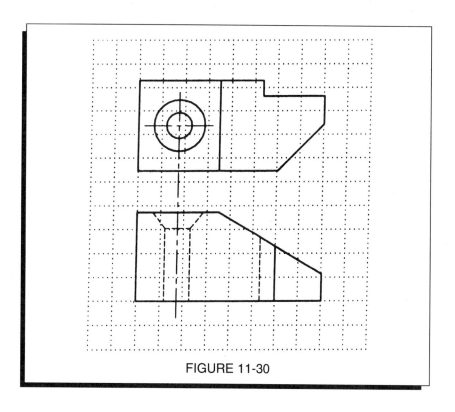

FIGURE 11-30

CHAPTER REVIEW

1. What is an orthographic projection?

2. What type of object can be described by only one projection?

3. What term is used to describe a drawing that contains several views of an object?

4. What are the three typical views used in orthographic projection?

5. What is an auxiliary view?

6. Why would you use an auxiliary view?

_____

_____

_____

7. What do hidden lines show in a drawing?

_____

_____

8. Name two ways a linetype can be designated in AutoCAD.

_____

_____

9. How would you control the length of individual segments in a dashed line?

_____

_____

10. Write a linetype pattern that contains a long line segment, three short segments, then repeats.

_____

_____

CHAPTER 12

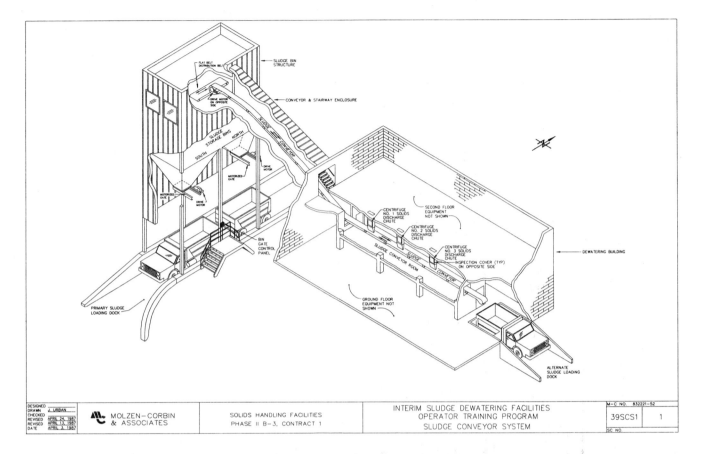

DESIGNED		MOLZEN-CORBIN	SOLIDS HANDLING FACILITIES	INTERIM SLUDGE DEWATERING FACILITIES	M-C NO. 832221-52	
DRAWN	J. URBAN	& ASSOCIATES	PHASE II B-3, CONTRACT 1	OPERATOR TRAINING PROGRAM	39SCS1	1
CHECKED				SLUDGE CONVEYOR SYSTEM		
REVISED	APRIL 24, 1987					
REVISED	APRIL 13, 1987				SC NO.	
DATE	APRIL 3, 1987					

Constructing Sectional and Patterned Drawings

OBJECTIVES

Sectional views are used to describe objects when other views are not sufficient. Computer aided design is an excellent tool for constructing sectional views. The objectives of this chapter are:

● To understand the many types of sectional views and their applications.

● Learning the techniques of constructing the crosshatching that is an integral part of sectional views.

● Creating the solid areas that can be used as part of sectional drawings.

SECTIONAL VIEWS

A view of an object or assembly that has been cut apart is called a section.

Many parts and assemblies can not be fully described by use of orthographic projection. It is often helpful to view the object as if it were cut apart. A view of an object or assembly that has been cut apart is called a *section*.

A section is used in many disciplines. The mechanical designer uses sections to show details that can not be described in other ways.

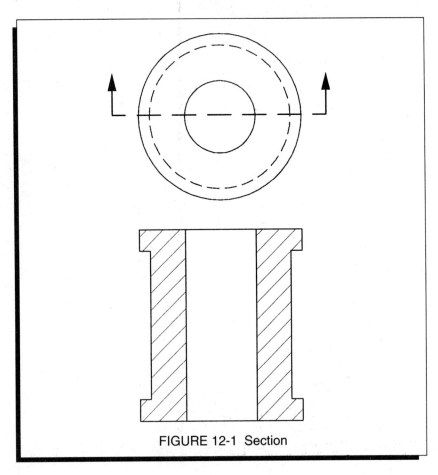

FIGURE 12-1 Section

Civil engineers detail roadway profiles by showing sections through the road.

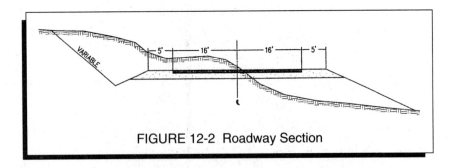

FIGURE 12-2 Roadway Section

Architects use sections frequently. Sections through entire structures show how a building structure is designed. Individual wall sections detail vertical measurements and delineate materials.

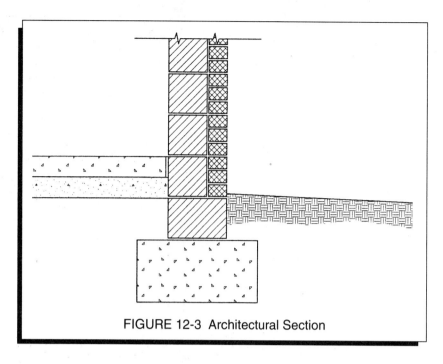

FIGURE 12-3 Architectural Section

TYPES OF SECTIONS

Depending on the desired information to convey, the designer uses different types of sections. Let's study each type of section and look at an example of each.

FULL SECTIONS

A full section is a section that is cut across the entire object.

A *full section* is a section that is cut across the entire object. Full sections are usually cut through the larger axis of the object.

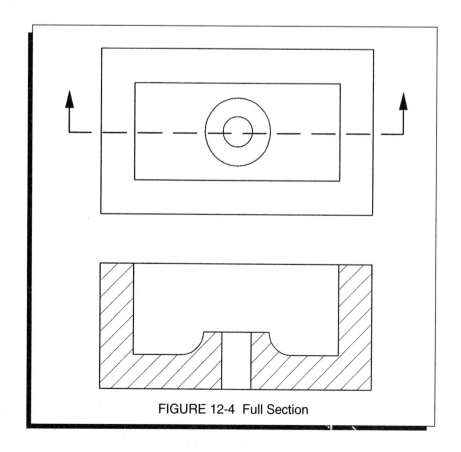

FIGURE 12-4 Full Section

Such a section cut along the longer axis is referred to as the longitudinal axis. If the section is cut along the minor axis, it is referred to as the latitudinal axis.

Parts of the object that are "cut" are shown with crosshatching.

REVOLVED SECTIONS

It is often helpful to view a section of a part of an object that is transposed on top of the point where the section was cut. Such a section is referred to as a *revolved* section. Figure 12-5 shows a revolved section.

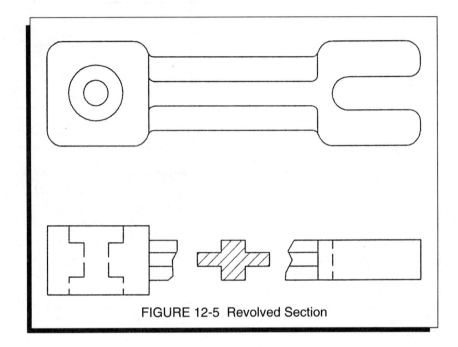

FIGURE 12-5 Revolved Section

REMOVED SECTIONS

A *removed section* is similar to a revolved section, except the section is not placed at the point that the section was cut.

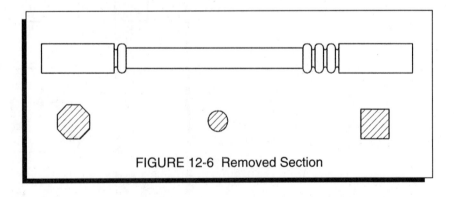

FIGURE 12-6 Removed Section

OFFSET SECTIONS

Offset sections *are sections that are cut along an uneven line.*

Offset sections are sections that are cut along an uneven line. Offset sections should be used carefully; changing the cutting plane only to show essential elements.

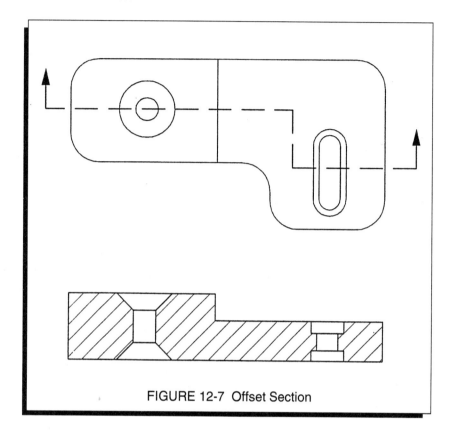

FIGURE 12-7 Offset Section

CROSSHATCHING SECTIONAL VIEWS

Crosshatching refers to placing a pattern within a boundary area. When drawing sections, it is customary to place crosshatching on the faces through the section cuts.

The spacing of the crosshatching should be relative to the scale of the section. The angle of the crosshatching should be oriented 45 degrees from the main lines of the cut area whenever possible.

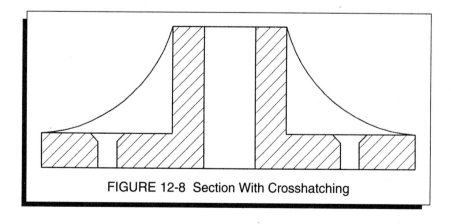

FIGURE 12-8 Section With Crosshatching

In most drafting applications, a simple crosshatch composed of parallel lines is used. In some applications, however, it is acceptable to show different materials with representative crosshatching. Figure 12-9 shows some standard hatch patterns for different materials.

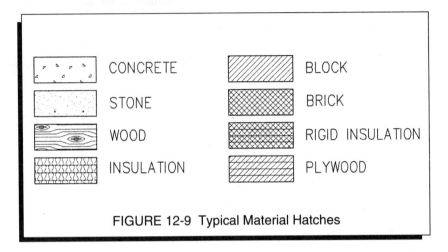

FIGURE 12-9 Typical Material Hatches

CREATING SECTIONAL VIEWS IN AUTOCAD

AutoCAD can be used to effectively create sectional views. You can draw the section, then render the cut areas with hatch patterns that are provided with the AutoCAD program. The following page shows all the patterns available in AutoCAD.

Hatches differ from other entities in that the entire hatch is treated as one entity. Because of this, you cannot edit a portion of it unless it is exploded. If you identify one line of a hatch to be erased, the entire hatch will be erased. Likewise, an entire hatch may be erased by the Erase-Last command.

Hatch patterns are placed with the Hatch and Bhatch commands. Let's look at how each command is used.

USING THE BHATCH COMMAND

The Bhatch (boundary hatch) command is used to create a boundary around an area, then place a hatch pattern within that area. The Bhatch command is controlled from a dialogue box. To use this command, select Draw/Bhatch from the screen menu, or Draw/Hatch from the pull-down menu.

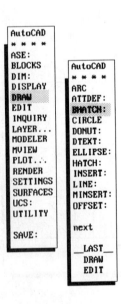

The Bhatch command displays a "Boundary hatch" dialogue box as shown in Figure 12-10. Let's look at how we can use the dialogue box to place a hatch.

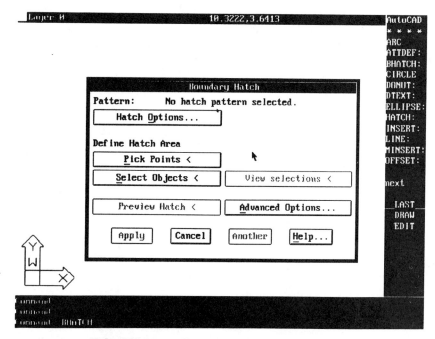

FIGURE 12-10 Boundary Hatch Dialogue Box

SELECTING A HATCH PATTERN AND STYLE

The first step in placing a hatch pattern is to select the pattern you want to use. If a selection has already been made in the current drawing session, its name is displayed to the right of the "Pattern:" listing at the top of the dialogue box.

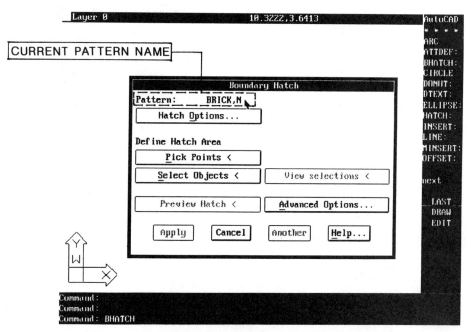

FIGURE 12-11 Current Hatch Pattern Name

If you wish to use the named pattern, it is not necessary to select it again. If you want to select a new pattern, select the "Hatch Options..." button. Selecting this button will display the "Hatch Options" dialogue box.

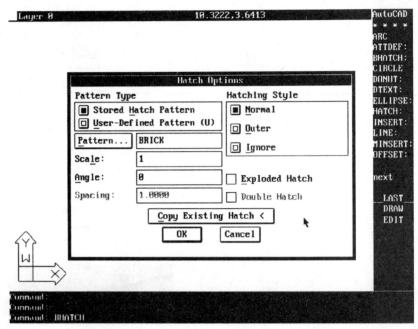

FIGURE 12-12 Hatch Options Dialogue Box

If we know the name of the pattern we wish to use, we can click in the text box next to the "Pattern..." button and type the name from the keyboard. If a name is already present, we can use the backspace key to erase it and type a new one.

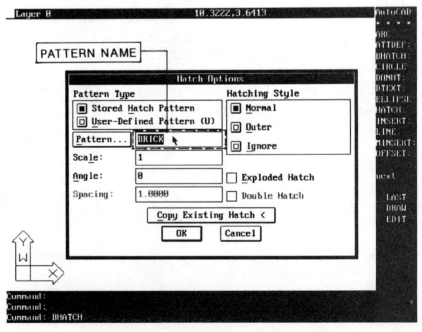

FIGURE 12-13 Hatch Pattern Name Text Box

Let's assume that we do not know the name of the pattern we wish to use. Click on the "Pattern..." button. A dialogue box containing slides of patterns is displayed.

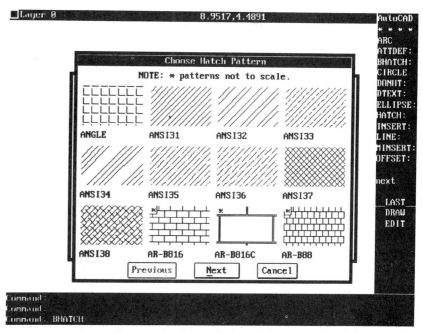

FIGURE 12-14 Pattern Selection Dialogue Box

Select the "Next" button to see more selections. You can use the "Next" and "Previous" buttons to flip back and forth through the hatch pattern slides. Notice that the listings are in alphabetical order.

Now flip to the page that has the "ANSI31" listing. Move the arrow pointer on top of the pattern and click. You are returned to the "Define Hatch Pattern" dialogue box. Notice how the name box contains the "ANSI31" hatch pattern name.

Selecting the Angle and Scale

Hatch patterns can be drawn at any angle and scale.

Hatch patterns can be drawn at any angle and scale. The angle of the hatch is specified in degrees and is true to AutoCAD's angle specifications (see Chapter 8). The angle of the hatch patterns shown in the dialogue box slides is zero. This is true even if the angle of the lines within the hatch are drawn at another angle.

To set the angle, click in the angle box and use the keyboard to specify the new angle.

The scale of the hatch pattern is defined as a numerical factor. The default scale is one. Setting the factor as two will create a hatch twice as large, while setting a factor of .5 will create a hatch half the size of the default.

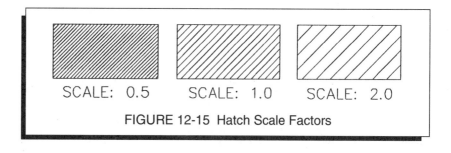

FIGURE 12-15 Hatch Scale Factors

Setting the Hatch Style

Hatch *styles* are used to determine the manner in which AutoCAD will place a hatch within a bounded area. Let's look at an example. Figure 12-16 shows an object that contains hatching in part of an area.

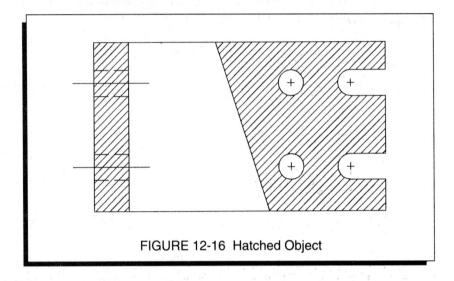

FIGURE 12-16 Hatched Object

To define the area that is to be hatched, a style is used to control the hatch. Let's look at how styles work.

If the area bounded by the identified entities have no objects within them, the hatch is filled with the selected pattern. If, however, the area contains other entities, the hatch works differently. You may choose the manner in which the hatch behaves. The following illustration shows a part called "PART A". Let's see how each hatch style would work.

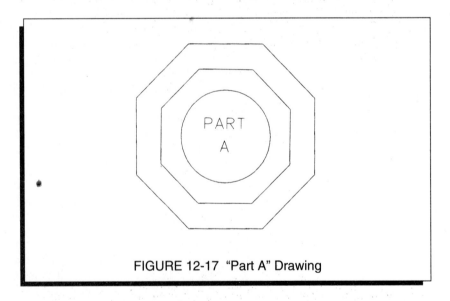

FIGURE 12-17 "Part A" Drawing

Normal Style

The default style of hatching is called Normal. The normal style will hatch inward from the first enclosed boundary, then skip the next enclosed boundary, and hatch the next. Notice how the text is hatched around. Text is protected by an invisible window. This ensures that the text is not obscured by the hatch pattern.

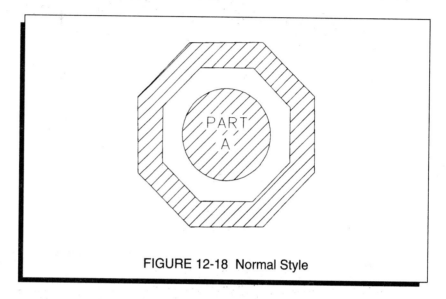

FIGURE 12-18 Normal Style

Outer Style

The Outer style option will cause the hatch pattern to hatch only the outermost enclosed boundary. The hatch continues until it reaches the boundaries and continues no further.

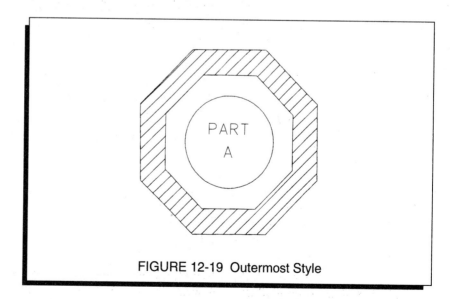

FIGURE 12-19 Outermost Style

Inner Style

The Inner style of hatching will hatch all areas which are defined by the identified boundary with no exceptions. This style also hatches through text.

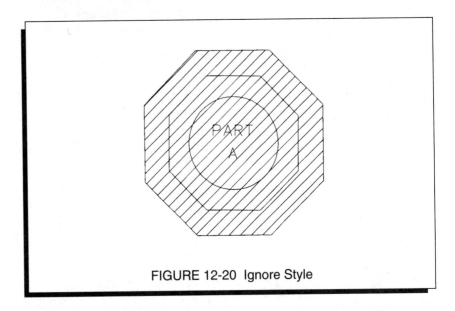

FIGURE 12-20 Ignore Style

SELECTING THE HATCH BOUNDARY

A hatch must be contained within a boundary that is made up of entities that form a closed polygon. The hatch may be contained by entities such as lines, polylines, circles, and arcs. To place a hatch, the entities that surround the area to be hatched must be identified. There are different ways to identify this boundary area. Let's look at each.

DEFINING A BOUNDARY BY PICKING OBJECTS

A hatch boundary can be selected by selecting the objects that surround the area to be hatched. Let's look at a simple example. Figure 12-21 shows a simple rectangle constructed by four line entities.

To place a hatch in the rectangle, select the Bhatch command. From the **Boundary Hatch** dialogue box, select the "Select objects" button.

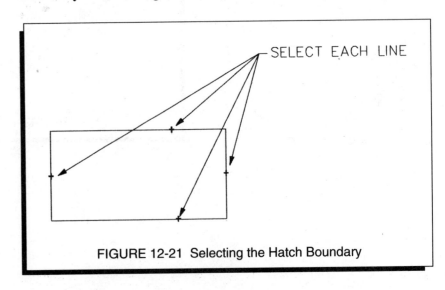

FIGURE 12-21 Selecting the Hatch Boundary

After you pick the select objects button, the dialogue box leaves the screen. If a hatch pattern has not been selected, the **Define Hatch Pattern** dialogue box will be displayed so you can choose a pattern. After a pattern has been selected, the dialogue box will be removed from the screen. Next, place the pickbox over each line and select. Now press Enter. You have just selected the objects that bound the area to be hatched.

Professional Tip

Use the window or crossing option to select all the sides of the boundary in one operation.

Now you can select the "Apply" button to complete the hatch. If you wish to see how the hatch will look without actually completing the hatch operation, select the "Preview hatch" button. The proposed hatch will be displayed, with the prompt:

> Press RETURN to continue

displayed on the command line.

If you wish to review the objects selected for the hatch boundary, select "View selections" from the dialogue box. The drawing will be displayed, with the boundary objects highlighted.

DEFINING A BOUNDARY BY SELECTING THE HATCH AREA

A simpler way to define a hatched area is to show AutoCAD the area inside a boundary that you wish to be hatched. Let's look at an example. Figure 12-22 shows an object with different areas that could be hatched. First select the Bhatch command. From the dialogue box, select the "Pick Points<" button. When the dialogue box is removed from the screen, place the crosshair into the area shown in the Figure 12-22; click, then press Enter. The dialogue box will again be displayed. Select "Apply" and the hatch will be completed.

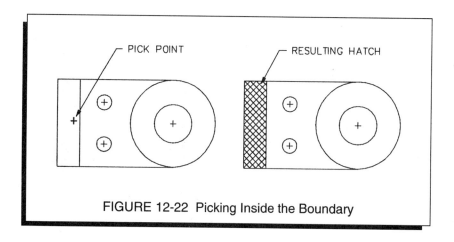

FIGURE 12-22 Picking Inside the Boundary

HATCH TUTORIAL

Let's look at a more complex example. Figure 12-23 shows an object that contains three areas that could be hatched. Let's suppose that we wanted to hatch the square and the circle, but not the triangle. Create a quick drawing similar to the one in the illustration.

This is a good example of how hatch *styles* can be used to control how a hatch pattern behaves. Let's start by choosing a hatch pattern. Select Bhatch, then "Hatch Options...", then select "Pattern..." from the next dialogue box. You should see a page of hatch patterns. Move the pointer over the hatch named "ANSI37" and select.

From under the "Hatching Style" heading, select the Normal style. Select "OK" to return to the previous dialogue box.

Next, select "Pick Points<". Click inside the right side of the box. Repeat the same steps for the triangle and circle as shown in Figure 12-23.

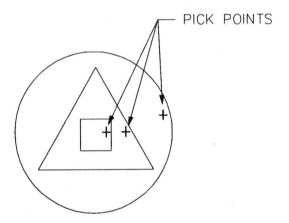

FIGURE 12-23 Selecting Pick Points

Next, select the "Apply" button. Your hatch should look similar to the one in Figure 12-24.

FIGURE 12-24 Hatched Drawing

ADVANCED HATCH BOUNDARY DEFINITIONS

Hatch boundary areas can also be described and stored. Selecting the "Advanced Options..." button will display the Advanced Options dialogue box.

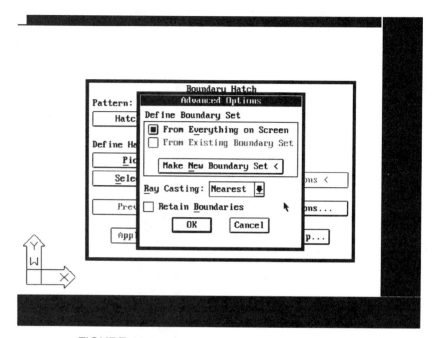

FIGURE 12-25 Advanced Options Dialogue Box

Let's look at each part of the dialogue box.

FROM EXISTING BOUNDARY SET

When you first define a hatch boundary, that boundary is stored for reuse. If the radio button next to the "From Existing Boundary Set" is checked, you can reuse the stored boundaries.

If you have not previously used a hatch boundary, this button is greyed out.

FROM EVERYTHING ON SCREEN

Selecting "From Everything On Screen" will choose all the entities currently visible on the drawing screen. If there is no current boundary stored, this is already checked. If a boundary is already stored, selecting this button will clear the stored set and reselect all the screen entities.

MAKE NEW BOUNDARY SET

Selecting the "Make New Boundary Set" radio button clears the existing set, then returns you to the drawing screen to select entities that will make up the new set.

RETAIN BOUNDARIES

If the hatch produces the desired results and you wish to retain the boundary as a polyline in the drawing, check the "Retain Boundaries" box.

RAY CASTING

The popup list box next to "Ray Casting:" is used to control the way that AutoCAD finds the boundary objects when you select a boundary with the "Pick Points<" option. When you pick a point inside of a boundary area, AutoCAD, by default, projects a "ray" to the nearest boundary and selects it. The Nearest setting is displayed by default.

You can control the direction that AutoCAD projects this ray by selecting the positive or negative direction in either the X or Y direction. The following illustration shows the areas of valid selection for each setting.

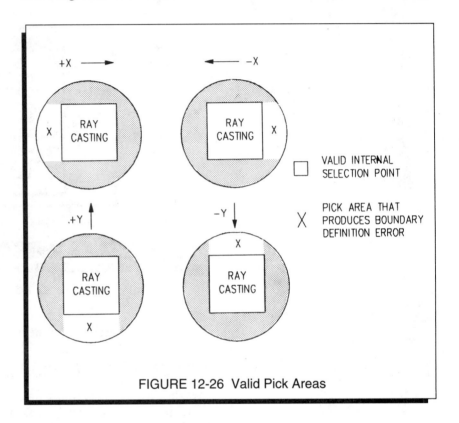

FIGURE 12-26 Valid Pick Areas

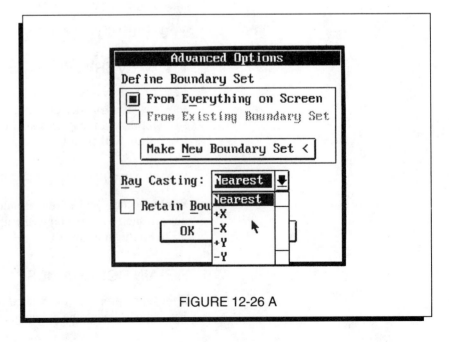

FIGURE 12-26 A

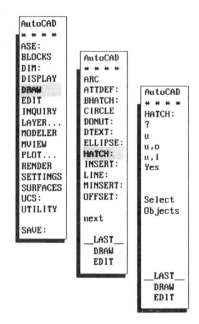

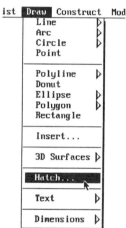

USING THE HATCH COMMAND

The Hatch command is used to place hatches from the command line. The result and principles are the same as a hatch placed with the Bhatch command, but the methodology is somewhat different. To use the Hatch command, enter Hatch at the command line.

> Command: <u>HATCH</u>
> (? or name/U,style) <*default*>:

HATCH COMMAND BOUNDARY DEFINITION

Before you can use the Hatch command to place a hatch in your drawing, you must first learn how to identify the hatch boundaries.

A hatch must be bounded by a closed polygon. The entities which create this boundary may be identified by the normal object selection process. There are, however, some tricks which make hatches constructed with the Hatch command work more smoothly.

The entities that bound the area should be perfectly joined at their intersections. If, for example, a line extends beyond the intersection, the hatch may not operate smoothly. In a situation such as that shown below, the line which runs past the intersection along the full length of the object can cause problems for the hatch.

In order to prevent incorrect hatching, the lines should be broken at the intersection. A good way to do this is to utilize the Break command with the First option to break the entity at the intersection as shown in the following illustration.

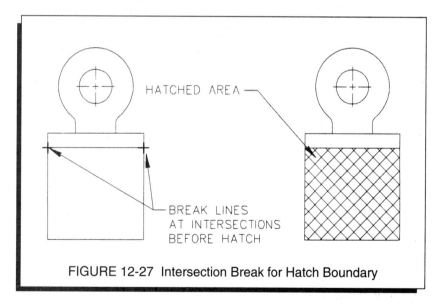

FIGURE 12-27 Intersection Break for Hatch Boundary

Now the entities which define the boundaries properly meet at their endpoints. Before we insert the Hatch, let's review the different styles utilized by the Hatch command. We will do this by creating some hatches with the Hatch command.

HATCH COMMAND TUTORIAL

Start a drawing called HATCH1. Set limits of 36 X and 24 Y. Draw the following object.

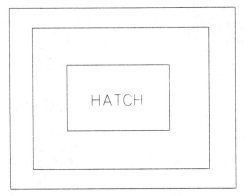

FIGURE 12-28 HATCH1 Drawing

We will start by using a Normal hatch style and the hatch pattern called ANSI31.

```
Command: HATCH
Pattern (? or name/U, style) <default>: ANSI31
Scale for pattern <default>: 1
Angle for pattern <default>: 0
Select objects: W
```

Place the window around the object and press Enter.

Your drawing should now look similar to the following illustration:

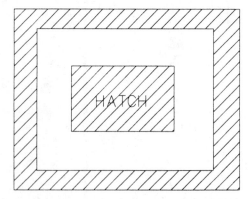

FIGURE 12-29 Normal Hatch Style

Let's now hatch the same drawing using the Outermost style. (Use the Erase-Last command to erase the hatch from your drawing and Redraw, if necessary).

```
Command: HATCH
Pattern (? or name/U, style) <default>: ANSI31,O
Scale for pattern:
Angle for pattern: 0
Select objects: W
```

Using the Outermost style, your drawing should look similar to the following illustration:

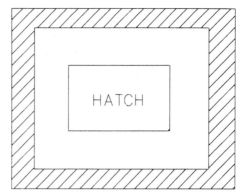

FIGURE 12-30 Outermost Hatch Style

Now, erase the hatch and use the Ignore style.

```
Command: HATCH
Pattern (? or name/U, style) <default>: ANSI31,I
Scale for pattern:
Angle for pattern: 0
Select objects: W
```

Notice how the hatch has ignored the boundaries and the text.

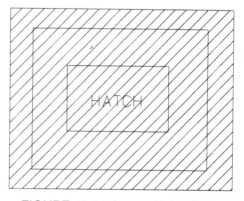

FIGURE 12-31 Ignore Hatch Style

DEFINING YOUR OWN

You may define your own hatches. If you choose the "U" option, AutoCAD will prompt you for the necessary information:

```
Angle for crosshatch lines <default>:
Spacing between lines <default>:
Double hatch area? <default>:
```

Simply respond to the prompts with the desired values. You then proceed as normal.

PATTERN ALIGNMENT

There may be times when you will place hatches adjacent to each other and will want them to line up. AutoCAD compensates for alignment problems by normally using the 0,0 point as the hatch origin for all hatches. This means that the hatches align properly. You can change the origin point by using the variable Snapbase to change the base point.

Hatches can be handled more easily if they are put on their own layer. They can also be turned off and frozen to speed redraw time. Be sure that the layer linetype is continuous. Even though the hatch pattern may contain dashed lines and dots, the linetype should be continuous to ensure a proper hatch.

CREATING A POLYLINE BOUNDARY

Since a polyline is a single entity, defining a hatch boundary as a polyline allows you to select a single entity as the boundary. A polyline can be composed of many segments, all functioning as a single entity.

To define an entire boundary as a single polyline, use the BPOLY command. When you select Bpoly, the "Polyline Creation" dialogue box is displayed.

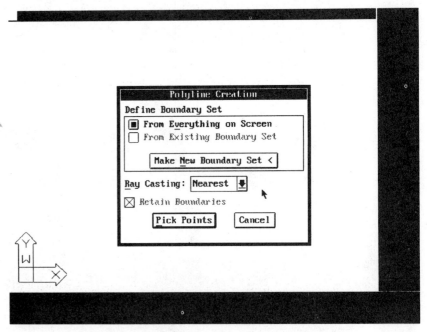

FIGURE 12-32 Polyline Creation Dialogue Box

This dialogue box is the same as the one displayed under the advanced options selection of the Bhatch command. The boundary is selected in the same manner. The difference is that the hatch is not placed within the boundary; just the boundary is constructed as a polyline.

Professional Tip

The Bpoly command has other options. Converting the outline of an object to a polyline allows you to select all parts of it as a single option when editing.

CREATING SOLID AREAS

Solids plot as solid ink areas.

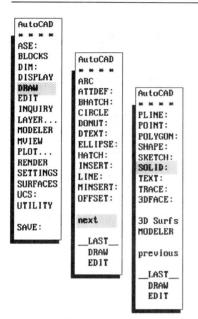

The Solid command allows you to fill areas with a solid color. Solids plot as solid ink areas.

NOTE: The solid areas are only displayed if the Fillmode is on.

To use the Solid command, enter:

> Command: <u>SOLID</u>
> First point:
> Second point:
> Third point:
> Fourth point:
> Third point:
> Fourth point:
> Third point:
> Fourth point:

This sequence will continue until you terminate it with a Enter. This allows you to solid polygons with any number of sides.

In some cases, the Solid command won't work properly if the points are not entered in the right sequence. For example, if you enter the points in the fashion shown in the following example, the solid will form a "bow tie".

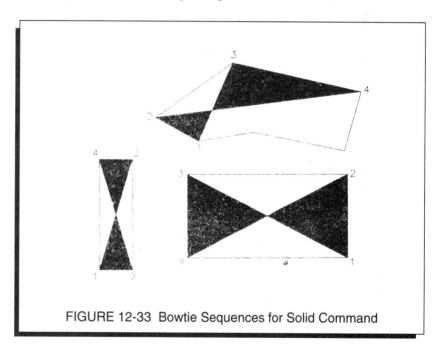

FIGURE 12-33 Bowtie Sequences for Solid Command

The following examples show the sequence to enter points for a correct solid fill. Draw each shape and enter the points as shown.

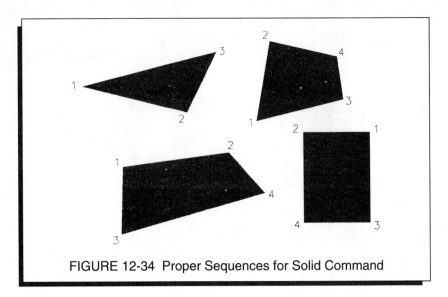

FIGURE 12-34 Proper Sequences for Solid Command

Turn off the fill after using the Solid command to speed up the regeneration process caused by zooms and pans, then turn the fill back on and Regen to redisplay filled solids.

SOLID EXERCISE

Use the work disk and start the drawing named "SOLIDS". The drawing shows several hot-air balloons. Use the Solid command to place solid areas in some of the balloon areas.

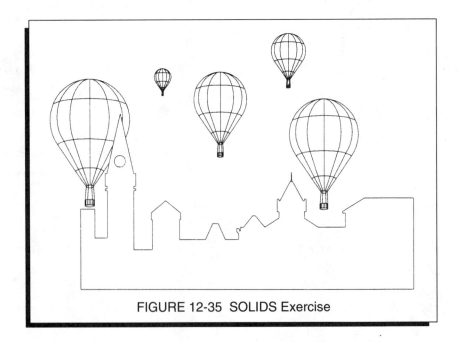

FIGURE 12-35 SOLIDS Exercise

CHAPTER EXERCISES

1. Start the drawing on the student work disk named "SOLIDS". This is the same drawing you used in the Solid command exercise. Use the Hatch command to place hatched areas in some of the balloons. Remember to use the Break command to make clean hatch boundaries.

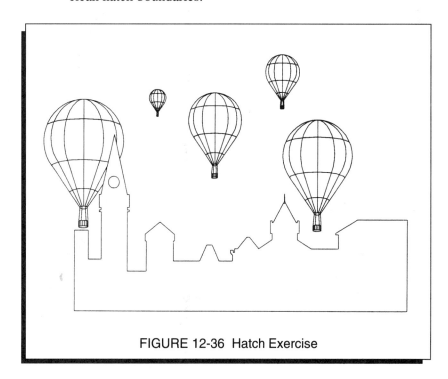

FIGURE 12-36 Hatch Exercise

2. Draw the following items, placing hatches in the areas shown.

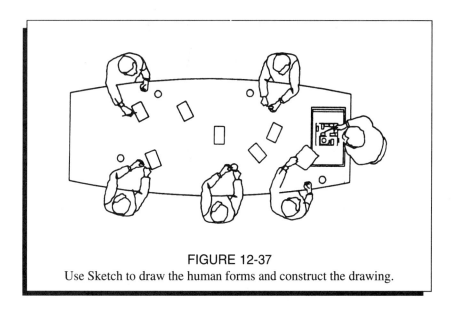

FIGURE 12-37
Use Sketch to draw the human forms and construct the drawing.

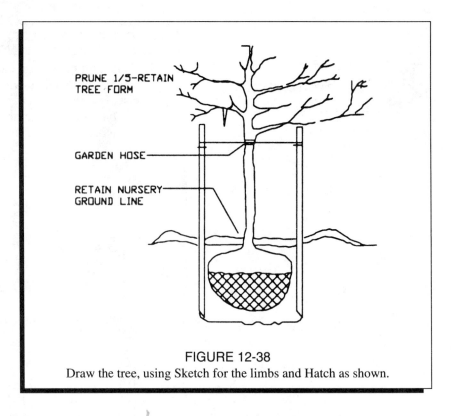

FIGURE 12-38
Draw the tree, using Sketch for the limbs and Hatch as shown.

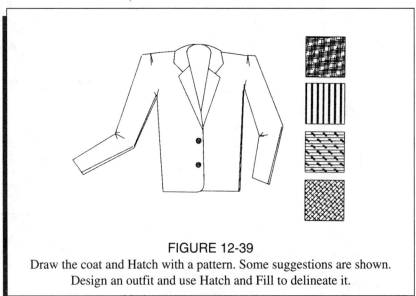

FIGURE 12-39
Draw the coat and Hatch with a pattern. Some suggestions are shown.
Design an outfit and use Hatch and Fill to delineate it.

CHAPTER REVIEW

1. Explain what the Fill command does.

2. If you did not want the solid filled areas in your drawing to plot, what could you do?

_____

_____

_____

3. What is a hatch boundary?

_____

_____

_____

_____

4. When using the Hatch command, why must a hatch boundary be perfectly constructed?

_____

_____

_____

5. How would you change the origin point of a hatch?

_____

_____

CHAPTER 13

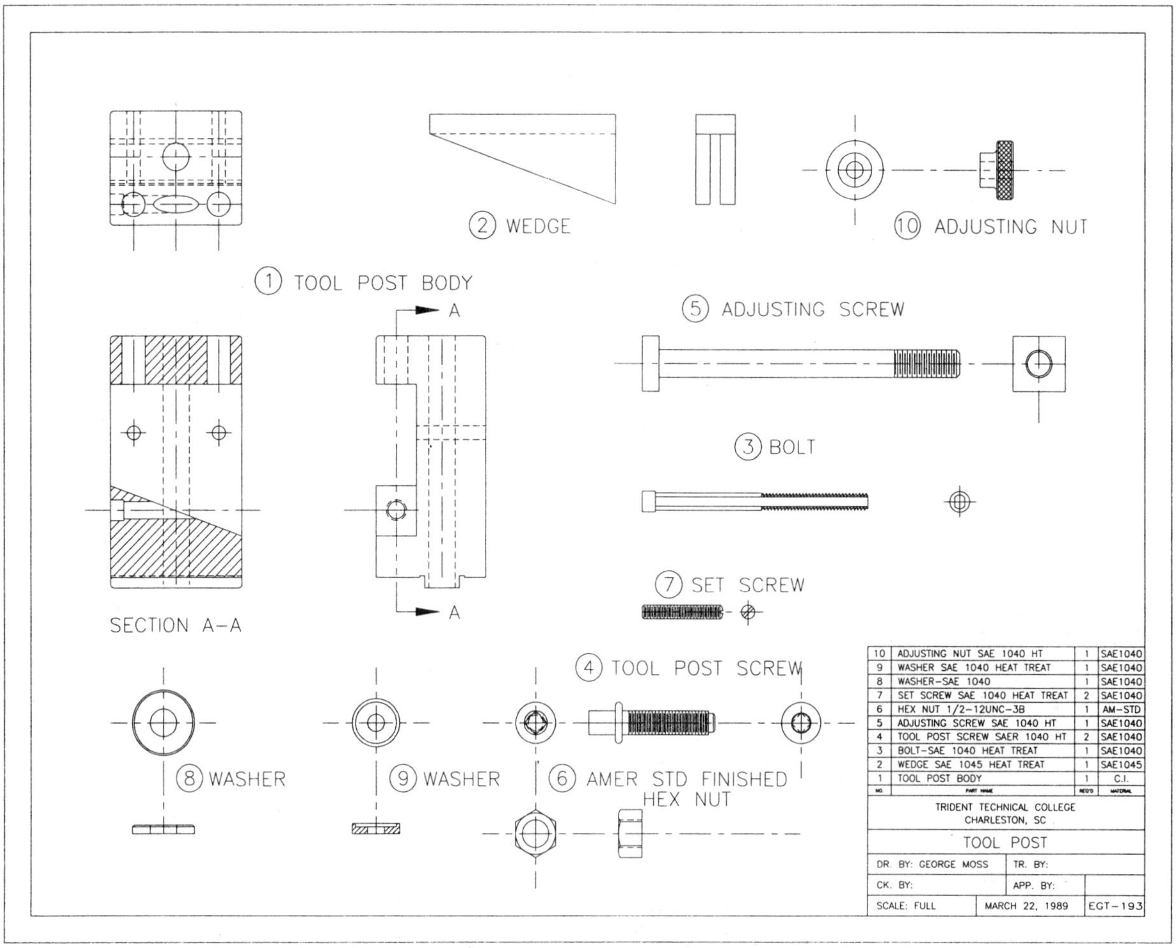
2 WEDGE
10 ADJUSTING NUT
1 TOOL POST BODY
A
5 ADJUSTING SCREW
3 BOLT
7 SET SCREW
SECTION A-A
A
4 TOOL POST SCREW
8 WASHER
9 WASHER
6 AMER STD FINISHED HEX NUT
10 ADJUSTING NUT SAE 1040 HT 1 SAE1040
9 WASHER SAE 1040 HEAT TREAT 1 SAE1040
8 WASHER-SAE 1040 1 SAE1040
7 SET SCREW SAE 1040 HEAT TREAT 2 SAE1040
6 HEX NUT 1/2-12UNC-3B 1 AM-STD
5 ADJUSTING SCREW SAE 1040 HT 1 SAE1040
4 TOOL POST SCREW SAER 1040 HT 2 SAE1040
3 BOLT-SAE 1040 HEAT TREAT 1 SAE1040
2 WEDGE SAE 1045 HEAT TREAT 1 SAE1045
1 TOOL POST BODY 1 C.I.
NO. PART NAME REQ'D MATERIAL
TRIDENT TECHNICAL COLLEGE
CHARLESTON, SC
TOOL POST
DR. BY: GEORGE MOSS
TR. BY:
CK. BY:
APP. BY:
SCALE: FULL
MARCH 22, 1989
EGT-193

Text, Fonts, and Styles

OBJECTIVES:

Drawings are a means of communication that uses both graphics and text. The proper use and placement of text in a drawing is an important aspect of constructing effective drawings. The objectives of this chapter are:

- To become familiar with AutoCAD's text capabilities.
- Learning how to create text styles that contain fonts and make modifications to those fonts.
- To learn the methods of placing text in a drawing.
- Familiarizing the user with the methods to handle text efficiently.

Kentucky's Vietnam Veterans Memorial
Thought-provoking design produced with AutoCAD®

In early 1987, the Kentucky Vietnam Veterans Memorial Fund announced a national competition seeking original drawings and scale models for a future Kentucky war monument. The design criteria stated that, "The monument should be distinct yet dignified. It should not seek to imitate other monuments, yet it should evoke an emotional remembrance while being aesthetically authentic as a work of art. The monument should display the names of all Kentuckians who died in the Vietnam Conflict...or who are still unaccounted for."

Helm Roberts answered the call with an innovative sundial design. The sundial would cast a shadow over the names of the 1,069 Kentuckians killed in Vietnam on the anniversary of their death. Only the names of the 23 Kentuckians classified as missing in action would not be darkened.

In June of 1987, the sundial design was unanimously selected as the winner of the memorial competition, but the committee was concerned that the design might not work. Roberts was convinced it would, with precise design on AutoCAD and excellent craftsmanship by stonemasons and contractors.

AutoCAD was used in several ways to design and build the elements of the memorial. It was used to determine the exact size of each granite slab and to create shop drawings for the sundial pointer, as well as for granite fabrication and name inscription. The plaza foundation was laid using AutoCAD dimensions in decimal feet to precisely locate the perimeter wall and more than 800 concrete piers. Each slab was placed without trimming or fabrication. This ease of assembly may be credited in part to the accuracy of the AutoCAD dimensioning system.

On November 12, 1988, over 7,000 people attended the dedication of the memorial by the Governor of Kentucky, Wallace G. Wilkinson. The names of the fallen soldiers will be etched in the granite for ages, just as the memory of the Vietnam War will remain etched in our minds forever.

Adapted with permission from an article by Helm Roberts. Excerpted from *CADENCE*, June 1989, copyright © 1989, Ariel Communications, Inc.

Photo by Helm Roberts

THE USE OF TEXT IN GRAPHIC DRAWINGS

While graphics are used in a drawing to convey information, the total description of an object often requires written words. Written words, or text, are easily placed in a drawing by AutoCAD. The traditional, laborious manner of placing text in a drawing by hand is made much easier with the use of CAD.

TEXT STANDARDS

The use of text in drawings is usually governed by standards. Many industries use the American National Standards Institute (ANSI) style of letters and numbers. Other companies and offices set standards of their own.

The most important aspect of lettering is that it is clear and concise.

The most important aspect of lettering is that it is clear and concise. The standards should be consistent. In general, note text should be ⅛" high. Headings should be 3/16" high. Note text is typically *left justified.* This means that each line of text is aligned at its left edge.

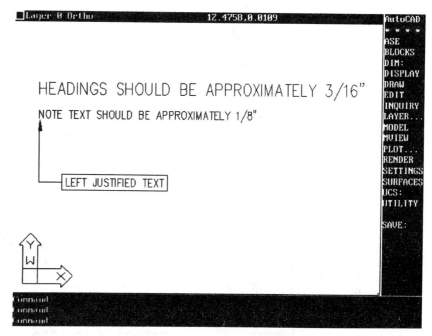

FIGURE 13-1 Text Size Standards

AUTOCAD TEXT COMPONENTS

AutoCAD provides many text tools for your use. You can use many different styles, create text in any size, slant, compress, rotate, and even tell AutoCAD how long any text line length should be.

A font is the "design" of the text letter.

Text can be a variety of different designs. These designs are called *fonts.* A font is the "design" of the text letter. Gothic, script, and bookface are types of fonts. See Figure 13-2.

Each font can be stretched, compressed, obliqued, mirrored, or drawn in a vertical stack. The text font, the text height, and its modifications are saved and stored as a *style.* The text style, including the font and style modifications, are created in AutoCAD prior to placing the text. Once created, a style file can be used as many times in the same drawing as you wish. AutoCAD provides many text fonts for your use. Figure 13-3 shows the fonts included with AutoCAD.

FIGURE 13-2 Text Fonts

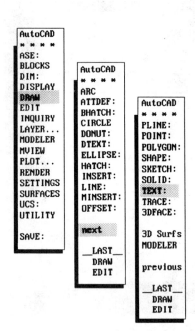

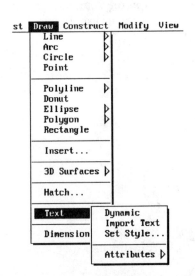

TEXT TUTORIAL

Let's place some simple text in a drawing. Start AutoCAD and start a new drawing named "TEXT". Next, select the Text command from the Draw/Next screen menu.

We will use the default style that is already contained in the drawing. When you choose the Text command, you will see the command prompt:

Command: <u>TEXT</u>
Justify/Style/<Start point>:

At this point, move your cursor into the drawing area and place a point on the screen. The command prompt will continue and AutoCAD will ask you for the text height:

Height <*default*>:

Let's just "show" AutoCAD how high the text should be. Move the crosshair up from the point you entered. The point will "rubber band" to the crosshair. Enter a point approximately ¼" (actual distance) above the first point you entered. AutoCAD will continue and prompt you for the:

Rotation angle <*default*>:

Enter zero (0) in response to the prompt. Now it's time to type the text. Type your name. If you make a mistake, use the backspace key to erase back and start again. Notice how the text shows up on the command line, but not on the screen. When you are finished typing your name, press Enter. You should now see your name on the screen!

txt	The quick brown fox jumped over the lazy dog.	ABC123
monotxt	The quick brown fox jumped over the lazy dog.	ABC123
romans	The quick brown fox jumped over the lazy dog.	ABC123
scripts	The quick brown fox jumped over the lazy dog.	ABC123
greeks	Τηε ϑυιχκ βροων φοξ ϑυμπεδ οϵερ τηε λαζψ δογ.	ABX123
romand	The quick brown fox jumped over the lazy dog.	ABC123
romant	The quick brown fox jumped over the lazy dog.	ABC123
italict	The quick brown fox jumped over the lazy dog.	ABC123
romanc	The quick brown fox jumped over the lazy dog.	ABC123
italicc	The quick brown fox jumped over the lazy dog.	ABC123
scriptc	The quick brown fox jumped over the lazy dog.	ABC123
greekc	Τηε ϑυιχκ βροων φοξ ϑυμπεδ οϵερ τηε λαζψ δογ.	ABX123
cyrillic	Узд рфивк бсоцн еоч йфмпдг охдс узд лащш гож.	АБВ123
cyriltlc	Тхе цуичк брошн фож щумпед овер тхе лазй дог.	АБЧ123
romanc	The quick brown fox jumped over the lazy dog.	ABC123
italicc	The quick brown fox jumped over the lazy dog.	ABC123
scriptc	The quick brown fox jumped over the lazy dog.	ABC123
greekc	Τηε ϑυιχκ βροων φοξ ϑυμπεδ οϵερ τηε λαζψ δογ.	ABX123
cyrillic	Узд рфивк бсоцн соч йфмпдг охдс узд лащш гож.	АБВ123
cyriltlc	Тхе цуичк брошн фож щумпед овер тхе лазй дог.	АБЧ123
gothice	The quick brown fox jumped over the lazy dog.	ABC123
gothicg	The quick brown fox jumped over the lazy dog.	ABC123
gothici	The quick brown fox jumped over the lazy dog.	ABC123
syastro	ΩϵU `↑→`∙ `˜¬∃∇ ⊃¬ℒ ↑↑∂´∪⊂ ¬‡∪˘ §ϵU ↓✳©® ⌒¬∩.	⊙♀♀123
symap		⊞△123
symath	⊂∞√		X′|123
symeteo		−123
symusic		⌐√123
cibt	The quick brown fox jumped over the lazy dog.	ABC123
cobt	The quick brown fox jumped over the lazy dog.	ABC123
rom	**The quick brown fox jumped over the lazy dog.**	**ABC123**
romb	**The quick brown fox jumped over the lazy dog.**	**ABC123**
sas	**The quick brown fox jumped over the lazy dog.**	**ABC123**
sasb	**The quick brown fox jumped over the lazy dog.**	**ABC123**
saso	***The quick brown fox jumped over the lazy dog.***	***ABC123***
sasbo	***The quick brown fox jumped over the lazy dog.***	***ABC123***
te	THE QUICK BROWN FOX JUMPED OVER THE LAZY DOG.	ABC123
tel	THE QUICK BROWN FOX JUMPED OVER THE LAZY DOG.	ABC123
teb	**THE QUICK BROWN FOX JUMPED OVER THE LAZY DOG.**	**ABC123**

FIGURE 13-3 AutoCAD Fonts

THE TEXT COMMAND AND ITS OPTIONS

When you enter the Text command, you see the following prompt:

Command: <u>TEXT</u>
Justify/Style/<Start point>:

The "start point" is the default. You used this in the previous exercise. Let's continue and look at the text options of Justify and Style.

PLACING JUSTIFIED TEXT

The Justify option is used to specify how the text will be aligned. If you respond to the prompt with a "J" (Justify), AutoCAD will respond with a prompt for the alignment options.

> Command: TEXT
> Justify/Style/<Start point>: J
> Align/Fit/Center/Middle/Right/TL/TC/TR/ML/MC/MR/BL/BC/BR:

Let's first look at the two letter abbreviated options. Don't worry about learning each of the abbreviated options. Let's stop and look at how text alignment options work and you will see that it's easy to remember.

Figure 13-4 shows the alignment modes for text. Notice that you can align text by both the vertical and horizontal alignments.

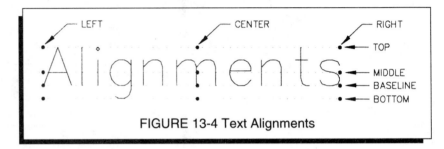

FIGURE 13-4 Text Alignments

Let's use single letter abbreviations to designate each alignment. Refer to Table 13-A.

ALIGNMENT	ABBREVIATION
Top	T
Middle	M
Bottom	B
Left	L
Center	C
Right	R

TABLE 13-A

You will notice in the last command prompt, there was a series of two letter options. To designate an alignment, simply use two letters; one to describe the vertical alignment, and one to designate the horizontal alignment.

If you know the type of alignment you desire, it is not necessary to enter the "J" option; just enter the two letters that describe the alignment you desire.

TEXT ALIGNMENT EXERCISE

We want to place the text "PART A" so that the text will be centered both vertically and horizontally on a selected point. We might choose this method of placement if we wanted to place text in the center of a space. Let's use the Text command to place the text. Refer to the following command sequence and Figure 13-5.

Command: <u>TEXT</u>
Justify/Style/<Start point>: <u>MC</u>
Middle point: (*SELECT POINT "A"*)
Height <*default*>: (*MOVE UP TO SHOW HEIGHT*)
Rotation Angle <*default*>: <u>0</u>

Text: <u>PART A</u>

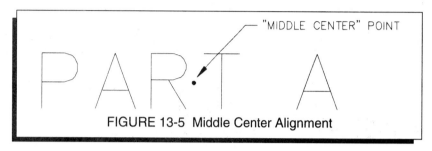

FIGURE 13-5 Middle Center Alignment

Notice how we simply entered "MC" instead of selecting the Justify option. It is not necessary to select Justify unless you want to see the options. We entered "MC" because we wanted to place the text vertically in the "Middle" and horizontally in the "Center" (see Figure 13-1 and Table 13-A).

For the height, we moved up and entered another point to "show" AutoCAD the height. We could have entered a value. The height of text is in <u>scale</u> units, not actual size.

TEXT ALIGNMENT EXERCISE

Figure 13-6 shows several text strings. The placement point is marked with a solid dot. Use the Text command to place the text as shown. If you need, refer back to Figure 13-4 and Table 13-A to identify the alignment mode abbreviations.

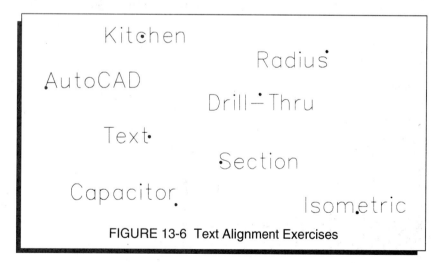

FIGURE 13-6 Text Alignment Exercises

ADDITIONAL ALIGNMENT OPTIONS

Several alignment modes listed under the Justify option are shown as full words. They are Align, Fit, Center, Middle, and Right. Let's take a look at each type of alignment.

PLACING ALIGNED TEXT

Align allows you to select two points that the text will fit between. AutoCAD will adjust the text height so the baseline of the text fits perfectly between the two points. Note that the two points may be placed at any angle in relation to each other.

```
Command: TEXT
Justify/Style/<Start point>: A
First text line point:
Second text line point:
Text:
```

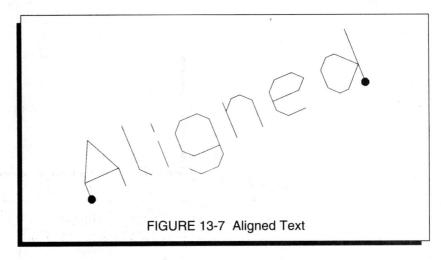

FIGURE 13-7 Aligned Text

PLACING CENTERED TEXT

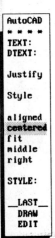

The Center option is used to center the baseline of the text on the specified point.

```
Command: TEXT
Justify/Style/<Start point>: C
Center point:
Height <default>:
Rotation angle <default>:
Text:
```

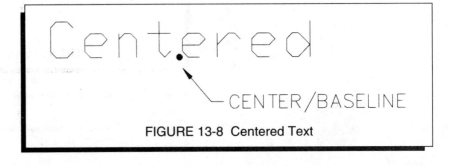

FIGURE 13-8 Centered Text

FITTING TEXT IN A SPECIFIED DISTANCE

The Fit option is similar to the Aligned option. You are prompted for two points to place the text between. With Fit, however, you are prompted for a text height. AutoCAD calculates only the text width and adjusts the width to fit perfectly between the two entered points.

> Command: <u>TEXT</u>
> Justify/Style/<Start point>: <u>F</u>
> First text line point:
> Second text line point:
> Height <*default*>:
> Text:

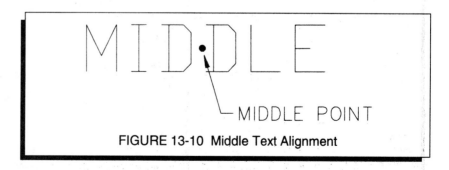

FIGURE 13-9 Text Option

PLACING MIDDLE ALIGNED TEXT

Middle is used as a shortcut when centering text both horizontally and vertically. It achieves the same result as the MC option.

> Command: <u>TEXT</u>
> Justify/Style/<Start point>: <u>M</u>
> Middle point:
> Rotation angle <*default*>:
> Text:

FIGURE 13-10 Middle Text Alignment

PLACING RIGHT ALIGNED TEXT

Using right justified text is similar to using "Start point", except the text ends at the reference point instead of beginning at it.

    Command: TEXT
    Justify/Style/<Start point>: R
    End point:
    Height <default>:
    Rotation angle <default>:
    Text:

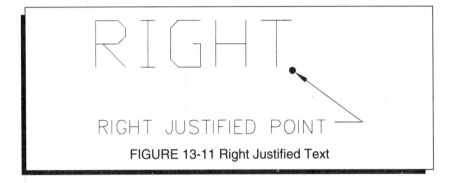

FIGURE 13-11 Right Justified Text

SELECTING DIFFERENT TEXT STYLES

The Style option is used to change between defined text styles. Note that you must first create a text style before you can use it. After the style is changed, the text command is repeated. Refer to the following command sequence that changes from the default style named "Standard" to a user-built style named "Bigtxt".

    Command: TEXT
    Justify/Style/<Start point>: S
    Style name (or ?) <Standard>: BIGTXT
    Justify/Style/<Start point>:

Note that the Style option under the Text command and the Style command are not the same.

Text can be placed at any angle in your drawing.

ROTATING TEXT

Text can be placed at any angle in your drawing. As you may have noticed, the previous command sequences included the prompt line:

    Rotation angle <default>:

You can specify the angle at which the text is drawn by designating the angle at this point in any text prompt. Note that the zero-angle direction set with the Units command affects which direction is zero. Unless changed, the default zero-angle in AutoCAD is to the right. Thus, a text angle of zero would place text that runs from the left to right. Figure 13-12 shows text placed at several angles.

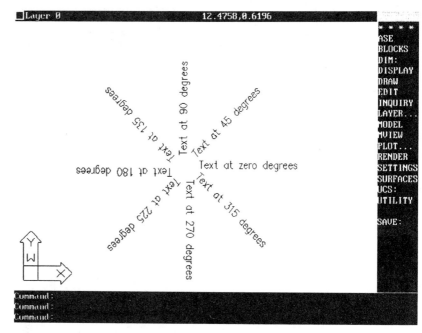

FIGURE 13-12 Rotated Text

Once the text angle is set, that angle remains the default angle until changed again.

TEXT ANGLE EXERCISE

Using the text angle prompt, place the following line of text at angles of 0, 45, 90, 135, and 180 degrees.

THIS IS ANGLED TEXT

Use the same text starting point for each line.

PLACING MULTIPLE TEXT LINES

Many times you may wish to place several lines of text.

You can use AutoCAD to place several lines of text at a time without repeated use of the Text command.

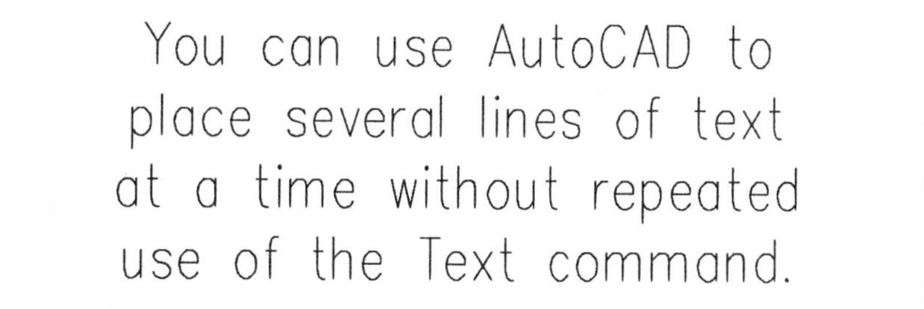

FIGURE 13-13 Placing Multiple Text Lines

To draw multiple text lines, place the first line of text, using the size and alignment you want for all the lines. Next, repeat the Text command. When AutoCAD prompts:

Justify/Style/<Start point>:

reply to the prompt by pressing the Enter key. AutoCAD will step down one line space and prompt for the text. The next line of text will be sized and aligned the same as the first line.

EXERCISE

Let's place some multiple lines of text. We will use the following lines of text:

THIS IS THE FIRST LINE OF TEXT
THIS IS THE SECOND & CENTERED LINE OF TEXT

Let's look at the command sequence used to do this.

Command: <u>TEXT</u>
Justify/Style/<Start point>: <u>C</u>
Center point: (*SELECT POINT "1"*)
Height <*default*>: (*MOVE UP AND PLACE A POINT TO DEFINE THE HEIGHT*)
Rotation angle <*default*>: <u>0</u>
Text: <u>THIS IS THE FIRST LINE OF TEXT</u>

Command: (*RETURN TO REPEAT THE TEXT COMMAND*)

TEXT Justify/Style/<Start point>: (*PRESS ENTER*)
Text: <u>THIS IS THE SECOND & CENTER LINE OF TEXT</u>

THIS IS THE FIRST LINE OF TEXT
THIS IS THE SECOND & CENTER LINE OF TEXT

FIGURE 13-14 Multiple Text Lines

You can repeat this procedure for as many lines of text as you want.

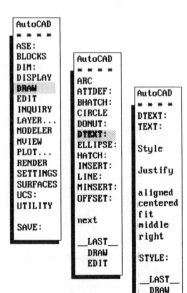

DRAWING TEXT DYNAMICALLY

Text can be placed into your drawings "dynamically". As you have already noticed, the text you enter is not displayed in your drawing until you press the Enter key after typing the string on the command line. Using dynamic text allows you to see the text in the drawing as you enter it. You can also place several strings of text at different positions in the drawing without exiting and reentering the text command again.

Dynamic text is placed with the Dtext command.

Command: <u>DTEXT</u>
Justify/Style/<Start point>:
Height <*default*>:

Notice how the command prompts are the same as the regular text command.

PLACING DYNAMIC TEXT

When you type the first string of dynamic text, you will notice that the text is displayed in the drawing as you are typing it. After you have placed a text string, you move the cursor to a new location, click, and start a new text string. To exit the Dtext operation, press the Enter key twice.

When you use dynamic text, you will notice some differences.

- As you place dynamic text, a *text box* is displayed at the text location. The size of the text box represents the height and width of the current text style.

- When you first enter Dtext, the last text string entered will be highlighted. If you press the Enter key instead of entering the text position with the cursor, the text box will be placed on the next line below the last text as though you had not previously exited Dtext. This is useful if you wish to go back and continue placing multiple text lines.

- When placing multiple lines of text, you can use the backspace key to backspace through all the text placed in that operation (even on previous lines).

- If you use text alignment codes other than "starting point", the text is not aligned properly until you finish the command.

- If you cancel the Dtext command at any time during the operation, <u>all</u> text placed during that operation will be canceled, not just the current line.

- All menu and tablet commands and options are "locked out". Only keyboard entry is permitted when placing dynamic text.

- When you use special text codes, the text codes are initially displayed instead of the effect. For example, if you enter:

    %%UTHIS IS UNDERLINED%%U

  the text codes will be shown in the drawing as you are entering the text. When the Dtext command is completed, the text will be redrawn showing the effect.

  <u>THIS TEXT IS UNDERLINED</u>

DYNAMIC TEXT EXERCISE

Use the Dtext command to place a line of text. Press the Enter key and place a second line of text.

Use the backspace key to "erase" the text on the second line, then continue to use the backspace key to erase text on the first line.

Place two more lines of text, then press the Enter key twice to end the Dtext command. Press the Enter key to repeat the Dtext command. Press the Enter key again and notice how the text box is placed on the next line below the last text string. Enter another line of text.

When you reach the end of the line, move the crosshairs and enter a new text location. Type a new line of text at this location.

TEXT STYLES

A style is a collection of modifiers that are applied to the font of your choice.

For instance, you may want your text to be slanted, or perhaps expanded so that it is longer than normal.

The style that you choose is stored under a name of your choice and can be applied to the font of your choice.

A text style is composed of the following information:

1. A style name. This name may be up to 31 characters in length.

2. A font file that is associated with the style. (You must have some pattern to modify.)

3. A fixed height. This height will be the text height. If you want to specify the height each time you place text, enter a "0" for this value.

4. A width factor. This factor is a numerical representation of the width. A width of 1 is the standard width factor. A decimal value creates text that is "narrower". For example, a width factor of .5 produces text one half the width of text created with a factor of 1.

5. An obliquing angle. This angle determines the slant. A positive angle is a forward slant; a negative angle is a backward slant.

6. A draw backwards indicator.

7. A draw up-side down indicator.

8. An orientation indicator to determine whether the text will be vertical (stacked), or horizontal.

After you have created a style, you can refer to it whenever you want that particular set of parameters. You do not have to go through a series of questions each time you want to define the "look" of your text!

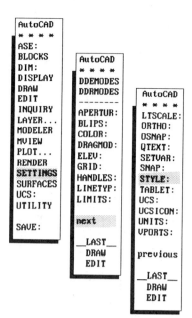

CREATING A TEXT STYLE

The Style command is used to create a style file. Note that the Style command is not the same as the Style option under the Text command. The Style command is used to *create* a text style while the Style option under the Text command is used to select a previously created text style for use.

To create a text style, select "Set Style..." from the Draw/Text pull-down menu. The following icon box is displayed.

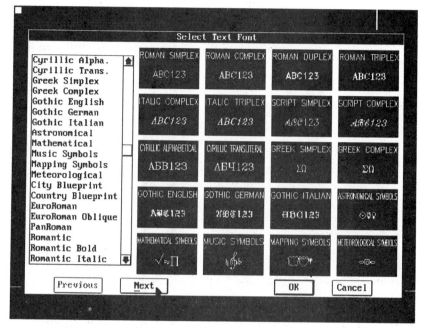

FIGURE 13-15 Set Style Dialogue Box

AutoCAD continues:

> Height *<default>*:
> Width factor *<default>*:
> Obliquing angle *<default>*:
> Backwards? <Y/N>:
> Upside-down? <Y/N>:
> Vertical? <Y/N>:

Let's look at each of the settings.

TEXT FONT FILE

There are many font files available for AutoCAD. The program comes with an excellent selection. Specialty fonts for map making (draws symbols instead of letters), cursive writing, and other applications are included with AutoCAD.

The font file should be appropriate for the application.

The font file should be appropriate for the application. Most mechanical applications use the ANSI type lettering. The Romans (roman, single stroke) font closely approximates this style. Architectural drawings typically use "hand lettered" fonts. Engineering applications often use the Romans font since it closely resembles a traditional font constructed with a lettering template.

TEXT HEIGHT

The text height represents the height, in *scale units*, that the text will be drawn. For example, if the drawing is plotted at ⅛"=1' 0" and the text height is 12, the plotted text will be ⅛" high on the paper. Because of this, you must first determine the scale of the drawing (see Chapter 8 on setting up a drawing) before you can set the final plotted text height.

Professional Tip

A standard architect's or engineer's drawing board scale can be used to "see" the size of the plotted text. Place the scale on a piece of paper, using the numerical scale that represents the final plotted scale and mark the height of the text.

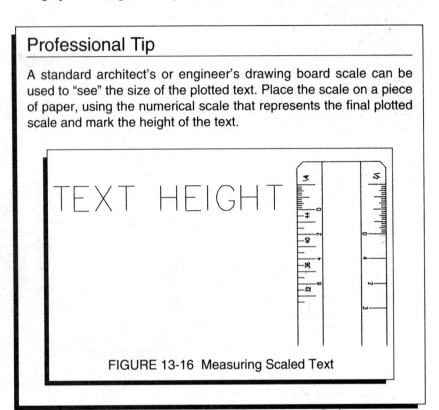

FIGURE 13-16 Measuring Scaled Text

TEXT WIDTH FACTOR

The width factor determines how wide the text will be drawn. A width factor of one can be thought of as a "standard" width. A decimal value will draw text that is narrower, resulting in condensed text. Values greater than one will create expanded text. The following figure illustrates the same text font with different scale factors applied.

SCALE: 0.5   SCALE 1.0   SCALE: 1.5

FIGURE 13-17 Text Width Factors

TEXT OBLIQUING ANGLE

A slant can be applied to a font with the obliquing angle setting. A zero obliquing angle draws text that is "straight up". Positive angles draw text that slants forward, while negative angles draw backward slants.

OBLIQUE −30°   OBLIQUE 0°   OBLIQUE 30°

FIGURE 13-18 Text Obliquing Angles

BACKWARDS TEXT

Text can also be drawn backwards. Backwards text is useful if you want to plot your drawing on the back side of film media.

TXET SDRAWKCAB

FIGURE 13-19 Backwards Text

UPSIDE DOWN TEXT

If you want the text drawn upside down, reply YES to the "Upside down:" prompt. Setting the value to NO will draw normal, right side up text.

UPSIDE DOWN TEXT

FIGURE 13-20 Upside Down Text

VERTICAL TEXT

Your text can be oriented so it draws vertically. This is not the same as text that is *rotated* 90 degrees. Vertically oriented text is drawn so that each letter within the text string is vertical and the text string itself is vertical.

Tip

Obliquing, underscoring, and overscoring should not be used with vertical text, since the result will not be correct.

V
E
R
T
I
C
A
L

T
E
X
T

FIGURE 13-21 Vertical Text

USING TEXT STYLES

The concept of fonts and styles is sometimes confusing to learn in the beginning. Remember that a style is a modification that is applied to a particular font (such as height, width factor, slant factor, etc.). You must first create a style in order to use a font. The first step is to choose the particular font that you would like to use in your drawing, then determine the modifications you would like to apply to it by using the Style command parameters.

You must first create a style in order to use a font.

You may have different styles applied to the same font. Just store them in a different style file with the name of your choice.

Professional Tip

"Fancy" styles (those created with multi-stroke fonts) are slow to regenerate and redraw. To speed your drawing operations, you can avoid such fonts, place the text in your drawing last, or use the Qtext command (covered later in this chapter) to make redraws and regenerations faster.

Multi-stroke fonts are identified as "duplex" or "complex". AutoCAD names fonts such as "Roman C" with the "D" and "C" denoting duplex and complex.

The Text command has a listing in the menu for Style. After you have stored your style file, this menu option will allow you to retrieve it.

The menu contains two listings for Style. The capitalized listing followed by a colon (STYLE:) is the style <u>command</u>. This is the command used to create a new text style. The second listing is a modifier under the Text command (Style). This lower case listing is used as a Text option to select the Current style.

SPECIAL TEXT CONSIDERATIONS

AutoCAD allows for special text operations. You can use text "codes" to create text that is underlined, place degree and plus/minus symbols, and other special text notations. This is accomplished by using a code consisting of a pair of percent characters (%%).

The following table shows the notations and their functions:

%%o	Toggle overscore mode on & off
%%u	Toggle underscore mode on & off
%%d	"Degrees" symbol
%%p	"Plus/minus" tolerance symbol
%%c	"Circle diameter" dimensioning symbol
%%%	"Percent" sign (think about it)
%%xxx	Draw a special character designated by "xxx"

Let's look at an example. The following text string:

If the piece is fired at 400%%d F for %%utwenty%%u hours, it will achieve %%p95%%% strength.

would be drawn as:

If the piece is fired at 400°F for twenty hours, it will achieve ±95% strength.

Notice that the underscore must be toggled on and off by typing "%%U" when you desire to start the underscore, and again when you desire to end the underscoring.

You may also "overlap" the symbols by using, for example, the degrees symbol between the underscore symbols.

The special characters refer to the ASCII (American Standard Code for Information Interchange) character set. This character set uses a number code for different symbols. The following table shows the ASCII character set. To use one of the characters, enter two percent signs (%%), followed by the ASCII character code. For example, to place a tilde (~) in your text, enter %%126.

32	space	56	8		80	P		104	h		
33	!	57	9		81	Q		105	i		
34	"	doublequote	58	:	colon	82	R	106	j		
35	#		59	;	semicolon	83	S	107	k		
36	$		60	<		84	T		108	l	
37	%		61	=		85	U		109	m	
38	&		62	>		86	V		110	n	
39	'	apostrophe	63	?		87	W		111	o	
40	(		64	@		88	X		112	p	
41	)		65	A		89	Y		113	q	
42	*		66	B		90	Z		114	r	
43	+		67	C		91	[		115	s	
44	,	comma	68	D		92	\	backslash	116	t	
45	-	hyphen	69	E		93	]		117	u	
46	.	period	70	F		94	^	caret	118	v	
47	/		71	G		95	_	underscore	119	w	
48	0		72	H		96	`	left apost	120	x	
49	1		73	I		97	a		121	y	
50	2		74	J		98	b		122	z	
51	3		75	K		99	c		123	{	
52	4		76	L		100	d		124	|	vert.bar
53	5		77	M		101	e		125	}	
54	6		78	N		102	f		126	~	tilde
55	7		79	O		103	g				

Courtesy of AutoDesk

TABLE 13-B ASCII Character Set

EXERCISE

Use text codes to construct the following text string in your drawing.

The story entitled <u>MY LIFE</u> is ±50% true.

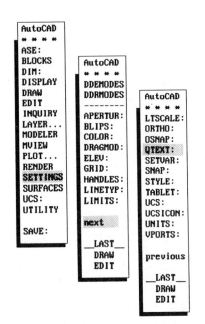

Qtext uses a rectangular box to represent the height and length of the text.

REDRAWING AND REGENERATING TEXT FASTER

Text strings redraw, regenerate, and plot slowly. As your drawings become more complex, the time required to handle text can slow down the drawing process. AutoCAD provides the Qtext (quick text) command to speed handling of text.

Qtext can be turned on or off by use of the Qtext command.

    Command: <u>QTEXT</u>
    ON/OFF <i><default></i>:

Qtext uses a rectangular box to represent the height and length of the text.

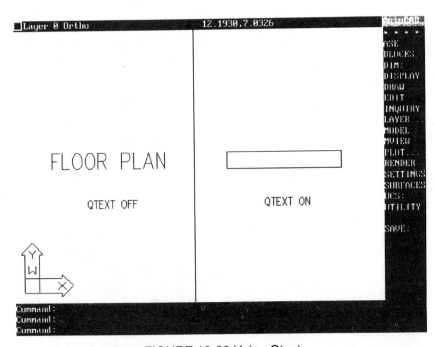

FIGURE 13-22 Using Qtext

The text boxes handle quicker when you perform redraws, regens, and plots. The change to text boxes will not take place until the next regeneration.

QUICK TEXT EXERCISE

Start a new drawing and use the Text command to place several lines of text on the screen. Now turn on the Qtext command.

  Command: QTEXT
  ON/OFF <OFF>: ON

Next use the Regen command to regenerate the drawing. You should see the text boxes.

EFFECTS OF QTEXT ON PLOTTING

The drawing will plot either text or quick text boxes. The display setting at the time of the plot determines the type of plot.

If you wish to plot the actual text, turn off the quick text, then regenerate the drawing with the Regen command before plotting.

SETTING QTEXT WITH A DIALOGUE BOX

You can use the drawing modes dialogue box to set quick text. This dialogue box is accessed by entering Ddrmodes at the command line or by selecting the "Settings/Drawing Modes..." pull-down menu.

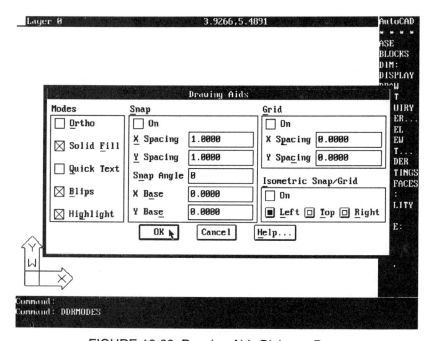

FIGURE 13-23 Drawing Aids Dialogue Box

Click on the "Quick text" check box in the "Modes" section of the dialogue box. An "X" in the box means the Quick text option is on.

Professional Tips

When a drawing contains a large amount of text, several techniques can be used to minimize the time required to display and plot the text.

1. Place the text in the drawing last. This eliminates having to regenerate text while you are constructing the drawing elements.

2. Create a special layer for text. Freeze the layer when you are not using the text (see Chapter 14).

3. Use Qtext if you want the text placements shown, but still need fast regenerations.

4. Plot *check* drawings with the Qtext option on. The text will plot as rectangles, greatly reducing plot time.

5. Whenever possible, avoid multi-stroke, "fancy" fonts. These fonts regenerate and plot more slowly than single stroke fonts. If you wish to use fancy fonts, the quick text option reduces the regeneration time.

IMPORTING TEXT INTO YOUR DRAWING

Some drawings require large amounts of text. It can be easier to type the text in a word processor, then import the file into your drawing.

Imported text must be in "ASCII" form.

Imported text must be in "ASCII" form. This means that it is free of internal word processing codes. Most word processing programs have an ASCII or "non-document" mode that can be used to create text files for import.

Tip

You can determine if a text file is in ASCII form by using the DOS Type command to display the file on the screen. For example, if the file is named TEXT1.DOC, enter the following at the DOS prompt:

C> TYPE TEXT1.DOC

If the text displays clearly (without unusual characters within the text), it is in ASCII format.

To import the text into the drawing, select the"Draw/Text/Import Text" pull-down menu. The following command sequence is used.

```
File to read (including extension):
Start point or Center/Middle/Right/?:
Height <default>:
Rotation angle <default>:
Change text options <N>:
```

The text is imported into the drawing using the current text style.

IMPORT TEXT EXERCISES

1. The electronic work disk contains a text file named "TEXTIMP.DOC". Use AutoCAD's import function to import the text into your drawing.

2. If you have a word processor capable of creating an ASCII file (or know how to use Edlin in DOS), create a text file that contains your name, address, city and state. Import the text file into your drawing.

CHAPTER EXERCISES

1. Use AutoCAD's text fonts to create styles you like and design your own business card.

2. Using the same font, create five different styles that represent very different text appearances, such as wide text, slanted, etc.

3. Use a combination of text and drawing commands to design a logo for a graphic design office.

CHAPTER REVIEW

1. How can you request a listing of stored style files?

_____

_____

2. What is a font?

_____

_____

_____

3. What text characteristics can be altered by means of the Style command?

_____

_____

_____

4. There are several methods of placing text. List them with a brief explanation of each.

_____

_____

_____

_____

_____

5. When an underscore or overscore is added to text, is an entire string altered, or can segments be treated separately? Explain.

_____

_____

6. When a text height is asked for, is a numerical entry required? Explain.

_____

_____

_____

7. List the alignment modes under the text command.

_____

_____

8. Can text be rotated at any angle?

_____

9. What is justified text?

_____

_____

_____

10. How can the text height be altered each time you enter text without redefining the style?

_____

_____

_____

11. How can you compress or expand text?

_____

_____

12. Style is listed in the menu twice. Show how each is listed and explain each meaning.

_____

_____

_____

13. What format must text be before importing into AutoCAD?

_____

CHAPTER 14

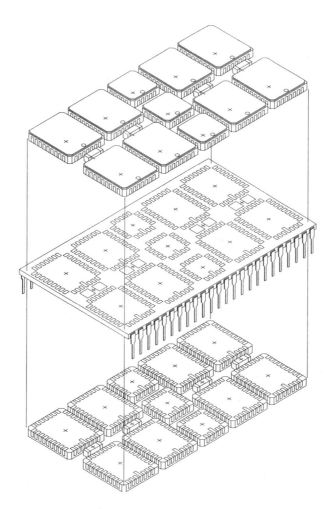

Layering Your Drawings

OBJECTIVES:

Professional CAD drawings are constructed on different layers that can be turned on and off or changed. Chapter 14 covers the methodology of using layers in your drawings. The objectives of this chapter are:

● Understanding the concept of CAD layering.

● Learning the methodology of using layers in your drawings.

● Becoming proficient in the use of layering.

LAYERS

Traditional drafting techniques often include a method of drawing called overlay drafting. This consists of sheets of drafting media that are overlaid so the drawing below shows through the top sheet. Items can be placed on the top sheet that line up with the drawing below. Both sheets can be printed together, resulting in a print that shows the work on both sheets.

The first sheet is typically referred to as the base drawing. Each additional sheet can be used to place different items.

As an example, if you draw a set of floor plans, you must prepare a separate drawing for the dimensioned floor plan, the plumbing plan, the electrical plan, and so forth. Since most of your drawing time is spent redrawing the floor plan, you spend a great amount of time doing repetitive tasks. The floor plan can be thought of as the base drawing, with each discipline such as electrical and plumbing being placed on overlay sheets.

AutoCAD provides capabilities that eliminate the repetition of redrawing the base drawing. You can use drawing *layers* to place different parts of your drawings.

You may think of layers as transparent sheets of glass that are stacked on top of each other.

You may think of layers as transparent sheets of glass that are stacked on top of each other. You may draw on each layer and see through all the layers so that all the work appears as though it were on one drawing.

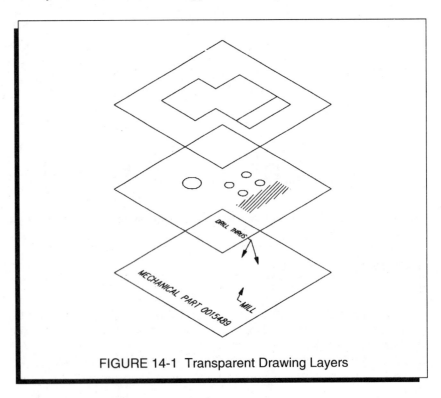

FIGURE 14-1 Transparent Drawing Layers

AutoCAD goes one step further. You may turn on or off each layer so that it is either visible or invisible!

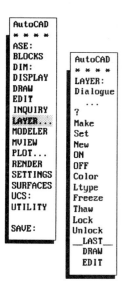

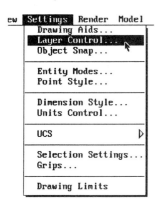

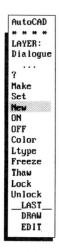

USING THE LAYER COMMAND

The Layer command is used to manipulate the layers in your drawing. Let's look at each option of the Layer command to learn how to use them.

LISTING LAYER INFORMATION

You may view a listing of the named layers and obtain a status report of each by entering a "?" in response to the prompt:

> Command: LAYER
> ?/Make/Set/New/ON/OFF/Color/Ltype/Freeze/Thaw/LOck/Unlock: ?
> Layer name(s) for listing <*>:

You may, at this point, enter any layer name to obtain a listing of the status. If you would like a listing of all the named layers, enter the wild card character "*". A typical listing would appear in the format shown in Figure 14-2.

Layer name	State	Color	Linetype
0	On	7 (white)	CONTINUOUS
FLOOR PLAN	On	1 (red)	CONTINUOUS
DIMENSIONS	On	2 (yellow)	CONTINUOUS
ELECTRICAL	On	3 (green)	CONTINUOUS
HEATING	On -L	4 (cyan)	CONTINUOUS
PLUMBING	On	5 (blue)	CONTINUOUS
DASHED_LINES	On	6 (magenta)	CONTI
OUS			
Current layer: 0			

FIGURE 14-2 Sample Layer Listings

Notice that the current layer is shown at the bottom.

NAMING A LAYER

Each layer may be named. You determine the name to be used. To establish the layer name, respond to the prompt with New.

> Command: LAYER
> ?/Make/Set/New/ON/OFF/Color/Ltype/Freeze/Thaw/LOck/Unlock: N
> Layer name(s) <default>: (name)

Professional Tip

Choose names for layers that describe the items drawn on that layer. For example, use DIM as the layer name to contain dimensions. Also, try to standardize your layer names for drawings that are always similar.

You have now set a new layer with the specified name. You may name several layers at once. To do so, separate each name with a comma. Each name may contain up to 31 letters, but no spaces. If you enter a space, AutoCAD will treat it the same as an Enter and terminate the sequence. You may use letter characters, the dollar sign ($), underlines, and hyphens. Lower case characters are converted to upper case.

You may only draw on the current *layer.*

MAKING A LAYER

The Make layer option allows you to make a new layer and simultaneously move to that layer. The new layer begins with a continuous linetype and a color assignment of 7 (white).

If the named layer already exists, AutoCAD makes it the current layer. If the named layer does not exist, it is created first, then becomes the current layer.

The option is selected while in the Layer command.

```
Command: LAYER
?/Make/Set/New/ON/OFF/Color/Ltype/Freeze/Thaw: M
New current layer <0>: (layer name)
?/Make/Set/New/ON/OFF/Color/Ltype/Freeze/Thaw/LOck/Unlock:
(Enter)
```

SETTING THE CURRENT DRAWING LAYER

You may only draw on the *current* layer. Even if other layers are on, the current layer is the only one that entities can be added to. The current layer name is displayed at the top of the screen. There can be only one current layer at a time.

There is no relationship to layers that are turned on and the current layer. If the current layer is turned off, your work can not be seen. Therefore, if you add a line, it will be placed on the drawing, but you will not be able to view it.

```
Command: LAYER
?/Make/Set/New/ON/OFF/Color/Ltype/Freeze/Thaw/LOck/Unlock: S
New current layer <current layer>: (layer name)
?/Make/Set/New/ON/OFF/Color/Ltype/Freeze/Thaw/LOck/Unlock:
(Enter)
```

TURNING LAYERS ON AND OFF

The visibility of each layer is determined by whether the layer is currently on or off.

If a layer is off, it is invisible. It is still a part of the drawing, you just can not see it. To turn a layer on or off, respond to the prompt with either "on" or "off". For example:

```
Command: LAYER
?/Make/Set/New/ON/OFF/Color/Ltype/Freeze/Thaw/Unlock/LOck: ON
Layer name(s) to turn On: NAME
```

```
AutoCAD
* * * *
LAYER:
Dialogue
...
?
Make
Set
New
ON
OFF
Color
Ltype
Freeze
Thaw
Lock
Unlock
__LAST__
DRAW
EDIT
```

LAYER COLORS

Each layer is associated with a color. The initial (default) color number is seven (white). AutoCAD sets the first seven color numbers and colors as follows:

1 — Red	5 — Blue
2 — Yellow	6 — Magenta
3 — Green	7 — White
4 — Cyan	

If you have a color monitor, the entities drawn on a layer will appear in the color assigned to that layer. If your monitor is monochrome, the colors still exist, but, of course, you will see them as shades of gray.

Professional Tip

Use colors to "code" different parts of your drawings. This will make recognition of the different parts easier.

You may set the color for each layer by responding to the prompt with "C".

Command: LAYER
?/Make/Set/New/ON/OFF/Color/Ltype/Freeze/Thaw/LOck/Unlock: C
Color: (select a color by name or number)
Layer name(s) for color n <current>:

```
AutoCAD
* * * *
LAYER:
Dialogue
...
?
Make
Set
New
ON
OFF
Color
Ltype
Freeze
Thaw
Lock
Unlock
__LAST__
DRAW
EDIT
```

LAYERS AND LINETYPES

Each layer can contain a certain linetype. Every entity that is placed on that layer will be shown on the drawing screen in that linetype.

Setting the *layer* linetype sets the default linetype that is used for each entity that is placed on that layer. You may also use the Change command to change one or more entities to different linetypes on any layer, regardless of the layer linetype setting.

Command: LAYER
?/Make/Set/New/ON/OFF/Color/Ltype/Freeze/Thaw/LOck/Unlock: LT
Linetype (or ?) <current linetype>:
Layer name(s) for linetype (selected linetype) <default>:
?/Make/Set/New/ON/OFF/Color/Ltype/Freeze/Thaw/LOck/Unlock:
(Enter)

FREEZING LAYERS

The Freeze option lets you turn off layers and eliminate them from subsequent regenerations. (See Regen command.) This can save time when performing operations that force regenerations. The current layer can not be frozen.

Command: LAYER
?/Make/Set/New/ON/OFF/Color/Ltype/Freeze/Thaw/LOck/Unlock: F
Layer name(s) to Freeze:

```
AutoCAD
* * * *
LAYER:
Dialogue
...
?
Make
Set
New
ON
OFF
Color
Ltype
Freeze
Thaw
Lock
Unlock
__LAST__
DRAW
EDIT
```

Tip

The Freeze option operates differently from the OFF option. When you turn a layer OFF, it is not displayed, but is regenerated by AutoCAD. A frozen layer is neither displayed nor regenerated. For faster regens, use the Freeze option.

THAWING LAYERS

The Thaw option is used to undo the effect of the freeze command.

> Command: <u>LAYER</u>
> ?/Make/Set/New/ON/OFF/Color/Ltype/Freeze/Thaw/LOck/Unlock: <u>T</u>
> Layer name(s) to Thaw:

Professional Tip

Use AutoCAD's layering ability to create a "base" drawing. Place specific parts of your drawing on other named layers. Freeze layers which you will not come back to. This will speed the drawing process, especially for complicated or "hatched" areas.

LOCKING AND UNLOCKING LAYERS

When a layer is locked, it can not be either edited or made current.

Layers can be *locked* so that they can be viewed but not edited. When a layer is locked, it can not be either edited or made current. You can, however, perform some operations such as object snap, color and line-type changes, and freezing locked layers.

> Command: <u>LAYER</u>
> ?/Make/Set/New/ON/OFF/Color/Ltype/Freeze/Thaw/LOck/Unlock: <u>L</u>
> Layer name(s) to Lock:
> ?/Make/Set/New/ON/OFF/Color/Ltype/Freeze/Thaw/LOck/Unlock:

Professional Tip

Lock the base drawing layer(s) when other CAD drafters will be performing specific discipline work on other layers in the drawing.

CONTROLLING LAYERS WITH A DIALOGUE BOX

Controlling layers is simplified by use of the Modify Layer dialogue box. There are four ways of displaying the dialogue box.

- Use the Ddlmodes command from the command line.
- Use the transparent command 'Ddlmodes during a current command.
- Select "Layer Control..." from the "Settings" pull-down menu.
- Select "Layer..." from the screen menu.

The following illustration shows the layer control dialogue box.

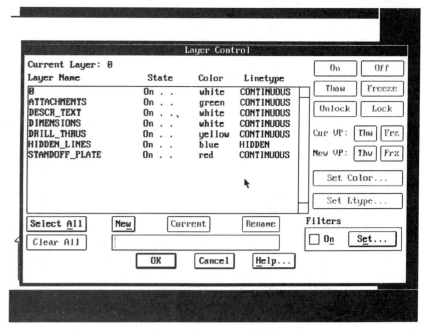

FIGURE 14-3 Layer Control Dialogue Box

The dialogue box can be used to perform all the operations possible with the Layer command plus a few more. Let's look at the methods used to manipulate layers with the **Modify Layer** dialogue box.

TURNING LAYERS ON OR OFF

To turn one or more layers on or off, first highlight the target layer(s) by clicking on the layer name, then click either the Qn or Off button. The "State" column will immediately reflect the change. If a layer is on, the word "On" appears. If off, a period (.) appears in the column.

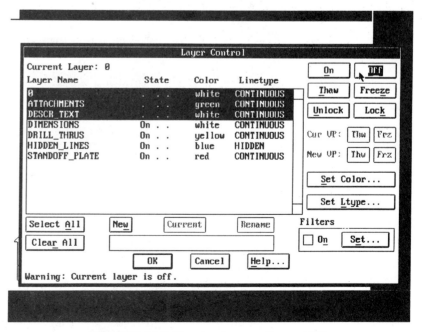

FIGURE 14-4 Turning Layers On and Off

FREEZING AND THAWING LAYERS

To freeze or thaw one or more layers, highlight the target layer(s), then click on the Freeze or Thaw buttons. A frozen layer is indicated by the letter "F" in the State column. A non-frozen or thawed layer is indicated by a period (.) in the column.

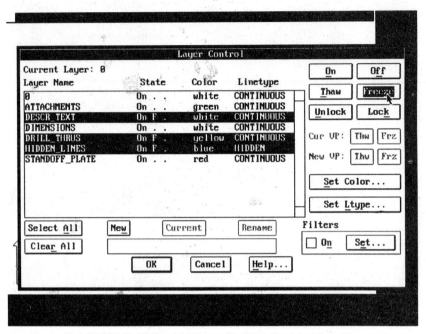

FIGURE 14-5 Freezing and Thawing Layers

LOCKING AND UNLOCKING LAYERS

To lock or unlock layers, select the target layer(s), then click on the Lock or Unlock buttons. The letter "L" listed in the State column denotes a locked layer. A layer that is not locked shows a period (.) in this position.

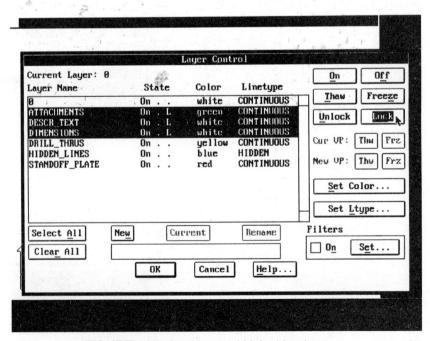

FIGURE 14-6 Locking and Unlocking Layers

SETTING THE LAYER COLOR

To set the layer color, first select the layer(s) to be modified, then click on the "Set Color..." button. A **Set Color** subdialogue box will be displayed as shown in Figure 14-7.

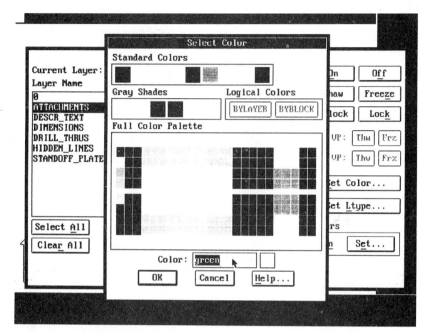

FIGURE 14-7 Select Color Subdialogue Box

To set the color, select a color from the color display chart. Note that this chart has the capability to display 255 colors. Not all display systems have the ability to use this many colors. The chart will display all the colors available with your display, with the remainder being displayed as gray. The color edit box will display either the name or number of the selected color. The first seven colors are listed by name, with the remaining colors listed by number. The first nine colors are displayed above the color edit box.

You may also enter the color name or number manually from the keyboard in the color edit box. After you have selected the color, click on the OK box to return to the **Modify Layer** dialogue box.

SETTING THE LAYER LINETYPE

You can set the linetype for all the entities residing on a layer. First pick the layer(s) for which you wish to set a linetype, then click on the "Set Linetype..." button. A **Select Linetype** subdialogue box is displayed as shown in Figure 14-8.

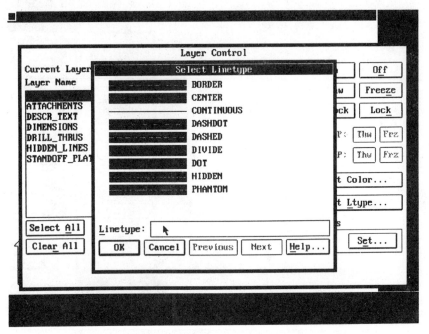

FIGURE 14-8 Select Linetype Subdialogue Box

The list box in the dialogue box displays the linetypes that have been loaded. As you select each linetype, it is displayed at the top of the dialogue box.

FILTERING THE LAYER LISTINGS

Some types of drawings may have a large number of named layers. Manipulating through the layer listings can become tedious. AutoCAD allows you to "filter" the listings so that only certain types of listings are displayed.

For example, you can filter the listing so that only layers that are not frozen will be displayed. The filter capabilities can be used to display or suppress layers that are on or off, frozen or thawed, locked or unlocked, and whether the layer is frozen in the current viewport.

You can also filter by name, color, and linetype. With these filters, you can use the DOS wildcard characters of question mark (?) and asterisk (*) to designate the layers.

To set the filter type, select the "Set..." button in the "Filters" section of the dialogue box. The following dialogue box is displayed.

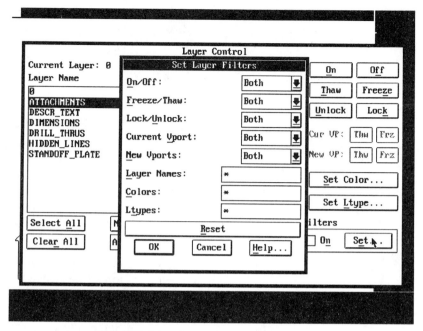

FIGURE 14-9 Layer Filter Dialogue Box

The first five filters listed (see Figure 14-9) use pop-up boxes to select between the settings of either selection listed, or both selections to be listed.

For example, if you select the Freeze/Thaw pop-up box, the selections are Both, Frozen, and Thawed.

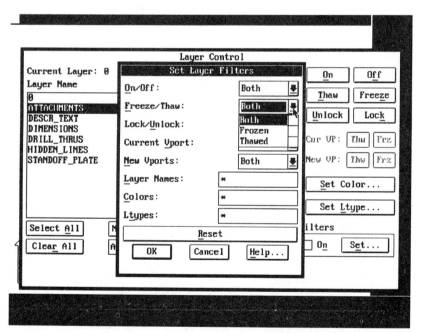

FIGURE 14-10 Filters Pop-Up Box

The last three selections require you to enter the filter type in the text box. The default listing is an asterisk (*), which means that all layer names will be listed.

Let's assume that you wanted to list all layers that started with the letters LEVEL and ended with any two characters. The filter would read:

LEVEL??

This would list layers that are named LEVEL21, LEVEL_A, and LEVEL2C. It would not list 1LEVEL, LEV21, or 3RD_LEVEL. If you do not remember how wildcard characters work, you may want to review the DOS section in this book.

You can reset the values so that all the layer names are listed by clicking on the "Reset" button.

LAYER EXERCISES

1. Create a layer named MYLAYER. Set MYLAYER as the current layer. Do you see the layer name on the status line at the top of the screen?

2. Set the layer color to green. Draw some objects on the layer.

3. Set the current layer to "0". Freeze the layer named MYLAYER. Did the objects you drew disappear? Select the layer dialogue box from the pull-down menu and Thaw MYLAYER. Did the objects reappear?

CHAPTER REVIEW

1. Why would a CAD drafter use layers?

2. What layer option would you use if you wanted to create a new layer and make that layer currently active?

3. How do you turn on a frozen layer?

4. What is the difference between turning layers off and freezing layers?

5. How would you obtain a listing of all the layers in your drawing?

_____

_____

6. Can you have objects of more than one color on the same layer? Explain.

_____

_____

_____

_____

CHAPTER 15

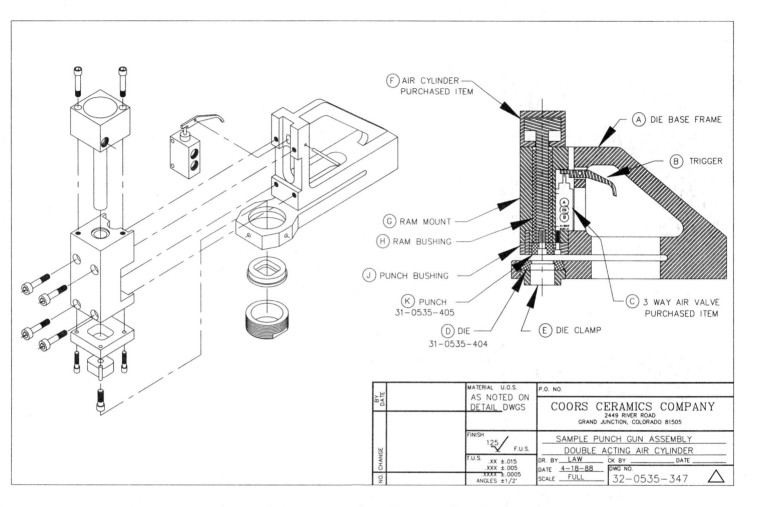

Introduction to Dimensioning

OBJECTIVES:

The ability to place dimensions into a drawing is one of the most essential elements of CAD drawing. In this chapter, the user will learn the basics of AutoCAD dimensioning. The objectives of Chapter 15 are:

● To acquaint the user with the basic elements of dimensioning.

● To learn the manner in which dimensions are placed in AutoCAD.

● To learn some of the special abilities of the dimensioning mode.

DIMENSIONING IN AUTOCAD

AutoCAD constructs dimensioning semi-automatically. That is, it can construct the dimensioning lines and measure the distances for you. All it needs is some basic information from you. This is a very powerful feature. If mastered, it can be a great time-saver and provide professional results.

DIMENSIONING COMPONENTS

Dimensioning is made up of several different parts. Before we try some dimensioning, you should know these parts. Let's look at each.

THE DIMENSION LINE

The dimension line is the line with the arrows or "ticks" at each end.

The dimension line is the line with the arrows or "ticks" at each end. The dimension text is either placed between this line, dividing it into two parts, or over the line.

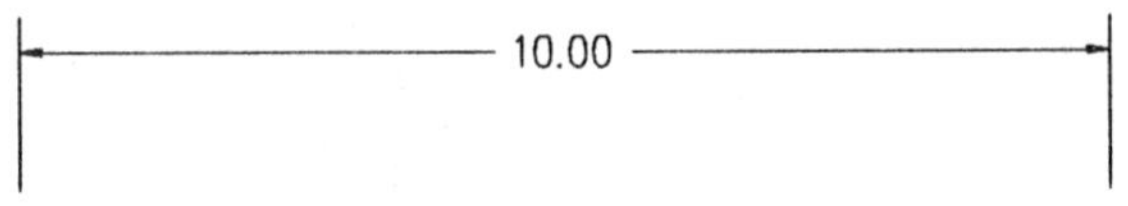

10.00

FIGURE 15-1 Dimension Line

When you are using angular dimensioning, the dimension line is an arc instead of a straight line.

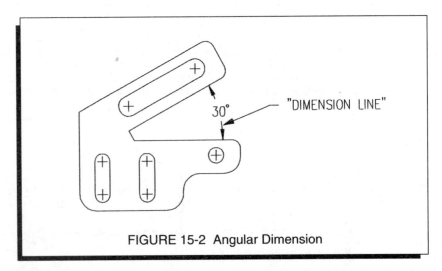

FIGURE 15-2 Angular Dimension

If you wish, the arrows at the end of the dimension line can be replaced with tick marks. The following examples show dimension lines with tick marks and arrows.

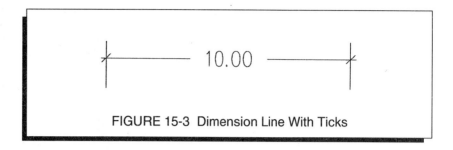

FIGURE 15-3 Dimension Line With Ticks

EXTENSION LINES

The extension lines (sometimes called "witness lines") are the lines constructed perpendicular to the dimension line and extending to the point that is being dimensioned to.

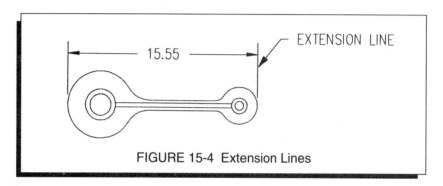

FIGURE 15-4 Extension Lines

DIMENSION TEXT

The dimension text is the text that appears at the dimension line.

The dimension text is the text that appears at the dimension line. You may allow AutoCAD to measure the distance and enter the text, you may specify the desired text, or you may suppress the text entirely by entering a space in place of the text.

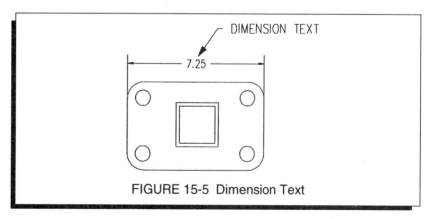

FIGURE 15-5 Dimension Text

The dimension text is drawn using the current text Style and font. The format used is determined by the current units. That is, if the units are set to architectural, you will receive an output of feet and inches. The smallest fraction displayed will be as chosen by the Units command, and so forth. You may, of course, enter any text if you choose the manual method of inserting the dimension text.

> **NOTE: You must use a horizontal text font when in the Dimension command. If the current text is vertical, you must change it before entering the dimensions.**

DIMENSION TOLERANCES

The dimension tolerances are the plus and minus amounts that are appended to the dimension text. These tolerances are added to the text that AutoCAD generates automatically. The plus and minus amounts are specified by you. They may be equal or unequal. If they are equal, they are drawn with a plus/minus symbol. If they are unequal, the tolerances are drawn one above the other. The following text shows examples of both equal and unequal tolerances.

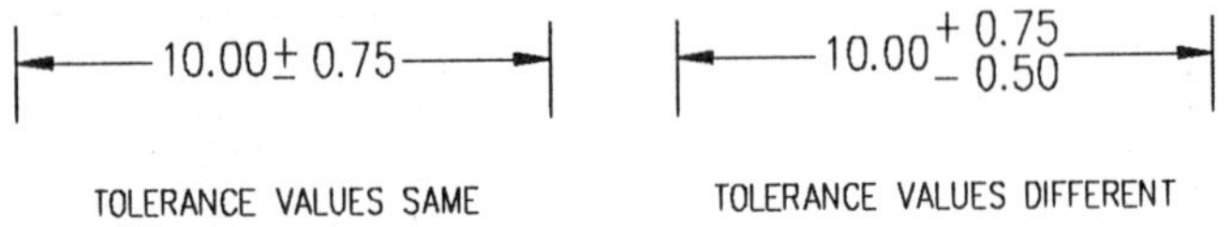

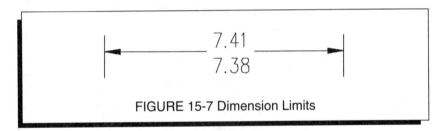

FIGURE 15-6 Dimension Tolerances

DIMENSION LIMITS

Instead of having the tolerance shown, you may choose to have them applied to the dimension. The example shown in the following illustration is a measurement of 7.4 units with a tolerance of +.01 and −02.

FIGURE 15-7 Dimension Limits

ALTERNATE DIMENSION UNITS

Alternate units can be used to show two systems of measurement simultaneously. For example, you can show English and metric units on the same dimension line.

FIGURE 15-8 Alternate Dimension Limits

LEADER LINES

Leader lines are "arrowed lines" with text at the end.

Leader lines are "arrowed lines" with text at the end. Leaders are often used to point out a specific part of a drawing to be noted.

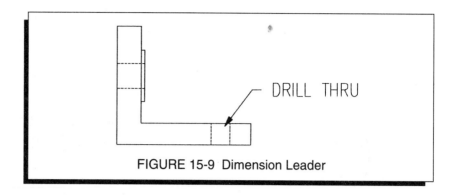

FIGURE 15-9 Dimension Leader

CENTER MARKS AND CENTER LINES

A center mark is a cross designating the center of a circle or arc. Center lines are lines that cross at the center of the circle or arc and intersecting the circumference. Examples of each are shown below.

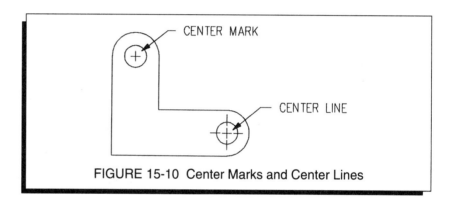

FIGURE 15-10 Center Marks and Center Lines

CHANGING THE LOOK WITH DIMENSION VARIABLES

Dimensioning variables determine the manner in which the dimension entities are drawn. Some variables are values and some are simply turned on and off. The variables may be changed by you to change the dimension "look" and function. Dimension variables are covered in Chapter 16.

ENTERING DIMENSIONING MODE

You begin dimensioning by selecting DIM: from the root screen menu, or Draw/Dimensions from the pull-down menu. When you do this, you will notice that the command line changes from "Command:" to "Dim:". This means that you are in dimensioning mode. *All dimensioning activities are performed in dimension mode.* While in the dimension mode, you can only use the dimension commands. You will see later that some commands such as Redraw are available while you are in the mode. You can exit the dimension mode by selecting "EX" or Ctrl-C, or by selecting another AutoCAD command from the menu.

When we enter the dimension mode, we first select the type of dimensioning we wish to perform, then use the associated commands to draw the dimensions.

Let's explore the different types of dimension commands.

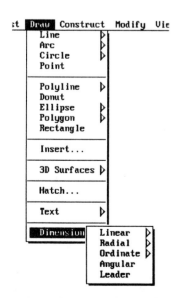

You begin dimensioning by selecting DIM: from the root screen menu.

DIMENSIONING COMMANDS

AutoCAD dimensioning commands can be grouped into four basic types of commands. These are:

>   Dimension *drawing* commands
>
>   Dimension *editing* commands
>
>   Dimension *utility* commands
>
>   Dimension *style* commands (covered in Chapter 16)

Let's now look at each of the types of dimensioning commands.

DIMENSION DRAWING COMMANDS

Dimension drawing commands are used to draw the different types of dimension lines. The following is a listing of dimension drawing commands.

Horizontal: Draws a dimension with a horizontal dimension line.

Continue: Continues a dimension line string after you have placed the first dimension. The continuing string uses the first dimension to determine the correct positioning of the next dimension.

Vertical: Constructs a dimension with a vertical dimension line.

Aligned: Draws a dimension line parallel to an entity or to the dimension extension line origins you specify.

Rotated: Constructs a dimension at a specified angle.

Baseline: Continues a dimension line (similar to the Continue command) in reference to the first extension line origin of the first dimension line in the string. The dimension line is offset to avoid conflict with the previous dimension line.

Angular: Dimensions the angle between two nonparallel lines. The dimension line is constructed as an arc, with the dimension value shown as the angle between the lines.

Diameter: Dimensions the diameter of a circle or arc.

Radius: Constructs a dimension line that shows the radius of an arc or circle.

Center: Places a center mark, or alternately, center lines, at the center point of a circle or arc.

Ordinate: Dimensions the X or Y coordinate, referenced to a specified point, of an object.

Let's look at each command and learn how to use each to place a dimension.

```
AutoCAD
* * *
DIM:
Aligned
Angular
Diameter
Horizntl
Leader
Ordinate
Radius
Rotated
Vertical
Edit
Dim Styl
Dim Vars
next
Exit
__LAST__
  DRAW
  EDIT
```

PLACING A HORIZONTAL DIMENSION LINE

The Horizontal dimension command creates the most common type of dimension line. The dimension line is drawn horizontally as shown below.

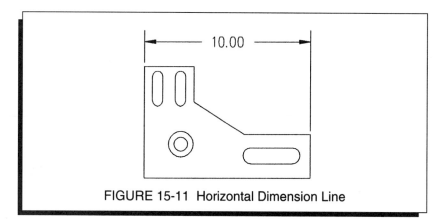

FIGURE 15-11 Horizontal Dimension Line

When placing a horizontal dimension, you can either specify an entity to dimension, or select the starting and ending points for the extension lines.

Let's place a horizontal dimension line. Draw a box as shown in Figure 15-12. Let's now enter the dimension mode. From the screen menu, select DIM:/HORIZNTL. Use the following command sequence and follow the instructions at the prompts. Refer to Figure 15-12.

Command: DIM
Dim: HORIZONTAL
First extension line origin or RETURN to select: (PRESS THE ENTER KEY)
Select line, arc, or circle: (SELECT THE TOP LINE OF THE BOX)
Dimension line location (Text/Angle): (MOVE THE CURSOR UP TO LOCATE THE DIMENSION LINE)
Dimension text <measured distance>: (PRESS RETURN TO ACCEPT THE MEASURED DIMENSION)

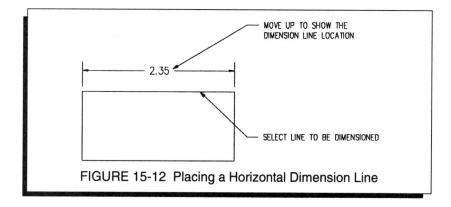

FIGURE 15-12 Placing a Horizontal Dimension Line

Note that you can also enter the extension line origin points. When AutoCAD prompts you for the first extension line origin, enter the actual point instead of pressing Enter. We will use this method in the next exercise.

Tip

Use object snap to set exact points for accurate dimensioning.

If you choose to select the object to be dimensioned by pressing the Enter key instead of specifying the extension line points, you can save the steps necessary for entering each beginning point.

This method works on lines, arcs, or circles and may be used with the Horizontal, Vertical, Aligned, and Rotated dimension commands. The following illustration shows a sample command sequence and a typical pick point for dimensioning the three entities using this method.

> Command: <u>DIM</u>
> Dim: <u>VERTICAL</u>
> First extension line origin or RETURN to select: *(RETURN)*
> Select line, arc, or circle: (*PICK ANY PART OF THE LINE, ARC, OR CIRCLE*)
> Dimension line location (Text/Angle): (*SELECT THE DIMENSION LINE LOCATION*)
> Dimension text <*default*>: (*RETURN*)

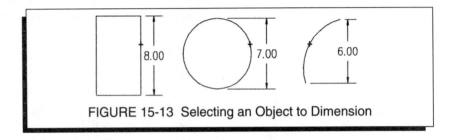

FIGURE 15-13 Selecting an Object to Dimension

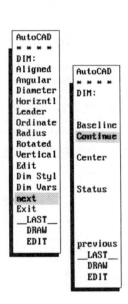

CONTINUING THE DIMENSION STRING

The Continue dimension command is used to place a dimension segment that follows the first dimension you place. The continued dimension is constructed by using the last extension line of the previous dimension as the first extension line point of the new dimension.

Construct the simple object shown in Figure 15-14. Place a horizontal dimension as shown.

Select NEXT from the screen menu, then click on CONTINUE. AutoCAD prompts:

> Dim: <u>CONTINUE</u>
> Second extension line origin or RETURN to select:

Let's use object snap to capture the upper right intersection. Type "INT" from the keyboard and press Enter. AutoCAD prompts you for the intersection point.

> of (*SELECT THE INTERSECTION*)
> Dimension text <*measured distance*>: (*PRESS RETURN TO ACCEPT THE MEASURED DISTANCE*)

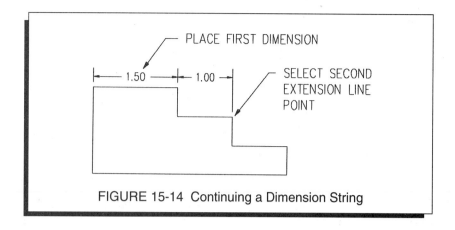

FIGURE 15-14 Continuing a Dimension String

It is not necessary to accept the actual measured distance. The default distance shown is the actual measurement that AutoCAD has measured between the extension lines.

To place your own measurement, just type in the distance from the keyboard instead of pressing Enter to accept the default measurement.

Professional Tip

There is no requirement for the dimension text to be a numerical value. You can type in any characters from the keyboard. For example, you may want to place a horizontal dimension and use the dimension text:

FIVE EQUALLY SPACED NOTCHES

HORIZONTAL DIMENSIONING EXERCISES

Draw the following objects and place the horizontal dimensions at the locations shown.

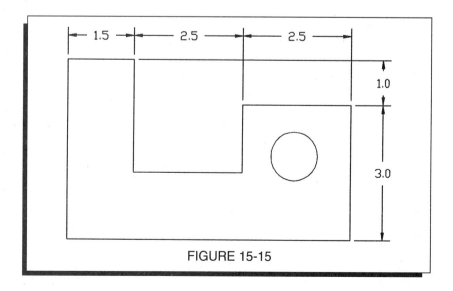

FIGURE 15-15

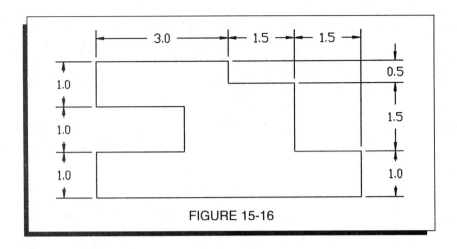

FIGURE 15-16

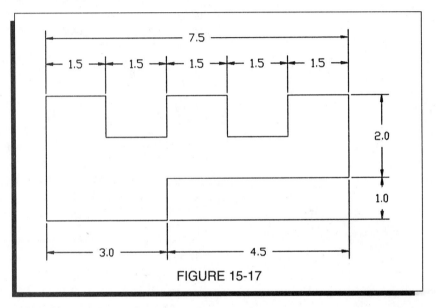

FIGURE 15-17

PLACING A VERTICAL DIMENSION LINE

The Vertical dimension command works the same as the horizontal command, except the dimension line is drawn vertically.

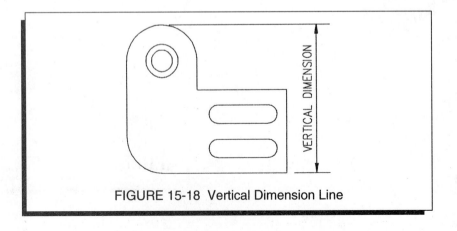

FIGURE 15-18 Vertical Dimension Line

To place vertical dimensions, either select an entity to dimension, or manually select the extension line origin points. Use the following exercise to place a vertical dimension line.

VERTICAL DIMENSIONING EXERCISE

Draw the following objects and use the vertical dimension command to place the vertical dimensions at the locations shown.

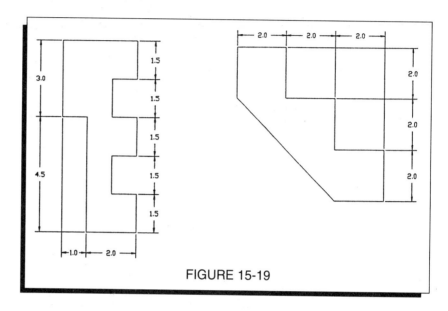

FIGURE 15-19

DIMENSIONING ANGLED SURFACES

Many times that you will be required to place dimensions that are constructed at an angle. AutoCAD provides two commands for placing angled dimensions. Let's see how each one works.

DRAWING ALIGNED DIMENSIONS

The Aligned dimension command draws the dimension line parallel to the extension line origin points.

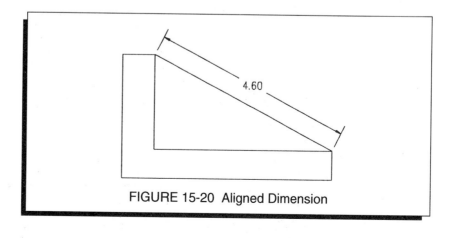

FIGURE 15-20 Aligned Dimension

AutoCAD
* * *
DIM:
Aligned
Angular
Diameter
Horizntl
Leader
Ordinate
Radius
Rotated
Vertical
Edit
Dim Styl
Dim Vars
next
Exit
__LAST__
  DRAW
  EDIT

To draw an aligned dimension, select either the entity that you want the dimension line to be parallel to, or manually select the extension line origins. The following exercise will guide you through the methodology of constructing an aligned dimension.

ALIGNED DIMENSION EXERCISE

Construct the following aligned dimension drawing and place all the dimensions as shown.

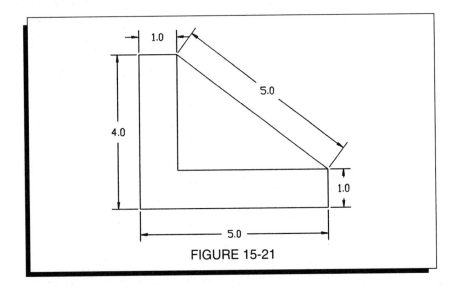

FIGURE 15-21

CONSTRUCTING ROTATED DIMENSIONS

The Rotated dimension command functions the same as the aligned command, except that you must first specify the angle. This is especially useful in situations where the extension line origins do not accurately describe the desired dimension line angle. The illustration below shows such a situation.

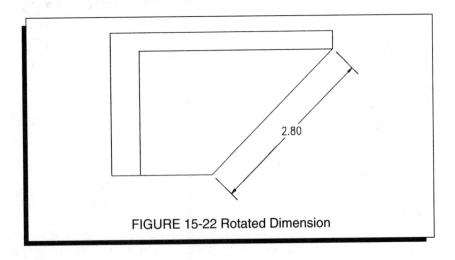

FIGURE 15-22 Rotated Dimension

AutoCAD
* * * *
DIM:
Aligned
Angular
Diameter
Horizntl
Leader
Ordinate
Radius
Rotated
Vertical
Edit
Dim Styl
Dim Vars
next
Exit
__LAST__
DRAW
EDIT

When you select the Rotated dimension command, AutoCAD prompts:

Dim: <u>ROTATED</u>
Dimension line angle <*default*>:

You can tell AutoCAD the angle you want to use in two ways. The first is to enter the angle from the keyboard. The angle is specified in AutoCAD's standard angle notation, with the zero angle to the right (east) direction.

The second way is to use two points to "show" AutoCAD the angle. To do this, respond with two points when prompted for the dimension line angle. AutoCAD will measure the angle between the two points and use that angle to construct the rotated dimension.

After you have specified the angle in either of the two ways, AutoCAD prompts you for the extension line origins.

ROTATED DIMENSION EXERCISE

Construct the following drawing and place all the dimensions shown.

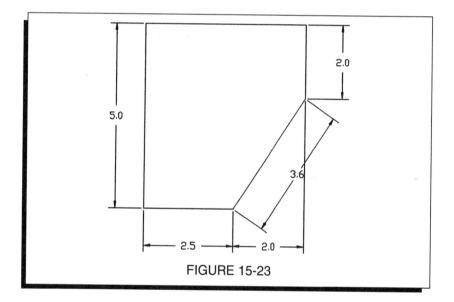

FIGURE 15-23

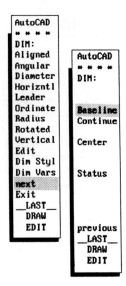

CREATING BASELINE DIMENSIONS

The Baseline dimension command creates continuous dimensions from the first extension line. The first extension line acts as a baseline from which the dimensions originate. AutoCAD offsets each new dimension line to avoid drawing on top of the first dimension line.

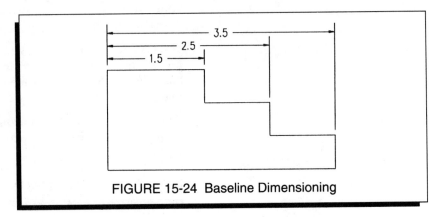

FIGURE 15-24 Baseline Dimensioning

To construct a baseline dimension, first construct an initial dimension line, then select Baseline from the menu. When AutoCAD prompts for the second extension line origin, select the next point. AutoCAD will construct the dimension line, using the first extension line origin of the first dimension line in the string as the first extension line origin, and the point you entered as the second extension line origin. AutoCAD also offsets the new dimension line so it is not constructed on top of the first.

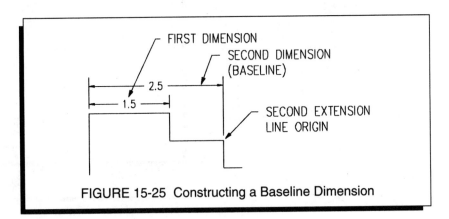

FIGURE 15-25 Constructing a Baseline Dimension

BASELINE DIMENSIONING EXERCISE

Construct the following object and place the baseline dimensions.

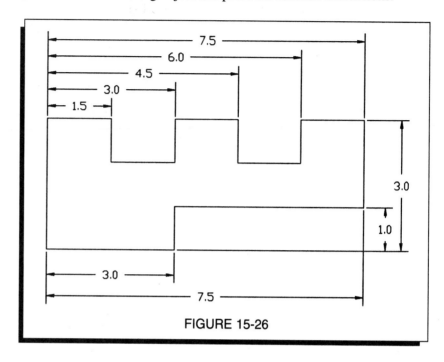

FIGURE 15-26

DIMENSIONING ANGLES

The Angular dimensioning command is used to dimension angles. There are four ways to specify an angular dimension:

Two non-parallel lines

An arc

A circle and another point

Three points

When you select Angular from the menu, AutoCAD prompts:

Dim: ANGULAR
Select arc, circle, line, or RETURN:

Let's look at how to place an angular dimension in each circumstance.

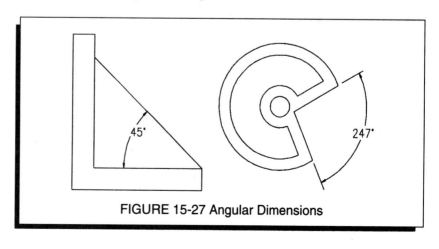

FIGURE 15-27 Angular Dimensions

```
AutoCAD
* * *
DIM:
Aligned
Angular
Diameter
Horizntl
Leader
Ordinate
Radius
Rotated
Vertical
Edit
Dim Styl
Dim Vars
next
Exit
__LAST__
DRAW
EDIT
```

ANGULAR DIMENSION EXERCISE

Let's place an angular dimension. Draw two lines as shown in Figure 15-28. Let's select DIM:/ANGULAR from the screen menu. Use the following command sequence and Figure 15-28.

Command: <u>DIM</u>
Dim: <u>ANGULAR</u>
Select arc, circle, line, or Return: (*SELECT "POINT 1"*)
Second line: (*SELECT "POINT 2"*)
Dimension arc line location (Text/Angle): (*MOVE THE DIMENSION ARC INTO PLACE AND CLICK*)
Dimension text <*default*>: (*PRESS ENTER*)

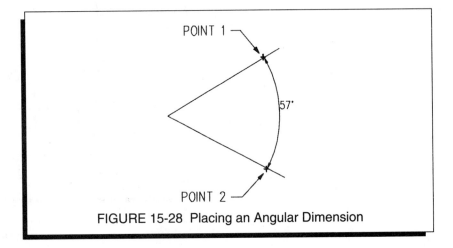

FIGURE 15-28 Placing an Angular Dimension

DIMENSIONING CIRCLES AND ARCS

Diameter and radius dimensioning of circles and arcs is easy with AutoCAD. The Diameter and Radius commands are used to place these types of dimensions. Let's see how each works.

DIMENSIONING THE DIAMETER OF A CIRCLE OR ARC

The Diameter dimension command draws dimensions of the diameter of either a circle or an arc. An example of each is shown in the following illustration.

```
AutoCAD
* * * *
DIM:
Aligned
Angular
Diameter
Horizntl
Leader
Ordinate
Radius
Rotated
Vertical
Edit
Dim Styl
Dim Vars
next
Exit
__LAST__
  DRAW
  EDIT
```

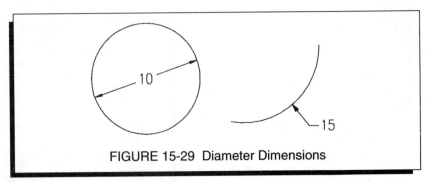

FIGURE 15-29 Diameter Dimensions

The dimension is placed according to the point you pick when selecting the arc or circle. The dimension line will intersect that point, passing through the center point of the arc or circle.

If the dimension line and text are too large to fit within the arc or circle, AutoCAD will place a leader line outside the circle or arc. The following illustration shows an example of such a leader line.

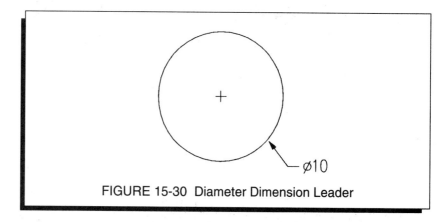

FIGURE 15-30 Diameter Dimension Leader

The length of the leader line is placed by you. AutoCAD asks for the leader length with the following prompt:

Enter leader length for text:

DIAMETER DIMENSIONING EXERCISE

Draw four circles on the screen. From the screen root menu, select DIM:/Diameter. When AutoCAD prompts for the arc or circle, select any part on the first circle. Accept the default dimension. Notice how the dimension line is located at the point where you selected the circle.

```
AutoCAD
* * * *
DIM:
Aligned
Angular
Diameter
Horizntl
Leader
Ordinate
Radius
Rotated
Vertical
Edit
Dim Styl
Dim Vars
next
Exit
__LAST__
  DRAW
  EDIT
```

DIMENSIONING THE RADIUS OF A CIRCLE OR ARC

The Radius dimension command draws the dimension of the radius from the center of a circle or arc.

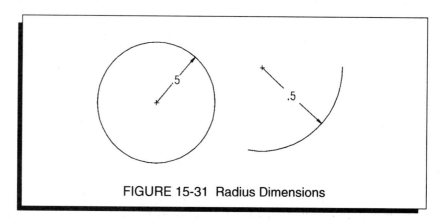

FIGURE 15-31 Radius Dimensions

The point at which the radius dimension line intersects the circle or arc is determined by the location of the pick point used when selecting the object to be dimensioned.

RADIUS DIMENSION EXERCISE

Draw the following object and use radius dimensioning to place the dimensions shown.

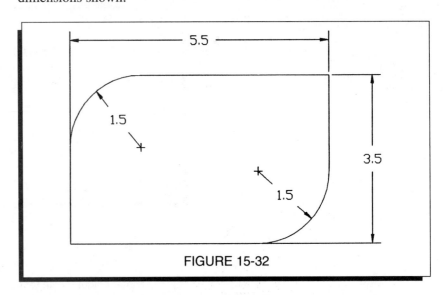

FIGURE 15-32

PLACING CENTER MARKS

You may place a center mark at the center point of an arc or circle. Center marks are drawn as an intersection cross as shown in the following figure.

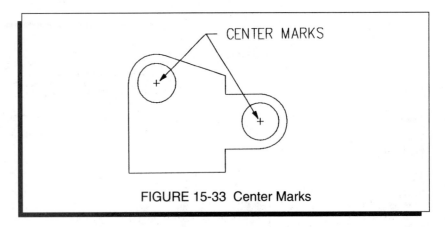

FIGURE 15-33 Center Marks

The center mark size is controlled by the Center Mark Size edit box and the Mark With Center Lines check box on the **Extension Lines** sub-dialogue box.

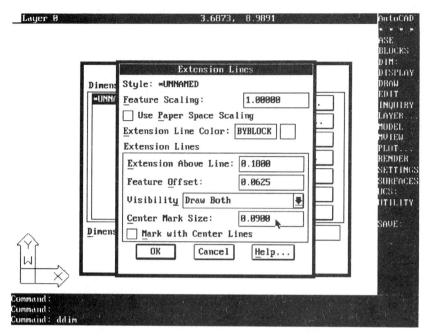

FIGURE 15-34 Extension Lines Dialogue Box

To place a center mark, select Center from the dimension menu.

> Dim: <u>CENTER</u>
> Select arc or circle:

ORDINATE DIMENSIONING

The Ordinate dimensioning command places dimensions that are relative to a reference point.

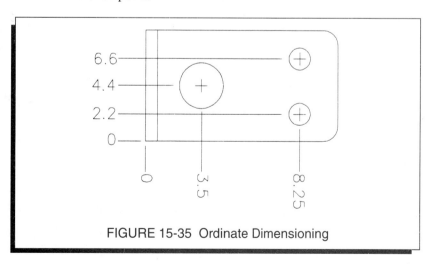

FIGURE 15-35 Ordinate Dimensioning

The reference point used is the current UCS origin. Values for ordinate dimensions are specified as either X or Y coordinates relative to the origin.

Tip

Always turn on the Ortho mode when placing ordinate dimensions.

The UCS origin is located, by default, in the lower left-hand corner of the screen (the 0,0 coordinate point). In most cases, you will want to relocate the UCS origin point so the ordinate dimensions will be referenced to a specific point. You can move the UCS origin by using the UCS command with the Origin option.

```
Command: UCS
Origin/Zaxis/3point/Entity/View/X/Y/Z/Prev/Restore/Save/Del/?/: O
Origin point <0,0,0>: (select the new origin point)
```

Ordinate dimension lines are shown as simple leader lines. AutoCAD asks for a feature location. This is the location to which the dimension is measured. You can either stipulate whether the point is to be measured along the X-coordinate or the Y-coordinate. When you select Ordinate from the dimensioning menu, AutoCAD prompts:

```
Dim: ORDINATE
Select feature: (enter the dimension location)
Leader endpoint (Xdatum/Ydatum): (enter either X or Y)
Leader endpoint: (enter the leader endpoint)
```

You can "shortcut" the process by entering a point on the drawing instead of specifying either a X or Y point. If you do this, AutoCAD will determine whether the measurement is along the X or Y direction by measuring between the two points.

DIMENSION EDITING COMMANDS

Dimension editing commands are used to alter a dimension after it has been placed in your drawing.

Dimension editing commands are used to alter a dimension after it has been placed in your drawing. AutoCAD's dimension editing commands are:

Hometext: Restores dimension text to its original position.

Newtext: Changes existing dimension text.

Oblique: Forces extension lines to a specified angle.

Tedit: Changes placement and orientation of dimension text.

Trotate: Rotates dimension text.

Update: Updates a dimension to the current settings.

Let's explore each function.

RESTORING DIMENSION TEXT TO ITS DEFAULT POSITION

If the dimension has been moved to a new location, it can be restored to its default position by using the Hometext command.

```
Dim: HOMETEXT
Select objects: (select the dimension)
```

AutoCAD
* * * *
DIM:

Hometext
Newtext
Oblique
TRotate
Tedit
Update

Select
Objects

Undo
REDRAW:
Dim Menu
__LAST__
  DRAW
  EDIT

CHANGING DIMENSION TEXT

In the normal course of dimensioning, some dimension values or dimension text are changed. Instead of erasing the dimension and replacing it with a new dimension containing the desired value or text, the Newtext command can be used.

    Dim: NEWTEXT
    Enter new dimension text: (*enter new text*)
    Select objects: (*select the desired dimension*)

If you press the Enter key when prompted for the new dimension text, AutoCAD measures the actual distance described by the dimension and uses that value as the dimension text.

OBLIQUING DIMENSION EXTENSION LINES

In some situations, the standard orientation of dimension extension lines can conflict with other dimensions. The conflict can be remedied by obliquing the extension lines. The following illustration shows an object with oblique extension lines.

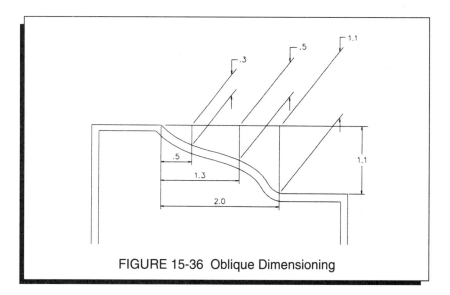

FIGURE 15-36 Oblique Dimensioning

Extension lines can be obliqued by using the Oblique dimensioning command.

    Dim: OBLIQUE
    Select objects: (*select dimension*)

Note that the dimension must first exist before the Oblique command can be used.

RELOCATING THE DIMENSION TEXT

Some situations require that you move the dimension text. For example, dimensions that cross sometimes have overlapping dimension text. You can move the dimension text by using the Tedit (text edit) dimension command.

When you select Tedit, AutoCAD displays the following prompt:

> Dim: <u>TEDIT</u>
> Select dimension: (*select a single dimension*)
> Enter text location (Left/Right/Home/Angle):

After selecting the dimension, moving the cursor dynamically moves the dimension text. Move the text to the desired location, click, and the text is repositioned. Let's look at how each of the options work.

LEFT

Selecting Left positions the dimension text to the left side of the dimension line.

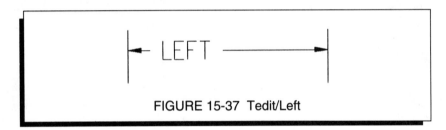

FIGURE 15-37 Tedit/Left

RIGHT

The Right option works the same as the Left option, except the dimension text is positioned to the right side of the dimension line.

FIGURE 15-38 Tedit/Right

HOME

If you select Home, the text is restored to its default position. The default position is determined by the dimension variable settings.

ANGLE

Selecting Angle allows you set the angle for the dimension text. You may set the angle in two ways. Entering an actual angle from the keyboard will cause the text to rotate to that angle. The default angle, with text reading from left to right, is 0. You can also enter two points to show AutoCAD the angle you wish to rotate the text.

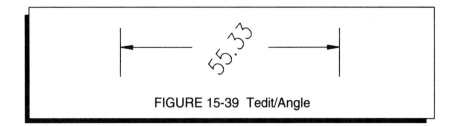

FIGURE 15-39 Tedit/Angle

```
AutoCAD
* * * *
DIM:

Hometext
Newtext
Oblique
TRotate
Tedit
Update

Select
Objects

Undo
REDRAW:
Dim Menu
__LAST__
  DRAW
   EDIT
```

ROTATING DIMENSION TEXT

The Trotate (text rotate) dimension command is used to rotate dimension text to a specified angle. Trotate functions similar to the Angle option of the Tedit command. The difference is that Trotate is used to rotate the dimension text of several dimensions.

> Dim: <u>TROTATE</u>
> Enter new text angle:
> Select objects:

You can either enter the actual angle or show two points to specify the angle. The Select objects prompt allows you to select several dimensions in one object selection process.

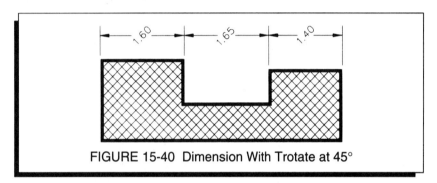

FIGURE 15-40 Dimension With Trotate at 45°

Tip

Use Trotate to change all the dimensions in your drawing by selecting the entire drawing with a window selection.

```
AutoCAD
* * * *
DIM:

Hometext
Newtext
Oblique
TRotate
Tedit
Update

Select
Objects

Undo
REDRAW:
Dim Menu
__LAST__
  DRAW
   EDIT
```

UPDATING DIMENSIONS

The Update dimension command updates the dimension components to reflect the current settings of the dimension variables. This is an easy way to make global changes in dimension components.

> Dim: <u>UPDATE</u>
> Select objects: (*select a dimension*)

Professional Tip

When you are using dimension variables to establish a dimension "look", first draw a dimension, then change the variables. Next, use the Update command to change the existing dimension to show the changes. Repeat the process until you achieve the desired dimension scale and appearance.

DIMENSIONING UTILITY COMMANDS

The dimensioning utility commands are used within the dimension mode for special purposes. Let's look at each of the utility commands.

EXITING DIMENSION MODE

As you know by now, all dimensioning takes place within the dimensioning mode. This mode is indicated by "Dim:" at the command line. You can exit dimension mode with the Exit command.

You may alternately exit dimension mode by entering Ctrl-C. Either method returns you to the "Command:" prompt.

REDRAWING WHILE IN DIMENSION MODE

Using most non-dimension AutoCAD commands will automatically exit you from the dimension mode. The Redraw command can be used while in the dimension mode without exiting the mode.

DISPLAYING THE DIMENSION STATUS

When you enter Status while in the dimension mode, AutoCAD displays the current dimension variable settings. If you working with a single-screen system, the listing is displayed on a text page. Press F1 to return to the drawing screen. On two-screen systems, the listing is displayed on the text monitor.

CHANGING THE DIMENSION TEXT STYLE

The dimension text style is drawn using the current text style. You can change the text style by using the Style command when in dimensioning mode.

    Dim: STYLE
    New text style <default>:

UNDOING A DIMENSION OPERATION

The Undo command can be used while within the dimensioning mode. Undo works the same as the standard Undo command. You can only undo back to the beginning of the current dimensioning session.

DEFINITION POINTS

When you create dimensions, AutoCAD places "definition points" in the drawing. These points are used as reference by AutoCAD in certain operations. The points are placed on a layer named "DEFPOINTS". If you do not wish to plot these points, freeze the layer named "DEFPOINTS".

ARROW BLOCKS

Many applications require specific icons at the end of the dimension line. AutoCAD provides arrows and tick marks for your use, but your application may specify other types of symbols (such as solid dots).

You can specify custom blocks to be used in place of the dimensioning arrows or ticks. The block reference must already exist in the drawing.

The following rules should be used when preparing a block for use as an "arrow".

1. The block should be prepared as the *right* arrow of a horizontal dimension line.

2. The insertion point (base point) should be placed at the point that would normally be the tip of the arrow.

3. The dimension line stops a distance from the tip of the arrow. Draw a small tail line to the left so it will connect to the dimension line.

4. In order for the arrow block to scale properly, draw the block exactly one drawing unit from the tip to the end of the tail line.

To select the block for use in dimensioning, select the Arrows subdialogue box, then the User radio button, and enter the name of the block. When you place a dimension, the arrow block will be used in place of arrows or ticks.

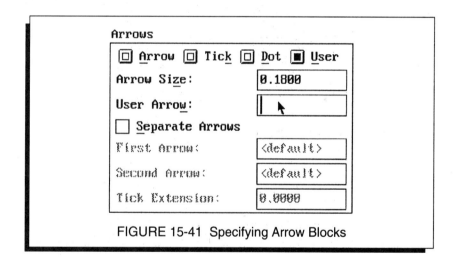

FIGURE 15-41 Specifying Arrow Blocks

SEPARATE ARROW BLOCKS

To create a separate arrow block at each end of a dimension line, select the **Arrows** subdialogue box, and check the Separate Arrows check box. Next, enter the names of the first and second arrow blocks in the edit boxes.

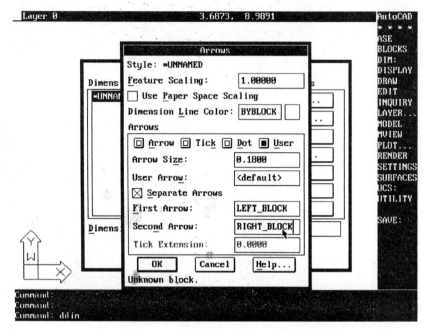

FIGURE 15-42 Creating Separate Arrow Blocks

DIMENSIONING EXERCISES

1. Draw a square approximately one-third the size of the screen. Select the DIM: command from the screen menu.

   Command: DIM

   From the DIM screen menu, select "Horizntl" from the menu.

   Dim: HORIZONTAL
   First extension origin or RETURN to select:

   Use object snap intersection to capture the lower left corner of the box you drew. The command sequence will continue.

   Second extension line origin:

   Use object snap intersection again to capture the lower right corner. The command sequence will respond:

   Dimension line location (Text/Angle):

   Enter a point on the screen approximately ¼" actual distance from the bottom line of the square. AutoCAD will display the measured length on the command line:

   Dimension text <*default*>:

   Press Enter to accept the measurement. You have just placed a dimension.

2. Repeat the same procedure for the upper line of the square. Instead of specifying the corners, however, just press Enter when prompted and select the upper line to dimension. The command sequence will appear as follows:

Dim: <u>HORIZONTAL</u>
First extension line origin or RETURN to select: (*RETURN*)
Select line, arc, or circle: (*select the line*)
Dimension line location (Text/Angle): (*enter a point where you want the dimension line*)
Dimension text <*default*>: (*type your name here*)

Notice how AutoCAD measured the selected line length, placing extension lines in the proper positions. For the dimension text, you entered your name. Notice that you can accept the default measurement, enter your own numerical value, or enter a text string (such as your name).

3. Select Vertical from the menu and dimension one of the vertical sides of the box you drew. The vertical dimension works the same as the horizontal dimension.

4. Draw a triangle. Let's use the aligned option to dimension one of the angled sides. Refer to the following command sequence.

Command: <u>DIM</u>
Dim: <u>ALIGNED</u>
First extension line origin or RETURN to select: (*Enter*)
Select line, arc, or circle: (*select an angled side*)
Dimension line location (Text/Angle): (*select a point*)
Dimension text <*default*>: (*Enter*)

AutoCAD will draw a dimension line parallel to the selected side.

5. Clear the screen and draw one horizontal dimension line. Accept the default dimension measurement. From the DIM:/Edit menu, select NEWTEXT. When prompted for the "new dimension text", enter "250". AutoCAD will ask you to "select objects". Select the dimension text of the dimension line you drew. The text will update to "250".

6. Select "Trotate" (text rotate). When prompted for the angle, enter "45" for 45 degrees. When instructed by AutoCAD to "select objects", select the dimension text. Did the text turn to a 45 degree angle?

7. Select "tedit" (text-edit). Select the dimension line. Now select "left" from the menu.

8. Select "tedit" again. When asked to "select dimension", select the dimension you drew. Now select "home" from the menu. The dimension text should return to its original position.

DIMENSIONING PROBLEMS

Use the dimension commands you have learned to draw and dimension the following objects.

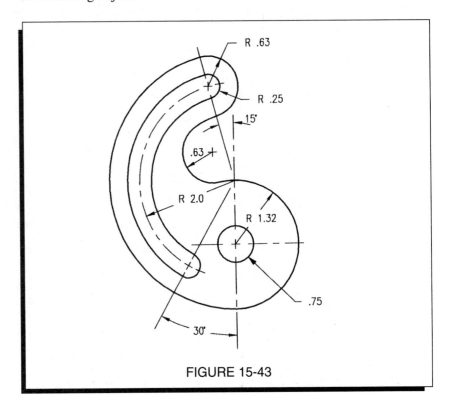

FIGURE 15-43

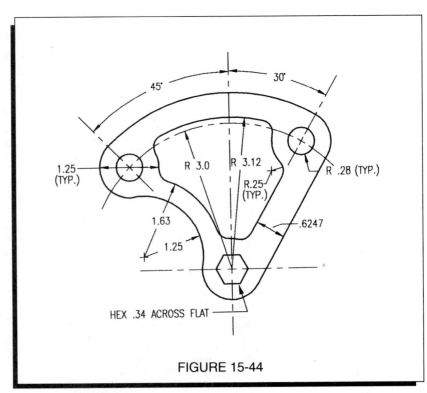

FIGURE 15-44

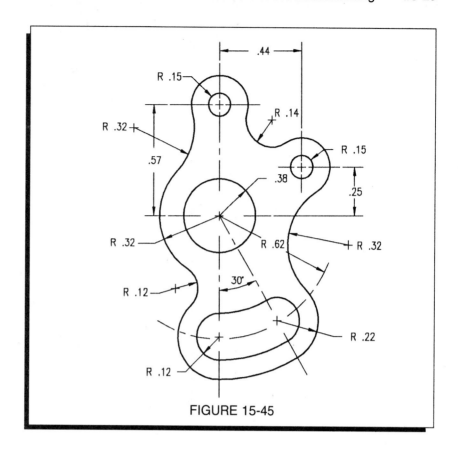

FIGURE 15-45

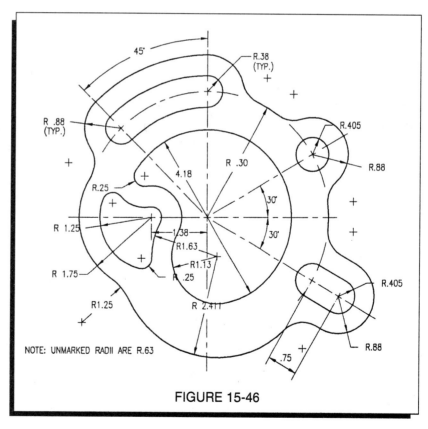

NOTE: UNMARKED RADII ARE R.63

FIGURE 15-46

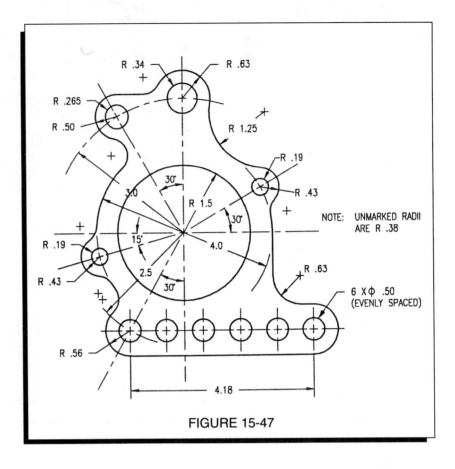

FIGURE 15-47

DIMENSIONING TUTORIAL

Electronic Work Disk Problem

Start the drawing named "DIMEN" that is on the work disk. We will dimension this drawing, using several of the dimensioning commands you have learned. The finished drawing will look like Figure 15-48.

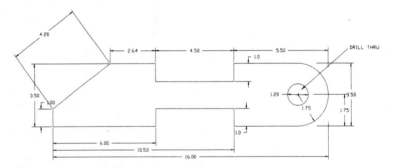

FIGURE 15-48 DIMEN Drawing

Let's start with linear dimensioning.

HORIZONTAL DIMENSIONING

From the root menu, choose DIM:. You will notice that dimensioning has its own menu. When you enter this menu, you are in the dimensioning mode. You may not use most "outside" menus without exiting the dimension menu.

From the dimension menu, choose Horizontl. Respond to the "First extension line origin" prompt by entering a point at the corner shown as "point 1" in the drawing below.

Respond to the "Second extension line origin" prompt by entering a point at the corner shown as "point 2" in the drawing below.

You should now be prompted with "Dimension line location". This is the distance above the object that the dimension line will be placed. Enter a point at the location of "point 3".

AutoCAD now has measured the distance and calculated it for you. It is displayed as "Dimension text value". You may, at this point, accept this text or enter your own. Let's accept the value calculated by AutoCAD by pressing Enter.

Isn't that easy? From now on, we will simply refer to the points labeled in the illustrations for each entry.

Let's continue this dimension line. From the menu, select "Next", then "Continue".

Respond to "Second extension line origin" with point 4. Enter a dimension text of 4.50 and Enter.

Repeat this procedure by choosing CONTINUE, selecting point 5 as the extension line origin and entering 5.50 as the dimension (don't forget to press Enter).

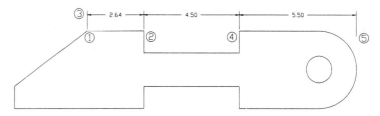

FIGURE 15-49 Linear Dimensioning (Continuing)

You have now completed a horizontal and a continuing dimension line.

BASELINE DIMENSIONING

Let's now do some baseline dimensioning.

This dimensioning method starts out the same way that continuing dimensioning does. From the menu, choose "Horizntl", then press the Enter key so you can select an object to dimension (you may first need to select "previous" from the menu to return to the previous menu). When prompted to select an entity, select the line defined by endpoints 6 and 7. Choose point 8 for the dimension line location. Enter 6.00 as the dimension text and press Enter.

Now, this is where we create the baseline dimensioning style. Choose "Next", then "Baseline" from the menu and enter point 9 as the second extension line origin. Enter 10.00 as the dimension text and press Enter.

Repeat the procedure by choosing "baseline" again, entering point 10 as the second extension line origin point and 15.50 as the dimension text.

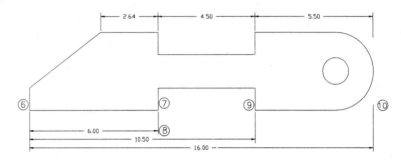

FIGURE 15-50 Linear Dimensioning (Baseline)

Notice that AutoCAD offset each dimension line the proper distance.

VERTICAL DIMENSIONING

Now let's draw the vertical dimensions.

Choose "Vertical" from the menu. Choose point 11 as the first extension line origin, point 12 as the second extension origin and point 13 as the dimension line origin. Notice that AutoCAD places the dimension text outside the dimension lines because there is not sufficient room inside the dimension lines.

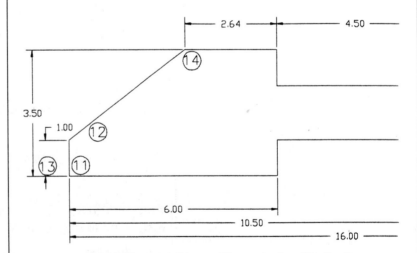

FIGURE 15-51 Linear Dimensioning (Vertical)

From the menu, choose "baseline", and enter point 14 as the second extension line origin. Enter 3.50 as the dimension text.

Repeat the procedure for the opposite end, using points 15 through 18 as the entered points. You can do this one on your own.

If you mess up, use the Undo command from the menu to eliminate the last dimension, or cancel if the dimension line is not yet drawn.

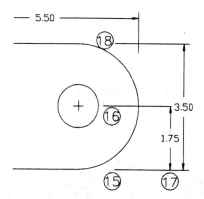

FIGURE 15-52 Completing the Vertical Dimension

LINEAR DIMENSIONING (ALIGNED)

Let's construct the dimension line which describes the angle at the left side of the part.

Choose "Aligned" from the menu, then press Enter. Select the angled line on the object. When prompted for the dimension line location, select point 21. Accept AutoCAD's measurement by pressing Enter in response to the "Dimension text" prompt.

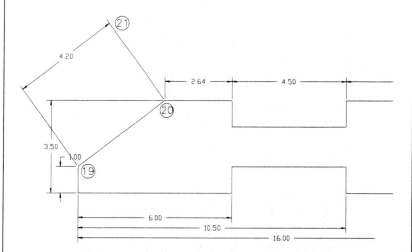

FIGURE 15-53 Linear Dimension (Aligned)

AutoCAD constructed the dimension line in alignment with the two extension line origin points.

DIAMETER DIMENSIONING

Select "Diameter" from the menu. You are prompted "Select arc or circle". Enter a point on the circle (point 22) to identify the object you want dimensioned. Press Enter to accept AutoCAD's measurement. Show point 23 as the distance for the leader line.

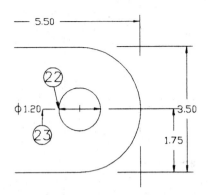

FIGURE 15-54 Diameter Dimensioning

Notice that AutoCAD used the point you entered on the circle as one of the endpoints of the dimension line. The other endpoint is positioned by drawing the dimension line from this point through the center of the circle to the opposite circumference. The extended text position is referenced beside the first point entered.

RADIUS DIMENSIONING

Now, let's dimension the arc which closes the right end of the object.

Select RADIUS from the menu. When prompted, choose the point on the arc which you want the dimension line to intersect (point 24). Enter 1.75 as the text dimension. Move the crosshair to place the dimension leader.

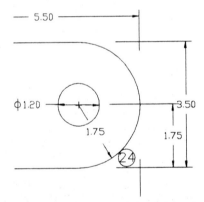

FIGURE 15-55 Radius Dimensioning

LEADER CONSTRUCTION

Let's construct a leader line and some text. Select LEADER from the menu.

Enter point 25 as the leader start and point 26 as the "to point". For the dimension text, let's put in some words (remember, we can use words instead of numerals for any dimension text). Enter "DRILL THRU" and press Enter.

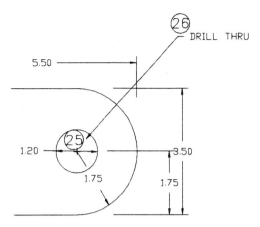

FIGURE 15-56 Constructing a Leader Line and Adding Text

Your dimensioned drawing should look like the one in Figure 18-57.

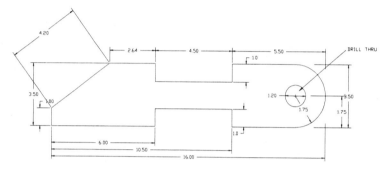

FIGURE 15-57 Completed Dimensioned Drawing

CHAPTER REVIEW

1. What is the dimension line?

2. What is the difference between the extension line and the witness line?

3. What is meant by "dimensioning mode"?

4. Draw an example of a baseline dimension.

5. Name the types of linear dimensions.

_____

_____

_____

_____

_____

6. What does the Diameter dimension command do?

_____

_____

7. What command would you use to tilt the dimension text?

_____

8. How would you apply new changes to an existing dimension?

_____

_____

9. What layer are the dimension definition points placed on?

_____

10. What are "arrow blocks"?

_____

_____

_____

CHAPTER 16

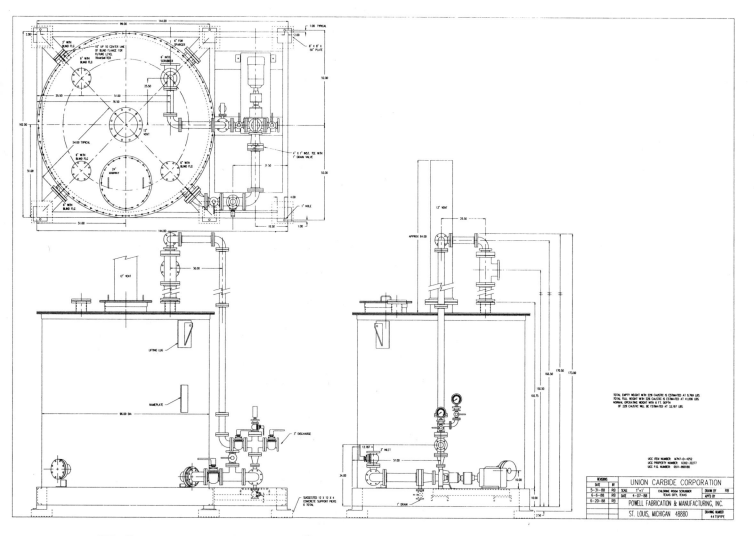

Dimension Styles and Variables

OBJECTIVES:

AutoCAD is rich in dimensioning capabilities. To obtain professional results, you must understand how to set the many dimension variables that control the dimension. The objectives of Chapter 16 are:

● To learn the different types of variables used to control the look and function of AutoCAD's dimensions.

● Learning how to use the dialogue boxes to set the many variables.

AutoCAD
In The
Real
World

Mapping the Alaskan Oil Spill
AutoCAD® and GeoREF to the Rescue

The grounding and rupture of the supertanker *Exxon Valdez* within Prince William Sound, Alaska, on the night of March 23, 1989, set in motion a series of events that has not been seen in the United States since the Santa Barbara oil spill of 1969. In the intervening months, the government and Exxon have spent more than a hundred million dollars and involved thousands of people in the response and cleanup effort.

A key part of this effort has been the production of maps indicating the location of surface oil and shoreline impacts. Teamed up with a geographic information system (GIS) and a relational database manager (RDMS), AutoCAD provided the graphical information needed to manage the cleanup effort. For over two months, geographic data collected through fly-overs, instruments, and sightings was used to direct AutoCAD's production of maps. These valuable progress reports, generated by a system that was built overnight, were used daily in operations meetings of the U.S. Coast Guard, NOAA, Exxon (ADEC) and representatives of state and federal agencies.

AutoCAD also helped set cleanup priorities. As the slick spread, it damaged the shoreline, first within the Sound and then along the Kenai Peninsula. Still later, it continued to strike major bird rookeries and seal haul-out areas across the Gulf of Alaska, extending several hundred miles away to past Kodiak Island and hitting the Alaska Peninsula and Katmai National Park. Determining the extent of light, moderate, and heavy shoreline impacts became the second major use of the system.

Shoreline impact data helped determine which beach or cove was the next priority in the cleanup effort.

Eventually, the system will be expanded to include other data sources that can be used to assess the impact of the spill on the natural resources of the area. A consultant will use the data collected to model the ways in which the ocean currents will pull and move the oil against the rocky shoreline in the future. Sampling sites and data for such things as water chemistry, intertidal biology, salmon-stream assessment, and cleanup will all potentially be linked within the system to provide a means of overlaying information for short and long-term assessments.

Adapted with permission from an article by Laurel Perkins. Excerpted from *CADENCE*, July 1989, copyright © 1989, Ariel Communications, Inc.

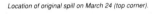

Location of original spill on March 24 (top corner).   By April 3, the spill had progressed south, nearing 59 .

DIMENSION STYLES AND VARIABLES

The manner in which dimensions look and act depend on the settings of dimension variables.

The manner in which dimensions look and act depend on the settings of *dimension variables*. The variables can control such characteristics as whether the dimension text is placed within or above the dimension line, whether arrows or ticks are used, and many other options.

After you set the variables for a dimension, you can store the settings in a file called a *style*. Storing dimension style files is similar to storing text style files. In both cases you can store many style files, then retrieve them for use.

In order to effectively use AutoCAD's dimensioning capabilities, you must become familiar with the variables available. The following sections show you what options are available and how to set and store them.

SETTING DIMENSION VARIABLES

AutoCAD's dimension variables are set through a dialogue box. To display the dialogue box, enter Ddim at the command line.

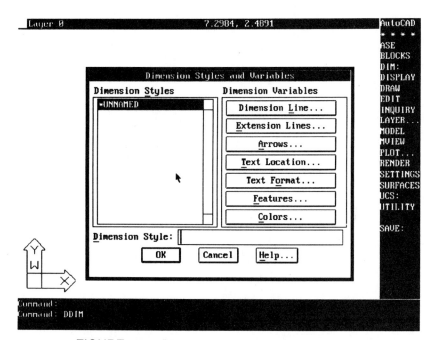

FIGURE 16-1 Dimension Variables Dialogue Box

The Ddim dialogue box contains two areas. The left side displays the available dimension styles. The right side displays categories of dimension characteristics. Each of these is listed on a button. Each button prompts a subdialogue box. The subdialogue boxes are where you set the dimension variables. Let's look at each category.

VARIABLES AFFECTING DIMENSION LINES

Variables affecting dimension lines are set from the **Dimension Line** subdialogue box. From the Ddim dialogue box, select the "Dimension Line..." button. The following dialogue box is displayed.

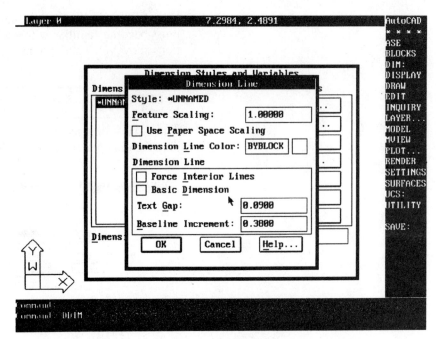

FIGURE 16-2 Dimension Line Subdialogue Box

Let's look at each of the settings and the dimension variables that are set from this subdialogue box.

SETTING THE CURRENT DIMENSION STYLE

The "Style" listing at the top of the subdialogue box displays the current dimension style. All changes made in the dialogue box will affect this style. If you wish to load a different style, the Ddim dialogue box contains the "Dimension Styles" box.

This feature is common in all dimension variable subdialogue boxes.

FEATURE SCALING

The *feature scaling* setting is a global scale factor used to enlarge or reduce the dimension line. To set the scale, enter a value in the text box next to the "Feature Scaling" listing. The default value is 1.00000. Use larger values to enlarge the dimension, and decimal values less than one to set smaller values.

This feature is common in all dimension variable subdialogue boxes.

Tip

To create a dimension style, first place a dimension line. Next, use the subdialogue boxes to create the appearance you want (zoom in to see the dimension better if necessary). You can use the dimension Update command to show the new settings. Then use feature scaling to scale the dimension to the proper size.

PAPER SPACE SCALING

If the "Use Paper Space Scaling" box is checked, AutoCAD computes a scale factor based on the scaling between the current model space viewport and paper space.

When checked, the Feature Scaling text box is grayed out.

SETTING THE DIMENSION LINE COLOR

To set a dimension line color, click on the color swatch that follows the "Dimension Line Color" listing. AutoCAD displays a color selection subdialogue box.

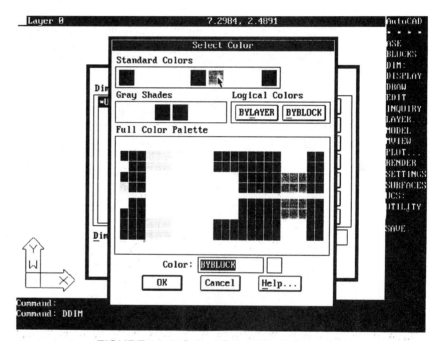

FIGURE 16-3 Select Color Subdialogue Box

The color chart displays the colors available with your graphics system. Select a color by clicking on a color block, then selecting "OK". You may also enter a number describing the color in the text block. Selecting "BYLAYER" or "BYBLOCK" will display that listing in the text box.

FORCE INTERIOR LINES

AutoCAD draws dimension lines and text inside the extension lines whenever space is available. In cases where the space between the extension lines is small, the lines or text are placed outside the extension lines.

The "Force Interior Lines" setting can be used to force the dimension lines between the extension lines even the text must be drawn outside. When the check box is selected, the variable is on.

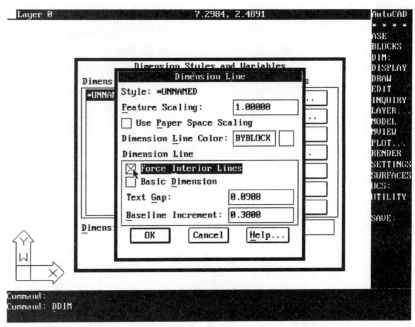

FIGURE 16-4 "Force Interior Lines" Setting

REFERENCE DIMENSIONS

A *reference dimension* (also referred to as a *basic dimension*) is a dimension with a box drawn around the dimension text.

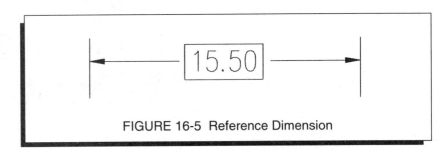

FIGURE 16-5 Reference Dimension

If the check box is selected, reference dimensioning is used. The distance between the text and the box is stored as a negative value in the DIMGAP variable.

SETTING THE TEXT GAP

The *text gap* is the distance between the dimension text and the dimension line when the text is placed within the line.

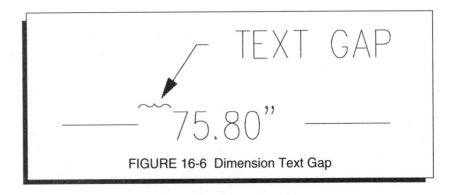

FIGURE 16-6 Dimension Text Gap

To set the text gap distance, enter the length in the edit box. The text gap distance is also used to specify the required length of dimension line segments. If a dimension line is broken for text, the remaining dimension line segments must be at least the text gap length. If the line length will be less than the text gap distance, the dimension is not broken and the text is placed outside the line.

SETTING THE BASELINE INCREMENT

The baseline increment is the distance maintained between baseline dimensions. The distance is provided so baseline dimensions do not overlap each other.

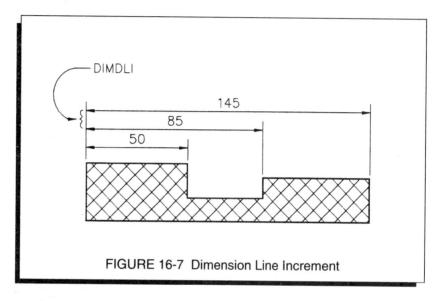

FIGURE 16-7 Dimension Line Increment

To set the baseline increment, enter the distance in the edit box next to the "Baseline Increment" listing.

VARIABLES AFFECTING EXTENSION LINES

Variables affecting extension lines are set from the **Extension Lines** subdialogue box. From the Ddim dialogue box, select the "Extension Lines..." button. The following dialogue box is displayed.

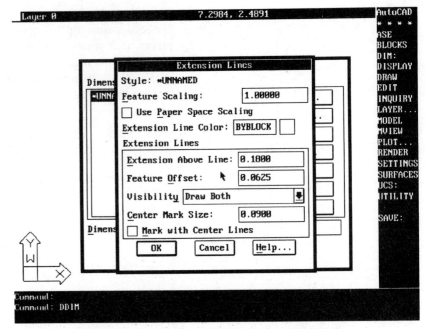

FIGURE 16-8 Extension Lines Subdialogue Box

Let's look at each of the settings and the dimension variables that are set from this subdialogue box.

EXTENSION LINE COLOR

The color of the extension line is assigned in the same manner as explained in the previous section.

EXTENSION ABOVE LINE

This setting determines the distance that the extension line extends past the dimension line. To set the distance enter the value in the text box next to the "Extension Above Line" listing.

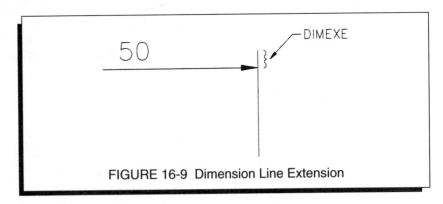

FIGURE 16-9 Dimension Line Extension

FEATURE OFFSET

The feature offset is the distance between the origin of the extension lines and the point you select.

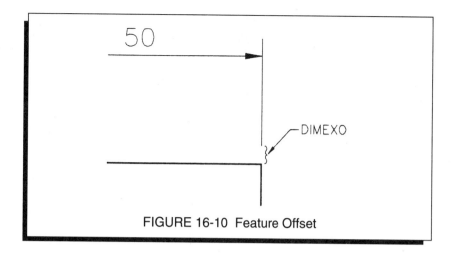

FIGURE 16-10 Feature Offset

VISIBILITY

The visibility setting determines whether the extension lines are displayed and drawn. Since a dimension has two extension lines, each must be stipulated as either on or off. You may also have both extension lines on or off.

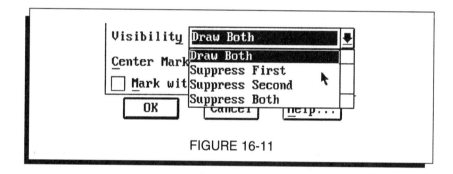

FIGURE 16-11

The extension line visibility is set with a popup list box. The box displays four choices that allow you to set any combination of visibility of the two extension lines.

CENTER MARK SIZE

Center marks are the small crosses that are placed at the center of a circle or arc when using the dimension Center command and in some cases when you use the Diameter and Radius dimensioning commands.

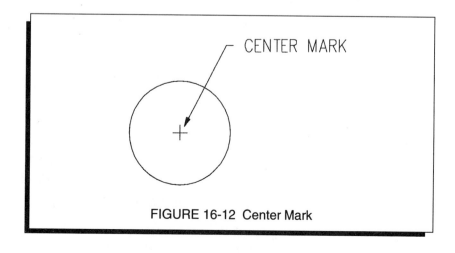

FIGURE 16-12 Center Mark

You can set the center mark size by entering the value in the text box next to the "Center Mark Size" listing.

MARK WITH CENTER LINES

Center lines are lines that extend from the endpoints of the center mark.

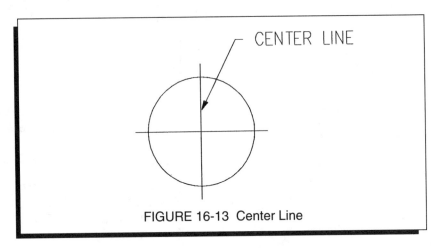

FIGURE 16-13 Center Line

If the "Mark with Center Lines" box is checked, center lines are added when a center mark is drawn.

VARIABLES AFFECTING DIMENSION ARROWS

Variables affecting dimension arrows are set from the **Arrows** sub–dialogue box. From the Ddim dialogue box, select the "Arrows..." button. The following dialogue box is displayed.

Let's look at each of the settings and the dimension variables that are set from this subdialogue box.

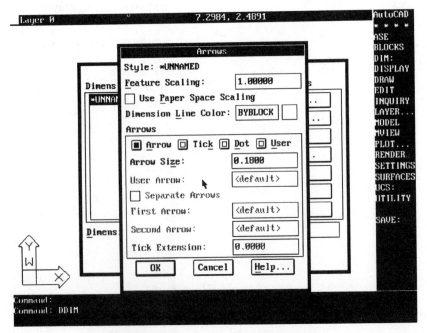

FIGURE 16-14 Arrows Subdialogue Box

ARROW

When the "Arrow" box is checked, AutoCAD uses arrows at the ends of the dimension lines. The arrow size is set by entering the value in the box to the right of the "Arrow Size" listing. The arrow size is the length from the base to the tip of the arrow when the feature scaling is set to a value of 1.0.

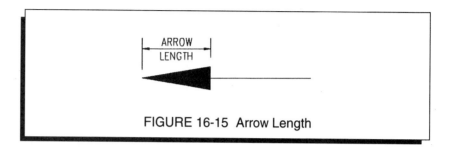

FIGURE 16-15 Arrow Length

Ticks are diagonal lines drawn through the intersection of the dimension line and extension line.

Ticks are diagonal lines drawn through the intersection of the dimension line and extension line. You can use ticks instead of arrows by selecting the check box next to the "Tick" listing.

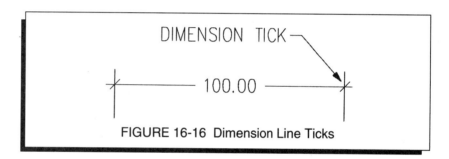

FIGURE 16-16 Dimension Line Ticks

The length of the tick is determined by the arrow size setting. You can specify the distance that the dimension line extends beyond the tick with the "Tick Extension" setting at the bottom of the subdialogue box.

DOT

The end of the dimension line can be defined by a dot. The dot is a solid circle drawn at the intersection of the dimension line and the extension line.

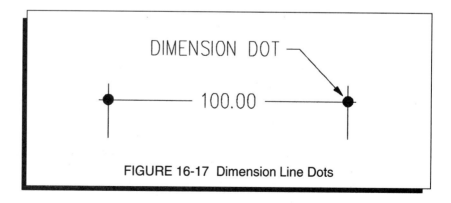

FIGURE 16-17 Dimension Line Dots

The size of the dot is determined by the value of the arrow size.

USER

You can draw an object, use AutoCAD's Block command to convert it to a symbol, and use the symbol as a custom arrow. The methodology is discussed in Chapter 15, "Arrow Blocks".

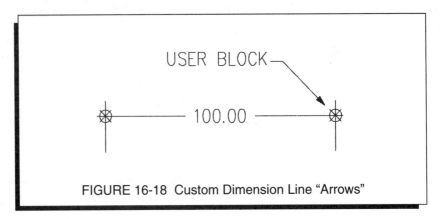

FIGURE 16-18 Custom Dimension Line "Arrows"

When you select "User", the "User Arrow" text box is used to enter the name of the block. You can specify separate symbols for the first and second "arrows" by clicking in the "Separate Arrows" check box. The text box to the right of each listing is used to list the blocks used for each respective arrow.

VARIABLES AFFECTING TEXT LOCATION

Variables affecting text location are set from the **Text Location** subdialogue box. From the Ddim dialogue box, select the "Text Location..." button. The following dialogue box is displayed.

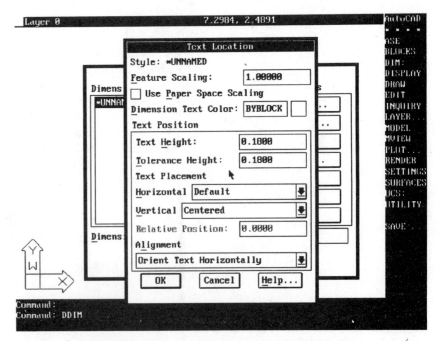

FIGURE 16-19 Text Location Subdialogue Box

Let's look at each of the settings and the dimension variables that are set from this subdialogue box.

TEXT HEIGHT

The "Text Height" edit box is used to set the dimension text height if the current text style does not have a specified height.

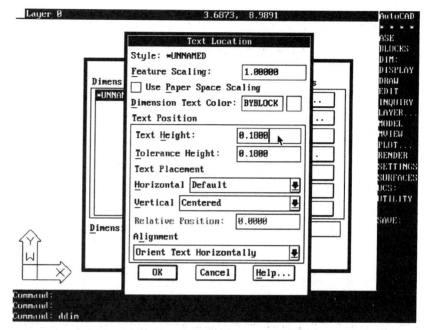

FIGURE 16-20 Text Location Dialogue Box

TOLERANCE HEIGHT

The "Tolerance Height" edit box specifies the height of the text used for dimension tolerances.

TEXT POSITION

The dimension text position is specified by the horizontal and vertical settings. Let's look at each type of setting.

Horizontal

The horizontal position of dimension text is determined by the *Horizontal* setting. The setting is accessed through a popup list box next to the "Horizontal" listing.

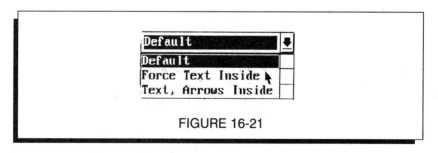

FIGURE 16-21

The popup list box contains the following settings.

Default: When "Default" is selected, the horizontal position of the text depends on the type of dimension. When placing linear or angular dimensions, the text is positioned inside the extension lines if room is available. Radius and diameter dimension text is placed outside the arc or circle.

Force Text Inside: Forces text to be located inside the extension lines.

Text, Arrows Inside: Forces the text and arrows to be placed inside the extension lines. If the text and arrows would normally be placed outside (as would be the case if there is not sufficient room), they will not be drawn.

Vertical

The vertical position of dimension text is determined by the *Vertical* setting. The setting is accessed through a popup list box next to the "Vertical" listing.

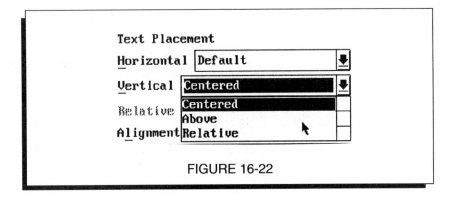

FIGURE 16-22

The popup list box contains the following settings.

Centered: Text is centered on the dimension line. The dimension line is broken where the text is located. Centered text is normally used for mechanical dimensioning.

Above: Text is positioned above the dimension line. The dimension line is drawn unbroken. The text is positioned at a distance equal to the text height above the dimension line. Text is normally positioned above the dimension line in architectural drawings.

Relative: Positions the text relative to the value entered in the "Relative position" text box. Let's continue and see how relative positioning works.

RELATIVE POSITION

The "Relative Position" settings controls the height of the text above the dimension line. It is referred to as the relative position because it is relative to a ratio of the relative position setting and the text height.

To determine the position, divide the relative position by the text height. For example, if you set the relative position to a value of 5 and the text height is .25, the position of the text is 2. The text height position would then be adjusted by two units.

ALIGNMENT

The *Alignment* settings control whether the text is vertical, horizontal, or inclined with the dimension line. Alignment settings are specified through a popup list box under the "Alignment" listing. There are four options listed in the list box.

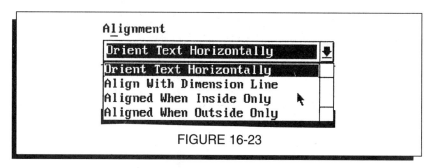

FIGURE 16-23

Align Text Horizontally: Causes text to be drawn horizontally, regardless of the alignment of the dimension line.

Align With Dimension Line: Aligns text with the dimension line, whether it is vertical, horizontal, or positioned at an angle.

Aligned When Inside Only: Text is aligned with the dimension line *only* if the dimension text is located <u>inside</u> the extension lines.

Aligned When Outside Only: Text is aligned with the dimension line *only* if the dimension text is located <u>outside</u> the extension lines.

VARIABLES AFFECTING TEXT LOCATION

Variables affecting dimension text format and measurement units are set from the **Text Format** subdialogue box. From the Ddim dialogue box, select the "Text Format..." button. The following dialogue box is displayed.

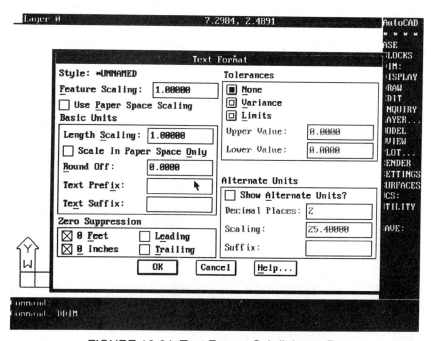

FIGURE 16-24 Text Format Subdialogue Box

Let's look at each of the settings and the dimension variables that are set from this subdialogue box.

LENGTH SCALING

Length scaling is used to adjust the measured length of a dimension by a specified factor. For example, if the length factor is 2, the length measured by AutoCAD for a dimension is multiplied by a factor of two.

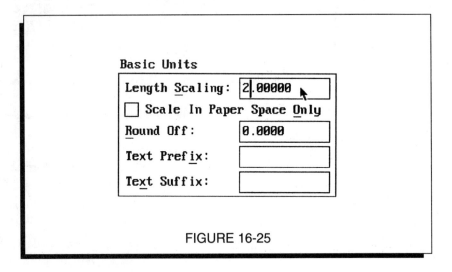

FIGURE 16-25

Professional Tip

You can use the length scaling feature to dimension a detail that has been enlarged on a drawing. For example, if the detail has been scaled to twice the size of the rest of the drawing, a length factor of .5 would adjust the dimensions to the proper measurement. Otherwise, the dimensions would be read twice the scale distance. This is very useful for enlarged details in a drawing.

SCALE IN PAPER SPACE ONLY

Clicking in this check box will cause AutoCAD to apply the length scale factor only to dimensions created in paper space. You can, thus, set the length scale factor equal to the zoom scale factor for objects in a model space viewport. Doing this allows you to construct dimensions in paper space that correctly denote model space geometry.

ROUND OFF

The round off value is the amount that AutoCAD will round off the measured distance. For example, if the round off value is .10, all measured distances will be rounded off to the nearest 0.10 unit.

TEXT PREFIX

You can add a prefix to the dimension text. For example, you may want to add the word *VERIFY* before the measured dimension.

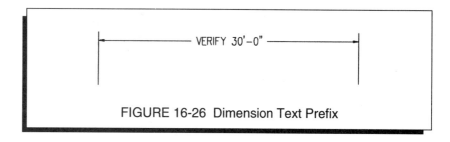

FIGURE 16-26 Dimension Text Prefix

To set a prefix, click in the text box next to the "Text Prefix", then type the prefix from the keyboard. A prefix will override any default prefix (such as the "R" used in radius dimensioning).

TEXT SUFFIX

The text suffix capability works the same as the text prefix function, except it adds a suffix. For example, you may want to add the word "(TYPICAL)" to the end of the measured distance.

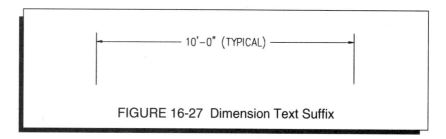

FIGURE 16-27 Dimension Text Suffix

ZERO SUPPRESSION

The check boxes listed under the Zero Suppression heading affects the manner in which dimensions are listed.

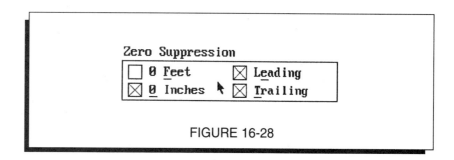

FIGURE 16-28

0 Feet: When dimensioning in feet and inches, suppresses the feet listing when the dimension is less than one foot. For example, 0'6" would become 6".

0 Inches: When dimensioning in feet and inches, suppresses the inches listing when the measured distance is whole feet. For example, 5'0" becomes 5'.

Leading: When dimensioning in decimal units, suppresses leading zeros. For example, 0.6500 would be drawn as .6500.

Trailing: When dimensioning in decimal units, suppress trailing zeros. For example, 0.6500 becomes 0.65.

TOLERANCES

The Tolerances box is used to control dimension tolerances. Tolerances are plus and minus values that are applied to a dimension text.

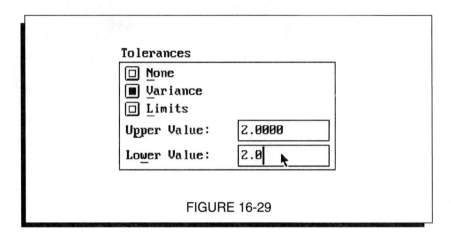

FIGURE 16-29

Variance: Selecting the Variance radio button causes the dimension to show the variance listed in the Upper and Lower Value edit boxes. The method of text display depends on whether the values are the same or different. Let's look at two examples.

Let's assume that the measured distance is 10.0 and the variances for the upper and lower value are both set to 2.0. Auto-CAD will draw the dimension text as the measured distance (10.0), followed by a plus/minus symbol and the variance (2.0).

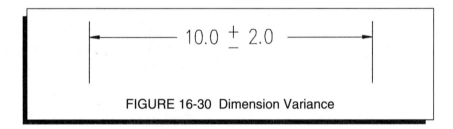

FIGURE 16-30 Dimension Variance

If the upper and lower values are different, the plus and minus distances will both be shown. In the following illustration, the measured distance is 10.0, and the upper and lower values are 1.5 and 2.5, respectively.

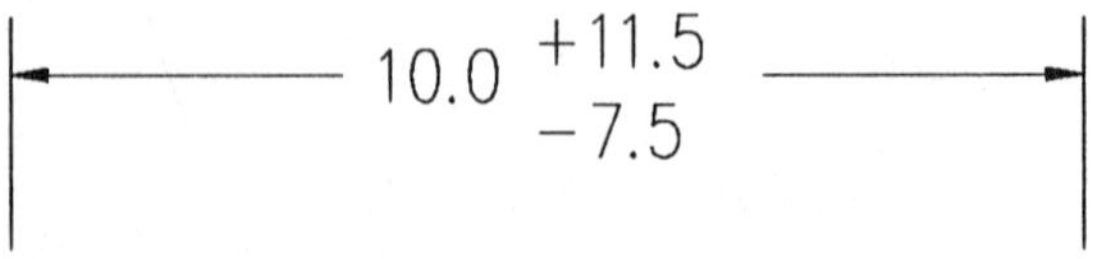

FIGURE 16-31 Tolerance Dimension With Different Values

Limits: Selecting "Limits" will cause AutoCAD to display the dimension as the measured distance, with the upper and lower values added and subtracted. For example, the following illustration shows the effects of a measured distance of 10.0, and upper and lower values of 1.5 and 2.5, respectively.

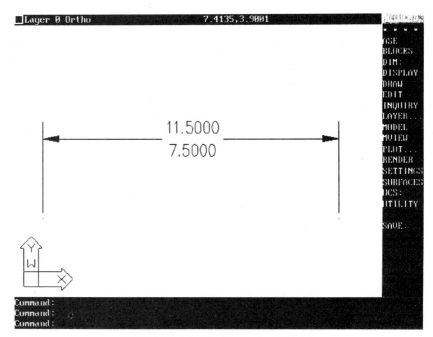

FIGURE 16-32 Dimension Limits

ALTERNATE UNITS

Alternate units measurement allows you to specify a multiplication factor to apply to the measured dimensioned. By applying the proper factor to multiply by, you can create measurements in different units. For example, you can apply a multiplication factor to convert architectural units to meters. When you select the check box next to the "Show Alternate Units?" listing, AutoCAD makes available three edit boxes.

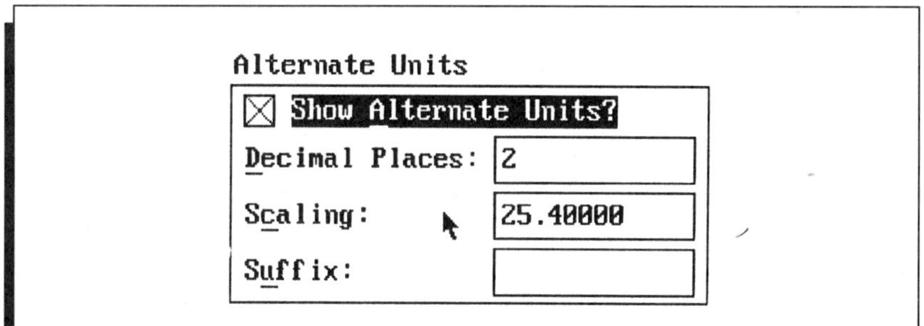

Alternate Units

☒ Show Alternate Units?

Decimal Places: `2`

Scaling: `25.40000`

Suffix:

FIGURE 16-33

Decimal places: Sets the number of decimal places used to calculate the alternate units.

Scaling: Specifies the factor to be used for conversion.

Suffix: Stipulates the suffix (if any) that should follow the alternate measurement.

DISPLAYING DIMENSION FEATURES

The *Features* subdialogue box displays all the settings created from the subdialogue boxes in one location. To display this dialogue box, select the "Features..." button.

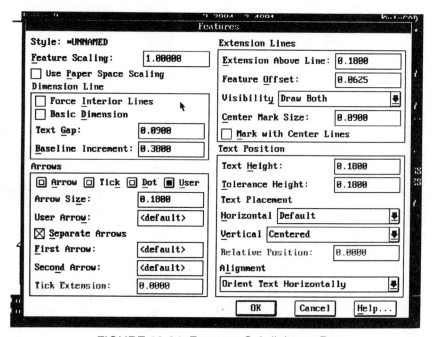

FIGURE 16-34 Features Subdialogue Box

Displaying the Features subdialogue box is a convenient way to display all the dimension style settings for inspection.

SETTING COLORS

Each of the subdialogue boxes contain a color section used to set the color for each of the individual dimension components. The **Colors** subdialogue box can be used to set colors for all the components. This eliminates the necessity to access each subdialogue box when setting several of the component colors. To access the **Colors** subdialogue box, select the "Colors..." button.

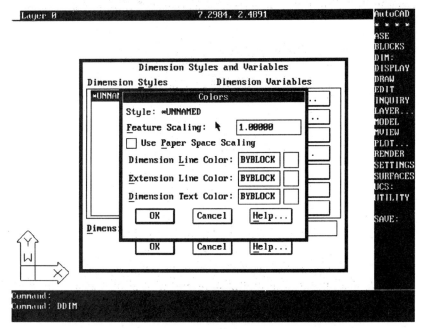

FIGURE 16-35 Dimension Colors Subdialogue Box

To access the color select palette, click on the color swatch next to the component you wish to assign a color.

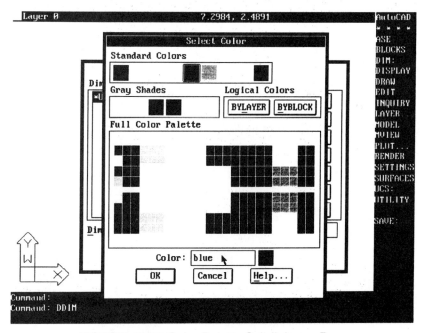

FIGURE 16-36 Color Palette Subdialogue Box

CHAPTER 17

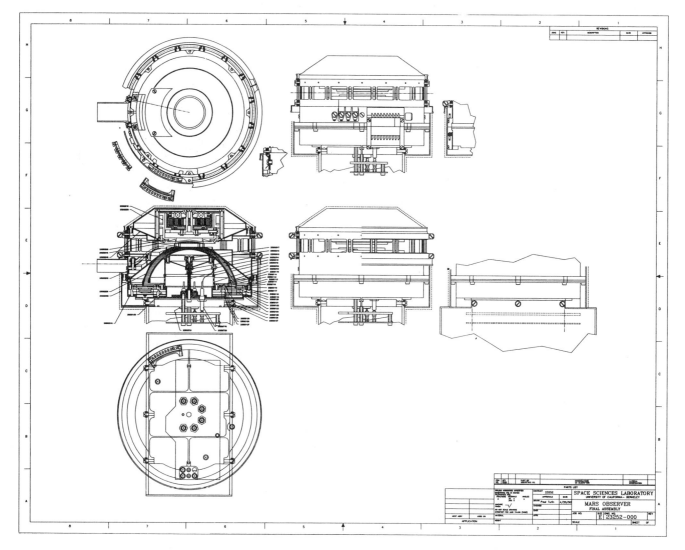

Dimensioning Practices

OBJECTIVES:

Establishing dimensions practices ensures clear and concise graphic instruction. The objectives of this chapter are:

● To explore standard dimensioning practices.

● To learn the dimensioning practices of different disciplines.

DIMENSIONING PRACTICES

The construction of an object can be pictorially shown by drawing methods. In order for the object to be constructed, it must also be described in terms of its dimensions. The combination of the pictorial representation and the dimensional information provides complete detail of the object that can be used for construction.

Proper dimensioning provides the necessary distances and notes to completely describe the object.

Proper dimensioning provides the necessary distances and notes to completely describe the object. The distances needed to draw the object are not necessarily those required for construction. Because of this, you must carefully select the dimensions you provide in your drawings. In order to properly dimension an object of any discipline, you should be familiar with the construction techniques used to build the object. It is helpful to mentally construct the object using the process that is common for building that object. Provide the dimensions that you would use when utilizing that method.

PLACING DIMENSIONAL INFORMATION IN A DRAWING

There are two methods of placing dimensional information in a drawing: a dimension and a note. Dimensions are used to stipulate distances between two points. The extension lines of the dimension designate the points to which the dimension is applied. The dimension line shows the direction of the dimension; the arrows or ticks the extent of the dimension, and the dimension text conveys the actual distance in numerical terms.

Dimensions are used to stipulate distances between two points.

Notes are used to indicate explanatory information that can not be properly conveyed with a dimension. Notes that are specific to a part of the object are indicated with a dimension leader.

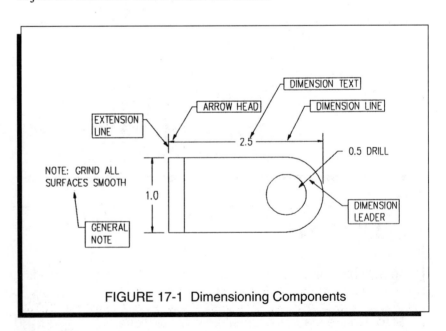

FIGURE 17-1 Dimensioning Components

The arrow of the leader points to the part of the object to which the note applies. General notes are used to give information that is applied to the drawing as a whole. General notes are drawn without a leader.

CONSTRUCTING DIMENSION COMPONENTS

Many disciplines use drawing as a means of conveying information. The dimensioning practices of each discipline vary. The objective, however, is always the same: to provide clear, concise information that can be used to construct the object. Because the information must be conveyed in such a concise manner, the methodology of dimensioning must be carefully considered. Let's look at some of the principles of dimensioning.

DIMENSION ARROWS

Dimension arrows are use to designate the extent of the dimension line. The length of the arrowhead will vary, depending on the scale of the drawing. Generally, arrowheads are ⅛" in length when used in small drawings, and ³⁄₁₆" in larger drawings. Arrowheads that are too large or small are either distracting or difficult to read.

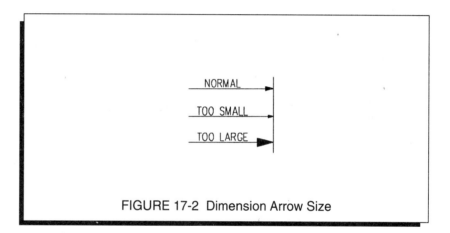

FIGURE 17-2 Dimension Arrow Size

CONSTRUCTING EXTENSION LINES

Extension lines designate the points to which the dimensions measure. The extension lines should not touch the points they reference. The normal offset from the reference points is ¹⁄₁₆". Extension lines should extend approximately ⅛" beyond the dimension line.

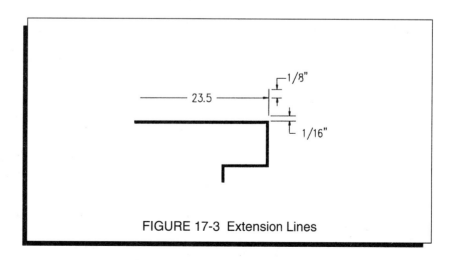

FIGURE 17-3 Extension Lines

CONSTRUCTING DIMENSION LINES

Dimension extension lines and their dimension lines should be drawn outside the object whenever possible. Dimensions should only be drawn within the object when no other option is available.

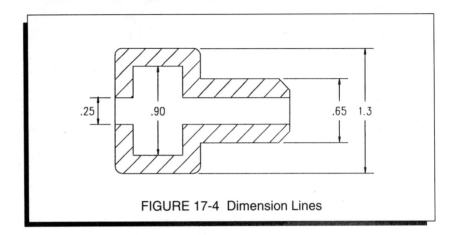

FIGURE 17-4 Dimension Lines

CONSTRUCTING DIMENSION TEXT

Dimension text is used to provide the actual distance described by the dimension components. Text used in dimensions is generally ⅛" for small drawings and ⁵⁄₃₂" for larger drawings. The location of dimension text is dependent on the discipline. In architectural and structural drawings, the dimension is placed on top of the dimension line. In mechanical drawings, the dimension is usually placed within the dimension line.

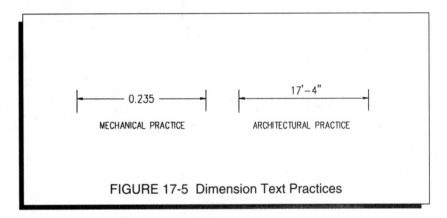

FIGURE 17-5 Dimension Text Practices

When stipulating distances, the text designating feet and inches is separated by a dash, such as 5'-4". If there are no inches, a zero is used; 6'-0". If dimensions are stipulated strictly in inches, the inch mark should be used to avoid confusion.

FRACTIONS

Fractions are given either as common fractions such as ½, ¾, etc., or as decimal fractions such as 0.50 and 0.75. Normally, inches and common fractions are stipulated without a dash between them. In CAD, however, many text fonts do not have "stacked" fractions. When fractions must be constructed from standard numerical text, you should use a dash to avoid confusion, such as 3-1⁄2.

DIMENSIONING THREE DIMENSIONAL OBJECTS

Three dimensional objects are generally dimensioned by stipulated rules. Let's look at some 3-D objects and the accepted methodology of dimensioning each.

DIMENSIONING WEDGES

Wedges are dimensioned in two views. The three distances that describe the length, width, and height are dimensioned in the two views.

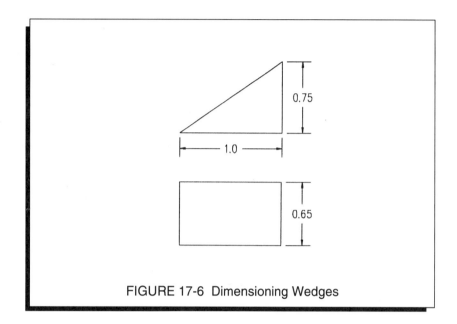

FIGURE 17-6 Dimensioning Wedges

DIMENSIONING CYLINDERS

Cylinders are dimensioned for diameter and height. The diameter is typically dimensioned in the non-circular view. If a drill-thru is dimensioned, it is described by a diameter leader.

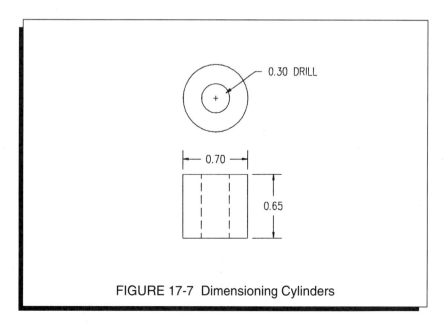

FIGURE 17-7 Dimensioning Cylinders

DIMENSIONING CONES

Cones are dimensioned at the diameter and the height. Some conical shapes require two diameter dimensions.

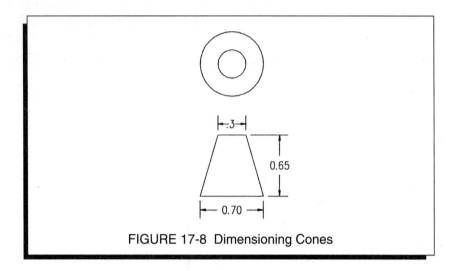

FIGURE 17-8 Dimensioning Cones

DIMENSIONING PYRAMIDS

Pyramids are dimensioned in a manner similar to cones.

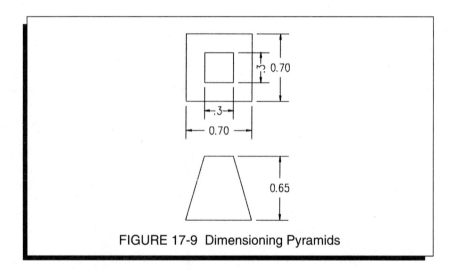

FIGURE 17-9 Dimensioning Pyramids

DIMENSIONING ARCS AND CURVES

Arcs are dimensioned as a radius. The dimension line should be placed at an angle, avoiding placement as either horizontal or vertical. The dimension text designating the radius value should be followed by the letter R, designating that it is a radius dimension.

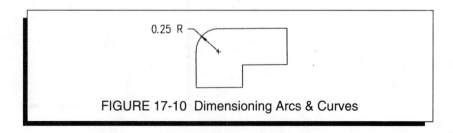

FIGURE 17-10 Dimensioning Arcs & Curves

An object constructed of several arcs is dimensioned by locating the center of the arcs with horizontal or vertical dimensions, and showing the radii with radius dimensioning.

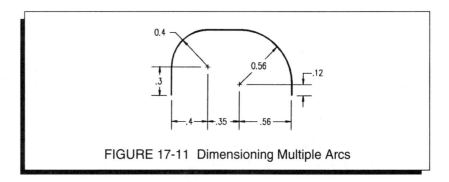

FIGURE 17-11 Dimensioning Multiple Arcs

Irregular curves are dimensioned with offset dimensions as shown in the following illustration.

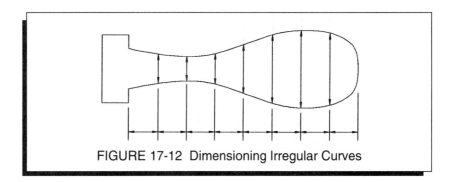

FIGURE 17-12 Dimensioning Irregular Curves

DIMENSIONING MECHANICAL COMPONENTS

The following sections illustrate the methodology of dimensioning mechanical components. Note that many techniques vary due to individual interpretation.

DIMENSIONING CHAMFERS

A *chamfer* is an angled surface applied to an edge. Chamfers of 45 degrees are dimensioned by a leader, with the leader text designating the angle and one (or two) linear distances.

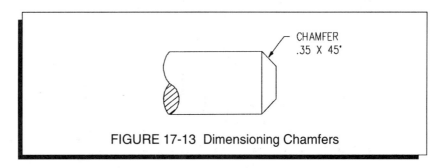

FIGURE 17-13 Dimensioning Chamfers

If the chamfer is not 45 degrees, the part is described by dimensions showing the angle and the linear distances.

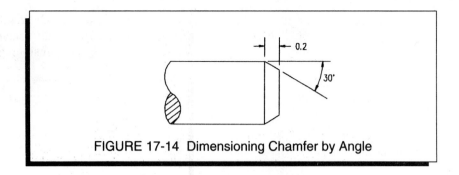

FIGURE 17-14 Dimensioning Chamfer by Angle

ENLARGING PARTS FOR DIMENSIONING

A portion of a part may be too small to properly dimension. To properly show the dimensions, a segment may be enlarged.

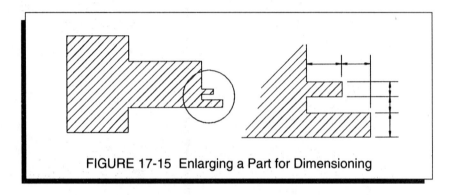

FIGURE 17-15 Enlarging a Part for Dimensioning

DIMENSIONING HOLES

Holes can be drilled, reamed, bored, punched, or cored. It is preferable to dimension the hole by note, giving the diameter, operation, and (if there is more than one hole) the number. The operation is used to describe such techniques as counterbored, reamed, and countersunk.

Standards dictate that drill sizes be designated as decimal fractions.

Whenever possible, point the dimension leader to the hole in the circular view.

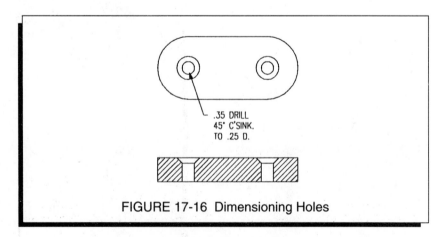

FIGURE 17-16 Dimensioning Holes

Holes that are made up of several diameters can be dimensioned in their section.

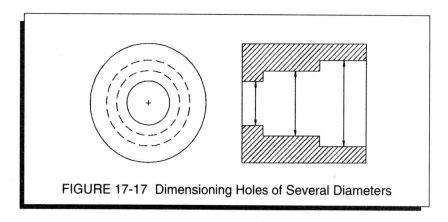

FIGURE 17-17 Dimensioning Holes of Several Diameters

DIMENSIONING TAPERS

A taper can be described as the surface of a cone frustum. Tapers are dimensioned by giving the diameters of both ends and the rate of taper, given as the distance of taper per foot.

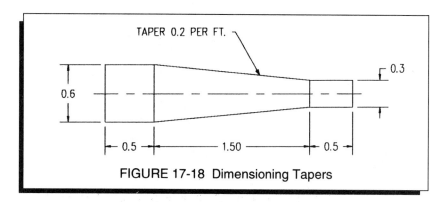

FIGURE 17-18 Dimensioning Tapers

CHAPTER PROBLEMS

Dimension the following drawings.

Electronic Work Disk Problem

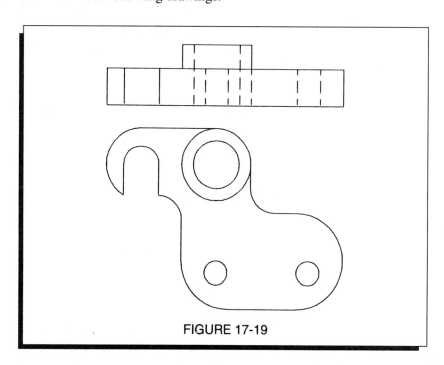

FIGURE 17-19

Electronic Work Disk Problem

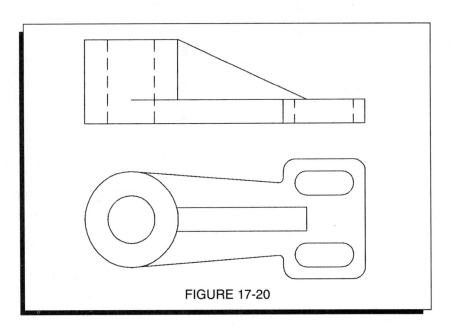

FIGURE 17-20

Electronic Work Disk Problem

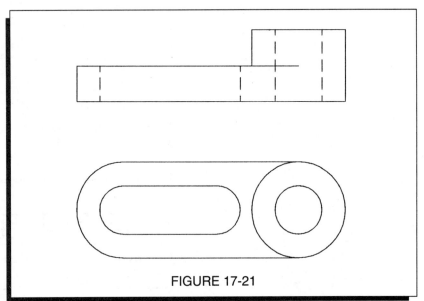

FIGURE 17-21

Electronic Work Disk Problem

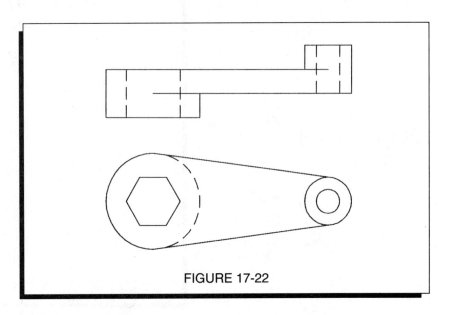

FIGURE 17-22

Electronic Work Disk Problem

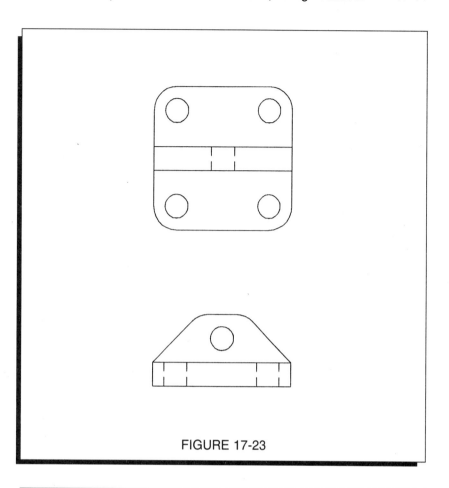

FIGURE 17-23

Electronic Work Disk Problem

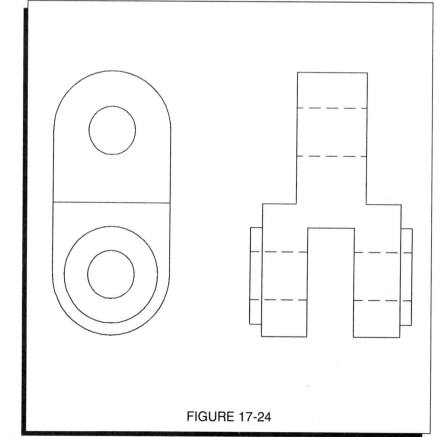

FIGURE 17-24

Electronic Work Disk Problem

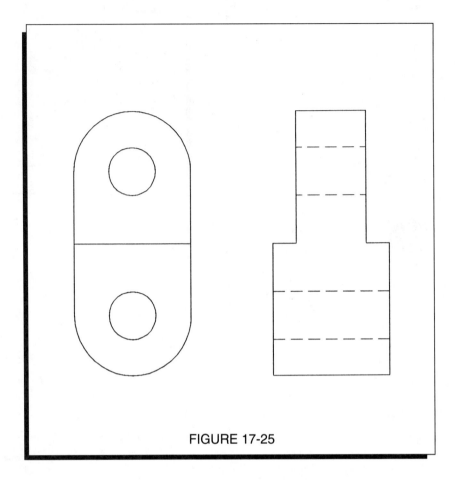

FIGURE 17-25

Electronic Work Disk Problem

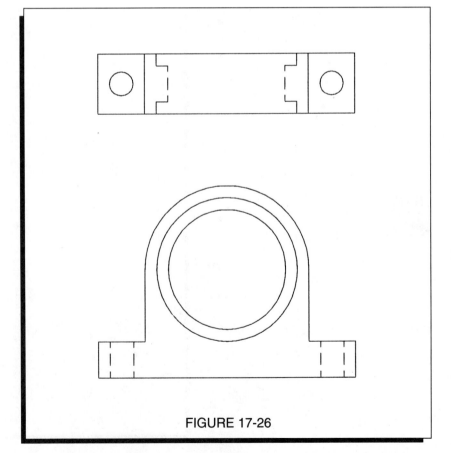

FIGURE 17-26

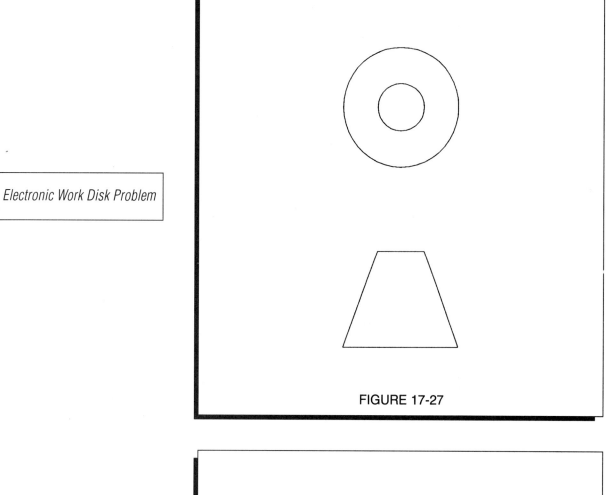

FIGURE 17-27

Electronic Work Disk Problem

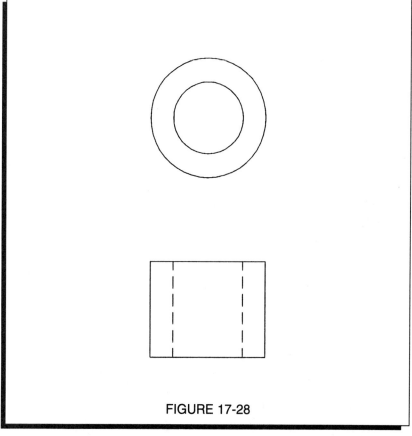

FIGURE 17-28

Electronic Work Disk Problem

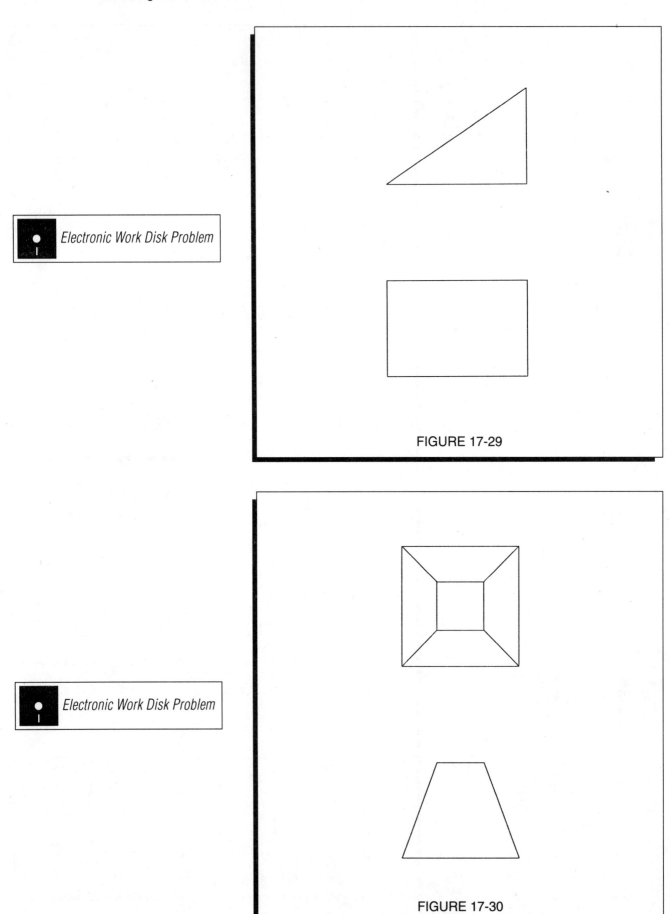

Electronic Work Disk Problem

FIGURE 17-29

Electronic Work Disk Problem

FIGURE 17-30

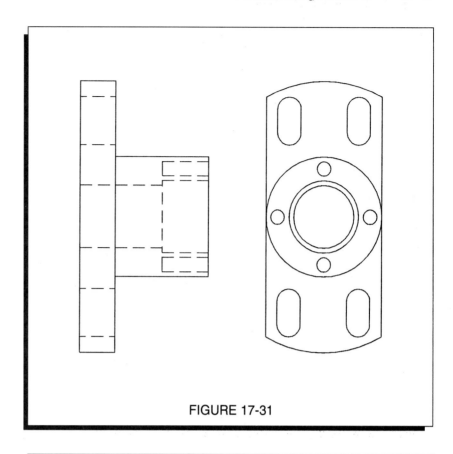

FIGURE 17-31

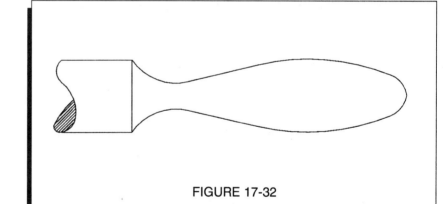

FIGURE 17-32

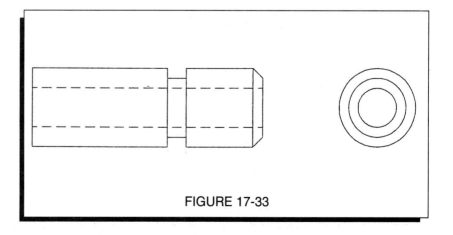

FIGURE 17-33

Electronic Work Disk Problem

Electronic Work Disk Problem

Electronic Work Disk Problem

Electronic Work Disk Problem

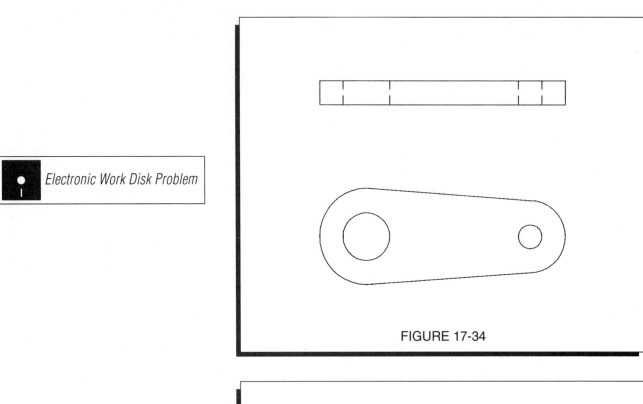

FIGURE 17-34

Electronic Work Disk Problem

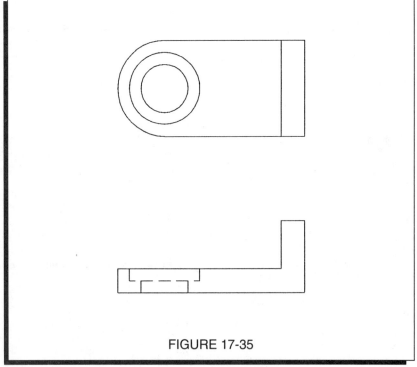

FIGURE 17-35

CHAPTER 18

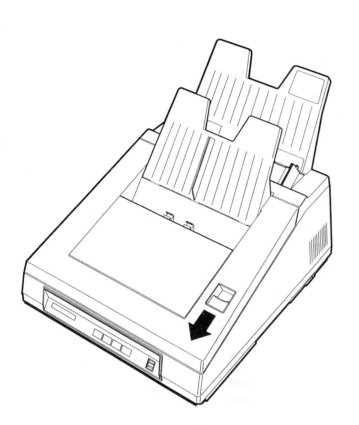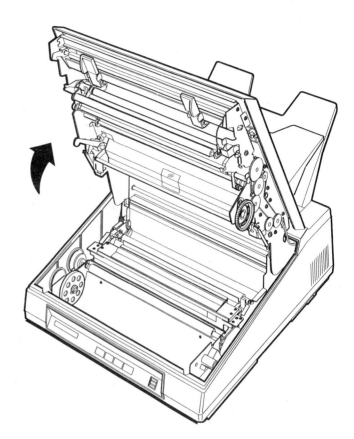

Plotting Your Work

OBJECTIVES:

The intended product of most CAD drawing products is to produce a hard copy of the work. In this chapter, you will learn how to plot your drawings. Chapter 18 objectives are:

● To understand the advantages and disadvantages of different types of plots.

● To understand how to initiate a plot.

● To learn to use AutoCAD's plot commands.

● To obtain an understanding of the relationship of plot scales and limits.

● To learn how to set up a drawing for a plot of a specified scale and paper space.

PLOTTING OVERVIEW

You have learned so far how to build and edit drawings using AutoCAD commands, but wouldn't you really like to see them on paper? After all, the end product is usually a finished drawing on paper.

AutoCAD allows you to plot your work on a plotter or printer (referred to as a "printer plot"). There are several other types of output devices. Before you can plot a drawing, the particular plotter and/or printer must be installed by using the Config command.

PRINTER PLOTS

Printer plots are excellent for check plots of your work.

Printer plots are easy (and cheap), but the line quality is usually not very good. Printer plots are excellent for check plots of your work. Some printer plotters have the ability to plot up to C-size drawings, while others can plot in color.

PLOTTER PLOTS

Plots produced from a pen plotter are very high quality. The plotter uses a technical or marker pen to actually "draw" your work.

Plotters use different sizes of paper. You will learn about this later in this chapter. The scale at which you plot is determined by your requirements and the paper size.

PLOTTING THE WORK

There are two basic ways to plot a drawing:

> By using AutoCAD's plot dialogue boxes
>
> From the command line

The Cmddia system variable determines whether the Plot command dialogue boxes or command line prompts. If Cmddia is set to 1, dialogue boxes are displayed. If set to 0, command line prompts are used. Let's see how AutoCAD's plot dialogue boxes are used to plot a drawing.

USING THE PLOT COMMAND DIALOGUE BOXES

To plot a drawing, enter the Plot command at the command line.

To plot a drawing, enter the Plot command at the command line. When you use the Plot command (and Cmddia is set to 1), the following dialogue box is displayed.

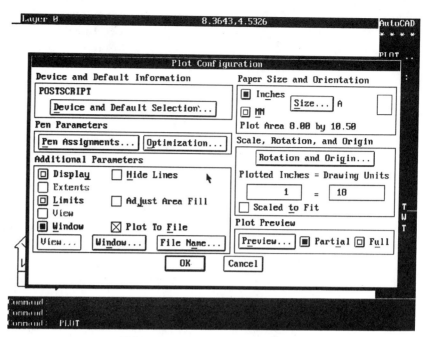

FIGURE 18-1 Plot Dialogue Box

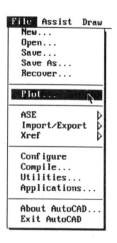

HOW TO PLOT

In order to plot a drawing, you must first determine several aspects concerning the plot. Let's take these in recommended order.

DETERMINE THE PROPER PLOTTING EQUIPMENT

AutoCAD can store several settings for different plot devices. For example, you may have two different types of plotters available to you. The "Device and Default Information" section of the plotting dialogue box displays the currently selected devices.

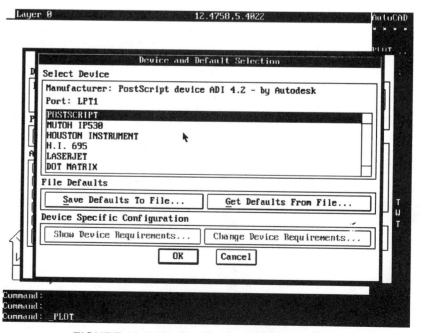

FIGURE 18-2 Plotting Device Subdialogue Box

To change the device, select the "Device and Default Selection..." button. AutoCAD displays a listing of the devices you have installed. To select a different plotter, click on the name of the device in the box, then select "OK".

SELECT PEN ASSIGNMENTS

Many plotters are capable of plotting with several pens. The pens can be different widths or colors. The pens are stored in a pen carousel or in a pen corral. Other plotters simulate a multi-pen device by stopping and prompting the user to install a different pen.

AutoCAD uses entity colors to assign pens. For example, the user can specify that all entities in the drawing that are red will be plotted with a certain pen, while those that are blue are plotted with a different pen. The pen used for each color is specified in the **Pen Assignments** dialogue box. This dialogue box is accessed by selecting "Pen Assignments.." from the plot dialogue box. The following subdialogue box is displayed.

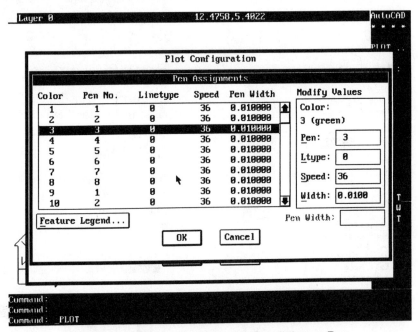

FIGURE 18-3 Pen Assignment Subdialogue Box

You can change the pen assignment, the linetype, the speed that the pen moves, and the width of the pen.

To make a change, first select the color number. For example, color number 1 represents red. The following listing shows the numbers AutoCAD uses to represent each color.

COLOR NUMBER	COLOR
1	RED
2	YELLOW
3	GREEN
4	CYAN
5	BLUE
6	MAGENTA
7	WHITE

Colors above 8 are listed by number only.

When you select a listing, the values in the "Modify Values" section of the dialogue box lists the values set for that color. To change a value, click in the edit box and enter the new value.

Let's continue and look a bit closer at each of the items you can change.

PEN

The pen number corresponds to the pen in a numbered carousel in the plotter. On single pen plotters that emulate a multipen plotter, AutoCAD will prompt for the pen by number.

Different pens can be used to plot drawings with different pen widths or colors. Using varying pen widths is common in complex drawings that are visually clearer when plotted in different line widths.

Some non-pen plotters (such as electrostatic) use the pen information to assign different line widths and/or colors.

Experienced CAD operators plan the drawing for the different pen widths as they construct the drawing. They draw objects in specified colors that correspond to pens they will use to plot the drawing. For example, all objects that will be plotted with a "wide" pen may be drawn in red. Entity colors can be assigned "BYLAYER" (see the Layer command), or by using the Color command to set all subsequent entity colors. The Change command can be used to change an entity color after it is constructed.

LINETYPE

The linetype setting stipulates the type of line that is drawn for entities drawn in the color listed. You can see the linetypes available by selecting the "Feature Legend..." button.

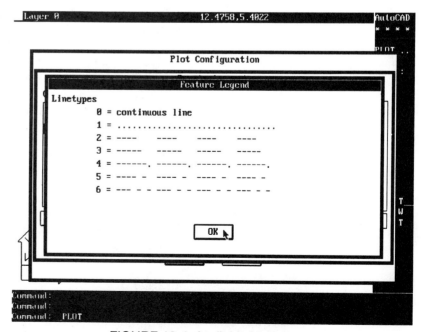

FIGURE 18-4 Available Linetypes

NOTE: You should not mix "onscreen linetypes" and plotter line-types. Either use onscreen linetypes or set the linetype by color. Using both will yield unsuitable linetypes.

SPEED

The Speed setting controls the speed at which the pen moves. This is useful if some of your pens skip when moved too quickly. Note that the speed of the pen movement is limited by the speed at which the plotter is capable of moving the pen.

WIDTH

The width setting specifies the actual linewidth drawn by the pen. The width should be set accurately since AutoCAD uses this information to calculate how much the pen is moved laterally when drawing in solids, polylines, and trace lines.

> ### Tip
>
> Most pens list the width somewhere on the pen. In most cases, these widths are in millimeters (for example, 0.5 mm). If you are drawing in inches units, be sure to convert the pen width to inches.

SELECT THE PART OF THE DRAWING TO PLOT

You can specify the portion of the drawing that you wish to plot. The choices are contained in the "Additional Parameters" box of the dialogue box. Let's look at the choices.

DISPLAY

Clicking in the Display checkbox will result in a plot of the current screen view. This is a "what you see is what you get" plot.

EXTENTS

The Extents option plots the portion of the drawing that contains any entities, eliminating "blank" areas. The plot would be the same as per-forming a Zoom Extents and then plotting that display.

If you choose the Extents option to plot a drawing that is in a perspec-tive view, and the camera position is in the drawing extents, the follow-ing message is displayed.

        PLOT/PRPLOT Extents incalculable, using display

The plot process will continue, but using the Display option instead of the Extents.

LIMITS

Plotting the Limits of a drawing uses the drawing limits as the border definition of the plot. This option will plot all areas of the drawing bounded by the limits, including "blank" areas.

VIEW

The View option plots a named view. The drawing that you stipulated to plot must contain a stored view. If you wish to plot a view, select the "View..." button. AutoCAD prompts you for the name of the view.

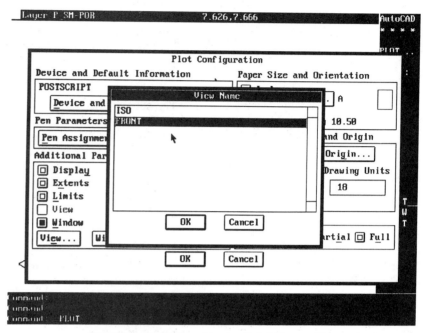

FIGURE 18-5 View Name Subdialogue Box

All the named views existing in the drawing are displayed in the sub-dialogue box.

WINDOW

Window allows you to plot any portion of your drawing by identifying it with a window. AutoCAD displays a **Window Selection** dialogue box.

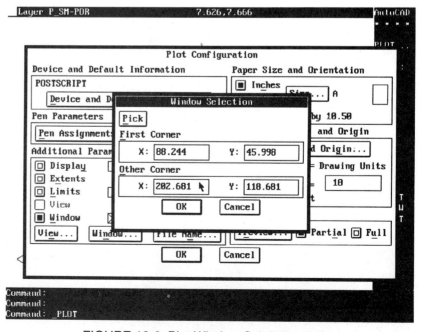

FIGURE 18-6 Plot Window Subdialogue Box

You can specify the drawing in two ways. The first is to use the text boxes to specify the X and Y coordinates of two corners of a window bounding the part of the drawing to be plotted.

> ## Professional Tip
>
> Use AutoCAD's ID command to determine exact coordinates for precise window placement when accuracy is of great importance.

The second way to specify a plotting window is to "show" the window on the drawing screen. Select "Pick" from the "Window Selection" subdialogue box. The drawing screen will be displayed. Enter a window on the screen in the same manner as an object selection window. When the second window corner is selected, the subdialogue box will be redisplayed. The actual coordinates of the window you picked will be displayed in the text boxes.

SELECT OTHER PARAMETERS

After selecting the portion of the drawing to plot, choose any other parameters that will affect the plot. Let's look at the choices. All selections are found in the "Additional Parameters" section of the dialogue box.

HIDE LINES

Selecting "Hide Lines" causes AutoCAD to process the drawing and remove hidden lines when plotting a 3-D drawing. Removing hidden lines from complex drawings can take a period of time and will slow down the plotting process.

> *NOTE: Using the Hide command to remove hidden lines on the drawing screen does not carry over to the plotting routine. The hidden lines must be removed at the time of the plot even if the display shows the hidden lines removed.*

The Hideplot option of the Mview command does not affect plots made from model space. You must select the Hide Lines check box if you want the plot to be drawn with hidden lines removed.

ADJUST AREA FILL

Selecting "Adjust Area Fill" causes AutoCAD to move the pen inward ½ pen width when plotting solids and filled areas. This results in very accurate fill areas. In most applications, this is not necessary. In some applications requiring extreme precision, such as printed circuit board design, this option should be used.

PLOT TO FILE

AutoCAD can write your plot to a file.

AutoCAD can write your plot to a file. The plot file can then be used to plot the drawing without AutoCAD actually being present.

This ability is very useful if you wish to continue drawing on one computer while plotting from another. In most cases, you will need a third-party program that allows you plot a plot file without AutoCAD.

To create a plot file, select the "Plot To File" check box. Next, select the "File Name..." button. A subdialogue box will be displayed.

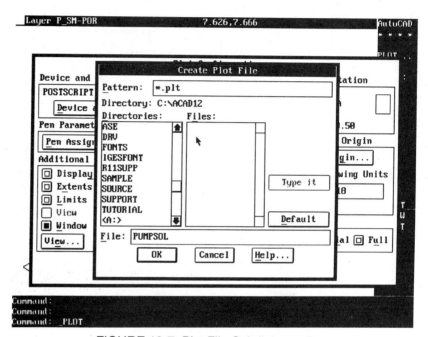

FIGURE 18-7 Plot File Subdialogue Box

The subdialogue box contains list boxes for the directory path (on the left), and the plot files (on the right). To enter a new plot file name, click in the "File" text box and enter the plot name.

The plot file name should be entered without a file extension. AutoCAD will append a file extension of .PLT for plot files.

A plotter file must be used with a plot file utility program supplied by a third party to plot the file.

In some cases, you can send a .PLT file to the "plotter" with the DOS COPY command. For example, some PostScript laser printers will allow you to send a .PLT file if you are configured for PostScript devices, and parallel (as opposed to a COM port) without a third-party plot utility program.

For example, if the plot file is named "WIDGET1.PLT", you can enter the following to send the plot file to the printer:

```
COPY WIDGET1.PLT LPT1:
```

This would send the file to the number one printer port (LPT1:).

SELECT PAPER SIZE AND ORIENTATION

CAD drawings are plotted on many different sizes of paper or film. AutoCAD allows you to select all the sizes available for your plotter, plus sizes that you can specify.

The plot size is determined by the **Paper Size** subdialogue box. To access this dialogue box, select "Size..." from the plot dialogue box. AutoCAD displays the following subdialogue box.

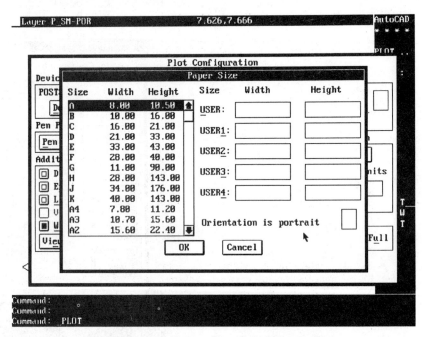

FIGURE 18-8 Paper Size Subdialogue Box

The list box displays the sizes available. Highlight the size you want by clicking on the entry. If you want to enter a custom size, click inside a text box next to one of the "USER" listings and enter the width and height of the custom plot size.

The orientation is listed below the user entries. The orientation listed is the normal direction of the plot for the plotter selected. You can rotate the plot if you want the orientation changed. Plot rotation is covered next in this chapter.

SELECT THE SCALE, ROTATION, AND PLOT ORIGIN

You can rotate the plotted drawing in 90-degree increments. This has the effect of "turning" the drawing on the paper. To rotate the plot, select the "Rotation and Origin..." button.

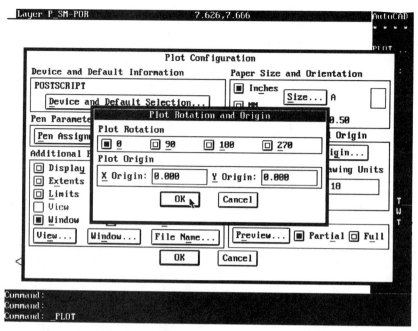

FIGURE 18-9 Plot Rotation Subdialogue Box

The degree of plot rotation is selected with the radio buttons at each rotation listing. The following illustration shows the effect of each rotation.

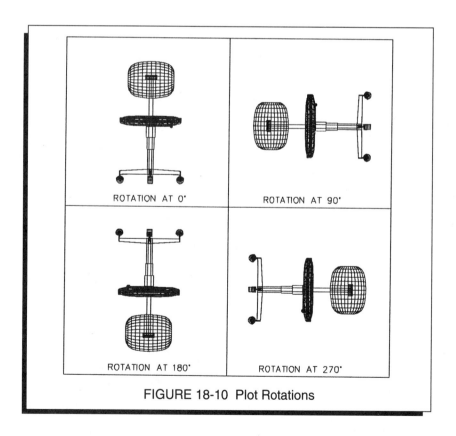

FIGURE 18-10 Plot Rotations

The plot origin is the distance that AutoCAD will offset the corner of the drawing from the origin corner of the paper. The origin point of the paper can be different for various devices. For most plotters, however, the origin point is the lower left corner.

For example, if you are using a pen plotter and plotting in inches, a plot origin of 6,4 would move the plot origin six inches to the right and four inches up the paper.

The distance that the plot is offset is set in the **Plot Rotation and Origin** subdialogue box. Click in the text boxes and enter the X and Y distances to offset the drawing. The offset distance is calculated in either inches or millimeters, depending on the setting in the "Paper Size and Orientation" box in the **Plot Configuration** dialogue box. The plot is <u>not</u> measured in drawing units.

SET THE PLOT SCALE

The plot scale is determined by setting the number of drawing units to be plotted on a specified number of inches or millimeters on the paper. For example, a scale of 1" = 8"-0" means that 1" of paper contains 8'-0" of drawing. This is the same, of course, as the scale ⅛" = 1'-0". To set this scale, enter 1" under "Plotted Inches" and 8'0" under "Drawing Units".

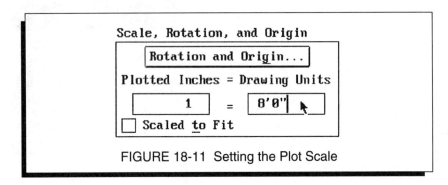

FIGURE 18-11 Setting the Plot Scale

You can also tell AutoCAD to plot the drawing to the maximum size allowed by the paper size you have selected. To do this, select the "Scaled to Fit" check box.

As unusual as it might seem, proper scaling begins at the time you set the drawing limits.

Many CAD operators initially calculate the proper plot scale. As unusual as it might seem, proper scaling begins at the time you set the drawing limits. The limits, paper size and the scale at which you intend to plot must all match for a properly scaled plot.

If you begin a drawing using traditional drafting techniques, you must know the size of paper on which you are drawing (of course), and the scale at which you are drawing. The same is true for CAD drafting. In fact, the limits determine the page size. But how do all these work together?

Let's first look at how the plotter translates the scale factor you give it. When you give the plot ratio, you are stipulating how many <u>units</u> will be contained in one inch on the paper that is being plotted on. (Or millimeters, if you choose that option.) For example, if you intend to plot the drawing at ¼" = 1'-0", and you have stipulated that one unit equals one foot, you may also say that ¼" = 1 unit. (One unit = 1 foot, remember?) We may take this further and say that 1" = 4 units, or there are four units in one inch. Let's review this process:

If   ¼" = 1'-0" & one unit = 1'
then   ¼" = 1 unit
then   1" = 4 units

Let's take this one step further. If 1" = 4 units, then each inch on the paper will contain 4 units. If you intend to plot your drawing on paper that is 36" wide by 24" high, you may multiply the number of inches in each direction of the paper by the number of units in one inch.

$$36" \times 4 \text{ units/inch} = 144 \text{ (X limit)}$$
$$24" \times 4 \text{ units/inch} = 96 \text{ (Y limit)}$$

Therefore, assuming the following parameters:

Intended scale: ¼" = 1'-0"
1 unit = 1 foot
Paper size = 36 × 24

the limits would be 0,0 and 144,96.

From this, we can derive a formula that will determine the proper limits when we have the other necessary information.

(No. of units/inch) × (paper width) = X limit
(No. of units/inch) × (paper height) = Y limit

When you are using architectural units, one unit = one inch.

If   ¼" = 1'-0" & 1 unit = 1"
then   ¼" = 12 units
then   1" = 48 units

therefore,

$$36" \times 48 \text{ units/inch} = 1728 \text{ (X limits)}$$
$$24" \times 48 \text{ units/inch} = 1152 \text{ (Y limits)}$$

You could also say that 1728 inches is equal to 144 feet and 1152 inches is equal to 96 feet. Therefore, you could enter either 1728,1152 or 144',96' as the upper right limits.

As you can see, calculating limits requires some basic mathematics skills. In fact, any type of drafting requires these types of skills. With practice, the process becomes easier.

The appendix has a chart that makes things quite a bit easier. This chart lists plot scales, paper sizes, and limits. You can use the chart to set up a drawing for a specific plot scale and paper size.

PREVIEW THE PLOT

You can preview the plot to see the area of the paper on which the plot will appear. Before doing this, you should first set the paper size, orientation, and scale. AutoCAD's plot preview allows two types of preview: partial and full. Let's look at each.

Tip

Use plot previews to discover plotting results before committing time, paper, and pens to plotting a drawing that may have been set up incorrectly for the plot.

PARTIAL PREVIEW

A partial preview shows the effective plotted area on the "page size" you have selected. On color displays, the plotted area is shown as a blue rectangle, and the paper area as a red rectangle. A partial preview does not show the drawing, but rather the position of the plot on the paper.

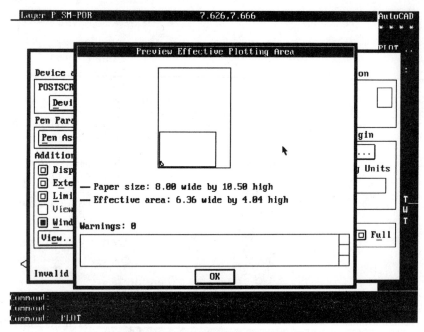

FIGURE 18-12 Partial Plot Preview

The plotted area also shows a rotation icon. This triangular icon represents the lower left corner of the drawing as it is positioned on the drawing screen. When the drawing is rotated to angle 0 on the paper, the icon appears at the lower left. At 90 degrees rotation, it is at the upper left. At 180, it appears at the upper right, and is positioned at the lower right at 270 degrees rotation.

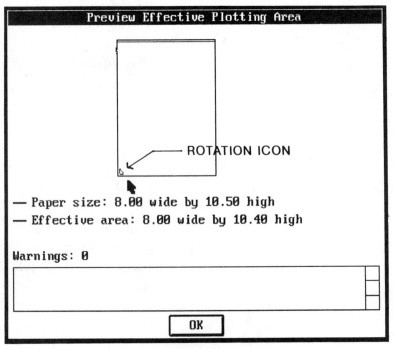

FIGURE 18-13

If the plotted area is entirely within the paper size, the plot area is slightly offset from the lower left corner so the plot area lines and the paper lines do not lie on top of each other. If the plotted area and the paper size are exactly the same, the lines are shown dashed, with the dashes alternating red and blue. If the plot origin is offset so that the plotted area extends outside the paper area, AutoCAD displays a green line at the clipped side and displays the following message:

Effective area clipped to display image

AutoCAD also uses the partial preview box to display warning messages such as "Plotting area exceeds maximum".

FULL PREVIEW

A full preview shows the drawing as it will appear as the final plot on paper.

A *full preview* shows the drawing as it will appear as the final plot on paper. When you select full preview, the drawing is regenerated to display the plot. Since the regeneration takes a period of time, AutoCAD displays a meter showing the percent of regeneration completed in the lower right corner of the plot dialogue box.

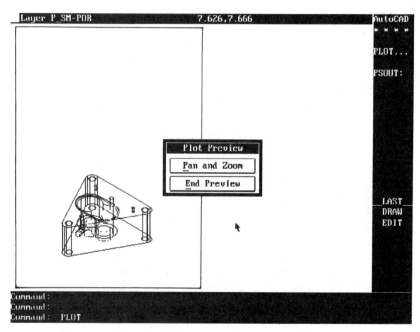

FIGURE 18-14 Full Plot Preview

When the full preview is displayed, AutoCAD places a small plot preview dialogue box on the screen. If you wish, you can move this box by placing the arrow pointer on the "Plot Preview" bar at the top of the dialogue box, and then clicking and holding as you move the box.

The dialogue box has two choices: "Pan and Zoom" and "End Preview". The pan and zoom is used to examine parts of the drawing to be plotted and works in the same way as the dynamic Zoom command. When you select Pan and Zoom, a zoom box is displayed with an "X" in the center. Move the box to a new location and press ENTER to pan. Clicking the pick button on the input device will display an arrow at the right side of the box. If you move the arrow, the box will change size, allowing you to zoom the display size. You can use pan and zoom in the same operation by clicking the input button to change between pan and zoom mode.

After you have panned or zoomed, the dialogue box displays a "Zoom Previous" button that will return the drawing to the previous zoom.

To end the preview, select the "End Preview" button. You will be returned to the plotting dialogue box.

FINALLY, PLOT THE DRAWING

When you have completed all the steps outlined, make sure the plotter is ready and select the "OK" button at the bottom of the plot dialogue box.

EXERCISES

1. If you have a printer plotter (most dot-matrix printers will work as a printer plotter), use the plotting dialogue box to verify the plotter is configured for use.

   Use the chart in the appendix to set the limits for an A-size drawing. Draw a simple drawing and save your work. Plot the drawing, using "Scaled to Fit" to scale the drawing.

2. Plot the drawing again, using the scale you configured from the chart in the appendix. After the drawing is plotted, use a draftsman's scale to check the scale of the drawing at a known dimension length. Did your drawing plot to scale?

3. Plot the drawing again, rotating the plot 90 degrees.

4. Enter the drawing you constructed. Select the Plot command. Plot the drawing, using a Window. Place a window around any part of the drawing. Set the plot units to Scaled to Fit. Plot the drawing.

5. Select the plot command again. Set the plot for Limits. Plot to a file. Select Scaled to Fit. Set the plot file name to "MYPLOT".

   After the plot has been written to file, use the Shell command to display the DOS prompt. Type the following:

   COPY MYPLOT.PLT LPT1:

   (If your printer is connected a second parallel port, you will need to specify LPT2.) You do not have AutoCAD running, or even installed on the computer, to printer plot a plot file.

PLOTTING FROM THE COMMAND LINE

If the Cmddia variable is set to 0, the plotting dialogue boxes will not be displayed. Instead, the plot information will be entered from the command line. Let's look at how AutoCAD prompts for the information. You may initiate a plot by entering:

AutoCAD prompts:

What to plot - Display, Extents, Limits, View, or Window <*default*>:

Choose the portion of the drawing to be plotted by entering the first letter of your choice and Enter.

AutoCAD then displays the default plot specifications. The following is an example of this listing (your listing may vary, depending on the equipment configuration, and if changes have been made to the defaults.)

```
Plotter port time-out = 30 seconds
Plot device is Houston Instruments ADI 4.2 - by Autodesk
Description: HOUSTON INSTRUMENT
Plot optimization level = 4
Plot will NOT be written to a selected file
Sizes are in inches and the style is landscape
Plot origin is at (0.00, 0.00)
Plotting area is 31.00 wide by 21.50 high (MAX) size)
Plot is NOT rotated
Pen width is 0.010
Area fill will NOT be adjusted for pen width
Hidden lines will NOT be removed
Plot will be scaled to fit available area

Do you want to change anything?
(No/Yes/File/Save) <N>:
```

The default settings for these values were set when you configured AutoCAD for the plotter you are using.

If the settings are correct for your use, press the Enter key to accept all the default values.

If you wish to change any part, enter a "Y". AutoCAD will prompt:

```
Do you want to change plotters <N>:
```

Responding "Yes" will display a listing of the installed plotters for choice. If you respond with "No", AutoCAD will prompt for the time-out period, then display a chart displaying the layer colors, pen numbers, linetypes, and pen speeds on the screen. Figure 18-15 is an example of the chart. Note that your listing may be different, depending on the type of plotter you have configured.

```
How many seconds should we wait for the plotter
port to time-out (0 means wait forever), 0 to 500 <7>:

Pen widths are in Inches.
Entity      Pen  Line   Pen     Entity      Pen  Line   Pen
Color       No.  Type   Width   Color       No.  Type   Width
1 (red)      1    0     0.010      9          1    0     0.010
2 (yellow)   1    0     0.010     10          1    0     0.010
3 (green)    1    0     0.010     11          1    0     0.010
4 (cyan)     1    0     0.010     12          1    0     0.010
5 (blue)     1    0     0.003     13          1    0     0.010
6 (magenta)  1    0     0.010     14          1    0     0.010
7 (white)    1    0     0.007     15          1    0     0.010
8            1    0     0.010     16          1    0     0.010

Linetypes
        0 = continuous line
        1 = ...............................
        2 = ----    ----    ----    ----
        3 = -----   -----   -----   -----
        4 = ------. ------. ------. ------.
        5 = ---- -  ---- -  ---- -  ---- -
        6 = --- - - --- - - --- - - --- - -
Do you want to change any of the above parameters? <N>
```

FIGURE 18-15 Plotting Pen Chart

If you would like to change anything, respond with a "Y" to the prompt:

> Do you want to change any of the above parameters? <N>

If everything is correct, press Enter to accept the default of "N" (NO).

If you answer "Y" to the prompt, AutoCAD will prompt:

> Enter values. blank=Next value, Cn=Colorn, S=Show current values, X=Exit

A listing will appear at the bottom of the screen, similar to the following:

Layer Color	Pen No.	Line Type	Pen Speed
1 (red)	1	0	16

> Pen number <1>:

You may flip through the listing of values for each color number and enter a change when you wish. You will first see the color number, then the pen number for color number 1, then the linetype for color number 1, then the pen speed for the pen set for color number 1. After that, the same sequence is displayed for color number 2, and so forth. AutoCAD uses the following entries to step through the choices:

Blank (space bar): Keeps the current value and advances to the next parameter. After you have advanced to color 15, AutoCAD returns to color 1.

Cn (color number): Proceeds directly to the color number entered. For example, if you want to proceed directly to color 12 to make a change, enter C12. This eliminates flipping through each color number.

S (Show current values): Entering an "S" redisplays the table, showing the changed values. Use this after changing any parameter to verify the change.

X (Exit): This entry will exit you from this portion of the listing and keep any changes made. This is the way you will exit the repeating sequence of color/pen/linetype/pen speed choices.

AutoCAD continues:

> Write the plot to a file <N>:

You are next prompted for the type of plotting units.

> Size units (Inches or Millimeters) <default>:

You may choose to plot in inches or millimeters by entering either "I" or "M".

Choosing either the "inches" or "millimeters" option will not change the units the drawing was drawn with.

Next you are prompted for the plot origin.

> Plot origin in Inches <0.00,0.00>:

The normal plot origin (home position) for a pen plotter is the lower left corner. For a printer plotter, it is usually the upper left corner.

You may set a new plot origin; that is, a specified position from the "home" position. The units used are either inches or millimeters, depending on which was specified in the previous plotting units option. The format is the coordinate type of X,Y entry.

Next you will be prompted for the plotting size. AutoCAD has to know the plot size you are using. Different plotters have the capability of plotting on various size sheets of paper. The standard paper sizes are A, B, C, D, and E (architectural sizes). The following table lists some paper sizes and the plot size for each. Notice that the plot size is less than the paper size.

	Paper		Plot	
Size	Width	Height	Width	Height
A	11.00	8.50	10.50	8.00
B	17.00	11.00	16.00	10.00
C	24.00	18.00	21.00	16.00
D	36.00	24.00	33.00	21.00
E	48.00	36.00	43.00	33.00

There are two other settings: MAX and USER. MAX is the largest plot that your plotter can plot. USER will describe the size if you enter anything other than a standard plot size (A, B, C, D, or E) by stipulating a width, height description. Note that not all plotters will plot all the sizes listed. Your display will vary, depending on the configured plotter.

The prompt for plot size is:

> Enter the Size or Width, Height (in units) <*default*>:

AutoCAD continues by prompting for the plot rotation.

Rotating a plot is especially useful when you are using printer plotters and wish to take advantage of the paper width. The prompt for plot rotation is:

> Rotate plot clockwise 0/90/180/270 degrees <0>:

Next, set the pen width. When AutoCAD is using the Fill mode to color in solids and traces, it needs to know the width of the pen used in the plotter. This allows for an appropriate offset for each pass of the pen to obtain a properly filled solid area. Pens are often marked with the width of the "nib". These widths are usually in mm. If the units are set to inches, be sure to convert the pen width to mm. The prompt for pen width is:

> Pen width in <*units*>: <*default*>:

If you are plotting drawings that require more accuracy than normal (such as printed circuit board drawings), AutoCAD will adjust the boundaries around filled areas one half pen width. Printer plotters do not display this option. The next prompt AutoCAD displays controls this adjustment:

> Adjust area fill boundaries for pen width? <N>:

For most applications, the response should be "N".

Next, determine whether AutoCAD will remove the hidden lines from the plot.

> Remove hidden lines? <N>:

Now set the scale. AutoCAD allows you to plot at a scale of your choice. The prompt from which the scale is set is:

> Specify scale by entering:
> Plotted units=Drawing units or Fit or ? <*default*>:

The Fit option will adjust the scale so that the drawing will fit the paper size. Thus, if you choose "F", the drawing will not be plotted to any standard scale.

Now, after all that, you are ready to plot. The following prompt will appear:

Effective plotting area: x wide by y high

Get your paper and pen or printer ready! AutoCAD continues:

Position paper in plotter
Press RETURN to continue or S to Stop for hardware setup.

The hardware setup option is required by some plotters as the time to perform certain preparation. If you are configured for a multi-pen plot, and your plotter is a single-pen plotter, AutoCAD will stop the plot at this point and ask for a specific pen. After everything is ready, press Enter and watch the plotter plot your work.

CHAPTER REVIEW

1. What is the advantage of a printer plot?

2. What part of the drawing would be plotted if you plotted the extents of the drawing?

3. How would you plot only a portion of a drawing?

4. How would you rotate the plot on the paper?

5. How would you write a plot file to a disk for a printer plotter?

6. What DOS command would you use to print a plot file named WIDGET3 to a printer connected to the second parallel port on the computer?

7. What is the "plot origin"?

_____

_____

_____

8. How would you offset the plot origin?

_____

_____

_____

9. What units does the plot origin use?

_____

_____

_____

10. Why does AutoCAD need to know the plotter pen width?

_____

_____

_____

11. What drawing limits would you set if you set up a drawing to be plotted in architectural units, with a scale of ¼ in. = 1 ft. -0 in., and on architectural C-sized paper?

_____

_____

_____

CHAPTER 19

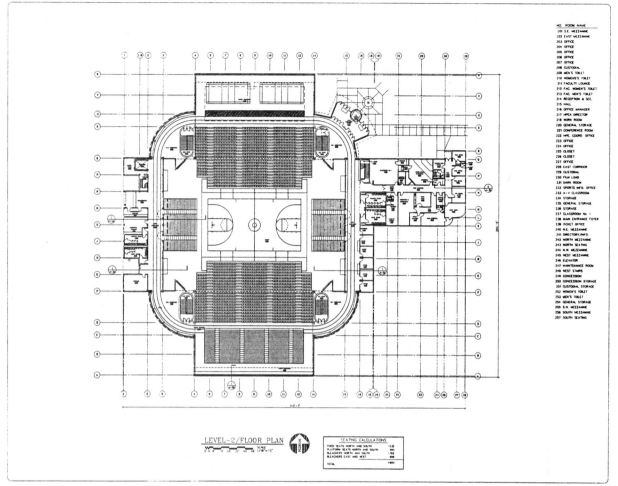

ROOM NAME

NO.	ROOM NAME
201	S.E. MEZZANINE
202	EAST MEZZANINE
203	OFFICE
204	OFFICE
205	OFFICE
206	OFFICE
207	OFFICE
208	CUSTODIAL
209	MEN'S TOILET
210	WOMEN'S TOILET
211	FACULTY LOUNGE
212	FAC. WOMEN'S TOILET
213	FAC. MEN'S TOILET
214	RECEPTION & SEC.
215	HALL
216	OFFICE MANAGER
217	HPEA DIRECTOR
218	WORK ROOM
220	GENERAL STORAGE
221	CONFERENCE ROOM
222	HPE. COORD OFFICE
223	OFFICE
224	OFFICE
225	CLOSET
226	CLOSET
227	OFFICE
228	EAST CORRIDOR
229	CUSTODIAL
230	FILM LOAD
231	DARK ROOM
232	SPORTS INFO. OFFICE
233	A-V CLASSROOM
234	STORAGE
235	GENERAL STORAGE
236	STORAGE
237	CLASSROOM No. 1
238	MAIN ENTRANCE FOYER
239	TICKET OFFICE
240	N.E. MEZZANINE
241	DIRECTORY/INFO.
242	NORTH MEZZANINE
243	NORTH SEATING
244	N.W. MEZZANINE
245	WEST MEZZANINE
246	ELEVATOR
247	MAINTENANCE ROOM
248	WEST STAIRS
249	CONCESSION
250	CONCESSION STORAGE
251	CUSTODIAL STORAGE
252	WOMEN'S TOILET
253	MEN'S TOILET
254	GENERAL STORAGE
255	S.W. MEZZANINE
256	SOUTH MEZZANINE
257	SOUTH SEATING

LEVEL-2/FLOOR PLAN
SCALE
0 4 8 24 32 40 48 1/16"=1'0"

SEATING CALCULATIONS

FIXED SEATS NORTH AND SOUTH	1232
PLATFORM SEATS NORTH AND SOUTH	984
BLEACHERS NORTH AND SOUTH	1792
BLEACHERS EAST AND WEST	896
TOTAL	4904

Inquiry and Utility Commands

OBJECTIVES:

When drawing with CAD, the user must be capable of obtaining drawing information. This chapter covers the Inquiry and Utility modes available to achieve this. The objectives of Chapter 19 are:

● To use the ID, List, and Dblist commands to obtain information on points and entities in the drawings.

● To learn to calculate areas within a drawing.

● To use AutoCAD's abilities to execute DOS commands while in the AutoCAD program.

● To learn the time-keeping function that is built into AutoCAD.

AutoCAD
In The
Real
World

Retail Store Planning With AutoCAD
AutoCAD gets retailer to market faster

The growth of a retail store chain, as with any chain store concept, can, at times, be fast paced. In the case of the Kobacker Company (Columbus, Ohio), this pace has been as rapid as 150 projects in a year, with as many as 40 stores opening in a month. To keep up with this vigorous expansion, the company's store planning and construction department (SPCD) is using AutoCAD.

When Kobacker committed to automating its drafting operations, it was able to keep the planning and construction department small. Ultimately, they reduced by 75 percent the time required to produce a typical store plan drawing.

Kobacker used AutoCAD to restructure construction documentation procedures, reducing the number of construction drawings per store to one or two documents.

AutoCAD's embedded programming language, AutoLISP, was used to streamline operation methods. Its custom menus provide easy access to frequently used commands and allow automation of routine procedures.

AutoCAD was also used for facility planning. Because the architectural firm provided the construction plans for an enlarged corporate office facility as AutoCAD drawings, the store planning and construction department was able to use them as a base layer for detailed layouts.

Some of the future applications Kobacker forsees for AutoCAD are 3-D modeling and image processing. Three-dimensional models of stores and display fixtures would provide a means for design continuity. These models could be combined with video image processing to generate realistic scenes of new design concepts in existing stores. This would eliminate the costly expense and timely delays involved in producing prototype stores, fixtures, and graphic packages.

Adapted with permission from an article by Mitchell Gruesen. Excerpted from *CADENCE*, October 1989, copyright © 1989, Ariel Communications, Inc.

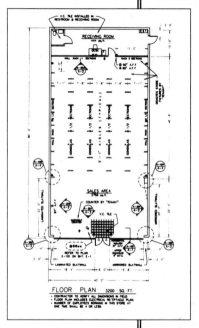

INQUIRY & UTILITY COMMANDS

AutoCAD's inquiry and utility commands allow you to obtain information and perform utility functions while working within your drawing. We will learn about the following commands:

ID: Identify a point

List: List information on one or more entities

Dblist: List information on all the entities in the current drawing

Dist: Compute distance between two points

Area: Compute area of a closed polygon

Files: On-line DOS capabilities

DOS Shell: External DOS commands while in AutoCAD

SH: Internal DOS commands while in AutoCAD

Time: Time management facility

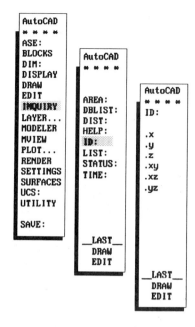

ID SCREEN COORDINATES

The ID command allows you to identify the coordinates of any point on the drawing. If you enter a location on the screen as the response to the prompt for a point, the coordinates of that location will be displayed on the command line.

The information displayed will contain the X-coordinate value, the Y-coordinate value, and the current Z-value elevation.

To execute the ID command, enter:

> Command: <u>ID</u>
> Point:
> X= <X-coordinate> Y= <Y-coordinate> Z= <current elevation>

You may also use the ID command to show a known point on the screen. If you enter a set of coordinates in response to the prompt, a marker blip will be displayed at that point on the screen.

For example, if you enter the ID command and enter the absolute coordinate value of 8,5 in response to the "Point:" prompt, a blip mark will be displayed at the X,Y coordinates of 8,5. Note that Blipmode must be "on" before marker blips are displayed.

ID EXERCISE

Start a new drawing named "INQUIRE". You can use this drawing for all exercises in this chapter. Draw a line, using the absolute endpoints of 2,2 and 6,6.

Select the ID command, then object snap ENDpoint. Select the first endpoint of the line with the object snap aperture. The command line should show the ID point as 2,2. Repeat the procedure with the other endpoint location of 6,6.

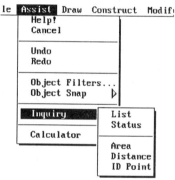

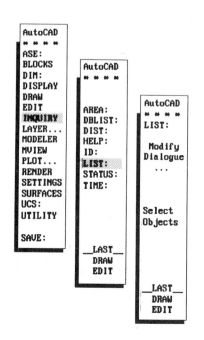

LISTING DRAWING INFORMATION

The LIST command is used to display the data stored by AutoCAD on any entity.

The format for List is:

> Command: <u>LIST</u>
> Select objects: (*SELECT*)

The information listed varies for each type of entity. For example, if you select a circle, you will obtain the layer the circle is drawn on, the radius, circumference, area, and center point of the circle.

If the object you select contains a lengthy amount of data, you can terminate the listing by using Ctrl-C.

The following shows a sample listing of a circle:

> CIRCLE   LAYER; 0
>   Space: Model space
> center point, X = 6.0264 Y= 4.8211 Z= 1.0239
> radius 1.7577
> Circumference = 11.0439,
> Area = 9.7059

LIST EXERCISE

Draw a line, circle, and arc on the screen. Use the List command to select the circle. You should obtain a listing of the circle similar to the one shown previously. Select each of the entities and notice the information displayed for each entity. The List command can be useful if you need to obtain information on a single entity in your drawing.

LISTING DRAWING DATABASE INFORMATION

Whereas the List command is used to obtain information on a single entity in a drawing, the Dblist command is used to display the data stored on <u>all</u> entities in a drawing.

This listing can be very long! You may pause the listing by using Ctrl-S. The listing will begin scrolling again if you strike any key. You may terminate the listing entirely by using Ctrl-C.

If you would like a printer copy of the data base, use Ctrl-Q (AutoCAD's printer echo) before issuing the Dblist command to send the output to your printer. Before you use Ctrl-Q, be sure your printer is hooked up and is turned on.

EXERCISES

1. Use the same drawing with the entities you used for the List exercise. Enter Dblist at the command line. Notice how the information scrolls on the screen. If you are using a single display system, you will need to use the F1 function key to switch back to the graphics display.

2. Use the Copy command to copy all the entities in the drawing three times. Use the Dblist command again and notice the length of the listing.

3. Use Dblist again and use Ctrl-S to stop the listing. If you are working on a fast computer, you will have to be quick! In some cases, turning off the turbo mode (if you have one on your computer) will allow you more time to stop the listing.

4. If you have a printer hooked up to your computer, turn it on. Press Ctrl-Q to turn on the printer echo. You will notice the following message on the command line:

    <Printer echo on>

    Enter the Dblist command again and watch the drawing database listing being printed on your printer. Be sure to turn the printer echo off again with Ctrl-Q.

COMPUTING DISTANCES

The Dist command computes the distance between two points, the angle created by the relative position of the points, and the difference of the X and Y values of the points. To invoke the Dist command, enter:

> Command: <u>DIST</u>
> First point: (*ENTER*)
> Second point: (*ENTER*)

The following is a sample listing of distance information:

> Distance=1.4971   Angle in X-Y Plane=45   Angle from X-Y Plane=0
> Delta X=1.0612   Delta Y=1.0560   Delta Z=0.0000

The following is an explanation of the listing:

> **Distance:** Distance between the two points in drawing units.
>
> **Angle in X-Y plane:** Angle created by relative position of the points in the 2-D X,Y plane.
>
> **Angle from X-Y plane:** Angle "up" from the paper into the Z-plane (used in 3-D construction).
>
> **Delta X:** Change in X-coordinate values between the points.
>
> **Delta Y:** Change in Y-coordinate values between the points.
>
> **Delta Z:** Change in Z-coordinate values between the points.

You may also show a desired distance on the screen by specifying a relative coordinate as the response to the "Second point" prompt.

For example, if you enter the first point on the screen and respond with a relative coordinate of @10,0 for the second point, AutoCAD will display a blip mark ten drawing units to the right (positive ten units X) of the first point.

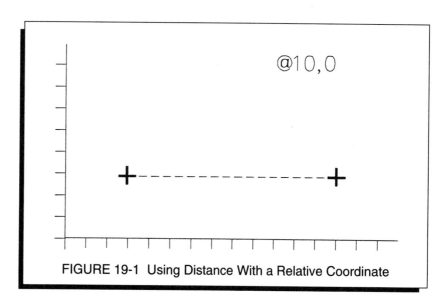

FIGURE 19-1 Using Distance With a Relative Coordinate

Note that Blipmode must be "on" before blip marks are displayed.

You may also use polar coordinates with the Dist command. For example, if you respond to the second point prompt with @15<45,

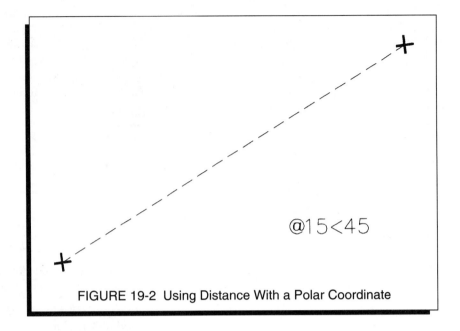

@15<45

FIGURE 19-2 Using Distance With a Polar Coordinate

AutoCAD will display a marker blip at a distance of fifteen drawing units and forty-five degrees from the point you entered in response to the "First point" prompt.

Tip

Use the Dist command and relative coordinate responses to set reference markers on the screen. You may then line up the cross-hairs on these markers. Remember, if you redraw the screen or use a command that forces a redraw (such as a zoom), the markers will be removed.

DISTANCE EXERCISE

Select the Dist command. Using object snap endpoint, select two endpoints of one of the lines on the screen. Notice how the length of the line is displayed on the command line.

CALCULATING AREAS IN YOUR DRAWING

The Area command is especially useful for roughcomputations of land bounded by property lines or calculating the areas of floor plans.

The Area command is used to calculate the area, in current drawing units, of a closed polygon.

The Area command is especially useful for rough computations of land bounded by property lines or calculating the areas of floor plans.

METHODS OF CALCULATING AREAS

The Area command permits different methods of calculating areas. The following explanations explain how to use the options in the Area command.

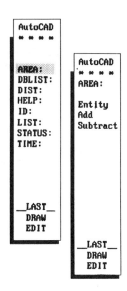

POINT METHOD

One method of calculating the area of an object is to simply enter points at the intersections of a polygon. The following example shows this method. Refer to Figure 16-3.

> Command: <u>AREA</u>
> First point/Entity/Add/Subtract: (*select point "1"*)
> Next point: (*select point "2"*)
> Next point: (*select point "3"*)
> Next point: (*select point "4"*)
> Next point: (*select point "5"*)

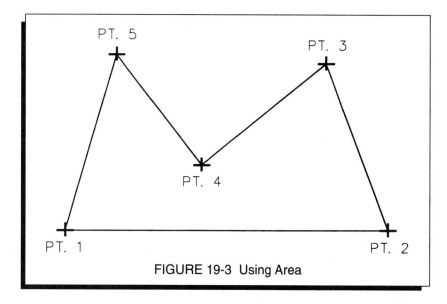

FIGURE 19-3 Using Area

Notice that the "Next point" prompt is repeated until you press Enter to tell AutoCAD that you have entered all the desired points. You do not have to "close" the polygon by entering the last point on top of the first point entered. AutoCAD will automatically close from the last point to the first point entered.

After you press Enter, you are shown the following information in the prompt area:

> Area=<calculated area>
> Perimeter=<calculated area>

ENTITY METHOD

If you select the Entity option under the Area command, you can compute the area of a circle or polyline. The following prompt appears:

> Select circle or polyline:

AutoCAD calculates each in the following manner.

Circle: Displays the area and the circumference.

Polyline: If the polyline is closed, the area and perimeter are calculated. If the polyline is open, the area and perimeter are calculated as though a line were drawn between the endpoints to close the polyline.

A wide polyline is calculated from the centerline of the polyline. An area for a polyline is valid only if the polyline can describe a closed area. In other words, you can not compute the area of a polyline of a single segment.

ADD AREAS

The Add option is used to calculate running totals of calculated areas. To use the Add option, select Add before calculating the areas. The prompt will be reissued after each calculation and AutoCAD will display the running total.

SUBTRACT

Subtract is used to subtract an area from the running total. Select Subtract before selecting the area(s) to be subtracted from the total.

ENTER

Pressing only Enter will exit the Area command.

AREA EXERCISES

1. Draw two boxes on the screen. Use the Area command to figure the area of one of the boxes. Be sure to use object snap INTersection to precisely capture the intersections of the box. Repeat the same procedure on the second box. Add the areas together to obtain the area total.

2. Use the Area command again to obtain the area of the first box. This time, use the Add option to add the area of the second box. Did the two areas add up to the same area you computed before?

3. Start the drawing named "AREA" from the work disk. Compute the area of each object and write down the figures.

Electronic Work Disk Problem

FILE UTILITIES

At times, you may have need to perform DOS functions while in your drawing. For example, you may want to list the directory of your disk. AutoCAD allows you to do this and other functions without having to exit your drawing by using the Files command.

The Files command allows you to:

1. Check your drawing files.
2. List any specified files on any disk.
3. Delete files from any disk.
4. Rename files on any disk.
5. Copy files.
6. Unlock files.

The Shell and Sh commands can also be used for DOS operations while in a current drawing. Shell and Sh commands are covered later in this chapter.

To use the Files facility, enter:

Command: FILES

AutoCAD displays a **File Utilities** dialogue box.

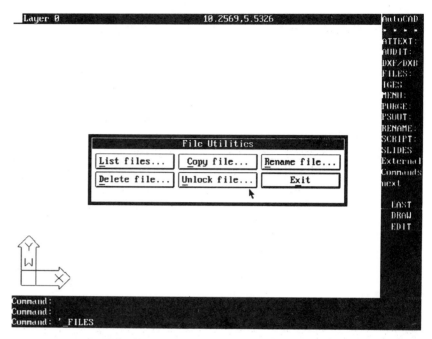

FIGURE 19-4 File Utilities Dialogue Box

Selecting any of the buttons causes AutoCAD to display a subdialogue box with a listbox containing file names. The following figure shows the **File List** subdialogue box.

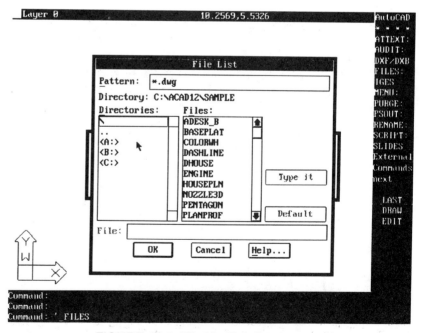

FIGURE 19-5 File List Subdialogue Box

Select the file name on which you wish to perform the operation.

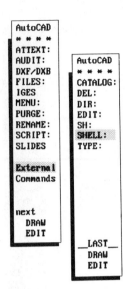

USING THE DOS SHELL

The Shell command allows you to perform normal DOS functions while still active in AutoCAD. To invoke the Shell command, enter:

    Command: SHELL
    DOS Command:

You can now issue a DOS command in the normal manner. After the DOS function is completed, you will be returned to AutoCAD.

If you wish to enter multiple DOS commands, enter a null response (press Enter) at the prompt "DOS command:". AutoCAD responds with the following message:

    Type EXIT to return to AutoCAD

then displays the DOS version's opening lines and the DOS prompt, (followed by two "prompts" instead of one):

    C>>

You may now enter as many DOS commands as you wish. When you are finished, you may return to AutoCAD by typing Exit. On some single-screen systems, you will be returned to the text screen. Pressing the F1 function key will return the drawing screen.

> **WARNINGS: Do not delete files with extension types of .AC, AC, or .$A. These are temporary files used by AutoCAD while a drawing is in progress. Do not delete files with file extensions matching ??K. These are lock files and should not be deleted.**
>
> **Do not use the /F option in Chkdsk. Using Chkdsk will display apparent errors while in the Shell utility. Attempting to correct these apparent errors will cause file damage.**
>
> **Do not run programs that reset the serial I/O ports on the computer. If you are not sure, play safe.**

SH COMMAND

The Sh command is used when there is not sufficient memory to execute the Shell command.

Sh uses less memory than the Shell command. The Sh command, however, can only execute internal commands such as Dir, Copy, and Type.

DOS SHELL EXERCISES

1. Let's use the operating shell commands to perform some DOS operations. If you are not familiar with DOS commands, you may want to review Chapter 5.

   Start a new drawing named "SHELLS". Enter the Sh command. You will see the prompt:

       DOS command:

   Respond to the prompt with "Dir". You will see a directory listing of the files in the current directory.

   Notice that after the directory listing is completed, the normal AutoCAD prompt returns.

2. Enter the Shell command. The prompt will say:

DOS command:

Press the Enter key again. AutoCAD will display the message:

Type EXIT to return to AutoCAD.

You will see a DOS "prompt", followed by a double ">>", similar to the following:

C:\ACAD>>

Enter the Dir command again. After the directory listing is complete, notice how the DOS prompt returns. You are still in the DOS shell. Type "Exit". The AutoCAD command prompt will be returned. You are now active in AutoCAD. If you are using a single-screen display system, you may have to press the F1 function key to return to the graphic drawing screen.

```
AutoCAD
* * * *
CATALOG:
DEL:
DIR:
EDIT:
SH:
SHELL:
TYPE:




__LAST__
DRAW
EDIT
```

AUTOCAD DOS COMMANDS

Certain DOS commands can be accessed straight from the command line in AutoCAD. These commands are contained in a file named ACAD.PGP. When you issue a command, AutoCAD looks for the command, and if it can not find a command by that name, it checks the ACAD.PGP file. Some of the commands included with AutoCAD include the following:

CATALOG (directory)
DIR (directory)
DEL (delete)
EDIT (Edlin)
TYPE (file listing)

The standard AutoCAD screen menu (ACAD.MNX) contains several standard operating system commands that can be invoked by simply choosing the command from the menu. These commands, as well as the Shell and Sh commands are found under the Utility/External Commands menu path.

EXTERNAL COMMANDS EXERCISES

1. Enter "Dir" at the command line. AutoCAD will respond with:

File specification:

Reply with "Dir C:\" and press Enter. You will see the directory listing of the root directory of the C-drive. Note that you did not "shell" out of AutoCAD to perform this operation.

2. Enter "Type" at the command line. AutoCAD responds with:

File to list:

Enter "ACAD.MSG". If the file named ACAD.MSG has not been deleted from the AutoCAD directory, you will see a listing of the contents of the file.

TIME COMMAND

The Time command uses the clock in your computer to keep track of time functions for each drawing. Some computers keep constant track of the date and time. This information must be entered on others at boot-up.

To obtain a listing of the time information for the current drawing, enter the Time command.

> Command: TIME

The following listing is displayed on a text screen as shown. The explanation of each follows:

Current time:	07 Aug 1990 at 07:15:50.860
Times for this drawing:	
Created:	07 May 1992 at 06:49:14.400
Last updated:	07 May 1992 at 06:49:14.400
Total editing time:	0 days 00:26:36:300
Elapsed timer (on):	0 days 00:26:36:300
Next automatic save in:	<no modifications yet>

Display/ON/OFF/Reset:

"Stopwatch" timer. You may turn this timer on or off. It is independent of the other functions.

Cumulative time spent on drawing. The Save command does not reset the time. If you exit the drawing by using Quit, the time does not count. (Printer and plotter time is not added.)

Last time the drawing was updated and saved using the Save or End command.

Date and time the current drawing was initially created. If the drawing was created using Wblock, the date of that execution is the creation time. If you edit a drawing created with a previous version of AutoCAD, the first edit time is used as the creation time.

The last line contains options for execution. The options are as follows:

Display: Redisplays the time functions with updated times.

On: Starts the "stopwatch" timer (the timer is initially on).

Off: Stops the "stopwatch" timer, freezing the display at the accumulated time.

Reset: Resets the "stopwatch" timer to zero.

If you do not wish to execute any of the options, enter a null response (Enter) or Ctrl-C (cancel).

DRAWING TIME EXERCISE

1. Use the Time command to check the current time in the drawing you are currently using.

2. Use the elapsed timer option in the Time command to time the period needed to draw a car.

WORK PROBLEMS

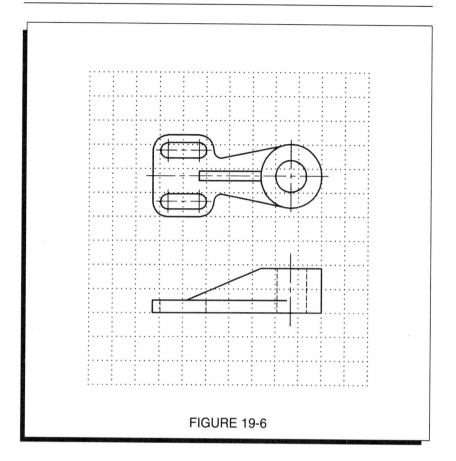

FIGURE 19-6

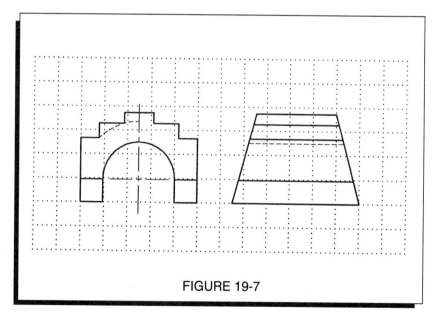

FIGURE 19-7

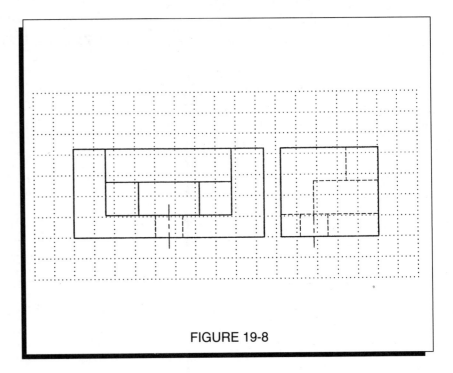

FIGURE 19-8

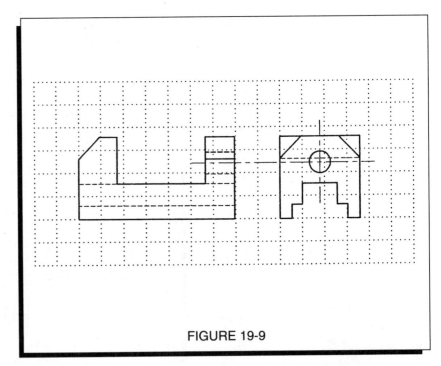

FIGURE 19-9

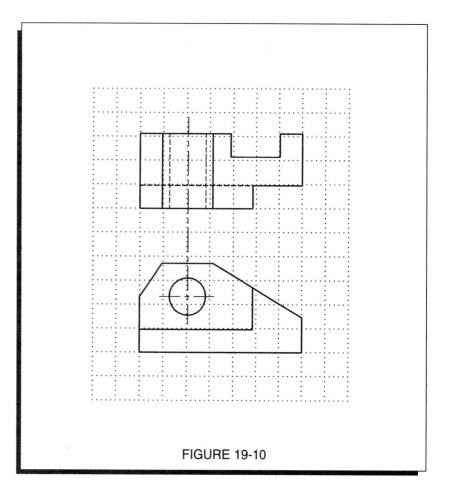

FIGURE 19-10

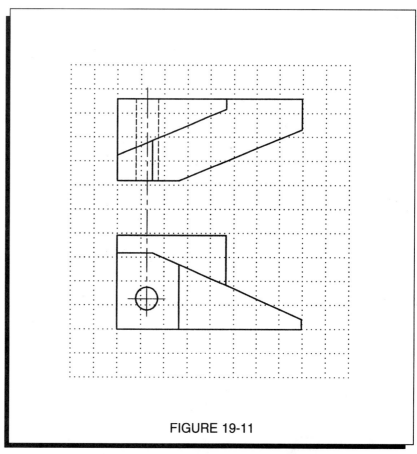

FIGURE 19-11

CHAPTER REVIEW

1. If you wanted to identify the coordinates of a specific point in a drawing, what command would you use?

   _____

2. What is displayed when you use the List command?

   _____

   _____

3. What is the difference between the List and the Dblist command?

   _____

   _____

   _____

   _____

4. How would you print the database of a drawing?

   _____

   _____

   _____

   _____

5. How can you stop the scrolling of the database when using the Dblist command?

   _____

   _____

6. What are the six distances returned by the Dist command?

   _____

   _____

   _____

   _____

   _____

7. What values are displayed when a circle is selected under the Area command?

   _____

   _____

8. What option under Area would you use if you wanted to calculate the area of a circle?

   _____

9. What are the six functions of the Files command?

_____

_____

_____

_____

_____

10. Why would you not want to delete a file with a .$AC file extension?

_____

_____

_____

11. What command allows you to access DOS for a single operation?

_____

12. What command allows you to access DOS for several operations?

_____

13. What DOS commands can be accessed from the AutoCAD command line?

_____

_____

_____

14. How would you determine the last time a drawing was updated?

_____

_____

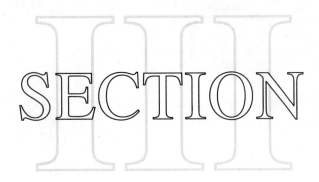

SECTION III

INTERMEDIATE AutoCAD

■ Intermediate Draw Commands
■ Isometric Drawings
■ Intermediate Edit Commands
■ Intermediate Operations

CHAPTER 20

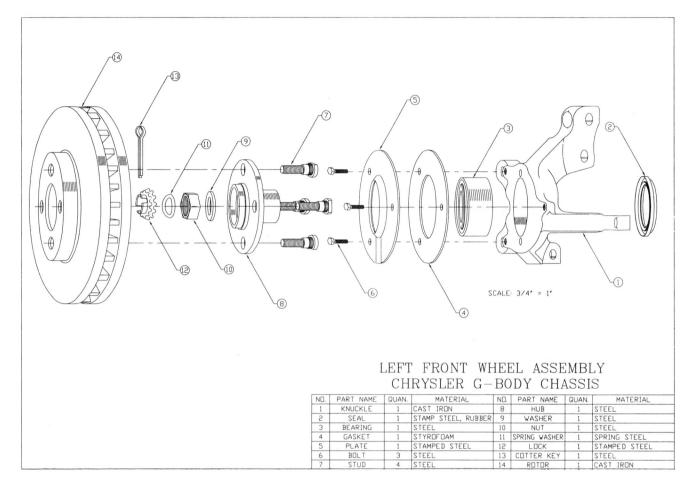

LEFT FRONT WHEEL ASSEMBLY
CHRYSLER G-BODY CHASSIS

SCALE: 3/4" = 1'

NO.	PART NAME	QUAN.	MATERIAL	NO.	PART NAME	QUAN.	MATERIAL
1	KNUCKLE	1	CAST IRON	8	HUB	1	STEEL
2	SEAL	1	STAMP STEEL, RUBBER	9	WASHER	1	STEEL
3	BEARING	1	STEEL	10	NUT	1	STEEL
4	GASKET	1	STYROFOAM	11	SPRING WASHER	1	SPRING STEEL
5	PLATE	1	STAMPED STEEL	12	LOCK	1	STAMPED STEEL
6	BOLT	3	STEEL	13	COTTER KEY	1	STEEL
7	STUD	4	STEEL	14	ROTOR	1	CAST IRON

Intermediate Draw Commands

OBJECTIVES:

After you have become proficient with the basic draw commands in AutoCAD, the next step is to master the intermediate commands. Learning the use of these commands will allow you to construct more complex drawings. Chapter 20 objectives are:

● To use commands for special objects such as ellipses and donuts.

● To construct new objects from existing ones with commands such as Offset and Minsert.

● To learn to use one of AutoCAD's most powerful features: object libraries. These are built with the Insert, Block, and Wblock commands.

DRAWING ELLIPSES

The Ellipse command is used to construct ellipses by specifying the axis endpoints, the axis center points, and the length of the axis. You may also place ellipses properly into any of the three planes of an isometric drawing.

An ellipse contains a major axis and a minor axis.

Before constructing an ellipse, let's look at the parts of an ellipse. An ellipse contains a major axis and a minor axis. The major axis consists of a line drawn along the longest direction of the ellipse. The minor axis consists of a line drawn along the shortest direction of the ellipse. The major and minor axes will intersect at the center point of the ellipse.

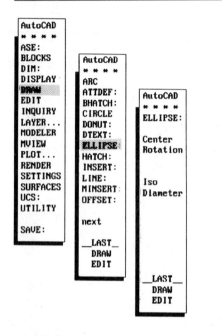

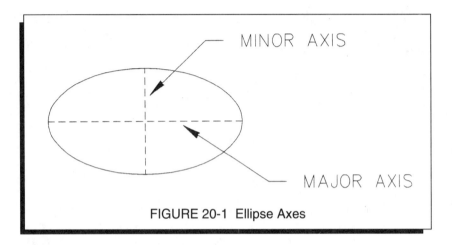

FIGURE 20-1 Ellipse Axes

You may specify these points in constructing an ellipse. Let's look at several ways to specify an ellipse.

SPECIFYING AN ELLIPSE BY AXIS AND ECCENTRICITY

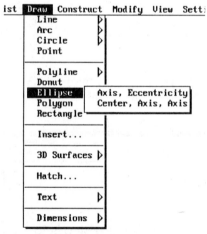

In the first example, we will construct an ellipse by showing AutoCAD the length of one axis, then the length of the other. First, enter the Ellipse command:

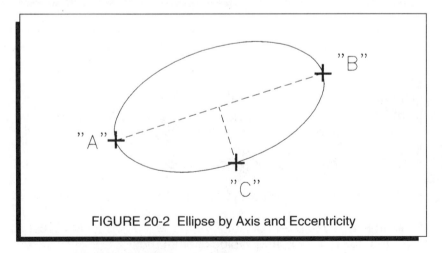

FIGURE 20-2 Ellipse by Axis and Eccentricity

Command: <u>ELLIPSE</u>
<Axis endpoint 1>/Center: (*enter point "A"*)
Axis endpoint 2: (*enter point "B"*)
<Other axis distance>/Rotation: (*enter point "C"*)

You may also specify point "C" by using a numerical distance.

The first two points entered may be either the major or minor axis. The distance specified for point "C" will determine which is the major axis. (Remember, the major axis is the longer axis.)

SPECIFYING AN ELLIPSE BY AXIS AND ROTATION

If you respond to the prompt "<Other axis distance>/Rotation:" with ROTATION (or "R"), you will be allowed to rotate the ellipse around the axis first specified. The ellipse will be considered as a circle, with the previously specified axis acting as a diameter line. The rotation will take place in the Z-plane. That is, it will be as though you rotated the circle "into" the screen. The circle may be rotated into the Z-plane at any angle from 0 to 89.4 degrees. Specifying a zero angle, however, will result in a full circle being drawn.

You may also show AutoCAD the angle by drag specification. The angle is relative to the midpoint of the ellipse.

The following illustrations show ellipses of varying rotation angles. Points "A" and "B" designate the endpoints of the major axis.

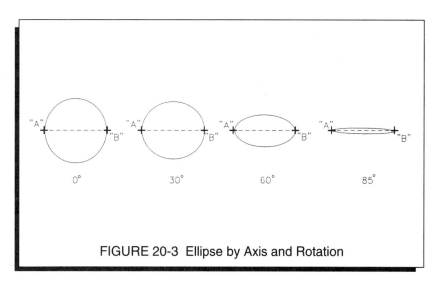

FIGURE 20-3 Ellipse by Axis and Rotation

SPECIFYING AN ELLIPSE BY CENTER AND TWO AXES

An ellipse may also be defined by specifying its center point, the end-point of one axis, and the length of the other axis.

Let's construct an ellipse by this method. Enter the Ellipse command:

```
Command: ELLIPSE
<Axis endpoint 1>/Center: C
Center of ellipse: (enter point "A")
Axis endpoint: (enter point "B")
<Other axis distance>/Rotation: (enter point "C")
```

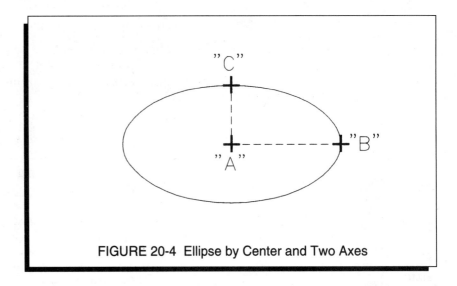

FIGURE 20-4 Ellipse by Center and Two Axes

Notice that the location of point "B" determines the angle of the ellipse. The prompt for "Axis endpoint" may be a numerical distance. This distance will be the distance from the center point, and perpendicular to the first axis specified by points "A" and "B." Note that a numerical distance represents one-half of the axis defined.

The following illustration shows the results of constructing ellipses by the center and two axes method. Note that the angle and the major axis is determined by the placement and distance of the points.

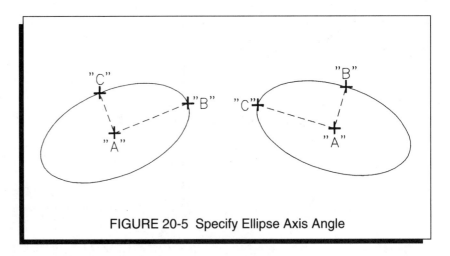

FIGURE 20-5 Specify Ellipse Axis Angle

You may also choose the "Rotation" option when constructing an ellipse using the center method. The following illustrations show the effects of this type of construction.

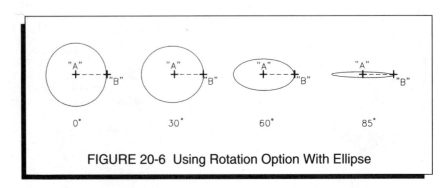

FIGURE 20-6 Using Rotation Option With Ellipse

CONSTRUCTING ISOMETRIC CIRCLES AND ELLIPSES

The Ellipse command allows you to correctly place circles in isometric drawings. You must be in "ISO" mode and execute the Ellipse command, the following prompt is issued:

Command: <u>ELLIPSE</u>
<Axis endpoint 1>/Center/Isocircle:

Responding with "Isocircle" from the screen menu, or "I" from the keyboard allows you to draw a circle in the current isometric plane. Let's look at an example of how isocircles work. First, use AutoCAD's Isometric Snap mode to construct a cube as shown in the following illustration. Then, enter the Ellipse command:

Command: <u>ELLIPSE</u>
<Axis endpoint 1>/Center/Isocircle: <u>I</u>
Center of circle: (*enter point "A"*)
<Circle radius>/Diameter: (*enter point "B"*)

Responding with "Isocircle" from the screen menu, or "I" from the keyboard allows you to draw a circle in the current isometric plane.

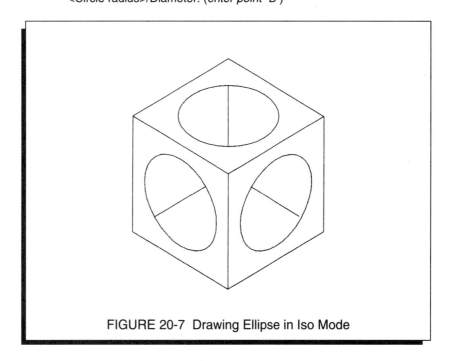

FIGURE 20-7 Drawing Ellipse in Iso Mode

You must be in the correct isometric plane to properly place an isocircle. Use Ctrl-E to toggle between the planes. (You may use this toggle while in the command without problem.) Chapter 21 covers isometric drawing in detail.

PROPERTIES OF ELLIPSES

Ellipses are constructed as polylines.

Ellipses are constructed as polylines. If you wish to edit the ellipse, use Pedit (polyline edit) and its associated commands. The commands of Trim, Extend, Offset, Break can also be used on ellipses.

EXERCISE

Let's use the Ellipse command to draw a can. Start by selecting the Ellipse command from the draw menu. Use the following illustration to draw the ellipse. Don't worry about the size.

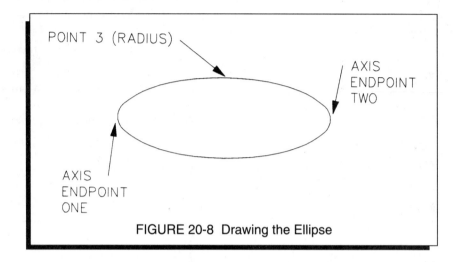

FIGURE 20-8 Drawing the Ellipse

Next, use the Copy command to copy the ellipse up to create the top of the can. Use function key F8 to turn on Ortho mode so the copy will align perfectly with the original ellipse.

Now use the Line command to draw lines between the two ellipses as shown in the following illustration. Use object snap QUADrant to capture the outer quadrant of the ellipses.

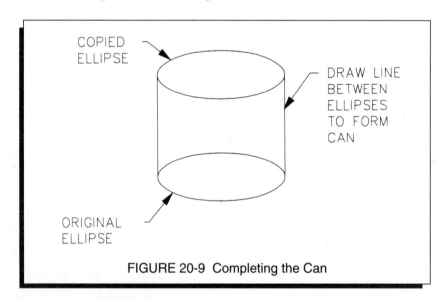

FIGURE 20-9 Completing the Can

DRAWING SOLID FILLED CIRCLES AND DONUTS

The Donut command constructs solid filled circles and donuts. The Donut command can be executed by entering either Donut or Doughnut. The following explanation uses both forms of the command.

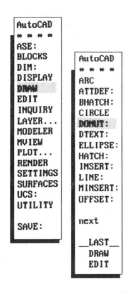

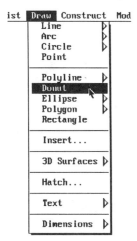

To construct a donut, you must tell AutoCAD both the inside and the outside diameters. If you wish to make a solid filled circle, specify an inside diameter of zero.

Let's first make a regular donut. Enter the Donut command:

> Command: <u>DONUT</u>
> Inside diameter <*default*>: <u>1.5</u>
> Outside diameter <*default*>: <u>3</u>
> Center of doughnut: (*pick point "A"*)
> Center of doughnut: (*ENTER*)

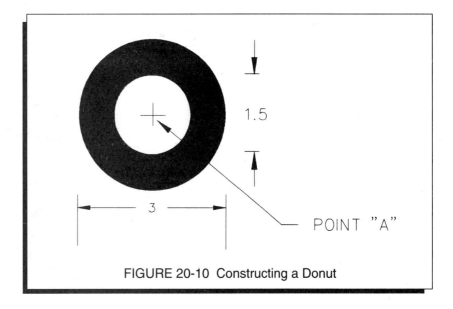

FIGURE 20-10 Constructing a Donut

Notice that the "Center of donut" prompt repeats to allow placement of several identical donuts. The default values are saved from the last values used.

Entering a value of zero (0) for the inside diameter results in a solid filled circle. Let's construct a solid filled circle using the Donut command.

> Command: <u>DONUT</u>
> Inside diameter <*default*>: <u>0</u>
> Outside diameter <*diameter*>: <u>3</u>
> Center of doughnut: (*pick point "A"*)
> Center of doughnut: (*ENTER*)

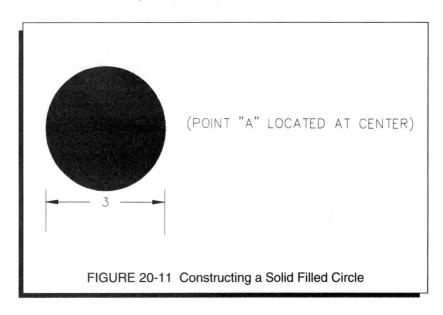

FIGURE 20-11 Constructing a Solid Filled Circle

Donuts are constructed as closed polylines using wide arc segments. To edit a donut, use the Pedit (polyline editing) or the edit functions.

The display of the solid fill in the donut is determined by the current setting of the Fill mode.

The display of the solid fill in the donut is determined by the current setting of the fill mode. If fill is on, the donut will be solid filled. If fill is off, only the outline of the donut will be displayed and plotted.

EXERCISE

Draw the bicycle as shown in Figure 20-12. Use Polylines for the frame, lines for the spokes, and donuts for the tires.

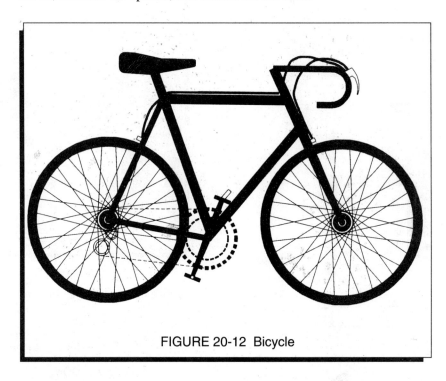

FIGURE 20-12 Bicycle

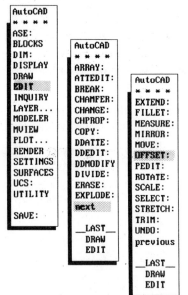

OFFSETTING ENTITIES

The Offset command allows you to construct a parallel copy to an entity or to construct a larger or smaller image of the entity through a point.

CONSTRUCTING PARALLEL OFFSETS

Let's first look at how to construct a parallel entity. First, construct a vertical line on the screen similar to the one shown in the following illustration. Now, enter the Offset command:

>   Command: <u>OFFSET</u>
>   Offset distance or Through <*default*>: <u>2</u>
>   Select object to offset: (*select the line*)
>   Side to offset? (*pick point "A"*)
>   Select object to offset: (*ENTER*)

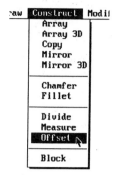

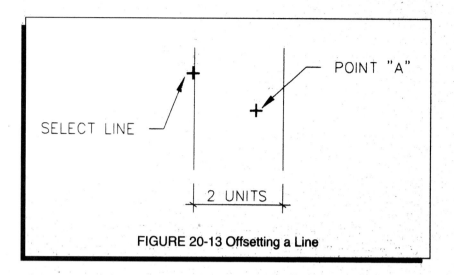

FIGURE 20-13 Offsetting a Line

The default value shown in the brackets will be either a numerical value or "Through," whichever was last chosen.

You may choose to show AutoCAD two relative points to designate the offset distance, instead of entering a numerical value.

The "Select object to offset:" prompt repeats to allow you to offset as many copies as you wish. Enter a null response (press Enter) to terminate the command.

The direction of the offset must be parallel to the Z-axis of the current user coordinate system (UCS systems are explained in Chapter 32). If it is not, AutoCAD will display the message:

> That entity is not parallel with the UCS.

The "Select object" prompt will then be repeated.

CONSTRUCTING "THROUGH" OFFSETS

The Through option allows construction of the image through a point.

The Through option allows construction of the image through a point. Let's create an offset to a circle. Draw a circle as in the following illustration. Enter the Offset command.

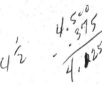

> Command: OFFSET
> Offset distance or Through <default>: T
> Select object to offset: (pick the circle)
> Through point: (pick point "A")
> Select object to offset: (ENTER)

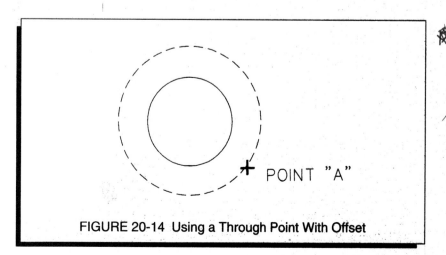

FIGURE 20-14 Using a Through Point With Offset

Tip

You may choose only one object at a time to offset. If you choose to offset a complex object, it must be one entity. Constructing objects with polylines will allow you to do this.

EXERCISE

Electronic Work Disk Problem

Let's use the Offset command to help draw a site plan. Start the drawing named "OFFSET" from the work disk. This is a drawing of a city scape. The edges of the streets are drawn with a different type of line called a polyline (polylines are covered in Chapter 24). Polylines can be joined so that each segment is "glued" to the other segments.

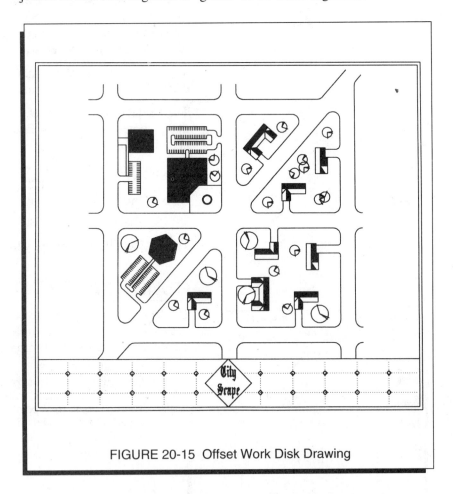

FIGURE 20-15 Offset Work Disk Drawing

Use the Offset command to offset a curb thickness (curbs are typically 6" thick). You can do this by using Offset/Through. Start by selecting the curb to be offset, then entering a relative coordinate to offset the 6". You may want to review relative coordinates in Chapter 6.

CHAMFERING LINES AND POLYLINES

The Chamfer command is used to trim segments from the ends of two lines or polylines and draw a straight line or polyline segment between them.

The amount to be trimmed may be specified by entering either a numerical value or by showing AutoCAD the distance using two points on the screen.

The distance to be trimmed from each segment may be different or the same. The two entities do not have to intersect, but should be capable of intersecting within the limits. If the limits are off, the segments should be capable of intersecting at some point.

The following example shows how the Chamfer command works. The following drawing will be used:

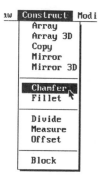

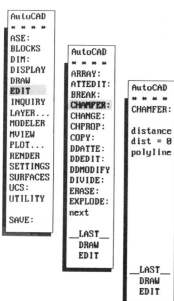

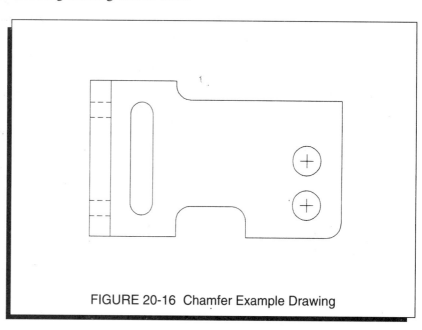

FIGURE 20-16 Chamfer Example Drawing

We will first set the Chamfer defaults:

    Command: <u>CHAMFER</u>
    Polyline/Distance/<*Select first line*>: <u>D</u>
    Enter first chamfer distance <0.0>: <u>2</u>
    Enter second chamfer distance <*default*>: <u>4</u>

You have now set the default chamfer distances. When you next enter the Chamfer command, the first line you choose will be trimmed by two units and the second by four units.

Reenter the command:

    Command: <u>CHAMFER</u>
    Polyline/Distance/<Select first line>: (*Select point 1*)
    Select second line: (*Select second line*)

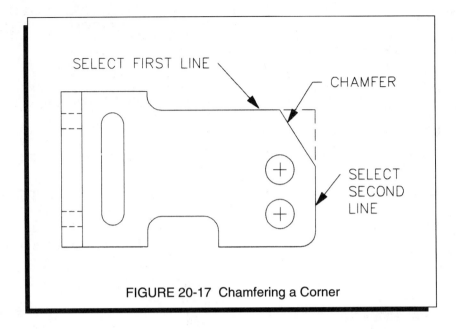

FIGURE 20-17 Chamfering a Corner

The default settings will remain until you reset them or you enter a new drawing. The initial setting is determined by the prototype drawing.

EXERCISE

Draw the object as shown on the left in the following illustration. Use the Chamfer command to edit the object so that it looks like the object on the right. Hint: You can set distances in AutoCAD by entering two points.

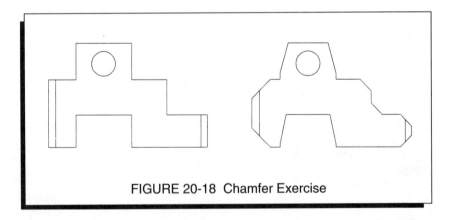

FIGURE 20-18 Chamfer Exercise

You may choose any number of sides from 3 to 1024.

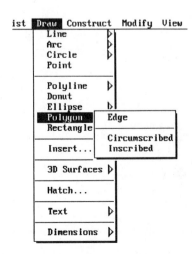

DRAWING POLYGONS

The Polygon command allows you to construct regular polygons (a closed object with all edges of equal length) with a specified number of sides. You may choose any number of sides from 3 to 1024.

There are three methods of constructing polygons: inscribed, circumscribed, and by specifying one edge of the polygon. Let's look at each method of constructing polygons.

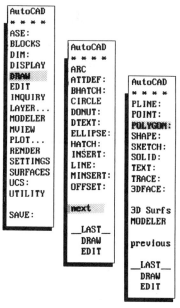

INSCRIBED POLYGONS

Inscribed polygons are constructed inside a circle of a specified radius (the circle is not drawn). The center point of the circle is first specified, followed by any point on the circumference of the circle. A vertex point of the polygon will start on the point chosen on the circumference, establishing the angle of the polygon. The following illustration shows a polygon constructed using the circumscribed method.

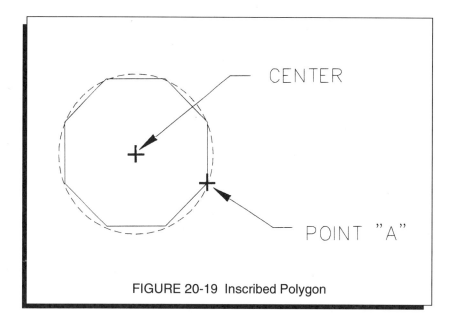

FIGURE 20-19 Inscribed Polygon

CIRCUMSCRIBED POLYGONS

Circumscribed polygons are constructed outside a circle of a specified radius. The center point of the circle is first specified, followed by any point on the circumference of the circle. The midpoint of one edge of the polygon will be placed on the point specified on the circumference, establishing the angle of the polygon. The following illustration shows a polygon constructed using the circumscribed method.

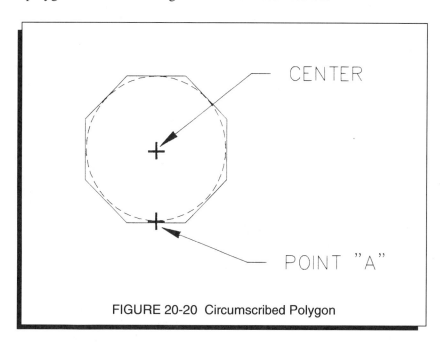

FIGURE 20-20 Circumscribed Polygon

EDGE METHOD OF CONSTRUCTING POLYGONS

You may also construct a polygon by specifying the length of one edge. Simply enter the endpoints of the edge. The angle of the two points specifies the angle of the polygon. The following illustration shows construction of a polygon using the "edge" method.

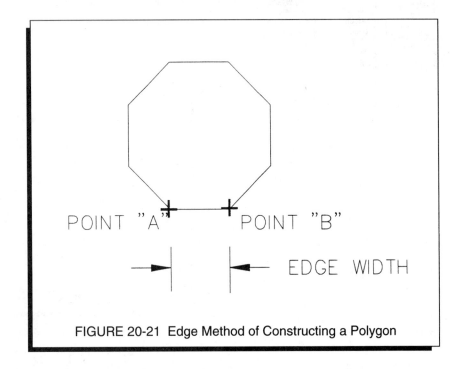

FIGURE 20-21 Edge Method of Constructing a Polygon

CONSTRUCTING POLYGONS

To construct a polygon using either the inscribed or circumscribed methods, enter the Polygon command:

    Command: POLYGON
    Number of sides: (enter number of sides)
    Edge/<Center of polygon>: C
    First endpoint of edge: (enter first edge point)
    Second endpoint of edge: (enter second edge point)

To construct a polygon using the edge method, respond to the "Edge/<Center of polygon>" prompt with "E" or choose "EDGE" from the screen menu.

    Command: POLYGON
    Number of sides: (enter number of sides)
    Edge/<Center of polygon>: E
    First endpoint of edge: (enter first edge point)
    Second endpoint of edge: (enter second edge point)

Polygons are constructed of closed polylines and may be edited using Pedit or edit commands.

EXERCISE

Use the Polygon command to draw the following object.

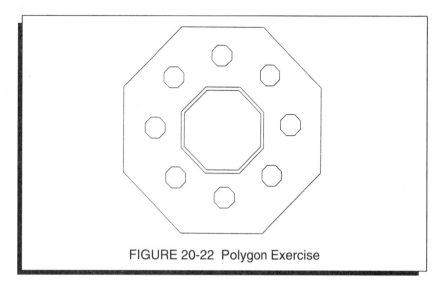

FIGURE 20-22 Polygon Exercise

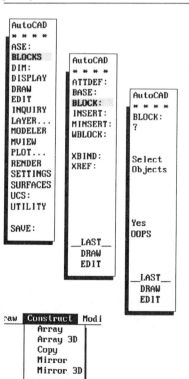

A block is considered as a single entity.

The insertion base point is the reference point for the block.

BLOCKS AND INSERTS

One of the most valuable parts of CAD drafting is the ability to library and reuse parts of drawings. AutoCAD provides commands to store such details and drawings. These commands are Block, Wblock and Insert.

The Block and WBlock commands are used to remove and store the drawing and the Insert command is used to place them in a drawing. Let's look at how to use the Block and Insert commands.

COMBINING ENTITIES INTO A BLOCK

A block is a group of entities that have been identified by a name. This grouping can be placed into a drawing. Blocks may be placed any place in the drawing, scaled, and rotated to your specifications.

A block is considered as a single entity. Because of this, you may move or erase a block as though it is a single entity.

To define a block, identify the entities on the current drawing that you wish to capture.

> Command: BLOCK
> Block name (or ?): NAME
> Insertion base point: (*ENTER*)
> Select objects: (*SELECT*)

The block name does not need a drive specifier since the block reference is stored with the drawing.

The insertion base point is the reference point for the block. The block will be placed into the drawing in reference to this point. To specify the base point, enter the point on the screen in the desired location.

Use the object selection process to identify the objects that make up the block.

After you capture the block, AutoCAD will erase the entities that make up the block from the screen. If you wish to keep the entities, use the Oops command to restore them to the drawing.

EXERCISE

Electronic Work Disk Problem

Let's capture a block from a drawing. Start the drawing from the work disk named "OFFICE". The following illustration shows the drawing. Execute the Block command and use the following command sequence. Refer to the following figure for the points to enter.

Command: <u>BLOCK</u>
Block name (or?): <u>SDESK</u>
Insertion base point: (*select point "1"*)
Select objects: <u>W</u> (*place a window around the desk*)

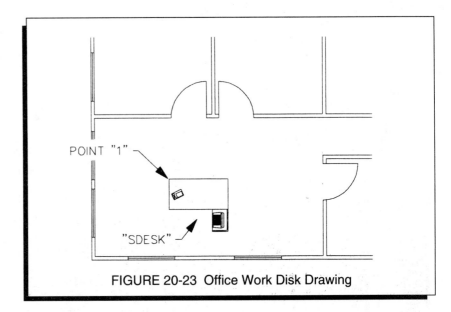

FIGURE 20-23 Office Work Disk Drawing

The block is now stored with the drawing and may be used as many times as you desire. Keep the drawing open or use End if you want to exit the exercise drawing now. We will use this drawing again for the Insert command which follows later in this chapter.

BLOCKS AND LAYERS

When inserted, a block retains its original layer definitions. That is, if an entity was originally located on a layer named "PCBOARD", it will be on that named layer when inserted. The exception is an entity which was originally on Layer 0. Entities on Layer 0 in the block are assigned to the layer on which the block is inserted.

NESTED BLOCKS

Blocks may be nested into each other. That is, you may place one block into another. Consider the following example. Each object is the same block and was inserted into another block. If you wish, you may "Block" the entire part (made up of other blocks) and have a new block which contains the original and the nested blocks together.

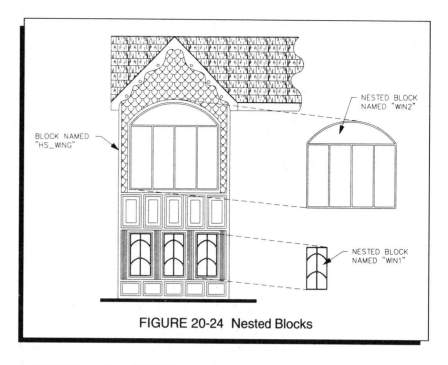

FIGURE 20-24 Nested Blocks

LISTING THE DEFINED BLOCKS

If you respond to the prompt with a "?", a listing of all the defined blocks which are associated with the drawing are displayed.

> Command: <u>BLOCK</u>
> Block name (or ?): ?

CREATING A DRAWING FILE FROM A BLOCK

The Wblock command can be used to capture a portion of a drawing and write it to the disk as a separate drawing.

To execute the WBlock command, enter:

> Command: <u>WBLOCK</u>
> File name: <u>NAME</u>
> Block name: <u>NAME</u>
> Insertion base point: (<u>SELECT</u>)
> Select Objects: (<u>SELECT</u>)

Notice that you must first have a named block. Let's suppose that you desire to save a part of a mechanical drawing and create a separate drawing on your disk that consists of those entities.

First you must designate the part of the drawing that you wish to capture. Designate this part as a block using the Block command. Let's use an example of a block named "PART-A".

Next, use the WBlock command to write the block named PART-A to the disk and call the drawing "GEAR".

> Command: <u>WBLOCK</u>
> File name: <u>GEAR</u>
> Block name: <u>PART-A</u>
> Insertion base point: (<u>SELECT</u>)
> Select Objects: (<u>SELECT</u>)

The block is now recorded to disk and has a file name of GEAR.DWG. Do not specify the file type (.dwg), since AutoCAD will attach the file extension for you.

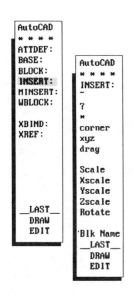

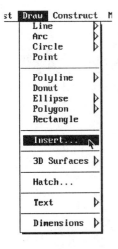

This method of storage must be used if you wish to utilize the block in other drawings. A separate drawing may be placed in any drawing, whereas one created "on the fly" as a block may only be used in the drawing in which it was created.

After you have placed the block in the drawing, the block may be used repeatedly without having the original (separate) drawing present from which the block was extracted.

A separate drawing may be used as part of any other drawing by simply inserting it with the Insert command.

INSERTING BLOCKS INTO YOUR DRAWING

The Insert command is used to place blocks or other entire drawings into your drawings. After inserting, the block becomes a part of the drawing.

To place a block or other drawing into your drawing, enter:

```
Command: INSERT
Block name (or ?): BLOCK OR DRAWING NAME
Insertion point: (ENTER)
X scale factor <<1>/Corner/XYZ: (select)
Y scale factor (default=X): (select)
Rotation angle: (ENTER)
```

Let's look at the options presented by the prompts.

INSERTION POINT

The insertion point is the reference point for the block. When you identified the base point for the block, you chose the reference point from which the block will be inserted. The block is inserted into the drawing so that the insert point and the base point of the block are the same.

SCALE FACTORS

AutoCAD automatically scales the inserted block to fit, regardless of the new drawing's limits. There are times, however, that you may want the block to be inserted at a different scale. The scale factor is a multiplier by which the block is scaled. The X and Y scales may be the same or different. The following examples show the same drawing inserted at different X and Y scales.

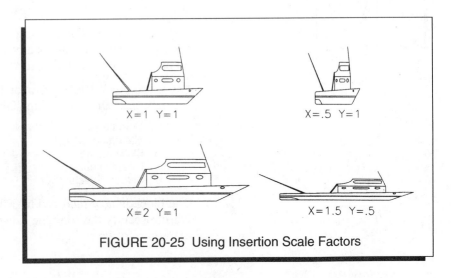

FIGURE 20-25 Using Insertion Scale Factors

NEGATIVE SCALE FACTORS

If you use negative scale factors, the drawing will be mirrored around the axis to which the negative factor is applied. The following example shows illustrations of negative scale factor combinations for each axis:

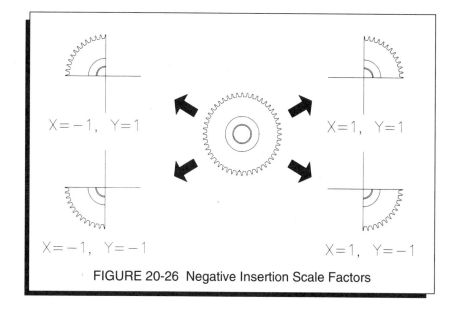

FIGURE 20-26 Negative Insertion Scale Factors

Note that the Mirror command is a more efficient manner of producing images of blocks and other entities than using negative scale factors. The Mirror command is covered in Chapter 22.

CORNER SPECIFICATION OF SCALE

You may specify the X and Y scales by responding to the scale prompt with the corners of a window. The X and Y dimensions of the window become the X and Y scales which are applied to the insert. If you enter a point in response to the prompt, AutoCAD will assume that you are showing the scale with a window. You may also enter a "C" and AutoCAD will prompt you with:

> Corner point:

You can then enter the first corner point of the window.

This method of scaling is very useful if you have a space of a certain size in which you wish to fit a block.

ROTATION ANGLE

The angle of the inserted block is specified in the current AutoCAD angle format. This angle is in reference to the original orientation of the drawn block. If you wish, you may enter a point showing the desired angle. This point will be entered immediately after you have been prompted for the insertion point. If you move the crosshairs, the point will rubberband between the previously set insertion point and the crosshair. Move the cursor until the rubberbanded line shows the desired angle and enter a point. The distance between the two points is irrelevant. The angle measured by the rubberbanded line between the insertion point and the angle point determines the angle of insertion.

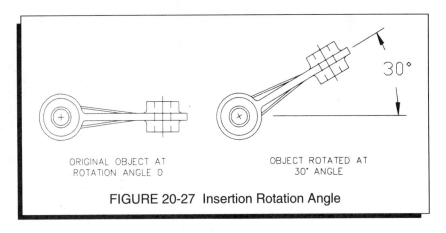

FIGURE 20-27 Insertion Rotation Angle

```
AutoCAD
* * * *
INSERT:
~
?
*
corner
xyz
drag

Scale
Xscale
Yscale
Zscale
Rotate

Blk Name
_LAST_
 DRAW
 EDIT
```

PRESET BLOCK VALUES

The rotation and scaling of a block are normally defined after the block's insertion point is specified. When using AutoCAD as a design tool, it is often desirable to "drag" the block into place at the desired scale and rotation to see the final results. By default, AutoCAD normally places the block into the drawing at a scale of 1 and a rotation of 0. Sometimes, it is helpful to drag the block at a size and/or rotation that is predetermined. To do this, first specify the block name you wish to insert. When AutoCAD prompts for the insertion point, select one of the following items to preset from the menu. Necessary information that is not preset will be prompted for after the insertion point is selected.

The following is an explanation of each menu item.

   Scale: Applies an overall (X,Y,Z) scale factor to the named block. The block is displayed at the specified scale as it is "dragged" into position.

   Xscale: Sets only the X scale factor of the block.

   Yscale: Sets only the Y scale factor of the block.

   Zscale: Sets only the Z scale factor of the block.

   Rotate: Presets the rotation angle of the block. The block is displayed at the specified rotation angle as it is "dragged" into position.

   PScale: Sets a temporary X,Y,Z scale. The block is displayed at the specified scale until the insertion point is selected, then AutoCAD prompts for the actual scale.

   PXscale: Same as Pscale, but only sets the X scale factor.

   PYscale: Same as Pscale, but only sets the Y scale factor.

   PZscale: Same as Pscale, but only sets the Z scale factor.

   PRotate: Similar to rotate. The rotation angle set is used temporarily to drag the object into the drawing area. After the insertion point is selected, AutoCAD prompts for the actual rotation angle.

WHOLE DRAWINGS AS INSERTS

You may insert an entire drawing into another drawing by using the Insert command. When you are prompted for the block name, specify the desired drawing name, including the drive specifier.

The drawing will be inserted using the 0,0 point of the original drawing as the insertion base point.

If you wish to have greater control over the insertion of the drawing, use the Base command. The Base command is executed in the drawing to be inserted before you wish to insert it into another drawing. In the drawing to be inserted, designate the Base command by entering:

> Command: <u>BASE</u>
> Base point <*default*>: (*select the point you desire for the insertion base point*)

Be sure to End the drawing to save the base point location. The point you stipulate will become the reference when you insert this drawing into another.

REDEFINING INSERTS

If you have used many inserts of the same block in a drawing, all the block duplications can be changed by "redefining" only one of the blocks. This is an especially powerful feature. Imagine being able to change one hundred drawing parts in a single operation!

There are two methods of redefining a block. If you inserted an entire drawing as a block, you may edit the original drawing. This alone will not redefine the block. You must then (while in the drawing in which the block was inserted) reissue the Block command. When you are prompted for the block name, use the

> Block name=file name

form of identification. This will force the regeneration of all instances of the inserted block and will result in your changes being incorporated in all of them!

If you defined the block "on the run" (that is, you defined a portion of your current drawing as a block), you may still redefine the block, but must use a different method.

Insert the block into the drawing using the *name method. Make the desired changes. Then re-block the edited block using the same block name. You will then be informed by AutoCAD that you already have an existing block by this name and will be asked whether or not you wish to redefine it. Respond to this prompt with Yes (Y) and press Enter. All instances of the block will be redefined (updated).

Another method of updating blocks is to use the "external reference" of specifying an insert. This method allows you to insert a separate drawing in a procedure similar to a standard insert. Instead of storing the inserted drawing in the database of the new drawing, however, an external reference to the original drawing is stored. If the original inserted drawing is changed, the changes will be loaded into the "second" drawing when it is next loaded.

External references are covered in Chapter 27.

ADVANTAGES OF BLOCKS

Using blocks in your drawings has several distinct advantages.

Libraries: Entire libraries of blocks can be built which can be used over and over again for repetitive details.

Time savings: Using blocks and nested blocks is an excellent method of building larger drawings from "pieces." (Nested blocks are blocks that are placed within each other.)

Space savings: Several repetitive blocks require less space than copies of the same entities. AutoCAD must only store information on one set of entities instead of several sets. Each instance of the block can be referred to as one entity (a Block reference). The larger the block, the greater the space savings. This can be very valuable if there are many occurrences of the block.

ATTRIBUTES

An attribute is a text record that is stored with a block.

An attribute is a text record that is stored with a block. The text can be set to be displayed or invisible. Attributes are "attached" to a block. These attributes can be loaded into database or spreadsheet programs or printed as a listing. This is useful in facilities management where there are multiple occurrences of items such as desks which may be stored as blocks and have attributes such as a person's name or telephone number associated with them.

Attributes are covered in Chapter 26.

INSERTING BLOCKS WITH A DIALOGUE BOX

You can use a dialogue box to insert blocks and drawing files into your drawing. To use a dialogue box, use the Ddinsert command.

Command: <u>DDINSERT</u>

AutoCAD displays the Insert dialogue box.

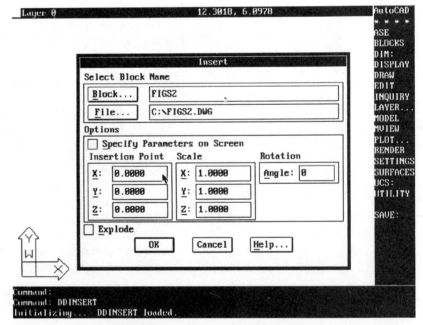

FIGURE 20-28 Insert Dialogue Box

INSERTING BLOCKS

A predefined block can be inserted in two ways. The first is click in the text box next to the "Block..." button, then enter a block name.

The second way to insert a block is to click on the "Block..." button to display a subdialogue box.

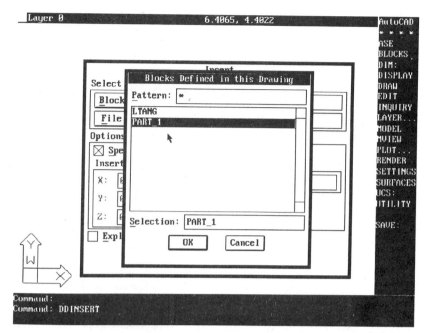

FIGURE 20-29 Defined Blocks Dialogue Box

The subdialogue box contains the names of all the predefined blocks in the drawing. Select a block, then click on the "OK" button.

INSERTING DRAWING FILES

The methods of inserting entire drawing files into your drawing are similar to inserting blocks. You can either enter a drawing name in the text box next to the "File..." button, or click on the "File..." button to display a drawing file subdialogue box.

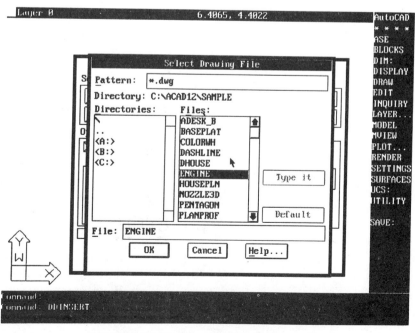

FIGURE 20-30 Drawing File Dialogue Box

You can select a drawing file from the list box displayed in the sub-dialogue box.

SETTING THE SCALE AND ROTATION

The scale factor and rotation can be "preset", or entered at the time of insertion in the traditional manner. To preset the scale factors and rotation angle, <u>deselect</u> the "Specify Parameters on Screen" check box. When the box is selected, the factors will be selected when the block is inserted and the scale factor text boxes will be "grayed out".

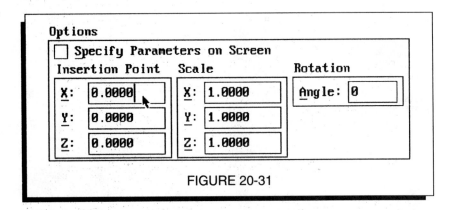

FIGURE 20-31

EXPLODING THE INSERTED ITEM

You can designate that the block or drawing file be automatically exploded. To do this, select the "Explode" check box.

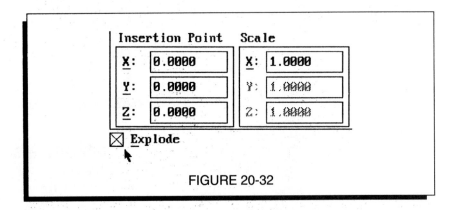

FIGURE 20-32

NOTE: You can not insert an exploded block unless the X,Y, and Z scale factors are equal and are a positive value.

EXERCISES

1. Use the work disk drawing named "OFFICE". This is the same drawing you captured a block from when we learned about the Block command earlier in this chapter. Use the Insert command to place the block "SDESK" into the drawing.

2. Use the work disk drawing named "INSERT". This is the site plan you used in the Copy exercise in Chapter 10. The landscape items have already been drawn and blocked and are contained as resident blocks in the drawing.

Use Insert/? to display the names of the blocks, then use Insert to insert the landscaping to create a design of your own.

MULTIPLE INSERTIONS

The Minsert (multiple insert) command is actually a single command that combines the Insert and Rectangular Array operations.

The sequence starts by issuing prompts in the same manner as the Insert command. You are then prompted for information to construct a rectangular Array. Let's step through the procedure.

EXERCISE

We will draw a box and perform a multiple insert containing four rows and six columns. We will use the "window" method of showing AutoCAD the column and row spacing. As you proceed, notice the similarities to the Insert and Rectangular Array commands.

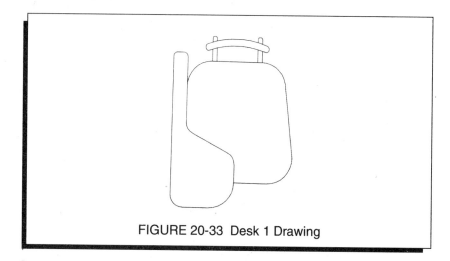

FIGURE 20-33 Desk 1 Drawing

Construct a box as shown on the illustration above. Block the box and name it "DESK1".

Now use the Minsert command:

```
Command: MINSERT
Block name (or ?) <name>: DESK1
Insertion point: (ENTER)
X scale factor <1>/Corner/XYZ: (ENTER)
Y scale factor (default=X): (ENTER)
Rotation angle <0>: (ENTER)
```

You have now placed the block "DESK1" in the drawing. (Notice, however, that you can not see it.) AutoCAD then continues and prompts:

Number of rows (---) <1>: <u>4</u>
Number of columns (|||): <u>6</u>
Unit cell or distance between rows (---): (*enter point "A"*)
Other corner: (*enter point "B"*)

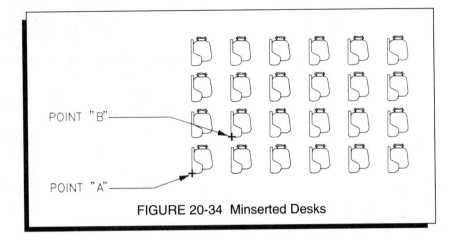

FIGURE 20-34 Minserted Desks

(Notice the notations in the rows and columns prompts that make it easy to remember which way rows and columns operate.)

MINSERT OPERATIONS

The Minsert command produces entire arrays that have many of the same properties as blocks, with some exceptions. The following qualities apply to Minserts:

1. The entire array reacts to editing commands as if it were one block. You may not edit each individual item. If you select any one object to move or copy, for instance, the entire array will be affected.

2. You may not use the "*" method of inserting blocks with individual entities.

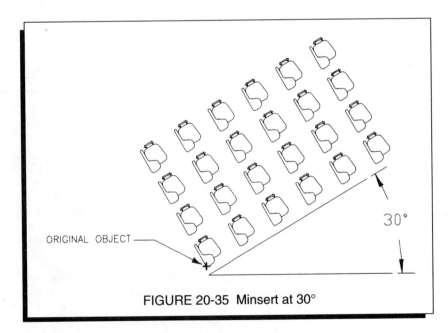

FIGURE 20-35 Minsert at 30°

3. You cannot "explode" the block into individual entities. (The Explode command is covered in Chapter 22.)

4. If the initial block is inserted with a rotation, the entire array will be rotated around the insertion point of the initial block. This creates an array in which the original object appears to have been inserted at a standard zero angle, then the entire array rotated. The following illustration shows the block inserted at a 30 degree angle using the Minsert command, with four rows and six columns.

USING MINSERT

If you wish to create a true horizontal and vertical array in which the objects are themselves rotated, block the original object in its desired rotation, or use the Insert and Array commands separately.

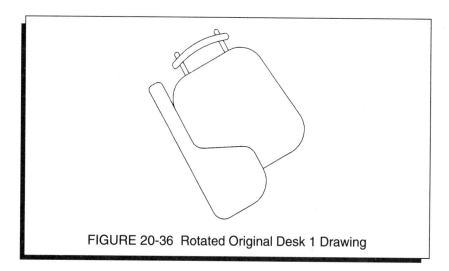

FIGURE 20-36 Rotated Original Desk 1 Drawing

The Minsert command can be used to save steps if you intend to array an inserted block by combining two command functions into one command.

Create arrays using the Minsert command if you may need to edit the array as a whole later. For example, a seating arrangement consisting of several rows of chairs may need to be moved around in a space for design purposes. Creating the arrangement by using the Minsert command would allow you to move and rotate the seating as a whole.

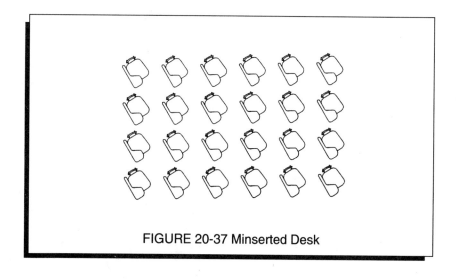

FIGURE 20-37 Minserted Desk

CHAPTER EXERCISES

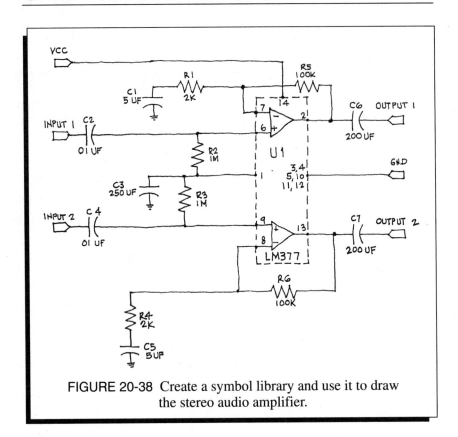

FIGURE 20-38 Create a symbol library and use it to draw
the stereo audio amplifier.

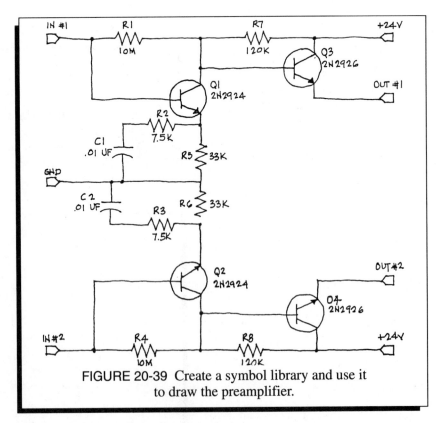

FIGURE 20-39 Create a symbol library and use it
to draw the preamplifier.

CHAPTER REVIEW

1. What are the two axes of an ellipse?

   _____

   _____

2. How would you draw an isometric circle?

   _____

   _____

   _____

3. What type of entity are ellipses constructed as?

   _____

   _____

   _____

4. What type of entities are constructed with the Donut command?

   _____

   _____

5. How do you control whether the solid filled areas of donuts are displayed and plotted?

   _____

   _____

6. How many entities can be offset at one time?

   _____

7. What does the Through option of the Offset command perform?

   _____

   _____

   _____

   _____

8. Draw an example of using the Offset option of Through.

9. What does the Chamfer command perform?

   _____

   _____

   _____

10. What is the procedure for setting chamfer distances?

_____

_____

11. The Polygon command constructs polygons of a specified number of sides. What is the minimum number of sides?

_____

The maximum?

_____

12. What is a Block?

_____

_____

_____

_____

13. What is the insertion base point of a block?

_____

_____

14. When placed into a drawing, how does a block handle its layer definitions?

_____

_____

_____

_____

15. What is a nested block?

_____

_____

_____

16. How would you create a separate drawing file from an existing block?

_____

_____

17. How do you place a block into a drawing?

_____

_____

_____

18. Can you place a block into another drawing?

_____

_____

19. When you place a block into the drawing, what is the insertion point?

_____

_____

20. Can you place one AutoCAD drawing into another AutoCAD drawing?

_____

21. Name two advantages of using blocks.

_____

_____

_____

_____

22. What commands are combined to create the Minsert command?

_____

_____

_____

CHAPTER 21

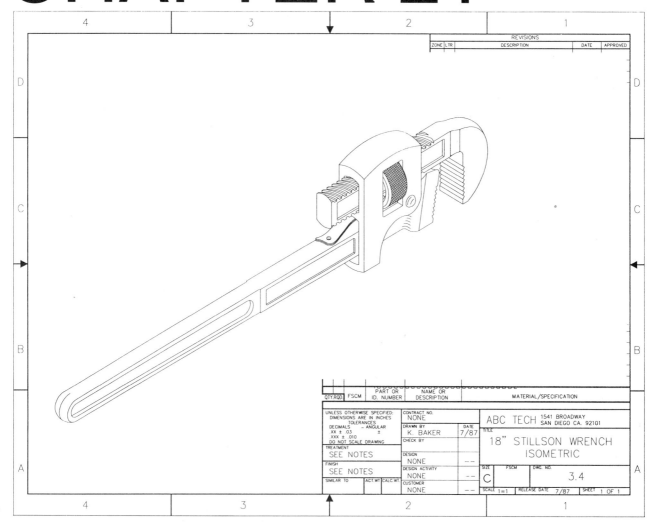

	PART OR	NAME OR		
QTY.RQD	FSCM	ID. NUMBER	DESCRIPTION	MATERIAL/SPECIFICATION

REVISIONS				
ZONE	LTR	DESCRIPTION	DATE	APPROVED

UNLESS OTHERWISE SPECIFIED:
DIMENSIONS ARE IN INCHES
TOLERANCES
DECIMALS – ANGULAR
XX ± .03 ±
.XXX ± .010
DO NOT SCALE DRAWING

TREATMENT
SEE NOTES

FINISH
SEE NOTES

SIMILAR TO

CONTRACT NO.
NONE

DRAWN BY
K. BAKER

CHECK BY

DESIGN
NONE

DESIGN ACTIVITY
NONE

CUSTOMER
NONE

DATE 7/87

ABC TECH 1541 BROADWAY
SAN DIEGO CA. 92101

TITLE
18" STILLSON WRENCH
ISOMETRIC

SIZE C   FSCM   DWG. NO. 3.4

SCALE 1=1   RELEASE DATE 7/87   SHEET 1 OF 1

Isometric Drawings

OBJECTIVES:

One of the standards in the drawing professions is the isometric drawing. This chapter covers the methodology of constructing isometric drawings with AutoCAD. Chapter 21 objectives are:

● To learn to recognize the three basic types of pictorial drawings.

● To learn the aspects of isometric drawing.

● To become proficient with the isometric drawing commands in AutoCAD. This is achieved by example and by tutorial.

ISOMETRIC DRAWINGS

AutoCAD provides a mode for drawing isometric drawings. This mode uses three drawing planes which you utilize to construct your drawings. The Snap and Grid commands are used to aid in the drawing process.

There are three basic types of engineering pictorial drawings: axonometric, oblique, and perspective. Isometric drawings are one type of axonometric drawings. Figure 21-1 shows examples of each type of pictorial drawing.

There are three basic types of engineering pictorial drawings: axonometric, oblique, and perspective.

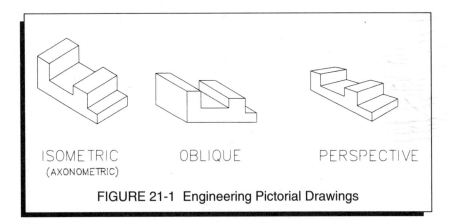

FIGURE 21-1 Engineering Pictorial Drawings

Axonometrics are mostly used for engineering drawings. Each face of the object is shown in true length, resulting in the ability to measure each length.

Oblique drawings are primarily used as quick design drawings, since the front face is shown in plane, and the sides are drawn back at an angle. This makes an oblique drawing easy to construct from an elevation view of the front face.

Perspectives are the most realistic types of drawings. Perspective drawings show the object as it would appear to the eye from a specified location and distance.

Perspectives are the most realistic types of drawings.

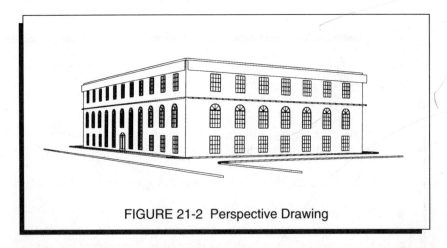

FIGURE 21-2 Perspective Drawing

This involves the use of vanishing points. (See Figure 21-2.) Although perspectives are the most realistic, most of the lengths in the drawing are not true lengths and can not be accurately measured.

PRINCIPLES OF ISOMETRICS

As mentioned earlier, isometric drawings are a type of axonometric drawing. In isometric, the lines that are used to construct a simple box are drawn at 30° from the horizontal. Figure 21-3 shows a box drawn in isometric.

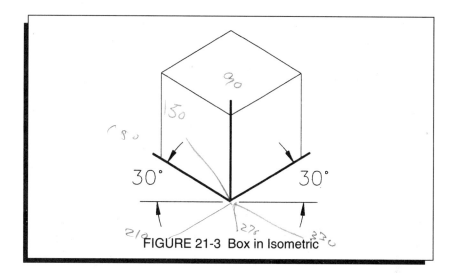

FIGURE 21-3 Box in Isometric

From this, we can derive an isometric axis as shown in Figure 21-4.

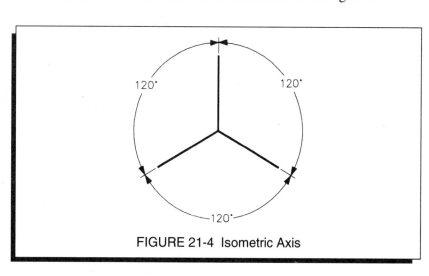

FIGURE 21-4 Isometric Axis

If we look at each of the isometric axes, we can identify a plane lying between each axis. These are referred to as isometric planes. There is a top, left, and right plane as shown in Figure 21-5.

As you draw in AutoCAD, you will be drawing in one of these three planes. Any lines that are parallel to one of the isometric axes are called isometric lines. Some objects are made up of lines that are not parallel to an axis. For example, a sloping surface will require lines to describe the slopes that are not parallel to any axis. These lines are called non-isometric lines. The endpoints of these lines, however, are derived from points determined by isometric lines.

Let's continue to learn how to create a drawing with AutoCAD's isometric capabilities.

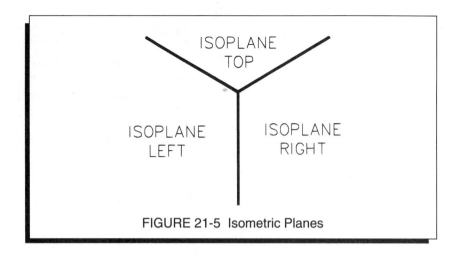

FIGURE 21-5 Isometric Planes

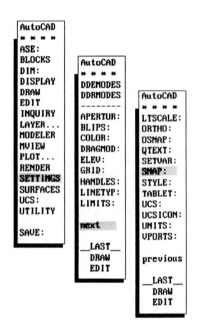

ENTERING ISOMETRIC MODE

The isometric mode is actually a Snap style. To enter isometric mode, enter the Snap menu and choose the Style option.

    Command: <u>SNAP</u>
    Snap spacing or ON/OFF / Aspect/ Rotate/Style <default>: <u>S</u>
    Standard/Isometric: <u>I</u>
    Vertical spacing <default>: (select)

You will notice that the crosshairs are displayed at angles. The particular angle depends on the current axis.

You may also use the pull-down menus to set Isometric mode. Select the Settings/Drawing Aids pull-down menu. A **Drawing Aids** dialogue box will be displayed on the screen as shown in Figure 21-6.

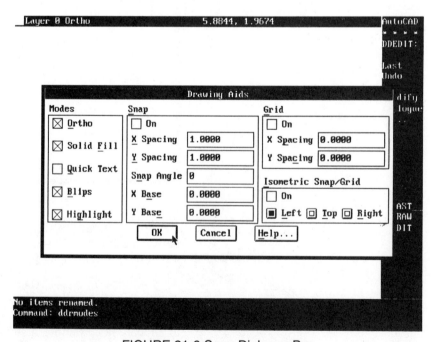

FIGURE 21-6 Snap Dialogue Box

Select the box next to Isometric to set the Isometric mode. You can also select the snap spacing and the isoplane setting from the dialogue box.

SWITCHING THE ISOPLANE

In order to draw in each axis, you must change between the axes. This is accomplished by using either the Isoplane command or by using Ctrl-E as a toggle. Let's look at how to use each.

The Isoplane command is used to toggle between the three isometric planes.

Command: <u>ISOPLANE</u>
Left/Top/Right/<*Toggle*>:

The following explains the options for the Isoplane command:

Left: Selects the left plane and uses axes defined by 90° and 150°.

Top: Selects the top plane and uses axes defined by 30° and 150°.

Right: Selects the right plane and uses axes defined by 90° and 30°.

Enter: Entering an Enter will toggle the current plane. The planes are displayed in a rotating fashion.

You may switch between the isoplanes transparently by using Ctrl-E. Each time you press Ctrl-E, the isoplane changes between the top, left, and right in a repeating order.

Figure 21-7 shows the crosshair configuration for each of the isoplane settings.

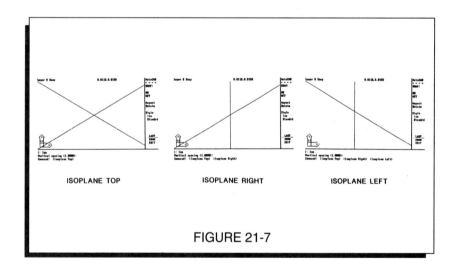

ISOPLANE TOP   ISOPLANE RIGHT   ISOPLANE LEFT

FIGURE 21-7

If you display a grid while in Isometric mode, the grid display will reflect the axis markings.

DRAWING IN ISOMETRIC

After you have set up the isometric mode, you may use AutoCAD's commands to construct and edit the drawing. An isometric drawing is constructed by first boxing in the general shape of the object. The boxing in process uses all isometric lines, creating the intersection points for nonisometric. Figure 21-8 shows the sequence for drawing an isometric object.

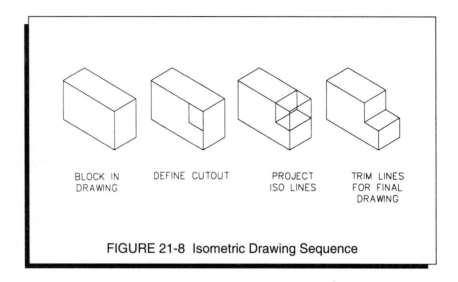

BLOCK IN DRAWING   DEFINE CUTOUT   PROJECT ISO LINES   TRIM LINES FOR FINAL DRAWING

FIGURE 21-8 Isometric Drawing Sequence

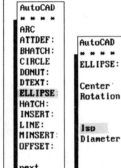

ISOMETRIC CIRCLES

Isometric circles are constructed with the Isocircle option under the Ellipse command.

Command: ELLIPSE
<Axis endpoint 1>/Center/Isocircle: I
Center of circle:
<Circle radius>/Diameter:

The isocircle will be drawn correctly for the current isoplane.

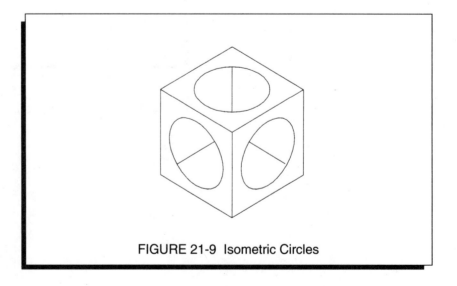

FIGURE 21-9 Isometric Circles

EXERCISE

Enter the isometric mode by selecting Snap from the Settings/Next menu. From the resulting menu, select Iso. At the prompt, enter .25 as the snap spacing.

Move the crosshairs into the screen area. Use Ctrl-E to switch the crosshairs between the three isoplanes.

Select the Ellipse command from the Draw menu. Choose the Isocircle option, then enter a point at the center of the screen. Move the crosshairs away from the center point and watch the isocircle dynamically drag into form. Use Ctrl-E to switch between the isoplanes. Note how the isocircle changes form for each isoplane.

ISOMETRIC TEXT

Text can be aligned with the isometric planes by creating text styles that align with the axes.

Text can be aligned with the isometric planes by creating text styles that align with the axes. This is achieved by creating three styles that have text rotation angles of 90°, 30°, and –30°. Figure 21-10 shows the use of three text styles used with the text rotation angles of 90°, 30°, and –30°.

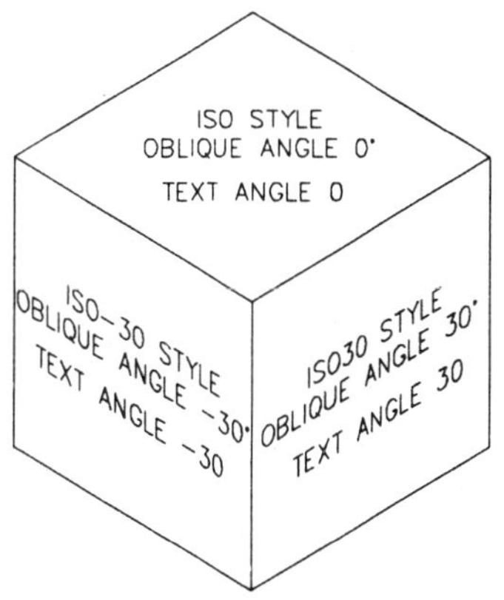

FIGURE 21-10 Isometric Text Styles

ISOMETRIC DIMENSIONING

Dimensioning an isometric object requires the dimension line, extension line, and text to sit properly in the isometric plane. To dimension an isometric drawing, the following steps are recommended.

1. Create three text styles of the desired text font and height. Set the text angle to 0°, 30°, and –30°. (You can use the same text styles for adding notes to the drawing.) You could name the style ISO, ISO30, and ISO-30 to denote the text rotation angles of 0°, 30°, and –30°, respectively.

2. Set the text style to the style that uses the proper text angle. (See Figure 21-11.)

3. Use either the aligned or vertical dimension style to place the dimension. The type selected depends on the plane in which the dimension is placed. (See Figure 21-11.)

4. Use the Oblique dimension option to change the extension lines to the proper angle. (See Figure 21-11.)

5. Use the Trotate dimension option to rotate the dimension text to the proper angle. (See Figure 21-11.)

Figure 21-11 shows the settings for each dimension placement.

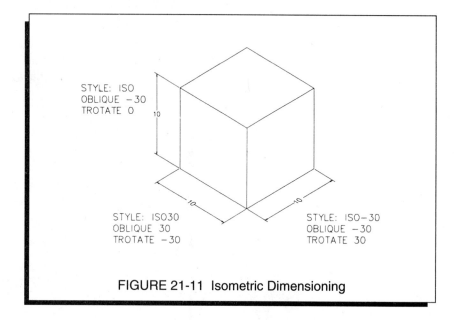

FIGURE 21-11 Isometric Dimensioning

CHAPTER EXERCISES

Draw the following isometric objects and dimension each. After you have drawn the objects, you may want to use the Color command to set different colors for each face and use the Solid command to make the faces solid.

You can make the isometric drawing process easier by setting the snap spacing to be an increment of the dimensions of the object. Also, using the Ortho mode will assist in drawing isometric lines perfectly along the isometric axes.

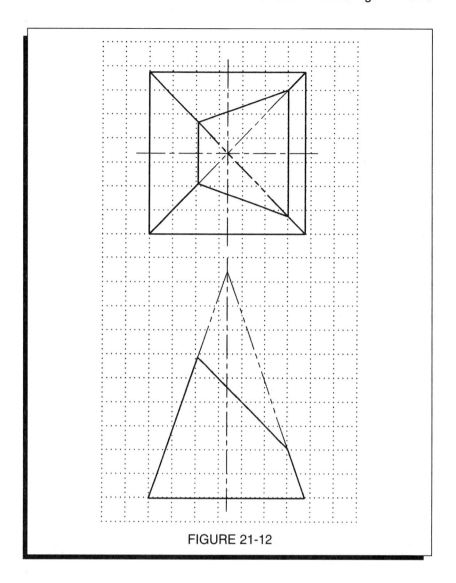

FIGURE 21-12

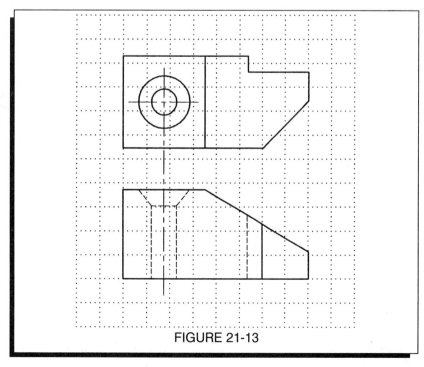

FIGURE 21-13

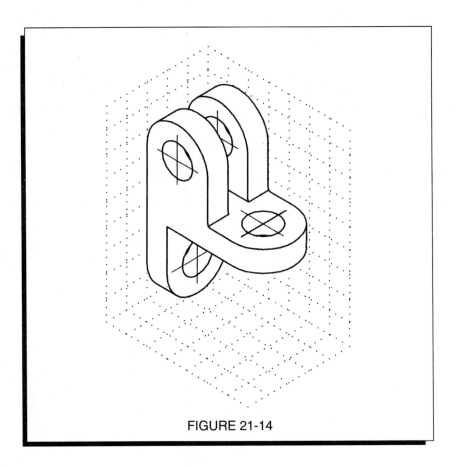

FIGURE 21-14

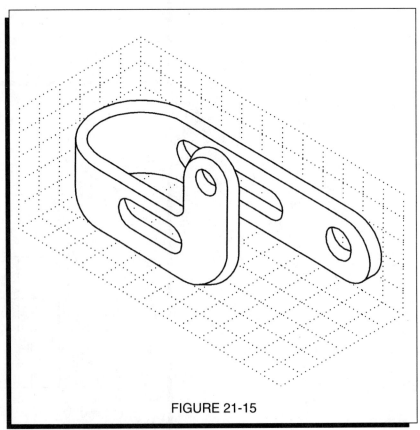

FIGURE 21-15

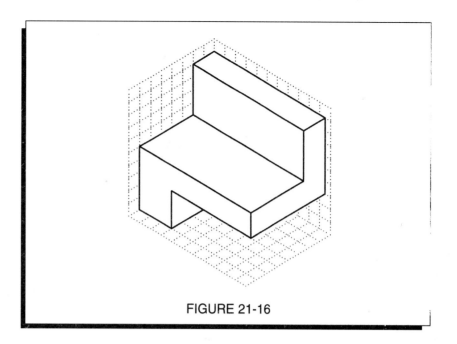

FIGURE 21-16

CHAPTER REVIEW

1. What are the three types of engineering pictorial drawings?

_____

_____

_____

2. Which type is the most realistic in appearance?

_____

3. What type of drawing is an isometric?

_____

_____

_____

4. How many axes are used in isometric drawing?

_____

_____

_____

5. How many degrees above horizontal are the isometric axes?

_____

6. What are the three isometric planes?

_____

_____

_____

7. How do you change between isometric planes in AutoCAD?

_____

8. What command is used to enter isometric mode?

_____

9. How would you set isometric mode from a pull-down menu?

_____

_____

_____

10. How would you draw a circle in isometric mode?

_____

_____

_____

_____

11. What command do you use to set up isometric text?

_____

12. What dimension commands are used to convert standard dimension components to isometric dimension components?

_____

_____

_____

_____

CHAPTER 22

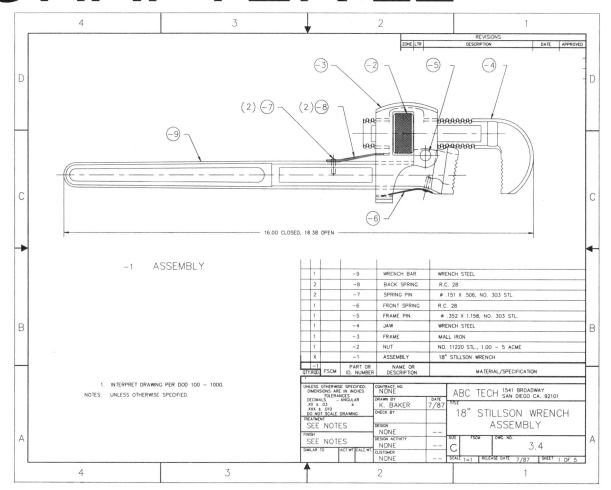

1		-9	WRENCH BAR	WRENCH STEEL
2		-8	BACK SPRING	R.C. 28
2		-7	SPRING PIN	ø .151 X .506, NO. 303 STL.
1		-6	FRONT SPRING	R.C. 28
1		-5	FRAME PIN	ø .352 X 1.158, NO. 303 STL.
1		-4	JAW	WRENCH STEEL
1		-3	FRAME	MALL IRON
1		-2	NUT	NO. 11220 STL., 1.00 – 5 ACME
X		-1	ASSEMBLY	18" STILLSON WRENCH
-1 QTY.RQD	FSCM	PART OR ID. NUMBER	NAME OR DESCRIPTION	MATERIAL/SPECIFICATION

-1   ASSEMBLY

16.00 CLOSED, 18.38 OPEN

1. INTERPRET DRAWING PER DOD 100 – 1000.
NOTES: UNLESS OTHERWISE SPECIFIED.

UNLESS OTHERWISE SPECIFIED:
DIMENSIONS ARE IN INCHES
TOLERANCES
DECIMALS   – ANGULAR
.XX ± .03   ±
.XXX ± .010
DO NOT SCALE DRAWING

TREATMENT
SEE NOTES

FINISH
SEE NOTES

SIMILAR TO   ACT.WT CALC.WT

CONTRACT NO.
NONE
DRAWN BY   DATE
K. BAKER   7/87
CHECK BY

DESIGN
NONE   – –
DESIGN ACTIVITY
NONE   – –
CUSTOMER
NONE   – –

ABC TECH 1541 BROADWAY
SAN DIEGO CA. 92101

TITLE
18" STILLSON WRENCH
ASSEMBLY

SIZE   FSCM   DWG. NO.
C   3.4

SCALE 1=1   RELEASE DATE 7/87   SHEET 1 OF 5

Intermediate Edit Commands

OBJECTIVES:

After you have become proficient with the basic edit functions in AutoCAD, you can learn more powerful edit commands. This chapter covers the intermediate edit commands. The objectives for Chapter 22 are:

● To learn how to change the properties of an existing object or objects.

● To learn how to produce multiple copies of an object or objects with the array functions.

● To edit existing objects by rotating, stretching, scaling, etc.

● To undo operations just performed with AutoCAD.

AutoCAD In The Real World

Ownership plats of the superconductor location site.

A base map of the Waxahachie area.

Mapping the Supercollider
How a large-scale GIS solution was developed using AutoCAD®

The supercollider is destined to become the next milestone in American science. The estimated $6 billion project will have a main accelerator ring of 53 miles in circumference. Two proton beams, steered and focused by superconducting magnets, will travel in opposing directions in an underground tunnel, intersecting in special chambers where scientists will study the particle collisions in detail. Energy levels are expected to be 20 times higher than ever reached before.

At a hearing conducted by the U.S. Department of Energy Site Selection Task Force to determine the environmental impacts of the SSC, landowners were able to view the system firsthand. Ken Dees, president of Datagraphics CADD Consultants of Richardson, Texas, explained how it works: "We can point at an entity, a pipeline, or a street or maybe a parcel of land, in AutoCAD and see the data associated with that entity in our database. We can point at a parcel of land, and then the owner's name, address, and phone number, maybe 100 bits and pieces of information associated with that graphic entity will come up on the screen."

To take care of all surveying and mapping concerns for the project, a Land Information System was developed with AutoCAD, a third-party geographic information system and relational database management software. Its primary function was to graphically display queries to the database of ownership and title information for 615 parcels of land located on the planned SSC ring.

In addition, AutoCAD generated a graphical map indicating where property or mineral rights had been purchased. It created a three-dimensional map indicating the appraised values of the property around the supercollider ring. It even calculated acreage affected by the SSC ring, which could be calculated to a precision exceeding 1:250,000.

Finally, AutoCAD was used to manage an inventory of rail lines, roads, power lines and pipelines so that right-of-ways could be acquired and easements could be negotiated.

The success of the superconducting supercollider project seems assured, with a portion of the funding, $225 million, recently guaranteed by the Texas legislature. Construction is set to begin this fall in Waxahachie, Texas.

Adapted with permission from an article by Ellen Adams. Excerpted from *CADENCE*, November 1989, copyright © 1989, Ariel Communications, Inc.

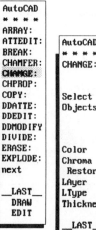

CHANGING ENTITY PROPERTIES

The Change command is used to modify existing entities.

    Command: CHANGE
    Select objects: (SELECT)
    Properties/<Change point>: (SELECT)

Enter the option desired. Notice the capitalized letters that denote the abbreviation that may be entered. If you are using the screen menu, it is not necessary to enter the "P" when choosing to change entity properties. Just choose the desired property from the menu. Let's look at the execution of each sub-option.

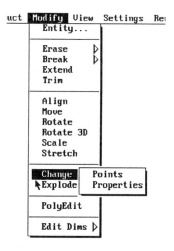

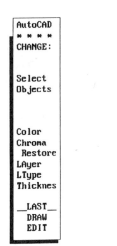

CHANGING PROPERTIES

The Change command allows changes in common entity properties. Each entity (line, circle, arc, etc.) has an associated layer on which it resides, a color, and a linetype. Let's step through the options in the Change command under the Properties sub-option. Choose Change from the Edit menu:

Command: <u>CHANGE</u>
Select objects: (*select entities to change*)
Properties/<Change point>: <u>P</u>
Change what property (Color/LAyer/ LType?/Thickness) ?

Following is an explanation of each option.

Color: Changes the color for the selected entity. You will be prompted:

New Color <current color>:

You may enter a color number, or choose a color name from the screen menu. If you have chosen entities of more than one color, the default will be:

New color <varies>:

If you wish the entity to be the color that is assigned to the layer on which it resides, enter "BYLAYER" in response to the prompt. If the object will be placed into a block and you wish it to inherit the color of the block, enter "BYBLOCK" in response to the prompt.

LAyer: Changes the layer on which the entity resides. The prompt is:

New layer <current>:

LType: Changes the linetype of the chosen entity or entities. The prompt is:

New linetype <current>:

You may only change the linetype of a line, arc, circle, or poly-line. All other entities are drawn in the continuous linetype.

Thickness: Changes the 3-D thickness of the chosen entity or entities. The prompt is:

New thickness <current>:

CHANGING PROPERTIES WITH A DIALOGUE BOX

If you wish to use a dialogue box to change entity properties, select the Change command from the Modify pull-down menu. Next, select Properties from the sub-menu.

AutoCAD will prompt:

Select objects:

Select the objects you wish to change and the following dialogue box will be displayed.

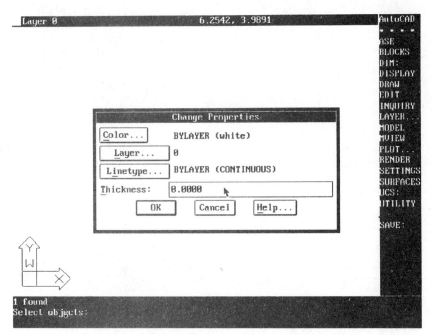

FIGURE 22-1 Change Properties Dialogue Box

Let's look at each part of the dialogue box.

CHANGING THE COLOR

You can change the selected entities' color by selecting the "Color..." button. A color selection subdialogue box is displayed.

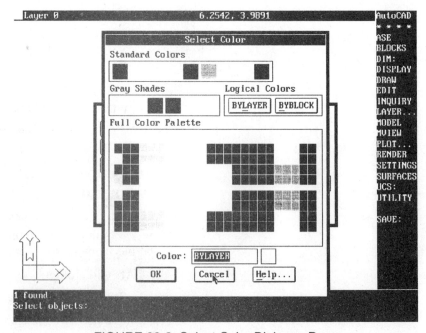

FIGURE 22-2 Select Color Dialogue Box

Select the desired color from the palette.

You can also set the color of the selected entities to be set to the layer color. Selecting the "BYLAYER" check box will set the selected entity color to the layer color.

CHANGING THE LAYER

To change the layer on which the selected entities reside, select the
"Layer..." button. The following subdialogue box is displayed.

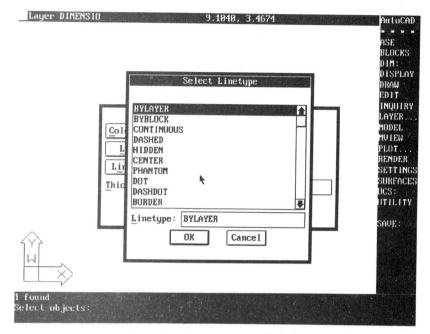

FIGURE 22-3 Select Layer Dialogue Box

To change the entities to a new layer, select the layer name from the
listing in the subdialogue box, then click on the OK button.

CHANGING THE LINETYPE

The linetype of the selected entities can be changed by selecting the
"Linetype..." button. The following subdialogue box is displayed.

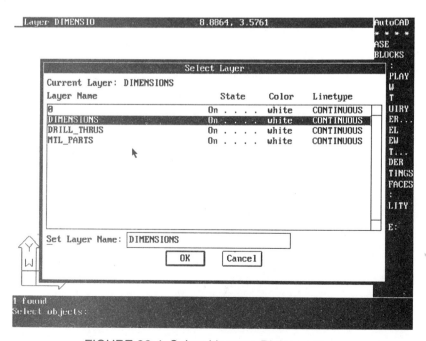

FIGURE 22-4 Select Linetype Dialogue Box

The subdialogue box displays the linetypes that have been loaded. Select the linetype that you desire and click on the OK button. If the linetype you want is not displayed, it must first be loaded with the Linetype command.

CHANGING THE ENTITY THICKNESS

The thickness of the selected entities can be changed in the "Thickness:" text box. Thickness settings are mostly used in 3-D drawings. To set the thickness, click in the box and enter the numerical value for the thickness.

CHANGING ENTITY POINTS

You can change the properties of existing lines, circles, text, attribute definitions, and inserted blocks by responding to the Change Point prompt with a new point. The effect is different on each entity.

The following describes the change for each:

> **Line:** The nearest endpoint of the line is changed to the change point. The line length will be modified if necessary.

Tip

Use the Change command to "grow" lines longer.

The following illustration shows an example of line modification using the Change command.

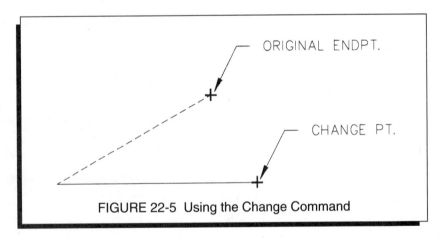

FIGURE 22-5 Using the Change Command

> **Circle:** The change point becomes a point on the circumference of the circle. The radius is changed accordingly. Thus, the distance from the original center of the circle to the change point becomes the new radius.

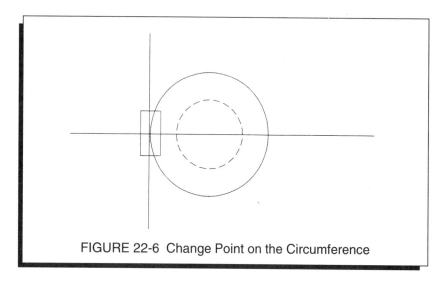

FIGURE 22-6 Change Point on the Circumference

Text: You may show a new text location by entering the change point at the desired point. You are then prompted for a new text style, height, rotation angle and text string.

You may leave the text string unchanged by pressing Enter when prompted for the "New text".

The height and angle of the text may be chosen by showing points relative to the change point or by entering numerical values.

If you only wish to change the text and not the location, press Enter in response to the Change Point prompt. You may then proceed to change either the text or the height or rotation angle. By using the Enter key to accept the parts of the text you do not wish to change, you may make only the desired changes.

Attribute Definition: Changes may be made in attribute definitions.

Blocks: When the Change command is used to change a block, the change point becomes the new insertion point. You are then prompted for a new rotation angle. The angle may be shown by entering a point at the desired angle from the change point.

If you do not want to relocate the insertion point, press Enter when prompted for the change point. The angle is then shown from the original insertion point (you may, of course, enter a numerical value for the angle).

CAUTION! Be sure that a block made up of several separate entities is really a block. If you select several separate entities in the object selection process and then enter a change point, you will scramble your drawing. Each entity will change separately as shown above!

CHANGING PROPERTIES WITH THE CHPROP COMMAND

If you wish to change properties (such as color, layer, etc.) of a drawing, the Chprop command is an efficient method.

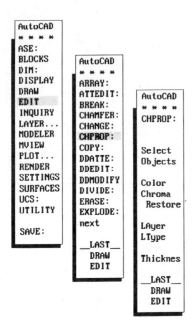

You could, of course, use the Change command to facilitate this. The Chprop command, however, functions in the same manner if you desire to only have the option to change entity properties.

The following properties may be changed with the Chprop command:

> Color of entities.
> Layer of entities.
> Linetype of entities.
> Thickness of entities.

The Chprop command dialogue is as follows:

> Command: CHPROP
> Select objects:
> Change what property (Color/LAyer/LType/ Thickness):

Notice that the options provided are identical to those under the "Properties" option of the Change command, with the exception of the Elev (elevation) option. The elevation may be changed with the single Elev command.

> **Tip**
>
> The Chprop command is a more efficient method of changing object properties than the multi-optioned Change command.

ARRAYING OBJECTS IN THE DRAWING

There are times that multiple copies of an object or objects are desirable. Consider the number of seats in a movie theater. Or the number of parking space lines in a shopping center parking lot. If you were using traditional drafting techniques, you would have to draw each one separately. AutoCAD uses the Array command to draw repeated objects.

The Array command is used to make multiple copies of one or more objects in rectangular or circular patterns.

The Array command is used to make multiple copies of one or more objects in rectangular or circular patterns. After you have arrayed the object, each one may be edited separately.

CONSTRUCTING RECTANGULAR ARRAYS

Let's first look at rectangular arrays. Rectangular arrays copy an object in a rectangular pattern that is made up of rows and columns.

The following example shows a rectangular array and identifies the parts which are defined as rows and columns:

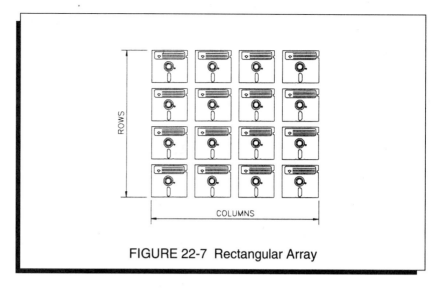

FIGURE 22-7 Rectangular Array

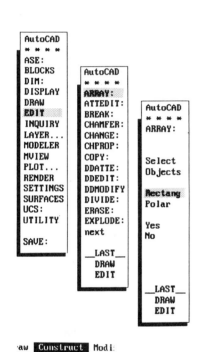

The first item of a rectangular array must occupy the most lower and left position. This is the object that will be identified as the selected object in the standard object selection process (notice how this process keeps showing up?).

Before invoking the Array command, this object must already be in existence. After you have this object in place, enter:

    Command: ARRAY
    Select objects:
    Rectangular or Polar array (R/P): R
    Number of rows (---):
    Number of columns (|||):
    Unit cell distance between rows (---):
    Unit cell distance between columns (|||):

The number of objects in the rows and columns should include the identified item(s).

The unit cell distances are "center to center". Many new CAD users make the mistake of thinking the unit cell distance is the distance between the items. It is not. The unit cell distance may be thought of as the distance from the center of one item to the center of the next item.

The unit cell distance is defined in the current drawing units. The distance between the items in the columns can be different from the distance between the items in the rows.

RECTANGULAR ARRAY EXERCISE

Let's try a rectangular array. Start a new drawing called "ARRAY". Set limits of 0,0 and 12,8. As an aid, display a grid with a value of one.

Draw a circle with the center point located at 1,1 and a radius of one.

Execute the Array command:

    Command: ARRAY
    Select objects: L
    Rectangular or Polar array (R/P): R
    Number of rows (---): 3
    Number of columns (|||): 5
    Unit cell or distance between rows (---): 2
    Unit cell distance between columns (|||): 2

Your array should look like the following illustration:

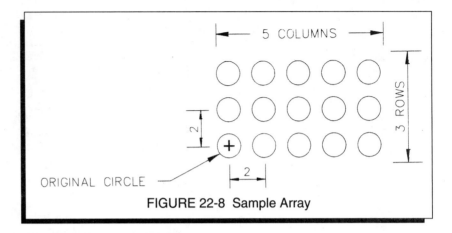

FIGURE 22-8 Sample Array

You may also use a window to specify the distances between the items. Simply enter a point when prompted for the first unit cell distance and enter a second point to define a window. The X and Y distances will be measured by AutoCAD and used as the values. The following illustration shows this method of distance definition:

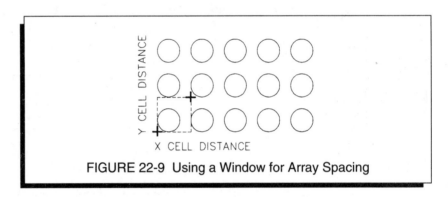

FIGURE 22-9 Using a Window for Array Spacing

Tip

Set your first point on the selected object so you may "see" the distances that the objects will be spaced.

ROTATED RECTANGULAR ARRAYS

A rotated rectangular array may be constructed by changing the Snap rotation angle. For example, if the snap angle is set to 30 degrees, the rectangular array will be rotated as a whole to a 30-degree angle.

CONSTRUCTING POLAR ARRAYS

Polar arrays are used to array objects in a circular pattern.

To construct a polar array, you must define the angle between the items (again, from center to center, not actually between) and either the number of items or degrees to fill.

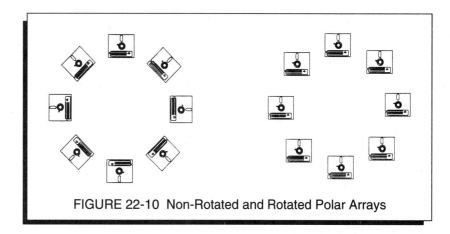

FIGURE 22-10 Non-Rotated and Rotated Polar Arrays

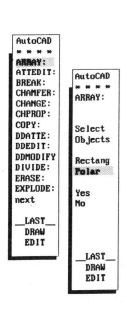

POLAR ARRAY EXERCISE

Let's start another drawing called "PARRAY" (for polar array). Set limits of 0,0 and 12,8. Place a square with sides that are one unit each.

Execute the Array command:

>   Command: ARRAY
>   Select objects: (SELECT)
>   Rectangular or Polar array(R/P): P
>   Center point of array: (ENTER)
>   Number of items: 7
>   Angle to fill (+=ccw, -=cw) <360>: 270
>   Rotate objects as they are copied? <default>: N

Your polar array should look like the one in the following illustration.

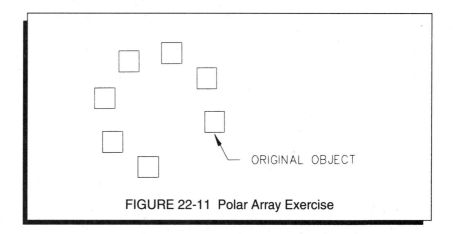

FIGURE 22-11 Polar Array Exercise

The item will be arrayed around the center point you chose.

A positive angle will cause the array to build in a counterclockwise direction; while a negative angle will cause the array to build in a clockwise direction from the selected object.

If the selected object is a circle or a block, you will be asked whether you wish the block to be rotated about the center point:

Rotate objects as they are copied <*default*>? (Y or N)

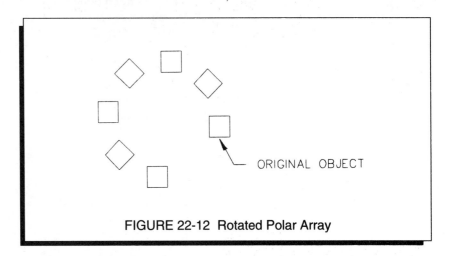

FIGURE 22-12 Rotated Polar Array

Respond with a "Y" or "N" (yes or no) to tell AutoCAD which you require. If the square you used in your circular array was a block and you responded with "Y", the block would be rotated around its base point. Other objects are rotated about specific points. The following table lists these points.

Point:	Insertion point
Circle, Arc	Center point
Block, Shape	Insertion base point
Text	Start point
Line, Trace	Nearest endpoint

TABLE 22-A

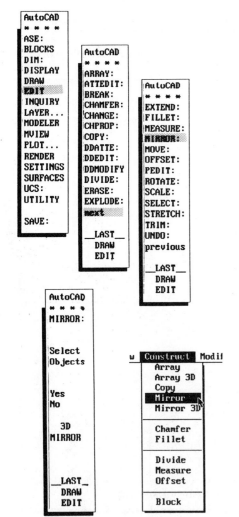

MIRRORING OBJECTS

The Mirror command is used to make a mirror image of objects. You may choose to retain or delete the original objects.

To use the Mirror command, enter:

Command: <u>MIRROR</u>
Select objects: (*SELECT*)
First point of mirror line: (*SELECT*)
Second point: (*SELECT*)
Delete old objects? <N>: <u>Y</u> or <u>N</u>

The mirror line is the line that the objects will be mirrored about.

MIRROR EXERCISE

Electronic Work Disk Problem

The following illustration shows how the Mirror command can be a great time-saver. Start the work disk drawing named "MIRROR1". Let's suppose that you are designing a house and you want to reverse the layout of the bathroom. The following drawing shows the room to be reversed.

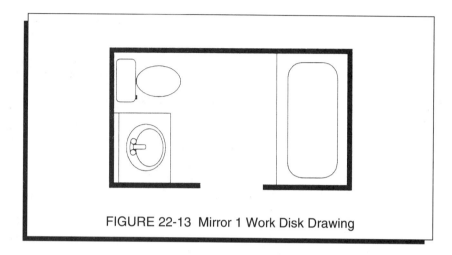

FIGURE 22-13 Mirror 1 Work Disk Drawing

Let's reverse the room:

```
Command: MIRROR
Select objects: (Select the fixtures)
First point of mirror line: (Enter point 1)
Second point: (Enter point 2)
Delete old objects? <N>: Y
```

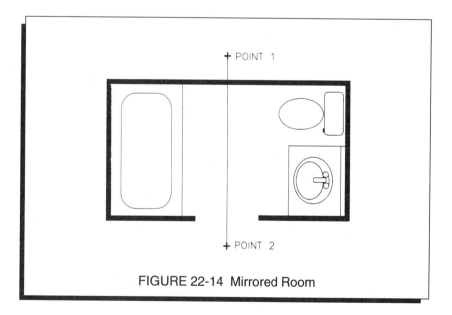

FIGURE 22-14 Mirrored Room

The mirror line may be placed at any angle in respect to the selected object.

MIRRORED TEXT

You may mirror objects with text (and attribute-associated text) without producing "backward" text in the image. This is achieved using the Mirrtext option under the Setvar (set variable) command. Enter Setvar:

    Command: SETVAR
    Variable name or ?: MIRRTEXT
    New value for MIRRTEXT <default>: 0

Setting the variable to zero produces non-mirrored text, while a variable setting of one produces a true mirror image of text.

The following illustration shows examples of text mirrored with the Mirrtext variable set to each variable.

The mirror command may be used to draw only a half or one fourth of

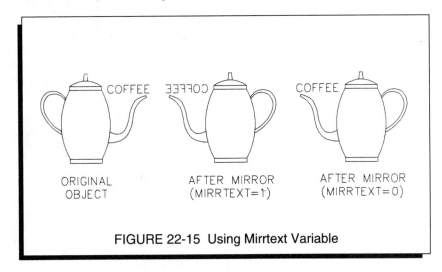

FIGURE 22-15 Using Mirrtext Variable

an object and construct the other parts by mirroring them.

DIVIDING ENTITIES

The Divide command divides an entity into an equal number of parts and places either a specified block or a point entity at the division points on the entity.

You may divide a line, arc, circle, or polyline. The crosshair pick selection process of object selection must be used to select the entity. You may not use Window, Crossing, or Last. Choosing an entity other than a line, arc, circle, or polyline will result in the message:

    Cannot divide that entity.

The current point setting will determine the type of point used at the divide points.

DIVIDE EXERCISE

Let's look at an example using a Pdmode of 34. First, draw a circle on the screen. Now, enter the Divide command:

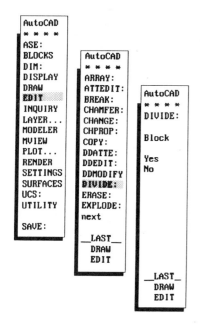

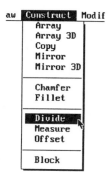

Command: <u>DIVIDE</u>
Select object to divide: (*select the circle*)
<Number of segments>/Block: <u>8</u>

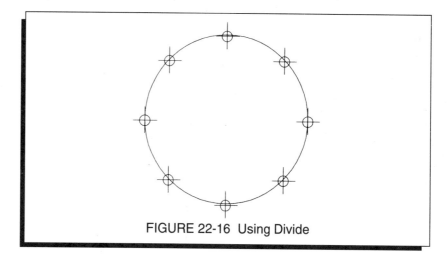

FIGURE 22-16 Using Divide

The circle should now be divided into eight equal segments as shown in the preceding illustration.

You may choose the number of divisions to be between 2 and 32767. The entity will be equally divided into the specified number of parts and a point entity will be placed at the division points.

USING BLOCKS TO DIVIDE

You may also place blocks of your own definition at the division points. The block reference must already exist in the drawing. If you are unsure whether a block reference exists, use the ? option from the Block command. Let's look at an example using a block for division markers.

DIVIDING WITH BLOCKS EXERCISE

First, draw a symbol similar to the one in the following illustration.

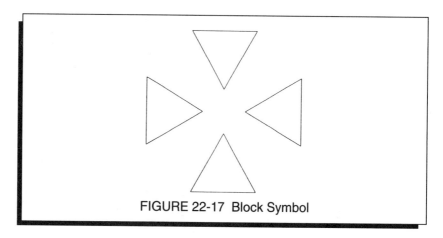

FIGURE 22-17 Block Symbol

Now, block the symbol and name it "SYMBOL1". Draw another circle on the screen. Enter the Divide command.

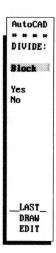

Command: <u>DIVIDE</u>
Select object to divide: (*select the circle*)
<Number of segments>/Block: <u>B</u>
Block name to insert: <u>SYMBOL1</u>
Align block with object? <Y>: <u>Y</u>
Number of segments: <u>8</u>

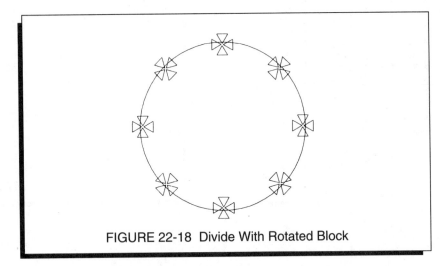

FIGURE 22-18 Divide With Rotated Block

If you respond to the "Align block with object?" prompt with "Y," the Divide command will rotate the block around its insertion point so that its horizontal lines are tangent to the object that is divided.

The following illustration shows the same procedure, except the block is not rotated:

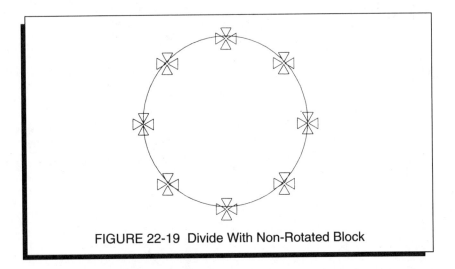

FIGURE 22-19 Divide With Non-Rotated Block

Tips

You may use the Divide command to divide an object into an equal number of parts, then snap to these points using the Node object snap.

Create custom blocks, used with the Divide command to place desired symbols at intervals along an entity.

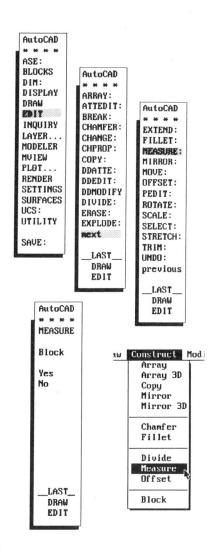

USING THE MEASURE COMMAND

The Measure command is similar to the Divide command, except that you may choose the length of segment that the points are spaced.

The rules for execution are the same as for the Divide command. You may only measure a line, arc, circle, or polyline. You must use only the single point method of object selection. The current point setting is the one used to place the point entities. If you use a block, the block reference must already exist in the drawing.

MEASURE EXERCISE

Let's perform a measure on an entity. Draw a horizontal line on the screen, 6 units in length. (A point setting of 34 is used to make the points visible.) Enter the Measure command:

> Command: MEASURE
> Select object to measure: (select the line)
> <Segment length>/Block: 1

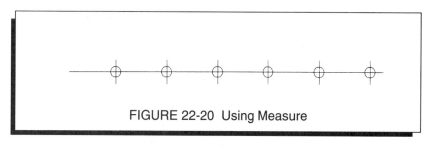

FIGURE 22-20 Using Measure

You may also show AutoCAD the segment distance by placing two points on the screen.

The measurements of lines and arcs start at the endpoint closest to the point used to select the entity.

The measurements of lines and arcs start at the endpoint closest to the point used to select the entity. The measurement of a circle starts at the angle of the center set by the current snap rotation. Measurements of polylines start at the first vertex drawn.

The Explode command breaks down the entities that make up a block.

EXPLODING BLOCKS

The Explode command breaks down the entities that make up a block. The block is replaced with the individual entities from which it was constructed. This command is similar to the *block method of inserting blocks as individual entities, except it is used after the block is inserted.

To explode a block into individual entities, enter the Explode command:

> Command: EXPLODE
> Select block reference, polyline or dimension: (select)

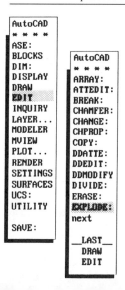

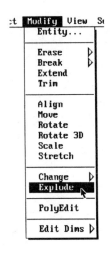

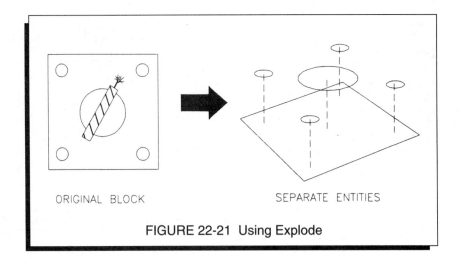

FIGURE 22-21 Using Explode

Explode breaks down the block one level at a time.

The Explode command breaks blocks into the simple entities that comprise the object. You can use Explode on polylines to break them down into simple lines and arcs. 3-D polygon meshes are replaced with 3-D faces and polyface meshes with 3-D faces, lines, and points.

Nested blocks must be exploded after the initial block is exploded. As you can see, some objects must be "exploded" several times to reduce them to the graphic primitives of lines, arcs, and circles.

The width and tangent information of polylines are discarded, and the resulting lines and arcs follow the center line of the old polyline. If the exploded polyline has segments of non-zero width or has been curve fitted, the following message appears:

> Exploding this polyline has lost (width/tangent) information.
> The UNDO command will restore it.

The new lines and arcs are placed on the same layer as the polyline and will inherit the same color.

Block attributes are deleted, but the attribute definitions from which the attributes were created will be redisplayed. The attribute values and changes made by using Attedit are discarded.

Blocks inserted with the Minsert command or with unequal X, Y, and Z scale factors may not be exploded.

If you explode a dimension, the dimension entities are placed on layer "0", with the color and linetype of each "BYBLOCK".

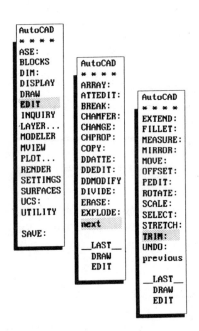

Tip

Explode standardized inserted objects into individual entities so they may be edited to suit the specific purposes for that drawing.

TRIMMING ENTITIES

The Trim command allows you to trim objects in a drawing by defining other objects as cutting edges, then specifying the part of the object to be "cut" from between them.

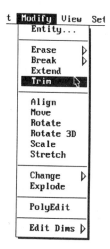

To use Trim, you must first define the object(s) to be used as the cutting edges, then the portion of the desired object to be removed. The cutting edges are defined by using the standard object selection process. The portion of the object to be trimmed must be specified by pointing to that part. Other types of object selection are not valid for this choice. Cutting edges may be lines, arcs, circles, and/or polylines. If you use a polyline with a non-zero width as a cutting edge, the center line of the polyline will be used as the point to trim to.

TRIM EXERCISE

Let's use the Trim command to trim an intersection. Draw four intersecting lines as shown in the following illustration. Now, enter the Trim command:

> Command: <u>TRIM</u>
> Select cutting edge(s)...
> Select objects: <u>W</u> (*window the four lines*)
> Select objects to trim: (*select points A,B,C, & D*)

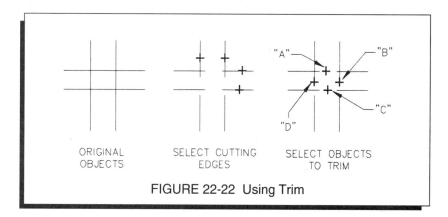

FIGURE 22-22 Using Trim

Notice that the "Select objects to trim" prompt repeats to allow multiple trimming. Entering a null response will return you to the command line.

The intersection will be trimmed and should appear as shown in the following illustration.

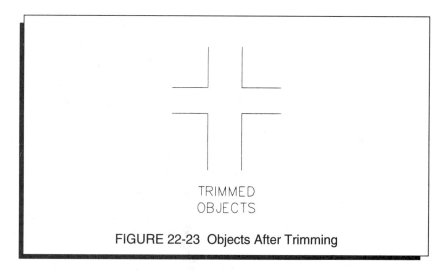

FIGURE 22-23 Objects After Trimming

Combinations of circles, arcs, and lines may be used as cutting edges. The following illustration shows how the Trim command can be used in a more complex manner.

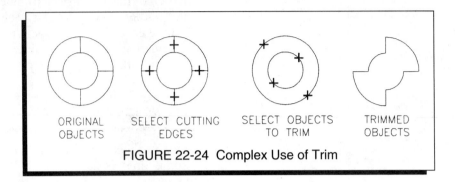

ORIGINAL OBJECTS   SELECT CUTTING EDGES   SELECT OBJECTS TO TRIM   TRIMMED OBJECTS

FIGURE 22-24 Complex Use of Trim

TRIMMING POLYLINES

Polylines are trimmed at the intersection of the center line of the polyline and the cutting edge (polylines are covered in Chapter 26). The trim is performed with a square edge. Therefore, if the cutting edge intersects a polyline of non-zero width at an angle, the square edged end may protrude beyond the cutting edge. The following illustration shows an example of such a situation.

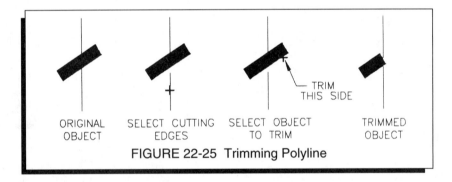

ORIGINAL OBJECT   SELECT CUTTING EDGES   SELECT OBJECT TO TRIM   TRIMMED OBJECT

TRIM THIS SIDE

FIGURE 22-25 Trimming Polyline

If you select entities that cannot serve as cutting edges, AutoCAD displays the message:

No edges selected.

If an entity is chosen that cannot be trimmed, AutoCAD displays:

Cannot TRIM this entity.

If the entity to be trimmed does not intersect a cutting edge, the following message is displayed:

Entity does not intersect an edge.

TRIMMING CIRCLES

In order to trim a circle, it must either intersect two cutting edges, or the same cutting edge twice (such as a line drawn through two points on the circumference). If the circle intersects only one cutting edge, AutoCAD displays the following message:

Circle must intersect twice.

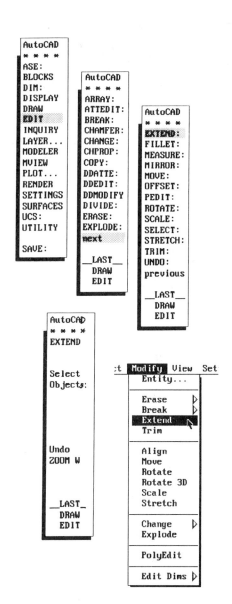

EXTENDING OBJECTS

The Extend command allows you to extend objects in a drawing to meet a boundary object. The Extend command functions very similar to the Trim command.

To use Extend, you must first specify the object(s) to be used as the boundary objects (the point to which a selected object will be extended), then the object to be extended.

You may use any type of object selection to choose the boundary objects. The selection of the object to be extended, however, must be performed by pointing to the end (or close to the end) of the part to be extended. This is the process by which you will tell AutoCAD which end of the object to extend. Let's look at an example.

EXTEND EXERCISE

Draw two vertical parallel lines and one horizontal line as shown in the following illustration. We will now extend the horizontal line to the vertical lines. Enter the Extend command.

    Command: EXTEND
    Select boundary edge(s)...
    Select objects: (*select the vertical lines & ENTER*)
    Select object to extend: (*select*)

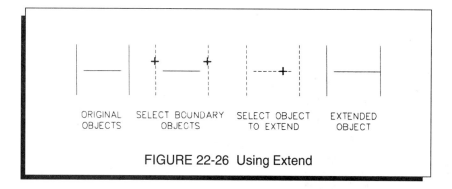

FIGURE 22-26 Using Extend

If you wish to extend the other end (remember, you chose both vertical lines as boundaries), simply respond to the repeating "Select object to extend" prompt by selecting a point at the other end of the horizontal line. Pressing the Enter key (null response) will return you to the command line.

If several boundary edges are selected, the object to be extended will be lengthened to meet the first boundary object encountered.

If several boundary edges are selected, the object to be extended will be lengthened to meet the first boundary object encountered. If none of the selected boundary objects can be met, AutoCAD displays the message:

    No edges selected.

If an object that cannot be lengthened is chosen, the following message is displayed:

    Cannot EXTEND this entity.

USING EXTEND WITH POLYLINES

Polylines are extended in much the same manner as lines and arcs. Polylines of non-zero width are extended until the center line meets the boundary object. Objects extended to a polyline used as a boundary are extended to the center line of the polyline.

Polylines of non-zero width are extended until the center line intersects the boundary. Therefore, if the wide polyline and the boundary intersect at an angle, a portion of the square end of the polyline may protrude over the boundary.

Extending tapered polylines results in a continuation of the existing taper. If the additional length causes the polyline to taper past the "zero point" and become a negative taper, the polyline stops the taper at zero. Examples of using the Extend command on tapered polylines follow.

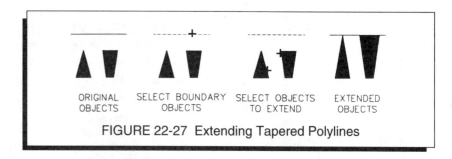

ORIGINAL OBJECTS   SELECT BOUNDARY OBJECTS   SELECT OBJECTS TO EXTEND   EXTENDED OBJECTS

FIGURE 22-27 Extending Tapered Polylines

Only open polylines may be extended. If you attempt to extend a closed polyline, the following message will appear:

Cannot extend a closed polyline.

ROTATING OBJECTS

The Rotate command allows you to rotate an entity or group of entities around a chosen base point. The entities are not required to be part of a block.

You may choose the angle at which the chosen object rotates by specifying the angle to rotate from its existing angle, by dragging the angle, or by choosing the angle of rotation from a reference angle. Let's look at examples of each type of angle rotation.

ROTATING BY SPECIFYING ANGLE

An object or a group of objects can be rotated by specifying an angle. You may specify a simple angle, or you may want to change one angle to another. For example, if an object is currently oriented at 58 degrees and you wish to rotate the object to 26 degrees, you could rotate the object the difference of −32 degrees. Let's use the Rotate command to rotate an object by specifying an angle.

ROTATE EXERCISE

Draw the object as shown in the following illustration. Enter the Rotate command:

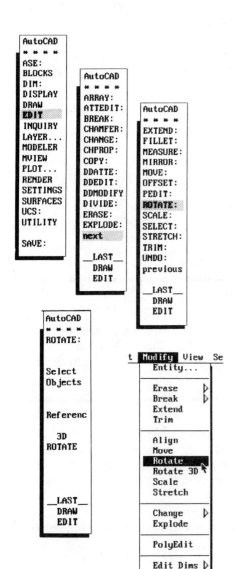

Command: <u>ROTATE</u>
Select objects: <u>W</u> (*window the entire object*)
Base point: (*Enter point "A"*)
<Rotation angle>/Reference: <u>45</u>

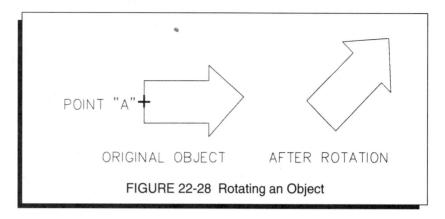

FIGURE 22-28 Rotating an Object

Entering a positive angle will result in a counterclockwise rotation of the object; a negative angle will result in a clockwise rotation.

ROTATING FROM A REFERENCE ANGLE

It is sometimes necessary to obtain a particular rotation angle. The Rotate command allows you to achieve this by using the Reference option.

In order to use the Reference option, you must first know the existing rotation angle of the object. Let's look at an example of rotating an object in reference to its existing angle.

REFERENCE ANGLE ROTATION EXERCISE

Draw an object similar to the one shown in the following illustration. Enter the Rotate command.

Command: <u>ROTATE</u>
Select objects: <u>W</u> (*window the object*)
Base point: (*Enter point "A"*)
<Rotation angle>/Reference: <u>R</u>
Reference angle <*default*>: <u>0</u>
New angle: <u>-45</u>

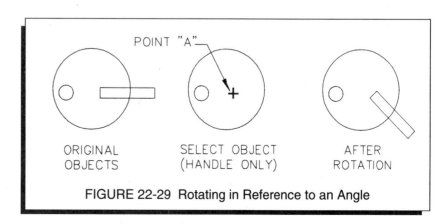

FIGURE 22-29 Rotating in Reference to an Angle

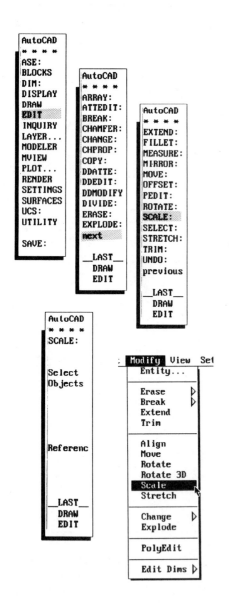

Tips

The List command is helpful in determining the existing angle of an entity when using the Reference option.

You may also rotate an object a specified number of degrees from its existing angle by entering the "Reference angle" as zero regardless of the actual angle.

ROTATING AN OBJECT BY DRAGGING

If you wish to drag-rotate an object, just move the cursor in response to the "<Rotation angle>/Reference:" prompt. If the updating screen coordinates are set for relative distance and angle, you may read the angle from the screen. Pressing the Enter key or the pick button on the input device will fix the object at the location currently shown on the screen.

You may rotate part of an object by choosing only the parts to rotate in response to the "Select objects:" prompt.

SCALING OBJECTS

The Scale command allows you to change the scale of an entity or entities. The X and Y scales of the object are changed equally. The entities are not required to be part of a block.

A base point is specified on the object. This point remains stationary, while the object is scaled from that point.

You may change the scale by a numerical factor, by dragging, or by referencing a known length, then entering a new length. Let's look at each method.

CHANGING SCALE BY NUMERICAL FACTOR

You may change the scale of an object by entering a numerical factor which serves as a "multiplier." Entering a positive number will have the effect of multiplying the size of the object by that number. For example, a factor of two will result in an object twice the original size.

The Scale command allows you to change the scale of an entity or entities.

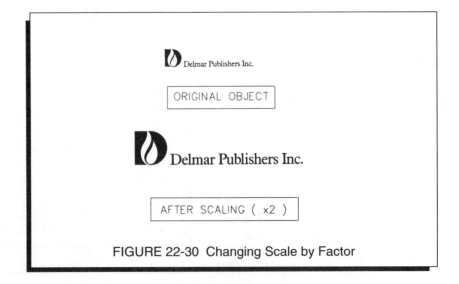

FIGURE 22-30 Changing Scale by Factor

Entering a decimal factor will result in an object smaller than the original. A factor of .25 will result in an object 25% of the original size.

CHANGING SCALE BY REFERENCE

You may change scale by specifying the known length of an entity, then choosing the desired length of that object. Let's look at an example of this method.

SCALE EXERCISE

Draw the object as in the following illustration. Enter the Scale command.

Command: SCALE
Select objects: (*select object*)
Base point: (*select point "A"*)
<Scale factor>/Reference: R
Reference length <default>: 2
New length: 4

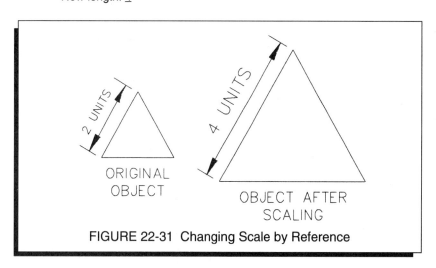

FIGURE 22-31 Changing Scale by Reference

Notice that AutoCAD rescales all the entities that make up the object, not just the length of the known entity.

STRETCHING OBJECTS

The Stretch command permits you to move selected objects while allowing their connections to other objects in the drawing to remain unchanged. As you will see, the Stretch command can be one of the most useful edit commands in AutoCAD.

There are several rules associated with the Stretch command that must be understood in order to execute it properly. Let's look at some of these rules.

Lines, arcs, solids, traces, and polylines may be stretched.

You may choose the objects to be edited by any combination of object selection options, but one of these options must be a window option such as "Window" or "Crossing."

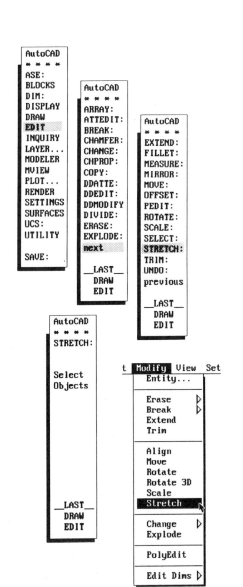

Any objects that are entirely within a window will be moved in the same manner as the Move command.

When stretching traces and solids, vertices that are outside of the Crossing window will remain fixed, while those inside will be moved.

Any objects that are entirely within a window will be moved in the same manner as the Move command.

If a line, arc, or polyline segment is chosen by using the "Crossing" method, the endpoints that are contained in the window will be moved, but those outside the window will remain "fixed."

When stretching traces and solids, vertices that are outside of the Crossing window will remain fixed, while those inside will be moved.

STRETCH EXERCISE

Before looking at more rules, let's use the Stretch command to move the location of a window in a wall. The following illustration shows a wall containing a window that we wish to move to the right. This is a work disk drawing. Start the drawing named "STRETCH1" and use the following command sequence. Let's enter the Stretch command and move the window.

    Command: <u>STRETCH</u>
    Select objects to stretch by window...
    Select objects: <u>C</u> (*AutoCAD enters this for you automatically if selected from the menu*).
    First corner: (*enter point "A"*)
    Other corner: (*enter point "B"*)
    Base point: (*enter point "C"*)
    New point: (*enter point "D"*)

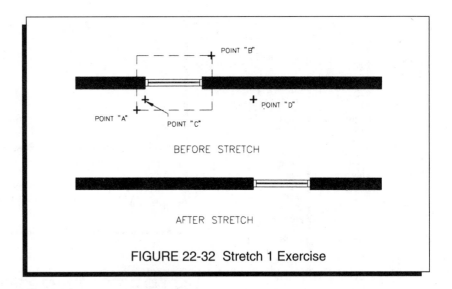

FIGURE 22-32 Stretch 1 Exercise

Tips

Turning Ortho mode on allows you to move the window along the wall perfectly.

You may enter a relative coordinate in response to the "New point:" prompt to move the object(s) an exact distance.

STRETCH RULES

Let's look at some other rules that apply to the Stretch command.

- Arcs are stretched similar to lines, except that the arc's center, start, and endpoints are adjusted so the distance from the midpoint of the chord to the arc is constant.

- Polylines are handled by their individual segments. The polyline width, tangent, and curve fitting are not affected.

- Some entities are just "moved" or left alone. The decision depends on the "definition point." If the definition point lies inside the window, the entity is moved. If it occurs outside the window, it is not affected. The definition point of certain entities is as follows:

  Point: Center of the point
  Circle: Center point of the circle
  Block: Insertion point
  Text: Left most point of the text line

- If more than one window specification is used in the object selection process, the last window used will be the one used for the Stretch.

- If you do not use a window selection, AutoCAD displays the message:

  You must select a window to stretch.

STRETCH EXERCISE

Electronic Work Disk Problem

Start the drawing from the work disk named "STRETCH2". This is a pencil as shown in the following illustration.

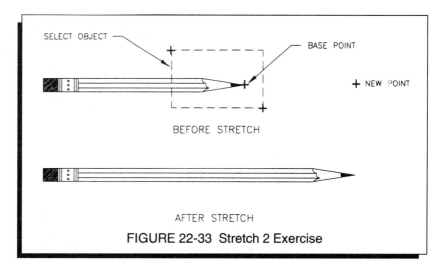

FIGURE 22-33 Stretch 2 Exercise

Use the Stretch command to make the pencil longer and shorter.

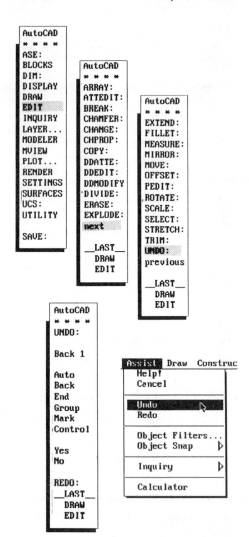

UNDOING DRAWING STEPS

The Undo command is used to undo several command moves in a single operation. You may also identify blocks of commands for reference later. To execute the Undo command, enter:

Command: <u>UNDO</u>
Auto/Back/Control/End/Group/Mark/<number>:

Responding to the prompt with a number will cause AutoCAD to undo the specified number of commands. This has the same effect as entering the U command the same number of times, except it is done in one operation, thus causing only one regeneration.

Let's look at the options for the Undo command.

Mark: Think of your drawing as a list of functions that is added to the drawing file, one at a time. If this list were on paper, you could place a mark at a certain point for reference. The Mark option allows you to do this. At a later time, you can use the Back option to undo everything back to the mark.

Back: The Back option will cause AutoCAD to undo all operations back to the preceding mark. Each operation will be listed and the message "Mark encountered" will be displayed. When the next marker back is encountered, it is removed. The next Undo will then undo all operations back to the previous marker, if any. If there is no preceding mark, AutoCAD displays the message:

This will undo everything. OK? <<Y>>

Entering "Y" will undo every operation since last entering the drawing editor. Answering "N" will cause the Back option to be ignored.

Multiple undos are stopped by a mark. Entering a number in response to the undo prompt that is greater than the number of operations since the last mark will have no greater effect than the Back option. The undo will still stop at the mark.

Group/End: The Group and End options cause all operations from the time Group is entered and the time End is entered to be treated as a single command. This means that all operations between the Group and End entries will be undone in a single step. For example, consider the following string of operations:

Circle
Arc
GROUP
    Line
    Line
    Fillet
END
Arc
U
U
U

The first U will remove the arc. The second U will remove all the operations between the Group/End entries (Line, Line, Fillet). The third U will remove the Arc. Only the first circle will remain.

If you enter the Group option while in a current group, the current group will be ended and a new one will be started.

The Back option will cause AutoCAD to undo all operations back to the preceding mark.

If a Group has been started, but not ended, and the U command is entered, it will undo one operation at a time, but cannot back up past the point where Group was entered. To continue back, the current group must be ended, even if nothing remains in the current group.

When using the Group option, Undo will not display each operation. The message "GROUP" will be displayed.

Auto: The Auto option causes macro commands from menus to be treated as single commands. Some menus combine several operations such as inserting a window in a wall of a floor plan by Breaking the wall and Inserting the window. If Auto is on, the entire command string will be undone as if it were a single command. Auto prompts with: "ON/OFF".

Control: The Control option limits the Undo commands or disables them entirely. This is sometimes necessary because of the large amount of disk space required if the Undo edit is extensive.

The Control option prompts:

All/None/One/ <<All>>:

Following is an explanation of the sub-options:

All: Enables all Undo commands and features.

None: Disables all Undo commands and features. Using None removes all markers, groups, and other stored information. If Undo is entered when the None sub-option is on, AutoCAD will display the Control prompt:

All/None/One <<All>>:

You may then enter the level of Undo performance that you desire.

One: Allows the Undo commands to function for one undo at a time. All markers, groups, and other stored information are removed. This frees disk space, making it a preferred setting for floppy-disk based systems. The Group, Mark, and Auto options are not available. The following prompt is displayed when Undo is executed:

Control/<<1>>:

GENERAL NOTES

Undo has no effect on the following:

AREA	HELP	REGENALL
ATTEXT	ID	RESUME
DBLIST	IGESOUT	SAVE
DELAY	LIST	SHADE
DIST	MSLIDE	SHELL
DXFOUT	PLOT	STATUS
END	QUIT	TEXTSCR
FILES	REDRAW	U
FILMROLL	REDRAWALL	UNDO
GRAPHSCR	REGEN	

Plotting clears the Undo information from the drawing.

The Undo command should not be confused with the Undo option contained in some menus such as the Line menu. Using the Undo option from the Line menu will remove one line segment at a time. If you use the Undo command, however, all line segments in the sequence will be undone in a single operation. For example, if you draw a box containing four lines, then exit the Line command and execute the Undo1 command, all four lines will be undone. If this does not produce the intended results, the Redo command will restore the lines.

EDITING WITH GRIPS

The grip boxes are generally placed at the positions avail-able with object snap.

In Chapter 10, you learned how to use the object selection process. This process is used to select objects for editing. AutoCAD provides a short-cut process to object selection and editing. You can set AutoCAD to display *grips* on the entities displayed on the screen. Grips are small rectangles that are placed on objects and can be used as "grip points" when editing. The grip boxes are generally placed at the positions available with object snap. The following illustration shows AutoCAD drawing objects with their grip locations.

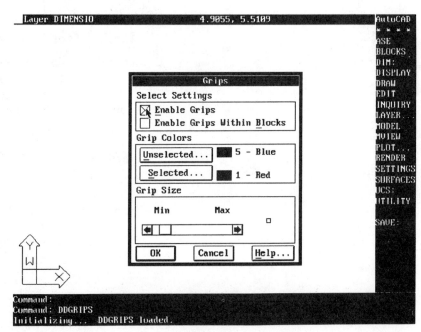

FIGURE 22-34

ENABLING GRIP EDITING

Grip editing is enabled or disabled by using the Ddgrips command to display the **Grips** dialogue box.

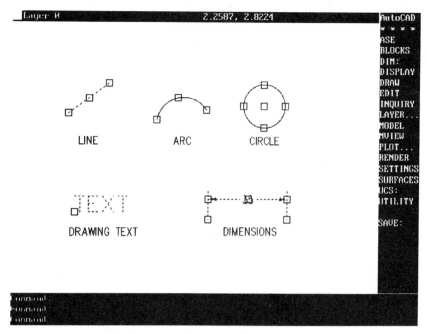

FIGURE 22-35 Grips Setting Dialogue Box

To enable grip editing, select the "Enable Grips" check box. Normally, a grip box is displayed at the insert point of an inserted block. If you wish to display grips on the entities *within* blocks, select the "Enable Grips Within Blocks" check box.

SETTING GRIP COLORS

As a visual aid, grip boxes can be assigned a color. If a grip box is selected, the interior of the box is filled with a solid color. Both the grip box and solid fill can be assigned a color through the dialogue box.

To set the colors, choose either the "Unselected" (grip box), or the "Selected" (solid fill) buttons. AutoCAD will display a **Select Color** subdialogue box.

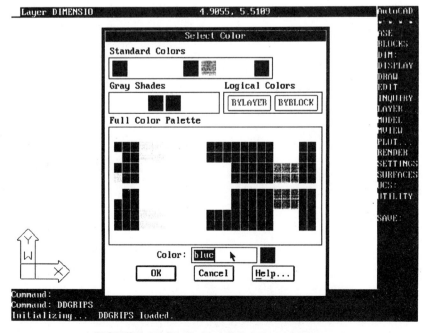

FIGURE 22-36 Select Color Dialogue Box

Select the desired color from the displayed palette, then click on the "OK" button to set the color.

SETTING THE GRIP SIZE

The size of the grip boxes is set with the slider bar in the dialogue box.

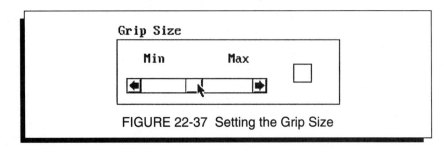

FIGURE 22-37 Setting the Grip Size

The panel to the right of the slider bar shows the current grip box size. As you move the slide bar, the grip box changes scale to indicate the actual grip box size. The grip box size can be set from 1 to 255 screen pixels.

USING GRIPS FOR EDITING

When grip editing is enabled, a grip selection box is displayed at the intersection of the crosshairs.

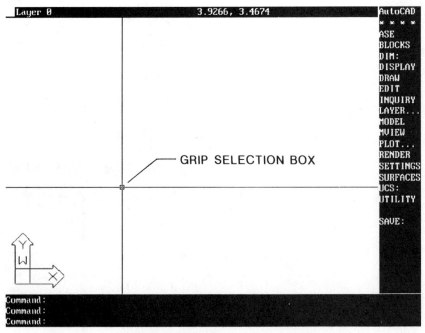

FIGURE 22-38 Grip Selection Box

To select an object for editing, place the selection box at any point on an object in the drawing and click. The object will be highlighted and grip boxes will be placed on the object. You can continue to select as many objects as you wish by selecting several times.

After you select the object(s) to be edited, you can select any of the displayed grip points as a base point for editing. As you move the selection over the grip points, the crosshairs will snap to the grip box in a similar manner as when using object snap. To select a grip box, move to it and click. The grip box will change colors to denote selection.

To select several grip boxes, hold down the shift key on the keyboard when selecting the grips.

Pressing Ctrl-C twice will clear all selected objects and their grips.

Pressing Ctrl-C twice will clear all selected objects and their grips. Using Ctrl-C once will clear the selected objects, but not the grips. This facilitates using a grip on a non-selected object as a base grip.

GRIP MODE

When you select a single grip, AutoCAD displays edit command options on the command line. The selections rotate as you press the space bar. The following command line listings show the options available as you "page" through with the space bar.

```
**STRETCH**
<Stretch to point>/Base point/Copy/Undo/eXit:

**ROTATE**
<Rotation angle>/Base point/Copy/Undo/Reference/eXit:

**SCALE**
<Scale factor>/Base point/Copy/Undo/Reference/eXit:

**MIRROR**
<Second point>/Base point/Copy/Undo/eXit:
```

Press the space bar until the desired edit command is listed, then proceed with the command. The selected grip point is used as a base point for the edit operations. You can alternately select one of the options listed on the command line. The commands and their options are covered later in this section.

When selecting several grip points by holding down the space bar, the base point grip is selected last. The base grip can be either a selected or nonselected grip. It is selected, however, after all the target grips are selected and the shift key is no longer held. It is only after the base grip is selected that the command options are displayed.

GRIP EDITING COMMANDS

The grip editing commands of Stretch, Move, Rotate, Scale, and Mirror are displayed on the command line when you enter grip mode. You can rotate through the edit command options by pressing the space bar. Let's look at each choice.

STRETCH MODE

Stretch mode functions similarly to the Stretch command, except that AutoCAD uses the selected grip points to determine the stretch results.

STRETCH
<Stretch to point>/Base point/Copy/Undo/eXit:

If you select the midpoint grip of a line or arc or the center of a circle, the object is moved, but not stretched. The following illustrations show some examples of using the Stretch mode.

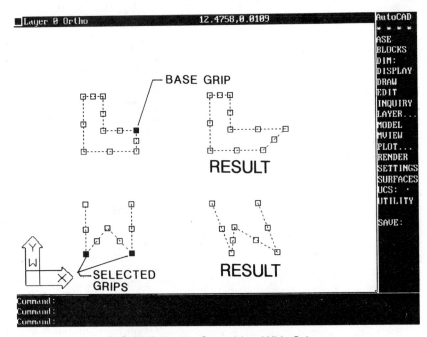

FIGURE 22-39 Stretching With Grips

Options:

Base point: Entering "B" at the command line allows you to use a base point other than a grip location.

Copy: Entering "C" (for Copy) makes copies from the stretch entities, leaving the original entities intact.

Undo: Performs an undo of the operation.

eXit: Exits grip editing.

MOVE MODE

If you press the space bar until the Move mode is displayed, you can use grip editing to move the selected objects.

MOVE
<Move to point>/Base point/Copy/Undo/eXit:

The distance the object(s) is moved is determined by the distance from the base grip to a point entered in response to AutoCAD's "Move to point" prompt. You can alternately enter either an absolute or relative coordinate to specify the distance and direction of the move.

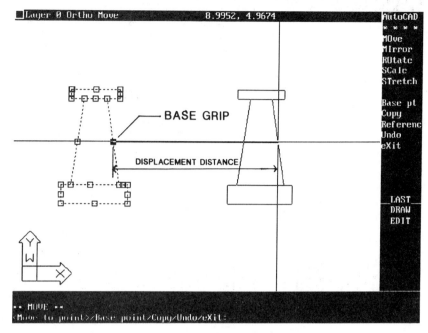

FIGURE 22-40 Moving With Grips

If you hold down the shift key after selecting the base grip and before placing the point designating the move distance and direction, AutoCAD places a copy of the object(s) at the new location, leaving the original object(s) unchanged. You can use this technique to place multiple copies. This functions similarly to the Copy option (explanation follows).

Options:

> **Base point:** Entering "B" at the command line allows you to use a base point other than a grip location.
>
> **Copy:** Entering "C" (for Copy) makes copies of the entities, leaving the original entities intact.
>
> **Undo:** Performs an undo of the operation.
>
> **eXit:** Exits grip editing.

ROTATE MODE

The Rotate option allows you to rotate the selected objects around the base point.

> ****ROTATE****
> <Rotation angle>/Base point/Copy/Undo/Reference/eXit:

Unless you use the "Base point" option to position the base point at a location other than a grip, the rotation will occur around the base grip.

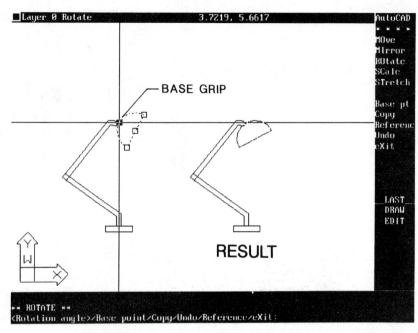

FIGURE 22-41 Rotating With Grips

When rotating, you can dynamically set the rotation angle by moving the crosshair, or you can specify a rotation in degrees.

Options:

Base point: Entering "B" at the command line allows you to use a base point other than a grip location.

Copy: Entering "C" (for Copy) makes copies of the rotated entities, leaving the original entities intact.

Undo: Performs an undo of the operation.

Reference: Allows you to set a reference angle. When you enter "R", AutoCAD prompts for the "Reference angle". This is the angle at which the entity is *currently* rotated. AutoCAD next prompts for the "New angle". The new angle is the actual angle you want the entity to be.

eXit: Exits grip editing.

SCALE MODE

If you wish to scale the selected objects, cycle through the mode list until the Scale mode is listed on the command line.

```
**SCALE**
<Scale factor>/Base point/Copy/Undo/Reference/eXit:
```

The scale mode is used to rescale the selected object(s). The base grip serves as the base point for the scaling operation. You can dynamically scale the objects by moving the crosshairs away from the base grip. You can also scale the selected objects by entering a scale factor. A scale factor greater than one scales the object by that factor. For example, a scale factor of two results in an object twice the size. Entering a decimal scale factor results in an object that is smaller than the original. For example, entering a scale factor of 0.5 scales the object to one-half size of the original.

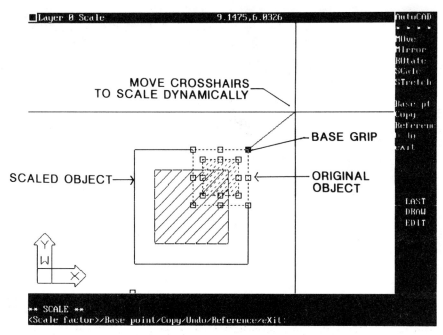

FIGURE 22-42 Scaling With Grips

Options:

> **Base point:** Entering "B" at the command line allows you to use a base point other than a grip location.
>
> **Copy:** Entering "C" (for Copy) makes copies of the scaled entities, leaving the original entities intact.
>
> **Undo:** Performs an undo of the operation.
>
> **Reference:** Allows you to set a reference scale. Let's look at an example. Let's suppose you have an object is 6 units in length and you wish to scale it to 24 units in length. Select the Reference option by entering "R" at the command line. AutoCAD prompts:
>
> > Reference length <1.0000>:
>
> Enter "6" and press Enter. AutoCAD then prompts for the new length.
>
> > <New length>/Base point/Copy/Undo/Reference/eXit:
>
> Enter "24" and press Enter. AutoCAD calculates the scale factor and applies the scale.
>
> **eXit:** Exits grip editing.

MIRROR MODE

Mirror mode is used to mirror the selected object(s) in a similar manner to the Mirror command.

> **MIRROR**
> <Second point>/Base point/Copy/Undo/eXit:

When using Mirror mode, the first point of the mirror line is stipulated as the point of the base grip. The second point of the mirror line is entered at any point on the drawing.

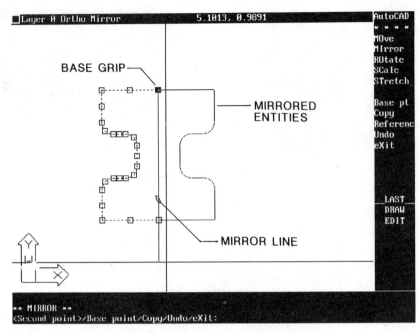

FIGURE 22-43 Mirroring With Grips

Options:

   Base point: Entering "B" at the command line allows you to use a base point other than a grip location.

   Copy: Entering "C" (for Copy) makes copies of the mirrored entities, leaving the original entities intact.

   Undo: Performs an undo of the operation.

   eXit: Exits grip editing.

CHAPTER REVIEW

1. What properties of an object can be altered with the Change command?

   _____

   _____

   _____

2. What is meant when you change an entity's color to "BYLAYER"?

   _____

   _____

   _____

3. Why would you use the Chprop command instead of the Change command?

   _____

   _____

   _____

4. What are the two types of arrays?

_____

_____

5. Using simple circles, draw an example of an array using 5 columns and 3 rows.

6. Using 4-sided boxes, draw an example of a polar array with 6 objects that are rotated.

7. What does the Mirror command perform?

_____

_____

_____

8. What variable controls whether text is mirrored?

_____

9. What is the "mirror line"?

_____

_____

_____

10. Use point type 34 to show a horizontal line divided with the Divide command into 4 segments.

11. Show a circle divided into 6 segments with the Divide command, using a small square as the block used with Divide. Show the same situation again, using the rotated block option.

12. What are the entities you can use with the Measure command?

_____

_____

_____

13. What is the result when you explode a block?

_____

_____

_____

14. What happens when you explode a polyline?

_____

_____

_____

15. What is a trim "cutting edge"?

_____

_____

_____

16. At what point is a polyline trimmed?

_____

_____

_____

17. What are the requirements for trimming a circle?

_____

_____

_____

18. What is the object called that is selected with the Extend command and acts as a borderline for the extended object?

_____

19. What are the three ways to rotate an object?

_____

_____

_____

20. Can an object be scaled differently in the X- and Y-axes with the Scale command?

_____

21. What value would you enter to scale an object to one-fourth of its original size?

_____

22. What entities can be stretched?

_____

_____

_____

23. When using the Stretch command, if you select objects with three window operations, which operation is used to determine the stretch?

_____

24. What does the Mark option of the Undo command do?

_____

_____

_____

25. What effect does plotting from the drawing have on the Undo command?

_____

_____

CHAPTER 23

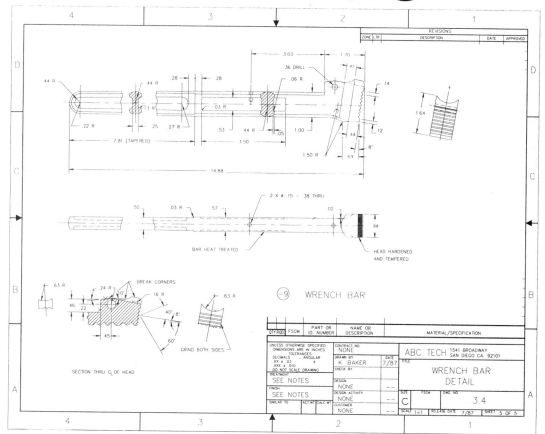

Intermediate Operations

OBJECTIVES:

Intermediate use of AutoCAD requires the CAD operator to possess knowledge of several operations. In Chapter 23 you will learn the following:

● To set and control the color of entities independent of the layer color settings.

● To store and retrieve drawing views and pictorial images.

● To save and view slide images of a drawing screen.

● To remove unwanted layers, blocks, styles, and other named objects from a drawing.

● To create a DOS shell while active within an AutoCAD drawing file.

● To import and export PostScript image files.

SETTING THE CURRENT COLOR

The Color command is used to set the color type for all subsequently drawn entities.

This differs from the Color option in the Layer command, which sets the color for entities drawn on that layer. The use of the Color command allows you to set colors that are contrary to the current color setting for the layer. Thus, it is possible that a layer will contain entities of different colors, regardless of the color set for that layer using the Layer/Color routine.

To set a new color for subsequently drawn entities, enter the Color command.

>Command: COLOR
>New entity color <current>:

You can set a new color by one of two methods. You can specify a number from 1 to 255 or enter a standard color name such as "BLUE". All new entities will be displayed in the designated color until a new color is selected by the Color command.

You may also enter "BYLAYER" or "BYBLOCK" in response to the prompt.

Entering BYLAYER will cause all subsequently drawn entities to inherit the layer's color, thus relinquishing control of entity colors to each layer's color setting.

Entering BYBLOCK causes all subsequent entities to be drawn in white until they are blocked. When the block is inserted, the entities will inherit the color of the block insertion.

COLOR EXERCISES

1. Set the current color to yellow and draw three circles. Next, set the current color to red. Draw three boxes. Did the objects appear in the correct color?

2. Use the Layer command to set the <u>layer</u> color to cyan. Draw some lines. Did the circles and boxes you drew change color? Notice that the Color command overrides the layer color setting.

3. Use the Change command and select all the objects on the screen. Select Properties, then Color. Select blue as the color. Did all the objects change to blue?

STORING AND DISPLAYING DRAWING VIEWS

Views are stored zooms that are identified by name. You may recall a view at any time in the drawing. This has the same effect as zooming to that location.

To invoke the View command, enter:

>Command: VIEW
>?/Delete/Restore/Save/Window:
>View name to save

The following is an explanation of the options to the View command.

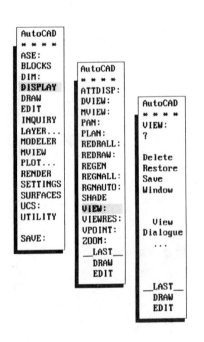

You may recall a view at any time in the drawing.

?: Entering a "?" will result in a listing of the previously named views. AutoCAD prompts:

View(s) to list <*>:

You can enter either a list of view names, separated by commas, or use DOS wildcard characters to list views. If you respond with an Enter, all the saved views will be listed.

D (Delete): Deletes a stored view.

R (Restore): Restores a saved view to the screen. You will be prompted for the name of the previously saved view.

S (Save): Selecting the "S" option saves the current screen view. You will be prompted for a name of the saved view. If you respond with a name of a view that is already saved, the present view will replace it.

W (Window): The window option works in the same manner as the Save option, except that you may show a window which describes the view. You do not have to be in the zoom that will be saved.

View names may be up to 31 characters in length but no spaces may be used. Some examples of named views would be "OFFICE_1", "BED-ROOM", and " LIVING_ROOM".

Tip
_____

Views are an invaluable aid in saving "zoom time" on complex drawings.

You may specify a view to be plotted from the Plot command (see Chapter 18).

STORING AND DISPLAYING DRAWING SLIDES

There may be times that you want to show several views of a drawing or several drawings to someone. You could, of course, take the time to load each one, but this would be very laborious. A much faster way to load pictures is the Vslide command.

The slide commands can capture a view of a drawing like a camera shot, then show it later. Think of it as making a slide with a camera, then showing the shot with a projector.

The slide commands are Mslide and Vslide. Let's look at how to use each.

MAKING A SLIDE

The Mslide (make slide) command is used to make a slide file. First, display the drawing or any part of the drawing you wish to make a slide of on the screen. Then enter:

Command: MSLIDE

AutoCAD displays a **Create Slide File** dialogue box. Enter the name you want the slide file to have. AutoCAD will add a file extension of .SLD to the slide name.

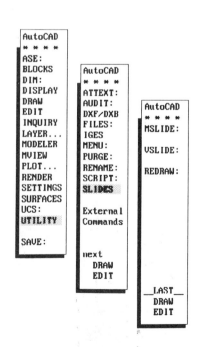

The Slide commands can capture a view of a drawing like a camera shot, then show it later.

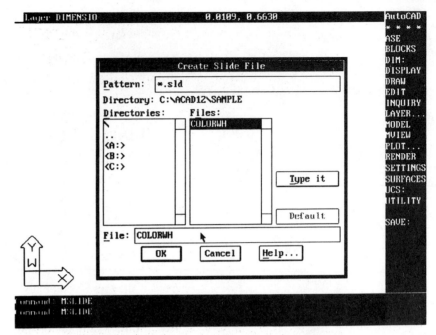

FIGURE 23-1 Create Slide File Dialogue Box

Portions of the drawing not currently displayed are not captured. The Mslide command operates as a "what you see is what you get" operation.

VIEWING A SLIDE

The Vslide command is used to view a slide. The following format is used to view a single slide.

> Command: <u>VSLIDE</u>

AutoCAD displays a **Select Slide File** dialogue box.

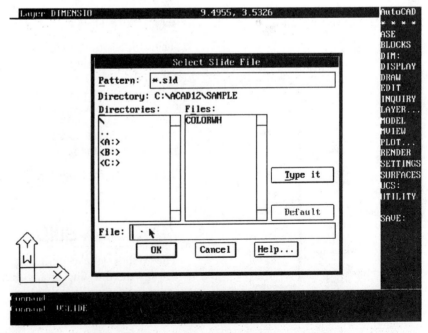

FIGURE 23-2 Select Slide File Dialogue Box

If you wish to view a slide that is part of a slide library, select the "Type it" button and enter the slide library name, followed by the slide file name. (See the next section for an explanation of slide libraries.) For example, if you wanted to view a slide named "sofa" from the "furnlib" library, the following format would be used.

```
Command: VSLIDE
Slide file name: furnlib(sofa)
```

It is not necessary to include the file extension. You may view the slide at any time and from any drawing. The current screen display is over-written by the slide file.

The current drawing is not affected by the Vslide command. To return to the original drawing, issue a Redraw command.

A slide may not be edited or zoomed. It is a fixed snapshot of the drawing.

SLIDE LIBRARIES

Slide libraries are a collection of slides stored in a special library format. Slide libraries are excellent for storing slides for use with icon menus.

To build a slide library, you must first prepare a text file (ASCII format) that contains the names of the slide files you wish to assemble into a library. List one slide file per line in the document. Next, use the Slidelib utility program included on the AutoCAD "Support" disk. The correct usage for the Slidelib program is as follows.

```
C>slidelib (library name) <(file list name)
```

Let's look at an example.

We want to prepare a slide library that contains names of furniture. First, we will prepare an ASCII text file that contains a list of the slide names, one to a line. Next, we use the Slidelib utility to assemble the slides into a library. If the text file is named FLIST (for furniture list) and we wish the library name to be FURNLIB (for furniture library), we would enter the following:

```
C>slidelib furnlib <flist
```

Once a library is built, you can not change a slide. If you wish to add or change a slide, you must rebuild the library.

SLIDE SHOWS

You may write a self-running script that presents a series of slides on the screen.

To do so, utilize the Script command. You can eliminate the required loading time by entering an "*" before the slide name, which makes AutoCAD "preload" the next slide while the current one is being displayed. The following is an example of a script for a self-running slide show:

```
VSLIDE SLIDE_A      (begin slide show)
VSLIDE *SLIDE_B     (preload slide B)
DELAY 5000          (insert a delay)
VSLIDE              (display slide B)
VSLIDE *SLIDE_C     (preload slide C)
DELAY 1000          (insert a delay)
VSLIDE              (display slide C)
DELAY               (insert a delay)
RSCRIPT             (recycle show)
```

Refer to the Script command for more information.

SLIDE EXERCISES

1. Start either an existing drawing you have completed or one of AutoCAD's sample drawings (you can use the Files command to display the available drawing files). Use a zoom window to select a part of the drawing.

   Use the Mslide command to capture a slide named "SLIDE1". Now use Zoom All to redisplay the entire drawing. Next, issue the Vslide command and respond to the prompt with "SLIDE1".

   Note that you can view a slide from any drawing, not just the one from which it was captured.

2. While the slide is displayed, issue a Redraw. Did the slide go away?

3. Use Vslide to display the slide again. Select the Line command and try to draw a line on the slide. What happens? You can not edit or zoom a slide. (Be sure to exit the drawing with Quit if you happen to edit the existing drawing and do not wish to save the edits.)

PURGING OBJECTS FROM A DRAWING

AutoCAD stores named objects (blocks, layers, linetypes, shapes, and styles) along with the drawing. When the drawing is loaded using the Open command, the drawing Editor determines whether each named object is referenced by other objects in the drawing. You may use the Purge command to delete any unused named objects.

You may use the Purge command to delete any unused named objects.

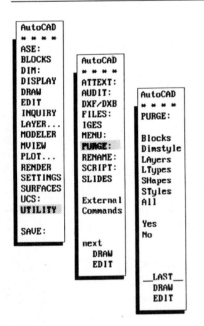

The Purge command can eliminate unused blocks, text styles, dimension styles, etc. This eliminates space-consuming parts of a drawing and can simplify drawing management. For example, you can purge unused layers so the dialogue box does not contain useless layers to filter through.

    Command: PURGE
    Purge unused Blocks/Dimstyles/LAyers/LTypes/SHapes/STyles/All:

You may use the capitalized letters to select any of the options or "A" to purge all the objects.

AutoCAD will prompt you with the name of each unused object and will ask if that object should be purged.

If you wish to purge objects that are present in the drawing, you must first erase them, then end the drawing. Then return to it, using Purge as the first command.

The Purge command can not be used after the drawing database (any part of the drawing) has been changed.

The Purge command can not be used to purge layer "0", the Continuous linetype, or the Standard text style.

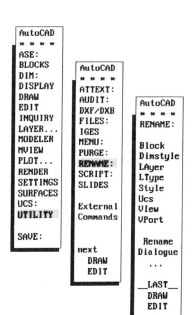

RENAMING PARTS OF YOUR DRAWING

The Rename command is used to rename certain parts of a drawing. These parts are as follows:

Blocks	Text styles
Dimension styles	Named user coordinate systems
Layers	Named views
Linetypes	Named viewports

To rename a part of the drawing, enter the Rename command.

Command: <u>RENAME</u>
Block/Dimstyle/LAyer/LType/Style/Ucs/VIew/VPort:
Old (object) name:
New (object) name:

Select the option that describes what you want to change. Then enter the existing (old) name in response to the prompt. You are then prompted for the new name. Names can be up to 31 characters in length.

There are items that can not be renamed. These are as follows.

Layer "0"
Linetype named "CONTINUOUS"
Names of shapes

USING A DIALOGUE BOX TO RENAME

You may use a Rename dialogue box to rename drawing objects. The dialogue box is displayed either by entering Ddrename from the keyboard or by selecting "Rename Dialogue" from the Utility/Rename screen menu.

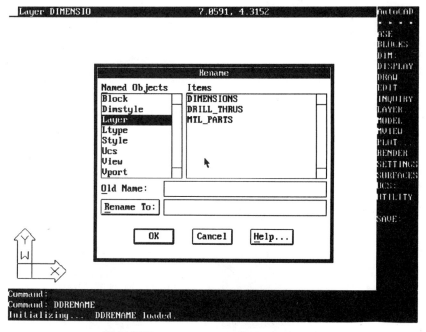

FIGURE 23-3 Rename Dialogue Box

PRODUCING AND USING POSTSCRIPT IMAGES

Images using the PostScript drawing format can be imported or exported within AutoCAD. PostScript images are universally used by desktop publishing packages and other types of drawing programs. The use of PostScript images allows a direct interface with these types of programs and makes AutoCAD an invaluable illustrating program for these programs.

EXPORTING A POSTSCRIPT IMAGE

You can export a drawing in PostScript format by using the Psout command. When you issue the Psout command, the following dialogue box is displayed.

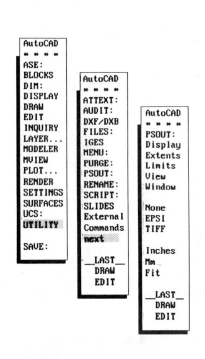

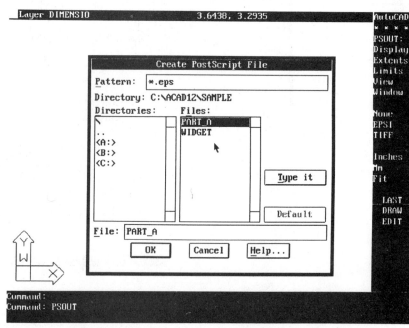

FIGURE 23-4 Create PostScript File Dialogue Box

The following series of prompts is displayed. Let's look at how each prompt controls the PostScript file.

DETERMINING WHAT PART OF THE DRAWING TO PLOT

You may plot any part of the drawing to a PostScript file.

You may plot any part of the drawing to a PostScript file. The following prompt is displayed.

        What to plot -- Display, Extents, Limits, View or Window <D>:

Enter the part of the drawing to export to the PostScript file. The choices are similar to the plot routine where you select the part of the drawing you want to plot.

ADDING A SCREEN PREVIEW

You are next prompted for the screen preview image.

        Include a screen preview image in the file? (None/ESPI/TIFF) <None>:

A screen preview image can be used by an external program to preview the image before placement. If you want to preview the image, select one of the image format options: ESPI or TIFF.

> **Tip**
>
> Check your desktop publishing or drawing program documentation to verify the use of either format with your program.

SETTING THE PREVIEW RESOLUTION

If you select either the ESPI or TIFF format, AutoCAD prompts for the pixel resolution to use.

> Screen preview image size (128x128 is standard)? (128/256/512) <128>:

> **Tip**
>
> Although higher resolution screen previews are clearer, they require larger file sizes and "drag" more slowly in your desktop publishing or drawing program. The lowest acceptable resolution is recommended.

After you enter the screen preview image size, AutoCAD displays the following message:

> Effective plotting area: ww by hh high.

where *ww* is the width and *hh* is the height in the current size units of either inches or millimeters.

SETTING THE OUTPUT UNITS

The output units of either inches or millimeters can be selected. AutoCAD prompts:

> Size units (Inches or Millimeters) <*current*>:

> **Tip**
>
> Set the size units to the same setting as the external program to which you will import the PostScript file.

SETTING THE OUTPUT FILE SCALE

The scale for the output file determines the final size of the drawing in the same manner as the plot scale function in the Plot command.

The scale is important if you will be printing the PostScript file to paper (see also the next section on output size). AutoCAD prompts:

> Specify scale by entering:
> Output *units*=Drawing units or Fit or ? <*default*>:

where *units* are either inches or millimeters (previously selected).

SETTING THE OUTPUT SIZE

The output size is the size to which the plot will be drawn. A listing similar to the following is displayed.

```
Standard values for output size
Size      Width      Height
A          8.00       10.50
B         10.00       16.00
C         16.00       21.00
D         21.00       33.00
E         33.00       43.00
F         28.00       40.00
G         11.00       90.00
H         28.00      143.00
J         34.00      176.00
K         40.00      143.00
A4         7.80       11.20
A3        10.70       15.60
A2        15.60       22.40
A1        22.40       32.20
A0        32.20       45.90
USER       7.50       10.50

Enter the Size or Width,Height (in Inches) <USER>:
```

FIGURE 23-5 Output Size Listing

AutoCAD will write the drawing to a file. Exported PostScript files contain a DOS file extension of .EPS (Encapsulated PostScript File).

IMPORTING A POSTSCRIPT IMAGE

PostScript images can be imported into AutoCAD with the Psin (PostScript in) command. When you enter the Psin command, AutoCAD displays the following dialogue box.

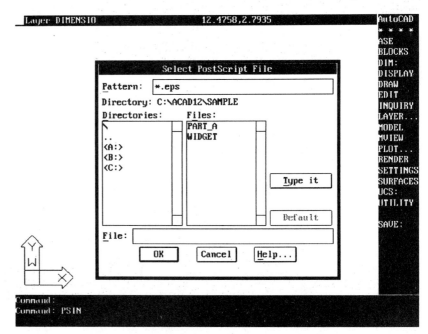

FIGURE 23-6 PostScript File Dialogue Box

The PostScript file is imported into the drawing as a block. The block can be exploded and edited with AutoCAD edit commands.

When you select a PostScript file to import, depending on the setting of the Psdrag command, AutoCAD displays a box representing the size of the file. The box contains the name of the PostScript file. AutoCAD then prompts:

> Insertion point <0,0,0>:
> Scale factor:

The insertion point and scale factor function in the same manner as when inserting a block. You may also visually place the file by moving the cursor around the screen, moving the representative box into position.

The scale can also be visually and dynamically set by moving the cursor away from the box.

SETTING THE PSDRAG

Psdrag controls how the PostScript image is displayed when it is imported into your drawing. The drag setting is controlled by the Psdrag command.

> Command: <u>PSDRAG</u>
> PSIN drag mode <0>:

If Psdrag is set to 0, the PostScript image is displayed as a box when imported. If set to 1, the actual image is displayed.

Tip

Setting Psdrag to 1 will cause the image to handle slowly. If your system works slowly, set Psdrag to 0.

SETTING POSTSCRIPT INPUT QUALITY

The quality of a PostScript image is determined by the Psquality command.

    Command: PSQUALITY
    New value for PSQUALITY <current>:

If Psquality is set to 0, the PostScript image is displayed only as a box with the file name enclosed within. The box is displayed even if the Psdrag setting is set to 1.

Any positive value sets the number of pixels per drawing unit. For example, a setting of 50 displays 50 pixels per drawing unit.

A negative value will display the drawing outline, but will not include the fills. The absolute value of the negative number controls the quality.

DISPLAYING A POSTSCRIPT FILL

AutoCAD allows you to fill a closed polyline boundary with any of several PostScript fill patterns. Although the fill patterns will not appear on the screen, the fill patterns will print when you output the drawing to a PostScript printer.

To place a PostScript fill, use the Psfill command.

    Command: PSFILL

AutoCAD prompts you to select the polyline border, then asks for the PostScript fill pattern.

    Select polyline:
    PostScript fill pattern (.=none) <.>/?:

To see the selections, enter a question mark (?). AutoCAD displays the following listing of patterns:

    Grayscale RGBcolor Allogo Lineargray Radialgray Square Waffle
    Zigzag Stars Brick Specks

then repeats the prompt.

    PostScript fill pattern (.=none) <.>/?:

The following illustration shows the available PostScript fills.

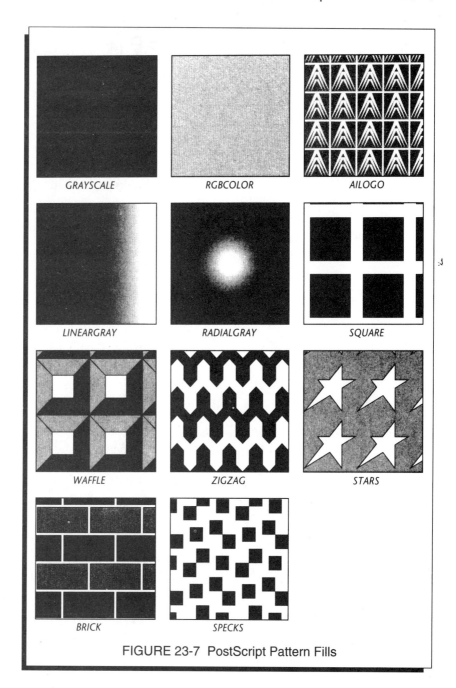

FIGURE 23-7 PostScript Pattern Fills

Enter the name of the desired PostScript fill. AutoCAD continues.

Scale <*default*>:

The scale factor works in a similar manner to a hatch pattern scale.

The remaining prompts are dependent on the pattern you select. When selecting grayscales, a value of 0 is white and 100 is black. Values between 0 and 100 represent the percent of black area of the grayscale.

CHAPTER REVIEW

1. When can you display a slide?

   _____

   _____

   _____

2. How do you "capture" and store a view?

   _____

   _____

   _____

3. Can a view be edited?

   _____

4. How do you make a slide?

   _____

   _____

   _____

5. Can you edit a slide?

   _____

6. What is the file extension of a slide file?

   _____

7. From where can you save a slide?

   _____

   _____

   _____

8. What can be purged with the Purge command?

   _____

   _____

   _____

9. When can you use the Purge command?

   _____

   _____

   _____

10. What items can not be purged?

   _____

   _____

11. What file extension is used with a PostScript file?

_____

_____

_____

12. Name some uses for PostScript export files.

_____

_____

_____

SECTION IV

ADVANCED AutoCAD

CHAPTER 24

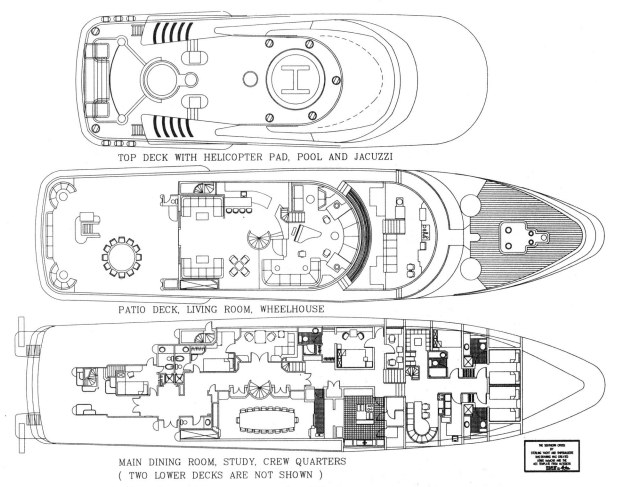

TOP DECK WITH HELICOPTER PAD, POOL AND JACUZZI

PATIO DECK, LIVING ROOM, WHEELHOUSE

MAIN DINING ROOM, STUDY, CREW QUARTERS
(TWO LOWER DECKS ARE NOT SHOWN)

Advanced Operations

OBJECTIVES:

Once you have become proficient with the draw, edit, and display commands of AutoCAD, you may want to use some of AutoCAD's advanced features. This chapter covers some of the advanced operations in AutoCAD. Chapter 24 objectives are as follows:

● To become proficient with the construction, editing, and special features of polylines.

● To learn the use of different types of spline curves.

● To learn to produce special output files from AutoCAD.

● To become familiar with the processes of recovering damaged AutoCAD drawing files.

AutoCAD In The Real World

The Role of Integration in Design and Drafting

How a consulting engineering firm integrated CAD into the design and drafting of a tank firing range

Fishbeck, Thompson, Carr & Huber, Inc. (FTC&H) is a 130-person multi-discipline consulting engineering firm in Ada, Michigan with heavy emphasis on civil and environmental engineering and hydrogeology. Major support services include structural, mechanical, and electrical engineering, and an extensive analytical laboratory. Approximately 90 percent of the drafting for the electrical, structural, and environmental departments is done on AutoCAD. They still depend on some degree of manual drafting in the other disciplines, but AutoCAD is gaining ground in those areas as well.

The projects FTC&H undertakes require the snythesis of data from many sources into a cohesive set of construction drawings. AutoCAD has streamlined this traditionally cumbersome process. They recently completed the design of a tank firing range (known as Multi-purpose Range Complex) in Northern Michigan that illustrates the degree to which CAD has been integrated into the design and drafting process complete with performing analytical functions.

In designing Camp Grayling, FTC&H faced the challenges of a target range with limited land space and a neighboring residential area. Target positions could not be obstructed and the residential area had to be protected.

A small portion of the Camp Grayling artillery range showing contours, maintenance, roads, trails, targets (enfilades) and firing locations (defilades).

AutoCAD was used to produce contour maps that plotted the land's topography. Civil engineers then used these maps to lay out the roads, foxhole locations, and target positions.

To avoid the residential area, precise calculation of angles and distances of the projectiles were used to assign the 300 targets' preliminary locations on the AutoCAD contour drawings. A database was extracted so the engineers could analyze any conflicts with the target positions and relocate them quickly and accurately. Once the targets were established, the roads, road profiles, and road cross sections were designed in AutoCAD using the contour drawings as a base layer.

FTC&H found that AutoCAD's intended use had been fulfilled: ease of revision, elimination of duplication and standardization of common design elements, resulting in a savings of untold hours.

Adapted with permission from an article by Don Potyraj and Kathleen Ivkovich. Excerpted from *CADENCE*, November 1989, copyright © 1989, Ariel Communications, Inc.

DRAWING POLYLINES

Polylines are similar to Trace lines, except that they can be used in a variety of ways.

Polylines have their own set of draw and edit commands.

A polyline can have a tapering width, curves, be made of arcs, be composed of different linetypes, and a variety of other configurations.

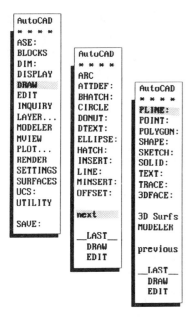

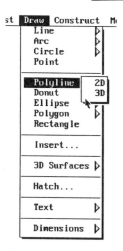

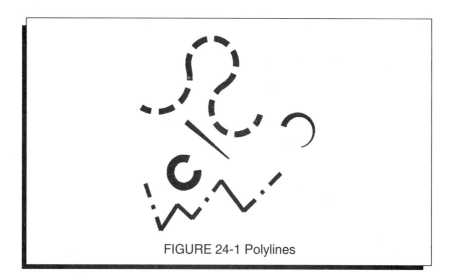

FIGURE 24-1 Polylines

Polylines have their own set of draw and edit commands. This chapter contains the draw commands first and the edit commands afterward.

Polylines are a bit more difficult to learn than most AutoCAD commands. You should practice each option of the Pline and Pedit commands until you become familiar with the characteristics of each.

USING THE PLINE COMMAND

To draw a polyline, the Pline (polyline) command is used:

> Command: <u>PLINE</u>
> From point:

You will always start a polyline by entering a "from point". After this point is entered, the following prompt is issued:

> Current line-width is <u>x</u>

The stated width is the width for all your polylines unless you make a change. This is followed by a rather long prompt:

> Arc/Close/Halfwidth/Length/Undo/Width/<Endpoint of line>:

This prompt contains all the options from which you can branch from this point. The following table explains each of these commands:

A (Arc): Switches to arc mode.

C (Close): Works the same as the Close option for line. A polyline will be drawn back to the starting point and the command will be terminated. The last width entered is used as the width for the closing polyline.

H (Halfwidth): Functions similar to the Width option, except that you can "show" AutoCAD the width by moving the crosshairs from the "from point" to one edge of the desired polyline width. This represents one-half the total width.

L (Length): Draws a line segment at the same angle as the previous segment. You must specify the length.

U (Undo): Works the same as the Undo command for line entities. The last polyline segment entered will be "undone".

W (Width): Selects the width for the succeeding polylines. A zero width produces a polyline like the Line command. A width greater than zero produces a line of the specified width similar to Trace lines. Polylines have both a starting and an ending width. You are prompted for both widths when choosing the Width option:

        Starting width <0.0000>:
        Ending width <0.0000>:

When you specify a starting width, that value becomes the default for the ending width. Setting both the starting and ending widths the same produces polylines of continuous width. If you specify different values, the polyline will be tapered with end widths of the specified values.

POLYLINE EXERCISE

Let's draw some basic polylines!

We'll start by drawing a box. Start a new drawing called "POLY". Set limits of 0,0 and 12,9.

        Command: PLINE
        From point: 1,2
        Current line width 0.0000
        Arc/Close/Halfwidth/Length/Undo/Width/ <Endpoint of line>: W
        Starting width: <0.0000>: .2
        Ending width: <0.2000>: (Enter)

This sets a polyline with a width of .2. Now let's draw the box:

        Arc/Close/Halfwidth/Length/Undo/Width/ <Endpoint of line>: 1,5
        Arc/Close/Halfwidth/Length/Undo/Width/ <Endpoint of line>: 3,5
        Arc/Close/Halfwidth/Length/Undo/Width/ <Endpoint of line>: 3,2
        Arc/Close/Halfwidth/Length/Undo/Width/ <Endpoint of Line>: CLOSE

This exits from the Polyline mode back into the command mode.

DRAWING ARCS WITH POLYLINES

To draw polyline arcs, you must enter the polyline arc mode. This is done by choosing the Arc option.

        Arc/Close/Halfwidth/Length/Undo/Width/<Endpoint of line>: A

AutoCAD then switches to the arc mode and displays the following (another long one) prompt:

        Angle/CEnter/CLose/Direction/Halfwidth/Line/Radius/Second
        pt/Undo/Width/<Endpoint of arc>:

The default is "Endpoint of arc". Therefore, if you enter a point, it is used as the endpoint of the arc.

The Halfwidth, Undo, and Width options are the same as for polylines. The Width and Halfwidth options determine the width of the polyline used to draw the arc and the undo removes the most recent arc.

AutoCAD
» » » »
PLINE:

Arc
Close
Halfwid
Length
Undo
Width

FILL ON
FILL OFF

__LAST__
DRAW
EDIT

The arc starts at the previous point and is tangent to the previous polyline segment. If this is the first segment, the direction will be the same as the direction of the last entity drawn. The options allow you to modify the manner in which the arc is drawn. The following table lists the options and their functions:

A (Angle): Permits you to specify the included angle. The prompt is:

Included angle:

Just like regular arcs, a polyline arc is drawn counterclockwise. If you desire a clockwise rotation, use a negative angle.

CE (Center): Polyline arcs are normally drawn tangent to the previous polyline segment. The CE option allows you to specify the center point for the arc. The prompt is:

Center point:

After the center point is entered, a second prompt is displayed:

Angle/Length/<End point>:

The Angle option refers to the included angle and Length refers to the chord length.

Notice that the CEnter option must be specified by entering "CE" in order to distinguish it from the CLose option.

CL (Close): Functions the same as the Close option for normal polylines, except that the close is performed using an arc.

D (Direction): As previously discussed, the starting direction is determined by the last entity's direction. The Direction option allows you to specify a new starting direction for the arc. You are prompted:

Direction from starting point:

You may then show AutoCAD the starting direction by entering a second point in the desired direction. The next prompt is:

End point:

H (Halfwidth): Same as straight line segments.

L (Line): Exits Arc mode and returns to regular Polyline mode.

R (Radius): Allows you to specify the radius of the arc. After choosing the Radius option, you are prompted with:

Radius:

Then with:

Angle/Length/<<End point>>:

S (Second pt): Using the Second pt option allows you to switch to a three-point type of arc construction. You are prompted:

Second point:
End point:

U (Undo): Same as for straight line segments.

W (Width): Same as for straight line segments.

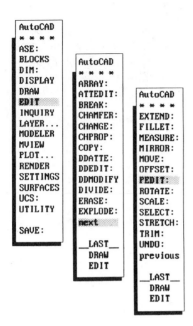

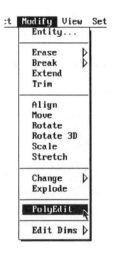

POLYLINE EDITING

The polyline editor is used to modify your polylines. The Pedit command is used to begin editing.

> Command: <u>PEDIT</u>
> Select polyline:

The desired polyline may be selected by any of the standard object selection processes. If the selected entity is not a polyline, AutoCAD prompts you with:

> Entity selected is not a polyline.
> Do you want it to turn into one?

If you respond with a "Y", the entity will be converted into a polyline.

After selecting a polyline, the following prompt is displayed:

> Close/Join/Width/Edit vertex/Fit/Spline/Decurve/Ltype gen/Undo/ eXit <X>:

NOTE: The "Close" option replaces the "Open" option, depending on whether the polyline is open or closed.

The following table describes each option and its function:

C (Close): Closes the polyline by connecting the last point with the first point of the polyline. This command performs the same function as the Close option in the Pline command, except it allows you to close the polyline after you have exited the Pline command.

O (Open): Opens a closed polyline by removing the segment created by the Close option. If the closing segment was not created by the Close option, the Open command will have no effect.

J (Join): The Join option is used to convert and connect non-polyline entities to a polyline. The string of connected entities becomes a polyline that is part of the original polyline.

When you enter the "J" option, AutoCAD prompts:

> Select objects or Window or Last:

You may then select the objects that you wish to join. Several objects may be selected in a continuous string. AutoCAD will then determine any arc, line, or polyline that shares a common endpoint with the current polyline and merge them into that polyline.

In order to be successfully joined, the entities must have a perfect endpoint match (pretty close doesn't count). Use Fillet, or Change and/or object snap to insure a perfect match.

The following example shows the use of the Join option:

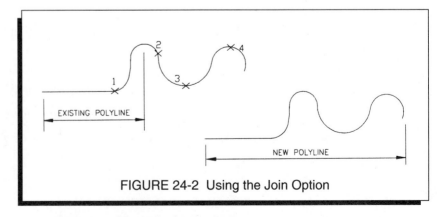

FIGURE 24-2 Using the Join Option

Command: <u>PEDIT</u>
Select polyline: *enter point "1"*
Close/Join/Width/Edit vertex/Fit curve/Decurve/eXit <X>: <u>J</u>
Select objects or Window or Last: *enter points 2, 3, & 4*

The objects picked by points 2, 3, and 4 will be converted into polylines and merged into the polyline selected by point 1.

W (Width): The "W" option allows you to choose a new line width for the entire polyline. When you choose the Width option, AutoCAD prompts:

Enter new width for all segments:

The new width may be entered by either a numerical value from the keyboard or by showing two points on the screen. The following example shows a polyline of varying widths and the same polyline after use of the Width option:

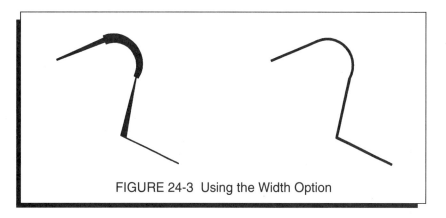

FIGURE 24-3 Using the Width Option

E (Edit vertex): The connecting points of the segments of a polyline are called a vertex. The "E" option allows you to edit a vertex and all the segments that follow it. Vertex editing is another mode, and is covered later in this chapter.

F (Fit curve): The fit curve option constructs smooth curves from the vertices in the polyline. Extra vertices are inserted by AutoCAD where necessary.

S (Spline curve): Creates a spline curve from the edited polyline. See the following section on spline curves.

D (Decurve): Negates the effects of the two curve options.

L (Linetype generation): Controls the generation of linetype through the vertices of the polyline. If the polyline linetype is set to other than continuous, the linetype dashes and dots are generated for each individual segment of the polyline. Depending on the linetype scale, some polyline segments will not show the linetype. If linetype generation is turned on, the polyline is considered as one segment when the linetype is applied, resulting in a uniform linetype pattern along the entire length of the polyline.

U (Undo): Reverses the last Pedit operation.

X (eXit): Exits the Pedit mode and returns to the command prompt.

CONSTRUCTING SPLINE CURVES

The Spline option of polyline editing is used to construct spline curves (specifically, cubic B-spline) from a polyline.

To construct the spline curve, select the Pedit command. Select the polyline to convert and select the "S" (Spline) option. Note that splined curves can only be constructed from polylines.

SPLINE ANATOMY

To properly construct spline curves, we must first understand the manner in which they work. The spline uses the original polyline as the frame of the spline curve.

This frame may be open or closed. In the case of the open frame, the spline is "connected" to the first and last vertex points (beginning and endpoints of the polyline). Each vertex point between these exerts a "pull" on the curve.

Notice that more central points about an area will exert more pull on the curve in that area.

The spline curve frame (original polyline) may be displayed or not, and consequently, plotted or not. The Splframe variable is used to control the visibility of the frame. If Splframe is set to 0, frames are not displayed. If set to 1, the frames will be displayed after a subsequent regeneration.

The Decurve option allows you to restore the polyline to its original configuration. Decurve may be applied to curves constructed with either the Curve or Spline options.

Polyarc segments are straightened for spline frame purposes. If the polyline contains differing line widths, a resulting spline curve will contain a smooth taper that begins with the width of the first endpoint and ends with the width of the last endpoint. This differs from a curve constructed with the Fit Curve option, which maintains width information for each segment.

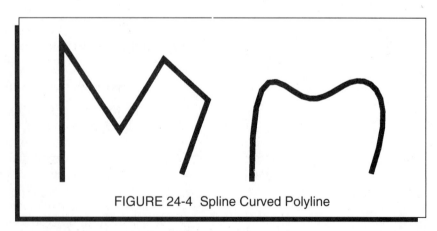

FIGURE 24-4 Spline Curved Polyline

The nature of the spline curve allows it to yield a more accurate curve with fewer central points.

Spline curves construct curves in a different manner than the Fit Curve method. Fit Curves constructs curves using a pair of arcs at each central point. More central points are required to obtain each central point. More central points are required to obtain a reasonably accurate curve. The nature of the spline curve allows it to yield a more accurate curve with fewer central points. The illustrations show the relationship of applying both the Fit Curve and Spline method of curve construction to the polyline shown on the left.

SPLINE SEGMENTS

Each spline contains a specified number of line segments used to construct the spline. These are the number of lines between each central point. The variable Splinesegs (spline segments) is used to control this number. The default is eight segments.

> Command: <u>SETVAR</u>
> New value for SPLINESEGS <8>:

Setting a larger Splinesegs value will yield a smoother curve. This should be balanced against the increased drawing size and longer regeneration times created by the larger number of segments. If a negative value is used for Splinesegs, the resulting curve will be constructed as a Fit Curve, with the number value determining the number of segments between central points.

EFFECTS OF EDIT COMMANDS ON SPLINES

Edit commands cause spline curves to react in different ways. The following describes the effects of each.

Move/Copy/Erase/Rotate/Scale/Mirror: Changes both the curve and the curve frame.

Explode/Break/Trim: Deletes the frame and creates a permanent change to the curve.

Decurve cannot be applied after using.

Offset: Copies only the curve (without the frame) for the new offset object.

Stretch: The frame itself is stretched and the curve is refitted to the new frame. The frame can be stretched whether it is visible or not.

Divide/Measure/Area (Entity)/Hatch/Chamfer/Fillet: Applies only to the curve and not the frame.

Pedit (Join): Decurves the polyline. After the Join process is completed, the Spline curve fit may be reconstructed.

Pedit (Vertex edit): Moves the markers (denoted by "x") to the vertices on the frame (whether visible or invisible). When the spline curve is edited with Inset, Move, Straighten, or Width, the curve is automatically refit. When the Break option is applied, the polyline is decurved.

Object Snap: Object snap recognizes only the curve.

IGES: IGESOUT translates only the curve information as a polyline.

POLYLINE VERTEX EDITING

Vertex editing is used to modify the vertices of a polyline. If you wish to edit the vertices in a polyline, choose the "E" (Edit vertex) option and you are presented with another option line.

> Next/Previous/Break/Insert/Move/Regen/Straighten/Tangent/Width/eXit <N>:

The first vertex is marked by an "X".

The first vertex is marked by an "X". If you have specified a tangent direction for that particular vertex, an arrow is displayed designating the direction.

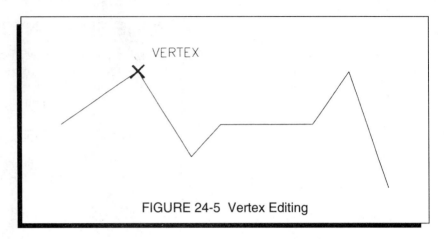

FIGURE 24-5 Vertex Editing

The following table explains the options on the vertex editing option line and their functions:

N (Next) & P (Previous): These options are used to move the identification marker "X". If you enter "N", you may then step through the vertices of the polyline by pressing the Enter key each time a move is desired. Choosing the P (Previous) option allows you to "back up" in the same manner. When you reach the last vertex in the polyline, you must back up to reach previous vertices. You may not wrap around the polyline, even if it is closed.

B (Break): The Break option performs the same function as the normal Break command, except that the break may only occur at vertices. To perform a break, move the marker to the vertices where you wish the break to begin and enter "B". The following prompt then appears:

Next/Previous/Go/eXit <N>:

Use the Next and/or Previous options to move to the end of the desired break and enter "Go". The segments between the points will be deleted. The example below shows the effects of the Break option:

If you wish to cancel the break while it is in progress, enter "X" (exit).

It is not possible to delete the entire polyline by entering break points at the first and last vertices.

If you break a closed polyline, it becomes "open" and AutoCAD removes the closing segment.

I (Insert): A new vertex may be added to the polyline by using the Insert option. The following prompt is displayed:

Enter location of new vertex:

The new vertex will be added at the location after the vertex that is currently marked by the "X". The following illustrations show a vertex insert.

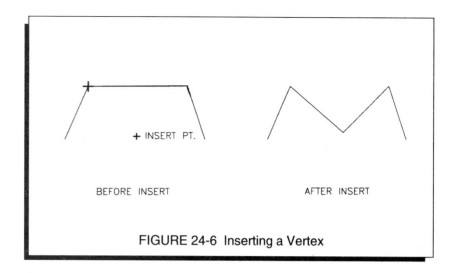

FIGURE 24-6 Inserting a Vertex

M (Move): Use the Move option to relocate a vertex. The following prompt appears:

Enter new location:

Enter the point that represents the new location for the current vertex.

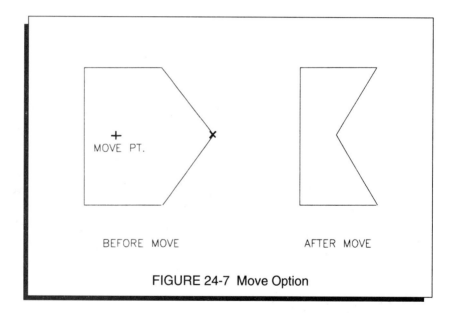

FIGURE 24-7 Move Option

R (Regen): Regenerates the polyline.

S (Straighten): The Straighten option is used in the same manner as the Break option described earlier, except the segments between the selected points are deleted and then replaced with a straight line segment. If you wish to straighten an arc segment, select the vertex immediately preceding the arc and enter both points on that vertex.

The illustrations below show the effect of the Straighten option:

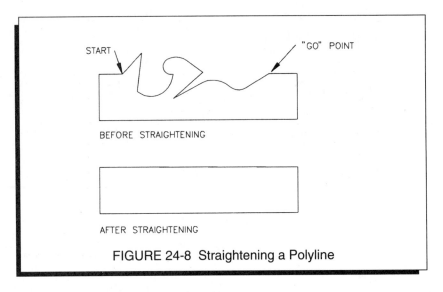

FIGURE 24-8 Straightening a Polyline

The eXit option cancels the operation if it is currently in progress.

T (Tangent): Used to assign a tangent direction to the current vertex for use at a later time in curve fitting. You are prompted:

Direction of tangent:

You may specify the direction by either entering a numerically described angle or showing AutoCAD the angle by entering a point in relation to the currently marked vertex.

W (Width): The Width option in the vertex editing portion of Pedit differs from the normal Width option. Whereas the normal Width command determines the width for the entire polyline (and all its segments), the Width option in the vertex editing option line changes the width of just the segment following the vertex currently marked by the "X". AutoCAD prompts:

Enter starting width <current>:
Enter ending width <start>:

The default starting width is equal to the current starting width for the segment being edited. As usual, the default ending width is shown equal to the starting width.

You must use the Regen option (see above) to redraw the screen and display the new segment width.

X (Exit): Exits vertex editing and returns to the Pedit option line.

EXCHANGE FILE FORMATS

AutoCAD drawing files may be converted to a form that can be read and used by external programs. For example, a database program can read a DXF (drawing interchange format file) and extract blocks for compilation. The file format is available to programmers for development purposes and is generated in ASCII format.

DXF and IGES files may also be produced by other programs for AutoCAD to read. Let's look at AutoCAD's file exchange formats.

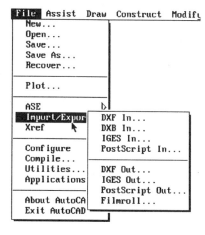

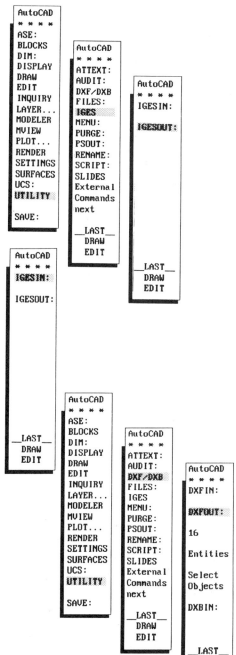

IGES FILE FORMAT

The Igesout and Igesin commands are used to produce and use IGES file formats compatible with IGES version 4.0.

CONVERTING TO A IGES FILE

An existing AutoCAD drawing may be converted to an IGES file by means of the Igesout command. This creates a file that can be read by certain other software programs. To create an IGES file, enter:

Command: IGESOUT

AutoCAD displays a **Create IGES File** dialogue box. If you enter a new file name, an ".IGS" extension will be added. It is not necessary to append the extension to the drawing name, since AutoCAD will add it automatically. If a file of the same name already exists, AutoCAD will delete it. If you add a file extension explicitly, AutoCAD will use that file extension instead of ".IGS".

USING AN EXISTING IGES FILE

An existing IGES file may be converted to an AutoCAD drawing by using the Igesin command. To use the Igesin command, begin a new drawing, Then execute the Igesin command.

Command: IGESIN

AutoCAD will display a **Select IGES File** dialogue box. Enter the name of the IGES file, then select the "OK" check box.

The file will then be converted. If AutoCAD encounters an error in conversion, the process is stopped and an error message is displayed.

DRAWING INTERCHANGE FILE FORMAT

Drawing interchange files (DXF) are a popular way to exchange graphics files between software programs. AutoCAD uses the Dxfin and Dxfout commands to use and produce DXF files.

PRODUCING A DXFOUTFILE

The Dxfout command produces a drawing interchange format file from an AutoCAD drawing for use by external programs. To produce a DXF file, issue the Dxfout command while in the drawing from which you wish to produce the file.

Command: DXFOUT

AutoCAD displays a **Create DXF File** dialogue box. Enter the name of the file you wish to produce and click the "OK" button. AutoCAD will prompt for the accuracy.

Enter decimal places of accuracy (0 to 16)/Entities/Binary <6>:

The file is written with a .DXF file extension (do not specify the extension, it is automatically appended).

The second prompt line permits the option of specifying Entities or Binary.

Selecting Entities will cause AutoCAD to request the entities that will be extracted. Block definitions will not be included.

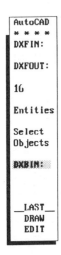

Selecting Binary causes the file to be in binary format, as opposed to ASCII format.

You are finally prompted for the precision of the output file (0 to 16 decimal places).

The output file will be a separate file from the drawing; it will not replace it.

USING AN EXISTING DXF FILE

A drawing interchange file may be converted to an AutoCAD drawing file by using the Dxfin command.

To convert a DXF file, first enter the drawing editor by starting a new drawing. The drawing may be of any name.

Next, issue the Dxfin command.

    Command: <u>DXFIN</u>

AutoCAD will display a **Select DXF File** dialogue box. Select the name of the DXF file and click on the "OK" button. It is not necessary to include the .DXF file extension.

If you wish to convert the entire drawing, only use the Dxfin command in a new drawing, before any entities are added. If a DXF file is loaded into a drawing that is not new, only the entities will be converted and the following message will be displayed:

    Not a new drawing -- only ENTITIES section will be input.

DRAWING INTERCHANGE BINARY FILES

Some programs, such as AutoSHADE that are executed through the external commands facility, can use an abbreviated form of a binary format file. This special type of format is called a binary drawing interchange file (DXB).

AutoCAD can load a binary drawing interchange file in the same manner as a DXF file by using the Dxbin command.

    Command: <u>DXBIN</u>

AutoCAD displays a **Select DXB File** dialogue box. Select the name of the DXB file and click on the "OK" button.

DRAWING FILE DIAGNOSTICS

The Audit command is used to examine an existing drawing for damage. This diagnostics tool can also be used to correct damage to a file. The command sequence for the Audit command is as follows.

    Command: <u>AUDIT</u>
    Fix any errors detected? <N>:

If you answer "No" to the "Fix any errors detected?" question, AutoCAD will display a report, but not fix the errors. Answering "Yes" will both display a report and fix the errors.

If a drawing contains no errors, AutoCAD will display a report showing the audit activity and the conclusion that no errors were found.

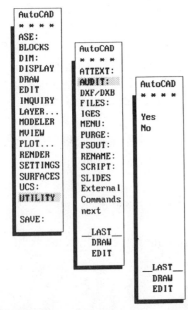

In addition to the screen report, the Audit command prints to file an audit report of the drawing file.

In addition to the screen report, the Audit command prints to file an audit report of the drawing file. This file has the same name as the drawing file with a file extension of ".ADT". You can read (with the DOS Type command, or a word processor) this file, or print it on a printer.

DRAWING FILE RECOVERY

In a perfect world, everything works as planned. In our real world, however, we sometimes encounter difficulties. One day you will see a message on the screen that says:

> INTERNAL ERROR (followed by a host of code numbers)

or

> FATAL ERROR.

This means that AutoCAD has encountered a problem and can not continue. You will usually be given a choice of whether or not you wish to save the changes you have made since the last time you saved your work. The following message is displayed:

> AutoCAD cannot continue, but any changes to your drawing made up to the start of the last command can be saved.
>
> Do you want to save your changes? <Y>:

If you select "Yes", AutoCAD will attempt to write the changes to disk. If it is successful, the following message will be displayed:

> DRAWING FILE SUCCESSFULLY SAVED

If the save is unsuccessful, one of the following messages are displayed:

> INTERNAL ERROR

or

> FATAL ERROR

If you see this, you can wave goodbye to all the changes made since you last saved your work. (Of course every good CAD operator saves their work regularly.)

You may manually recover damaged drawing files by using the Recover command. When you use the Recover command, AutoCAD displays the **Open Drawing File** dialogue box. Pick the damaged drawing file and click on the "OK" button. AutoCAD will attempt to recover the damaged file. If successful, the drawing will be displayed.

If a drawing file is detected as damaged when you open it with the Open command, AutoCAD will perform an automatic audit of the drawing. If the audit is successful, the drawing is loaded for use. If it is not, the drawing will usually be unrecoverable.

If you exit the drawing without saving, the "repair" performed by AutoCAD will be discarded. If the recovery is successful and you save the drawing, you can load it normally the next time.

CHAPTER REVIEW

1. What does the Pline option "Close" perform?

   _____

   _____

   _____

2. What option is used to create a tapered polyline?

   _____

3. What mode controls the display of solid areas in polylines?

   _____

4. What command is used explicitly to edit polylines?

   _____

5. What is a polyline vertex?

   _____

   _____

   _____

6. How do you edit a polyline vertex?

   _____

   _____

   _____

7. What types of vertex editing can you perform?

   _____

   _____

   _____

8. Can a spline curve be used on an entity other than a polyline?

   _____

9. What variable setting controls the number of segments used in a spline curve?

   _____

10. What is an IGES file?

   _____

   _____

   _____

11. How do you create a DXF file?

_____

_____

_____

12. What is the Audit command used for?

_____

_____

_____

CHAPTER 25

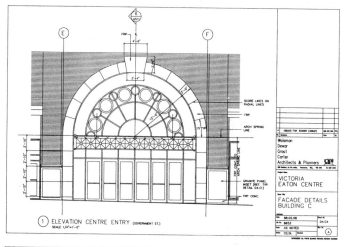

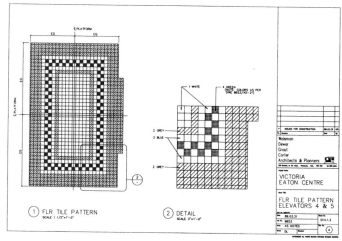

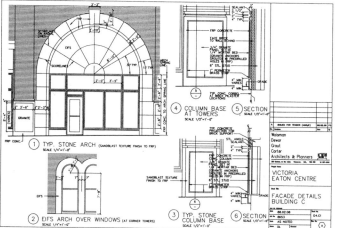

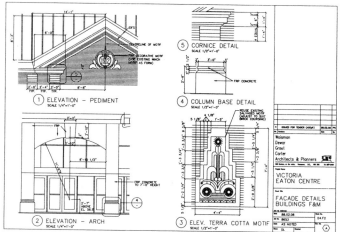

Viewports and Working Space

OBJECTIVES:

One of the most interesting aspects of AutoCAD is the viewports and working space capability. Learning to use these can be very helpful in many types of work. Chapter 25 objectives are:

● To learn how to construct and use multiple viewports.

● To save and retrieve viewport configurations.

● To learn the aspects of the two types of working spaces in AutoCAD.

● To become proficient with the use of viewports and working spaces by example and tutorial.

USING VIEWPORTS IN AUTOCAD

The AutoCAD drawing editor screen may be divided into several "windows", called *viewports*. Each viewport may display a different view or zoom of the current drawing.

The following illustration shows a four-viewport screen, with different views and zooms of the same drawing.

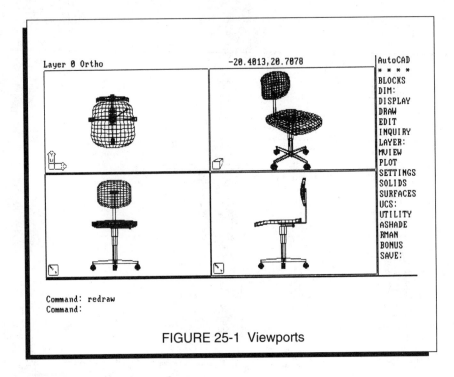

FIGURE 25-1 Viewports

THE CURRENT VIEWPORT

Only one viewport may be active at one time.

Each viewport may be drawn in individually. However, only one viewport may be active at one time. When drawing in the active viewport, the crosshair will be displayed in that viewport, and all command activities are performed in the normal manner.

If the crosshair is moved into another view window, it becomes an arrow. To change another viewport to the active viewport, move the arrow into it and click the left button on the input device. The crosshairs will then be displayed and normal drawing activities may be performed.

You may alternately change the current viewport by pressing Ctrl-V on the keyboard. As the active viewport is changed, the border around the viewport is highlighted.

DRAWING BETWEEN VIEWPORTS

It is sometimes helpful to draw between viewports. For example, you may want to zoom in to a particular area of a drawing and connect a line to another area of the drawing that is not displayed in the current viewport. You may start the line in the current viewport, then move the cursor into the other viewport and click the input device. You have now changed the current viewport. The crosshair is displayed in the new current viewport and you may continue the Line command by connecting to the desired point that is displayed in the new current viewport.

> ## Tip
>
> Drawing between viewports is especially helpful when drawing in 3-D. You may display a 3-D view in one viewport, and the plan view in another.

You can not change viewports while some commands are active. These commands are as follows.

Dview	Vpoint
Grid	Vport
Pan	Zoom
Snap	

SETTING VIEWPORT WINDOWS

You may create from one to sixteen viewport displays, depending on the type of operating system and display system.

To set the number and design of viewports displayed on the screen, use the Viewport command.

Command: <u>VIEWPORTS</u> (*you may alternately use the command VPORTS*)
Save/Restore/Delete/Join/?/2/<3>/4:

Let's look at each option.

Save: A current viewport configuration may be named and saved. It may then be recalled at any time in the future (you must, of course, be in the same drawing). The following information is stored with the Save option.

Number of viewports
Viewport positions
Grid and snap modes and spacings for each
Viewres mode
Ucsicon settings
Views set by either the Dview or Vpoint commands
Dview perspective mode
Dview clipping planes

The saved viewport configuration name may be up to 31 characters in length. You may use any letter and the special characters of dollar ($), hyphen (-), and underscore (_).

Restore: After one or more viewport configurations are saved, a desired configuration may be recalled by using the Restore option. The prompt will ask for the name of the configuration to restore. You may enter a question mark (?) in response to the prompt to obtain a listing of the saved viewport configurations.

Delete: Deletes a saved viewport configuration.

Join: Permits merging one viewport with another. One of the viewports to be merged is identified as the "dominant" viewport. The dominant viewport's display will inherit the new viewport created by the merging of the two.

When the Join option is selected, the following prompt is displayed:

Select dominant viewport <current>:
Select viewport to merge:

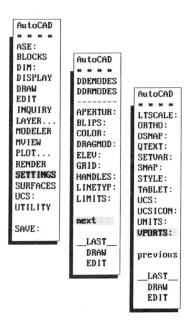

Select each viewport by moving the cursor into it and clicking. You may select the current viewport as the dominant viewport by pressing Enter in response to the prompt for the dominant viewport.

If you select viewports that will not merge into one rectangular viewport, an error message will be displayed. AutoCAD then reissues the prompt.

SI: Returns to a single viewport display. The viewport that is current will be displayed in the single viewport.

?: Each viewport is identified by a number. Responding to the prompt with a question mark (?) displays a listing of the viewport numbers, with the following information.

Coordinates of each display window of the current configuration

Names of each saved configuration

Coordinates of each display window in the saved configurations (viewport identification numbers are not displayed for saved coordinates)

The number and coordinates of the currently active window are displayed first. The coordinates are not true absolute coordinates. The lower left of the screen is designated by the coordinates of 0,0. However, the upper right coordinates are always identified as a value up to 1,1.

2, 3, 4: To set the number of viewports, enter the desired number (2, 3, or 4) in response to the prompt. You are then prompted for the desired placement of the windows. The subsequent prompts depend on the number of viewports you request. The following illustrations show some possible placements.

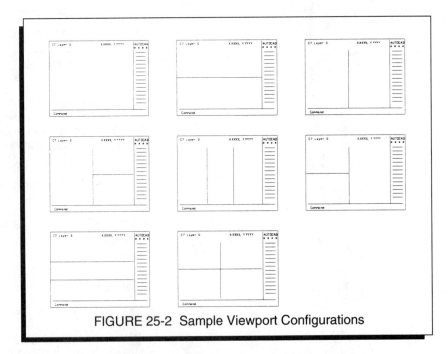

FIGURE 25-2 Sample Viewport Configurations

Let's look at how the selected number of viewports and placements are controlled.

2: Splits the screen in half, displaying two windows. You are prompted to designate whether the screen is divided horizontally or vertically.

3: Creates three windows: two small windows and one large, or three equal windows. You are prompted:

Horizontal/Vertical/Above/Below/Left/<Right>:

The Horizontal and Vertical options display three equal windows, situated either horizontally or vertically. The other options are used to create one large and two small windows. The selected option determines the location of the large window. For example, selecting Above places one large window above two small ones.

4: Creates four windows of equal size.

When multiple viewports are selected, each window initially displays the current view of the previous single-screen display. If the previous display contained multiple viewports, each of the windows in the new configuration will initially display the view of the previously current window.

REDRAWS AND REGENERATIONS IN VIEWPORTS

The Redraw and Regen (regeneration) commands affect only the current viewport. If you wish to perform either a redraw or regeneration on all viewports simultaneously, use Redrawall or Regenall, respectively.

VIEWPORTS EXERCISE

Start a new drawing named "PORTS". Let's use the Vports command to set up four viewports.

Command: <u>VPORTS</u>
Save/Restore/Delete/Join/SIngle/?/2/<3>/4: <u>4</u>

You should now see four viewports on the screen as shown in the following illustration.

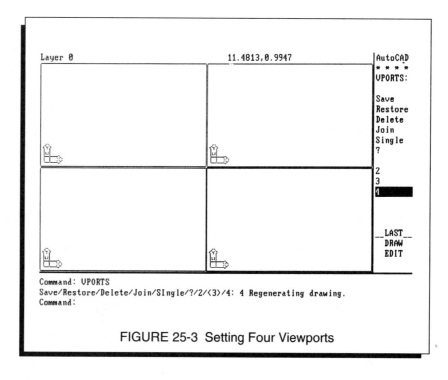

FIGURE 25-3 Setting Four Viewports

Move the crosshairs between the viewports. Notice how the crosshairs only show up in one of the viewports. When you move into the other viewports, the crosshairs turn into an arrow. Move into one of the viewports where an arrow is displayed and click the button on your input device. You should now see crosshairs in that viewport. This is how you change active viewports.

If you are not there now, move into the upper left viewport and make it active. Draw several circles in the drawing area. Notice how the circles appear in all the viewports.

Move to the upper right viewport and make it active. Use the Zoom command to zoom in on one of the circles. Next, move to the lower left viewport and zoom in on another circle. Now select the Line command and with object snap, select the center of the circle. Before placing the second endpoint of the line, move to the upper right viewport and click to make it active. With object snap CENter, place the line's second endpoint at the center of the circle on the screen. Notice how you can monitor the activity of the entire screen on the viewport at the upper left, since it is in a "zoom all" display.

WORKING SPACES

In AutoCAD, you can work in either model space or paper space. Model space is the space you are used to working in now. Most of your work will still be performed in model space.

Paper space is used to arrange, detail, and plot views of your work. You arrange views in paper space by moving and sizing viewports. In paper space, viewports are handled as entities and can be edited with AutoCAD's standard edit commands. This allows you to place and plot different views of your work on the same drawing sheet (you can only plot the currently active viewport from model space).

In order to use paper space, you must first set the system variable Tilemode to zero.

In order to use paper space, you must first set the system variable Tilemode to zero (or "off"). You can do this by either entering the Setvar command, then entering Tilemode as the system variable to change or issue Tilemode as a command at the command prompt.

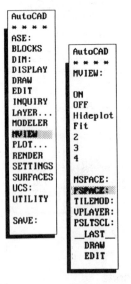

MODEL SPACE AND PAPER SPACE

You switch between paper space and model space with the Pspace and Mspace commands, respectively. Let's look at each command and how it works.

SWITCHING TO PAPER SPACE

Use the Pspace command to switch to paper space. Before you can do this, the system variable Tilemode must be set to zero. The Pspace command has no options.

Command: PSPACE

PAPER SPACE ICON

When you are in paper space, AutoCAD displays an icon at the lower left of the screen. A "P" is also displayed on the status line at the top of the screen.

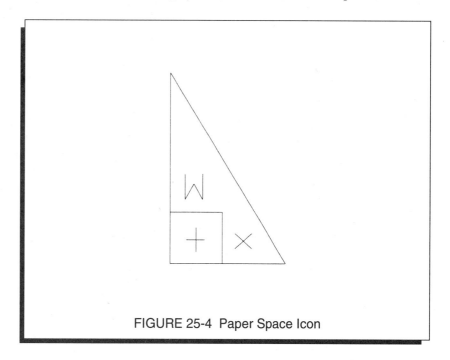

FIGURE 25-4 Paper Space Icon

SWITCHING TO MODEL SPACE

You switch to model space by issuing the Mspace command. Model space is the space you were used to working in before now. There are no options for Mspace.

Command: MSPACE

MVIEW COMMAND

The Mview command is used to create and manage viewports in paper space. Mview only works in paper space. If you select Mview while in model space, AutoCAD automatically switches to paper space, while issuing a message to inform you of the change.

Command: MVIEW
Switching to Paper Space
ON/OFF/Hideplot/Fit/2/3/4/Restore <First Point>:

When you switch to paper space, you will not initially see any of your drawing. Before you do, you must first create a viewport with the Mview command. Your drawing will be displayed in this viewport. The drawing will be displayed in the last zoom or viewpoint (if in 3-D).

In paper space, you can edit the viewports you created with the Mview command with AutoCAD's edit facilities. Let's look at the Mview command's options, then look at an example of using paper space.

Mview only works in paper space.

MVIEW OPTIONS

When you issue the Mview command, you are presented with a selection of options.

```
Command: MVIEW
Switching to Paper Space
ON/OFF/Hideplot/Fit/2/3/4/Restore <First Point>:
```

Let's look at each of the options.

<First point>: This is the default. If you simply enter a point on the screen, you will set the first corner of a box that will become a new viewport. AutoCAD will prompt you for the other corner. Move the cursor away from the first point and you will see a box forming. Enter the second point and you will see the viewport form with your drawing contained within the viewport.

ON/OFF: Used to turn off or on the contents of a viewport. This is helpful if you do not want to regenerate all the viewports as you edit.

If you turn off all the viewports, you will not be able to work in model space.

If you create and attempt to turn on more viewports than the maximum number, AutoCAD will turn on the maximum number of viewports. The rest will be marked ON and will be plotted, but will not display.

The maximum number of viewports is determined by the operating system and your display system. The maximum number (up to the possible maximum) is set with the Maxactvp system variable.

Hideplot: This option allows you to specify which viewports will be plotted with the hidden lines removed. You can either choose to have the hidden lines removed in all the viewports or just in the ones you choose.

This is especially useful if you are plotting a sheet that contains a 3-D view of an object in one of the viewports. When you select Hideplot, you can turn the Hideplot function either on or off. If you turn it off, you can choose individual viewport(s) to be plotted with hidden lines.

```
Command: MVIEW
Switching to Paper Space
ON/OFF/Hideplot/Fit/2/3/4/<First Point>: H
ON/OFF: OFF
Select objects:
```

You can now select the viewports to be plotted with hidden lines.

Note that the selection of a viewport does not create a hidden line view. It will only plot with hidden lines. If you wish to display a hidden line view, use the Hide command.

Fit: Selecting Fit will create a new viewport that will fill the current graphics screen. Note that this will not fill the entire limits of the drawing if you are zoomed in to a part of the drawing. It will fill the currently displayed area.

2, 3, 4: Creates either two, three, or four viewports. The use of this option is similar to setting a specified number of viewports with the Vports command, except the viewports are created to fill the currently displayed screen area or an area you specify by building a box by placing two corner points. If you select either 2, 3, or 4, AutoCAD responds with:

Fit/<first point>:

Fit will fill the currently displayed screen area with the specified number of viewports, while "<first point>" (the default) allows you to specify the area for the viewports by selecting two corner points that define the area.

Since the choices can conceivably build configurations of different arrangements (for example, side by side or over and under for two viewports), AutoCAD prompts for the arrangement.

The following is an overview of the prompts and responses used with each choice.

2: A prompt asks if you want a horizontal or vertical division. Vertical is the default.

3: The following prompt is displayed:

Horizontal/Vertical/Above/Below/Left/<Right>:

4: Creates four equally spaced viewports automatically.

Restore: Permits you to create a new set of viewports based on a previously saved configuration. AutoCAD prompts:

?/Name of window configuration to insert <*default*>:

Entering a question mark (?) will display the names of saved viewport configurations. Enter the name of the saved configuration and press Enter and AutoCAD prompts:

Fit/<first point>:

As before, Fit fills the entire currently displayed area with the viewports, while "<first point>" permits you to define an area for the viewports by creating a box with two corner points.

CREATING RELATIVE SCALES IN PAPER SPACE

The obvious primary use of AutoCAD's paper space is to create drawings with various views and details in a single, plottable drawing. Many times this requires that part of the drawing be plotted at a different scale. Let's look at an example.

Suppose that we have a floor plan of a house. The scale of the floor plan is ¼" = 1'0". We want to place an enlarged plan of a bath, with dimensions, on the same drawing sheet. We could switch to paper space and create a new viewport. We can then switch back to model space, zoom into the bath area, and dimension it. The problem is that we wish the bath area to be plotted at a scale of ½" = 1'0".

We can create this scale by using a function of the Zoom command. If we are in model space, we can make a viewport active, then zoom at a factor of the paper scale. Let's look at an example.

Electronic Work Disk Problem

WORKING SPACE TUTORIAL

Start the drawing from the work disk named "PSPLAN". This is a drawing of a floor plan as shown in the following illustration.

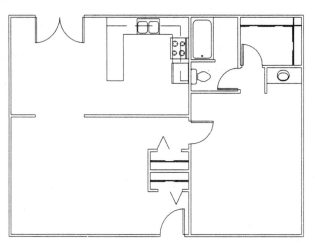

FIGURE 25-5 PSPlan Work Disk Drawing

The drawing is drawn in architectural units with limits of 0,0 and 96',72'. This is set up to be plotted at ¼" = 1'0" on a C-size (24" × 18") sheet of paper.

We wish to enlarge an area containing the bath and show this area at a scale of ½" = 1'0". Let's look at the steps for doing this.

First, let's set the Tilemode to 0.

    Command: TILEMODE
    New value for TILEMODE <1>: 0

AutoCAD will now switch to paper space automatically, displaying a message telling you it is doing so.

The limits for the model space have been set, but they have not been set for paper space. Let's set the limits.

    Command: LIMITS
    Reset paper space limits:
    ON/OFF/<Lower left corner> <default>: 0,0
    Upper right corner <default>: 96',72'

Now perform a Zoom All to display the entire drawing area.

Let's now build the first viewport, using the Mview command.

    Command: MVIEW
    ON/OFF/Hideplot/Fit/2/3/4/Restore/<First Point>: F

Your drawing should now be present on the screen. Next, use the Mview command again to place a new viewport in the upper right area of the drawing. Use the following command sequence and Figure 25-6 to place the viewport.

    Command: MVIEW
    ON/OFF/Hideplot/Fit/2/3/4/Restore/<First Point>: (enter point "1")
    Other corner: (enter point "2")

Notice how the entire floorplan is contained in the viewport. Let's switch to model space.

    Command: MSPACE

Move the cursor into the new viewport and click to make it the active viewport. Now zoom into the area of the bath.

Let's now use AutoCAD's Zoom command to zoom and scale the contents of the new viewport in relation to the paper space units.

Command: ZOOM
All/Center/Dynamic/Extents/Left/Previous/Vmax/Window/<Scale (X/XP)>: 2XP

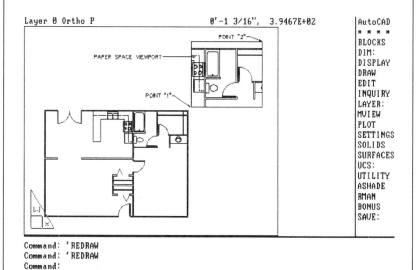

FIGURE 25-6 Completed Paper Space Drawing

Notice how the scale of the viewport changes. The area of the plan you wanted to show may not be correctly centered. While in model space, use the Pan command to reposition the drawing. After you have finished, change to paper space.

Command: PSPACE

Now that you are in paper space, the viewports themselves are entities. Note that you can not edit the actual floor plan, but work with the viewports. The viewport may be too large or small. Use the Stretch command to stretch the viewport (don't worry about getting the crossing window over the floor plan). You can stretch the viewport to the correct size to show the area of the bath you want.

After the bath area is properly positioned, use the Text command to create titles for each drawing. If this is performed in paper space, the text can be placed anywhere on the screen, even outside of the viewports.

You may want to dimension the floor plan. If you do, switch back to model space so you can edit the floor plan drawing.

CHAPTER REVIEW

1. How many viewports can be active at one time?

2. Can you switch between viewports while in a draw command?

_____

3. How would you save a viewport configuration that you wanted to use again?

_____

_____

_____

4. When you join two viewports, what is meant by the term "dominant" viewport?

_____

_____

_____

5. How would you regenerate all the viewports in one operation?

_____

_____

_____

6. What must the Tilemode variable be set to before you can enter paper space?

_____

_____

_____

7. When can the Mview command be used?

_____

_____

_____

8. How would you place a new viewport that would fill the entire screen in paper space?

_____

_____

_____

9. Do model space and paper space have different limits?

_____

10. How do you switch from paper space to model space?

_____

_____

_____

CHAPTER 26

Attributes

OBJECTIVES:

Many types of CAD drawings can be used with attributes. Attributes are often avoided because they look difficult to work with. Once you are familiar with the concept and learn the use of some basic commands, attributes can be very helpful and rewarding. Chapter 26 objectives are:

● To understand what attributes are and how they are used.

● To learn the anatomy of attributes.

● To become proficient with the use of AutoCAD commands used with attributes.

● To learn how to produce attribute output files for printing and use with other computer programs.

AutoCAD
In The
Real
World

Designing Disk Heads

AutoCAD® is used to design disk-head suspension systems and manage their manufacture

Today's CAD users are demanding larger capacities and faster access times from their disk drives. A critical component in the hard drive is the suspension assembly. This component floats the read/write head just above a spinning magnetic disk, maintaining a gap of air that separates a routine AutoCAD session from a disk "crash." For a hard drive to meet these demands of capacity and speed, stringent product designs and tight manufacturing tolerances are required from the suspension assemblies.

Hutchinson Technology, Inc. (HTI) is the world's largest manufacturer of suspension assemblies. HTI also manufactures flexible circuits and other precision components for use in a number of electronic applications.

Hutchinson uses AutoCAd in a wide range of applications: to design the die and fixture tooling used in the manufacture of various products, to maintain over 380,000 square feet of facilities, to design manufacturing equipment, to design new products, and to design suspension assemblies and flexible circuits.

AutoCAD is used because, with this large number of diverse needs, HTI needed the software that could best meet the requirements of each discipline.

HTI feels the most important contribution AutoCAD makes to the final product is the improved interface between design and manufacturing functions. For example, AutoCAD can create a design from the customer's specs and provide the geometric information needed to manufacture the customer's circuits. In addition, NC programs, used to manufacture a circuit are generated from an AutoCAD model. Then these drawings are used by the tool design department to create the tooling needed to manufacture the circuit in mass quantities.

AutoCAD's integration capabilities are responsible for HTI's designs to build a CAD network that includes not only CAD but CAM and CAE as well.

Adapted from an article by David Makig in *CADalyst*. Copyright © 1990 by CADalyst Publications, Ltd.

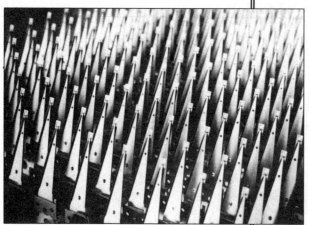

Suspension assemblies for disk drives manufactured by Hutchinson Technology, Inc.

ATTRIBUTES

An attribute may be considered as a "label" that is attached to the block.

AutoCAD allows you to add *attributes* to a block. An attribute may be considered as a "label" that is attached to the block. This label contains any information you desire.

The information from each block may be taken from AutoCAD's database file and used in other places such as database programs.

Attributes are placed in the drawing with the block they are attached to. When the block is inserted, the values for the attributes are requested by AutoCAD. You determine what information is requested, the actual prompts, and the default values for the information requested.

TUTORIAL

Let's look at an example of using attributes. You are now the manager of an engineering department that utilizes CAD (see how CAD has already helped your career?). The department contains several CAD workstations, each with an employee, a computer, and a telephone. You use attributes to keep information on each of these items contained in the floor plan of the department.

Start a new drawing called OFFICE. Set limits of 0,0 and 24,18. Draw walls as shown below:

FIGURE 26-1 Office Walls

First, you must draw the desk. (Do this now.) It might help to zoom a bit. Now to set up the attributes.

DEFINING ATTRIBUTES

The ATTDEF command is used to set up a template for the attribute (or label). Each label is made up of different bits of information. Your attribute will include the name of employee, the type of computer used, and the telephone extension number of that station. These items are called *tags*.

ATTRIBUTE TAG

A tag is the name of a part of an attribute. The following tags will be used in your attribute:

    EMPLOYEE_NAME:
    COMPUTER:
    EXT._NO.:

Notice that we used underlines instead of spaces. Blank spaces are not allowed in tag names. You may also use a backslash (\) as a leading character in lieu of spaces.

Let's jump in and execute the Attdef command:

    Command: ATTDEF
    Attribute modes - Invisible:N Constant:N Verify:N Preset:N
    Enter (ICVP) to change, RETURN when done:

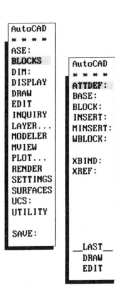

Let's look at the options for the attribute modes:

Invisible: The "I" option determines whether the labeling is visible when the block containing the attribute is inserted. If you later want to visibly display the attribute, you may use the ATTDISP command.

Constant: The "C" option gives every attribute the same value. This might be useful if every computer on every desk is the same. Beware! If you designate an attribute to contain a constant value, you can not change it later.

Verify: If you use the "V" option, you will be asked to verify that every value is correct.

Preset: Allows presetting values that are variable, but not prompted when the block is inserted. The values are automatically set to their preset values. The preset option is not active if the attributes are entered via the attribute dialogue box.

Each preset option is either activated (Y) or not activated (N). To change the current setting for each, enter I, C, V or P. The corresponding setting will toggle between N and Y, and the "Attribute modes" line will be redisplayed, reflecting the change. When you have set each option as desired, press the ENTER key.

Let's leave the modes as they are for now, so press the ENTER key.

You are then prompted for the:

Attribute tag:

The attribute tag is the name of the attribute. We first enter the tag of "EMPLOYEE_NAME".

You are then prompted for the:

Attribute prompt:

The prompt is the text that will appear on the text line when the block containing the attribute is inserted. If you want the prompt to be the same as the tag name, enter a null response (press ENTER). If the Constant mode was specified for the attribute, a default prompt is not requested. For the default prompt, we will use "ENTER EMPLOYEE NAME".

You are then prompted for the:

Default Attribute value:

The Attribute default value is the name that will be displayed on the default prompt line. If you have specified the Constant option, you are instead prompted with:

Attribute value:

The response to this prompt will determine the constant value. Let's respond with an ENTER, since we do not want a default value to be listed.

After you have provided AutoCAD with the requested information, AutoCAD begins a series of prompts that are similar to the text prompts, except that the text string is not requested. The attribute information is used as the text string. The location and text size you specify will become the location of the information in the inserted block. Enter a text height of 0.25 and a rotation of 0.

Continue by entering the ATTDEF command again:

```
Command: ATTDEF
Attribute modes - Invisible:N Constant:N Verify:N Preset:N
Enter (ICVP) to change, RETURN when done: ENTER
```

This time we want to enter the tag for the computer. The following responses will be entered:

```
Attribute tag: COMPUTER
Attribute prompt: ENTER COMPUTER NAME:
Default attribute value: IBM-XT
```

Notice that we used IBM-XT as the default attribute value. Every time the block is inserted, AutoCAD will show this as the default.

Now, for the telephone extension number. Enter the ATTDEF command again:

```
Command: ATTDEF
Attribute modes - Invisible:N Constant:N Verify:N Preset:N
Enter (ICVP) to change, RETURN when done: ENTER
```

Enter the following:

```
Attribute tag: EXT NO.:
Attribute prompt: ENTER TELEPHONE EXTENSION NUMBER:
Default attribute value: ENTER
```

Again, we did not specify a default value. Now, to block the desk:

```
Command: BLOCK
Block name (or ?): STATION
Insertion base point: POINT A
Select objects: W
First corner: CHOOSE
Second corner: CHOOSE
Select objects: ENTER
```

You are now ready to insert your block with its attributes!

Insert the block named "STATION" and answer the prompts with different names, computer types, and extension numbers.

SUPPRESSION OF ATTRIBUTE PROMPTS

The system variable ATTREQ is used to suppress attribute requests. If ATTREQ is set to 0, no attribute values are requested, and all attributes are set to their default values. A setting of 1 causes AutoCAD to prompt for attribute values.

DEFINING ATTRIBUTES WITH A DIALOGUE BOX

Attribute values may be set by use of a dialogue box. The DDATTDEF command is used to display the dialogue box.

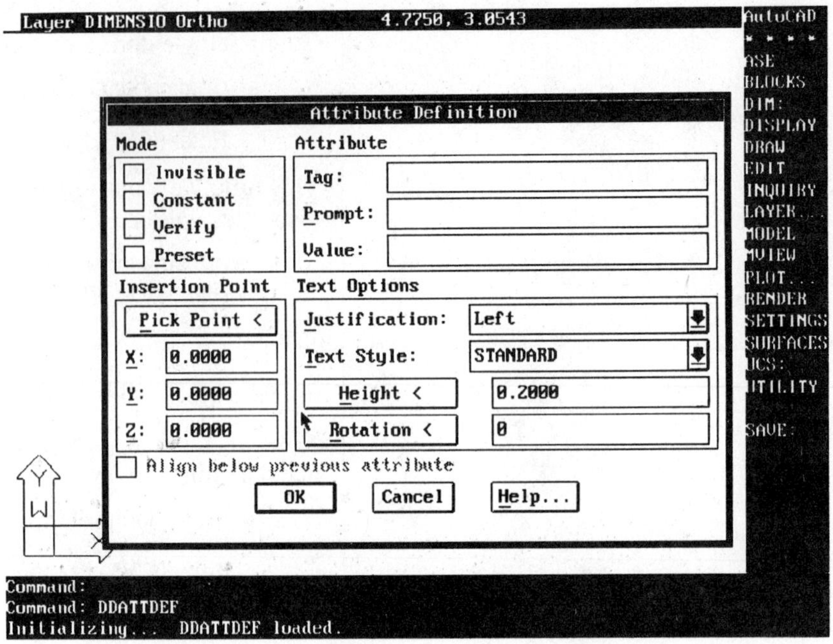

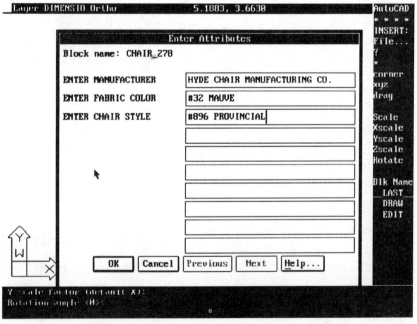

FIGURE 26-2 Attribute Definition Dialogue Box

ENTERING ATTRIBUTES WITH A DIALOGUE BOX

You are prompted for the attribute values when you insert the block. If the system variable ATTDIA is set to 1, AutoCAD will display a dialogue box that contains the tags you defined. You can use this dialogue box to enter the attribute values.

FIGURE 26-3 Enter Attributes Dialogue Box

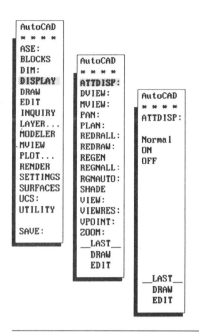

You can use the ATTDISP (attribute display) to determine the visibility of the attributes.

CONTROLLING THE DISPLAY OF ATTRIBUTES

You don't want the attributes to always show up on the display screen. You can use the ATTDISP (attribute display) to determine the visibility of the attributes.

> Command: ATTDISP
> Normal/ON/OFF/<current value>

The options are listed below:

> **Normal:** Attributes are visible, unless you specified them to be invisible on the attributes modes line in the original Attdef command when they were formed. This option is useful if you want some attributes displayed and not others.

> **On:** All attributes are visible.

> **Off:** All attributes are invisible.

After changing the Attdisp, the display is regenerated to show the new state (unless the REGENAUTO is off).

EDITING ATTRIBUTES

Now that everything is all set up properly, John Smith leaves and Andy Cadman is hired to take his place. You have to make a change in your attribute base. The ATTEDIT command is used to make changes in attributes.

> Command: ATTEDIT
> Edit attributes one at a time? <Y>

The response determines the string of options which will follow:

> **Yes:** Selects <u>individual</u> (one by one) editing. The attributes that are currently visible on the screen may be edited. The attributes to be edited may be further restricted by object selection or block names, tags, and values of the attributes to be edited.

> **No:** Used for <u>global editing</u> of attributes (all). You may also restrict the editing to block names, tags, values, and on-screen visibility.

You will next be asked to select the method of editing. You may choose the attributes to be edited by global (*), or using the ? symbol to replace common characters. AutoCAD prompts for the parts of the attributes to be edited:

> Block name specification <*>:
> Attribute tag specification <*>:
> Attribute value specification <*>:

Your reply to each prompt will determine the parts of the attribute that may be edited.

You may choose to edit individual attributes or all attributes.

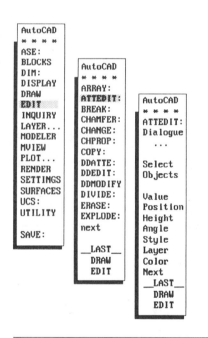

The ATTEDIT command is used to make changes in attributes.

INDIVIDUAL EDITING

You may choose the individual attributes to be edited by using the object selection process. The prompt issued after you have selected the block, tag, and values that are possible to edit is:

Select Attributes:

Use the standard object selection process to choose the attributes to be edited. (The attribute set selection will limit the attributes to be selected. If you entered an ENTER to each prompt at that time, all attributes will be edited.)

After you have selected each attribute to be edited with the object selection process, an "X" will mark the first item that may be edited. The "X" marks the current spot to be edited until you enter Next (or ENTER) and a new spot is marked. You are then prompted:

Value/Position/Height/Angle/Style/Layer/Color/Next <N>:

The options are:

Value — attribute value
Position — text position
Height — text height
Angle — text angle
Style — text style
Layer — layer
Color — color
Next — next

The first letter may be used to select the appropriate option or press CTRL-C to cancel.

If you enter Value, AutoCAD will prompt with:

Change or Replace? <R>

Change is used to change a few characters, such as for a misspelling. If you choose C, the following prompt appears:

String to change:
New string:

You should respond to the first string with the string of characters to be changed and to the second string with the string you want it replaced with.

Replace is used to change the attribute value. You are prompted:

New Attribute value:

Responding with Position, Height, Angle, Style, Layer, or Color, will result in prompts which request the new text parameters and layer location.

EDITING ATTRIBUTES WITH A DIALOGUE BOX

Attribute values may be edited by use of a dialogue box. The DDATE command is used to access the dialogue box.

Command: DDATE
Select block:

Select the block with attributes to be edited and the dialogue box is displayed.

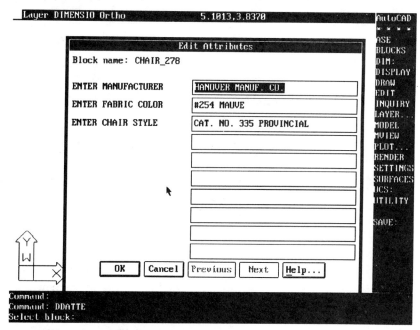

FIGURE 26-4 Edit Attributes Dialogue Box

Several blocks may be edited successively with the dialogue box. To do this, the following command is used.

Command: <u>MULTIPLE DDATE</u>

The DDATE process will automatically repeat until you cancel the command.

EXAMPLE

Consider the following workstations and their corresponding attribute values:

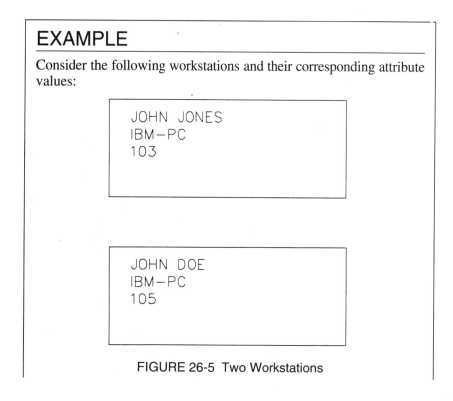

FIGURE 26-5 Two Workstations

Let's assume that we want to change John Doe's name to Jane Doe. Execute the ATTEDIT command:

```
Command: ATTEDIT
Edit Attributes one by one? <Y>: ENTER
Block name specification <*>: ENTER
Attribute tag specification <*>: ENTER
Attribute value specification <*>: ENTER
Select Attributes: SELECT

Val/Val/Hgt/Ang/Style/Lay/Nxt <N>: V
Change or Replace <R>: C
String to change: JOHN DOE
New string: JANE DOE
```

The name change will automatically be reflected on the screen

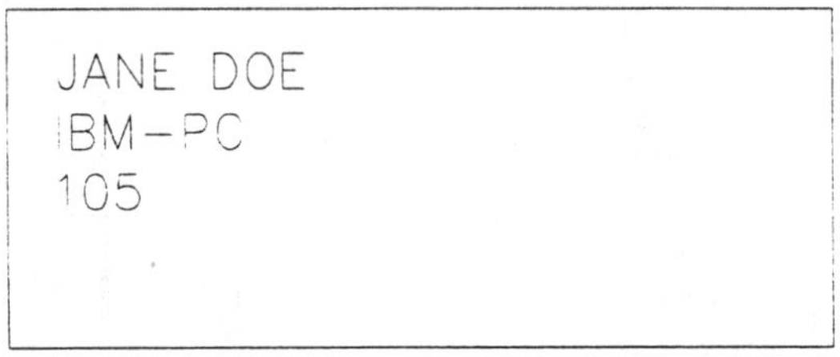

```
JANE DOE
IBM-PC
105
```

FIGURE 26-6 New Workstation Name

GLOBAL EDITING

Global editing is used to edit all the attributes at one time.

Global editing is used to edit all the attributes at one time. As usual, the limits you set for editing will be used.

You may choose global editing by responding to the initial prompt:

```
Command: ATTEDIT
Edit Attributes one at a time? <Y>: N
```

AutoCAD then prompts:

```
Global edit of attribute values.
Edit only Attributes visible on screen? <Y>
```

A "N" response to this prompt will result in the comment:

```
Drawing must be regenerated afterwards.
```

All this means is that your changes will not be immediately shown on the screen. You will have to Regen to see them.

You must then restrict the set of attributes to be edited to the specific tags, values, or blocks.

VISIBLE ATTRIBUTES

If you responded with a "Y" to the prompt, you will only edit visible attributes. You are prompted:

```
Select Attributes:
```

Use the standard object selection process to choose the group of attributes to edit. An "X" is displayed at the starting point of the selected attributes. You are then prompted:

```
String to change:
New string:
```

Respond to the prompts with the string you wish to change and the changes you wish to make.

EXAMPLE

The two workstations below show IBM-PC as the type of computer. We want to change it to IBM-XT. Let's use global editing to do this.

Command: ATTEDIT
Edit Attributes one by one? <Y>: N
Global edit of Attribute values.
Edit only Attributes visible on ? <Y>: RETURN
Block name specification <*>: STATION
Attribute tag specification <*>: COMPUTER
Attribute value specification <*>: RETURN
Select Attributes or Window or Last: W
First point: SELECT
Second point: SELECT
String to change: IBM-PC
New string: IBM-XT

Each station should now contain the attribute value of IBM-XT in place of IBM-PC.

```
JOHN  JONES
IBM—XT
103
```

```
JOHN  DOE
IBM—XT
105
```

FIGURE 26-7 Workstation With IBM-XT

The ATTEXT command is used to extract data base information from the drawing in a specified form.

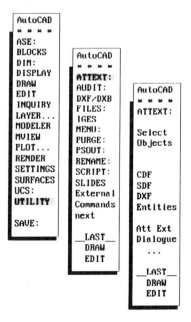

ATTRIBUTE EXTRACTIONS

Attributes are a great feature for keeping records of your inserted blocks. You could maintain a database on furniture; model and cost figures on parts used in a design; or the number, type and cost of windows in a plan.

It would be useful if you could print out all these items in a report. The ATTEXT command can!

The ATTEXT (ATTribute EXTract) command is used to extract database information from the drawing in a specified form.

Command: ATTEXT
CDF, SDF or DXF Attribute extract(or Entities)?<C>:
Template file <*default*>:
Extract filename <name>:

The attributes may be extracted in three formats:

CDF: The CDF (Comma Delimited Format) produces a file that contains delimiters (commas) that separate the data fields. The character fields are enclosed in quotes. This format may be read directly by some database programs.

SDF: The SDF (Space Delimited Format) format is similar to the CDF form, except it does not use commas and requires fixed field lengths. The SDF format is the standard for input to database systems on mini-computers.

DXF: Similar to the AutoCAD drawing interchange file. This format contains the block reference, attribute, and end-of-sequence entities only.

Entities: Allows you to select the specific blocks whose attributes you wish to extract.

We use the SDF format to prepare an attribute extraction of information from our drawing.

USING A DIALOGUE BOX TO EXTRACT ATTRIBUTES

The DDATTEXT command displays a dialogue box for use in extracting attribute values.

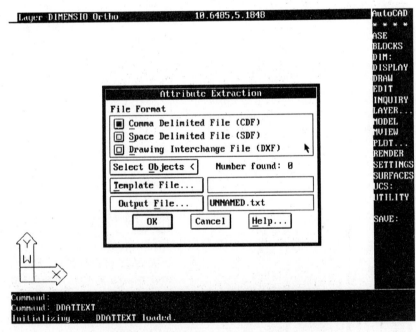

FIGURE 26-8 Attribute Extract Dialogue Box

CREATING TEMPLATE FILES

A template file is a guide by which the information is extracted from the drawing.

To extract our information, we must first prepare a template file. A template file is a guide by which the information is extracted from the drawing.

You may use a word processor or the appropriate commands from a database program to prepare the template file. Each line of the template represents one field to be listed in the extract file. You may also specify the width of the field (in characters), and the number of decimal places to be displayed in numerical fields. Each field will be listed in the order shown in the template file. The following table shows the possibilities of field choices:

BL:LEVEL	Nwww000	Block nesting level
BL:NAME	Cwww000	Block name
BL:X	Nwwwddd	X-coordinate of block
BL:Y	Nwwwddd	Y-coordinate of block
BL:NUMBER	Nwww000	Block counter
BL:HANDLE	Cwww000	Block's handle
BL:LAYER	Cwww000	Block insertion layer name
BL:ORIENT	Nwwwddd	Block rotation angle
BL:XSCALE	Nwwwddd	X scale factor of block
BL:YSCALE	Nwwwddd	Y scale factor of block
BL:ZSCALE	Nwwwddd	Z scale factor of block
BL:XEXTRUDE	Nwwwddd	X component of extrusion
BL:YEXTRUDE	Nwwwddd	Y component of extrusion
BL:ZEXTRUDE	Nwwwddd	Z component of extrusion
tag	Cwww000	Attribute tag (character)
tag	Nwww000	Attribute tag (numeric)

TABLE 26-A

Each field may be a character field (C) or a numerical field (N). The first character designates the type. The next three numbers represent the field width. The last three represent the number of decimal places in a numeric field. Thus, a character field representing a tag with a field spacing of 18 characters would be represented as "C018000".

EXAMPLE

Let's use our OFFICE drawing to extract the attributes from. We want to obtain the block name, X-scale factor, Y-scale factor, employee name, computer type, and telephone extension number.

First, we must prepare a template file. Use a text editor or word processor to prepare a template like the one shown in Table 26-B. Call the file TEMPLATE.TXT. The template file must have a file extension of "TXT".

BL:NAME	C010000
BL:XSCALE	N006002
BL:YSCALE	N006002
EMPLOYEE	C018000
COMPUTER	C010000
TELEPHONE	N005000

TABLE 26-B

Notice that the tag listings in the template file must exactly match the tag names in the attribute.

Now, proceed to AutoCAD and obtain your drawing called OFFICE. Execute the Attext command:

```
Command: ATTEXT
CDF,SDF or DXF Attribute extract <C>?: SDF
Template file <default>: TEMPLATE
Extract filename <default>: EXTRACT1
```

You have now created an extract file with the name EXTRACT.TXT. You may use the print utility of your word processor to obtain a copy of the listing. Your listing should be similar to the following:

STATION	1.00	1.00	JOAN JONES	IBM-PC	103
STATION	1.00	1.00	JOHN DOE	IBM-PC	105
STATION	1.00	1.00	JANE BROWN	IBM-XT	107
STATION	1.00	1.00	ANDY CADMAN	TEXAS INST	110
STATION	1.00	1.00	SARAH DOS	COLUMBIA	112
STATION	1.00	1.00	RANDY RAM	COMPAQ	115
STATION	1.00	1.00	HARRY HEADMAN	IBM-AT	120

TABLE 26-C

CHAPTER REVIEW

1. What is an attribute?

_____

_____

_____

2. What is an attribute tag?

_____

_____

_____

3. What command do you use to create attributes?

_____

4. What is the attribute prompt?

_____

_____

_____

5. How would you suppress attribute prompts?

_____

_____

_____

6. How do you control whether the attribute dialogue box is displayed?

_____

_____

_____

7. What determines whether attributes are displayed in the drawing?

_____

_____

_____

8. How are attributes edited?

_____

_____

_____

9. What parts of an individual attribute can be changed with the attribute edit capabilities?

_____

_____

_____

10. What command will prompt the attribute edit dialogue box?

_____

_____

_____

11. How could you efficiently edit successive blocks with attributes?

_____

_____

_____

12. How would you globally edit all the attributes?

_____

_____

_____

13. How would you obtain a file of all the attribute values in your drawing?

_____

_____

_____

_____

14. What is a template file?

_____

_____

_____

15. What are the three types of attribute extract file formats?

_____

_____

_____

CHAPTER 27

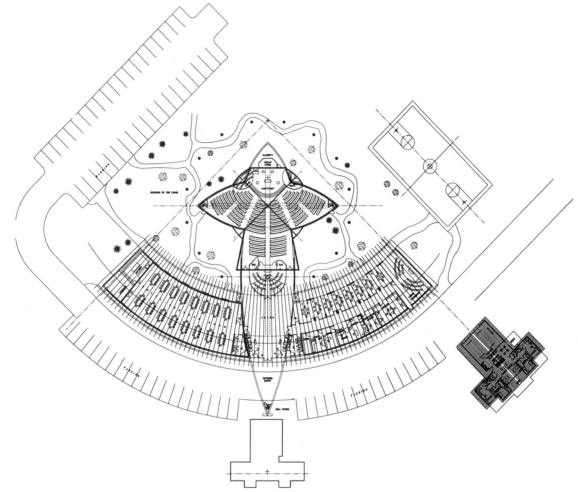

External Reference Drawings

OBJECTIVES:

External reference drawings are extremely useful for certain types of CAD work. Anyone who assembles a large part of their work from library symbols and other drawings should consider the use of external reference drawings. The objectives of Chapter 27 are as follows:

● To understand the concept and use of external reference drawings.

● To become proficient with the AutoCAD commands used with the external reference functions.

● To learn to manage externally referenced files.

OVERVIEW

One of the strengths of CAD drafting is the ability to draw small components, then assemble them into a larger, more complex drawing. In Chapter 20 you learned how to do this with the Block and Insert commands. The Insert command allows you to merge a drawing into another drawing, controlling the placement and scale of the insertion.

When you insert a drawing, AutoCAD creates a block reference of that drawing in the destination drawing file. If you insert that drawing again, AutoCAD uses the block reference to obtain a copy of the previously inserted drawing. It is not an easy task to change the part of the drawing that was inserted. You can delete all copies of the block, then use the Purge command to delete the block reference and reinsert the drawing with the changes, or you can use the Explode command to break the inserted block into its simple entities, then edit the entities. This means that any changes made to a component drawing must also be changed in the drawing into which it was previously inserted.

AutoCAD's external reference capabilities can be useful when you have a situation such as this. The external reference capabilities allow you to insert a drawing into another in a similar way as you would with the Insert command. If the drawing is inserted as an external reference drawing, however, AutoCAD does not load a block reference. Each time the master drawing is loaded, the component drawing is scanned, then loaded at that time. Thus, any changes made to the component drawing will be updated in the master drawing automatically.

Any changes made to the component drawing are automatically updated in the master drawing.

Let's look at an example. Let's suppose that you have a design firm that designs machinery. Your machinery drawings are made up of many standard and nonstandard parts. You normally insert the parts (created and stored as component drawings) into a master drawing to create the finished machine drawings. One day you decide that one of the component parts would be better if a change was made. The problem is that you have 25 master drawings that contain that part. If you used the Insert command to place the component drawings into the master drawings, you have 25 master drawings to correct. If you use external references, each master drawing will be automatically updated when they are next started or plotted.

External references can be useful for any type of application that uses component drawings, or even for multi-station offices that have several people drawing parts of the work. There are several particular features of external references that we need to be aware of. Let's review these. ·

- The Xref command is used to insert a drawing as an external reference. The process is very similar to the Insert command.

- An external reference drawing is not stored as a block reference in the master drawing. Because of this, the original component drawing must be available for AutoCAD to scan and load into the master drawing. The drive and path to the component must be either maintained, or redefined if it is moved.

- Since no block reference is loaded, the master drawing can have many inserted drawings without the disadvantage of excessive single drawing file size. Note, however, that the component drawing must also reside on disk or network for the master drawing to load.

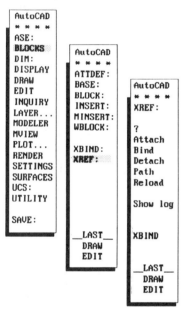

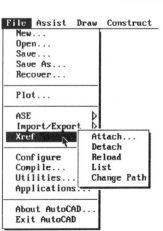

- You can choose to "bind" the externally reference drawing into the master drawing. This has the effect of turning the component drawing into a block, with all the standard aspects of a block.

- AutoCAD codes the external referenced drawing's layers for identification. Let's look at an example. Let's assume that we have a component drawing named "WIDGET." The Widget drawing has a layer named "DETAILS." If we insert the Widget drawing into a master drawing, a layer will be created with the name "WIDGET|DETAILS." This is a combination of the component drawing name and its layer name, separated by the vertical bar (|). This allows layers of the same name to coexist with other component drawings.

- External reference drawings may themselves contain other referenced drawings. For example, the Widget drawing may contain an external reference to another drawing named "COG." Thus, if you place the Widget drawing into a master drawing, you will also include the Cog drawing as an external reference. Both drawings will have to be "available" to the master drawing whenever it is started or plotted.

- Changes made in externally referenced drawings will be reflected in the master drawing either the next time it is started, or at the time it is updated if the master drawing is current. This will continue until you bind the externally referenced drawing.

Let's look at the commands used with external references.

XREF COMMAND

The XREF command is used to insert externally referenced drawings into a master drawing. It is also used to bind a referenced drawing, remove a referenced drawing, reset the path to a referenced drawing, and update a referenced drawing.

When you select the Xref command, the following prompt is displayed:

    Command: XREF
    ?/Bind/Detach/Path/Reload/<Attach>:

Let's look at each of the Xref command's options and see how they work.

ATTACH (ADDING AN EXTERNAL REFERENCE)

Attach is the default when you use the Xref command. Attach is used to insert a drawing. If you select Attach, AutoCAD prompts:

    Xref to Attach <*default*>:

The default is the last drawing attached. If you would like to use a dialogue box from which to choose the drawing name, enter a tilde (~) at the prompt. If AutoCAD detects a block name that matches, it issues an error message and terminates, since you cannot have a block reference and an external reference by the same name.

If AutoCAD detects that an external reference by that name is already present, it alerts you and proceeds. For example, the following command sequence shows an external drawing named "FLANGE" being reloaded as an external reference drawing.

```
Command: XREF
?/Bind/Detach/Path/Reload/<Attach>: ATTACH
Xref to Attach <FLANGE>: FLANGE (or ENTER)
Xref FLANGE has already been loaded.
Use Xref Reload to update its definition.
Insertion point:
```

? (LIST EXTERNAL REFERENCE INFORMATION)

Entering a question mark (?) in response to the prompt allows you to display a list of existing external references. AutoCAD prompts:

Xref(s) to list <*>:

The listing will include the name of the external reference, the path-name for the reference, and the total number of external references. The following is a sample listing.

Xref Name	Path
SPROCKET	/ACAD/DWGS/SPROCKET
COG21	/ACAD/PARTS2/COG21

Total Xref(s): 2

BIND (BIND AN XREF TO THE DRAWING)

Using Bind will bind the external reference drawing to the master drawing, causing it to become a regular block. AutoCAD prompts:

Xref(s) to bind:

List the name(s) of the external references to bind.

> **Tip**
>
> You can bind all the external references by responding to the prompt with the DOS wildcard asterisk (*).

If there are nested Xrefs (Xrefs to Xrefs), they will also be bound.

DETACH (REMOVE AN XREF FROM THE DRAWING)

The Detach option allows you to remove an external reference from the master drawing. This is the equivalent to erasing all occurrences of a block, then purging its reference. When you select Detach, AutoCAD prompts:

Xref(s) to detach:

Enter the name(s) of the Xrefs to detach. You can also respond with an asterisk (*) to detach all Xrefs.

PATH (CHANGE PATH TO AN XREF)

The Path option is used to either view the path of an existing Xref, or to specify a new path for an Xref. As we learned earlier, an attached Xref must remain on the disk drive and directory where it was located when it was attached. The Path option lets you review or change it.

When you select the Path option, AutoCAD displays the prompt:

Edit path for which Xref(s):

You can enter a single Xref name or a list of names. If you enter an asterisk (*), AutoCAD lists all the Xrefs. If you respond with an ENTER, the command is canceled and you will be returned to the "Command:" prompt.

Let's look at how you would change the path for an Xref.

Command: XREF
?/Bind/Detach/Path/Reload/<Attach>: P
Edit path for which Xref(s): TEE?
Xref name: TEE7
Old path: C:\DWGS\PARTS\TEE7
New path: D:\NEWDWGS\PARTS\TEE7

After you are finished, AutoCAD performs an automatic reload of Xrefs and updates the drawing.

RELOAD (UPDATE EXTERNAL REFERENCES)

When you first start a drawing that contains external references, each Xref is automatically reloaded. The Reload option is used to update one or more Xrefs without exiting and reentering the drawing. When you select the Reload option, AutoCAD prompts:

Xref(s) to reload:

You can enter a single Xref or a list. Entering an asterisk (*) reloads all the attached Xrefs. When you reload an Xref, AutoCAD scans the Xref(s), looking for updates. This can take a period of time. AutoCAD displays the message "Scanning..." while the scanning process is in progress.

EXERCISE

Electronic Work Disk Problem

Let's use an external reference. The work disk contains a drawing named "PARTA." Figure 27-1 shows the drawing.

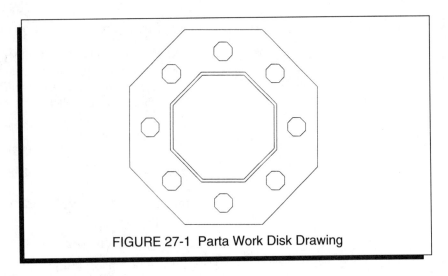

FIGURE 27-1 Parta Work Disk Drawing

Let's start a new drawing first. Begin a new drawing named "MAS-TER1." Set the units to decimal, and the limits to 24,18. Let's now attach the "PARTA" drawing as an external reference. Use the Xref command as follows.

Command: XREF
?/Bind/Path/Reload/<Attach>: A
Xref to Attach<default>: PARTA (be sure to include any drive specifier and directory)
Insertion point: (place anywhere in drawing)
X scale factor <1>/corner/XYZ: (ENTER)
Y scale factor (default=X: (ENTER)
Rotation angle <0>: (ENTER)

The externally referenced drawing is now attached to the "MASTER1" drawing.

Now use the End command to save and exit the drawing. Start the drawing named "PARTA." This is the externally referenced drawing. Use the Erase command to erase the hexagons so the drawing looks like Figure 27-2.

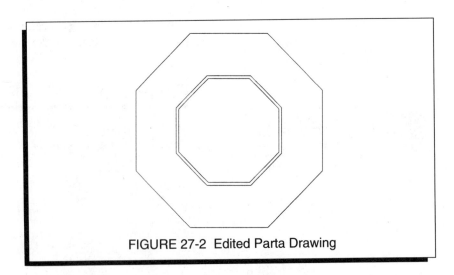

FIGURE 27-2 Edited Parta Drawing

Use the End command to save and exit the drawing. Now start the "MASTER1" drawing again. Notice the messages about scanning the xref PARTA. When the drawing appears on the screen, you will notice that the edits you performed in the "PARTA" drawing were scanned and incorporated into the "MASTER1" drawing.

Continue and use the Xref/Bind command to bind the xref drawing "PARTA." End the drawing and start the "PARTA" drawing. Edit the drawing again in any way you want. End the drawing and start the "MASTER1" drawing again. Were the last edits incorporated?

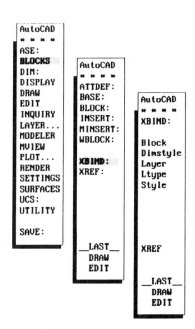

XREF LOG

Your xref operations are recorded in a log that is kept by AutoCAD. The log file is written to disk as an ASCII file. You can view this log by using the DOS TYPE command, or with a word processor. (You can also use the Utility/External Commands/Type facility in the screen menu.) The log file is named the same as the drawing file, except it has a file extension of .XLG. Thus, if your drawing file is named "MASTER1," the log will be named "MASTER1.XLG."

XBIND COMMAND

You have learned how to use Xref/Bind to bind an Xref drawing to a master drawing. There are times, however, when you may only want to bind a part of a drawing. For example, you may want to bind a linetype of layer to the drawing, without binding the rest of the externally referenced drawing. You can do this with the XBIND command.

When you select the Xbind command, AutoCAD prompts:

> Command: XBIND
> Block/Dimstyle/LAyer/LType/Style:

Enter the capitalized letter of the part of the Xref you wish to bind. When prompted for the name of the symbol, style, etc., you can enter a single name, or several names, separated by commas.

The items are renamed when they are bound. You learned earlier how AutoCAD lists xref items, such as layers, with a vertical bar (|). AutoCAD removes the vertical bar and replaces it with two dollar signs ($) and a number that is usually 0. For example, a layer named "PARTA|HEXAGONS" will be named "PART0HEXAGONS." If there is already a layer by that name, AutoCAD will try "PARTS1-HEXAGONS," and so forth. The number of characters must be 31 or less, or AutoCAD will terminate the command and undo the effects of the Xbind command.

CHAPTER REVIEW

1. Explain the difference between an inserted drawing and one placed as an external reference.

_____

_____

_____

_____

2. Is an external reference stored as a block?

_____

3. Can an external reference contain another external reference?

_____

4. What are some advantages of using external references?

_____

_____

_____

_____

5. What command is used to place an external reference drawing?

_____

6. How would you obtain a listing of the external references placed in a drawing?

_____

_____

7. How would you convert an external reference to a block?

_____

_____

8. Under what conditions would you want to convert the external references to blocks?

_____

_____

_____

9. How would you remove an external reference from a drawing?

_____

_____

_____

10. Why must an externally referenced drawing remain in its original drive and directory?

_____

_____

_____

_____

11. How would you change the drive and directory of an externally referenced drawing?

_____

_____

12. What option is used to update externally referenced drawings in the master drawing?

_____

13. How would you write a log file that describes the external reference activity to disk?

_____

_____

14. Can you bind only part of an externally referenced drawing to the master drawing? Explain.

_____

_____

_____

CHAPTER 28

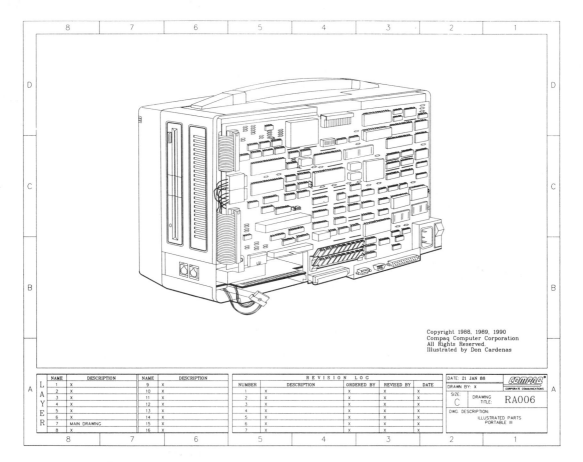

NAME		DESCRIPTION	NAME		DESCRIPTION
1	X		9	X	
2	X		10	X	
3	X		11	X	
4	X		12	X	
5	X		13	X	
6	X		14	X	
7		MAIN DRAWING	15	X	
8	X		16	X	

REVISION LOG

NUMBER	DESCRIPTION	ORDERED BY	REVISED BY	DATE
1	X	X	X	X
2	X	X	X	X
3	X	X	X	X
4	X	X	X	X
5	X	X	X	X
6	X	X	X	X
7	X	X	X	X

DATE: 21 JAN 88
DRAWN BY: X
SIZE: C
DRAWING TITLE: RA006
DWG. DESCRIPTION: ILLUSTRATED PARTS PORTABLE III

Customizing AutoCAD

OBJECTIVES:

At some point in time, all serious AutoCAD users will want to learn to customize their program. Increased drawing ease and performance will result in a properly customized system. Chapter 28 objectives are:

● To control the look and performance of the AutoCAD program with the many variable settings.

● To control many of the display and adjustment settings such as the display of drawing blips, and the target box sizes.

● To control display characteristics such as the view resolution and regeneration rules.

● To redefine existing commands.

AutoCAD
In The
Real
World

Ride the Wave

Inflatable rescue craft goes faster with AutoCAD®

How does a West Coast boat builder evolve from manufacturing simple pleasure crafts to servicing military and government contracts that require up to 58 sheets of detailed drawings? With AutoCAD, of course.

Zodiac Hurricane produces all the Zodiac rigid-hull pleasure boats to North America and exports a small number to Australia and Europe. The manufacturing facility in Vancouver produces 400 to 500 recreational crafts a year.

The company's expanding customer base includes the government, military and industry—customers with stringent requirements for rescue and liberty boats.

The industrial boats range from a 24-foot inflatable assault boat to the 47-foot rigid-hull inflatable boats (RIB) that the Canadian Coast Guard is thinking about using to replace some of its older cutters.

Constructed of fiberglass hulls and neoprene hypalon tubes, RIBS are ideal as rescue boats. They have soft sides so they can come up along side other boats and, with their reserve buoyancy, they are difficult to capsize or swamp. The inflatable collar acts as an energy sink, making the ride fairly soft.

The traditional methods of boat building involves the hull being hand drawn and faired by a drafter, generally a process of trial and error. It's done at a scale of one inch to the foot, and you end up with a table of coordinates for various points on the hull. These are redrawn at full size and the boat is built using the full-size drawings.

AutoCAD's design capabilities were used for the craft's structural systems, mechanical systems and all metalwork. With AutoCAD, it took two drafters eight months to produce what would have taken six drafters the same amount of time by hand. And designs for subsequent military and government contracts, which were take-offs of the original design, took even less time to draft.

Adapted with permission from an article by Sharon Arsenault in *CADalyst*. Copyright © 1990, by CADalyst Publications, Ltd.

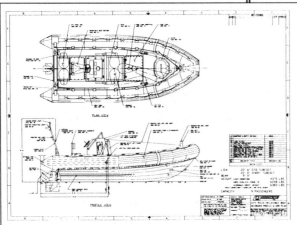

AutoCAD makes it easy to design new boats based on older plans.

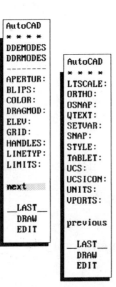

SETTING SYSTEM VARIABLES

The SETVAR (Set System Variables) command allows you to change AutoCAD's system variables.

The system variables control default settings for the drawing editor. Values for such items as default aperture size, global linetype scale factor, and other items are stored here. Some variables are changed by commands, some are "read only", and some may be set by using the Setvar command.

To change a setting, issue the Setvar command.

Command: <u>SETVAR</u>
Variable name or ? <*default*>: (*enter variable name*)

Tip

Many variables can be executed directly from the command line without using the Setvar command first. This can be performed with variables that do not match AutoCAD command names.

After entering the variable name, you may enter a new value. If you respond to the prompt with a "?", AutoCAD prompts:

> Variable(s) to list <*>:

System variables control default settings for the drawing editor.

If you respond with an ENTER, all the variables are displayed. Some values are defined as "read only". Entering one of these values will result in a response in the form of:

> variable-name = current (read only)

An example of this would be:

> Command: SETVAR
> Variable name or ?: AREA
> AREA = 0.0000 (read only)

If you enter a changeable variable, AutoCAD will prompt:

> New value for (variable name) <*default*>:

USING SETVAR WHILE IN A COMMAND

There are times when it is desirable to change a system variable while in a current command. AutoCAD allows you to do this by issuing the special code of an apostrophe (').

An example would be:

> Command: LINE
> From point: 'SETVAR
> >>Variable name or ?: TRACEWID
> >>New value for TRACEWID <*default*>: (*enter new value*)

You may maintain the default value by entering a null response to the prompt.

After you have entered the new value, AutoCAD returns you to the current command:

> Resuming LINE command.
> From point:

You may now resume the current command.

Blips do not plot.

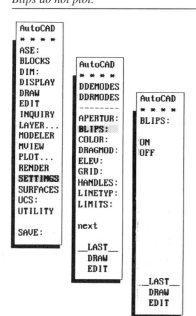

DISPLAYING BLIP MARKS

The marker that is left on the screen by your drawing activity is called a *blip*. Blips do not plot and may be thought of as "push pin" reference points to aid you. You turn the drawing of blips on and off by using the BLIPMODE command. To use the command, enter the following:

> Command: BLIPMODE
> On/Off <current>:

If the blipmode is on, you may remove blips on the screen by issuing a Zoom, Pan, Redraw, or Regen command.

The initial setting of the Blipmode command is determined by the prototype drawing. You may change the setting at any time and as often as you desire. AutoCAD remembers the setting when you end the drawing and retains it as the initial setting when you reenter the drawing at a later time.

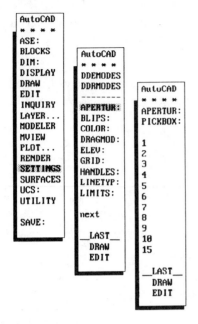

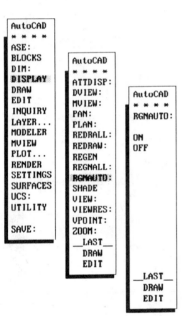

SETTING APERTURE SIZE

The APERTURE command is used to adjust the size of the target box used in object snap modes.

The box size is described by the number of screen pixels specified. To set this number, enter:

> Command: <u>APERTURE</u>
> Object snap target height (1-50 pixels) <i><default></i>:

The last aperture size will be remembered when you reenter the drawing.

The aperture is only used with Object Snap and is not the same as the pickbox used with object selection. The pickbox can be changed by using the PICKBOX system variable.

CONTROLLING DRAWING REGENERATIONS

Some functions performed with AutoCAD cause an automatic regeneration. This regeneration reorganizes the data on the screen to ensure that all information is current. It is possible that you may have need to perform several operations at one time that will force a regeneration each time. Since each regeneration takes some time to perform, AutoCAD provides a command to warn you before regenerations are performed by some operations.

> Command: <u>REGENAUTO</u>
> On/Off <current>:

The initial status of the Regenauto mode is determined by the prototype drawing. You may change it at any time and as many times as necessary. The last setting is remembered by AutoCAD and is restored when you reenter the drawing at a later time.

If Regenauto is Off and a regeneration is required, AutoCAD will prompt:

> About to regen — proceed? <Y>

SETTING THE VIEW RESOLUTION

The VIEWRES command controls the fast zoom mode and resolution for circle and arc regenerations.

AutoCAD regenerates most zooms, pans, and view restores. This regeneration can sometimes, depending on the complexity of the drawing, take a great amount of time. The Fast Zoom mode allows AutoCAD to simply redisplay the screen wherever possible. This redisplay is performed at the faster redraw speed. (Some zooms that are more extreme still require a regen.)

AutoCAD also calculates the number of segments that is required to make circles and arcs "smooth" at the current zoom. (Circles and arcs are made up of many short line segments.) The Viewres command allows you to control the number of segments used. Using fewer segments speeds regeneration time, but trades off screen resolution. Although the displayed circles and arcs are not as smooth, plotter and printer plots are not affected.

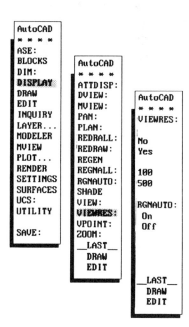

To use the Viewres command, enter:

Command: <u>VIEWRES</u>
Do you want fast zooms? <Y>: (*choose Y or N*)
Enter circle zoom percent (1-20000) <*default*>:

Entering "N" to the first prompt will cause all zooms, pans, and view restores to regenerate.

The default value for the circle zoom percent is 100. A value less than 100 will diminish the resolution of circles and arcs, but will result in faster regeneration times. A value greater than 100 will result in a larger number of vectors than usual to be displayed for circles and arcs. This is not important unless you zoom in a great amount.

For example, if you will be zooming in at a factor of 10, setting the circle zoom percent to 1,000 will result in smooth circles and arcs at that zoom. If you want to maintain a smooth display and still achieve the optimum regeneration speed, set the percent equal to the maximum zoom ratio you intend to use.

Regardless of the setting, AutoCAD will never display a circle with fewer than eight sides. On the other hand, AutoCAD will not display any more circle or arc segments than it calculates to be necessary for the current zoom. If the circle uses less than two screen pixels at the maximum zoom magnification that does not require a regeneration, the circle will be displayed as a single pixel.

If you wish to show the drawing to others at the maximum resolution, use a smaller percentage while drawing, then change the percentage and perform a regen. This allows you to perform the drawing at fast regeneration times, then redisplay the drawing at its optimum resolution for presentation.

REDEFINING COMMANDS

An existing AutoCAD command may be redefined to suit customized purposes. The UNDEFINE command is used to facilitate this. Undefine is used extensively by AutoCAD third-party programmers to create new commands for their applications. You may want to use Undefine to customize some existing commands, making the use of AutoCAD more applicable to your particular tasks. Let's look at an example of using the Undefine command.

EXERCISE

Let's say you want to add a line to remind one of your CAD operators to place blocks in the proper subdirectory. You could use AutoLISP and the Undefine command to accomplish this. Let's see how this would work. Start a new drawing of any name. From the "Command" prompt, enter the following:

Command: <u>(defun c:BLOCK ())</u>
<u>1>(princ "Remember to specify the correct subdirectory\n")</u>
<u>1> (command ".BLOCK"))</u>
C:BLOCK
Command:

The Block command has been redefined to display the reminder message. The original Block command is not actually destroyed. You may still use it by simply preceding it with a period, such as ".BLOCK." NOTE: After the above message was prompted, the original Block command was initiated ".BLOCK".

Now undefine the Block command.

> Command: <u>UNDEFINE</u>
> Command name: <u>BLOCK</u>

Now issue the Block command to see the message.

> Command: <u>BLOCK</u>
> Remember to specify the correct subdirectory
> .BLOCK Block name (or?): nil
> Block name (or?):

Let's now redefine the Block command. This will return it to its original form.

> Command: <u>REDEFINE</u>
> Command name: <u>BLOCK</u>
> Command:

The Block command is now redefined to its original form and the message will not be displayed if it is subsequently issued.

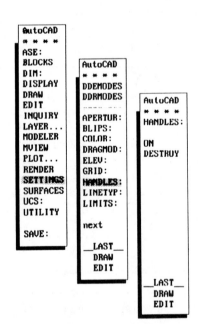

ENTITY HANDLES

Each entity in the drawing possesses an identifier called a "handle". Whether AutoCAD assigns a handle to entities is controlled by the Handles command.

The handles assigned to entities can be used in a variety of application programs that access the drawing database. Thus, the absence of handles can render such applications useless.

To enable or disable the handles assignments, issue the Handles command.

> Command: <u>HANDLES</u>
> ON/DESTROY

Let's look at the two options.

On: Causes AutoCAD to assign handles to all subsequent entities added to the drawing.

Destroy: Deletes all the handles in the drawing. You must type the entire word "DESTROY". If you select this option, AutoCAD responds with the following message:

WARNING: Completing this command will destroy ALL database handle information in the drawing. Once destroyed, links into the drawing from external database files cannot be made.

If you really want to destroy the database handle information, please confirm this by entering <string> to proceed or "NO" to abort the commands.

Proceed with handle destruction <NO>:

where <string> is one of six messages randomly selected by AutoCAD.

CHAPTER REVIEW

1. What command can be used to set AutoCAD's system variables?

2. Under what condition can variables be entered directly from the command line?

3. How could you change a variable while actively in a command?

4. What is a blip?

5. How do you turn the blips on or off?

6. In what increment is the aperture setting measured?

7. Why would you sometimes want to set a low Viewres value?

8. What difference in the displayed drawing would you notice if you set the Viewres low?

9. Describe a good example of redefining a command.

10. What could be the risk of destroying entity handles?

CHAPTER 29

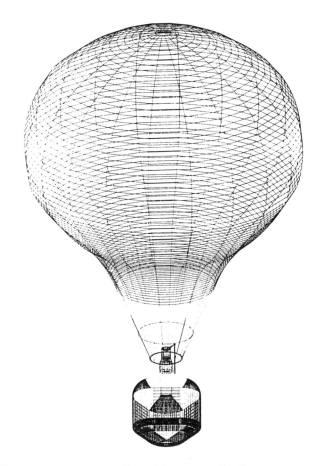

Customizing Menus

OBJECTIVES:

Using custom menu systems can multiply the productivity of any CAD system. You can buy expensive systems or you can become proficient with the techniques of designing your own. The objectives of Chapter 29 are:

● To learn the concept of AutoCAD menu systems.

● To learn and understand the anatomy of a menu system.

● To learn to write the files necessary for the different types of AutoCAD menus.

● To learn to construct special types of AutoCAD menus such as icon boxes and custom pull-down menus

CUSTOM MENUS

Custom menus are an exciting part of AutoCAD. You may prepare a menu that is particular to your type of work, or one that just suits your style (or both!).

A menu is nothing more than a text file.

A menu is nothing more than a text file. AutoCAD reads the item from the menu and executes it as though it were entered from the keyboard. Before we jump all the way in, let's learn two basic rules and look at a simple menu.

SIMPLE MENUS

Menu items are arranged one to a line. Each line contains one or more items that will be "typed" if chosen.

Menus are constructed with a word processor in non-document mode or a line editor. The file must have a .MNU extension in order to be loaded by AutoCAD. The following is a simple menu that could be written for AutoCAD:

```
LINE
ARC
CIRCLE
TRACE
REDRAW
ZOOM
COPY
MOVE
```

If you choose any of these from the screen, it will be executed as though you typed it from the keyboard.

SCREEN DISPLAY

Sometimes it is desirable for the menu item to have a special listing on the screen menu. Consider the case of the Quit command. You may want the screen to display "DISCARD" instead of "QUIT".

You may include text that AutoCAD will not execute by enclosing them in brackets ([ ]). The first eight characters within the brackets will be displayed on the menu screen and the items immediately following the closing bracket will be executed. Consider the following menu items:

```
[FAT LINE]TRACE
[TARGET]APERTURE
[RULER]AXIS
[BACKWARD]MIRROR
```

In the second line, "TARGET" will appear on the screen and "APER-TURE" will be executed. Be sure that you do not put a space between the second bracket and the command, otherwise AutoCAD will interpret the space as if you had pressed the ENTER key.

MULTIPLE MENUS

AutoCAD allows you to store, concurrently, several device menus in one menu file. Each device menu is compartmented in its own section and marked by a beginning label. The following table shows the section labels and the associated devices:

***SCREEN	Menu area on screen
***BUTTONS	Pointing device buttons
***TABLET1	Tablet menu area one
***TABLET2	Tablet menu area two
***TABLET3	Tablet menu area three
***TABLET4	Tablet menu area four
***AUX1	Auxiliary device
***ICON	Icon menu area
***POPn	Pull-down menu (where n is a number between 1 and 16).

Each label starts with three asterisks.

Notice that each label starts with three asterisks. The asterisks, along with the label name, tell AutoCAD that this is the start of the menu items for that particular menu area or device.

The items that follow will be contained in the associated section until another label is listed or the end of the file occurs. The following short menu shows two sections: a screen menu and an auxiliary menu for a device such as a function box:

```
***SCREEN
LINE
ARC
CIRCLE
[BACKWARD]MIRROR
***AUX1
LINE
TRACE
ZOOM
```

SUBMENUS

You have already noticed that the default AutoCAD menu is actually made up of many menus that are displayed almost magically on the screen as you make your choices. Consider what occurs when you choose Line from the screen menu. You must first choose Draw from the Main Menu. You are then presented with a special Draw menu. You then choose Line from this menu and are presented with a special Line menu. These menus are called submenus.

In order to construct a submenu, you must use another section label. The structure for a submenu is:

```
**name
```

Every menu item that is listed after the submenu section label through the next section label belongs to that section. Each submenu label must be named differently, even though it occurs under a different menu or device label.

When a submenu is displayed, it will replace every item of the currently displayed menu down to the end of the submenu file. It is therefore possible that a submenu may only replace a part of the previous menu. At times, this may be desirable. If you do not want this to occur, fill up the number of screen items on your display with blank lines.

You may specify which item number (down from the top) that the submenu replaces by designating a number describing the position after the submenu name. For example:

**SUB-A 5

will display the submenu labeled "**SUB-A" starting at the fifth position down on the currently displayed menu, replacing the remaining items to the bottom of the submenu file. Using a negative number will cause the same result, except from the bottom of the displayed menu.

LINKING MENUS

You have learned about section labels that separate menus in the same file and submenus that are separate screen lists. Now we need to learn how to navigate.

All those submenus are nice, but you need a way to get between them. If you select the Circle command from the screen menu, you will then want a submenu that contains all the commands for working with circles.

AutoCAD provides a way to "jump" to a named submenu. The following format is used:

$section=submenu

The section refers to the section label. The sections may be referenced by using the following letters:

    S   SCREEN menu
    B   BUTTONS menu
    T1   TABLET area one
    T2   TABLET area two
    T3   TABLET area three
    T4   TABLET area four
    A1   AUXILIARY device
    Pn   POPDOWN menu n

If you wanted to access a submenu named "**subline" in the Screen section, the correct entry would be:

$S=SUBLINE

Notice that the double asterisk is not used when referring to the submenu.

AutoCAD also provides a way to return to the last menu. The format for this is:

$S=

This returns you to the last screen menu item. The number of "last" (nested) menus allowed is eight.

At first, submenus can be confusing. You may use a word processor to print out AutoCAD's menu for an example. The name of the file is ACAD.MNU. If you do not have a word processor, use the print echo from DOS (CTRL-PrtSc) and enter TYPE ACAD.MNU to print the menu. (Be sure to turn off the echo by entering "CTRL-PrtSc" again after finishing.)

MULTIPLE COMMANDS IN MENUS

Commands may be linked together to perform several functions at once.

Commands may be linked together to perform several functions at once. This is called a macro. To do this, you must have a good understanding of AutoCAD's command sequences. The following special input items are used for this purpose:

Space: A space (or blank) is read as an ENTER.

End of line: AutoCAD automatically inserts a blank at the end of each menu line. A blank is used interchangeably with the ENTER in most commands.

Semi-colon (;): The semi-colon is used if an ENTER is desired instead of a blank.

Backslash (\): A backslash is used where user input is desired. The command will pause and await your input.

Plus mark (+): A plus mark is used to continue a long command string to the next line. If a plus mark is not present at the end of the line, AutoCAD will insert a blank.

Let's look at an example. Suppose you wanted to set up a new drawing by setting limits of 0,0 and 36,24, perform a zoom-all, and turn the grid on. The following menu sequence would perform this:

[SET LIM]LIMITS 0,0 36,24 ZOOM A GRID ON

AutoCAD would read this as:

LIMITS<enter>0,0<enter>36,24<enter>ZOOM<enter>A<enter> GRID<enter>ON<enter>

Special functions may also be performed. Let's suppose that you wanted to insert a window in a solid wall made of a Trace line. The window is a drawing called "WIN-1" and is stored in the C: drive. The window is 36 units in length, and the base point is at the right end of the window and 4 units down.

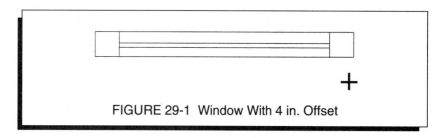

FIGURE 29-1 Window With 4 in. Offset

The following menu string could be used to insert the window in the wall:

[36" WIN]BREAK \@36,0 INSERT C:WIN-1 @ 1 1 0

AutoCAD would break the wall, leaving a 36-unit opening and insert the window in it.

LOADING MENUS

To load a menu, use the Menu command:

Command: MENU

A "Select Menu File" dialogue box is displayed.

AutoCAD
* * * *
ASE:
BLOCKS
DIM:
DISPLAY
DRAW
EDIT
INQUIRY
LAYER...
MODELER
MVIEW
PLOT...
RENDER
SETTINGS
SURFACES
UCS:
UTILITY

SAVE:

AutoCAD
* * * *
ATTEXT:
AUDIT:
DXF/DXB
FILES:
IGES
MENU:
PURGE:
PSOUT:
RENAME:
SCRIPT:
SLIDES
External
Commands
next

__LAST__
DRAW
EDIT

A menu has a file extension of .MNU until the first time it is loaded. When loaded, AutoCAD compiles a menu for faster operation. A new copy of the menu is made with a .MNX file extension. This is the menu used by AutoCAD. If you edit the menu, you will need to edit the one with the .MNU extension. To use the reedited menu, you do not need to delete the menu of the same name with the .MNX extension. AutoCAD senses the change and automatically recompiles the menu.

TABLET MENUS

A digitizer pad may be used with a tablet menu. You may specify up to four tablet menus and a drawing area. Figure 29-2 shows a typical tablet menu set up.

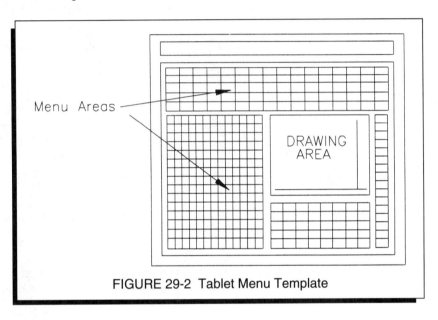

FIGURE 29-2 Tablet Menu Template

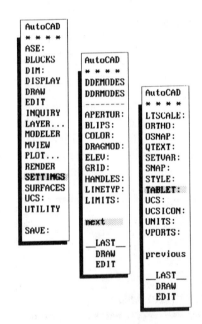

The four menu areas are designated TABLET 1 through 4. The menus are made up of smaller boxes of equal dimension in rows and columns. The menu boxes are labelled from left to right and top to bottom. The label corresponds to the item in the menu under the appropriate section label. That is, the first command to appear will be contained in box A1, and so forth. You may arrange the menus in any fashion you wish. The CFG option in the TABLET command is used to configure the menus and drawing.

```
Command: TABLET
Option (ON/OFF/CAL/CFG): CFG
Enter number of tablet menus desired (0-4) <default>:
```

If you have already used the tablet menu, AutoCAD will prompt:

```
Do you want to realign tablet menu areas? <N>
```

AutoCAD will proceed and prompt:

```
Digitize upper left corner of menu area x:
Digitize lower left corner of menu area x:
Digitize lower right corner of menu area x:
```

After entering the descriptive points, AutoCAD prompts:

```
Enter the number of columns for menu area x:
Enter the number of rows for menu area x:
```

You may now define the drawing area. You are prompted:

> Do you want to respecify the screen pointing area? <N>

If you reply "Y", AutoCAD prompts:

> Digitize lower left corner of screen pointing area:
> Digitize upper right corner of screen pointing area:

PULL-DOWN MENUS

Pull-down menus may be written that are accessed from the top screen menu bar. These are obtained by moving the cursor to the status line area at the top of the screen. When you do this, the status lines are replaced by a listing of menus across the top of the screen. Placing the cursor over one of these and clicking pulls down the corresponding menu.

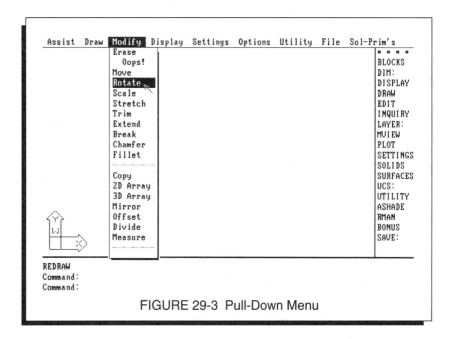

FIGURE 29-3 Pull-Down Menu

Some graphic systems are not capable of displaying pull-down menus. There will be no display or effect on these systems. Other graphic systems simultaneously display the status line and pull-down menus.

Pull-down menus are designated as "POP1" through "POP16." They are written in the same fashion as screen and tablet menus, with some exceptions. Each menu is handled as a separate menu; using, for example, ***POP1 as the menu area for the first pull-down menu. The equivalent to the $S= command in the pull-down menu is the $Pn= command, where "n" is the name of the pull-down menu to access. In addition, the special command $Pn=* line is used to automatically pull down the menu desired.

Let's look at an example of a pull-down menu (designated as POP3) that is to be automatically pulled down when accessed from a screen menu. You could use the following line in the screen menu area.

> [PARTS]$p3=parts $p3=*

This would pull down the submenu named "PARTS" from the POP3 menu (listed in the written menu under "***POP3"). The menu would then be forced down by the "$p3=*" command.

When writing the POPn menu sections, the first line under each area is used as the header bar title (listing in the top screen area). These listings will be displayed across the top of the screen. The menu under each will be as wide as the longest item in the corresponding menu. Keep in mind that lower resolution screens are capable of displaying only 80 columns in width. If the total width of the menus are longer, they will be truncated.

You may provide separation between items in the menu by placing a separator line between them. This is done by placing a line as follows.

[--]

The two hyphens expand to the width of the menu and provide the separator line.

A menu item label may be displayed as "grayed out" by beginning it with a tilde (~). A grayed out item typically denotes an item that is not currently active. This could be used if a menu is in progress and will be completed at a later time. It could also be used for minor selections. If the item is followed by a valid string, it will execute normally.

ICON MENUS

Icon menu listings are placed under a "***ICON" heading in the menu text file.

Icon menus use slides to display the graphic part of the icon box.

Icon menus use slides to display the graphic part of the icon box. The slides are normal AutoCAD slides made with the Mslide command. Some displays are not capable of displaying icon boxes on the screen. On these systems, selecting a box will have no effect.

The first line of the icon menu will be the title of the icon box. The title is displayed at the top of the box.

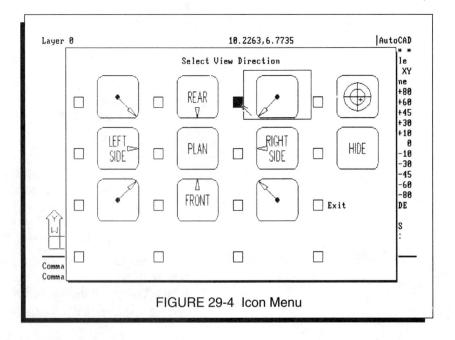

FIGURE 29-4 Icon Menu

Let's look at an example of a menu text listing for an icon menu.

```
***ICON
**FURNTURE
[Living Room]
[sofa]^Cinsert sofa
[lchair]^Cinsert lchair
[ctable]^Cinsert ctable
[lamp]^Cinsert lamp
[bookcase]^Cinsert bcase
[ Cancel]^C
[ Bedroom]$i=bdrm $i=*

**BDRM
[Bedroom]
[Bed]^Cinsert bed
```

Notice how the format is similar to the standard screen menus and icon menus. Submenus are used to create different icon boxes under the main icon heading of "***ICON." The slide names of the items to be displayed in the icon box are enclosed in brackets ([]). The slide names should be the same as the name listed if it were viewed with the Vslide command. An executable string may be prefaced by ^C (executes as CTRL-C) to cancel any command that is in progress when the item is selected.

If the first character of an item is blank, the balance of the string in the brackets will be displayed as text characters instead of a slide. Thus, the lines in the preceding sample menu listed as "Cancel" and "Bedroom" will be displayed in the icon box as text items. You may want to use "Cancel," "Exit," "Next," "Previous," or the name of another icon box in the design of an icon box and display only text for that purpose.

The special string $i=* causes the icon box to be displayed on the screen. A prompt to display an icon box may be placed in any menu section (***SCREEN, ***POPn, etc.), but may not be executed from the keyboard. For example, the following line could be placed in a pull-down menu to execute the icon box described by the previous menu.

[Living Room]$i=furniture $i=*

The number of items displayed in the icon box is dependent on the number of items in the menu section for that box. You may have 4, 9, or 16 items displayed. A selector box will be displayed next to each item in the icon box. When an icon box is displayed, an arrow appears. The arrow may be moved by the input device. Moving the arrow over a selector box causes a frame to be displayed around the item. Clicking the input device causes the item to be selected and the corresponding text string in the text menu is executed.

SELECTING SLIDES FROM LIBRARIES

Slides for icon menus may be selected from slide libraries. This is an efficient way to manage groups of slides for icon menus.

In order to select a slide from a slide library, the name of the library must be listed in the menu before the slide name. Let's assume the slides for the icons we used in the earlier menu were stored in a library named "FURNLIB" (furniture library). The same menu listing would look like the following.

```
***ICON
**FURNTURE
[Living Room]
[furnlib(sofa)]^Cinsert sofa
[furnlib(lchair)]^Cinsert lchair
[furnlib(ctable)]^Cinsert ctable
[furnlib(lamp)]^Cinsert lamp
[furnlib(bookcase)]^Cinsert bcase
[Cancel]^C
[Bedroom]$i=bdrm $i=*

**BDRM
[Bedroom]
[furnlib(Bed)]^Cinsert bed
```

DESIGNING ICON BOXES

There are several guidelines that insure good icon box design.

First, always be sure to design a way out. If an icon box is displayed by mistake, or you change your mind about making a selection, you need to be able to cancel the box.

If there are more selections under a heading than an icon box has room for (the maximum icons in one box is 16), you may place a "Next" button to display a subsequent box with more choices. In this case, you may also want to put a "Previous" choice.

When preparing slides, keep the slides simple. The icon box will take less time to generate onto the screen. You may want to construct outline frames of complex slides just for this purpose. You can also turn off the fill when preparing the slides to cut down on display time.

Make the slides as large as possible. The screen area for the slide is very small. Keeping the slide big and simple makes selection easier.

CHAPTER REVIEW

1. How many characters can be displayed on a single line on an AutoCAD screen menu?

   _____

2. How many different drawing devices can be served by an AutoCAD menu?

   _____

3. How do you designate a submenu within the menu file?

   _____

4. What is a macro?

   _____

   _____

   _____

   _____

5. What command is used to load a new menu?

_____

6. What is a tablet menu?

_____

_____

_____

7. What are the maximum menu areas on a tablet menu?

_____

8. How are the graphics in an icon menu produced?

_____

_____

_____

9. What is meant if a pull-down menu selection is "grayed" out?

_____

_____

_____

10. What is the range of drawings that can be displayed in an icon box?

_____

SECTION V

*Auto*CAD
3-D

CHAPTER 30

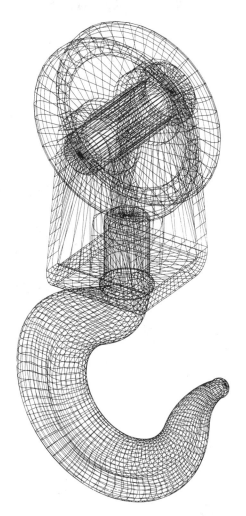

Introduction to AutoCAD 3-D

OBJECTIVES:

One of the most exciting parts of AutoCAD is 3-D. Before you can start constructing 3-D drawings, you must first become familiar with the many concepts of three-dimensional drawing construction. Chapter 30 objectives are:

● To become familiar with the three-dimensional coordinate system.

● To understand the differences between 3-D and perspective.

● To understand the concepts used with clipping planes.

INTRODUCTION TO AUTOCAD 3-D

AutoCAD contains the capabilities to produce true 3-D and perspective models. These capabilities may be used interactively with 2-D drawings.

This section explains the use of AutoCAD 3-D. It is divided into four chapters. Chapter 30 introduces you to 3-D drawing. Chapter 31 covers the methods of constructing views. This is important both while constructing the drawing and for modeling a final product. Chapter 32 covers the User Coordinate System. This is an important principle in creating 3-D drawings. Finally, chapter 33 explores the many methods of drawing in 3-D.

This section has been organized in a learning order. The best results will be achieved by reviewing the information in the order presented. For example, you will need to become skillful in creating 3-D views before learning to draw in 3-D, since much of the drawing construction process is performed while in 3-D views.

HOW TO APPROACH 3-D

It is first assumed that you have a good working knowledge of the 2-D drawing functions of AutoCAD. Using AutoCAD 3-D requires expertise in many of the commands you have learned in the previous chapters. If you are not familiar with some of the commands or concepts in certain areas, review these in the previous chapters.

Although AutoCAD 3-D uses many of the commands you are familiar with, the approach to 3-D drawing requires knowledge of some unique concepts. The primary difference is the X,Y,Z coordinate system. Other concepts such as camera positions, target points, clipping planes, and the User Coordinate System are used to create and view your 3-D drawings.

Take time not only to read and study these concepts, but to understand them. Practice each concept with simple shapes before proceeding to more advanced problems.

Three-dimensional drawing takes time and practice to learn, but with time the results will be well worth the effort.

3-D THEORY

Let's look at some of the concepts associated with three-dimensional drawing.

COORDINATE SYSTEM

In order to comprehend the construction of 3-D drawings, the concept of the X,Y,Z coordinate system must be understood. This is the same X,Y coordinate system you work with when constructing a 2-D drawing, with the Z-axis representing the "height" of the entity added.

Before we proceed to learn about the Z-axis, it is necessary to understand that the 2-D drawings you have constructed have used the X,Y,Z coordinate system all along. You have only drawn in the X,Y plane of this system. We will now expand to also draw in the Z-axis planes.

It is easy to understand the X,Y,Z coordinate system if you think of the "plan" view of your drawing as lying in the X,Y plane. Figure 30-1 shows the different axes.

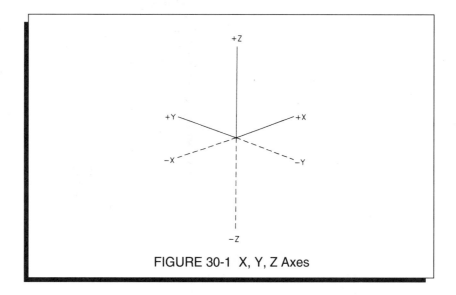

FIGURE 30-1 X, Y, Z Axes

You may, at this point, wish to review the section on coordinates in Chapter 9.

When working with a 3-D drawing, you must also draw in a manner that can be thought of as "up from the page." Let's take an example of a box with dimensions of 4 × 3 × 2 (in current units). Figure 30-2 shows the box sitting in the positive quadrants of an X,Y,Z coordinate system, with 4 units along the X-axis, 3 units along the Y-axis and 2 units along the Z-axis.

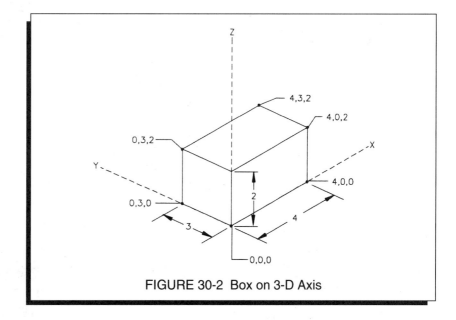

FIGURE 30-2 Box on 3-D Axis

As in 2-D drawing, each intersection has coordinates. In the case of a 3-D drawing, the coordinates are represented in an X,Y,Z format. Notice the coordinates listed in the previous illustration.

EXERCISE

Refer to Figure 30-3 and write the coordinates for each corner in the space provided.

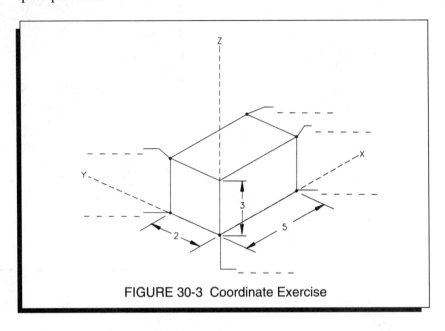

FIGURE 30-3 Coordinate Exercise

3-D VERSUS PERSPECTIVE

AutoCAD is capable of displaying your drawings in either 3-D or 3-D perspective views.

AutoCAD is capable of displaying your drawings in either 3-D or 3-D perspective views. A 3-D view may be perspective or non-perspective. A perspective view shows the drawing in 3-D form with faces diminishing to a vanishing point and all forms shortened in distance. This is similar to the way the human eye perceives forms in the environment.

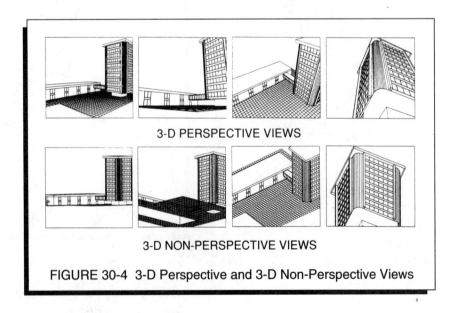

3-D PERSPECTIVE VIEWS

3-D NON-PERSPECTIVE VIEWS

FIGURE 30-4 3-D Perspective and 3-D Non-Perspective Views

A non-perspective view displays the drawing with "true lengths" for all lines in the drawing, similar to an isometric drawing. The previous illustrations show the same drawing displayed in both 3-D perspective and 3-D non-perspective views.

CLIPPING PLANES

Some applications require that a "cut-away" type of view be displayed for the purpose of showing parts of the drawing that may otherwise be concealed. This can be accomplished by a clipping plane.

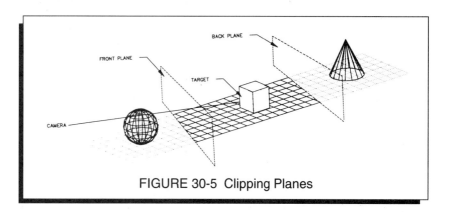

FIGURE 30-5 Clipping Planes

You can think of a clipping plane as an imaginary plane or surface that can "cut" through the drawing and eliminate every part of the drawing either in front or behind the plane.

You can think of a clipping plane as an imaginary plane or surface that can "cut" through the drawing and eliminate every part of the drawing either in front or behind the plane. Figure 30-6 illustrates the effect of the clipping plane shown in Figure 30-5.

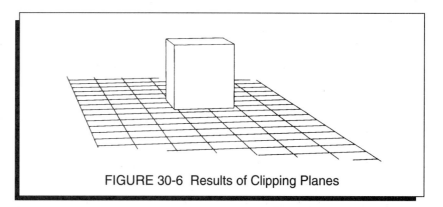

FIGURE 30-6 Results of Clipping Planes

CHAPTER REVIEW

1. What are the axes in the cartesian coordinate system?

_____

2. From which direction from a page would the Z-axis normally project?

_____

3. What is the difference between normal 3-D and perspective?

_____

_____

_____

_____

4. What is a "clipping plane"?

_____

_____

_____

_____

5. How many clipping planes are in AutoCAD? Name each.

_____

_____

6. What form of 3-D most closely approximates the view of the human eye?

_____

7. In AutoCAD, how would you show a coordinate that has values of X = 3, Y = 5, Z = 9?

_____

8. Which axes are two-dimensional drawings constructed in?

_____

9. Which axis would normally represent the "height" of an object?

_____

10. What is meant by "true lengths" when referring to a 3-D drawing?

_____

_____

_____

CHAPTER 31

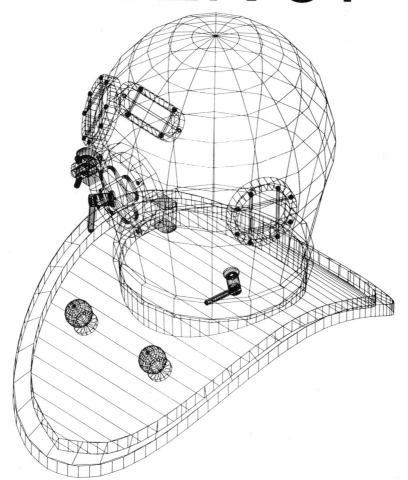

Viewing 3-D Drawings

OBJECTIVES:

To construct a 3-D drawing, you must be capable of manipulating the drawing in the three planes so you can work with the different parts. After the drawing is completed, you can use the viewing commands to observe the drawing from different viewpoints. Chapter 31 objectives are:

● To learn the use of the two commands used to view AutoCAD 3-D drawings.

● To become proficient in placing the imaginary camera and target to obtain the view you desire.

● To learn to use the Dview command options to control the look of the 3-D view.

● To produce hidden line and shaded views of the 3-D objects in the drawing.

AutoCAD In The Real World

On and Off the Road to CAM

AutoCAD®'s flexibility pays off for a manufacturer of injection-molded parts

If you've ever seen an off-road vehicle, you've probably seen some of Daystar's products: the red, white, blue or yellow protective boots on the shock absorbers. Daystar, Inc. of Glendale, Arizona, manufactures flexible automotive boots and bellows for both original-equipment and after-market applications. By utilizing injection-molding and CAD/CAE/CAM technology, they have established themselves as the people to go to for boots and bellows.

Daystar is a family business. Dick and Jean Goodman founded Daystar in 1978 when they acquired a small injection-molding company that made boots and bellows for motorcycles. This was, to the best of their knowledge, the first application of injection-molding to a flexible boot or bellows.

When Daystar began to move beyond motorcycles into the off-road industry, the engineering and volume requirements of their customer base increased a notch. It was the off-road industry that provided Daystar with the impetus to go to CAD. When they were dealing with motorcycle products. Daystar supplied only the product itself to its distributors. The off-road manufacturers, on the other hand, had engineering departments that demanded drawings and specifications.

Daystar simply did not have the resources to hire a draftsperson or an engineer to sit down and create these drawings. They concluded that the logical thing to do was leap into the 20th century. Rather than establish an engineering department with people and pens and paper and pencils, they decided to go directly to an electronic system.

Daystar needed to figure the stretch capability of the boot or bellows it designs, as well as clearances to the device the boot or bellows is protecting. Also, by calculating the material required to mold the part, their engineers could accurately estimate material costs. They needed a system that would take engineering inputs, perform calculations and predict the performance. When the performance was satisfactory, it would produce an engineering drawing.

Daystar selected AutoCAD because its open architecture allowed it to be customized to precisely fit their application. A program to do this was developed using AutoLISP, AutoCAD's embedded programming language.

When Daystar decided to add CAM to its CAD/CAE system, this same open architecture made it easy to tailor NC programming software to their specific need—having the part go directly from AutoCAD to the NC machine, substantially cutting the lead time for producing new products. They were successful with this, in fact, for one special project, they were able to design and produce a boot in only nine days.

Adapted from an article by Phil Kreiker in *CADalyst*, Copyright © 1990 by CADalyst Publications, Ltd.

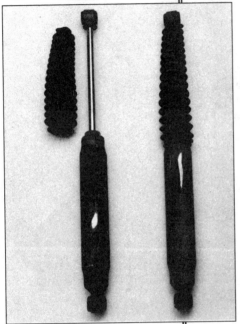

Two shock absorbers taken from a Ford truck. The units were in place for two years, 80,000 miles.

VIEWING 3-D DRAWINGS

Learning the methods to model your drawing in 3-D is not only important for presentation purposes but is important during the drawing process. In this chapter, we will review the methods of displaying a drawing in 3-D.

METHODS OF VIEWING 3-D DRAWINGS

The Vpoint command may be referred to as a "static" method, while the Dview command is a "dynamic" method of viewing.

There are two methods of creating views of your drawings. These are with the VPOINT or DVIEW commands. The Vpoint command may be referred to as a "static" method, while the Dview command is a "dynamic" method of viewing. The Dview's dynamic method allows you to see the drawing as it is being rotated into view. The Vpoint's static method is a simpler shortcut method for creating quick view points. Let's look at each method of creating views.

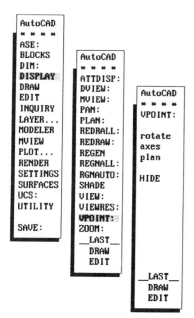

SETTING THE 3-D VIEWPOINT

The Vpoint command is used to select a viewpoint for the current viewport by setting a direction and elevation of view.

When you select the Vpoint command, the following prompt appears:

Command: <u>VPOINT</u>
Rotate/<View point> <current>:

The coordinates listed as <current> show the current view coordinates.

You can construct the viewpoint in three ways. Let's look at each way.

CREATING A VIEW BY COORDINATES

You may enter an X,Y,Z coordinate in response to the prompt to stipulate a point from which to view the drawing. The coordinate will be the point to look from, with the coordinate of 0,0,0 always the point to look at.

A viewpoint of 0,0,1 looks at the drawing in plan view (directly down along the Z-axis). A negative coordinate value places the viewpoint at the negative end of the axis. Thus, a viewpoint of 0,0,-1 would look at the drawing directly from below.

CREATING A VIEW BY AXES

If you respond to the prompt by selecting AXES from the screen menu or pressing ENTER on the keyboard, the drawing screen will temporarily display a special axes diagram. The visual diagram consists of a tripod, representing the X, Y, and Z axes and a flattened globe. Figure 31-1 shows the tripod and globe.

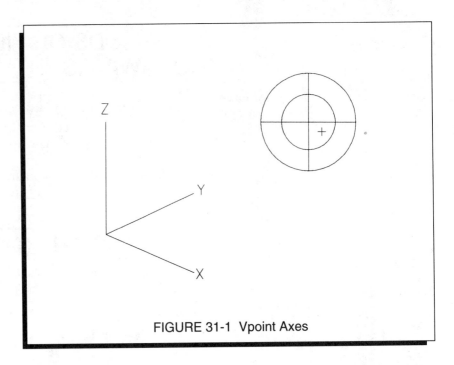

FIGURE 31-1 Vpoint Axes

To set the desired view, move the input device. This causes the tripod to rotate, representing the rotation of each axis. It helps to think of your drawing as lying in the X,Y plane of the tripod when visualizing the desired view.

The compass-appearing icon to the right is a two-dimensional representation of a globe. The center point of the crosshairs is the north pole, the middle circle is the equator, and the outer circle is the south pole. The four quadrants of the globe may be thought of as the direction of the view. For example, the lower right quadrant would produce a view that is represented from the lower left of the plan view. Moving above the equator produces an "above ground" view; below the equator, a "below ground" view.

When you wish to return to the plan view, enter Plan from the screen menu.

Don't be afraid to experiment with different views. Try to associate the globe and tripod with the results of the 3-D view. With a little practice, you will be able to obtain whatever results you desire.

SETTING VIEW BY DIALOGUE BOX

You can use a dialogue box to set standard views of your 3-D drawing. Select "View/SetView/Viewpoint/Presets..." from the pull down menus. Click on the degree settings shown in the dialogue box illustration to change the degrees. You may alternately set the degrees in the text box.

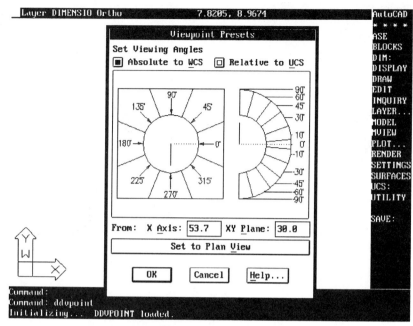

FIGURE 31-2 Vpoint Dialogue Box

DYNAMIC VIEWING

The DVIEW command is a very useful tool for modeling the drawing dynamically. This means you can rotate the drawing and see the results as you go.

The Dview command is also used to set clipping planes, set the distance from which the drawing is to be viewed, and other functions that allow you to precisely control the appearance of the 3-D view.

DVIEW OPTIONS

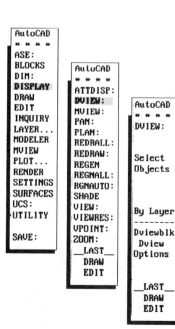

When you issue the Dview command, the following prompt is displayed:

Command: DVIEW
Select objects: (select)
CAmera/TArget/Distance/POints/PAn/Zoom/TWist/CLip/Hide/Off/Undo/
<eXit>:

You must have selected objects and be in the Dview command in order to use any of the options listed.

If you do not select objects and just press ENTER, AutoCAD displays a house (derived from a block named "DVIEWBLOCK") and displays it for a viewing model.

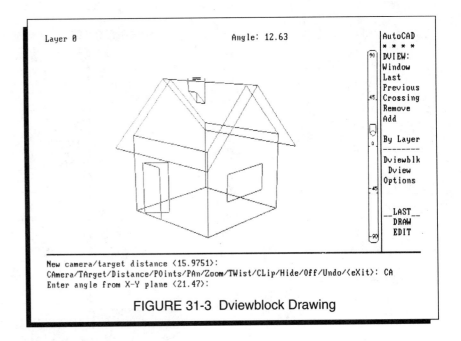

```
Layer 0                              Angle: 12.63              AutoCAD
                                                               * * * *
                                                          90   DVIEW:
                                                               Window
                                                               Last
                                                               Previous
                                                          45   Crossing
                                                               Remove
                                                               Add

                                                          0    By Layer
                                                               ---------
                                                               Dviewblk
                                                               Dview
                                                          45   Options


                                                               __LAST__
                                                          90   DRAW
                                                               EDIT

New camera/target distance <15.9751>:
CAmera/TArget/Distance/POints/PAn/Zoom/TWist/CLip/Hide/Off/Undo/<eXit>: CA
Enter angle from X-Y plane <21.47>:
```

FIGURE 31-3 Dviewblock Drawing

The following is a brief description of the options.

CAmera: Dynamically sets a camera position. This is the position from which you will view the drawing.

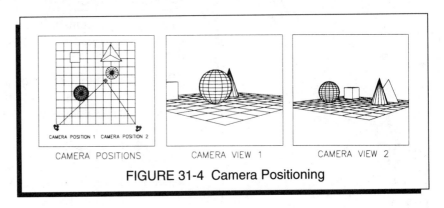

FIGURE 31-4 Camera Positioning

TArget: Dynamically sets a target position. This is the point in the drawing the camera will look at.

Distance: Moves the camera closer or further from the target along a path. This path is defined by a line between the camera and target point known as the "sight line."

POints: Allows you to position the camera and target points using X,Y,Z coordinates.

PAn: Pans the camera from its present position.

Zoom: If in perspective mode, Zoom is used to change the focal length of the camera. This is similar to changes in a camera image created by different lenses. For example, a wide angle or telephoto-type lens could be used to obtain different results.

If perspective mode is off, the Zoom option is used similarly to the standard Zoom command.

TWist: Tilts the 3-D view around the line of sight.

CLip: Sets clipping planes in the view. This has the effect of a cut-away type of view.

Hide: Creates a hidden line view.

Off: Turns off the perspective mode.

Undo: Reverses the previous command; same as the standard U command.

eXit: Exits the Dview command.

Let's learn how to use Dview to dynamically view your drawings.

CAMERA AND TARGET POSITIONING

When you view objects in 3-D, there is a point you look from and a point you are looking to. AutoCAD uses a camera and target imagery to assist in placing these points. Figure 31-5 shows a camera location and view of the resulting 3-D viewpoint.

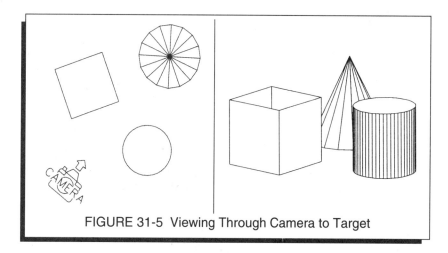

FIGURE 31-5 Viewing Through Camera to Target

POSITIONING THE CAMERA AND TARGET

The Dview command is used to place the camera and target. Let's look at how to do this. Choose the Dview command.

```
Command: DVIEW
Select objects: (select)
CAmera/TArget/Distance/POints/PAn/Zoom/TWist/CLip/Hide/Off/Undo/
<eXit>:
```

You must first select the entities that will be dynamically moved. The failure to select entities will not exclude them from the subsequent change of view, but will exclude them from being displayed dynamically. Selecting too many entities to be dynamically viewed will result in slow operation. It is prudent to select representative "frame" entities in the amount suitable for visualizing the overall view. When you accept the final view, the entire drawing will be generated in that view.

If you respond to the prompt with a null response (ENTER), a house will be displayed for viewing purposes only. You may also select DVIEWBLK from the screen menu in response to the "Select objects" prompt to display the house.

After the desired entities for dynamic viewing are selected, choose the CAmera option. Only the selected entities are displayed. The command line displays:

Toggle angle in/Enter angle from XY plane <>*default*>:

You may set the angle in two ways. This prompt is asking for the angle "up or down". You can set the angle, in degrees, by entering the numerical degrees from the keyboard. You may also set the angle "dynamically" by moving the crosshairs around the screen, rotating the selected entities of the drawing.

The selected entities change as you move the crosshairs, showing the new camera position. Although the drawing appears to be actually rotating, the effect is caused by the "camera" moving around the entities in the drawing.

When you are satisfied with the vertical view rotation, press the ENTER button on your input device.

If you enter the number of degrees from the keyboard, AutoCAD continues and prompts you for the number of degrees of rotation "around" drawing made up from the selected entities.

Toggle angle from/Enter angle in XY plane <>*default*>:

You can toggle between the two prompts by entering a "T" (for *toggle*) from the keyboard.

If you choose to dynamically set the camera angle by moving the crosshairs, AutoCAD will not display the second prompt, since both display angles are set at one time.

After you have set the new camera angle, AutoCAD redisplays the Dview prompt.

CAmera/TArget/Distance/POints/PAn/Zoom/TWist/CLip/Hide/Off/Undo/ <eXit>:

You may now select another option and continue to model the drawing. If you wish to reposition the camera or target, select the desired option. It is not necessary to reselect objects unless you exit the Dview command and the Dview prompt is no longer displayed.

You can set the camera target by selecting the TArget option.

CAmera/TArget/Distance/POints/PAn/Zoom/TWist/CLip/Hide/Off/Undo/ <eXit>: TA

Remember, the target is the point at which the camera is pointed. The TArget option and the CAmera option perform in the same manner.

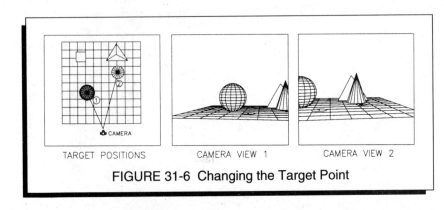

TARGET POSITIONS   CAMERA VIEW 1   CAMERA VIEW 2

FIGURE 31-6 Changing the Target Point

SETTING THE DISTANCE TO VIEW FROM

When the camera and target are placed, the line extending between them is called the "line of sight." The Distance option moves the camera along the line of sight, changing the distance between it and the target point. To select the Distance option, enter "D" in response to the prompt.

CAmera/TArget/Distance/POints/PAn/Zoom/TWist/CLip/Hide/Off/Undo/ <eXit>: <u>D</u>

Selecting Distance also activates the perspective mode, causing the view to appear in perspective form.

Selecting Distance also activates the perspective mode, causing the view to appear in perspective form. A perspective icon appears in the lower left corner of the screen to denote this.

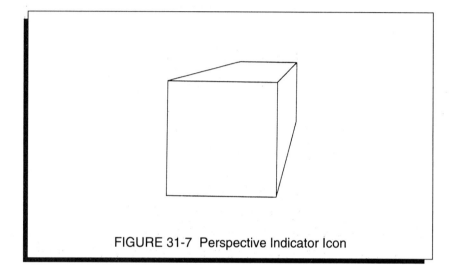

FIGURE 31-7 Perspective Indicator Icon

A single slider bar is used to dynamically set the camera-to-target distance. The slider bar contains graduations from 0× to 16×. This represents the distance factor, relative to the current distance between the camera and target. The current distance is, of course, represented by the value of 1. Moving the diamond marker to 4×, for example, would move the camera four times as far from the target point. This would have the visual effect of moving away from the objects in the view. Moving the slider bar to a value less than zero will shorten the distance, as though you approached the objects in the view.

When you are satisfied with the view distance, press the ENTER button on the input device.

Certain commands cannot be used in perspective mode. If you use one of these commands with Regenauto turned off, AutoCAD will display the message:

About to regen with perspective off — proceed?<Y>

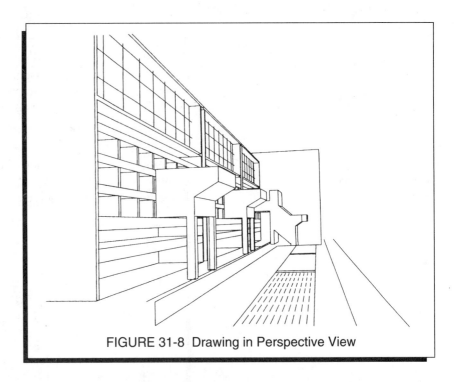

FIGURE 31-8 Drawing in Perspective View

Entering a "Y" or pressing ENTER will turn perspective mode off and continue the command. Entering an "N" will cancel the command and leave perspective mode on.

You may manually turn perspective mode off (and return to non-perspective mode) by selecting the Off option from the Dview prompt.

PANNING THE VIEW

Selecting the PAn option allows you to pan the camera from its present location. You can think of this as a "look around" option.

The operation is very simple. Just enter two points on the screen, in the same manner as a 2-D pan, and the scene will change accordingly. If you are not in perspective mode, you may alternately enter keyboard coordinates.

ZOOMING THE VIEW

The Zoom option operates differently, depending on whether the perspective mode is on or off.

The Zoom option, like the PAn option, operates differently, depending on whether the perspective mode is on or off.

If perspective mode is off, a slider bar is displayed at the top of the screen, allowing you to move the marker and view the resulting zoom. The slider bar is marked in graduations from 0 to 16×, with 1× representing the current zoom level.

If perspective mode is on, you may either use the slider bar, or stipulate the camera lens focal length. Changing the focal length is an interesting feature. The effect on the view is the same as if you changed the actual camera lens. For example, a 28mm setting displays a wide angle shot and a 100mm setting displays a telephoto shot towards the target point. The default is 50mm, which closely resembles the view from the human eye.

Figure 31-9 shows the effects of changing the focal length of the lens.

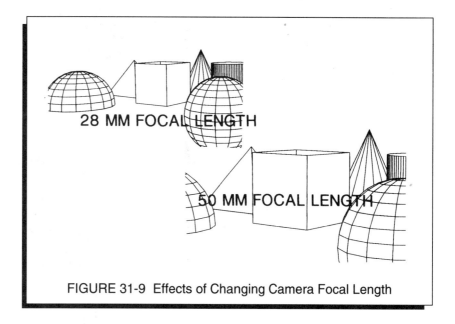

FIGURE 31-9 Effects of Changing Camera Focal Length

TWISTING THE VIEW

The TWist option is used to "twist" the view around the current line of sight. You can dynamically twist the view by entering a point on the screen, or by entering a twist angle.

When you select TWist, a rubber-banded line is drawn from the center of the screen to the crosshairs. Moving the cursor allows you to dynamically twist the view.

You may alternately enter the twist angle from the keyboard. The angle is measured counterclockwise, with 0° to the right at 3 o'clock.

SETTING CLIPPING PLANES

Clipping planes are used to cut away a part of the drawing. For example, you may want to cut away part of a building to see the interior.

You can think of clipping planes as transparent walls that slice through part of the drawing and remove everything that is either in front of or behind them.

There is a front and a back clipping plane. Either or both of these planes can be positioned in the drawing. Positioning is accomplished by either specifying a distance from the target point, or dynamically with slider bars.

The clipping planes may be positioned in either perspective or non-perspective mode. When perspective mode is activated by using the Distance option, the front clipping plane is automatically turned on and positioned at the location of the camera by default.

Figure 31-10 shows a perspective view. The clipping planes are shown as dashed "walls." The dotted parts of the drawing are the areas in front of the front clipping plane and to the rear of the back clipping plane. The second illustration shows the effect of placing the clipping planes at these locations.

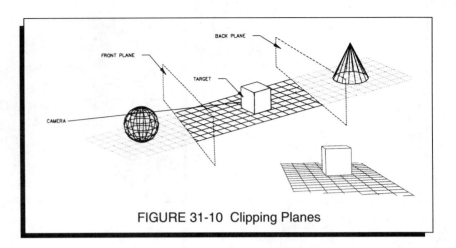

FIGURE 31-10 Clipping Planes

To set one or both clipping planes, select the CLip option from the Dview menu.

> CAmera/TArget/Distance/POints/PAn/Zoom/TWist/CLip/Hide/Off/Undo/ <eXit>: CL

The following prompt appears:

> Back/Front/<Off>:

Let's look at each of the Clip options.

Back: Sets the location of the back clipping plane.

Selecting the Back option displays the prompt:

> ON/OFF/distance from target <current>:

If you enter a positive numerical value, the back plane is placed at that distance (in current units) in front of the target point. A negative value places the plane that distance behind the target point.

A slider bar is also displayed that alternately allows dynamic placement. You can see the effects of the clipping plane on the drawing as you move it with the slider bar.

The ON/OFF options allow you to turn the effects of the plane on or off. The ON option uses the current distance value.

FRont: Sets the location of the front clipping plane.

The front clipping plane is positioned in the same manner as the back clipping plane.

Selecting the FRont option displays the prompt:

> ON/OFF/Eye/distance from target <current>:

The Eye option simply places the front plane at the current camera position.

PRODUCING HIDDEN LINE VIEWS

The Hide option is used to produce hidden line drawings of the current view. A similar Hide command is available when using the Vpoint command to produce a 3-D view.

The 3-D views are drawn and modeled in "wire frame."

The 3-D views are drawn and modeled in "wire frame." A wire frame is a drawing that you can see through the sides of. (Think of your object being made of wires.) The Hide command removes the parts of the drawing that you normally would not see in a three-dimensional view.

> **Tip**
>
> Start experimenting with the Hide command by using simple drawings to reduce the time required for regeneration.

You may instruct AutoCAD to display the hidden lines in a different color. To do so, use the Layer command to create layers of the same names as those in your drawing, but with the prefix "HIDDEN" added. For example, if you have a layer called "PARTS," create a separate

> **Tip**
>
> Use the layer color and linetype command to achieve different display appearances between visible and hidden lines.

layer called "HIDDENPARTS."

Hidden lines must be regenerated at the time of the plot if you wish to obtain a hard copy drawing with hidden lines removed. This is performed in the plot routine. See Chapter 18 for detailed instructions on plotting.

PRODUCING SHADED IMAGES

The SHADE command is used to produce shaded images, similar to AutoShade, of your drawing. To use Shade, enter the Shade command:

Command: <u>SHADE</u>

There are no options with the Shade command; the shading process begins immediately.

AutoCAD processes the shaded image in two steps. The first removes hidden lines. The second process produces the shaded image. On machines with limited memory, AutoCAD will produce the shaded image with several passes.

SHADING TYPES

The normal method of shading produces an image with one light source from the eyepoint. The shading type is controlled by the Shadedge and Shadedif system variables.

If Shadedge is set to 0 or 1, the faces are shaded based on the angle the faces form with the viewing direction. The percentage of diffuse reflection and ambient light level is set with the Shadedif variable. Shadedif is set to 70 by default. This means that 70 percent of the light is diffused light from the light source and 30 percent is ambient (overall general level) light. These numbers will always add to 100 percent of the light. The Shadedif variable sets the diffused light, while the balance of 100 percent is ambient light. Higher diffused light levels produce more contrast in a shaded image.

Table 31-A lists the four settings for the Shadedge variable and their effects.

SHADEDGE setting	Rendering Type
0	Shaded faces, no edge highlighting.
1	Shaded faces, edges highlighted in screen background color (requires 256 color display).
2	Simulates hidden line rendering. Centers of polygons are painted in background color. The color of visible edges is determined by the entity color.
3	Faces are drawn in original color but not shaded. Hidden faces are hidden, the visible edges displayed in the background color.

TABLE 31-A

CHAPTER REVIEW

1. What commands are used to generate a third dimension of a drawing?

   _____

   _____

2. What is meant by "dynamic modeling"?

   _____

   _____

   _____

   _____

3. What does the Dview/TArget command do?

   _____

   _____

   _____

   _____

4. How do you turn on perspective mode?

   _____

   _____

5. What are the conditions under which you could set either the zoom or camera lens when using Dview/Zoom?

_____

_____

_____

_____

6. Why would you only select part of the drawing in the Dview selection set?

_____

_____

_____

_____

7. In the Dview command, how would you display a model house for viewing?

_____

_____

8. What Dview option would you use to specify X,Y,Z coordinates to set a view from?

_____

_____

9. How does setting a smaller millimeter camera lens affect the view?

_____

_____

_____

_____

10. What is meant by "wire frame"?

_____

_____

_____

_____

11. What does the Shade command do?

_____

_____

12. What is the sum of the ambient light and diffused light levels in AutoCAD?

_____

CHAPTER 32

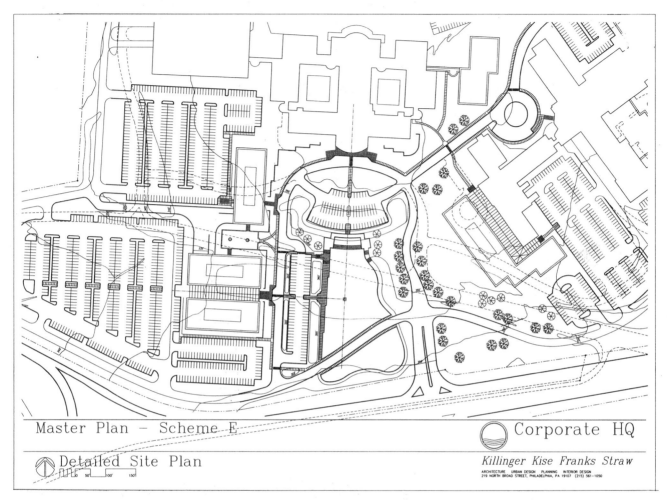

Master Plan – Scheme E

Detailed Site Plan

0 50' 100' 150'

Corporate HQ

Killinger Kise Franks Straw

ARCHITECTURE   URBAN DESIGN   PLANNING   INTERIOR DESIGN
219 NORTH BROAD STREET, PHILADELPHIA, PA 19107 (215) 561–1050

The User Coordinate System

OBJECTIVES:

To effectively construct a 3-D drawing, you must become proficient with the use of the User Coordinate System. Chapter 32 objectives are:

● To understand the concept and use of the User Coordinate System.

● To learn to manipulate the UCS.

● To understand the effects of the UCS on AutoCAD commands.

● To learn to save, restore, and manage UCS systems you create.

THE USER COORDINATE SYSTEM

When you are drawing in 2-D plan, you are working in the X,Y plane. Drawing is simplified, since you are working in a single plane. Drawing in 3-D, however, is more complicated. There may be many planes in which you wish to work. The User Coordinate System is designed to make this process simpler. We'll refer to the User Coordinate System as the "UCS."

In order to effectively draw in AutoCAD 3-D, it is essential to understand the UCS.

In order to effectively draw in AutoCAD 3-D, it is essential to understand the UCS. The primary purpose of the UCS is simplification of the 3-D process. Mastering the use of this system will allow you to construct 3-D drawings efficiently.

Let's consider the example of a sloped barn roof that has a graphic painted on it. It would be simple to draw the graphic in plan view, but placing it on the slope of the roof is quite different. Being able to draw on the slope of the roof as if it were in plan would be quite efficient.

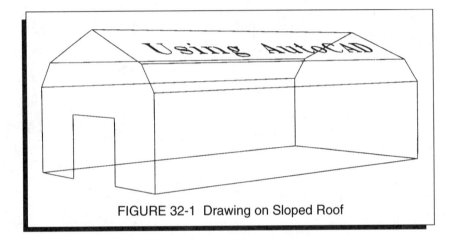

FIGURE 32-1 Drawing on Sloped Roof

The UCS allows you to do this. You may slope and rotate the UCS to change the plan view to match the slope of the roof. It may help to think of the UCS as the X,Y plane that you are used to seeing when you draw in 2-D plan view. Then imagine the ability to move, turn, and/or rotate it to any position on the 3-D object you are drawing. Now you can redisplay the drawing with the new plan view "flat on the paper" and draw on it as though you were in plan.

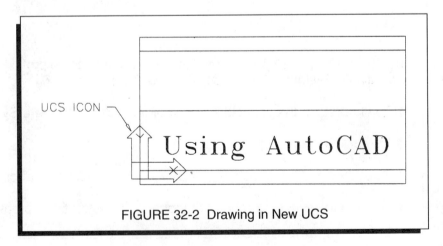

FIGURE 32-2 Drawing in New UCS

Actually, this is exactly what you are doing. You can always return to "true" plan. The true plan is called the World Coordinate System. The User Coordinate System is a temporary, user-defined drawing plane to make drawing on the sides, slopes, etc. of the 3-D object simpler. Let's continue and see how to manipulate the UCS to make 3-D drawing simple.

THE UCS ICON

The UCS icon is used to denote the orientation of the current UCS. The icon is displayed at the lower left of the drawing screen.

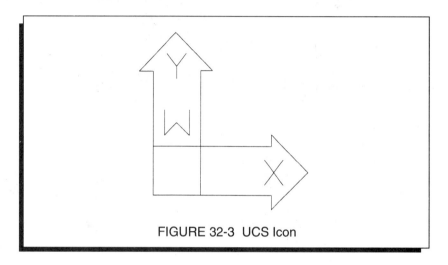

FIGURE 32-3 UCS Icon

The icon indicates the current UCS axes orientation, the origin of the UCS, and the viewing direction.

The icon indicates the current UCS axes orientation, the origin of the UCS, and the viewing direction. If the icon contains a "W," the World Coordinate System is in effect. The box indicates plan view. A plus (+) indicates the drawing is being viewed from above. If the plus is absent, the drawing is being viewed from below. The UCSicon command is used to control certain display characteristics of the icon. We will learn about the command later in this chapter.

HEAD-ON INDICATOR

It is possible to rotate the UCS, or the view relative to the current UCS, to a position that looks head-on into the edge of the drawing.

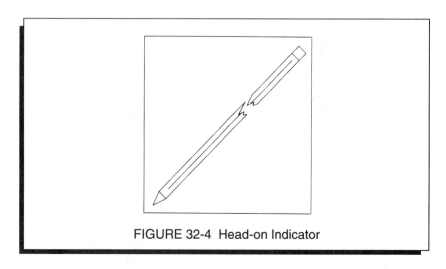

FIGURE 32-4 Head-on Indicator

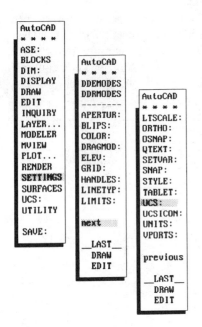

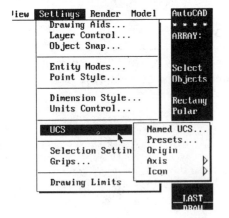

Such a position is almost useless as a drawing view. When such a view is current, AutoCAD displays a "head-on" indicator.

CHANGING THE UCS

The UCS command is used to change the current UCS. When you issue the UCS command the following prompt is displayed.

> Command: UCS
> Origin/ZAxis/3point/Entity/View/X/Y/Z/Prev/Restore/Save/Del/?/<World>:

Let's look at each option under the UCS command. It may be helpful to use a work disk drawing to practice each option as you study it.

Origin: Used to change the origin of the UCS. The axes are left unchanged. (The location of the icon will not change unless the Origin option of the UCSicon command is on. The UCSicon command is covered later in this chapter.) When you select the Origin option under the UCS command, the following prompt is displayed:

> Origin/ZAxis/3point/Entity/View/X/Y/Z/Prev/Restore/Save/Del/?/<World>: O
> Origin point <0,0,0>:

Enter an X,Y,Z coordinate point to describe a new origin point. If you enter only an X,Y point, the Z coordinate will be equal to the current elevation.

You may alternately enter a point on the screen to designate the new origin.

Object snap is especially useful in placing the new origin at a 3-D point that can be described by a point on an entity.

Tip

The use of object snap is very helpful when using many of the UCS options.

ZAxis: Used to define a new UCS defined by an origin point and a point along the Z-axis.

AutoCAD prompts:

> Origin point <0,0,0>:
> Point on positive portion of the Z axis <default>:

Responding to the second prompt will cause the Z-axis of the new origin to be parallel to the previous system.

3point: Aligns the UCS by placing three points that define the origin and rotation of the X,Y plane of the new UCS. This is particularly helpful when you align the UCS with existing entities using object snap. Selecting the 3point option displays the following prompts.

Origin/ZAxis/3point/Entity/View/X/Y/Z/Prev/Restore/Save/Del/
?/<World>: <u>3</u>
Origin point <0,0,0>:
Point on positive portion of the X axis <*default*>:
Point on positive-Y portion of the UCS X-Y plane <*default*>:

The point given for each may be either a numerical coordinate entered from the keyboard, or a point entered on the screen.

The point entered for the origin point prompt designates the new origin point. The second point defines the direction of the X-axis. The third point will lie in the X,Y plane and define the direction of the positive Y-axis. Simply entering an ENTER in response to any of the prompts will designate a value equal to the existing origin or direction.

Figure 32-5 shows the points entered to align the UCS with our barn roof.

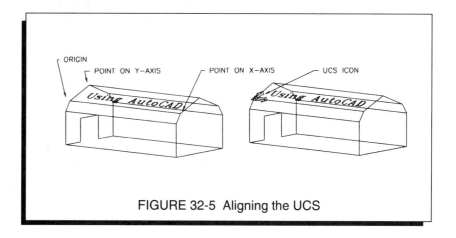

FIGURE 32-5 Aligning the UCS

Entity: Places the UCS relative to an existing entity. Selecting Entity results in the following prompt.

Origin/ZAxis/3point/Entity/View/X/Y/Z/Prev/Restore/Save/Del/
?/<World>: <u>E</u>
Select object to align UCS:

You must use object pointing to select the entity. No other object selection method is allowed.

Using this option will position the X,Y plane of the UCS parallel to the entity selected. The direction of the axes, however, will depend on the object selected. Table 32-A explains the effect of each.

Arc	The center of the arc becomes the new UCS origin with the X-axis passing through the point on the arc visually closest to the pick point.
Circle	The circle's center becomes the new UCS origin, with the X-axis passing through the point on the arc visually closest to the pick point.
Dimension	The new UCS origin is the middle point of the dimension text. The direction of the new Y-axis is parallel to the X-axis of the UCS in effect when the dimension was drawn.
Line (2-D and 3-D)	The endpoint visually nearest the pick point becomes the new UCS origin. The X-axis is chosen such that the line lies in the X,Z plane of the UCS (i.e., its second endpoint has a Y coordinate of zero in the new system).
Point	The new UCS origin is the point's location. The X-axis is derived by an arbitrary but consistent algorithm.
Polyline (2-D, 3-D, and polygon mesh)	The polyline's start point is the new UCS origin, with the X-axis extending from the start point to the next vertex.
Solid	The first point of the solid determines the new UCS origin. The new X-axis lies along the line between the first two points.
Trace	The "from" point of the trace becomes the UCS origin, with the X-axis lying along its center line.
3-D Face	The UCS origin is taken from the first point, the X-axis from the first two points, and Y positive side from the first and fourth points. The Z-axis follows by application of the right-hand rule. If the first, second, and fourth points are collinear, no new UCS is generated.
Shape, Text, Block Ref., Attribute, Attribute Def.	The new UCS origin is the insertion point of the entity, while the new X-axis is defined by the rotation of the entity around its extrusion direction. Thus, the entity you pick to establish a new UCS will have a rotation angle of 0° in the new UCS.

TABLE 32-A

View: It is often convenient to set the current UCS to be oriented to the current view. This view may have been set by using either the Vpoint or Dview commands. Selecting the View option resets the UCS to be perpendicular to the current viewing direction. That is, the current view will become the plan view under the new UCS created by the option. This results in a new UCS that is parallel to the computer screen.

Origin/ZAxis/3point/Entity/View/X/Y/Z/Prev/Restore/Save/Del/
?/<World>: <u>V</u>

X/Y/Z: Used to rotate the UCS around any of the three axes. This is actually three options. You may enter either X, Y, or Z in response to the UCS command prompt. Entering any of the three will result in the following prompt:

    Origin/ZAxis/3point/Entity/View/X/Y/Z/Prev/Restore/Save/Del/
    ?/<World>: (n)
    Rotation angle about n axis <0.0>:

The "n" is either X, Y, or Z. Entering an angle will cause the current UCS to rotate about the specified axis the designated number of degrees. You may also enter a point on the screen to show the rotation. AutoCAD provides a rubber-band line from the current origin point to facilitate this.

The direction of the angle is determined by the standard engineering "right hand rule" method of determining positive and negative rotation angles.

The direction of the angle is determined by the standard engineering "right hand rule" method of determining positive and negative rotation angles. Figure 32-6 shows the method of determining angle directions.

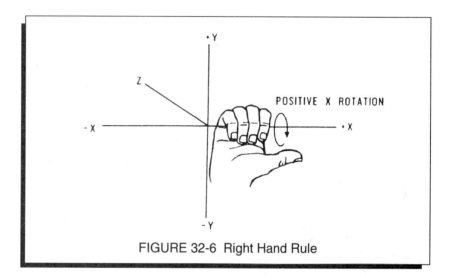

FIGURE 32-6 Right Hand Rule

Imagine placing your right hand around the axis which the UCS is to rotate, with the thumb pointing in the positive direction. The direction your curled fingers point is the direction of positive angle of rotation of that axis. (Be especially careful of the angle settings under the Units command, since they affect this procedure.)

If Tilemode is off, the last ten coordinate systems in both paper space and model space are saved. The "previous" coordinate system derived depends on the space in which you use the Previous options.

Previous: Returns the last UCS setting. Up to ten settings are stored. When repeatedly selected, the Previous option will "step back" through each. The operation of this option is similar to the Zoom Previous function.

    Origin/ZAxis/3point/Entity/View/X/Y/Z/Prev/Restore/Save/Del/
    ?/<World>: P

Restore: Restores a UCS saved with the Save option (explained next). The following prompt is displayed:

    Origin/ZAxis/3point/Entity/View/X/Y/Z/Prev/Restore/Save/Del/
    ?/<World>: R
    ?/Name of UCS to restore:

Enter the name of the desired UCS to be restored. The named UCS then becomes current.

If you enter a question mark (?), AutoCAD prompts:

UCS name(s) to list <*>:

Press ENTER to display all the saved coordinate systems.

Tip

The previously saved UCS becomes current, but the previous view does not. You may want to use the Plan command (explained later in this chapter) to restore the plan view of the now current UCS.

Entering a question mark (?) in response to the prompt will display a list of the saved coordinate systems.

Save: Permits naming and saving of the current UCS and return to it using the Restore option. The name may be up to 31 characters in length and may contain letters, numbers, dollar signs ($), hyphens (-), and underscores (_).

Tip

Use names that describe the location of the UCS, such as "ROOF-TOP" or "FRONT-SIDE."

```
Origin/ZAxis/3point/Entity/View/X/Y/Z/Prev/Restore/Save/Del/
?/<World>: S
?/Desired UCS name:
```

Del: Deletes a previously saved UCS name. The following prompt is issued:

```
Origin/ZAxis/3point/Entity/View/X/Y/Z/Prev/Restore/Save/Del/
?/<World>: D
UCS name(s) to delete <none>:
```

The DOS-similar wildcard characters of "?" and "*" may be used to delete several UCS names at a time. Entering the name of a single UCS name will delete only that system. Several names may be entered by separating them with commas.

?: Lists the saved coordinate systems. This performs the same function as the ? option under Restore. A listing of each saved UCS and the coordinates of the origin and X,Y,Z axes is displayed.

```
Origin/ZAxis/3point/Entity/View/X/Y/Z/Prev/Restore/Save/Del/
?/<World>: ?
UCS name(s) to list <*>:
```

World: Resets the UCS to the World Coordinate System.

```
Origin/ZAxis/3point/Entity/View/X/Y/Z/Prev/Restore/Save/Del/
?/<World>: W
```

UCSFOLLOW SYSTEM VARIABLE

The UCSFOLLOW system variable allows you to set the UCS plan view to follow a newly set User Coordinate System. Normally, when you set a new UCS, you will select the Plan command to reset the display to align in true plan view with the new coordinate system. Turning on (setting to "1") UCSFOLLOW will cause the plan view to be set automatically each time the UCS is changed.

UCSICON COMMAND

The UCS icon is different for model space and paper space.

The UCSICON command is used to control the display of the icon indicator. The icon is located, by default, at the lower left corner of the drawing screen. The UCS icon is different for model space and paper space. Figure 32-7 shows the UCS icon for each.

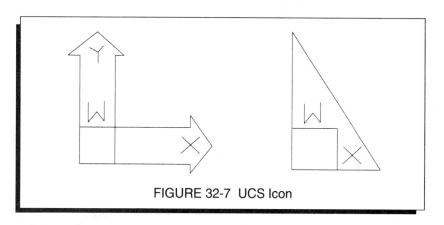

FIGURE 32-7 UCS Icon

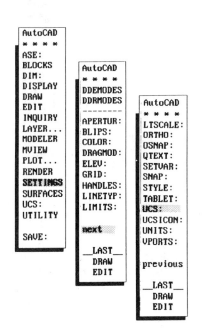

Issuing the UCSicon command results in the following prompt.

    Command: UCSICON
    ON/OFF/All/Noorigin/ORigin <ON>:

The following is a listing of the options for the UCSicon command.

OFF: Turns off the display of the icon.

ON: Turns on the icon display if it is off.

All: Selecting the All option allows you to simultaneously apply the changes made to the UCS icon to all the viewports currently in effect. Normally, the UCS icon only affects the icon in the current viewport.

To use the All option, first select All. The prompt will repeat, allowing the choice of the option that will affect the icons in each viewport.

Noorigin: Causes the icon to be displayed at the lower left of the drawing screen, without respect to the actual current UCS origin (default setting).

ORigin: Causes the icon to be displayed at the actual UCS origin point of 0,0,0. If the origin point is not within the screen display, the icon is displayed at the lower left of the screen.

DDUCS COMMAND (UCS DIALOGUE BOX)

The DDUCS command displays a dialogue box that assists management of the UCS system.

The dialogue box contains a listing of the coordinate systems that have been defined (saved), as well as the World Coordinate System, the previous system, and the current system, if it has not been saved and named. Figure 32-8 shows a typical DDUCS dialogue box.

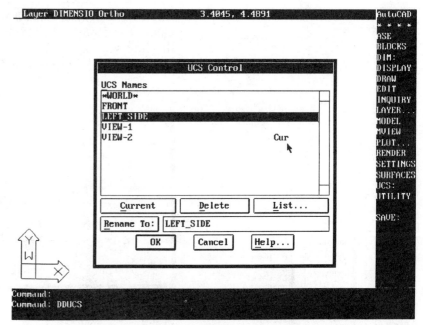

FIGURE 32-8 UCS Control Dialogue Box (DDUCS)

The dialogue box contains "scroll bars" that allow the listing to be scrolled if there are more listings than the box can display at one time. The UP and DOWN buttons scroll the list continuously, while the PAGE UP and PAGE DOWN buttons scroll the listing a page at a time. If there is less than one page of listings, the buttons have no effect. To operate the scroll buttons, place the arrow marker over the box and press the input key.

The first entry in the dialogue box is always the World Coordinate System and is listed as *WORLD*. If you have changed the UCS, a listing named *PREVIOUS* is shown. A current listing that has not been named is shown as *NO NAME*. Additional listings show the name of each saved UCS.

CHANGING THE CURRENT UCS

The current UCS is noted with "Cur" in the listing. To select a new UCS, click on another name.

LISTING UCS INFORMATION

You may obtain UCS information by clicking on the "List..." button in the dialogue box.

The List subdialogue box displays the X,Y,Z vectors of the origin and each axis.

Tip

Deleting a UCS that is no longer in use makes UCS management easier.

DELETING A UCS

You may delete a UCS by selecting the UCS name, then the Delete button.

You cannot delete either the World or Previous UCS listings.

CHAPTER REVIEW

1. In what plane does the User Coordinate System exist?

   _____

2. What is the World Coordinate System?

   _____

   _____

   _____

   _____

3. What does the "head-on indicator" mean?

   _____

   _____

   _____

   _____

4. What command is used to manipulate the UCS?

   _____

5. What command is used to display the UCS icon?

   _____

6. What UCS option would you use to align the UCS with the current drawing rotation, placing the UCS parallel with the view?

   _____

7. What rule is used to determine the rotation of axes?

_____

_____

8. How would you store and recall a UCS?

_____

_____

_____

9. What is the function of the UCSFOLLOW system variable?

_____

_____

_____

_____

10. What are the two possible positions for the UCS icon?

_____

_____

CHAPTER 33

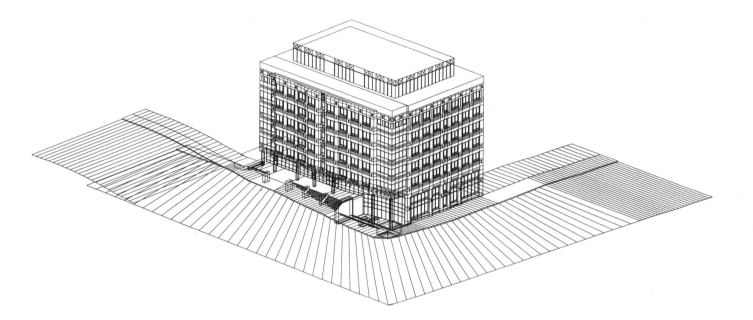

Drawing in 3-D

OBJECTIVES:

After you have become proficient with the use of 3-D viewing and UCS commands, you must learn the methodology of constructing 3-D drawings in AutoCAD. Chapter 33 objectives are:

● To understand the concepts of elevation and thickness.

● To become proficient with drawing in different UCS systems.

● To create solid faces for objects.

● To learn to construct various types of 3-D surface meshes.

● To learn to use AutoCAD's functions to create basic 3-D objects.

AutoCAD In The Real World

What Goes Down Should Come Up

AutoCAD® is used on a project that's hardly child's play

It is said that life goes in circles and there is nothing new under the sun. John Schaefer disagreed with that philosophy until recently, when something made him stop and think. "Here we are in an age where we can design practically everything on the computer, and it occurred to me to apply a little modern technology to an idea that first became popular back in 1929."

It was then that Donald Duncan, Sr. invented the string that allowed a yo-yo to "sleep" (or continue to spin and stay down after it reached the end of its length). The whole world was hooked and soon another fad was born. Today, the yo-yo has recaptured our attention, so Schaefer decided to redesign it using current technology.

Product Design

The product design of a yo-yo has a few restrictions. It must be round and needs a shaft surrounded by two hubs that will cause a string to wind up around the shaft as the unit rotates. Outside of that, there are many variations that can go into the redesign of this product.

Through third-party applications, AutoCAD provided an integrated CAD/CAM environment for the design and manufacture of the yo-yo.

The yo-yo is experiencing a new wave of popularity. The key to selling yo-yos successfully is building them for peak performance at the lowest cost. For better performance, the design required that as much material mass go to the outer edges as possible. Decreasing the part costs required sophisticated design and manufacturing.

Enter the computer-design yo-yo. The design was made easier with AutoCAD which let the designer experiment easily with modifications. Low production cost was made possible with the right choice of plastic and designing the most efficient mold with AutoCAD and an injection mold design system. Once designed, the mold was developed with CNC software which read the AutoCAD file information. Computers were used to monitor the molding presses and the yo-yo was recreated with very few problems. This toy, originally developed in 1929, is ready to spin anew.

Adapted with permission from an article by John R. Schaefer. Excerpted from *CADENCE*, November 1989, copyright © 1989, Ariel Communications, Inc.

DRAWING IN 3-D

Now that you have learned about the User Coordinate System and how to set up views of 3-D drawings, it is time to learn the components of 3-D drawing construction.

There are several manners in which to construct the components that make up a 3-D drawing. Some are used to draw a unique shape, while some are basic shapes that can be placed in the drawing. Many drawings are composed of a combination of specially drawn objects and basic shapes.

The first step in constructing a new 3-D drawing is studying the shapes to be drawn. Determine the best method of approach. It is often easier to construct each individual shape, than to insert it into a master drawing which is composed of many objects.

The ways to construct a 3-D drawing that we will study are as follows:

- Elevation and thickness to create extruded entities.
- Standard drawing methods in different coordinate systems.
- 3-D polygon meshes
- 3-D objects

Let's look at how we can use each of these to create 3-D drawings.

EXTRUDED ENTITIES

An extrusion may be thought of as applying a thickness to an entity.

This method of placing 3-D shapes forms the components by applying extrusions to drawing entities. An extrusion may be thought of as applying a thickness to an entity. Think of the entity as "growing" up or down from the flat drawing plane (X,Y drawing plane).

Thus, a line appears as a sheet of paper on edge. A circle appears as a tube, etc. Figure 33-1 shows several drawing entities on the left and the same entities in extruded form on the right.

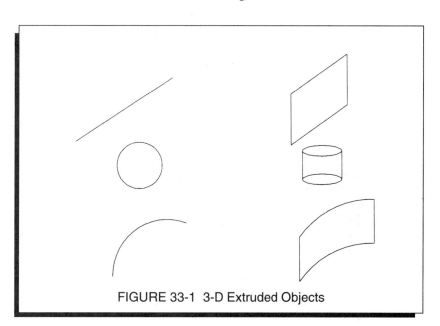

FIGURE 33-1 3-D Extruded Objects

ELEVATION

The base, or bottom, of the extrusion can be set at different elevations. Consider an extruded tube (made from a circle) sitting on a table top. The top of the table could be considered as zero elevation. If you placed the bottom of the tube above the zero elevation, the tube would appear to be hovering above the table top. If the elevation is negative, the tube will appear to be shoved downward through the table top.

Of course, the floor on which the table sits could be placed at the zero elevation. If the table was 30 in. to the top, the table top elevation would be 30 in. If you wanted the tube to sit on the table, the elevation of the tube would also be 30 in.

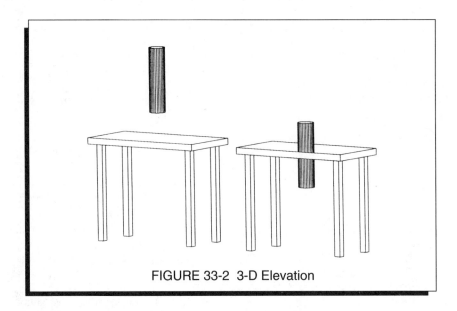

FIGURE 33-2 3-D Elevation

THICKNESS

The thickness of an extruded entity is the distance from the base elevation of the entity. For example, a thickness of 6 in. would make our tube 6 in. high. The thickness is measured from the base elevation of the entity. Note that this is not necessarily zero, as in the previous example of the tube sitting on a table top with a 30 in. elevation.

SETTING ELEVATION AND THICKNESS

To draw an entity with a specified elevation and/or thickness, the ELEVATION command is used. This command presets both values, and every entity that is subsequently drawn has these values. The default value in the ACAD prototype drawing is zero for each, resulting in a flat entity in 3-D.

When you issue the Elevation command, the following prompts are displayed:

> Command: <u>ELEV</u>
> New current elevation <current>:
> New current thickness <current>:

Setting new values only affects the entities drawn after the change. It is not retroactive, and changing either setting has no immediate visual effect on the drawing at the time the change is made.

CHANGING EXISTING ENTITIES

In order to create several entities of different elevations and/or thicknesses, the Elevation command is used to change each value before drawing the new entities.

Many times, entities are drawn with an incorrect thickness. If this happens, it is not necessary to erase the entities and redraw them with a new thickness. The CHANGE command is very convenient for changing this.

Simply issue the Change command.

> Command: <u>CHANGE</u>
> Select objects: (*select*)
> Properties/<Change point>:

At the last prompt, you may choose "Thickness" from the screen menu. If you are typing the commands from the keyboard, enter "P" to select the Properties option, and the following prompt appears.

Change what property (Color/Elev/LAyer/LType/Thickness)?

Enter either "E" or "T" (for Elevation or Thickness) and you are prompted for the new thickness for the entity or entities you selected.

Tip

It is often easier to construct all or part of a drawing at a single thickness, than use the Change command to reset one entity or groups of entities when you are through.

TUTORIAL

Let's try constructing a simple drawing using the Elevation command to set the base elevation and the thickness of the extrusion.

Begin a new drawing called "3-D." Set limits of 0,0 and 12,8.

Now let's set the first elevation and thickness.

```
Command: ELEV
New current elevation <current>: 0
New current thickness <current>: 4
```

Draw a box (see Figure 33-3) using the Line command.

FIGURE 33-3 Box

Now change the thickness again:

```
Command: ELEV
New current elevation <0>: (ENTER)
New current thickness <4.00>: 10
```

Notice how the currently set values show up as defaults. We pressed ENTER to accept the current elevation of zero but changed the thickness to 10.

Now use the Circle command to draw a circle like to the one shown in Figure 33-4.

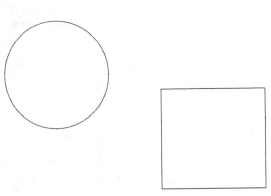

FIGURE 33-4 Circle and Box

Use either the Vpoint or Dview command to view the 3-D shapes!
Your drawing (depending on the viewpoint) should appear similar to
the one in Figure 33-5.

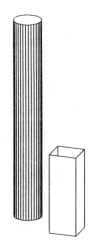

FIGURE 33-5 3-D View

Try changing the elevation and thickness with the Change command.

DRAWING IN COORDINATE SYSTEMS

If we wish to draw more complex objects, we must use the User
Coordinate System to relocate the current system. This allows you to
draw in a stipulated plane, as defined by the current UCS, as though
you were in plan view.

This is especially useful, since most 3-D drawings require detailing on
the different faces (planes) of the objects in the drawing.

In addition to drawing in different planes, the thickness and elevation
settings may be used. Note that these are relevant to the current UCS
when the entity is drawn.

Let's look at an example of drawing in 3-D by using different coordinate systems.

TUTORIAL

Let's draw a small shop building so we can become familiar with the techniques of drawing in AutoCAD 3-D.

STARTING THE DRAWING

Start a new drawing called "SHOP." Create the following setup parameters.

     Units: Architectural
     Limits: 0,0 / 80 ft.,50 ft. (remember to Zoom All)
     Snap: 1 ft.
     Grid: 10 ft. (initially)

In Release 12, the coordinates are set for relative display by default. Use CTRL-D to toggle between the modes.

DRAWING THE BASIC SHAPE

Select Line and draw the outline of the floor. The dimensions are 50 ft. in length and 30 ft. in width. Figure 33-6 shows the dimensioned plan. Do not dimension the plan.

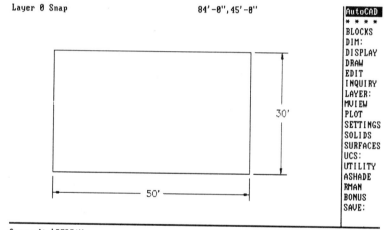

FIGURE 33-6 Floor Outline

Use the Vpoint command to create a view similar to the one shown in Figure 33-7.

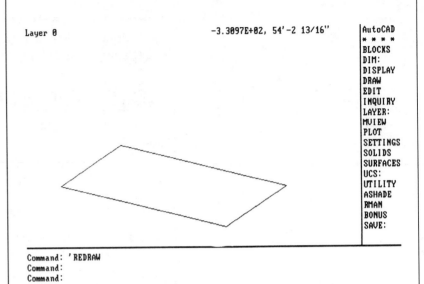

FIGURE 33-7 VPoint View

Let's save this view for recall later. Select View/Save. Enter the name "VIEW1" for this view.

We will now set the UCS icon so that it moves to each new origin as we set it. Select UCSicon/ORigin.

Let's set the first UCS. Select UCS/Entity. Select the nearest end wall line. Notice how the UCS icon moves to the corner of the building. Observe the orientation of the axes.

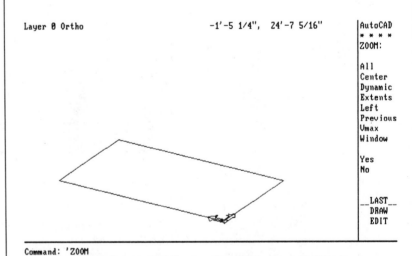

FIGURE 33-8 New UCS Origin

Let's now draw the first vertical corner line. Select Line, then choose the .XY filter from the menu. Now select INTERSECtion snap. Snap to the intersection of the front corner. When the "need Z" prompt appears, enter a Z (height) value of 12 ft.

Use the Copy command and Osnap to copy the vertical line to the other end wall corner.

Let's now rotate the UCS so we can draw directly on the end wall.

Select UCS/X. The "X" option is used to rotate the UCS around the X-axis. By the right hand rule, we want to rotate the UCS –90°. Enter –90 in response to the prompt. Notice how the UCS icon rotates.

We may want to save this UCS for recall later. Select UCS/Save. Enter the name END_WALL.

Let's now change to the plan view for the current UCS. Select Plan. Press RETURN to default to the plan view for the current UCS.

We want to construct the roof angles as shown in Figure 33-9.

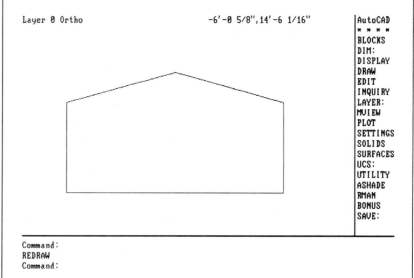

FIGURE 33-9 Endwall

You may want to zoom to a comfortable working size.

Select Line and use object snap to connect to the top of the left vertical line. Enter the polar coordinate of "@16'<15" to define the endpoint. Connect a line to the other vertical line and enter the polar coordinate of "@16'<165". Finish by Filleting the ridge point to form a perfect intersection at the peak of the roof.

Restore the previously stored view by selecting View/Restore, then responding "VIEW1" to the prompt. Copy the end wall "panel" to the opposite end (using object snap aids in exact placement).

Now use the Line command and object snap to connect the ridge points and the edges of the roof as shown in Figure 33-10.

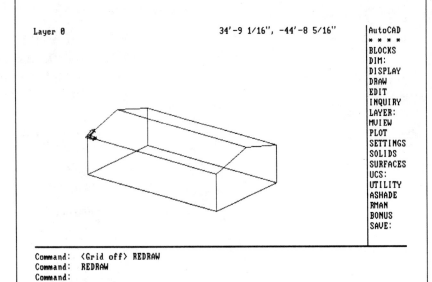

Layer 0   34'-9 1/16", -44'-8 5/16"

Command: <Grid off> REDRAW
Command: REDRAW
Command:

FIGURE 33-10 Main Building Lines

DRAWING ON THE ROOF

Let's now draw some lines on the slope of the roof to represent siding. Select UCS/3point. Use object snap to snap to the origin, X-axis line, and Y-axis line as shown in Figure 33-11. Notice how the UCS icon relocates to the edge of the roof and rotates to match the slope.

Select Plan and Return to display the plan view of the new UCS. The plan view should look similar to the following illustration. You may want to zoom to a comfortable working size.

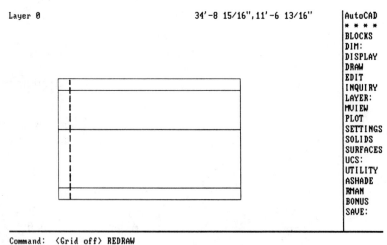

Layer 0   34'-8 15/16",11'-6 13/16"

Command: <Grid off> REDRAW
Command: REDRAW
Command:

FIGURE 33-11 Roof in Plan View

Array the edge line (shown dotted in the previous illustration). Select Rectangular array, 1 row, 26 columns, and 24 in. between columns.

Select View/Restore/VIEW1 to restore the previously saved 3-D view.

Select UCS/3point and reset the UCS to the opposite roof in accordance with the points shown in Figure 33-12.

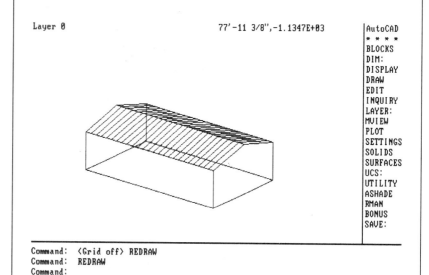

```
Layer 0                          77'-11 3/8",-1.1347E+03      AutoCAD
                                                              * * * *
                                                              BLOCKS
                                                              DIM:
                                                              DISPLAY
                                                              DRAW
                                                              EDIT
                                                              INQUIRY
                                                              LAYER:
                                                              MVIEW
                                                              PLOT
                                                              SETTINGS
                                                              SOLIDS
                                                              SURFACES
                                                              UCS:
                                                              UTILITY
                                                              ASHADE
                                                              RMAN
                                                              BONUS
                                                              SAVE:

Command:   <Grid off> REDRAW
Command:   REDRAW
Command:
```

FIGURE 33-12 Roof Lines

Select Plan and Return to default to the plan view of the new UCS. Array the roof line in the same manner as the opposite side of the roof.

Select View/Restore/View1 to restore our standard working view.

DRAWING DOORS ON THE WALLS

Let's now proceed and draw some doors on one wall. Select UCS/3point. Select points as shown in the following illustration to set a new UCS. Select Plan, then press ENTER to set the plan view for the new UCS. The new plan view should look like Figure 33-13.

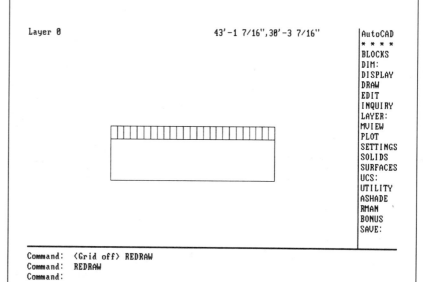

```
Layer 0                          43'-1 7/16",30'-3 7/16"      AutoCAD
                                                              * * * *
                                                              BLOCKS
                                                              DIM:
                                                              DISPLAY
                                                              DRAW
                                                              EDIT
                                                              INQUIRY
                                                              LAYER:
                                                              MVIEW
                                                              PLOT
                                                              SETTINGS
                                                              SOLIDS
                                                              SURFACES
                                                              UCS:
                                                              UTILITY
                                                              ASHADE
                                                              RMAN
                                                              BONUS
                                                              SAVE:

Command:   <Grid off> REDRAW
Command:   REDRAW
Command:
```

FIGURE 33-13 New UCS Plan View

Use the Line command to draw doors on the side wall of the shop. You can draw any type of doors and/or windows you wish. Figure 33-14 shows some doors as you may want to draw them.

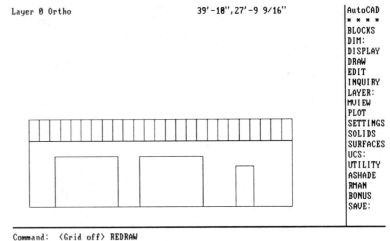

```
Layer 0 Ortho                           39'-10",27'-9 9/16"        AutoCAD
                                                                   * * * *
                                                                   BLOCKS
                                                                   DIM:
                                                                   DISPLAY
                                                                   DRAW
                                                                   EDIT
                                                                   INQUIRY
                                                                   LAYER:
                                                                   MVIEW
                                                                   PLOT
                                                                   SETTINGS
                                                                   SOLIDS
                                                                   SURFACES
                                                                   UCS:
                                                                   UTILITY
                                                                   ASHADE
                                                                   RMAN
                                                                   BONUS
                                                                   SAVE:

Command:  <Grid off> REDRAW
Command:  REDRAW
Command:
```

FIGURE 33-14 Doors in Wall

Let's now set the UCS system back to the World system before we model the drawing. Select UCS/World, then Plan/ENTER.

MODELING THE DRAWING IN 3-D

Use the Vpoint or Dview commands to model the drawing. This is a good time to also practice using the Dview options such as Camera, Target, and Distance.

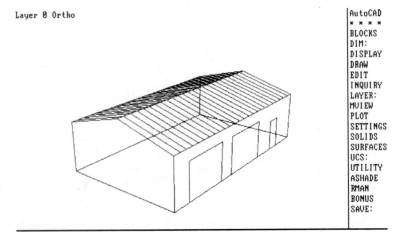

```
Layer 0 Ortho                                                     AutoCAD
                                                                   * * * *
                                                                   BLOCKS
                                                                   DIM:
                                                                   DISPLAY
                                                                   DRAW
                                                                   EDIT
                                                                   INQUIRY
                                                                   LAYER:
                                                                   MVIEW
                                                                   PLOT
                                                                   SETTINGS
                                                                   SOLIDS
                                                                   SURFACES
                                                                   UCS:
                                                                   UTILITY
                                                                   ASHADE
                                                                   RMAN
                                                                   BONUS
                                                                   SAVE:

CAmera/TArget/Distance/POints/PAn/Zoom/TWist/CLip/Hide/Off/Undo/<eXit>:
Regenerating drawing.
Command:
```

FIGURE 33-15 3-D View

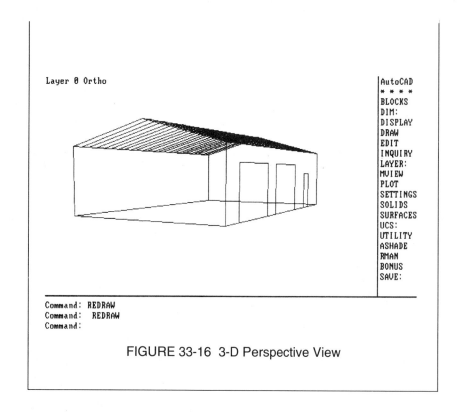

Layer 0 Ortho

AutoCAD
* * * *
BLOCKS
DIM:
DISPLAY
DRAW
EDIT
INQUIRY
LAYER:
MVIEW
PLOT
SETTINGS
SOLIDS
SURFACES
UCS:
UTILITY
ASHADE
RMAN
BONUS
SAVE:

Command: REDRAW
Command: REDRAW
Command:

FIGURE 33-16 3-D Perspective View

CREATING SOLID 3-D FACES

It is often desirable to create solid faces on objects that will obscure objects behind them when the Hide command is used.

As you have already learned, many types of extruded entities naturally create solid faces. When you are drawing single entities (such as lines, circles, arcs, etc.), however, solid faces are not automatically formed.

3DFACE COMMAND

The 3DFACE command is used to create solid faces. The 3Dface command is similar to a solid face in that it creates a "face plane." It is dissimilar, however, because it can be defined with different Z coordinates for each corner of the face, creating the possibility of a nonplanar or warped plane. It is also void of solid fill, although an external program such as AutoShade may be used to create colors on the faces.

PLACING 3-D FACES

The method of placing 3-D faces is similar to that used with the Solid command. When stipulating the corner points, however, the points are entered in a consecutive clockwise or counterclockwise fashion. This differs from the method of entry for a solid, where such a sequence would create a "bow-tie" effect.

The placement of 3-D faces creates a visual "edge frame." This can be undesirable in some situations. Take, for example, an area of irregular shape. Placing a 3-D face creates several planes that fill in the irregular area. Normally, each frame would contain an edge that is visible in the drawing. Figure 33-17 shows the same drawing with and without edge frames on the 3-D faces.

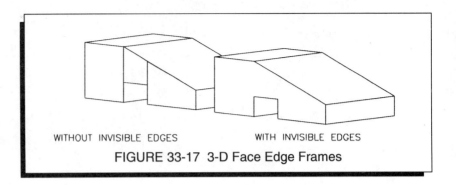

WITHOUT INVISIBLE EDGES   WITH INVISIBLE EDGES

FIGURE 33-17 3-D Face Edge Frames

The 3Dface command uses an option called "invisible" as a modifier to delete the appearance of the edge frame. Let's look at an example of both placing a 3-D face and making part of the frame area invisible.

3DFACE TUTORIAL

Use the Line command to draw the polygon shown in Figure 33-18. Issue the 3Dface command and enter the following sequence.

```
Command: 3DFACE
First point: (enter point 1)
Second point: (enter point 2)
Third point: I (ENTER)
Fourth point: (enter point 4)
Third point: (enter point 5)
Fourth point: (enter point 6)
```

After the final ENTER, the second 3-D face plane is closed.

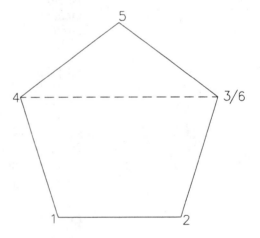

FIGURE 33-18 3-D Face Sequence

Notice how the I (invisible) option is entered prior to the segment of the frame you wish to be invisible. Of course, all frame segments may be stipulated to be invisible.

The frame segments that are constructed with the "I" option may be changed to visible with the use of the Splframe system variable. A zero setting maintains invisibility, while a nonzero (such as 1) setting makes them visible. This is convenient when you wish to edit sections that were constructed as invisible. The change is not apparent until the next regeneration is performed.

3-D POLYGON MESHES

A 3-D polygon mesh can be thought of as a "blanket" type of entity that can be curved and warped into shapes that can not be described by other entities.

MESH DENSITY

There are several methods of constructing polygon meshes. All the methods of construction create a mesh that is defined by a density. The density is the number of vertices used to describe the surface of the mesh. Figure 33-19 shows an object described by a mesh in two different densities.

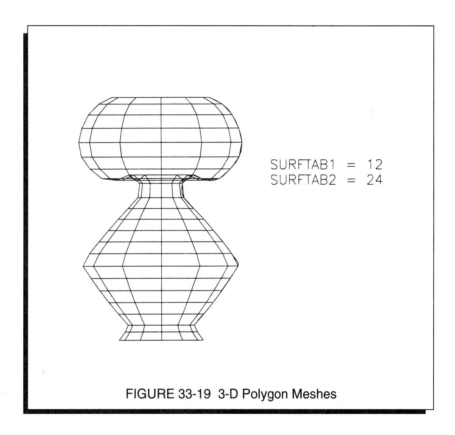

SURFTAB1 = 12
SURFTAB2 = 24

FIGURE 33-19 3-D Polygon Meshes

The density is described by the system variables named Surftab1 and Surftab2.

The density is described by the system variables named Surftab1 and Surftab2. One-directional meshes are controlled by Surftab1, while two-directional meshes are controlled by both variables; one for each direction. The directions are defined in AutoCAD as "M" and "N."

The methods of mesh construction are as follows:

    3DMESH
    PFACE
    RULESURF
    TABSURF
    REVSURF
    EDGESURF

Let's look at each and study the construction method of each.

3DMESH COMMAND

A 3DMESH is constructed by stipulating the number of vertices in each (M and N) direction, then specifying the X,Y,Z coordinate of each of the vertices.

It should be noted at this time that construction of 3-D meshes is very tedious. In most situations, it is more efficient to construct a mesh of the same type with one of the other construction methods. The use of the 3Dmesh command is best utilized in LISP routines. With this in mind, let's proceed to study the method by which it works.

CONSTRUCTING A 3-D MESH

To construct a 3-D mesh, first issue the 3Dmesh command, then the number of vertices in the M and N directions, and finally the vertex coordinate of each. Let's look at an example.

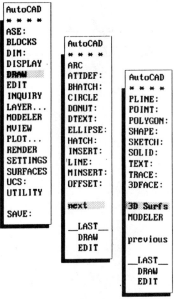
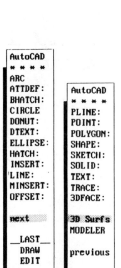

```
Command: 3DMESH
Mesh M size: 3
Mesh N size: 3
Vertex (0,0): 10,10,-1
Vertex (0,1): 10,20,1
Vertex (0,2): 10,30,3
Vertex (1,0): 20,10,1
Vertex (1,2): 20,20,0
Vertex (1,3): 20,30,-1
Vertex (2,0): 30,10,0
Vertex (2,1): 30,20,1
Vertex (2,2): 30,30,2
```

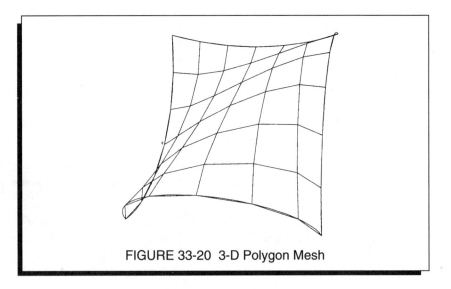

FIGURE 33-20 3-D Polygon Mesh

The order of entry is one column at a time, then to the next column and up.

3-D meshes are displayed as wireframes; when they are coplanar, they are considered opaque when the Hide command is used. 3-D meshes cannot be extruded.

PFACE COMMAND (POLYFACE MESH)

A mesh constructed with the PFACE command will draw a polygon mesh that is independent of a continuous surface. Pface meshes are defined by entering individual vertex values in X,Y,Z format.

Selecting the Pface command results in the prompt:

```
Command: PFACE
Vertex 1:
Vertex 2:
Vertex 3:
Vertex 4:
```

and so forth, until you press ENTER on a blank line to close the mesh. Pressing ENTER again will terminate the construction of the mesh.

Polyface meshes can be used for simple mesh construction or be incorporated in a program to automatically enter many data points for a specialized application.

RULESURF COMMAND (RULED SURFACE)

A mesh created by the RULESURF command creates a mesh that represents a ruled surface between two entities. The entities may be lines, points, arcs, circles, 2-D and 3-D polylines.

A similar effect could be achieved on a drawing board by dividing two entities into the same number of segments and drawing a line between the corresponding segments. Figure 33-21 shows ruled surfaces between entities.

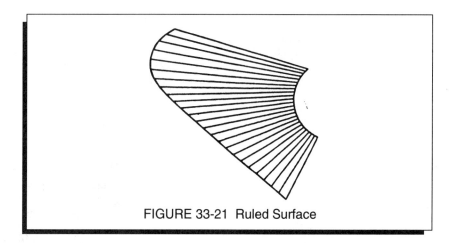

FIGURE 33-21 Ruled Surface

CONSTRUCTING RULED SURFACES

To construct a ruled surface, select the Rulesurf command, then select the two entities you wish the surface to be drawn between.

```
Command: RULESURF
Select first defining curve: (select)
Select second defining curve: (select)
```

AutoCAD draws the ruled surface from the endpoint nearest to the selection point on the entity. Thus, selecting opposite ends of the entities will create a ruled surface that is crossed.

If an entity is a circle, the selection point has no special effect. The ruled surface will begin at the 0° quadrant point. If a point is selected, the mesh lines will be drawn from the single location of the point. Thus, a circle and a point would create a cone-type object as in Figure 33-22.

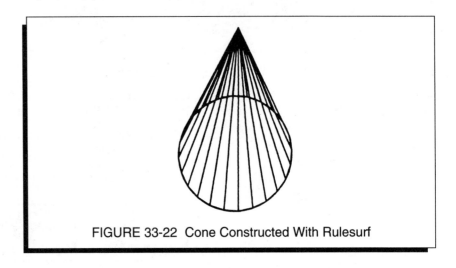

FIGURE 33-22 Cone Constructed With Rulesurf

TABSURF COMMAND (TABULATED SURFACE)

The TABSURF command constructs a mesh surface that is defined by a path and a direction vector.

The effect is similar to an extrusion, except for the mesh surface.

CONSTRUCTING TABULATED MESH SURFACES

To construct a tabulated surface, select a path curve (entity from which the surface will be calculated) and a direction vector (entity describing the direction and length of the mesh from the path curve).

The following command sequence is displayed.

    Command: TABSURF
    Select path curve:
    Select direction vector:

The path curve may be a line, arc, circle, 2-D or 3-D polyline. The direction vector may be either a line or open polyline (2-D or 3-D).

Use object pointing to identify each. The closest end to the pick point on the direction vector defines the direction in which the mesh is projected. Picking the direction vector at one end causes the mesh to project in the direction of the opposite endpoint. Figure 33-23 shows the curve path, direction vector, and the pick point on the direction vector for the result shown.

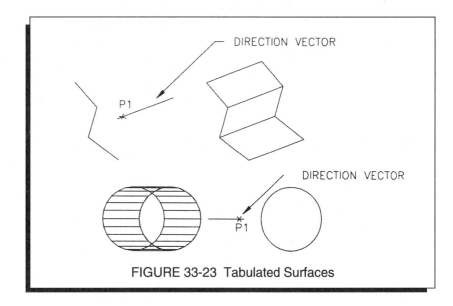

FIGURE 33-23 Tabulated Surfaces

The heavier line identifies the original path curve.

REVSURF COMMAND (REVOLVED SURFACE)

The REVSURF command is used to create meshes from entities revolved around an axis.

CREATING REVOLVED SURFACES

To create a revolved surface, you must first have a path curve (entity to be revolved) and an axis of revolution (an entity that defines an axis around which the entity will revolve). The path curve can be a line, circle, arc, 2-D or 3-D polyline. The axis of revolution may be a line or open polyline (2-D or 3-D).

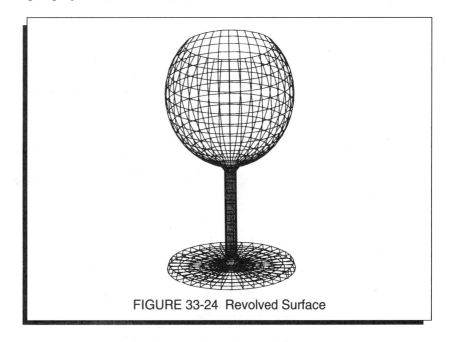

FIGURE 33-24 Revolved Surface

```
AutoCAD
* * * *
EDGSURF:
REVSURF:
RULSURF:
TABSURF:

Surftb1:
Surftb2:

3DFACE:
3DMESH:
PFACE:
3DPOLY:

3d
objects
__LAST__
 DRAW
 EDIT
```

The displayed command prompts are:

```
Command: REVSURF
Select path curve:
Select axis of revolution:
Start angle <0>:
Included angle (+=ccw, -=cw) <Full circle>:
```

The start angle point of zero is defined by the location of the path curve. If you specify a start angle other than zero, the starting point of the revolution will offset the specified number of degrees from the path curve.

The included angle designates the degrees of rotation of the path curve around the axis of revolution and from the start point.

The direction to which the revolution emanates is dependent on the pick point when the axis of revolution is selected. The right hand rule is used to determine the direction. The revolution is in a positive rotation direction around the axis of revolution; the positive direction of the axis defined as being from the end nearest the pick point to the following end. Thus, if your right hand is curved around the axis of revolution, with the thumb pointing toward the end of the axis furthest from the pick point, the direction of your fingers designates the positive rotation angle.

Figure 33-25 shows the effect of the location of the pick point on the axis of revolution in determining the direction of revolution. Each revolution has a starting angle of 0° and an included angle of 90°.

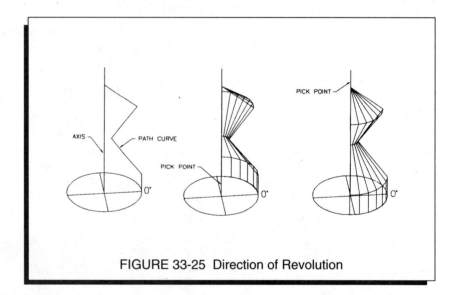

FIGURE 33-25 Direction of Revolution

EDGESURF COMMAND (EDGE-DEFINED SURFACE)

The EDGESURF command is used to construct a Coons surface patch from four edge surfaces. Figure 33-26 shows a Coons surface patch.

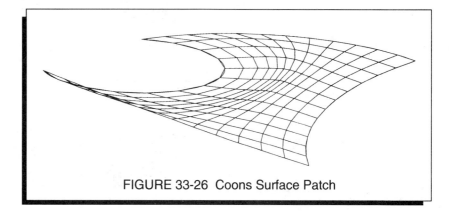

FIGURE 33-26 Coons Surface Patch

The patch follows the contour of each edge surface, forming a mesh that approximates a surface attached to all points of each edge.

CONSTRUCTING EDGE-DEFINED SURFACES

To construct a Coons patch, you must first have four edges. These edges may be lines, arcs, or open 2-D or 3-D polylines. They must connect at their endpoints. The command sequence is as follows:

Command: <u>EDGESURF</u>
Select edge 1:
Select edge 2:
Select edge 3:
Select edge 4:

If one edge is not connected to the adjacent edge, the message

Edge x does not touch another edge

is displayed, where *x* defines the number of the edge that does not touch.

3-D OBJECTS

Several basic object shapes have been included for convenient use in drawings. These objects are actually constructed from the tools you have already learned to use. The sequence to construct them has been preprogrammed. Prompts question you for pertinent information for proper construction to your specifications. The following objects are included for your use.

BOX
CONE
DOME
DISH
SPHERE
TORUS
WEDGE

Let's look at each of these and the information you will need to provide.

AutoCAD
* * * *
EDGSURF:
REVSURF:
RULSURF:
TABSURF:

Surftb1:
Surftb2:

3DFACE:
3DMESH:
PFACE:
3DPOLY:

3d
objects
__LAST__
DRAW
EDIT

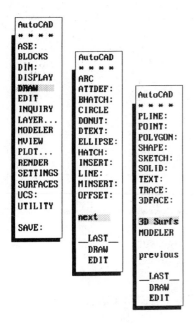

BOX

The BOX command constructs a box of given length, width, and height, or a cube of a given edge dimension. The command sequence is as follows:

```
Command: BOX
Starting point of box:
Length:
Cube <Width>:
Height:
```

Figure 33-27 shows the components of box construction.

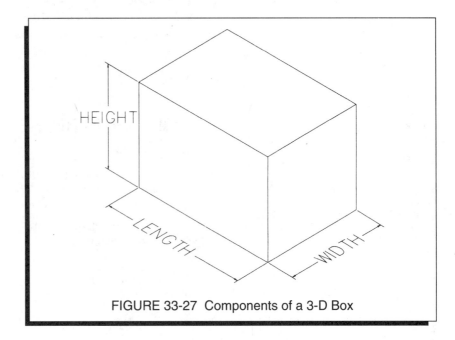

FIGURE 33-27 Components of a 3-D Box

If you select the Cube option from the fourth prompt line, a cube will be constructed with the edge length equal to the length you previously defined.

CONE

The CONE command is used to construct cones. You define a cone by specifying the radius or diameter of the top and bottom and the height.

The command prompts are:

```
Command: CONE
Base center point:
<Base radius>/Diameter:
<Top radius>/Diameter <0>:
Height of cone:
Number of segments <16>:
```

Figure 33-28 labels the parts of a cone.

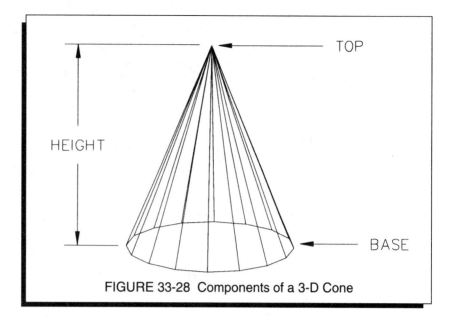

FIGURE 33-28 Components of a 3-D Cone

DOME

Use the DOME command to create domes for your drawing.

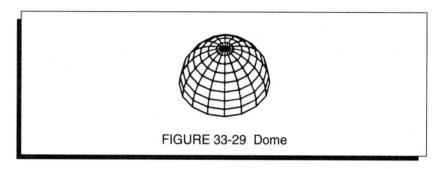

FIGURE 33-29 Dome

The command sequence is as follows.

```
Command: DOME
Center of dome:
Diameter/<Radius> of dome:
Included angle of dome in degrees (1-359) <180>:
Number of segments <16>:
```

DISH

A dish is simply an inverted dome. The construction of a dish is similar to that of a dome.

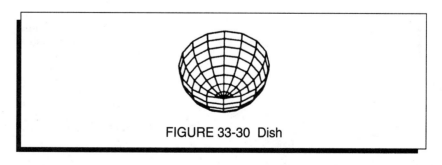

FIGURE 33-30 Dish

AutoCAD
* * * *

Box
Cone
Dish
Dome
Mesh
Pyramid
Sphere
Torus
Wedge

__LAST__
DRAW
EDIT

The following command sequence is displayed.

> Command: <u>DISH</u>
> Center of dish:
> Diameter/<Radius>of dish:
> Included angle of dish in degrees (1-359) <180>:
> Number of segments:

SPHERE

Spheres are created with the Sphere command.

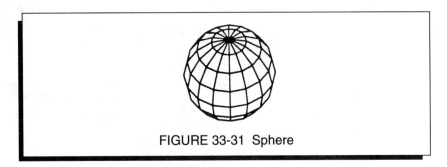

FIGURE 33-31 Sphere

The command sequence is as follows:

> Command: <u>SPHERE</u>
> Center of sphere:
> Sphere <Radius>/Diameter:
> Number of segments <16>:

TORUS

A torus is a closed tube, rotated around an axis.

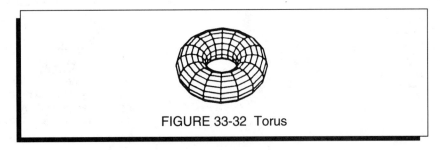

FIGURE 33-32 Torus

The command sequence for a torus is:

> Command: <u>TORUS</u>
> Center of torus:
> Torus <Radius>/Diameter:
> Tube <Radius>/Diameter:
> Number of segments <16>:

If you enter a tube radius or diameter that is greater than the torus radius or diameter, the following message is displayed:

> Tube radius cannot exceed torus radius

You will then be given the opportunity to reenter the data.

WEDGE

A wedge could be thought of as a block, cut diagonally along its width.

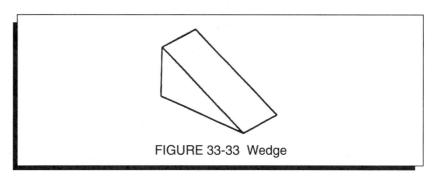

FIGURE 33-33 Wedge

The command sequence when constructing a wedge is:

    Command: WEDGE
    Starting point of wedge:
    Length:
    Width:
    Height:

SUMMING IT UP

Mastering the principles of 3-D drawing takes time and effort. Try to simulate the examples in the text and experiment on projects of your own interest to build expertise in each area of 3-D drawing.

Understand the principles of 3-D, as discussed in Chapter 30.

Master the principles of viewing 3-D drawings covered in Chapter 31. This is not only important for viewing, but to display the drawing for effective 3-D drawing construction while the drawing is in progress.

The User Coordinate System explained in Chapter 32 is extremely important, since it is one of the primary methods of construction used in 3-D drawings. You can not obtain the ultimate results from AutoCAD 3-D without a complete understanding of this system.

The drawing methods described in Chapter 33 should be considered as a tool box to be used for 3-D construction. Study each drawing to determine the best method of creating the objects in your drawing.

And most of all, have fun!

CHAPTER REVIEW

1. What is an extrusion?

_____

_____

_____

2. Which axis direction is an extrusion normally projected into?

_____

_____

3. What is meant by the elevation and thickness of an entity?

_____

_____

_____

_____

_____

4. How could you change the thickness of an existing entity?

_____

_____

5. How do you return to the plan view after rotating your drawing?

_____

_____

6. What does the 3Dface command perform?

_____

_____

_____

7. Compare the placement of a 3-D face with a solid's face that would be placed with the Solid command.

_____

_____

_____

_____

_____

8. What is the procedure used if you want to place a 3-D face without showing the edges?

_____

_____

_____

_____

9. Describe a use for the Rulesurf method of constructing a surface.

_____

_____

_____

10. The density of a two direction 3-D surface is described by the values of M and N. Which system variable controls the values of each?

_____

_____

CHAPTER 34

Using AutoShade for Release 11

For Release 12 users, use the AVERender facility built into AutoCAD R12.

OBJECTIVES:

After you are proficient with the use of AutoCAD 3-D, the next step is to master the use of AutoShade. Our objectives in Chapter 34 are:

- To understand the use and concept of the AutoShade program.

- To learn to create an AutoShade file in AutoCAD.

- To understand and use the functions to prepare a scene for shading and viewing.

- To create an output file from AutoCAD for AutoShade.

AUTOSHADE OVERVIEW

AutoShade is a rendering program designed for use with AutoCAD. Existing AutoCAD drawings are rendered with solid faces. Lighting and other effects are applied to create a more realistic view of the objects in the drawing.

You first create your drawing with AutoCAD, then insert lights and cameras to set up the "photo shot" you desire.

AutoShade is a separate, stand-alone program. You first create your drawing with AutoCAD, then insert lights and cameras to set up the "photo shot" you desire. A shot (or many shots) is made in preparation for use with the AutoShade program. The drawing is then loaded in AutoShade for embellishment.

The locations of solid faces are determined by placement of 3-D faces in the AutoCAD drawing. The solid face colors in AutoShade are dependent on the entity colors used when the drawing and its 3-D faces are created.

CREATING A DRAWING FOR USE WITH AUTOSHADE

Let's start a drawing to be viewed in AutoShade. To make it easy, we will use the 3-D objects in AutoCAD. The objects are automatically created with 3-D faces. Figure 34-1 shows our goal.

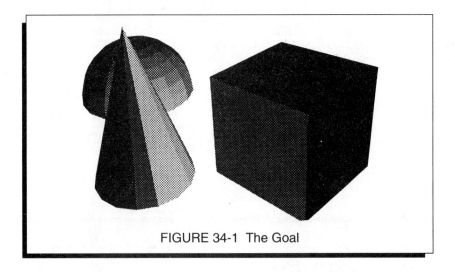

FIGURE 34-1 The Goal

Let's begin by starting a new drawing called "SHADPLAN." Set limits of 12,9 and a snap increment of 1.

Now it is time to create some objects. We want to create a red box. From the Color menu, select RED. Next, from the root menu, select 3-D, then 3-D objects. Wait for a moment as AutoCAD loads the LISP routines necessary for creating 3-D objects. From the 3-D objects menu, select BOX. Respond to the prompts as follows.

```
Command: BOX
Corner of box: (place at 2,2)
Length: 2
Cube/Width: C
Rotation angle about Z axis: 0
```

Let's add a yellow cone. From the Color menu, select YELLOW. Go back to 3-D objects menu and select CONE.

```
Command: CONE
Base center point: (place at 5,5)
Diameter/<radius> of base: 1
Diameter/<radius> of top <0>: 0
Height: 3
Number of segments <16>: (RETURN)
```

Next we will place a green dome in the drawing. From the Color menu, select GREEN. Choose DOME from the 3-D objects menu.

```
Command: DOME
Center of Dome: (place at 8,3)
Diameter/<radius>: 1.5
Number of longitudinal segments <16>: (RETURN)
Number of latitudinal segments <8>: (RETURN)
```

Your drawing should now look similar to Figure 34-2.

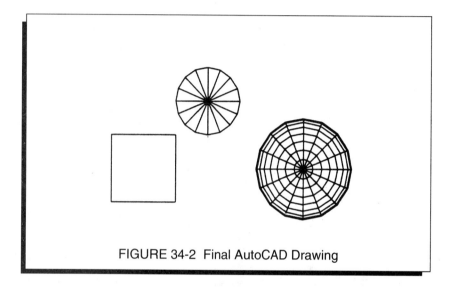

FIGURE 34-2 Final AutoCAD Drawing

PLACING LIGHTS AND CAMERAS

It is helpful to think of AutoShade as a photography studio.

It is now time to place lights and cameras in the drawing. It is helpful to think of AutoShade as a photography studio. The studio has lights, camera(s) and film. How we situate the lights and camera determines the result of the final product on film. Let's see how to set up our CAD "studio." First, load the AutoShade support commands.

```
Command: (LOAD "ASHADE")
```

PLACING THE CAMERA

Enter Camera at the command line.

```
Command: CAMERA
Enter Camera name: CAM1
Enter target point: .XY
of (select 6,3)
(need Z): 1
Enter camera location: .XY
of (select 1,7)
(need Z): 4
```

AutoCAD draws a camera on the screen. The camera is located at the camera location specified. The camera is pointed at the selected target point.

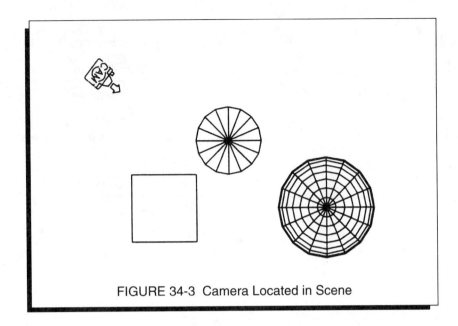

FIGURE 34-3 Camera Located in Scene

Note that we used point filters to locate both the camera and target point. The camera is located 4 units above the "floor" (0° Z elevation). The place the camera is pointing to (target point) is 1 unit high. Let's now place some lights in the drawing.

PLACING LIGHTS

There are two types of lights in AutoShade: point and directed.

There are two types of lights in AutoShade: point and directed. Point lights are similar to overhead lights in a home. They provide overall lighting (or ambient) light. Point lights may be located at any place and height (Z elevation) in a drawing. A directed light may be thought of as a spotlight. Directed lights have both a location and a target (aim) point.

Let's first place a directed light in the drawing.

```
Command: LIGHT
Enter light name: LT1
Point source or Directed <P>: D
Enter light aim point: .XY
of 7,3
(need Z): 1
Enter light location: (select 3,3)
```

AutoCAD will now place a directed light icon in the drawing at the point specified. Notice how the light points in the direction of the aim point. The light's name (LT1) is displayed on the icon.

Next we will place a point light in the drawing.

```
Command: LIGHT
Enter light name: LT2
Point source or Directed <P>: P
Enter light location: (place at 3,5)
```

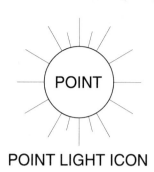

POINT LIGHT ICON

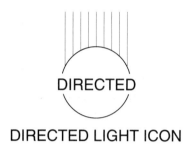

DIRECTED LIGHT ICON

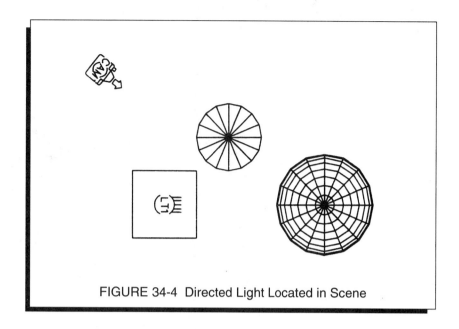

FIGURE 34-4 Directed Light Located in Scene

A point light source is now placed in the drawing. We placed this one "on the floor" (Z elevation of 0°). The point light source looks like the sun with the light name on it.

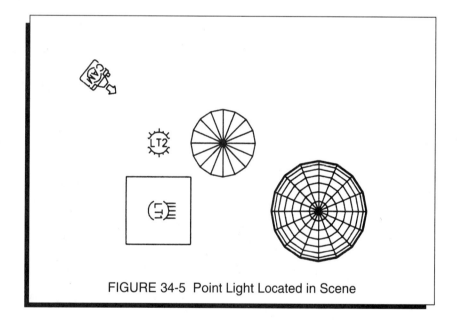

FIGURE 34-5 Point Light Located in Scene

Now it is time to view our drawing. Before we go to AutoShade, however, let's preview the shot. After all, any decent photographer would look through the camera lens before taking a shot. Let's look through our CAD "camera lens." Select Camview from the Ashade menu. You may get a message explaining that the flatland variable must be set to zero. If this message is displayed, use the Setvar command and enter Flatland as the variable. Enter the value as 0 and execute the Camera command again.

Command: CAMVIEW
Select camera: (select CAM1)

After a moment's wait, the following scene (Figure 34-6) is displayed.

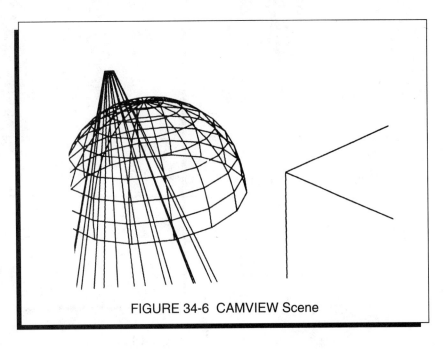

FIGURE 34-6 CAMVIEW Scene

Well, that is a little close to the subject, but we did this intentionally. AutoShade has some good tools to manipulate the shot with (something you can't do with a "standard" studio).

Time to take the shot. Use the Plan or Undo command to return to the plan view.

SCENES AND FILMROLLS

The selected arrangement is called a "scene."

It is possible in AutoShade to have several lights and cameras. You may select any combination of a camera and lights. The selected arrangement is called a "scene." Let's define a scene for our drawing. Start by selecting Scene from the Action menu.

> Command: <u>SCENE</u>
> Enter scene name: <u>SCENE1</u>
> Select the camera: (*select CAM1 from the drawing*)

Select the camera by placing the pick box over the camera. The command prompts continue:

> Select a light: (*select LT1*)

The light name LT1 is named on the command line. Continue and select the light named LT2.

> Select a light: (*select LT2*)

The light name LT2 is named on the command line.

Press ENTER to end the selection process for the scene. AutoCAD then prompts for the "scene location."

> Enter scene location:

The scene location is where a "clapper board" is placed. The clapper board shows the names of the scene, camera, and lights. Like the camera and lights, the clapper board is not part of the "photo" that AutoShade produces. Just select an empty space in the drawing for the clapper board. The final drawing looks like Figure 34-7.

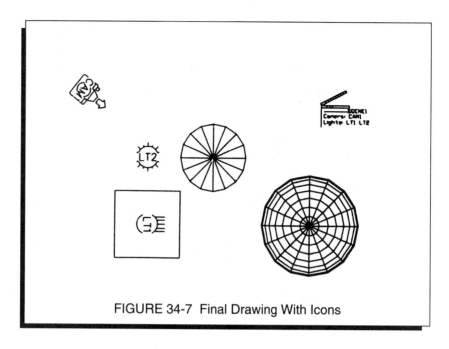

FIGURE 34-7 Final Drawing With Icons

A filmroll, like its studio counterpart, can contain several scenes.

It is now time to take the shot. Select Filmroll from the menu. A filmroll, like its studio counterpart, can contain several scenes. We will only put one shot on it right now.

Command: <u>FILMROLL</u>

A "Create Filmroll File" dialogue box is displayed. Enter "SHAD-PLAN" as the filmroll file name.

That's it! You have now shot your first "roll of film." Now it's time to move to AutoShade and develop (and manipulate) it. Exit AutoCAD and start AutoShade.

CHAPTER 35

The AutoShade Program for Release 11

For Release 12 users, use the AVERender facility built into AutoCAD R12.

OBJECTIVES:

Once you have prepared a file for AutoShade, the next step is to start the AutoShade program and use its many functions to create a shaded drawing. The objectives for Chapter 35 are as follows:

● To learn the basic use of the AutoShade program.

● To learn how to load AutoCAD output files.

● To learn the functions used to manipulate the drawing.

● To learn the shading options available within the program and how they affect the appearance of the final drawing.

● To learn to fine tune the appearance of the shaded model.

THE AUTOSHADE PROGRAM

When AutoShade is first started, a blank screen is displayed as shown in Figure 35-1.

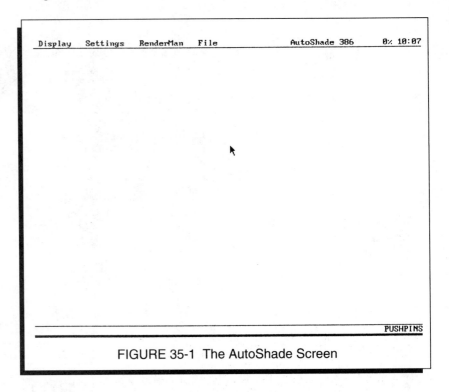

Display   Settings   RenderMan   File   AutoShade 386   0% 10:07

PUSHPINS

FIGURE 35-1 The AutoShade Screen

The top line shows a menu bar. The left part of the menu bar is the pull-down menu area. This area contains the listings of Display, Settings, Renderman, and File.

The right side of the bar shows the percent of system memory used and a digital clock.

The bottom line is the status line. The name of the Filmroll file is displayed on the right. The left side of the status line functions similarly to the AutoCAD program status line. Progress of operations is displayed here.

The center of the screen is the display area. The wireframe and shaded models are displayed here.

SELECTING MENU ITEMS

When you first move your input device, you will notice an arrow on the screen. The arrow is moved by the input device (such as a mouse). A pull-down menu can be accessed by placing the arrow over the desired menu name and pressing the button on the device. A choice may be made from the menu by moving the input device up or down the menu until the desired item is highlighted, and pressing the button on the device. If an item is grayed out, it is unavailable at the time. If you wish to put away the menu without making a choice, simply move outside the menu area and click the input button.

DIALOGUE BOXES

Many of AutoShade's choices are made through dialogue boxes. These boxes are similar in operation to AutoCAD's dialogue boxes.

LOADING THE FILMROLL AND DISPLAYING THE SHOT

Let's get started and "process" our shots taken in AutoCAD.

From the File menu, select Open Filmroll. The Select Filmroll dialogue box is displayed. The dialogue box may contain several filmroll selections. If more files than can be displayed on the screen are available, the up/down and page up/page down buttons will scroll the choices up or down one line or one page at a time.

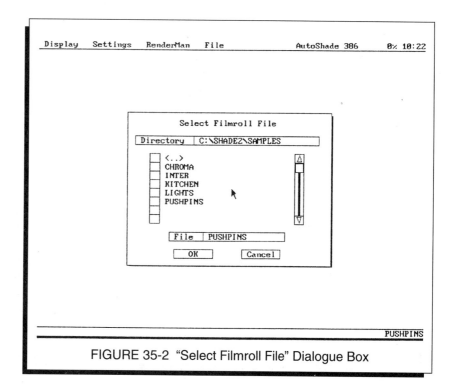

FIGURE 35-2 "Select Filmroll File" Dialogue Box

Scroll the choices until the Filmroll file named SHAD1 is displayed. Select SHAD1, then select the OK button. Notice the name of the Filmroll file name is displayed in the "file box." Now select OK from the box at the bottom of the dialogue box. You could choose cancel if you decided not to choose a Filmroll file.

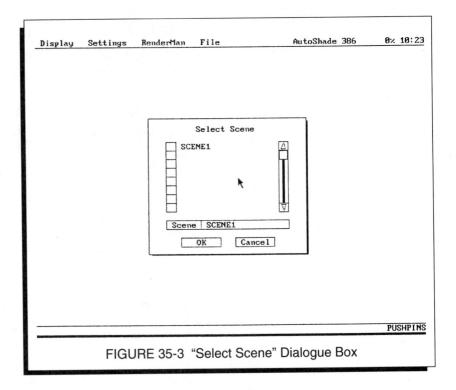

FIGURE 35-3 "Select Scene" Dialogue Box

When the Select Scene dialogue box appears, choose SCENE1 and OK. Note that the scene is displayed yet.

DISPLAYING THE SHOT

You have now loaded the filmroll and selected the scene. It is time to look at the shot. Before we shade the scene, let's first verify that the shot is what we want. From the Display menu select Wireframe. After a moment, a wireframe is shown in the display area. This is the same shot you saw when you selected Camview in AutoCAD. We thought the shot was a little close then, and it still appears that way now. Let's manipulate the shot to see if we can get better results.

SETTING THE CAMERA LENS

A 50mm lens closely approximates the field of view, or peripheral vision, of the human eye.

The display you see through a camera lens depends on the focal length of the camera lens. The focal length is measured in millimeters. A 50mm lens closely approximates the field of view, or peripheral vision, of the human eye. As the focal length increases, the view becomes telescopic. For example, a 150mm lens would simulate a view through a medium powered telescope. As focal length decreases, the angle of view widens. If a field of view is too wide, the shot is distorted. This point occurs at approximately 28mm. An extremely wide shot using a 15mm lens would result in a "fish eye" view.

Although photographers are limited by the number of lenses they possess, an AutoShade user has the luxury of defining the focal length by simply entering the focal length number. You have hundreds of camera lenses!

Our shot is too close. Let's widen the field of view by changing the lens. Note that the camera doesn't move. We are simply changing the lens to a wider angle lens.

Pull down the Settings menu and select Camera. The Camera Specifications dialogue box is displayed. Change the box entitled Lens IN MM to show a 28mm lens. Be sure to select OK to confirm the new setting. Select OK again to put away the dialogue box.

Now pull down the Display menu and select Wireframe. The shot is displayed with the wider angle.

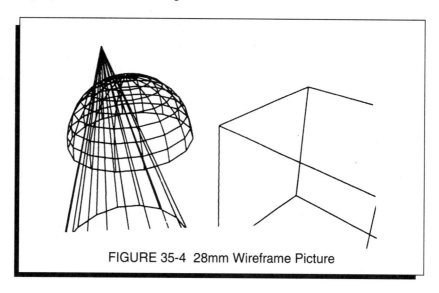

FIGURE 35-4 28mm Wireframe Picture

That is a better shot, but it still doesn't quite measure up to what we had in mind. Let's move the camera back just a bit.

MOVING THE CAMERA

Select Settings/Camera again. Change the Distance setting to 10. Now redisplay the wireframe view again. That's better. Now let's do some shading.

SHADING THE PHOTO

The fast shade function is useful when several light or position adjustments are being made.

The Display menu shows three types of shading: quick shade, fast shade and full shade. A fast shade will shade the picture the same as the full shade function, but skips complex calculations required to achieve a perfect shade. The fast shade function is useful when several light or position adjustments are being made.

The full shade function performs all the necessary calculations required for a correct, fully shaded shot.

Let's first do a fast shade. From the Display menu, select Fast Shade. After a few moments the picture is displayed in its fast shaded form.

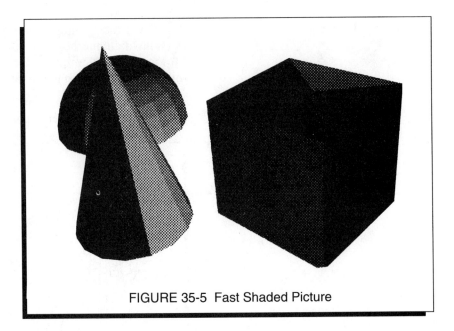

FIGURE 35-5 Fast Shaded Picture

Notice how the top surface of the cube is shaded incorrectly. This is typical of fast shade inaccuracy. Let's now do a full shade and compare the results. Select Full Shade from the Display menu. The full shade process takes a bit longer. A graphic is displayed showing a running man. The distance the man runs across the screen represents the approximate percent of completion of the fully shaded model.

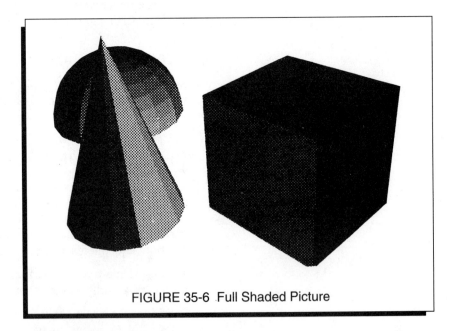

FIGURE 35-6 Full Shaded Picture

After the fully shaded model is displayed, we can see that the shading on the cube is now correct.

ADJUSTING LIGHTS

If we like, we can adjust the lighting levels to achieve different results. Let's do this and use fast shade to view the results.

From the Settings menu, select Lights. The Set Light Intensities dialogue box is displayed. The light intensity for each light (LT1 and LT2) is set to 1. This is the initial default value for all lights in the scene. The light levels are set relative to each other only. Increasing or decreasing each light intensity the same amount will not result in a change.

Set the point light (LT2) to 0 and the directed light (LT1) to 10. Now perform a fast shade to see the results. Note how the directed light illuminates surfaces it hits. However, since the point light now has an intensity of 0, there is no ambient light to illuminate the general scene. Thus, the surfaces of the cube that are not lit by the point light are dark and appear undetailed. Let's try a new light setting.

Select Settings/Lights again. This time, set the point light (LT2) to level 4 and leave the directed light (LT1) at level 10. Perform another fast shade to view the results.

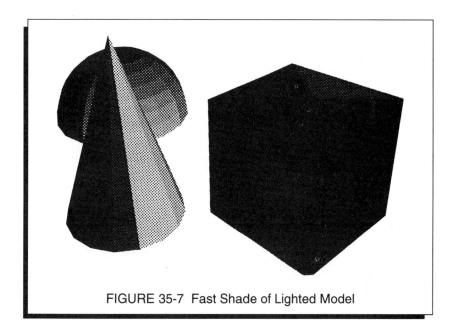

FIGURE 35-7 Fast Shade of Lighted Model

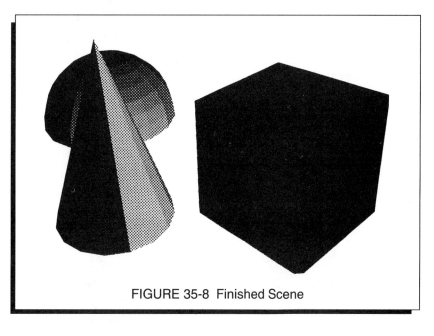

FIGURE 35-8 Finished Scene

That's better. With a little experimentation you will get very good at lighting a scene. This would be a good time to do another full shade to see the finished product.

PANNING THE CAMERA

Sometimes it is desirable to rotate the camera to a new position. You have already learned how to move the camera closer to or away from the items in the shot. Let's see how to rotate it around the items.

The camera position can be rotated either in the X,Y plane or up in the Z-axis direction. Select Camera from the Settings menu. The Camera Specifications dialogue box is displayed. The camera is moved in the X-, Y-axis (around the scene) with the box labeled DEGREES RIGHT. The measurement, in degrees, is calculated from the default AutoCAD 0° setting at 3 o'clock in the plan view. Figure 35-9 shows how this works.

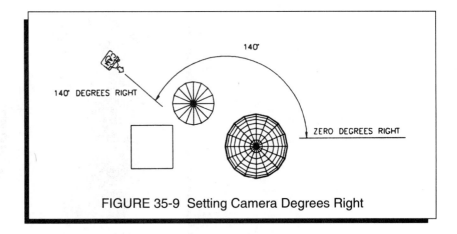

FIGURE 35-9 Setting Camera Degrees Right

The camera may be angled up toward the Z-axis with the Degrees Up box. If the camera is angled up to 90°, a plan view will result.

Let's enter a new setting and look at the results. Set the degrees right to 270°. Redisplay the shot in wire frame to see the results. Note that the change in camera setting affects AutoShade and does not change the AutoCAD drawing with the light and camera placements.

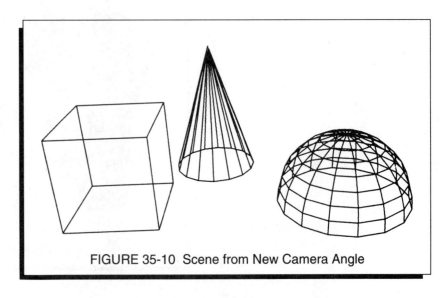

FIGURE 35-10 Scene from New Camera Angle

Now perform a full shade. Note how the lighting is poor! We did not place the lights to make a pleasing shot from this angle. Reset the degrees right to 141.34° and redisplay the shot in full shaded form.

This has been a tour through AutoShade's basic operation. Experimentation will make you a better CAD photographer.

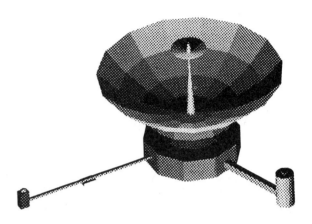

Courtesy of AutoDesk   FIGURE 35-11 AutoShade Sample Drawing

SECTION VI

PROFESSIONAL
AutoCAD

- Introduction to Solid Modeling
- Constructing Solid Primitives
- Creating Custom Solids
- Modifying Solid Objects
- Creating Composite Solid Models
- Displaying and Representing Solid Models
- Introduction to AutoLISP
- Programming in AutoLISP

CHAPTER 36

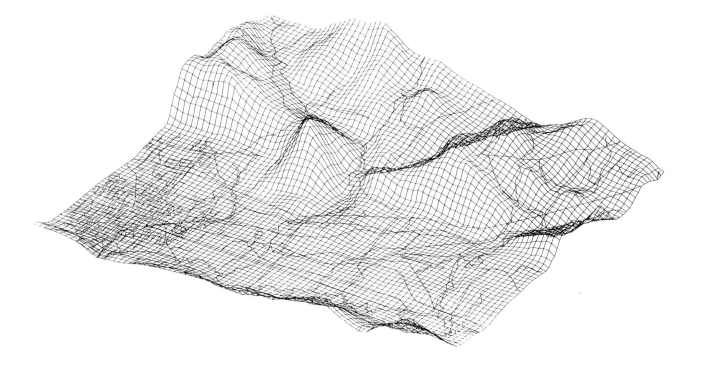

Introduction to Solid Modeling

OBJECTIVES:

Solid modeling can be easy, fun, and useful. This chapter introduces you to the fundamentals of solid modeling. The objectives of this chapter are:

● To understand the purpose and use of the AutoCAD AME (Advanced Modeling Extension).

● To differentiate the differences between solid models and 3-D models.

● To learn the ways a solid model can be displayed.

● To gain a general understanding of the methods of constructing solid objects.

Profile of an AEC Firm
Innovative approach combines freehand art with AutoCAD® graphics

Water features is an unusual area for engineers and designers to specialize in. But Pacific Aquascape, Inc. undertakes many projects that include scaled, free-form sketches of lakes, waterfalls, and pools. When Aquascape, Inc. began to use AutoCAD, they found it worked well for drawing the mechanical details. Their in-house design artist, however, was skeptical about using AutoCAD to produce full drawings. He considered computer-generated art, though technically accurate, to lack the vitality that he and the company had come to expect and demand from their drawings.

To avoid the "etch-a-sketch" look in the designs they were producing on their CAD system, they used AutoCAD as a springboard to explore various third-party graphics packages, music boards, printers, scanners, programming utilities, animation, and software packages.

Experimenting led to discoveries, discoveries paved the way to better-looking drawings, and better-looking drawings inspired more experimenting.

Pacific Aquascape, Inc. became much more efficient as they combined manual and AutoCAD drafting techniques. Now they are able to use stylized fonts, to vary line widths, and to insert their own original drawing blocks.

Understanding the advanced fields of engineering, treating drafting and CAD as a form of art, and unlocking the secrets of computers have all had an impact on Aquascape. They consider speed, low memory requirements, and high-quality graphics to be their signature.

Adapted with permission from an article by Corey Comstock and Rick McGuire. Excerpted from *CADENCE*, January 1989, copyright © 1989, Ariel Communications, Inc.

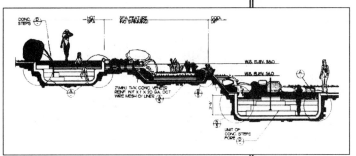
Spa cross section partly hand drawn, scanned, finished in ACAD, and PBrushed.

OVERVIEW

AutoCAD's Advanced Modeling Extension is another way to create solid three dimensional (3-D) objects. The solid objects created are similar in appearance to wireframe models created in AutoCAD 3-D. Solid models, however, contain more information than a wireframe model. Let's look at some of the differences.

Wireframe models created in AutoCAD 3-D are composed of solid faces. Imagine a cube that is constructed from thin pieces of board. The cube has six faces, but no solid interior. A solid model, however, is not constructed of faces; it is a solid object. The same cube constructed with a solid modeling program would have a solid interior.

Creating objects as solids allows you to scientifically analyze the object. Object properties such as center of gravity, mass, surface area, and moments of inertia can be calculated. Since different materials (such as steel, aluminum, etc.) differ in their properties, AutoCAD includes several material definitions. Each definition can be assigned as the material for the solid model. In addition, you can create a new definition by entering the material properties of any material.

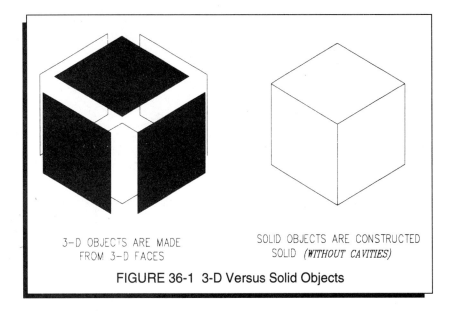

FIGURE 36-1 3-D Versus Solid Objects

WHO USES SOLID MODELING?

Solid modeling is useful to many disciplines. The mechanical engineer who needs to calculate properties of objects will find the ability to scientifically analyze an object of different materials invaluable.

Architects can use solid modeling to visually represent complex intersections of building roofs. After the model is constructed, the drawing can be converted to a "standard" 3-D form and embellished for presentation purposes.

Those who model the objects they create will find that solid modeling offers the very useful possibilities of intersection construction, scientific analysis, and the simplicity of "building block" construction.

DRAWING WITH SOLIDS

Solid models are created from solid three dimensional shapes. This "building block" approach is different from the method used with the AutoCAD 3-D program. Objects created in 3-D, however, can be converted to a solid. This allows the flexibility to create an object in the most efficient manner. Before you begin your work with solid modeling, you should be proficient with the use of the AutoCAD 3-D program.

SOLID PRIMITIVES

AutoCAD provides commands that create basic building block shapes referred to as solid "primitives." These simple 3-D solid shapes are the box, wedge, cone, cylinder, sphere, and donut. These shapes can be "added" or "subtracted" from each other to create more complex shapes. In addition, you can edit with commands that revolve, extrude, chamfer, or fillet the shapes.

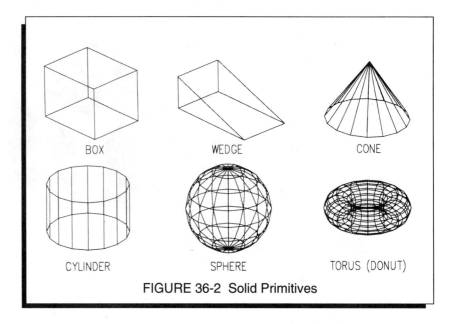

FIGURE 36-2 Solid Primitives

COMPOSITE SOLIDS

When you create a solid object from several primitives, it is referred to as a composite solid. The primitives that combine to make the object can be consolidated to create a single object, enclosing the entire volume as one solid.

You may also add or subtract solids from each other. For example, a drill hole can be created from a cylinder that has been placed in a solid plate. Subtracting the cylinder from the plate creates the "drill hole."

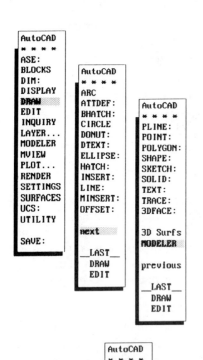

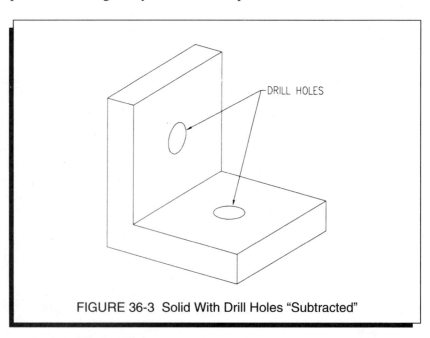

FIGURE 36-3 Solid With Drill Holes "Subtracted"

SOLID MODELING COMMANDS

AutoCAD's solid modeling commands are distinguishable from other commands by the "SOL" prefix. For example, to draw a box, you use the SOLBOX command. The same prefix is also used for commands used under the Modify, Inquiry, Display, and Utility submenus under the Solids menu heading in the AutoCAD root screen menu.

The menu tree to the left shows the solids menus and their command selections.

DISPLAYING SOLIDS

Solids may be displayed either as wireframe or mesh representations.

WIREFRAME REPRESENTATION

The wireframe representation is similar in appearance to the 3-D wireframe display appearance. Each edge of the object is shown with a line. The curved surfaces are displayed with tessellation lines. These are lines that are displayed along a curved surface to assist in visualization of a nonplanar surface. Wireframe representation is the default display method. Wireframe representations cannot be displayed as hidden line or shaded models.

MESH REPRESENTATION

Mesh representation creates a display made up of solid 3-D Pface entities. Mesh displays can be used to create a hidden line model with the Hide command, or a shaded model with the Shade and Render commands.

CHAPTER REVIEW

1. What is the primary difference between an object created with 3-D and one created as a solid model?

2. What is meant by a "building block" approach?

3. What is a "solid primitive"?

4. What is a "composite solid"?

5. Which display representation can be rendered as either hidden line or shaded?

CHAPTER 37

Constructing Solid Primitives

OBJECTIVES:

Solid primitives are used to create solid models from building block shapes. Many solid models can be mostly created from these basic shapes. In order to become proficient with the use of the solid modeling program, you should master the construction of each of these primitive shapes. The objectives of this chapter are:

● To learn the methods of loading the AutoCAD AME program into memory for use.

● To become familiar with the AME command name logic.

● To understand the AME menu organization.

● To learn to use each of the solid primitive construction commands.

SOLID PRIMITIVES

Solid primitives are the "building blocks" of solid modeling. The solid primitives available are as follows:

Box & Cube
Cone
Cylinder
Sphere
Torus
Wedge

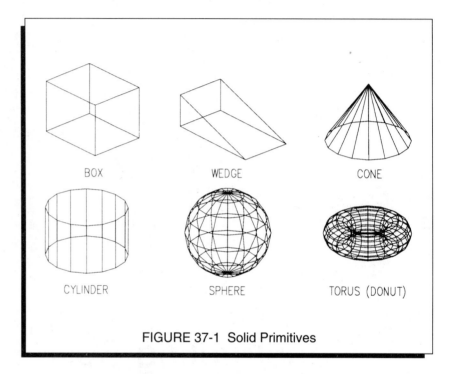

FIGURE 37-1 Solid Primitives

Solid primitives are created by providing the dimensions of the object. Let's draw each of the primitives. Start a new drawing of any name and follow the short tutorial for each.

DRAWING SOLID PRIMITIVES

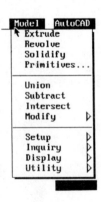

The solid modeling commands are contained in a screen menu under MODEL. Note how the solid modeling command names are designed. Each command starts with a SOL prefix. It is helpful to associate a command function with the name occurring after this prefix. Thus, SOLBOX is the SOLid BOX command. The menu selections for AME are shown in the menus displayed at the left.

If you are using a digitizer tablet with the AutoCAD tablet overlay, the AME commands can be accessed from the tablet. Figure 37-2 shows the tablet area containing the AME commands.

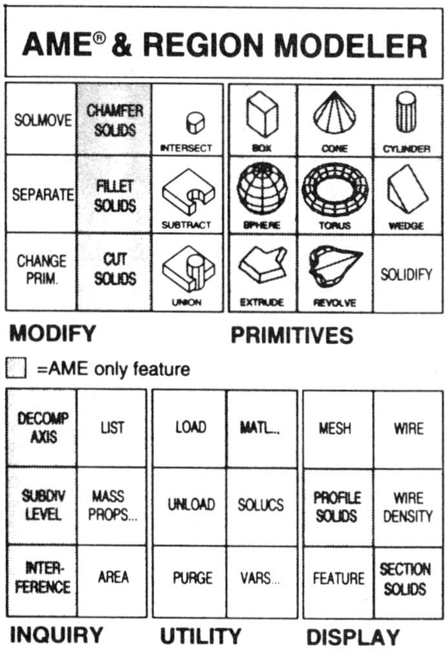

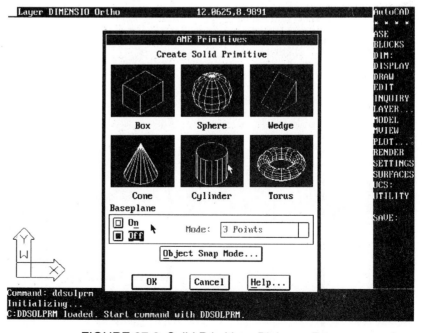

AME® & REGION MODELER

FIGURE 37-2 AME Tablet Overlay

Note also that you can use the "MODEL" pull-down menu at the far right of the pull-down menu bar. We will use these menus to select the commands to construct our solid primitives. Solid primitives are found under the "Model/Prims" screen menu and the "Model/Primitives..." pull-down menu. Using the pull-down menu selection will display a dialogue box that contains all the solid primitive choices. You may also display the dialogue box by selecting "MODEL/DDSOLPRM" from the screen menu.

FIGURE 37-3 Solid Primitives Dialogue Box

Let's use the solid primitive commands to construct some solid objects. Let's start with the Solbox command.

DRAWING A SOLID BOX

The Solbox command is used to draw a solid 3-D box.

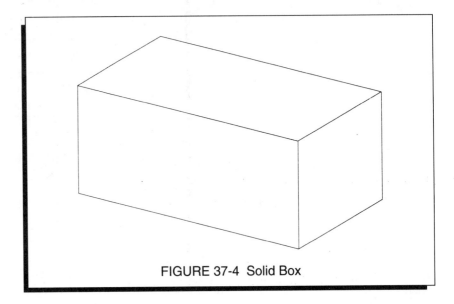

FIGURE 37-4 Solid Box

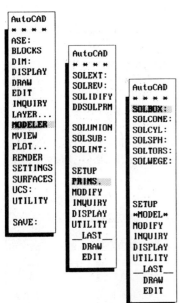

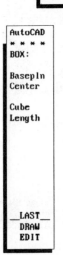

There are three methods of creating a box with this command. Let's look at each separately.

CREATING A SOLID BOX SPECIFYING OPPOSITE CORNERS AND HEIGHT

This is the default method of creating a box. Start by selecting the Solbox command. Enter the first point, then the opposite corner. Refer to the following command sequence and Figure 37-5.

```
Command: SOLBOX
Baseplane/<Corner of box>: (enter point "1")
Cube/Length/<Other corner>: (enter point "2")
```

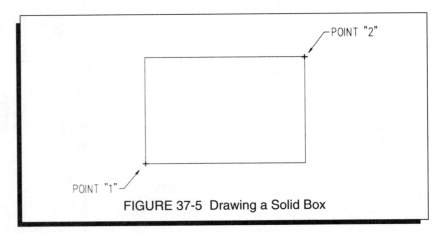

FIGURE 37-5 Drawing a Solid Box

The two points you have just entered specify the length and width of the box. You must now specify the height. You could also enter a relative coordinate to locate the opposite corner of the box after entering the first corner. The command line will now prompt you for that height. In this example, let's make our box 3 units high.

```
Height: 3
Phase I - Boundary evaluation begins.
Phase II - Tessellation computation begins.
Updating the Advanced Modeling Extension database.
```

The last three lines shown in the command sequence are displayed as the box is constructed. We will not show these lines after this point.

You may want to stop at this point and use AutoCAD's Vpoint command to display a 3-D representation of the box. Return to the Plan view and use a Zoom All after you are finished.

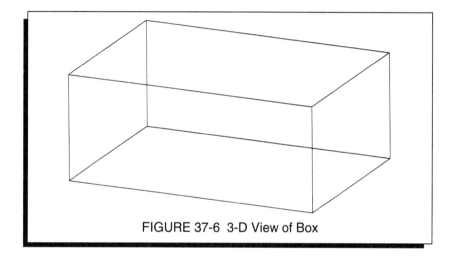

FIGURE 37-6 3-D View of Box

Note that the length and width of the box are constructed relative to the current UCS and the height is perpendicular to the current UCS.

Let's continue and look at the other two ways to construct a solid box.

LENGTH OPTION OF CONSTRUCTING A SOLID BOX

The Length option allows you to construct a box by designating the actual length, width, and height of a box in numeric values. Let's construct a box that is 4 units long, 3 units wide, and 2 units high. The following command sequence will guide you through the process.

```
Command: SOLBOX
Corner of box: (enter a point on the screen)
Cube/Length/<Other corner>: LENGTH
Length: 4
Width: 3
Height: 2
```

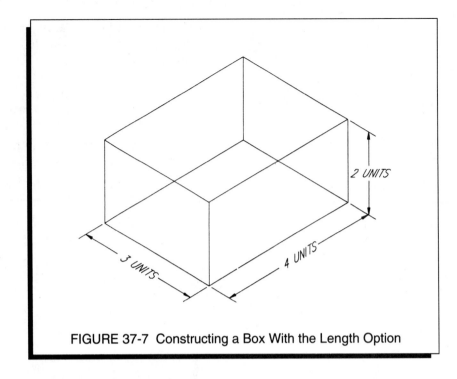

FIGURE 37-7 Constructing a Box With the Length Option

CREATING A SOLID CUBE

The Cube option is used to create a solid cube. Let's draw a cube.

```
Command: SOLBOX
Corner of box: (enter a point showing the corner of the box)
Cube/Length/<Other corner>: CUBE
Length: 3
```

AutoCAD will now construct the cube, using the value entered for the length (in this case, the value of 3 you entered) to construct a cube with all sides equal to the entered value.

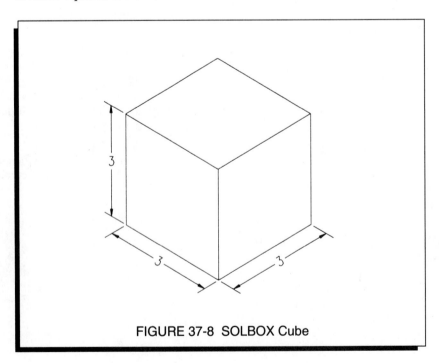

FIGURE 37-8 SOLBOX Cube

CREATING A SOLID CONE

The Solcone command is used to create a solid cone.

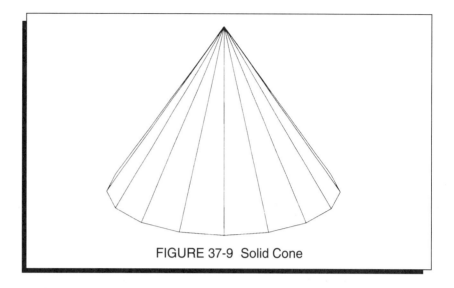

FIGURE 37-9 Solid Cone

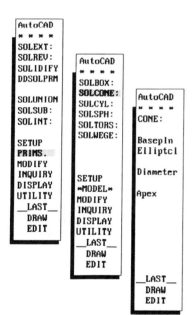

A cone can be constructed with either a circular or elliptical base. The cone's base will lie in the X,Y plane of the current UCS. The height describes the distance between the base and the point, and is perpendicular to the current UCS.

Let's construct a cone with a circular base. Select the Solcone command and use the following command sequence.

> Command: SOLCONE
> Baseline/ Elliptical/<Center point>: (enter a point on the screen)
> Diameter/<Radius>: 2

Note that you can construct the base by specifying either the diameter or the radius of the base. In our case, we entered a value of 2 units for the radius, since the radius is the default (in <brackets>). If you wish to enter the diameter, enter "D" at this prompt and you will be prompted for the diameter. Let's continue with the command sequence:

> Apex/Height: 3

Figure 37-10 shows the completed cone in 3-D.

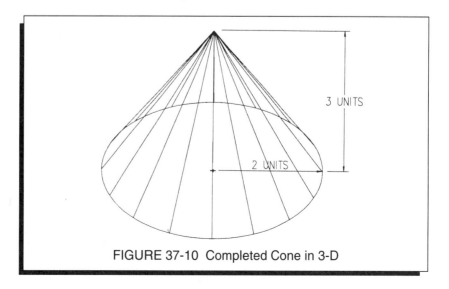

FIGURE 37-10 Completed Cone in 3-D

CONSTRUCTING A CONE WITH AN ELLIPTICAL BASE

The Elliptical option allows you to construct a cone with an elliptical base. Let's look at an example. Refer to Figure 37-11.

Command: <u>SOLCONE</u>
Elliptical/<Center point>: <u>ELLIPTICAL</u>
<Axis endpoint 1>/Center: (*enter a point for the first axis endpoint - shown as "Point 1"*)
Axis endpoint 2: (*enter "Point 2"*)
Other axis distance: (*enter "Point 3"*)
Apex/<Height>: <u>3</u>

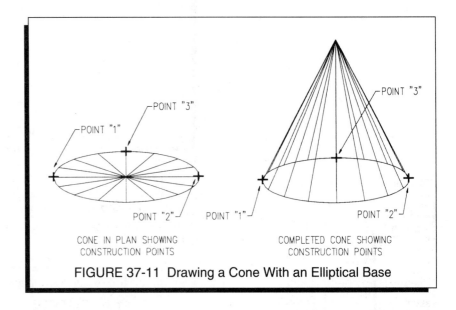

CONE IN PLAN SHOWING
CONSTRUCTION POINTS

COMPLETED CONE SHOWING
CONSTRUCTION POINTS

FIGURE 37-11 Drawing a Cone With an Elliptical Base

The base ellipse is constructed in the same manner as a standard ellipse when using the AutoCAD Ellipse command. You can also construct an ellipse using the Center option (see the third line of the previous command sequence). The following command sequence shows the prompts for this type of solid cone construction:

Command: <u>SOLCONE</u>
Elliptical/<Center point>: <u>ELLIPTICAL</u>
<Axis endpoint 1>Center: <u>CENTER</u>
Center of ellipse:
Axis endpoint:
Other axis distance:
Apex/<Height>:

Notice, again, the similarity to the AutoCAD Ellipse command.

CREATING A SOLID CYLINDER

The Solcyl command is used to construct solid cylinders.

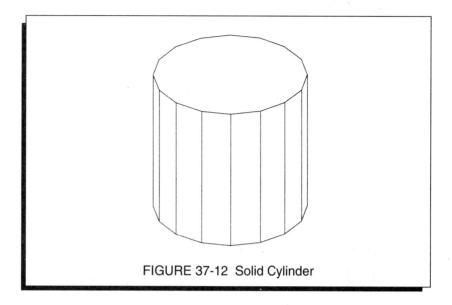

FIGURE 37-12 Solid Cylinder

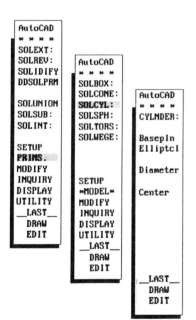

Solid cylinders are constructed in exactly the same manner as solid cones. The difference, of course, is that the cylinders are not tapered to a point.

Cylinders can be constructed with either circular or elliptical bases. Elliptical base cylinders are also constructed in the same manner as cones with elliptical bases.

Let's construct a solid cylinder with a circular base. Refer to Figure 37-13 for the points to enter.

Command: SOLCYL
Baseline/ Elliptical/<Center point>: (enter "Point 1")
Diameter/ <Radius>: (enter "Point 2")
Center of other end<Height>: 3

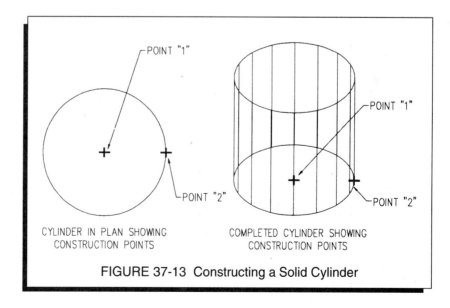

FIGURE 37-13 Constructing a Solid Cylinder

CREATING A SOLID SPHERE

The Solsphere command is used to create a solid 3-D sphere (ball).

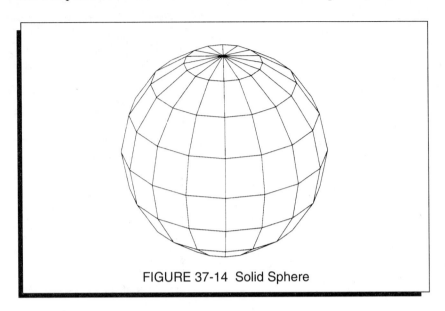

FIGURE 37-14 Solid Sphere

Constructing a solid sphere is very simple. You first designate the center point of the sphere, then either the radius or diameter. Let's construct a sphere. Use Figure 37-15 for the points to enter.

Command: <u>SOLSPHERE</u>
Baseline/<Center of sphere>: (*enter "Point 1"*)
Diameter/<Radius> of sphere: (*enter "Point 2"*)

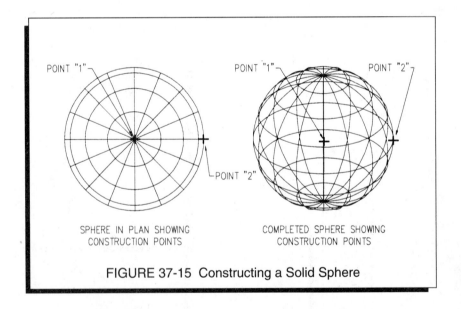

SPHERE IN PLAN SHOWING
CONSTRUCTION POINTS

COMPLETED SPHERE SHOWING
CONSTRUCTION POINTS

FIGURE 37-15 Constructing a Solid Sphere

The sphere is constructed with the center point you entered on the X-Y axis of the current UCS. The circle described by the two entered points is then rotated about the center point to construct the sphere. The vertical axis of the sphere is perpendicular to the X-Y plane of the UCS.

AutoCAD
* * * *
SOLEXT:
SOLREV:
SOLIDIFY
DDSOLPRM

SOLUNION
SOLSUB:
SOLINT:

SETUP
PRIMS.
MODIFY
INQUIRY
DISPLAY
UTILITY
__LAST__
DRAW
EDIT

AutoCAD
* * * *
SOLBOX:
SOLCONE:
SOLCYL:
SOLSPH:
SOLTORS:
SOLWEGE:

SETUP
MODEL
MODIFY
INQUIRY
DISPLAY
UTILITY
__LAST__
DRAW
EDIT

AutoCAD
* * * *
SPHERE:

Basepln

Diameter

__LAST__
DRAW
EDIT

CONSTRUCTING A SOLID TORUS

The Soltorus command is used to create a solid torus. A torus is a circle rotated about a point to create a tube, like a donut. The Soltorus allows some variations of the traditional torus object. Figure 37-16 shows a solid torus.

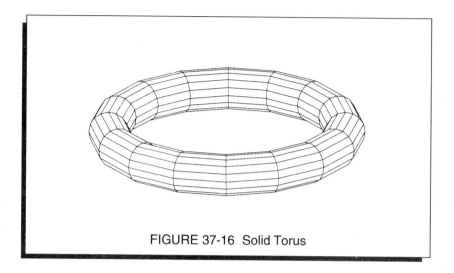

FIGURE 37-16 Solid Torus

Before we construct a solid torus, let's look at the components of a torus. Figure 37-17 shows plan views of a torus with the components listed.

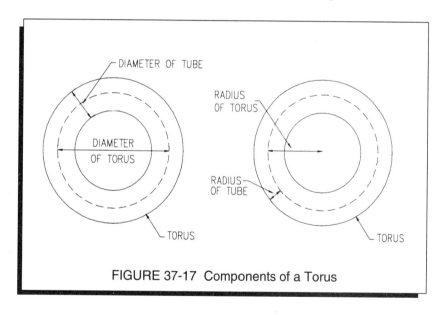

FIGURE 37-17 Components of a Torus

Let's construct a standard torus. Use the following command sequence and Figure 37-18.

    Command: SOLTORUS
    Baseline/<Center of torus>: (enter "Point 1")
    Diameter/<Radius> of torus: (enter "Point 2")
    Diameter/<Radius> of tube: (enter "Point 3")

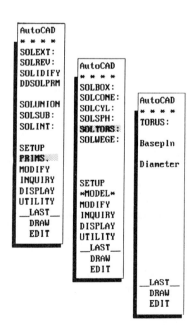

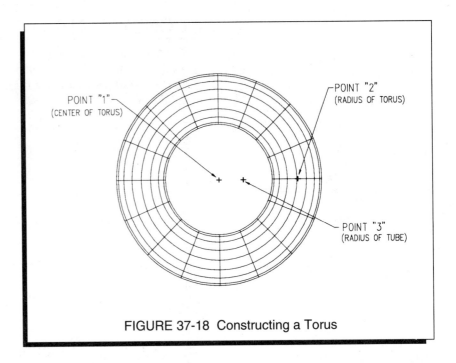

FIGURE 37-18 Constructing a Torus

It is possible to construct a torus with a tube radius that exceeds the radius of the torus. Take a moment to create a torus that has a radius of 2 and a tube radius of 5. View the torus in 3-D with the Vpoint command. Notice how the tubes intersect around the center point of the torus.

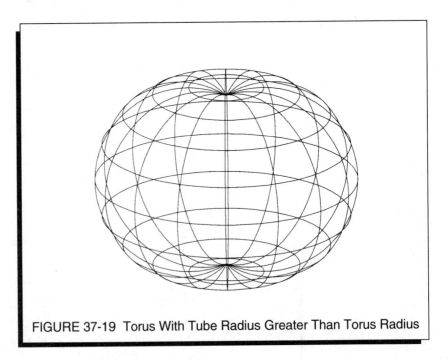

FIGURE 37-19 Torus With Tube Radius Greater Than Torus Radius

You can also use a negative value for the torus radius. This value, however, must be a positive number of greater value. For example, if the torus radius is −3, the tube radius must be greater than 3. Construct a torus with a torus radius of −3 and a tube radius of 4.

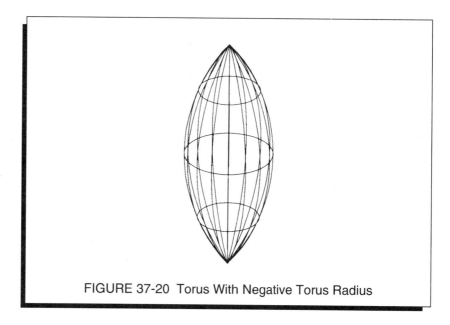

FIGURE 37-20 Torus With Negative Torus Radius

If you have used the Vpoint command to view your torus, select the Plan command to return to the plan view and Zoom All before proceeding.

CONSTRUCTING A SOLID WEDGE

The Solwedge command is used to create a solid wedge.

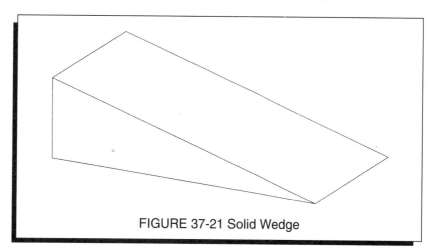

FIGURE 37-21 Solid Wedge

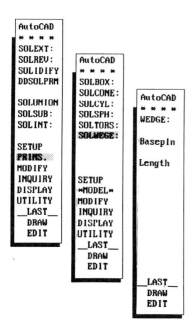

The wedge is constructed by specifying the dimensions of the base, then the height of the end of the wedge. You may alternately enter the length, width, and height in numeric values. Let's construct a wedge. Refer to Figure 37-22.

    Command: <u>SOLWEDGE</u>
    Baseline/<Corner of wedge>: (*enter "Point 1"*)
    Length/<other corner>: (*enter "Point 2"*)

Notice how the base of the wedge is "rubber-banded" from the first point. Let's continue in the command sequence.

    Height: <u>2</u>

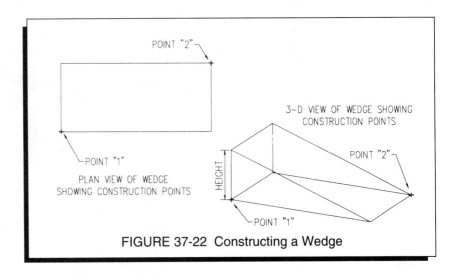

FIGURE 37-22 Constructing a Wedge

If you view the wedge in 3-D, you will notice the height is applied to the end described by the first point entered, and the "point" of the wedge is placed at the end of the base described by the second point.

LENGTH OPTION OF CONSTRUCTING A SOLID WEDGE

If you wish to construct a wedge by entering the actual dimensions as numeric values, simply select the "Length" option. The following command sequence shows the prompts displayed when you select Length.

```
Command: SOLWEDGE
Corner of wedge: (enter a point)
Length/<Other corner>: LENGTH
Length: (enter a numeric value)
Width: (enter a numeric value)
Height: (enter a numeric value)
```

CHAPTER REVIEW

1. What are some solid primitive objects?

_____

_____

_____

_____

_____

_____

_____

2. What is the prefix for solid modeling commands?

_____

3. What are the ways to access the AutoCAD solid modeling program?

_____

_____

_____

_____

4. What are the two types of solid cone bases that can be constructed?

_____

_____

5. What is a torus?

_____

_____

_____

CHAPTER 38

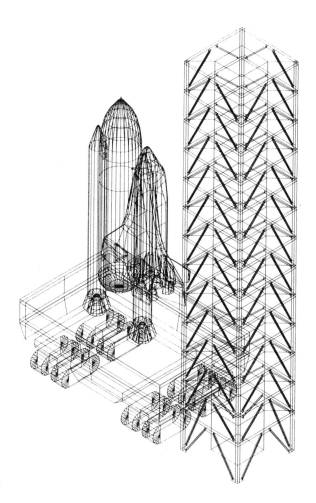

Creating Custom Solids

OBJECTIVES:

In Chapter 37, you learned how to construct solid primitives. In this chapter, you will practice the techniques necessary to create solid objects of your own design. The objectives of this chapter are:

● To learn the use of the commands used to create custom solid objects.

● To become familiar with the rules and limitations of the commands.

● To learn the technique for transforming your 3-D drawings to 3-D solid object shapes.

AutoCAD In The Real World

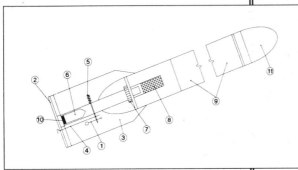

A schematic view of an Avalauncher projectile shows the safety pin (1), base plate (2), tail-fin assembly (3), base-plate arming wire (4), bore rider pin (5), striker pin (6), primer (7), blasting cap (8), explosive (9), magnet (10), and nose cone (11).

AutoCAD® Top Gun
AutoCAD® is used to design an avalanche-destroying gun to make recreational skiing safer

Under a blue-black sky, two figures move across the snow in the early light. Ahead, the monster waits. The only sound is their breathing. The only tracks in the freshly-fallen snow are their own. Below, the village sleeps. But here, at 9,000 feet, there's work to do.

"Seat piston," calls out the first, and his partner adjusts the long gun. "Set pressure. Set elevation. Place shot. Pull safety pin. Seat shot. Close barrel. Lock barrel. Aim. Ready to fire. Fire!"

A dull thud and the shell arcs through the air. Seconds later, a louder explosion echoes across the valley. The monster is loosed: tons of snow cascade down the mountainside. In less than a minute, it's over.

Avalanche control at Whistler and Blackcomb mountains in British Columbia is the job of specially-trained members of the ski patrol. They rely on their knowledge of snow conditions and computerized weather reports to predict when an avalanche risk exists. When danger threatens, the teams go up the mountain to set off the moving masses of snow before they threaten the thousands of recreational skiers heading for the slopes later that day. The future tools of their trade will be a special projectile and launcher designed using AutoCAD.

As early as the 1940s, people determined that ski areas would be safer if avalanches were set under controlled conditions. Back then, some ski areas used slingshots made from inner-tubes to hurl sticks of dynamite at starting zones.

Design for avalanche-starting guns has gained sophistication since then. A company called Avalanche Control Systems, currently manufactures and markets the Avalauncher. The system consists of a gun with a 12-foot long barrel, a firing cylinder activated by pressurized nitrogen, and a projectile consisting of a solid explosive, a nose cone, and a fixed fin-tail housing a contact detonator. Each gun is mounted at a fixed position within range of avalanche-prone terrain and has a range of 1,635 yards.

A new avalanche-destroying gun and projectile have been designed with AutoCAD by Sear Search and Rescue Equipment Ltd. "Superlauncher," a more powerful version of the current technology, delivers a larger projectile at a greater distance with improved accuracy.

Adapted with permission from an article by David Cohn in *CADalyst*, Copyright © 1990 by CADalyst Publications, Ltd.

CREATING SOLIDS

You can use AutoCAD commands to create virtually any custom solid object you wish. The following is a listing of AME commands and their functions that we will explore in this chapter.

Solext command: Creates solid extrusions from circles and polylines. You may also create tapered extrusions.

Solrev command: Creates solid revolutions by revolving a polyline around an axis.

Solidify command: Creates solids by solidifying certain objects and 3-D shapes.

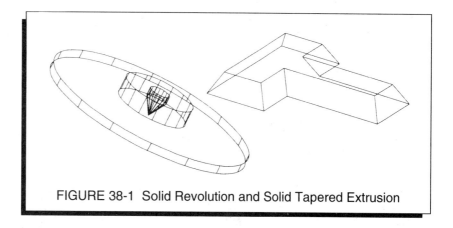

FIGURE 38-1 Solid Revolution and Solid Tapered Extrusion

Let's use these commands to create some solids. First, start a new drawing of any name. Let's get going and create some interesting solids!

CREATING SOLID EXTRUSIONS

The SOLEXT (solid extrusion) command is used to create solid objects by extruding existing polylines and circles. The following objects can be extruded:

> Polylines
> Polygons
> Circles
> Ellipses
> 3Dpoly entities

The effect of the Solext command is similar to extruding an object in 3-D by specifying a thickness. The difference, of course, is that Solext creates a solid extrusion as opposed to a basic 3-D extrusion. The object created is extruded perpendicular to its X-Y plane.

SOLID EXTRUSION RULES AND LIMITATIONS

In order to be extruded, a polyline must have at least 3 vertices, and no more than 500 vertices.

The polyline must either be closed or be capable of being closed without crossing over another polyline. If the polyline is not closed, AutoCAD will attempt to close it by adding a segment between the endpoints. If that (or any existing) segment crosses over another segment, the polyline can not be extruded.

You can extrude several polylines in one operation. If any selected polylines are not capable of being extruded, they are ignored. If a polyline with a non-zero width is selected, it is extruded with a zero width at the center line of the polyline.

Extrusions are created perpendicular to the X-Y plane of the object.

CREATING AN EXTRUSION WITH SOLEXT

Use the Pline command to draw an object similar to the one shown in Figure 38-2. Be sure to close with either the Close option or with object snap ENDpoint.

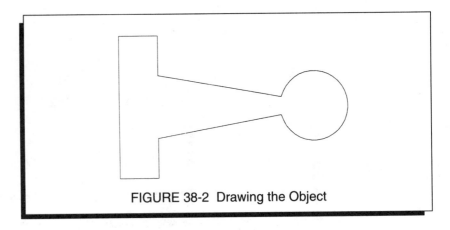

FIGURE 38-2 Drawing the Object

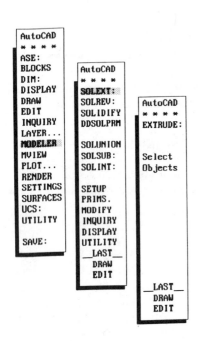

Now use the Solext command to create an extrusion that is 3 units "thick". Use the following command sequence.

    Command: <u>SOLEXT</u>
    Select regions, polylines and circles for extrusion... (*select the objects*)
    Select objects: (*select the object to extrude*)
    1 selected 1 found
    Select objects: (*press ENTER*)
    Height of extrusion: <u>3</u>
    Extrusion taper angle: (*press ENTER to accept 0*)

Now use the Vpoint command to view the object in 3-D. When you are finished, use the Plan command to return to the plan view and Zoom All.

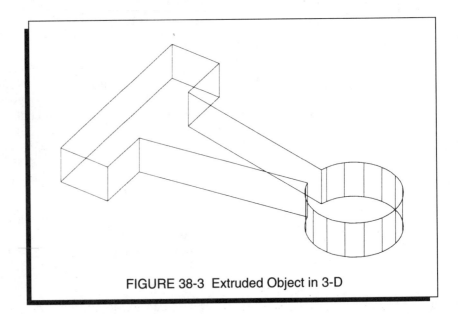

FIGURE 38-3 Extruded Object in 3-D

CREATING A TAPERED EXTRUSION

Let's use Solext to create a tapered extrusion. Use the Pline command to draw an object similar to the one shown in Figure 38-4.

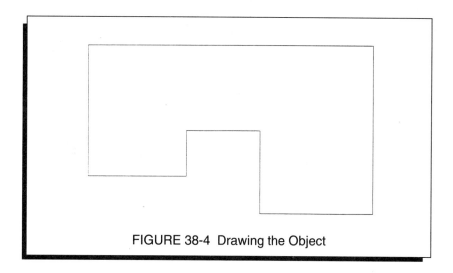

FIGURE 38-4 Drawing the Object

Now use the Solext command to create an extrusion 5 units "thick", with a taper of 30 degrees.

```
Command: SOLEXT
Select polylines and circles for extrusion... (select the polyline)
Select objects:
1 selected, 1 found
Select objects: (press ENTER)
Height of extrusion: 5
Extrusion taper angle (0): 30
```

Now use the Vpoint command to view the object as before. Notice how the sides of the polyline segments taper 30 degrees.

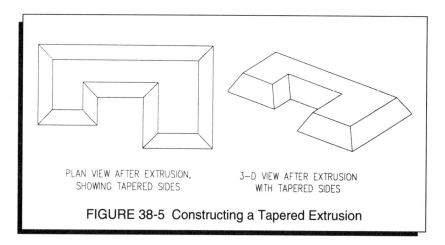

PLAN VIEW AFTER EXTRUSION, SHOWING TAPERED SIDES

3-D VIEW AFTER EXTRUSION WITH TAPERED SIDES

FIGURE 38-5 Constructing a Tapered Extrusion

The degree of taper specified must be greater than zero, but less than 90 degrees. You can not use negative values to create an "outward" taper. Extrusions can only taper inward from the original object.

CREATING A SOLID REVOLUTION

The SOLREV command is used to create solid revolutions. This is similar to the 3-D Revsurf command.

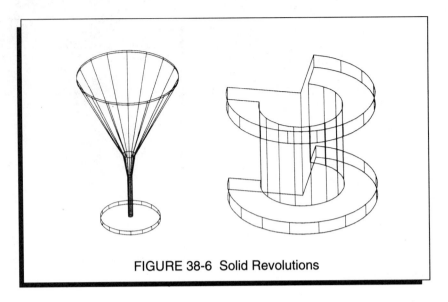

FIGURE 38-6 Solid Revolutions

Revolved solids are created by revolving an object about a specified axis. The following objects may be revolved:

Polylines	Ellipses
Polygons	3-D poly objects
Circles	

REVOLVED SOLIDS RULES AND LIMITATIONS

In order to be revolved, a polyline must have at least 3 vertices, but no more than 500 vertices. Polylines with non-zero width are changed to zero width. You can only revolve one object at a time.

The closed polyline rules apply as with the Solext command. You must be able to close the polyline without crossing another polyline segment.

CREATING A REVOLVED SOLID

Let's use the Solrev command to create a revolved solid. Use the Pline command to draw an object similar to the one shown in Figure 38-7. Omit the notations shown.

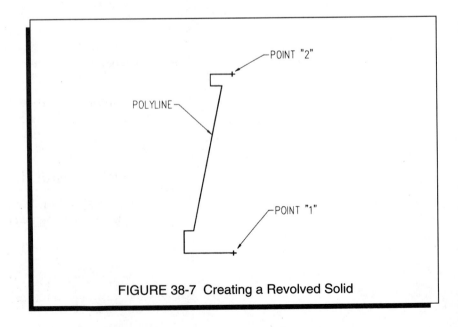

FIGURE 38-7 Creating a Revolved Solid

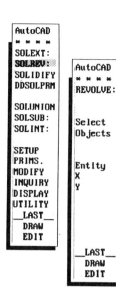

Use Figure 38-7 and the following command sequence to create the solid.

> Command: <u>SOLREV</u>
> Select region, polyline or circle for revolution... (*select the polyline*)
> Select objects: (*select the object*)
> 1 selected, 1 found
> Select objects: (*press ENTER*)
> Axis of revolution - Entity/X/Y/<Start point of axis>: <u>ENDpoint</u>
> of (*select "Point 1"*)
> Endpoint of axis: (*select "point 2"*)
> Angle of revolution <full circle>: (*press ENTER to accept a full circle revolution*)

Now use the Vpoint command to view the object in 3-D.

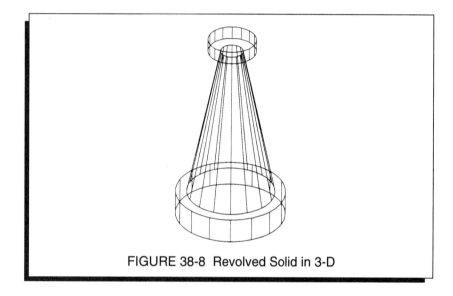

FIGURE 38-8 Revolved Solid in 3-D

After you have viewed the solid object, use Undo to return to the original polyline. Try a new revolved solid, using 180 degrees as the included angle.

REVOLVING AROUND AN ENTITY

You can use a separate entity as the axis to revolve a polyline around. Use Undo to return the drawing to the original polyline. Draw a line in the position shown in Figure 38-9.

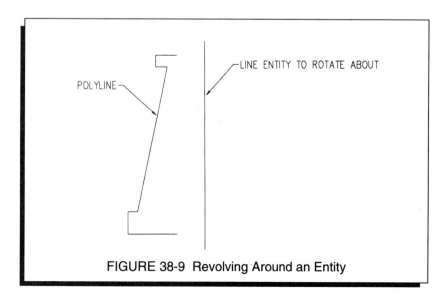

FIGURE 38-9 Revolving Around an Entity

Now let's create a solid object with an open shaft along its central axis.

> Command: <u>SOLREV</u>
> Select region, polyline or circle for revolution... (*select the polyline*)
> Select objects: (*select the object*)
> 1 selected, 1 found
> Select objects: (*press ENTER*)
> Axis of revolution - Entity/X/Y/<Start point of axis>: <u>ENTITY</u>
> Pick entity to revolve about: (*select the line*)
> Angle of revolution <full circle>: (*press ENTER to accept a full circle revolution*)

View the object in 3-D and notice the central shaft created by the location of the line from the polyline.

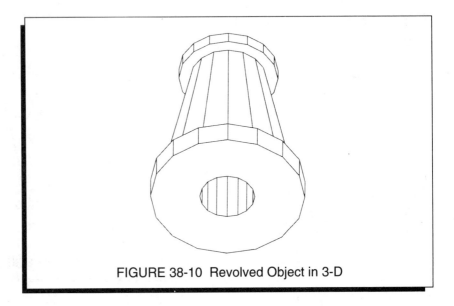

FIGURE 38-10 Revolved Object in 3-D

X AND Y ROTATION OPTIONS

The X and Y options of the Solrev command use either the X-axis or Y-axis of the current UCS as the axis of revolution. The following illustrations show the effects of using each with a full circle revolution.

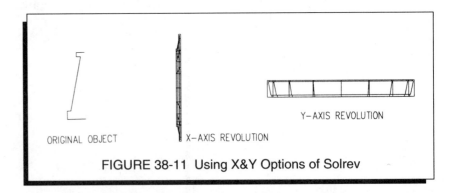

FIGURE 38-11 Using X&Y Options of Solrev

CONVERTING EXISTING OBJECTS TO 3-D SOLIDS

The SOLIDIFY command converts certain objects into 3-D solids. Using the Solidify command allows you to create a custom 3-D object with the extensive AutoCAD 3-D commands, then convert the object to a solid.

The following objects can be converted:

Polylines	Traces
Polygons	Donuts
Circles	2-D entities (if they have a non-zero thickness)
Ellipses	

The following objects can not be solidified:

Lines	3-D faces
3-D lines	3-D polys

SOLIDIFY RULES AND LIMITATIONS

A polyline must have at least three vertices to be solidified. The same closure rules for Solext and Solrev apply to Solidify. That is, you must be able to close the polyline without crossing another polyline segment.

If a polyline or trace of non-zero width is selected, the width is ignored and the solid is created from zero width lines along the center point of the trace or polyline.

SOLIDIFYING OBJECTS

To solidify an existing 3-D object, use the Solidify command.

    Command: SOLIDIFY
    Select objects:

Select the 3-D object to be solidified. There are no options for the Solidify command.

The Solidify command is very useful if the 3-D solid object you wish to create can not be created by other solid commands. The extensive capabilities of the AutoCAD 3-D commands allow you to create virtually any object you wish. After creating the 3-D object, just use the Solidify command to convert it to a solid object.

CHAPTER REVIEW

1. What command is used to create a solid object from a standard 3-D shape?

   _____

2. What is an extrusion?

   _____

   _____

   _____

3. What objects can be extruded?

   _____

   _____

4. What is created with the Solrev command?

   _____

5. In order to be solidified, how many vertices must a polyline have?

   _____

CHAPTER 39

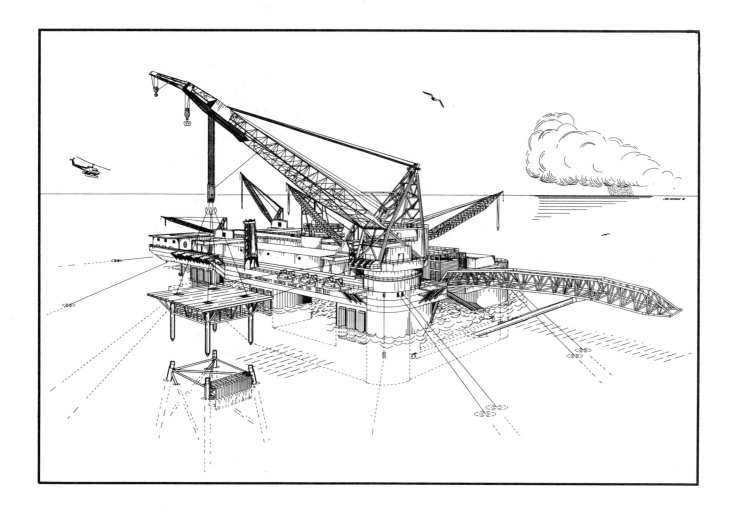

Modifying Solid Objects

OBJECTIVES:

To create solid objects of any design, you must be able to modify basic solid shapes. The objectives of this chapter are as follows.

● To understand the methods of editing solid shapes.

● To become familiar with the commands used to modify existing solid models.

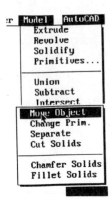

MODIFYING SOLID SHAPES

Solid models can be constructed by the combination of custom and primitive shapes. You can intersect, combine, and subtract shapes to achieve the model you desire. Then you can chamfer and fillet edges, move, rotate, and change the properties of the model and its parts. Solid modifier commands are used to modify solid models in these ways.

Let's look at the commands used to modify solid shapes.

CREATING SOLID INTERSECTIONS

The SOLINT (solid intersection) command is used to create a solid from the intersection of two solids. The resulting solid is created from the common volume occupied by both solids. Figure 39-1 shows the result of using the Solint command with two spheres.

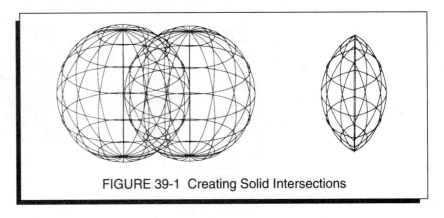

FIGURE 39-1 Creating Solid Intersections

When you select the Solint command, you are prompted to choose the objects that are to be used for the operation.

    Command: SOLINT
    Select objects:

SUBTRACTING SOLIDS

The SOLSUB (solid subtraction) command is used to subtract one solid shape from another, creating a new solid. Figure 39-2 shows a box with four cylinders. The Solsub routine has been used to subtract the cylinders from the box.

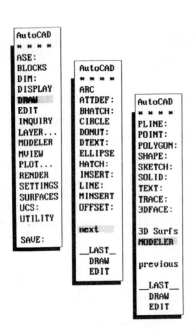

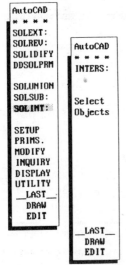

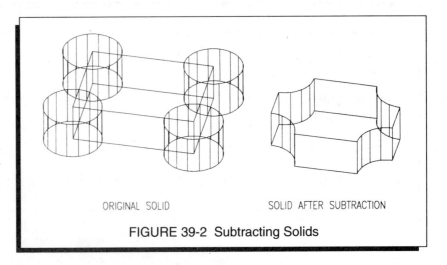

ORIGINAL SOLID   SOLID AFTER SUBTRACTION

FIGURE 39-2 Subtracting Solids

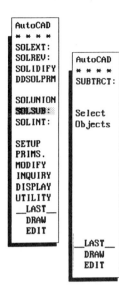

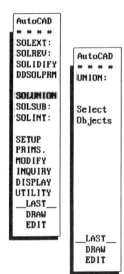

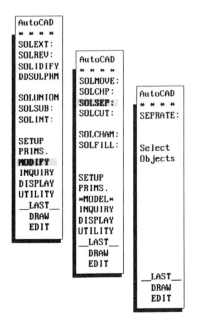

Let's look at how the Solsub command prompts for the solids you will modify. Solsub first asks for the objects that will be subtracted from them. The subtracted object(s) can be one or more objects. When you select the subtracted object(s), AutoCAD automatically performs a union of the selected objects.

> Command: SOLSUB
> Source objects...
> Select objects:

AutoCAD then prompts for the solid objects to be subtracted from the source object:

> Objects to subtract from them..
> Select objects:

AutoCAD then subtracts these objects from the source object, creating a new solid.

JOINING SOLID OBJECTS

The SOLUNION (solid union) command joins two solid objects together as a single object. The new solid encloses both objects and their common space (if they overlap).

> Command: SOLUNION
> Select objects:

SEPARATING SOLID OBJECTS

The SOLSEP (solid separate) command is used to separate composite solids created by the Solint, Solsub, and Solunion commands.

> Command: SOLSEP
> Select objects:

The separation is performed one level at a time. That is, the operations that created the selected composite solid are "undone" in reverse order.

CHAMFERING A SOLID

The SOLCHAM (solid chamfer) command is used to create chamfered edges on existing solid objects.

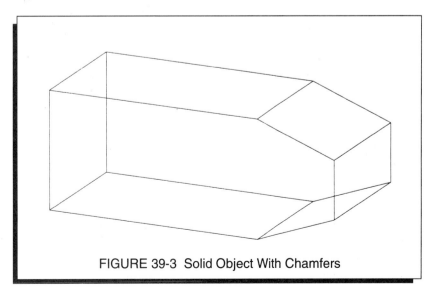

FIGURE 39-3 Solid Object With Chamfers

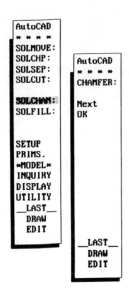

The chamfer is achieved by first selecting a "base surface," then the edges of the base surface to be chamfered. Finally, the chamfer dimension is specified. Let's look at how the Solcham command sequence is used.

Command: <u>SOLCHAM</u>
Pick base surface:
Next/<OK>:

When you select a base surface, one of the surfaces around the edge you selected is highlighted. If this is the correct surface, press ENTER to accept the default <OK>. If you want to designate another surface, respond with Next. Adjacent surfaces will blink to show the selected surface. When the correct surface is selected, press ENTER. Next, you will choose the edges common with the base surface that are to be chamfered. Let's continue with the command sequence.

Pick edges of this face to be chamfered (Press ENTER when done):

Select the edges to be chamfered as the response to this prompt. If the edge you select is not adjacent to the base surface, it will not be chamfered. You may select as many edges as you wish.

Next, specify the chamfer distances.

Enter distance along base surface <*default*>:
Enter distance along an adjacent surface <*default*>:

You may enter a numeric value or show AutoCAD the distance by picking two points on the drawing.

FILLETING A SOLID

The SOLFILL (solid fillet) command is used to create a filleted edge on a solid object.

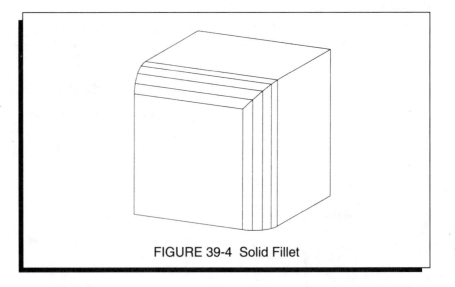

FIGURE 39-4 Solid Fillet

Solfill can create concave or convex fillets. The fillet is created by selecting the edges to be filleted.

Command: <u>SOLFILL</u>
Pick edges of solids to be filleted (Press ENTER when done):
Diameter/<Radius> of fillet <*default*>:

The radius or diameter can be specified by either entering a numeric value or showing AutoCAD the distance by entering two points on the drawing.

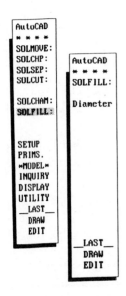

```
AutoCAD
* * * *
SOLMOVE:
SOLCHP:
SOLSEP:
SOLCUT:

SOLCHAM:
SOLFILL:


SETUP
PRIMS.
*MODEL*
INQUIRY
DISPLAY
UTILITY
__LAST__
DRAW
EDIT
```

```
AutoCAD
* * * *
CHPRIM:

Color
Delete
Evaluate
Instance
Move
Next
Pick
Replace
Size
eXit


__LAST__
DRAW
EDIT
```

CHANGING PROPERTIES OF SOLIDS

The SOLCHP (solid change property) command is used to change certain properties of a solid object. The changes can be applied to a primitive even if it is part of a composite solid. When you select a solid, an evaluation is performed, then you are prompted to select a primitive.

Command: SOLCHP
Select a solid or region:
Color/Delete/Evaluate/Instance/Move/Next/Pick/Replace/Size/eXit <N>:

Let's look at each option.

Color: Changes the primitive's color. Enter the AutoCAD color number you desire. The basic AutoCAD color numbers are:

1: Red
2: Yellow
3: Green
4: Cyan
5: Blue
6: Magenta
7: White

Delete: Erases the selected primitive. If the selected primitive is not part of a composite solid, it is completely erased. If it is part of a composite solid, you have the choice of either deleting it completely, or retaining it as a separate primitive. That is, it will appear in the same position, but will not be an attached part of the composite solid it was originally a part of. In this case, AutoCAD prompts:

Retain detached primitive? <N>:

Responding with "Yes" will retain the primitive, but as an unattached part. Entering "No" will delete the primitive entirely.

Evaluate: Forces an evaluation of the selected solid.

Instance: Produces a copy of the selected primitive. The copy is not visually evident since it is created at the same position as the original. The original primitive is not detached from the composite solid (if it is a part of one). You can use the Move option (explanation follows) to move the copy to another location.

Move: Moves the selected primitive. The move process is the same as the standard AutoCAD Move command. That is, you can specify the distance to move by showing two points on the drawing.

Next: Used to select another primitive in a composite solid. Each selection of Next will highlight a new primitive for change.

Pick: Used to select another primitive in a composite solid by object selection picking. Selecting Pick will display a pick box that is used to select the desired primitive.

Replace: Replaces the selected primitive with another primitive. You are asked to choose another primitive to replace the selected primitive.

If the replacement primitive is part of a composite solid, you must first use the Instance option to make a copy of the primitive. If the original primitive is part of a composite solid, you can choose whether the replacement will be an attached or a separate part of the composite. In this case, AutoCAD will prompt:

Retain detached primitive? <N>:

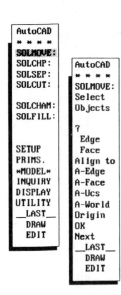

Answering "Yes" will create a separate primitive. Responding "No" will make the replacement a part of the composite solid.

Size: Changes the size of the selected primitive. When you select Size, the solid axes icon like the one used with the Solmove command (explanation follows) is displayed. The current dimension for each axis is displayed, one at a time. You can enter a new value for each to specify the new dimensions of the primitive.

MOVING AND ROTATING SOLID OBJECTS

The SOLMOVE (solid move) command is used to move and rotate solid objects. When you select Solmove, you are prompted to select the solid object(s) to move or rotate.

Command: <u>SOLMOVE</u>
Select objects:

After you select the object(s) to be moved or rotated, a solid axes icon is displayed. The axis shows the X, Y, and Z axes. The X-axis is designated by a single cone, the Y-axis by a double cone, and the Z-axis with three cones.

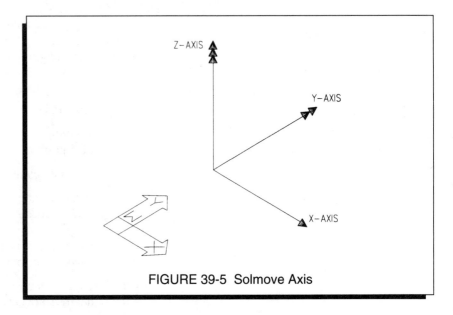

FIGURE 39-5 Solmove Axis

The intersection of the axes is the origin of the axis. You are then prompted for the "motion description."

<Motion description>/?:

Entering a question mark (?) will display a listing of the motion description codes.

A motion description is a code that moves the object, or relocates the origin of the solid axes icon. Motion descriptions can be entered one at a time, or several at a time if they are separated by commas. The codes designate a specific action and are reduced to a single letter. The following lists the basic codes.

A: Align (aligns objects with a coordinate system)
R: Rotate (rotates objects around an axis)
T: Translate (moves [translates] an object along an axis)

These codes describe the three major functions of the Solmove command. In addition, the following codes are also used:

E: Sets axes to edge coordinate system
F: Sets axes to face coordinate system
U: Sets axes to the current UCS
W: Sets axes to the World Coordinate System
O: Restores the object to the original position and rotation

The codes can be used together to combine operations. For example, if you responded with "AU", the selected objects and the solid axes icon are moved so they align with the UCS.

You can also rotate the object a specified number of degrees about an axis. For example, entering "RX30" rotates the object(s) 30 degrees around the X-axis.

To translate (move) an object, use the translate code (T), the axis, and the distance to move along that axis. For example, specifying "TZ20" moves the object(s) 20 units along the Z-axis.

CHAPTER REVIEW

1. Describe the function of the Solsub command.

2. Which command is used to create a new solid from the common area described by two overlapping solids?

3. How would you join two existing solids?

4. When chamfering a solid object, what is meant by the "base surface"?

5. How would you make a copy of a solid primitive that is a part of a composite solid?

6. What is the motion description code to move a solid 35 units along the Y-axis of the solid axes icon?

CHAPTER 40

William Taylor

Creating Composite Solid Models

OBJECTIVES:

To effectively use AutoCAD's Advanced Modeling Extension (AME), you must practice using the commands in actual modeling conditions. The objectives of this chapter are:

● To gain familiarity with the modeling commands through use with an actual solid model.

● To learn the procedures of drawing and editing a solid model.

DRAWING A COMPOSITE SOLID MODEL

Let's start a solid model drawing. We will construct the model, edit it, and display it as both a hidden line and solid object. Figure 40-1 shows the finished model.

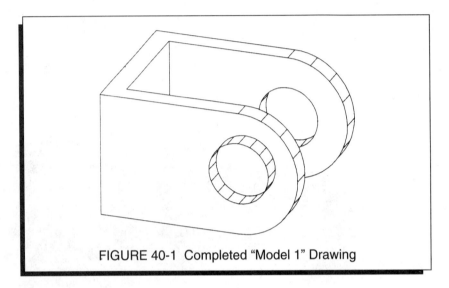

FIGURE 40-1 Completed "Model 1" Drawing

BEGINNING THE MODEL

Let's start by beginning a new drawing. Use the NEW command to start a new drawing. Enter MODEL1 as the drawing name. This tutorial uses the default prototype drawing settings. If this file has been changed, the actual results or display may vary from those shown.

Figure 40-2 is a dimensioned drawing of the object we will draw. You may want to refer to it as we are constructing the base model from solid primitives.

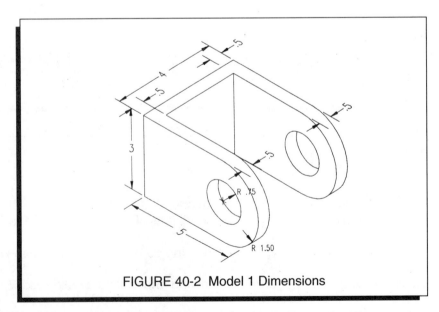

FIGURE 40-2 Model 1 Dimensions

Let's begin our drawing by using these commands to construct our basic model shape. Figure 40-3 shows the building block components we will use to "assemble" our model.

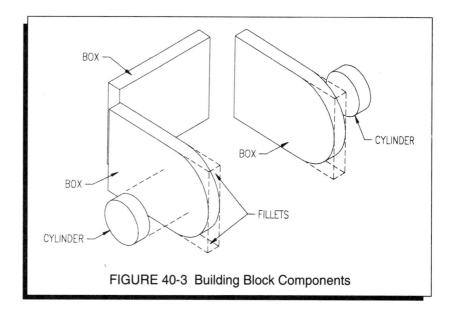

FIGURE 40-3 Building Block Components

Before starting any drawing, you should analyze the object to determine the best primitives to use. We are going to use both solid commands and some 3-D principles to construct our model. Let's get started.

CREATING THE FIRST BOX

Select the SOLBOX command from the menu and enter the points indicated in the following command sequence. We will discuss each step as we perform it.

> Command: SOLBOX

Select the first corner of the box.

> Baseplane/Center/<Corner of box>: 3,2

Next, define the opposite corner of the box.

> Cube/Length/<Other corner>: @5,0.5

Now define the height of the box.

> Height: 3

You will see some message prompts as AutoCAD processes the construction of the box. Select the Solbox command again. Refer to Figure 40-4 for the points to enter.

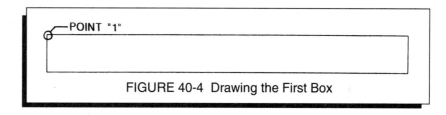

POINT "1"

FIGURE 40-4 Drawing the First Box

Command: SOLBOX
Corner of box: <u>INTERSEC</u>
of (*select point "1"*)
Cube/Length/<Other corner>: <u>@0.5,3</u>
Height: <u>3</u>

CREATING THE SECOND BOX

Let's use the Solbox command one more time. Refer to Figure 40-5.

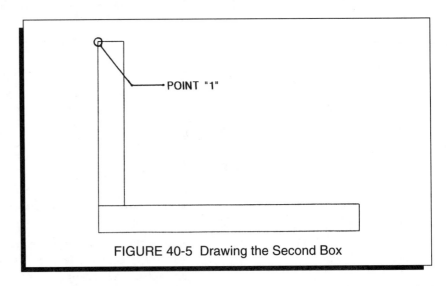

FIGURE 40-5 Drawing the Second Box

Command: <u>SOLBOX</u>
Corner of box: <u>INTERSEC</u>
of (*select point "1"*)
Cube/Length/<Other corner>: <u>@5,0.5</u>
Height: <u>3</u>

Your drawing should look like the one in Figure 40-6.

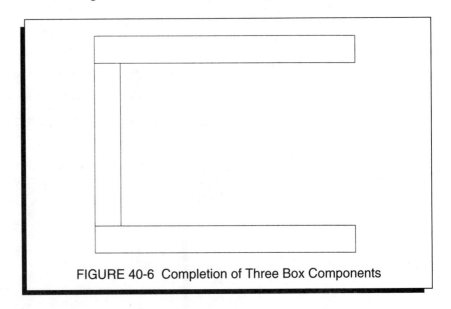

FIGURE 40-6 Completion of Three Box Components

ROTATING THE OBJECT

Let's use the Vpoint command to rotate the object so we can complete our work.

Command: VPOINT
Rotate/<View point> <0.0000,0.0000,1.0000>: R
Enter angle in X-Y plane from X axis <270>: 290
Enter angle from X-Y plane <90>: 23

Let's use a zoom factor to "zoom out" the display of our drawing.

Command: ZOOM
All/Center/Dynamic/Extents/Left/Previous/Vmax/Window/<Scale(X/XP)>: .6X

Your drawing should look similar to Figure 40-7.

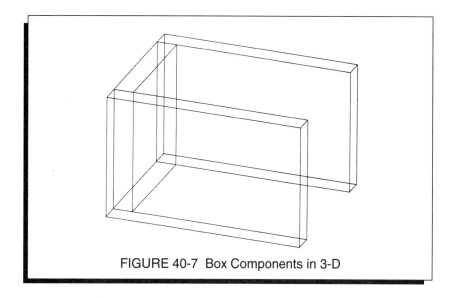

FIGURE 40-7 Box Components in 3-D

ADDING THE DRILL HOLES

We want to add a drill hole to the side of the object. Let's begin by setting our UCS icon so we can see the origin of the UCS we will be working in.

Command: UCSICON
ON/OFF/All/Noorigin/ORigin <ON>: OR

Now let's change the UCS. Refer to the following command sequence and Figure 40-8.

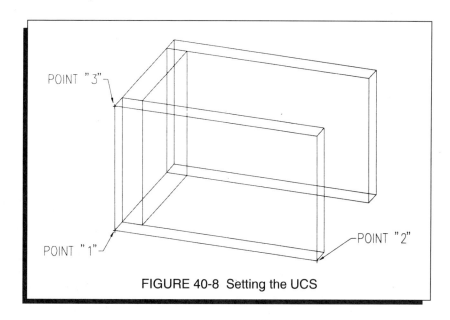

FIGURE 40-8 Setting the UCS

Command: UCS
Origin/ZAxis/3point/Entity/View/X/Y/Z/Prev/Restore/Save/Del/?/
<World>: 3
Origin point <0,0,0>: INTERSEC
of (select point "1")
Point on positive portion of the X-axis <1.0000,0.0000,0.0000>:
INTERSEC
of (select point "2")
Point on positive-Y portion of the UCS X-Y plane <0.0000,1.0000,
0.0000>: INTERSEC
of (select point "3")

It is now time to add the drill hole. We will construct this with the Solcyl (solid cylinder) command. Let's walk through each step of this command. Refer to Figure 40-9.

Command: SOLCYL

Next, specify the center point of the cylinder. Note that the absolute coordinates we use are relative to the origin of the new UCS.

Elliptical/<Center point>: 3.5,1.5

Now specify the radius of the cylinder.

Baseplane/Diameter/<Radius>: .75

Finally, we will designate the extrusion height of the cylinder. Since we want the extrusion to extend in a negative direction, the value will be negative.

Center of other end/<Height>: -0.5

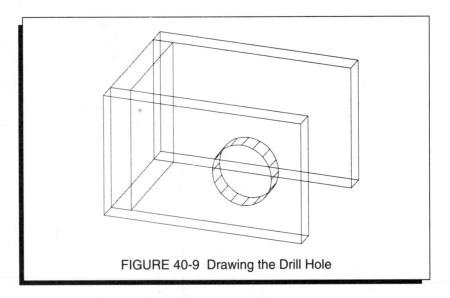

FIGURE 40-9 Drawing the Drill Hole

ADDING THE SECOND DRILL HOLE

Let's use the Vpoint command to rotate the object so we can add the second drill hole.

Command: VPOINT

Rotate/<View point> <default>: R
Enter angle in X-Y plane from X axis <290>: 330
Enter angle from X-Y plane <23>: (ENTER)

Now zoom out again.

Command: ZOOM
All/Center/Dynamic/Extents/Left/Previous/Vmax/Window/<Scale(X/
XP)>: .6X

Next, move the UCS to the opposite side of the object. Refer to the following command sequence and Figure 40-10.

Command: <u>UCS</u>
Origin/ZAxis/3point/Entity/View/X/Y/Z/Prev/Restore/Save/Del/?/
<World>: <u>O</u>
Origin point <0,0,0>: <u>INTERSEC</u>
of (*select point "1"*)

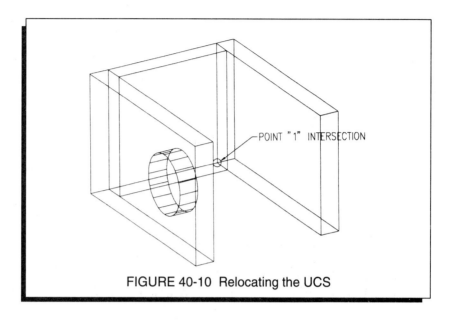

FIGURE 40-10 Relocating the UCS

Let's draw this cylinder a different way. We will use a circle, change it to a cylinder, then solidify the cylinder into a solid object. Use the following command sequence and Figure 40-11.

Command: <u>CIRCLE</u>
3P/2P/TTR/<Center point>: <u>3.5,1.5</u>
Diameter/<Radius>: <u>.75</u>

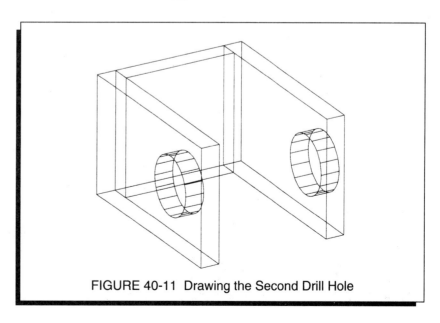

FIGURE 40-11 Drawing the Second Drill Hole

Now use the Chprop command to extrude the circle into a cylinder.

```
Command: CHPROP
Select objects: L
1 found
Select objects: (ENTER)
Change what property (Color/LAyer/LType/Thickness) ? T
New thickness <0.0000>: -.5
Change what property (Color/LAyer/LType/Thickness) ? (ENTER)
```

Next, use the Solidify command to change the cylinder into a solid cylinder.

```
Command: SOLIDIFY
Select objects: L
1 found
Select objects: (ENTER)
```

CONVERTING TO A COMPOSITE SOLID

Before we convert our object, let's change back to the view we previously saved.

```
Command: VIEW
?/Delete/Restore/Save/Window: R
View name to restore: V1
```

Let's now create a composite solid. To do this, we must change the three boxes into a single solid object, then subtract the cylinders that make the drill holes. We will first use the Solunion (solid union) command to combine the boxes. Use the following command sequence.

```
Command: SOLUNION
Select objects: (select each of the three boxes and press ENTER)
```

AutoCAD will now go to work and perform all the necessary calculations to combine the boxes into a single solid object. You will notice when the drawing is redisplayed that the edge lines between the boxes are no longer a part of the object.

SUBTRACTING THE CYLINDERS

Let's continue and subtract the cylinders from the object. We will use the Solsub (solid subtract) command.

```
Command: SOLSUB
Source objects...
Select objects: (select the boxes)
Select objects: (ENTER)
1 solid selected

Objects to subtract from them...
Select objects: (select each of the cylinders, then press ENTER)
Select objects: (ENTER)
```

AutoCAD will now evaluate the object and remove the cylinders from the solid object created by the union of the three boxes. Note that you will not notice a visual difference after this step. Your drawing should now look similar to Figure 40-12.

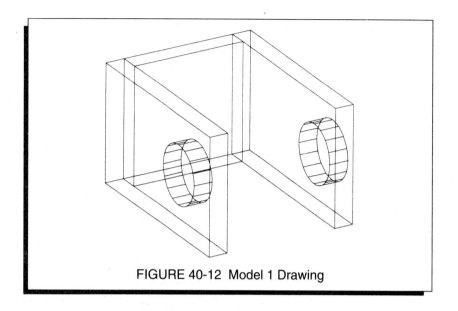

FIGURE 40-12 Model 1 Drawing

FILLETING THE CORNERS

Next we will use the Solfill (solid fillet) command to fillet the corners. Refer to the following command sequence and Figure 40-13. We will discuss each step as we proceed.

Command: <u>SOLFILL</u>
Select edges to be filleted (press Enter when done): (*select points "1" and "2", then press ENTER*)
Diameter/<Radius> of fillet <0.0>: <u>1.5</u>

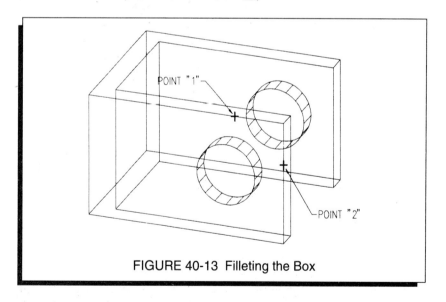

FIGURE 40-13 Filleting the Box

Your drawing should look similar to Figure 40-14.

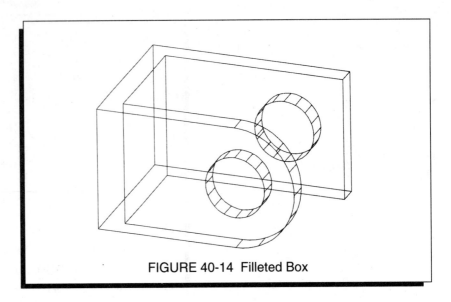

FIGURE 40-14 Filleted Box

Now use the Solfill command again to fillet the back leg of the object in the same manner. When completed, your drawing should look like Figure 40-15.

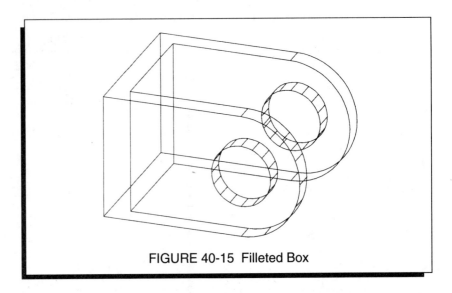

FIGURE 40-15 Filleted Box

SOLID MODEL ANALYSIS

Now that you have completed your solid model, you can use AutoCAD's AME capabilities to analyze the model. To do this, we will use the Solmassp command.

        Command: SOLMASSP
        Select objects: (*pick the model*)

Figure 40-16 shows a listing of the calculated mass properties.

```
Ray projection along X axis, level of subdivision: 3.
Mass:           8.135 gm
Volume:         1.035 cu cm   (Err: 0.1089)

Bounding box:           X: 1.9   --   4.327 cm
                        Y: 1.108  --   3.067 cm
                        Z: -1.384  --   1.099 cm

Centroid:               X: 2.883  cm    (Err: 0.3605)
                        Y: 2.213  cm    (Err: 0.2706)
                        Z: -0.301  cm    (Err: 0.1193)

Moments of inertia:     X: 44.39  gm sq cm (Err: 6.455)
                        Y: 74.41  gm sq cm (Err: 10.96)
                        Z: 112.5  gm sq cm (Err: 15.9)
Products of inertia: XY: 52.08  gm sq cm (Err: 7.431)
                     YZ: -6.106  gm sq cm (Err: 2.189)
                     ZX: -7.703 gm sq cm (Err: 2.985)

Radii of gyration:      X: 2.336  cm
                        Y: 3.024  cm
                        Z: 3.719  cm

Principal moments(gm sq cm) and X-Y-Z directions about centroid:
                        I: 3.468 along [0.8826 0.1805 -0.4342]
                        J: 6.426 along [0.05003 0.882 0.4685]
                        K: 5.064 along [0.4675 -0.4352 0.7694]
```

FIGURE 40-16 Mass Properties Listing

DISPLAYING YOUR MODEL

We can produce hidden line and shaded models of our model. The model is currently displayed in wireframe representation. To perform a hidden line or shaded model, we must first convert the model to a mesh representation. Let's use the Solmesh command to do this.

Command: <u>SOLMESH</u>
Select objects: (*select the model*)

Now perform the hidden line removal.

Command: <u>HIDE</u>

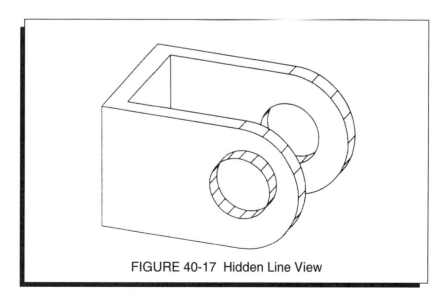

FIGURE 40-17 Hidden Line View

You may want to use the Shade command to produce a shaded model.

Command: <u>SHADE</u>

If you choose to convert back to wireframe representation, Regenerate the drawing, then use the Solwire command.

CHAPTER 41

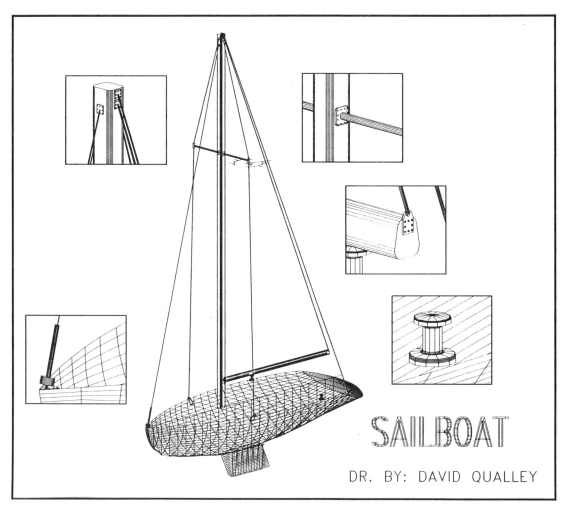

SAILBOAT

DR. BY: DAVID QUALLEY

Displaying and Representing
Solid Models

OBJECTIVES:

The objectives of this chapter are:

● To learn the principles involved in representing and displaying three-dimensional representations of solid models.

● To learn the commands used to display solid models.

VISUAL REPRESENTATION OF SOLIDS

Solid models are either displayed as wireframe or mesh representations. The default representation is as a wireframe. The type of representation can be changed by the Solmesh and Solwire commands.

You can display the solid model in either representation, but you can only use one or the other at a time. If you explode a wireframe model, the result is individual line and polyline entities. If you explode a mesh model, it is reduced to pface entities.

To display a hidden line or shaded model, you must first use the Solmesh command to convert it to a mesh representation.

Let's look at the commands that control the representation of your solid models.

DISPLAYING SOLIDS AS WIREFRAMES

The SOLWIRE (solid wireframe) command is used to display a model in wireframe form. Solid models start out as wireframes by default. You cannot display your model in either a hidden or shaded form in wireframe.

To use the Solwire command, simply select the object(s) to be converted to wireframe.

    Command: SOLWIRE
    Select objects:

In most cases, there will be no visual effect on the model.

DISPLAYING SOLIDS IN MESH FORM

The SOLMESH (solid mesh) command is used to display a model in mesh form. You must first convert the solid model to a mesh representation before performing a Hide or Shade operation.

To use the Solmesh command, select the solid(s) to be converted to mesh form.

    Command: SOLMESH
    Select objects:

CONTROLLING TESSELLATION LINES

The SOLWDENS (solid wire density) command is used to control the number of tessellation lines displayed on the curved surfaces of wireframe models. The number of lines can be 1 to 12. The higher number of tessellation lines produces a higher visual image level, but takes longer to calculate.

    Command: SOLWDENS
    Wireframe mesh density (1 to 12) <default>:

Solwdens can be used either as a command or as an option under the Solvars command (explanation follows). When used as an option, it can be accessed by the abbreviation "WDENS".

SOLVAR COMMAND (AME/AMElite)

The SOLVAR (solid variables) command is used to assign values to variables that affect solid models.

        Command: SOLVAR
        Variable name or ?:

To obtain a listing of the variables, enter a question mark (?). Figure 41-1 shows the variable listing displayed.

```
SOLAMECOMP    AME2          Script compatibility
SOLAMEVER     R2.1          AME release  (read only)
SOLAREAU      sq cm         Area units
SOLAXCOL      3             Solid axes color
SOLDECOMP     X             Mass property decomposition direction
SOLDELENT     3             Entity deletion
SOLDISPLAY    wire          Display type
SOLHANGLE     45.000000     Hatch angle
SOLHPAT       U             Hatch pattern
SOLHSIZE      1.000000      Hatch size
SOLLENGTH     cm            Length units
SOLMASS       gm            Mass units
SOLMATCURR    MILD_STEEL    Current material (read only)
SOLPAGELEN    25            Length of Text Page
SOLRENDER     CSG           Rendering type
SOLSECTYPE    1             Cross section representation type
SOLSERVMSG    3             Solid Server message display level
SOLSOLIDIFY   3             Automatic solidification
SOLSUBDIV     3             Mass property subdivision level
SOLUPGRADE    0             Upgrade solids to double precision
SOLVOLUME     cu cm         Volume units
SOLWDENS      1             Mesh wireframe density
```

FIGURE 41-1 Listing of Solid Variables

CHAPTER REVIEW

1. What is the default display representation of a solid model?

   _____

2. What type of representation must a solid model be in order to produce a hidden line drawing of the model?

   _____

   For a shaded model?

   _____

3. What is the result of exploding a wireframe model?

   _____

   _____

4. How do you set the variables that affect the appearance of solid models?

_____

5. What does Solwdens control?

_____

_____

_____

CHAPTER 42

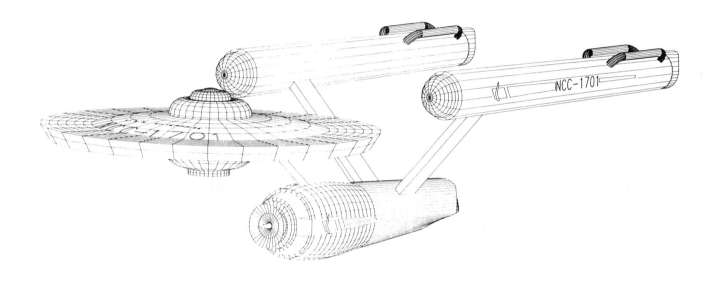

Introduction to AutoLISP

OBJECTIVES:

AutoLISP is a powerful programming tool that is a part of AutoCAD. The objectives of this chapter are:

● To become acquainted with the nature and purpose of the AutoLISP programming language.

● To learn how to load and use existing AutoLISP routines.

AutoCAD In The Real World

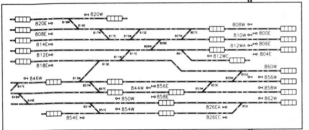

AutoCAD® on Track

AutoCAD®'s been working on designing signaling systems and other facilities for leading railroads.

CP Consulting used AutoCAD to produce a detailed signal system design for the 6.1 mile Northeast Extension of the Calgary, Alberta Light Rapid Transit System. For the Long Island Railroad West Side Storage Yard, a detailed yard signaling system was designed with AutoCAD. The package of approximately 600 drawings was plotted in-house over a period of a few weeks. Time, effort and money were saved because there would be extensive changes over the three years of design and construction process.

Signal design lends itself to CAD. The basic design unit, the interlocking, contains many repeated drawings, so prototypes are created and a script file written in AutoCAD's AutoLISP is used to make the changes that create the specific switch machine circuit.

CAD is also being used in track design. For New York City's Grand Central terminal, with its double-level arrangement of 67 tracks, AutoCAD was used to raise the speed through the interlock on as many routes as possible and incorporate them in the new signal route and aspect design. The tunnel was accurately surveyed and the appropriate information read into AutoCAD where track realignments were constructed, turnouts and curves were drawn, and tunnel clearances were checked.

These and the many CAD applications that CP Consulting has developed have not only reduced design time significantly, but have helped them inject fresh ideas into their design approach.

Adapted with permission from an article by Jeffrey Smith in *CADalyst*, Copyright © 1990 by CADalyst Publications, Ltd.

USING AUTOLISP

AutoCAD is a powerful drawing and design program. While many people use this program for various purposes, most have implemented CAD for a specific discipline. While the "generic" form of AutoCAD contains all the command routines needed to construct any type of drawing, most users can benefit from the custom programming capabilities within AutoCAD.

In Chapter 29 we learned how to customize menus and write macros to combine several steps into one. A more powerful method of customization is the use of the LISP programming language embedded within the AutoCAD package. This feature, referred to as AutoLISP, allows you to set and recall points, mix mathematical routines within a list of instructions, and perform many other routines.

WHY USE AUTOLISP?

AutoLISP allows the AutoCAD user to customize new commands that perform one or many functions. For example, third-party programmers have used AutoLISP to create packages that can automatically create a 3-D contour map from site data, create "unfolded" patterns from three dimensional objects, and construct a drawing from a list of dimensions that describes an object (parametric drawing construction).

Using AutoLISP to customize routines for your work creates a more efficient drawing system. Whether you continue to increase your knowledge of LISP programming and write extensive routines, or just gain a general understanding and write simple time-saving routines, you will find that AutoLISP will enhance your AutoCAD work!

USING AN AUTOLISP PROGRAM

Electronic Work Disk Problem

You don't have to be a LISP programmer to use AutoLISP routines. AutoCAD contains many LISP routines for your use. Let's look at one of these programs, then learn how to load and use it.

The electronic work disk contains a LISP file named "AXROT.LSP". This is an AutoLISP program used to rotate an object around any of its axes. Before starting, make sure this program is in the directory in which you have placed your AutoCAD files. Table 42-1 is a listing of the program.

```
;;; -------------------------------------------------------------
;;; AXROT.LSP
;;;   Copyright (C) 1990 by Autodesk, Inc.
;;;
;;;   Permission to use, copy, modify, and distribute this software and
;;;   documentation for any purpose and without fee is hereby granted.
;;;
;;;   THIS SOFTWARE IS PROVIDED "AS IS" WITHOUT EXPRESS OR IMPLIED WAPP
;;;   ALL IMPLIED WARRANTIES OF FITNESS FOR ANY PARTICULAR PURPOSE AND
;;;   MERCHANTABILITY ARE HEREBY DISCLAIMED.
;;;
;;;   By Jan S. Yoder                                         May 11,
;;;   Modified for AutoCAD Rel 11                             July
;;; -------------------------------------------------------------
;;; DESCRIPTION
;;;
;;;   A routine to do 3 axis rotation of a selection set.
;;;
;;; ----------------------- Main program -----------------------

(defun c:axrot (/ axerr s olderr obpt oce ogm ohl oucsf ssel kwd dr bpt
  (if (and (= (getvar "cvport") 1) (= (getvar "tilemode") 0))
    (progn
      (prompt "\n *** Command not allowed in Paper space ***\n")
      (princ)
    )
    (progn
      ;; Internal error handler

      (defun axerr (s)                   ; If an error (such as CTRL-C) oc
        ;; while this command is active...
        (if (/= s "Function cancelled")
          (princ (strcat "\nError: " s))
        )
        (setq *error* olderr)            ; restore old *error* handler
        (setvar "gridmode" ogm)          ; restore saved modes
        (setvar "highlight" ohl)
        (setvar "ucsfollow" oucsf)
        (command "ucs" "restore" "_AXROT_")
        (command "ucs" "del" "_AXROT_")
        (command "undo" "e")             ; complete undo group
        (setvar "cmdecho" oce)
        (princ)
      )

      (setq olderr *error*
            *error* axerr)
      (setq oce (getvar "cmdecho")
            ogm (getvar "gridmode")
            ohl (getvar "highlight")
            oucsf (getvar "ucsfollow")
      )
      (setvar "cmdecho" 0)
      (command "undo" "group")
      (command "ucs" "save" "_AXROT_")
      (setvar "gridmode" 0)
      (setvar "ucsfollow" 0)
      (setq ssel (ssget))

      (if ssel
        (progn
          (setvar "highlight" 0)
          (initget 1 "X Y Z")
          (setq kwd (getkword "\nAxis of rotation X/Y/Z: "))
          (setq dr (getreal "\nDegrees of rotation <0>: "))
          (if (null dr)
            (setq dr 0)
          )
          (setq bpt (getpoint "\nBase point <0,0,0>: "))
          (if (null bpt)
            (setq bpt (list 0 0 0))
          )
          (setq bpt (trans bpt 1 0))
          (cond ((= kwd "X") (command "ucs" "Y" "90"))
            ((= kwd "Y") (command "ucs" "X" "-90"))
            ((= kwd "Z") (command "ucs" "Z" "0"))
          )
          (setq bpt (trans bpt 0 1))
          (command "rotate" ssel "" bpt dr)
          (command "ucs" "p")              ;restore previous ucs
          (command "'redrawall")
        )
        (princ "\nNothing selected. ")
      )
      (setvar "gridmode" ogm)            ;restore saved modes
      (setvar "highlight" ohl)
      (setvar "ucsfollow" oucsf)
      (command "ucs" "del" "_AXROT_")
      (command "undo" "e")               ;complete undo group
      (setvar "cmdecho" oce)
      (princ)
    )
  )
)
(princ "\n\tC:AXROT loaded.  Start command with AXROT.")
(princ)
;;; -------------------------------------------------------------
```

TABLE 42-1 AutoLISP Program Listing

DRAWING THE BOX

Let's start a new drawing and try out this program. Start a new drawing named "LISPTST". Use AutoCAD's 3-D capabilities to draw a cube similar to the one shown in Figure 42-1. You can do this by using the BOX command under the screen menu path, or the Draw/Surfaces.../3D Objects pull-down menus (the last is an icon box). As you draw the cube, you will notice that it appears only as a square in plan.

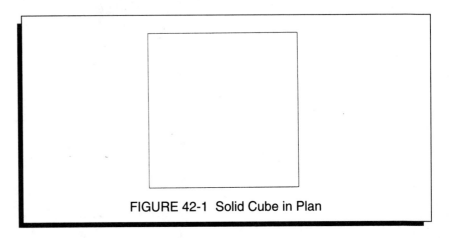

FIGURE 42-1 Solid Cube in Plan

```
Command: BOX
Corner of box: (enter a point on the screen)
Length: (move the crosshairs to show a length and press ENTER)
Cube/<Width>: C
Rotation angle about Z axis: 0
```

USING THE AXROT.LSP PROGRAM

Now let's use the Axrot LISP program. The first thing we have to do is load the program. You can load a LISP program in different ways. We will load this one from the command line. Enter the following exactly as listed, including the quotes and parentheses.

```
Command: (LOAD "AXROT")
```

If you entered the line correctly, you will see a short message that the program was loaded. Now that it is loaded, we can use the program as a command. Let's do this now.

```
Command: AXROT
Select objects: (select the cube)
Select objects: 1 selected, 1 found
Select objects: (press ENTER)
Axis of rotation X/Y/Z: X
Degrees of rotation <0>: 30
Base point <0,0,0>: (select a point about the center of the cube)
```

The box has rotated 30 degrees about the X-axis. Let's perform one more rotation. Press the ENTER key to repeat the command.

```
Command: AXROT
Select objects: (select the cube)
Select objects: 1 selected, 1 found
Select objects: (press ENTER)
Axis of rotation X/Y/Z: Y
Degrees of rotation <0>: 30
Base point <0,0,0>: (select a point about the center of the cube)
```

Your cube should now look similar to the one in Figure 42-2. Notice how you can see the rotations performed around the X- and Y-axes.

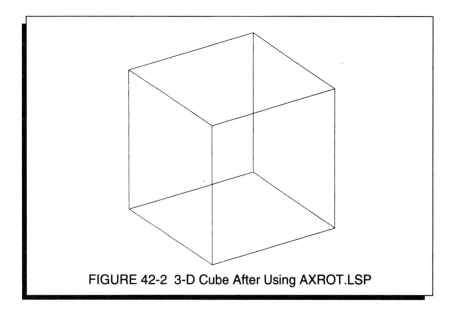

FIGURE 42-2 3-D Cube After Using AXROT.LSP

Now perform a Hide to see the cube more clearly.

CHAPTER REVIEW

1. Why would you program in AutoCAD with AutoLISP?

_____

_____

_____

2. What are some uses for AutoLISP?

_____

_____

_____

3. How would you load a LISP file named 3DARRAY.LSP while within an AutoCAD drawing?

_____

4. Describe an AutoLISP program that would be useful for you.

_____

_____

_____

CHAPTER 43

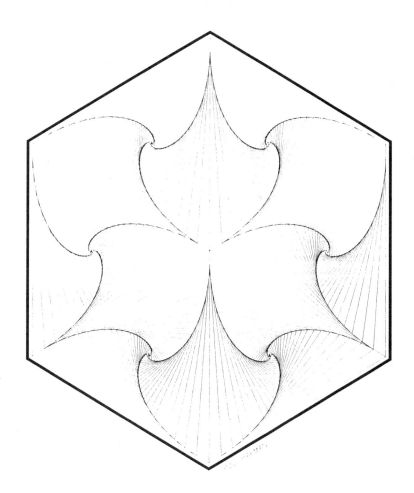

Programming in AutoLISP

OBJECTIVES:

To use AutoLISP, you must learn the available AutoLISP functions and the basics of programming in AutoLISP. The objectives of this chapter are:

● To learn the basics of programming in AutoLISP.

● To analyze a LISP program file.

● To learn how to use a LISP file inside of AutoCAD.

AUTOLISP BASICS

AutoLISP programming can range from the very simple to very complex functions. A LISP program is nothing more than a list of instructions. The LISP program embedded in AutoCAD contains many functions that can be used to perform the tasks you desire. Let's take a look at some of these.

ARITHMETIC FUNCTIONS

You can use LISP to perform math functions. Start an AutoCAD program of any name. We are going to enter some LISP routines directly at the command line.

At the command line, enter the following exactly. Be sure to include the parentheses.

> Command: (+ 5 4)
> 9

Notice how AutoCAD "returns" the value of 9. This simple routine adds the values of 5 and 4, then prints the sum of these to the screen. Continue and enter the following and notice the results of addition, subtraction, multiplication, and division.

> Command: (- 100 40)
>
> Command: (* 5 6)
>
> Command: (/ 100 20)

Notice how the LISP routine is entered at the command line using parentheses. The opening and closing parentheses are used to tell AutoLISP what is an AutoCAD or AutoLISP expression. If AutoCAD detects an opening parenthesis, the following expression is passed to AutoLISP. The expression ends with a closing parenthesis. The expressions you entered at the command line were started with an opening parenthesis, so AutoCAD knew it was an AutoLISP expression. The closing parenthesis denoted the end of the expression. Note how you could use a space between parts of the expression. If you were in AutoCAD, you could not do that.

If you get a "1>" return from AutoCAD, enter a closing parenthesis, then ENTER. This code means that there is not a closing parenthesis to match an opening parenthesis. There must always be an equal number of opening and closing parentheses. If you want to test this situation, re-enter one of the previous expressions, leaving off the closing parenthesis.

AUTOLISP AND AUTOCAD COMMANDS

An AutoCAD command can be used within an AutoLISP routine. To place a command with the routine, use the COMMAND function, followed by the AutoCAD command name in parentheses, then the proper "arguments." The arguments are the responses to the command prompts.

If the command requires user input, a pause can be placed within the routine. For example, if you wanted to draw a circle with the center at the absolute coordinate of 5,5 and then drag the circle to the desired radius, the following routine could be used.

> (command "circle" "5,5" pause)

If you try this routine, you will notice that the Circle command's prompts are "echoed" (displayed) to the command line. Notice also that the coordinate of 5,5 is placed in quotes. This is because it is the actual value and not a variable. There may be times that you do not wish to display these prompts. For example, if the routine contains all the inputs for the prompts, it is useless to show them.

The prompts can be suppressed by setting the CMDECHO variable within the expression. The following line can be included within a LISP routine to do this.

> (setvar "cmdecho" 0)

This line sets the AutoCAD variable Cmdecho to zero, which suppresses the command prompts. Appendix C contains a listing of AutoCAD variables.

SETQ FUNCTION

The SETQ function is used to assign a value. For example, we could assign values for A and B as follows.

> Command: (setq A 10)

Continue and assign a value for B.

> Command: (setq B 25)

Now let's use an arithmetic expression to use the values set for A and B.

> Command: (+ A B)
> 35

Notice how AutoCAD returned the value 35 for the sum of A and B.

GETTING AND STORING POINTS IN AUTOLISP

You can use AutoLISP to store a point that you enter as a coordinate or as a point selected on the drawing screen. For example, you may want to store a point with the Setq function for later use in the routine. You can do this with the GETPOINT function. We will use this function in an example later.

You can also get and store a distance. The GETDIST function is used to obtain a distance. The distance can either be entered as a numeric value or by showing AutoCAD two points on the drawing screen.

PLACING COMMAND PROMPTS WITHIN AUTOLISP

If you write your own LISP command routines, you may wish to create your own prompts. Prompts are placed within quotes (") inside the LISP routine. For example, the following line would prompt REFERENCE POINT: at the command line.

> (setvar "lastpoint" (getpoint "REFERENCE POINT:"))

USING NOTES WITHIN A ROUTINE

As you write LISP routines, you may want to include notes for your own purposes. A line that starts with a semicolon will not be executed as a part of the routine.

It is sometimes helpful to include a heading that describes the routine you are writing. We will use a decription when we write a LISP routine later in this chapter.

There are many more functions available in AutoLISP, but we will stop here and use the ones we have learned about. If you want to learn all the available functions, the AutoLISP Programmer's Reference contains a complete listing.

WRITING AND USING LISP

It's time to write, store, and use a simple LISP routine. Let's assume that you are a machine parts designer. You frequently draw parts that have drill holes of different diameters at a certain position on a plate. The position is always relative to a corner of the plate. You want to write a custom AutoCAD command to streamline your drawing process. The following LISP routine could be used. Let's look at the routine and analyze the functions.

```
;-------------------------------------------------------------
;DPCIR.LSP
;-------------------------------------------------------------
;DESCRIPTION
;
;Constructs a circle of a specified radius at a designated
;point from a reference position.
;-------------------------------------------------------------
;
  (defun C:DPCIR()
    (setvar "CMDECHO" 0)
    (setvar "lastpoint" (getpoint "Select Corner of box:"))
    (setq p1 (getpoint "\nEnter X,Y distance (using @):"))
    (setq p2 (getdist "\nEnter radius:"))
    (command "CIRCLE" p1 p2))

                        DPCIR.LSP
```

This routine is a simple ASCII text file. The file was arbitrarily named DPCIR.LSP for Designated Point Circle. Note that all LISP files have a .LSP file extension. The file is simply a collection of lines of LISP instructions. Let's discuss each section of the routine.

The first nine lines are preceded by a semicolon. This means they will not be processed as part of the routine. We used these lines to print a description of the file. This might be useful if we looked through a library of LISP routines later.

We then used Define Function (Defun) to define a new command named DPCIR. This will allow us to use the routine as we would a regular AutoCAD command.

The next line sets the variable Cmdecho to 0. We did this because we do not want the prompts for the Circle command, which occurs later, to be displayed.

Next we used the system variable LASTPOINT (see Appendix C for explanations of this and all system variables) to set a reference point to locate our circle. If you remember, this reference point is to be the corner of the plate. We used the Getpoint function to obtain this point and included the prompt: "Select Corner Of Plate:".

We next used the Setq function to store a value of a point we arbitrarily named "p1". The point for p1 was obtained with the Getpoint function and we included a prompt for a relative coordinate.

Next we used Setq again to store a value for the point named "p2". This time we used the Getdist function to obtain this distance. We also included a prompt for the radius distance.

Finally, we used the Circle command. The values p1 and p2 are the arguments for the prompts that the Circle command issues (center point and radius).

If we wanted to enhance the routine, we could have used the Setvar routine to set the object snap to INTersection when we captured the plate corner, then set the object snap back to NONE. The great part of LISP programming is that you can write the command to suit yourself!

USING THE LISP ROUTINE

Let's try the LISP program we just looked at. The first step is to create a file named DPCIR.LSP. To do this, use a text processor in "non-document" mode. This means that the file must be all ASCII text. You can also use Edlin. Name the file DPCIR.LSP. Type each line exactly as it is printed, then save the file and copy it to the directory where you have stored the AutoCAD program.

Next, enter AutoCAD and start a drawing of any name. Let's now load the LISP program.

> Command: (LOAD "DPCIR")

If you get an error message, go back and check the contents of your file to verify that you copied it exactly as written. If the loading was successful, AutoCAD should return "C:DPCIR".

Now let's use the program. Draw a square that is 5 units on each side. Now let's place our drill hole. Use your DPCIR routine as a regular command.

> Command: DPCIR
> Select corner of box: (*select the lower left corner*)
> Enter X,Y distance (using @): @2,2
> Enter radius: .5

IN CONCLUSION

Writing routines in AutoLISP takes time and practice to learn. The effective use of the LISP programming techniques can be further explored in many excellent books dedicated to this purpose.

CHAPTER REVIEW

1. Write a LISP routine that will multiply 2 times 4.

   _____

2. What does "n>" mean when "n" is a number?

   _____

   _____

3. How can an AutoCAD command be used within a LISP routine?

   _____

   _____

   _____

4. How would you suppress the command prompts from an AutoCAD command contained within a LISP file?

   _____

   _____

   _____

5. What does the Setq function do?

   _____

   _____

   _____

SECTION VII

APPENDICES

APPENDIX A—PROFESSIONAL CAD TECHNIQUES

Studying and learning the commands in this book are only a start toward becoming a professional CAD operator. Using the proper techniques is just as important. The following is a list of items which should be followed to obtain the most from your expertise.

Learn every command. Most CAD operators tend to learn just enough to get by. If this is your intention, stick with your pencil. You will not realize the full benefits of time savings and more professional results. Force yourself to use each command. This is best accomplished by introducing yourself to each new command and using it until you are comfortable with it. Some of the parts of AutoCAD that appear the hardest to learn become easy with just a little practice!

Practice, Practice, Practice! Efficiency on a CAD system comes with practice. (Doesn't it also take practice to perform good board drafting?) Never pass up the opportunity to spend time with a system. After you are comfortable with the commands you are presently using, try new ones. Before long, you will be constructing drawings with ease!

Plan your approach. Never just start drawing. There are hundreds of approaches to every drawing when you are using CAD. The time savings you will realize will come from your technique, not your speed. Drawing faster dosen't mean working harder or faster, it means working smarter. This program has some amazing capabilities, let it work for you!

Use layers. If you are drawing a set of house plans, don't draw the floor plan more than once. Use the layering system to use the plan for each drawing that requires it. The electrical, plumbing, HVAC, lighting, framing, dimensions, furniture, and other plans can exist on each layer.

Use blocks. Never draw anything twice! If you have drawn it once, write-block it. Before long, you will have a nice library to draw from. The drawings may be transferred onto a library disk for later use. If you build a large enough library of the drawings of your trade, you will soon be assembling more than you will be drawing.

Set up a tablet menu. Set up a tablet menu that contains all the commands that you normally use in your work. Be sure to include any blocks that are normally utilized in your work. This allows you to choose the commands and drawing parts quickly.

Buy proper equipment. Don't try to save money on brain surgery and CAD equipment. You will purchase a CAD station to save time (i.e., money). If the equipment doesn't suit the job, you won't obtain the savings and may end up not using it at all. It is cheaper to buy the proper equipment than it is to replace it later!

Set up a proper workstation. Like any other type of job, the proper work setup is essential. If you have purchased the right equipment, plan a proper setting for it. A little planning will make your work day (or those of your employees) more efficient.

Be patient. Your first few months with CAD won't save you all the time that you had anticipated. It will come! After a while, you will notice that your speed has increased dramatically. This time period will vary with each individual and each task. It is normal to experience a learning curve, but don't get discouraged, it shouldn't last too long.

Designate a key operator. If you are using a multi-station CAD setup, assign one person the task of coordinating all operations. This person will emerge soon after you install the system. Some people just seem to gravitate to the position. This will soon become a very valuable employee.

Keep pushing! Don't ever stop experimenting with ways to streamline your graphics procedures. Every task is different, with many ways to approach it. One of the advantages of a CAD system is the ability to customize it to your specific needs. With the ability of AutoCAD, your real challenge is to discover the ways it can serve you best!

Use Zooms. Zoom in to a drawing to perform detail work. Don't attempt to draw complicated parts when the display shows the work in small scale.

Run check plots. Run periodic check plots to check your work. You will also obtain a feel for the scale of the finished work. Use the dot matrix printer for inexpensive plots. Use a pen plotter with a felt tip pen for a "dress rehearsal" before plotting the final work.

Use both CAD and traditional techniques. You will soon learn which work CAD is best for and which work traditional methods are best for. Use a combination of both by hand drafting over plots. Sometimes it is best to lay out your drawing in rough form by hand, then digitizing the base drawing in and finishing with CAD.

Use Copy and Array. Use the Copy and Array commands for repeated work. Never, never draw the same thing twice!

Standardize. Standardize your own procedures and those of your office for CAD use. Create standards for base drawing layers, text sizes, fonts, linetypes, and other operations. Not only will your work be consistent, but your drawing operations will be easier to perform.

APPENDIX B — COMMAND SUMMARY

About
Displays AutoCAD information dialogue box that includes version and serial numbers, Acad.Msg text, and other information.

Aperture
Adjusts the size of the target box used with object snap.

Arc
Permits drawing of arcs using different parameters.

Area
Computes area and perimeter of a polygon.

Array
Makes multiple copies of an object or group of objects.

Attdef
Creates an attribute definition.

Attdisp
Controls whether the attributes are displayed.

Attedit
Used for editing attributes.

Attext
Allows attribute entities to be removed from a drawing and written to another disk for use with another program.

Audit
A diagnostic command used to examine and/or correct errors in a drawing file.

Base
Specifies point of origin for insertion into another drawing.

Bhatch
Used to fill an automatically defined boundary; the use of a dialogue box allows preview and adjustment without starting over.

Blipmode
Controls whether a marker blip is displayed on the screen when picking a point.

Block
Forms a complex object from a group of separate entities in a drawing.

Bpoly
Draws a closed boundary polyline.

Break
Erases part of an entity or breaks it into two entities.

Chamfer
Trims two intersecting lines and connects the two trimmed lines with a chamfer line.

Change
Permits modification of an entity's characteristics.

Chprop
Similar to the Change command, except only the properties (linetype, color, etc.) of the entity are affected.

Circle
Draws any size circles.

Color (or Colour)
Used to set a new color for all subsequently drawn entities.

Compile
Used to compile shape and font files.

Config
Allows configuration of peripheral devices and operating parameters.

Copy
Copies selected objects.

Dblist
Provides database information of a drawing.

Ddattdef
Displays attribute definition dialogue box.

Ddatte
Displays attribute editing dialogue box.

Ddattext
Displays attribute extraction dialogue box.

Ddchprop
Displays change properties dialogue box.

Ddedit
Displays attribute edit dialogue box.

Ddemodes
Displays current properties dialogue box.

Ddgrips
Displays grips dialogue box.

Ddim
Displays a series of dimension control dialogue boxes.

Ddinsert
Displays insert dialogue box.

Ddlmodes
Displays the layer control dialogue box.

Ddosnap
Displays running object snap dialogue box.

Ddrename
Displays rename dialogue box.

Ddrmodes
Displays drawing aids and modes dialogue box.

Ddselect
Displays entity selection dialogue box.

Dducs
Displays UCS dialogue box.

Ddunits

Displays units control dialogue box.

Delay

Allows for delay between operations in a script file.

Dim

Semi-automatic dimensioning capabilities.

Dim1

Enters a single dimension then exitsback to the Command: prompt.

Dist

Computes the distance between two points.

Divide

Divides an entity into an equal number of parts and places either a specified block or a point entity at the division points on the entity.

Donut (or Doughnut)

Constructs solid filled circles and doughnuts.

Dragmode

Permits dynamic dragging of an entity to the desired position on the display.

Dtext

Allows you to place text on the screen and view it in place as it is entered.

Dview

Used to display a 3-D view dynamically.

Dxbin

Creates binary drawing interchange files.

Dxfin

Converts an interchange file into an AutoCAD file.

Dxfout

Allows an AutoCAD file to be reformatted for use with another program.

Edgesurf

Draws an edge-defined surface.

Elev

Sets current elevation and thickness.

Ellipse

Used to construct ellipses.

End

Saves the drawing file and exits the drawing editor.

Erase

Removes entities from a drawing.

Explode

Breaks down a block into the individual entities from which it was constructed; breaks down a Polyline into lines and arcs.

Extend

Used to extend objects in a drawing to meet a boundary object.

Files
Allows user to perform file utility tasks while in the drawing editor.

Fill
Creates solid fill in a closed polygon.

Fillet
Connects two lines with an arc.

Filmroll
Produces a filmroll file for AutoShade.

Graphscr
Display control function for single-screen systems which allows user to toggle to graphics screen.

Grid
Displays grid of specified spacing.

Handles
Turns on or off the assignment of unique "handle" numbers for each entity.

Hatch
Performs crosshatching of an area with a specified pattern.

Help (or ?)
Displays a list of AutoCAD commands with detailed information available.

Hide
Removes hidden lines from the currently displayed view.

Id
Displays the position of a point in X,Y coordinates.

Igesin
Converts an existing IGES file to an AutoCAD drawing.

Igesout
Converts an AutoCAD drawing to an IGES file.

Insert
Inserts a block or another drawing into the current drawing.

Isoplane
Allows user to select another isoplane.

Layer
Creates or switches drawing layers and assigns linetypes and colors to them.

Limits
Sets the drawing boundaries.

Line
Draws a straight line.

Linetype
Lists, creates, or modifies linetype definitions or loads them for use in a drawing.

List
Displays database information for a single entity in a drawing.

Load
Loads a shape file into a drawing.

Ltscale
Specifies a scale for all linetypes in a drawing.

Measure
Places point entities at a specified distance on an object.

Menu
Loads a menu of AutoCAD commands into the menu area.

Minsert
Used to make multiple inserts of a block.

Mirror
Creates a mirror image of an entity.

Move
Moves an entity from one location to another.

Mslide
Creates a slide of the current display.

Mspace
Used to switch to model space.

Multiple
When used before a command, causes the command to repeat after each use.

Mview
Used in paper space to create and manipulate viewports.

New
Used to create a new drawing.

Offset
Constructs a parallel copy to an entity or constructs a larger or smaller image of the entity through a point.

Oops
Restores entities that were accidentally erased with the previous command.

Open
Used to open an existing drawing.

Ortho
Causes all lines to be drawn orthogonally with the set snap rotation angle.

Osnap
Allows geometric points of existing objects to be easily located.

Pan
Moves the display window for viewing a different part of the drawing without changing the magnification.

Pedit
Permits editing of polylines.

Pface
Constructs a polygon mesh that is defined by the location of each vertex in the mesh.

Plan
Returns to the current UCS plan view.

Pline

(Polylines) Lines of specified width which can be manipulated.

Plot

Plots a drawing with a pen printer plotter.

Point

Draws a specified point.

Polygon

Used to draw a regular polygon with a specified number of sides.

Psdrag

Controls the scale and position of an imported PostScript image that is being dragged into place.

Psfill

Allows 2-D polylines to be filled with PostScript fill patterns.

Psin

Used to import EPS (Encapsulated PostScript) files.

Psout

Used to export the current view of a drawing to an EPS (Encapsulated PostScript) file.

Pspace

Used to switch to paper space.

Purge

Selectively deletes unused blocks, layers, or linetypes.

Qsave

Command that saves the drawing without requesting a file name.

Qtext

Permits text entities to be drawn as rectangles.

Quit

Exits the drawing editor without saving the updated drawing.

Recover

Used to attempt recovery of corrupted or damaged files.

Redefine

Restores AutoCAD's definition of a command.

Redo

Restores operations deleted by the Undo command.

Redraw

Cleans up the display.

Redrawall

Performs a redraw in all viewports.

Regen

Causes the entire drawing to be regenerated and redraws the screen.

Regenall

Performs a regeneration in all viewports.

Regenauto

Allows the user to control whether the drawing is automatically regenerated.

Reinit

Reinitializes the I/O ports, digitizer, display, plotter, and PGP file.

Rename

Allows name changes of blocks, linetypes, layers, or text style.

Revsurf

Draws a revolved surface.

Rotate

Rotates an entity or a group of entities around a specified center point.

Rscript

Forces a script to be restarted from the beginning.

Rulesurf

Draws a ruled surface.

Save

Saves an updated drawing without exiting out of the drawing editor.

Saveas

Saves the current drawing under a different specified name.

Scale

Changes the scale of an entity or entities.

Script

Allows user to invoke a script file while in the drawing editor.

Select

Used to preselect objects to be edited.

Setvar

Used to change AutoCAD's system variables.

Sh

Used to execute external commands when there is not sufficient memory to execute the Shell command.

Shade

Creates a fast shade of a 3-D object, similar to the fast shade option in AutoShade.

Shape

Places shapes from a shape file into a drawing.

Shell

Permits the execution of utility commands while in the drawing editor.

Sketch

Allows freehand sketching as a part of the drawing.

Snap

Allows user to turn snap on or off, change the snap resolution, set different spacing for the X and Y axis, or rotate the grid, and set isometric mode.

Solid

Draws filled in polygons.

Status

Displays a status screen containing information about the current drawing.

Stretch
Move selected objects while allowing their connections to other objects in the drawing to remain unchanged.

Style
Creates and modifies text styles.

Tablet
Permits alignment of digitizer with existing drawing coordinates.

Tabsurf
Draws a tabulated surface.

Text
Allows text to be entered into a drawing.

Textscr
Display control function for single-screen systems which allows user to toggle to text screen.

Time
Keeps track of time functions for each drawing.

Trace
Draws lines of a specified width.

Treestat
Displays drawing information on the current spatial index.

Trim
Trims objects in a drawing by defining other objects as cutting edges then specifying the part of the object to be cut from between them.

U
Used to undo the most recent command.

UCS
Used to manipulate the User Coordinate System.

UCSicon
Controls the on-screen display of the UCS icon indicator.

Undefine
Disables a command.

Undo
Used to undo several command moves in a single operation.

Units
Allows the user to select display format and precision of that format.

View
Saves the display as a view or displays a named view.

Viewres
Controls the fast zoom mode and resolution for circle and arc regenerations.

Vplayer
Controls the visibility of the individual viewport layers.

Vpoint
Sets the view point from which the user will see the drawing.

Vports (or Viewports)
Sets the number and configuration of viewports displayed on the screen.

Vslide
Allows user to view a slide file.

Wblock
Writes entities to a new drawing file.

Xbind
Binds externally referenced drawings, converting them to blocks in the master drawing.

Xref
Used to place an externally referenced drawing into a master drawing.

Zoom
Allows user to increase or decrease the size of the display for viewing purposes.

3Dface
Creates a solid face in a defined plane.

3Dmesh
Draws a 3-D mesh.

3Dpoly
Draws a three-dimensional polyline.

Variable name	Type	Saved in	Meaning
ACADPREFIX	String		The directory path, if any, specified by the ACAD environment variable, with path separators appended if necessary (read-only)
ACADVER	String		This is the AutoCAD version number, which can have values like "12" or "12a" (read-only). Note that this differs from the DXF file $ACADVER header variable, which contains the drawing database level number
AFLAGS	Integer		Attribute flags bit-code for ATTDEF command (sum of the following): 0 = No Attribute mode selected 1 = Invisible 2 = Constant 4 = Verify 8 = Preset
ANGBASE	Real	Drawing	Angle 0 direction (with respect to the current UCS)
ANGDIR	Integer	Drawing	1 = clockwise angles, 0 = counterclockwise (with respect to the current UCS)
APERTURE	Integer	Config	Object snap target height, in pixels (default value = 10)
AREA	Real		Last area computed by AREA, LIST, or DBLIST (read-only)
ATTDIA	Integer	Drawing	1 causes the Insert command to use a dialogue box for entry of Attribute values; 0 to issue prompts
ATTMODE	Integer	Drawing	Attribute display mode (0 = off, 1 = normal, 2 = on)
ATTREQ	Integer	Drawing	0 assumes defaults for the values of all Attributes during Insert of Blocks; 1 enables prompts (or dialogue box) for Attribute values, as selected by ATTDIA
AUDITCTL	Integer	Config	Controls whether an *.adt* log file (audit report file) is created 0 = Disables (or prevents) the writing of *.adt* log files 1 = Enables the writing of *.adt* log files by the AUDIT command
AUNITS	Integer	Drawing	Angular units mode (0 = decimal degrees, 1 = degrees/minutes/seconds, 2 = grads, 3 = radians, 4 = surveyor's units)
AUPREC	Integer	Drawing	Angular units decimal places
BACKZ	Real	Drawing	Back clipping plane offset from the target plane for the current viewport, in drawing units. Meaningful only if the Back clipping bit in VIEWMODE is on. The distance of the back clipping plane from the camera point can be found by subtracting BACKZ from the camera-to-target distance (read-only)
BLIPMODE	Integer	Drawing	Marker blips on if 1, off if 0
CDATE	Real		Calendar date/time (read-only) (special format; see later)

Variable name	Type	Saved in	Meaning
CECOLOR	String	Drawing	Sets the color for new entities
CELTYPE	String	Drawing	Sets the linetype for new entities
CHAMFERA	Real	Drawing	Sets the first chamfer distance
CHAMFERB	Real	Drawing	Sets the second chamfer distance
CIRCLERAD	Real		Sets the default circle radius. To specify no default, enter 0 (zero)
CLAYER	String	Drawing	Sets the current layer
CMDACTIVE	Integer		Bit-code that indicates whether an ordinary command, transparent command, script, or dialogue box is active (read-only). It is the sum of the following: 1 = Ordinary command is active 2 = Ordinary command and a transparent command are active 4 = Script is active 8 = Dialogue box is active
CMDDIA	Integer	Config	1 = Use dialogue boxes for PLOT command; 0 = don't use dialogue boxes for PLOT command
CMDECHO	Integer		When the AutoLISP (command) function is used, prompts and input are echoed if this variable is 1, but not if it is 0
CMDNAMES	String		Displays in English the name of the command (and transparent command) that is currently active. For example: LINE'ZOOM indicates that the ZOOM command is being used transparently during the LINE command
COORDS	Integer	Drawing	If 0, coordinate display is updated on point picks only. If 1, display of absolute coordinates is continuously updated. If 2, distance and angle from last point are displayed when a distance or angle is requested
CVPORT	Integer	Drawing	The identification number of the current viewport
DATE	Real		Julian date/time (read-only) (special format; see later)
DBMOD	Integer		Bit-code that indicates the drawing modification status (read-only). It is the sum of the following: 1 = Entity database modified 2 = Symbol table modified 4 = Database variable modified 8 = Window modified 16 = View modified
DIASTAT	Integer		Dialogue box exit status. If 0, the most recent dialogue box was exited via "CANCEL." If 1, the most recent dialogue box was exited via "OK" (read-only)

Variable name	Type	Saved in	Meaning
DIMxxx	Assorted	Drawing	All the dimensioning variables are also accessible as system variables. See chapter 11 for descriptions of these variables
DISTANCE	Real		Distance computed by DIST command (read-only)
DONUTID	Real		Default donut inside diameter, can be zero
DONUTOD	Real		Default donut outside diameter. Must be nonzero. If DONUTID is larger than DONUTOD, the two values are swapped by the next command
DRAGMODE	Integer	Drawing	0 = no dragging, 1 = on if requested, 2 = auto
DRAGP1	Integer	Config	Regen-drag input sampling rate; (default value = 10)
DRAGP2	Integer	Config	Fast-drag input sampling rate; (default value = 25)
DWGCODEPAGE	String	Drawing	Drawing code page. This variable is set to the system code page when a new drawing is created, but otherwise AutoCAD doesn't maintain it. It should reflect the code page of the drawing and you can set it to any of the values used by the SYSCODEPAGE system variable (see page 585) or "undefined." It is saved in the header
DWGNAME	String		Drawing name as entered by the user. If the drawing hasn't been named yet, DWGNAME reports that it is "unnamed". If the user specified a drive/directory prefix, it is included as well (read-only)
DWGPREFIX	String		Drive/directory prefix for drawing (read-only)
DWGTITLED	Integer		Bit-code that indicates whether the current drawing has been named. (read-only) 0 = The drawing hasn't been named 1 = The drawing has been named
DWGWRITE	Integer		Controls the initial state of the read-only toggle in the OPEN command's "Open Drawing" standard file dialogue box 0 = Opens the drawing for reading only 1 = Opens the drawing for reading and writing. The default is 1
ELEVATION	Real	Drawing	Current 3D elevation, relative to the current UCS for the current space
ERRNO	Integer		Code for errors caused by on-line programs such as AutoLISP and ADS applications (see *ADS Programmer's Reference Manual*)
EXPERT	Integer		Controls the issuance of certain "Are you sure?" prompts, as indicated next: 0 = Issues all prompts normally 1 = Suppresses "About to regen, proceed?" and "Really want to turn the current layer off?" 2 = Suppresses the preceding prompts and BLOCK's "Block already defined. Redefine it?" and SAVE/WBLOCK's "A drawing with this name already exists. Overwrite it?"

Variable name	Type	Saved in	Meaning
			3 = Suppresses the preceding prompts and those issued by LINETYPE if you try to load a linetype that's already loaded or create a new linetype in a file that already defines it
			4 = Suppresses the preceding prompts and those issued by "UCS Save" and "VPORTS Save" if the name you supply already exists
			5 = Suppresses the preceding prompts and those issued by "DIM SAVE" and "DIM OVERRIDE" if the dimension style name you supply already exists (the entries are redefined)
			When a prompt is suppressed by EXPERT, the operation in question is performed as though you had responded Y to the prompt. In the future, values greater than 5 may be used to suppress additional safety prompts. The setting of EXPERT can affect scripts, menu macros, AutoLISP, and the command functions. The default value is 0
EXTMAX	3D point	Drawing	Upper-right point of drawing extents. Expands outward as new objects are drawn, shrinks only by ZOOM All or ZOOM Extents. Reported in World coordinates for the current space (read-only)
EXTMIN	3D point	Drawing	Lower-left point of drawing extents. Expands outward as new objects are drawn, shrinks only by ZOOM All or ZOOM Extents. Reported in World coordinates for the current space (read-only)
FILEDIA	Integer	Config	1 = Use file dialogue boxes if possible; 0 = don't use file dialogue boxes unless requested via ~ (tilde)
FILLETRAD	Real	Drawing	Fillet radius
FILLMODE	Integer	Drawing	Fill mode on if 1, off if 0
FRONTZ	Real	Drawing	Front clipping plane offset from the target plane for the current viewport, in drawing units. Meaningful only if the front clipping bit in VIEWMODE is On and the Front clip not at eye bit is also On. The distance of the front clipping plane from the camera point can be found by subtracting FRONTZ from the camera-to-target distance (read-only)
GRIDMODE	Integer	Drawing	1 = grid on for current viewport; 0 = grid off
GRIDUNIT	2D point	Drawing	Grid spacing for current viewport, X and Y
GRIPBLOCK	Integer	Config	Controls the assignment of grips in blocks 0 = Assigns grip only to the insertion point of the block. The default value is 0 1 = Assigns grips to entities within the block
GRIPCOLOR	Integer (1–255)	Config	Color of nonselected grips; drawn as a box outline. Its default value is 5
GRIPHOT	Integer (1–255)	Config	Color of selected grips; drawn as a filled box. The default value is 1

Variable name	Type	Saved in	Meaning
GRIPS	Integer	Config	Allows the use of selection set grips for the Stretch, Move, Rotate, Scale, and Mirror modes 0 = Disables grips. 1 = Enables grips. The default value is 1. To adjust the size of the grips, use the GRIPSIZE variable. To adjust the effective pick area used by the graphics cursor when you snap to a grip, use the GRIPSIZE system variable
GRIPSIZE	Integer (1–255)	Config	The size in pixels of the box drawn to display the grip. The default value is 3
HANDLES	Integer	Drawing	If 0, entity handles are disabled. If 1, handles are on (read-only)
HIGHLIGHT	Integer		Object selection highlighting on if 1, off if 0. HIGH-LIGHT does not affect objects selected with grips
HPANG	Real		Default hatch pattern angle
HPDOUBLE	Integer		Default hatch pattern doubling for "U" user-defined patterns. 0 = Disables doubling 1 = Enables doubling
HPNAME	String		Default hatch pattern name. Up to 34 characters, no spaces allowed. Returns "" if there is no default. Enter . (period) to set no default
HPSCALE	Real		Default hatch pattern scale factor. Must be nonzero
HPSPACE	Real		Default hatch pattern line spacing for "U" user-defined simple patterns. Must be nonzero
INSBASE	3D point	Drawing	Insertion base point (set by BASE command) expressed in UCS coordinates for the current space
INSNAME	String		Default block name for DDINSERT or INSERT. The name must conform to symbol naming conventions. Returns "" if there is no default. Enter . (period) to set no default
LASTANGLE	Real		The end angle of the last arc entered, relative to the XY plane of the current UCS for the current space (read-only)
LASTPOINT	3D point		The last point entered, expressed in UCS coordinates for the current space. Referenced by @ during keyboard entry
LENSLENGTH	Real	Drawing	Length of the lens (in millimeters) used in perspective viewing, for the current viewport (read-only)
LIMCHECK	Integer	Drawing	Limits checking for the current space. On if 1, off if 0
LIMMAX	2D point	Drawing	Upper-right drawing limits for the current space, expressed in World coordinates
LIMMIN	2D point	Drawing	Lower-left drawing limits for the current space, expressed in World coordinates
LOGINNAME	String		Displays the user's name as configured or input when AutoCAD is loaded (read-only)

Variable name	Type	Saved in	Meaning
LTSCALE	Real	Drawing	Global linetype scale factor
LUNITS	Integer	Drawing	Linear units mode (1 = scientific, 2 = decimal, 3 = engineering, 4 =architectural, 5 = fractional)
LUPREC	Integer	Drawing	Linear units decimal places or denominator
MACROTRACE	Integer		Debugging tool for DIESEL expressions (see the *AutoCAD Customization Manual* for details) 0 = Disables MACROTRACE. Default is 0 1 = Displays an evaluation of all DIESEL expressions in the command line area, including an evaluation of expressions used in menus and the status line
MAXACTVP	Integer		Maximum number of viewports to regenerate at one time
MAXSORT	Integer	Config	Maximum number of symbol/file names to be sorted by listing commands. If the total number of items exceeds this number, then none of the items are sorted (default value=200)
MENUCTL	Integer	Config	Controls the page switching of the screen menu 0 = Screen menu doesn't switch pages in response to keyboard command entry 1 = Screen menu switches pages in response to key-board command entry. The default value is 1
MENUECHO	Integer		Menu echo/prompt control bits (sum of the following): 1 = Suppresses echo of menu items (^P in a menu item toggles echoing) 2 = Suppresses printing of system prompts during menu 4 = Disables ^P toggle of menu echoing 8 = Debugging aid for DIESEL macros. Prints input/-output strings The default value is 0 (all menu items and system prompts are displayed)
MENUNAME	String	Drawing	The name of the currently loaded menu file. Includes a drive/path prefix if you entered it (read-only)
MIRRTEXT	Integer	Drawing	MIRROR command reflects text if nonzero; retains text direction if 0
MODEMACRO	String		Allows you to display a text string in the status line, such as the name of the current drawing, time/date stamp, or special modes. You can use MODEMACRO to display a simple string of text, or use special text strings written in the DIESEL macro language to have AutoCAD evaluate the macro from time to time and base the status line on user-selected conditions. See the *AutoCAD Customization Manual* for details
OFFSETDIST	Real		Sets the default offset distance. If you enter a negative value, it defaults to Through mode
ORTHOMODE	Integer	Drawing	Ortho mode on if 1, off if 0

Variable name	Type	Saved in	Meaning
OSMODE	Integer	Drawing	Sets object snap modes using the following bit codes. To specify more than one osnap, enter the sum of their values. For example, entering 3 specifies the Endpoint (1) and Midpoint (2) osnaps 0 = None 32 = Intersection 1 = Endpoint 64 = Insertion 2 = Midpoint 128 = Perpendicular 4 = Center 256 = Tangent 8 = Node 512 = Nearest 16 = Quadrant 1024 = Quick
PDMODE	Integer	Drawing	Point entity display mode
PDSIZE	Real	Drawing	Point entity display size
PERIMETER	Real		Perimeter computed by AREA, LIST, or DBLIST (read-only)
PFACEVMAX	Integer		Maximum number of vertices per face (read-only)
PICKADD	Integer	Config	Controls additive selection of entities 0 = Disables PICKADD. The most recently selected entities, either by an individual pick or windowing, become the selection set. Previously selected entities are removed from the selection set. You can add more entities to the selection set, however, by holding down [Shift] while selecting 1 = Enables PICKADD. Each entity you select, either individually or by windowing, is added to the current selection set. To remove entities from the selection set, hold down [Shift] while selecting. The default value of PICKADD is 1
PICKAUTO	Integer	Config	Controls automatic windowing when the Select objects: prompt appears. 0 = Disables PICKAUTO. 1 = Allows you to draw a selection window (both window and crossing window) automatically at the Select objects: prompt. The default is 1
PICKBOX	Integer	Config	Object selection target height, in pixels
PICKDRAG	Integer	Config	Controls the method of drawing a selection window 0 = You draw the selection window by clicking the mouse at one corner, and then at the other corner. The default value is 0 1 = You draw the selection window by clicking at one corner, holding down the mouse button, dragging, and releasing the mouse button at the other corner
PICKFIRST	Integer	Config	Controls the method of entity selection so that you can select objects first, and then use an edit/inquiry command 0 = Disables PICKFIRST 1 = Enables PICKFIRST. The default value is 1

Variable name	Type	Saved in	Meaning
PLATFORM	String		Read-only message that indicates which version of AutoCAD is in use. This is a string such as one of the following: Microsoft Windows Sun4/SPARCstation 386 DOS Extender DECstation Apple Macintosh Silicon Graphics Iris Indigo
PLINEGEN	Integer	Drawing	Sets the linetype pattern generation around the vertices of a 2D Polyline. When set to 1, PLINEGEN causes the linetype to be generated in a continuous pattern around the vertices of the Polyline. When set to 0, Polylines are generated with the linetype to start and end with a dash at each vertex. PLINEGEN doesn't apply to Polylines with tapered segments
PLINEWID	Real	Drawing	Default polyline width. It can be zero
PLOTID	String	Config	Changes the default plotter, based on its assigned description
PLOTTER	Integer	Config	Changes the default plotter, based on its assigned integer (0–maximum configured). You can create up to 29 configurations
POLYSIDES	Integer		Default number of sides for the POLYGON command. The range is 3–1024
POPUPS	Integer		1 if the currently configured display driver supports dialogue boxes, the menu bar, pull-down menus, and icon menus. 0 if these features are not available (read-only)
PSLTSCALE	Integer	Drawing	Controls paper space linetype scaling 0 = No special linetype scaling 1 = Viewport scaling governs linetype scaling
PSPROLOG	String	Config	Assigns a name for a prologue section to be read from the *acad.psf* file when using the PSOUT command. See the *AutoCAD Customization Manual* for details
PSQUALITY	Integer	Config	Controls the rendering quality of PostScript images and whether they are drawn as filled objects or as outlines. A zero setting disables PostScript image generation and a nonzero setting enables PostScript generation Positive setting: Sets the number of pixels per AutoCAD drawing unit for the PostScript resolution Negative setting: Still sets the number of pixels per drawing unit, but uses the absolute value. Causes AutoCAD to show the PostScript paths as outlines and doesn't fill them
QTEXTMODE	Integer	Drawing	Quick text mode on if 1, off if 0
REGENMODE	Integer	Drawing	REGENAUTO on if 1, off if 0
RE-INIT	Integer		Reinitializes the I/O ports, digitizer, display, plotter, and *acad.pgp* file using the following bit codes. To specify more than one reinitialization, enter the sum of their values, for example, 3 to specify both digitizer port (1) and plotter port (2) reinitialitzation

Variable name	Type	Saved in	Meaning
			1 = Digitizer port reinitialization
			2 = Plotter port reinitialization
			4 = Digitizer reinitialization
			8 = Display reinitialization
			16 = PGP file reinitialization (reload)
SAVEFILE	String	Config	Current auto-save filename (read-only)
SAVENAME	String		The filename you save the drawing to (read-only)
SAVETIME	Integer	Config	Automatic save interval, in minutes (or 0 to disable automatic saves). The SAVETIME timer starts as soon as you make a change to a drawing, and is reset and restarts by a manual SAVE, SAVEAS, or QSAVE. The current drawing is saved to *auto.sv$*.
SCREENBOXES	Integer	Config	The number of boxes in the screen menu area of the graphics area. If the screen menu is disabled (configured off), SCREENBOXES is zero. On platforms that permit the AutoCAD graphics window to be resized or the screen menu to be reconfigured during an editing session, the value of this variable might change during the editing session. (read-only)
SCREENMODE	Integer	Config	A (read-only) bit code indicating the graphics/text state of the AutoCAD display. It is the sum of the following bit values: 0 = text screen is displayed 1 = graphics mode is displayed 2 = dual-screen display configuration
SCREENSIZE	2D point		Current viewport size in pixels, X and Y (read-only)
SHADEDGE	Integer	Drawing	0 = faces shaded, edges not highlighted 1 = faces shaded, edges drawn in background color 2 = faces not filled, edges in entity color 3 = faces in entity color, edges in background color
SHADEDIF	Integer	Drawing	Ratio of diffuse reflective light to ambient light (in percent of diffuse reflective light)
SHPNAME	String		Default shape name. Must conform to symbol naming conventions. If no default is set, it returns a "". Enter . (period) to set no default
SKETCHINC	Real	Drawing	SKETCH record increment
SKPOLY	Integer	Drawing	SKETCH generates lines if 0, Polylines if 1
SNAPANG	Real	Drawing	Snap/grid rotation angle (UCS-relative) for the current viewport
SNAPBASE	2D point	Drawing	Snap/grid origin point for the current viewport (in UCS X,Y coordinates)
SNAPISOPAIR	Integer	Drawing	Current isometric plane (0 = left, 1 = top, 2 = right) for the current viewport
SNAPMODE	Integer	Drawing	1 = snap on for current viewport; 0 = snap off

Variable name	Type	Saved in	Meaning
SNAPSTYL	Integer	Drawing	Snap style for current viewport (0 = standard, 1 = isometric)
SNAPUNIT	2D point	Drawing	Snap spacing for current viewport, X and Y
SORTENTS	Integer	Config	Controls the display of entity sort order operations using the following codes. To select more than one, enter the sum of their codes, for example, enter 3 to specify codes 1 and 2. The default, 96, specifies sort operations for plotting and PostScript output 0= Disables SORTENTS 1= Sort for object selection 2= Sort for object snap 4= Sort for redraws 8= Sort for MSLIDE slide creation 16=Sort for REGENs 32=Sort for plotting 64=Sort for PostScript output
SPLFRAME	Integer	Drawing	If = 1: • The control polygon for spline fit Polylines is to be displayed • Only the defining mesh of a surface fit polygon mesh is displayed (the fit surface is not displayed) • Invisible edges of 3D Faces are displayed If = 0: • Does not display the control polygon for spline fit Polylines • Displays the fit surface of a polygon mesh, not the defining mesh • Does not display the invisible edges of 3D Faces
SPLINESEGS	Integer	Drawing	The number of line segments to be generated for each spline patch
SPLINETYPE	Integer	Drawing	Type of spline curve to be generated by PEDIT Spline. The valid values are: 5 = quadratic B-spline 6 = cubic B-spline
SURFTAB1	Integer	Drawing	Number of tabulations to be generated for RULESURF and TABSURF. Also mesh density in the M direction for REVSURF and EDGESURF
SURFTAB2	Integer	Drawing	Mesh density in the N direction for REVSURF and EDGESURF
SURFTYPE	Integer	Drawing	Type of surface fitting to be performed by PEDIT Smooth. The valid values are: 5 = quadratic B-spline surface 6 = cubic B-spline surface 8 = Bezier surface
SURFU	Integer	Drawing	Surface density in the M direction
SURFV	Integer	Drawing	Surface density in the N direction

Variable name	Type	Saved in	Meaning
USERS1–5	String		Five variables for storage and retrieval of text string data. Accepts strings with embedded blanks. To discard the existing text string, enter ".". The maximum string length is platform-dependent, and can be as low as 460 characters. Intended for use by third-party developers
VIEWCTR	2D point	Drawing	Center of view in current viewport, expressed in UCS coordinates (read-only)
VIEWDIR	3D vector	Drawing	The current viewport's viewing direction expressed in UCS coordinates. This describes the camera point as a 3D offset from the TARGET point (read-only)
VIEWMODE	Integer	Drawing	Viewing mode bit-code for the current viewport (read-only). The value is the sum of the following: 1 = perspective view active 2 = front clipping on 4 = back clipping on 8 = UCS follow mode on 16 = Front clip not at eye. If On, the front clip distance (FRONTZ) determines the front clipping plane. If Off, FRONTZ is ignored and the front clipping plane is set to pass through the camera point (i.e., vectors behind the camera are not displayed). This flag is ignored if the front clipping bit (2) is off
VIEWSIZE	Real	Drawing	Height of view in current viewport, expressed in drawing units (read-only)
VIEWTWIST	Real	Drawing	View twist angle for the current viewport (read-only)
VISRETAIN	Integer	Drawing	If = 0, the current drawing's On/Off, Freeze/Thaw, color, and linetype settings for Xref-dependent layers take precedence over the Xref's layer definition. If = 1, (the default value), these settings don't take precedence
VSMAX	3D point		The upper-right corner of the current viewport's virtual screen, expressed in UCS coordinates (read only)
VSMIN	3D point		The lower-left corner of the current viewport's virtual screen, expressed in UCS coordinates (read only)
WORLDUCS	Integer		If = 1, the current UCS is the same as the World Coordinate System. If = 0, it is not (read-only)
WORLDVIEW	Integer	Drawing	DVIEW and VPOINT command input is relative to the current UCS. If this variable is set to 1, the current UCS is changed to the WCS for the duration of a DVIEW or VPOINT command. Default value = 1
XREFCTL	Integer	Config	Controls whether .xlg files (external reference log files) are written 0 = Xref log (.xlg) files not written 1 = Xref log (.xlg) files written

APPENDIX D—ACAD PROTOTYPE DRAWING SETTINGS

The setup for each new drawing is determined by the settings in a "prototype" drawing. (See Chapter 7.) The default drawing is named "ACAD". Following is a listing of the settings for the ACAD drawing file. See Chapter 7 for an explanation of how to create custom prototype drawings.

APERTURE	<u>10</u> pixels
Attributes	Visibility controlled individually, entry of values during DDINSERT or INSERT permitted (using prompts rather than dialogue box)
BASE	Insertion base point (0.0, 0.0, 0.0)
Blipmode	On
CHAMFER	Distance 0.0
COLOR	Entity color "BYLAYER"
Coordinate display	Updated on point entry
DIM variables	

DIMALT	Off	DIMRND	0.00
DIMALTD	2	DIMSAH	Off
DIMALTF	25.40	DIMSCALE	1.00
DIMAPOST	(None)	DIMSE1	Off
DIMASO	On	DIMSE2	Off
DIMASZ	0.18	DIMSHO	On
DIMBLK	(None)	DIMSOXD	Off
DIMBLK1	(None)f	DIMSTYLE	Unnamed
DIMBLK2	(None)	DIMTAD	Off
DIMCEN	0.09	DIMTFAC	1.0
DIMCLRD	BYBLOCK	DIMTIH	On
DIMCLRE	BYBLOCK	DIMTIX	Off
DIMCLRT	BYBLOCK	DIMTM	0.00
DIMDLE	0.00	DIMTOH	On
DIMDLI	0.38	DIMTOFL	Off
DIMEXE	0.18	DIMTOL	Off
DIMEXO	0.0625	DIMTP	0.00
DIMGAP	0.09	DIMTSZ	0.00
DIMLFAC	1.00	DIMTVP	0.00
DIMLIM	Off	DIMTXT	0.18
DIMPOST	(None)	DIMZIN	0

DRAGMODE	Auto
ELEV	Elevation 0.0, thickness 0.0
FILL	On
FILLET	Radius 0.0
GRID	Off, spacing (0.0, 0.0)
HANDLES	Off
Highlighting	Enabled
ISOPLANE	Left
LAYER	Current/only layer is "0", On, with color 7 (white) and linetype "CONTINUOUS"
LIMITS	Off, drawing limits (0.0, 0.0) to (12.0, 9.0)
LINETYPE	Entity linetype "BYLAYER", no loaded linetypes other than "CONTINUOUS"
LTSCALE	1.0
MENU	"acad"
MIRROR	Text mirrored with other entities

Object selection	Pick box size 3 pixels
ORTHO	Off
OSNAP	None
PLINE	Line-width 0.0
POINT	Display mode 0, size 0
QTEXT	Off
REGENAUTO	On
SKETCH	Record increment 0.10, producing lines
SHADE	Rendering type 3, percent diffuse reflection 70
SNAP	Off, spacing (1.0, 1.0)
SNAP/GRID	Standard style, base point (0.00, 0.00), rotation 0.0°
SPACE	Model
Spline curves	Frame off, segments 8, spline type = cubic
STYLE	One defined text style ("STANDARD"), using font file "txt", with variable height, width factor 1.0, horizontal orientation.
Surfaces	6 tabulations in M and N directions, 6 segments for smoothing in U and V directions, smooth surface type = cubic B-spline
TABLET	Off
TEXT	Style "STANDARD", height 0.20, rotation 0.0°
TILEMODE	On
TIME	User elapsed timer on
TRACE	Width 0.05
UCS	Current UCS equivalent to World, auto plan view off, coordinate system icon on (at origin)
UNITS (angular)	Decimal degrees, 0 decimal places, angle 0 direction is to the right angles increase counterclockwise
UNITS (linear)	Decimal, 4 decimal places
Viewing modes	One active viewport, plan view, perspective off, target point (0, 0, 0), front and back clipping off, lens length 50mm, twist angle 0.0, fast zoom on, circle zoom percent 100, worldview 0
ZOOM	To drawing limits

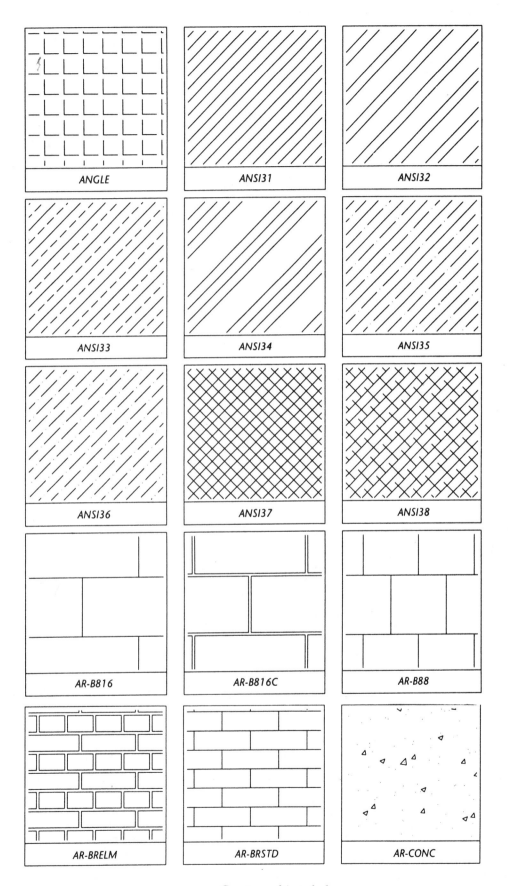

ANGLE ANSI31 ANSI32 ANSI33 ANSI34 ANSI35 ANSI36 ANSI37 ANSI38 AR-B816 AR-B816C AR-B88 AR-BRELM AR-BRSTD AR-CONC

APPENDIX E—HATCH PATTERNS

Courtesy of Autodesk

E-1

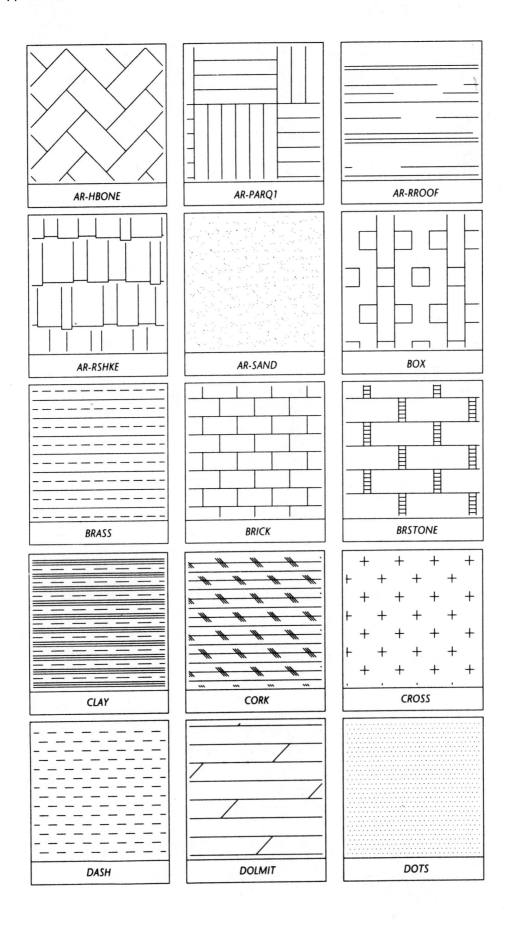

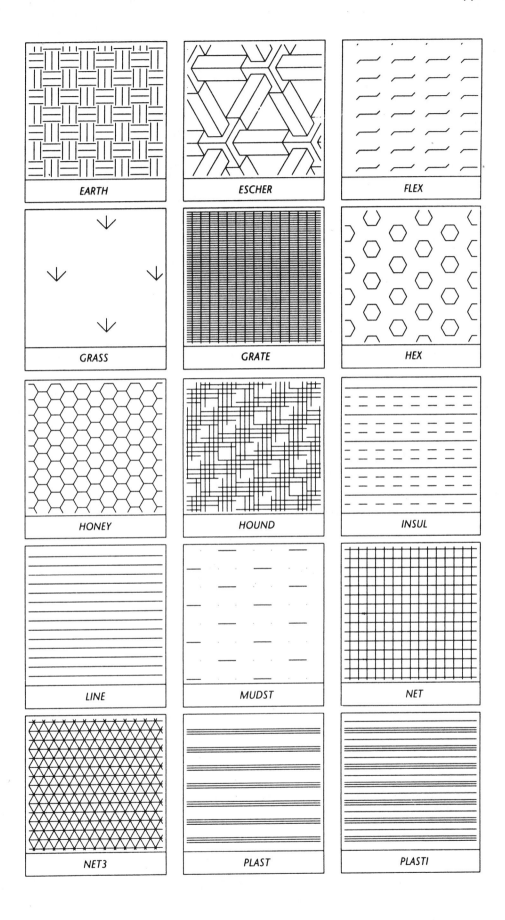

EARTH

ESCHER

FLEX

GRASS

GRATE

HEX

HONEY

HOUND

INSUL

LINE

MUDST

NET

NET3

PLAST

PLASTI

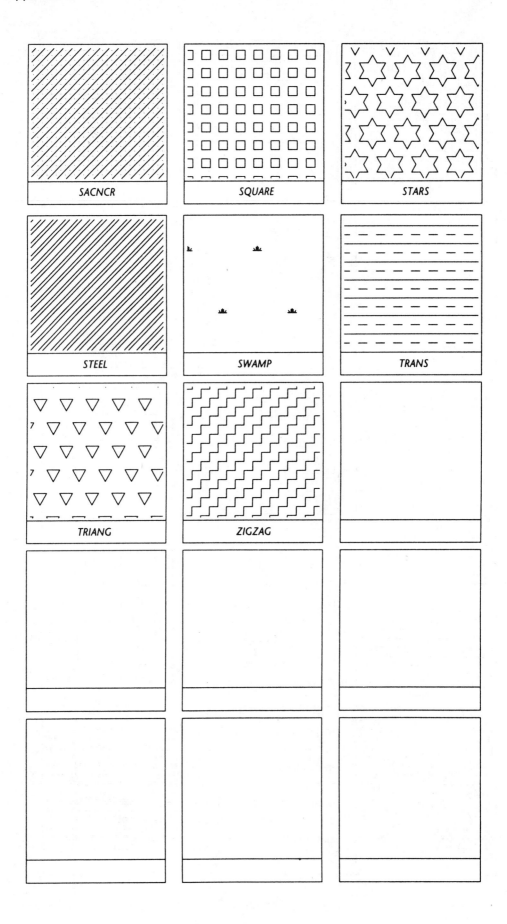

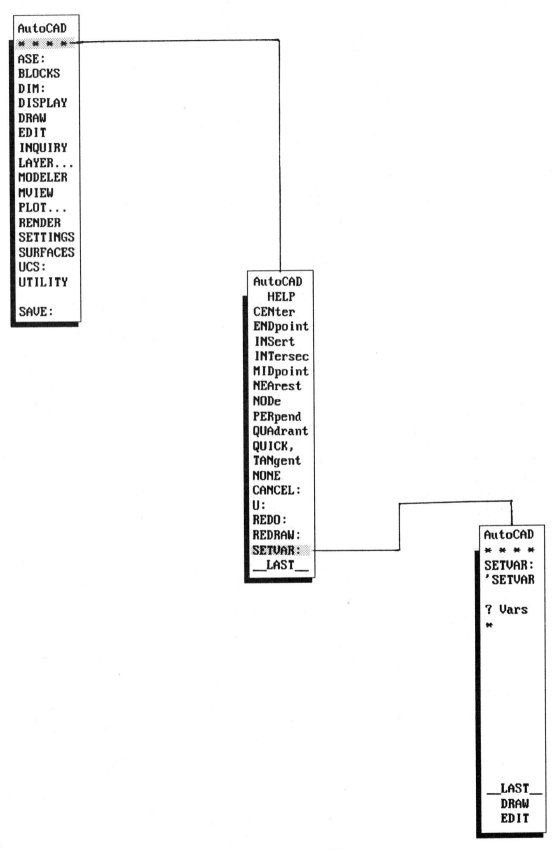

Osnap and Setvar Menus

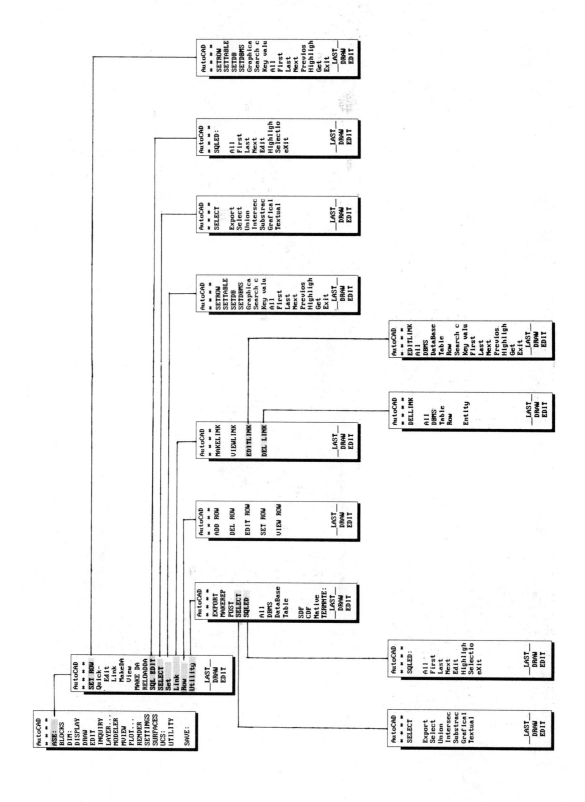

ASE Menus

Blocks Menus

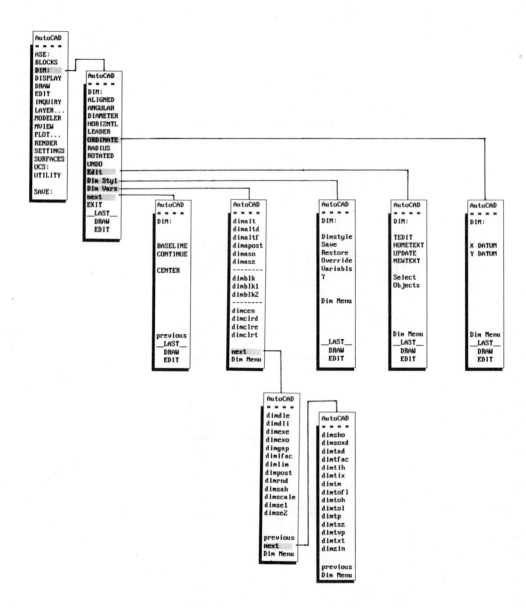

Dimension Menus

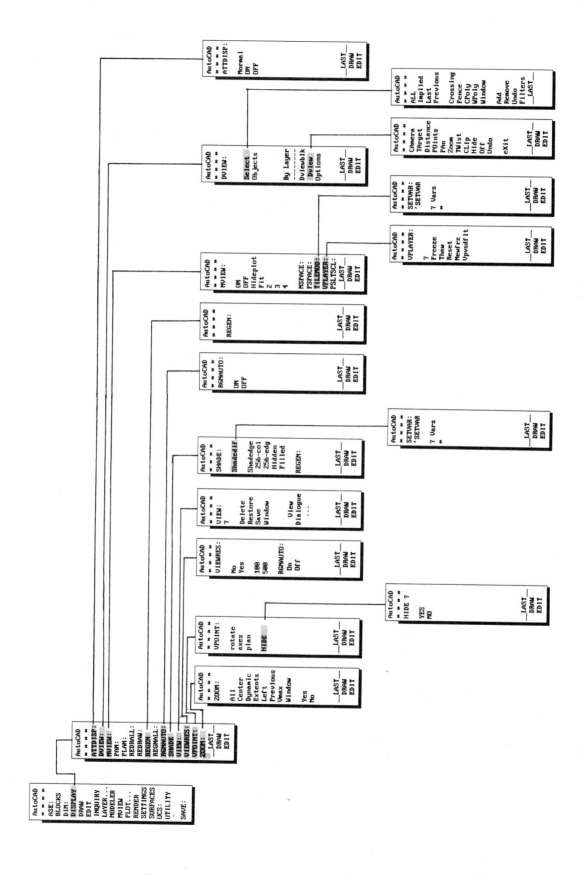

Display Menus

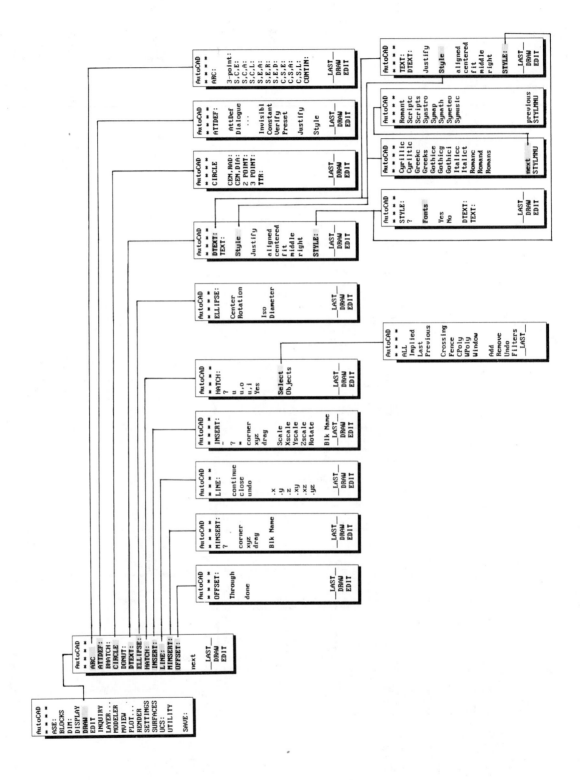

Draw Menus

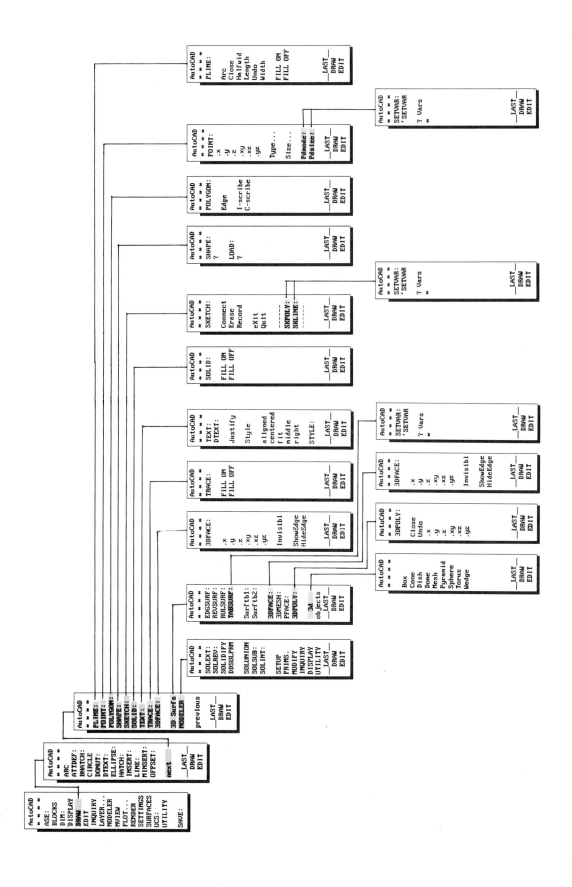

Draw Menus (Next)

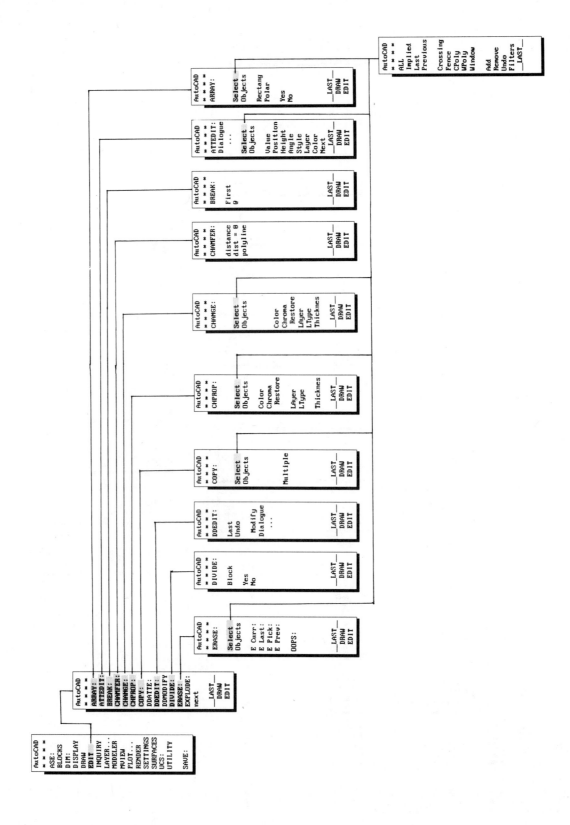

Edit Menus

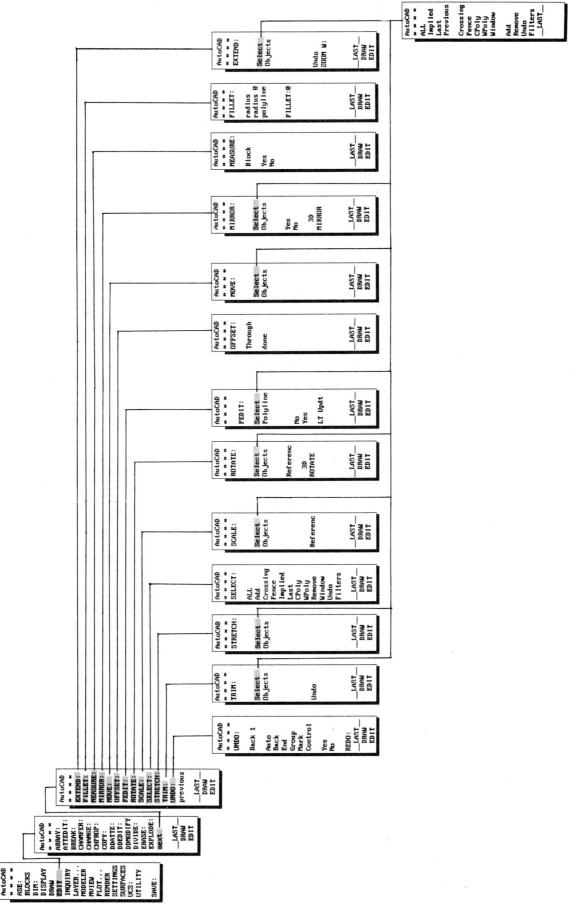

Edit Menus (Next)

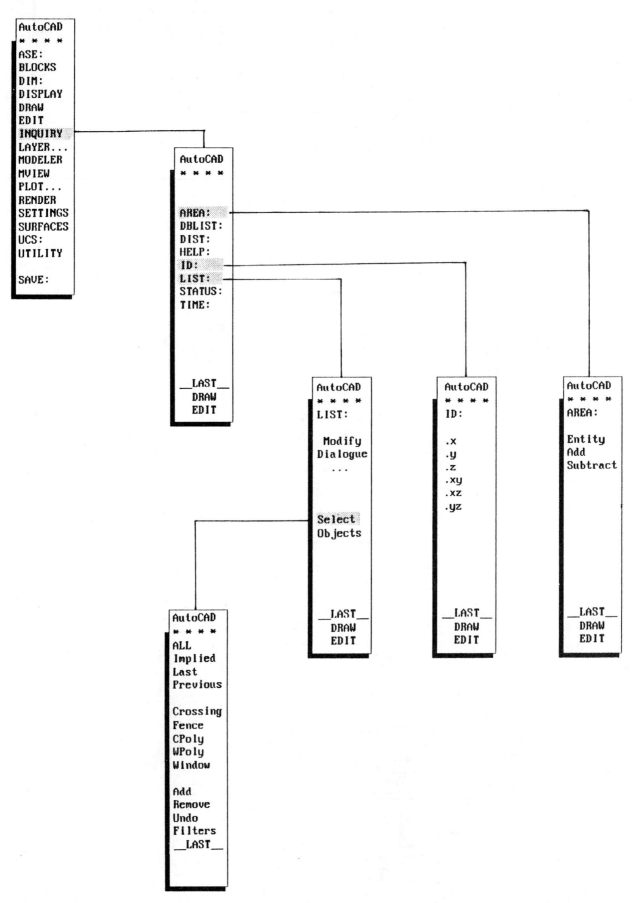

Inquiry Menus

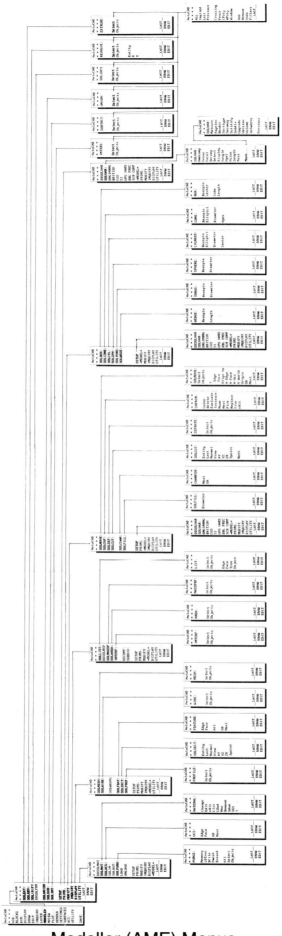

Modeller (AME) Menus

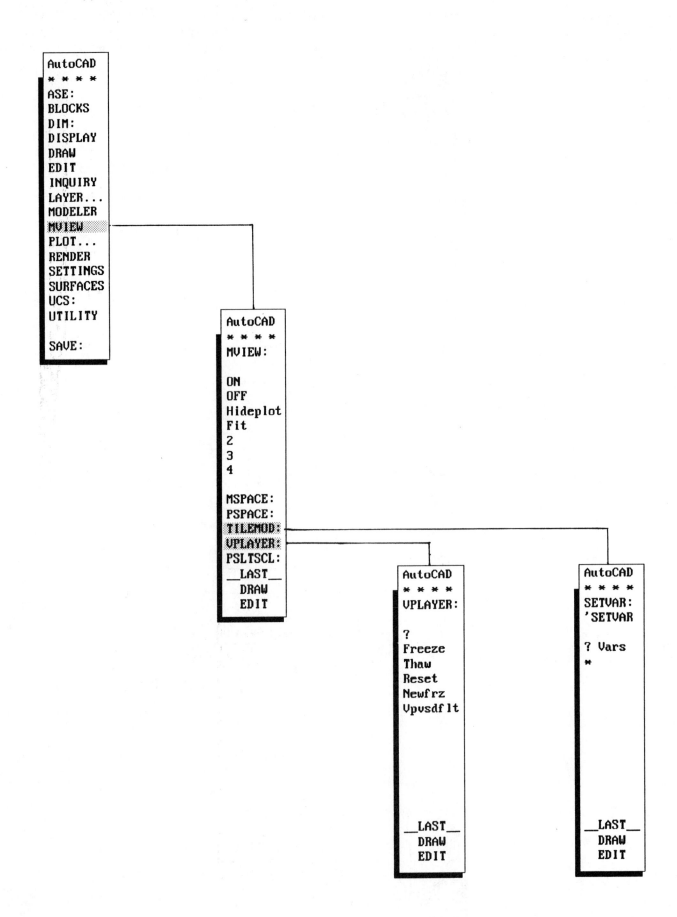

Mview Menus

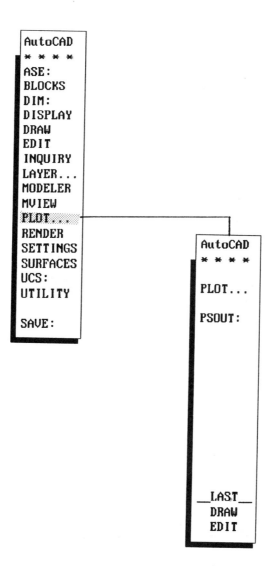

Plot Menus

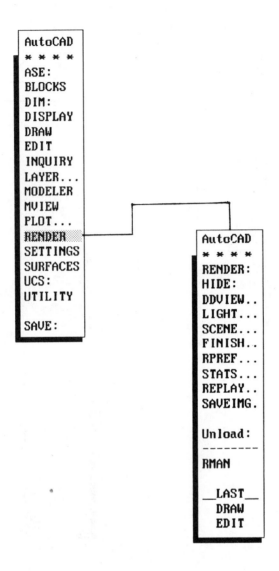

Render Menus

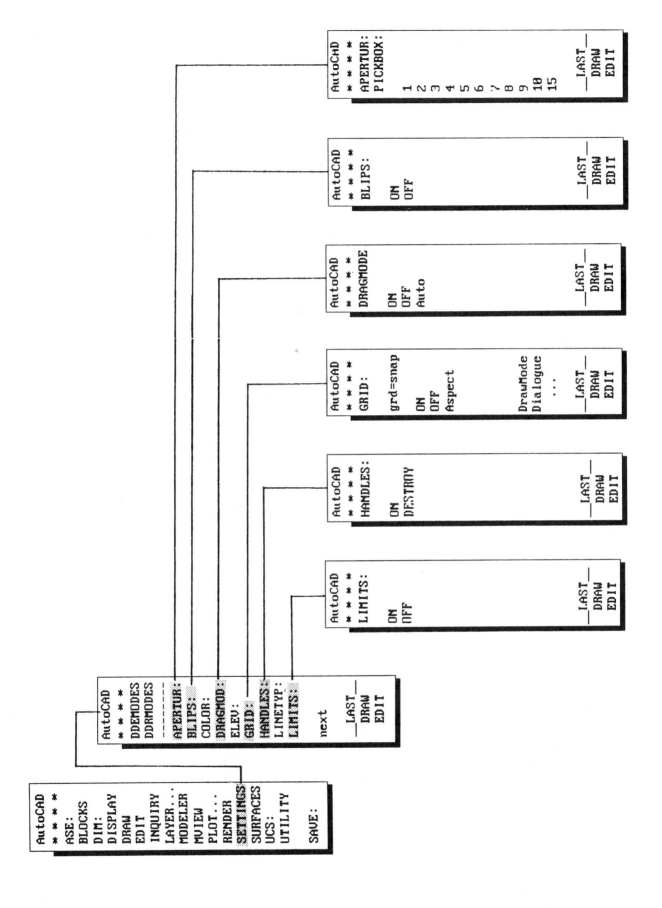

Settings Menus

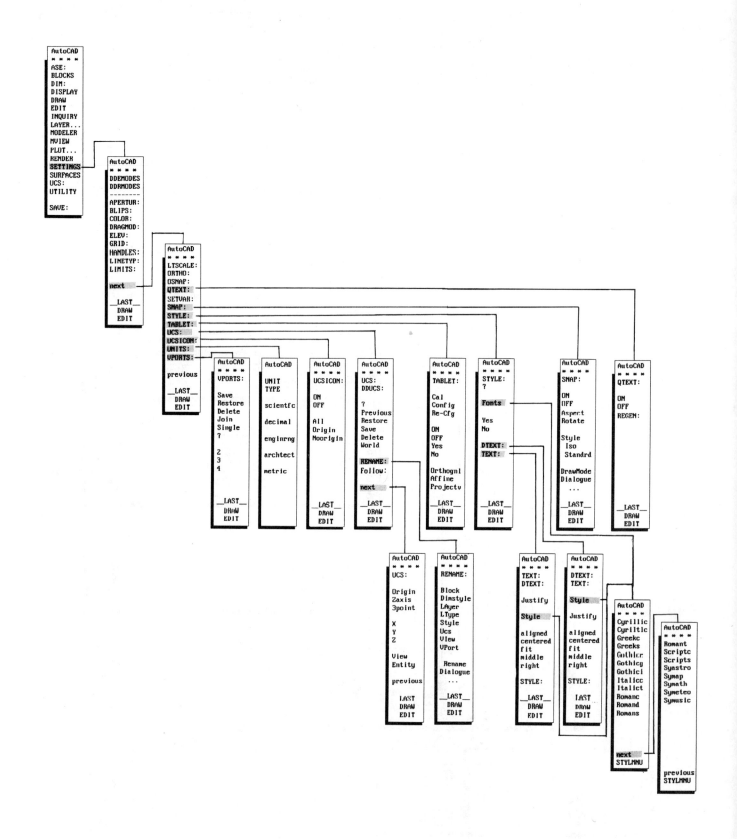

Settings Menus (Next)

Surfaces Menus

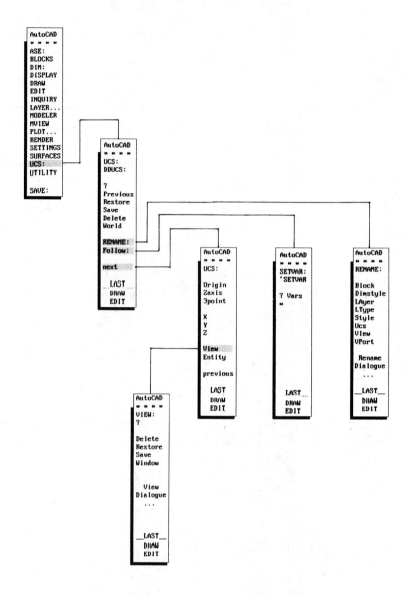

UCS Menus

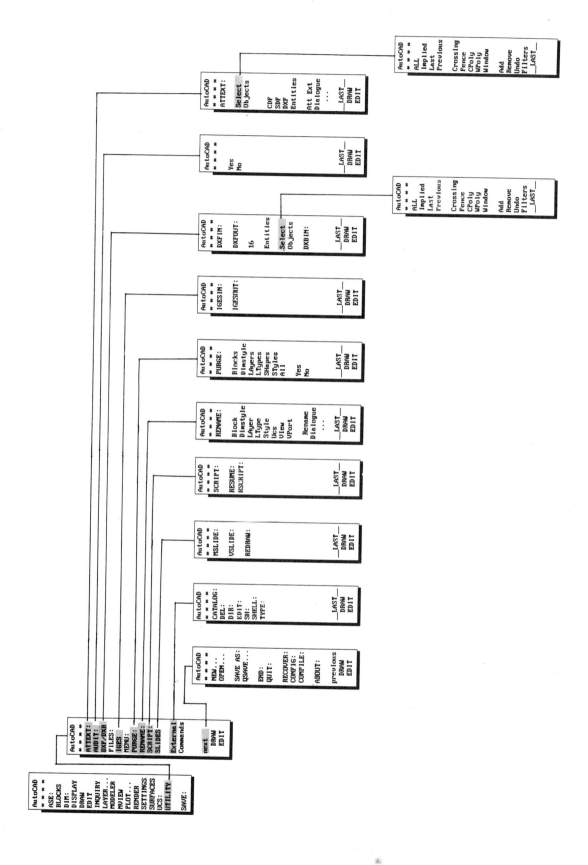

Utility Menus

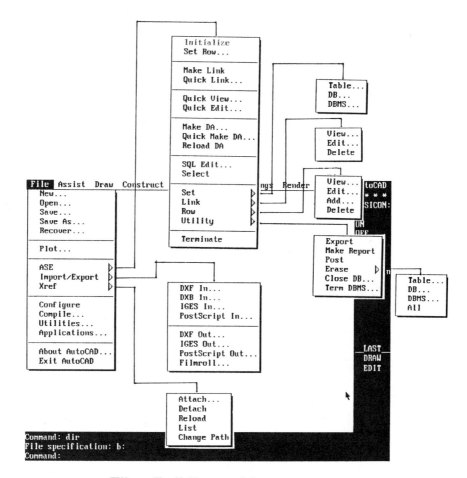

Files Pull-Down Menus

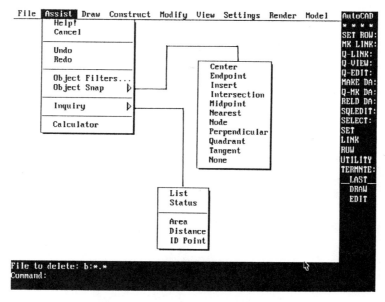

Assist Pull-Down Menus

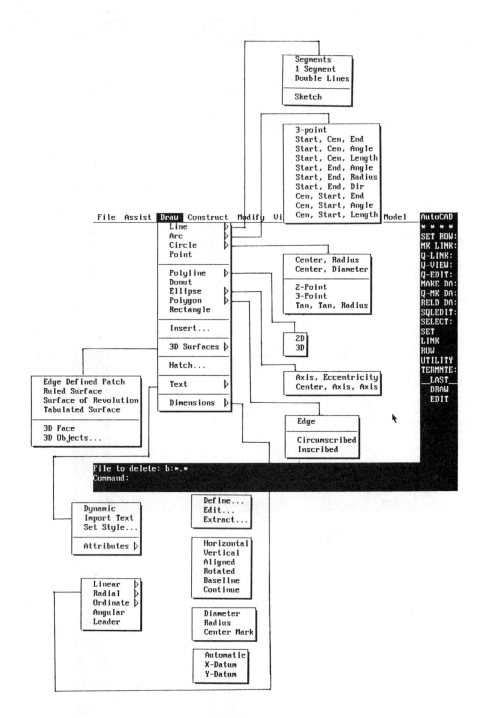

Draw Pull-Down Menus

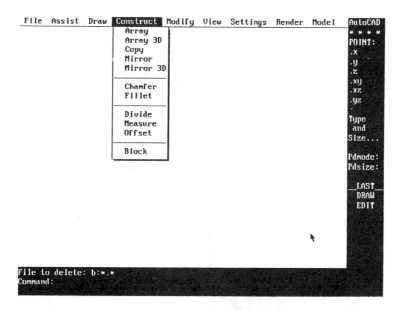

Construct Pull-Down Menus

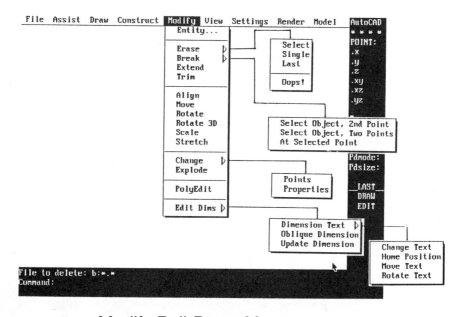

Modify Pull-Down Menus

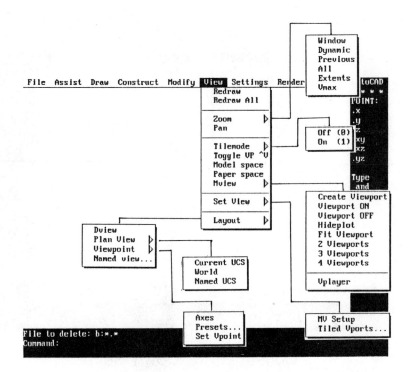

View Pull-Down Menus

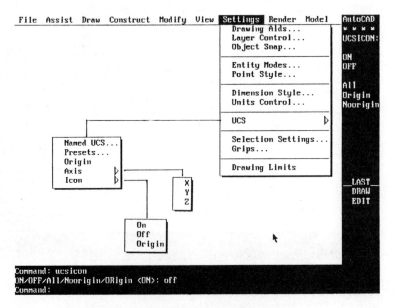

Settings Pull-Down Menus

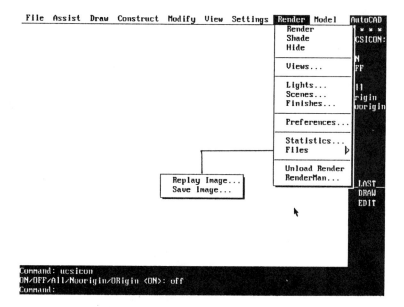

Render Pull-Down Menus

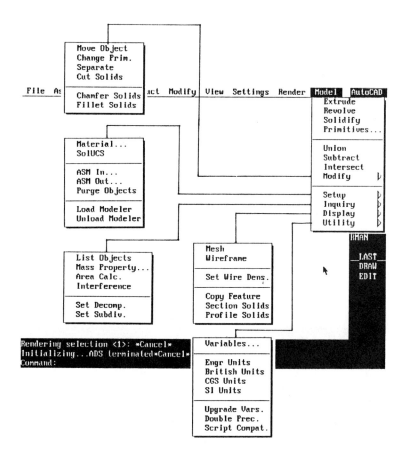

Model Pull-Down Menus

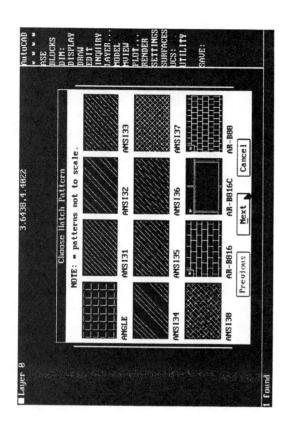

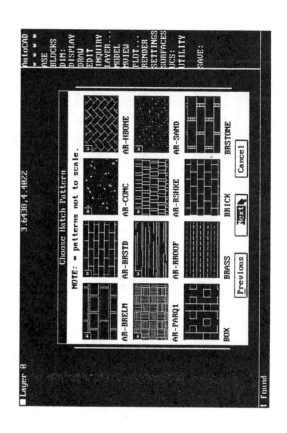

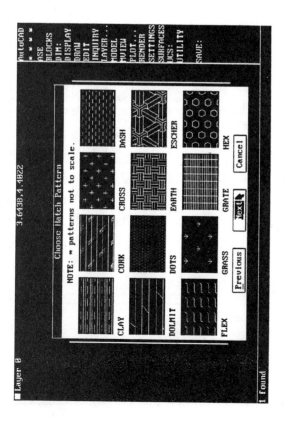

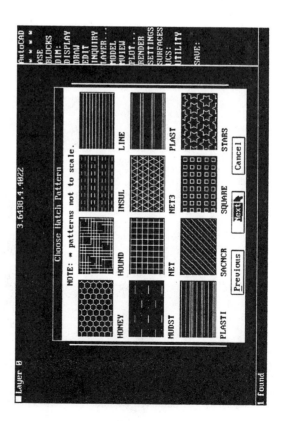

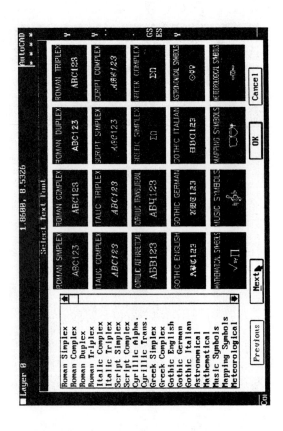

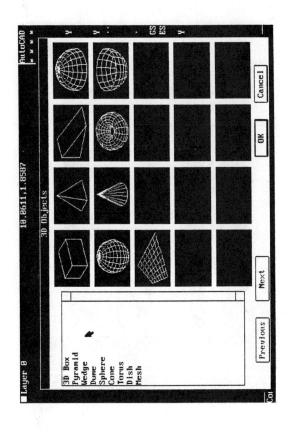

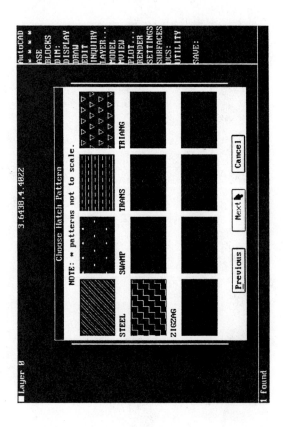

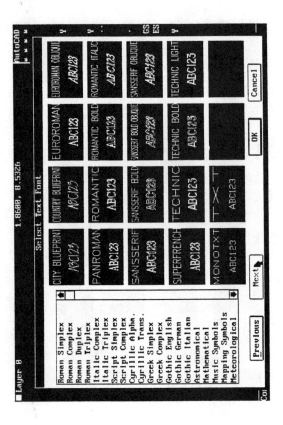

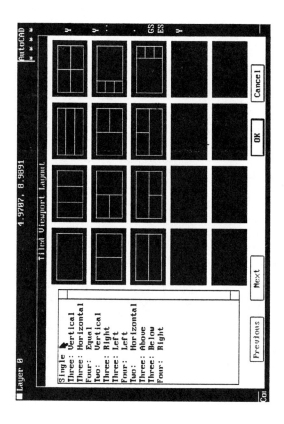

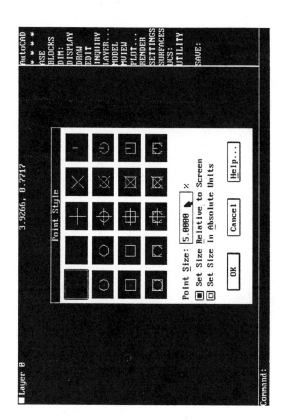

APPENDIX I—DIALOGUE BOXES

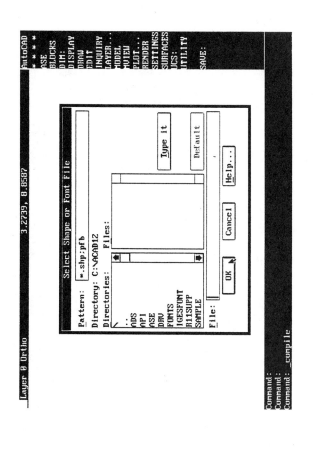

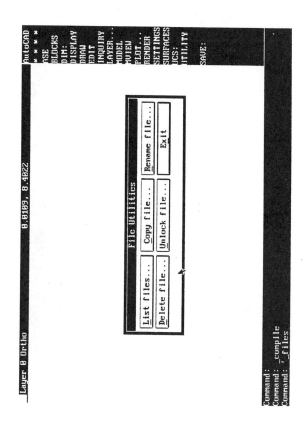

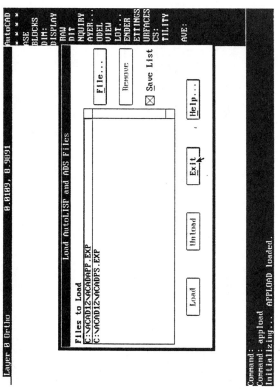

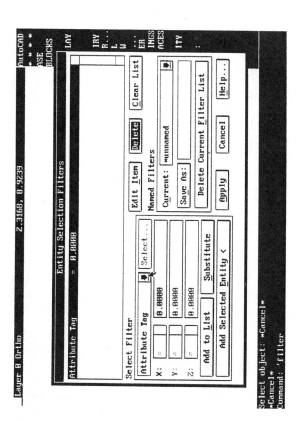

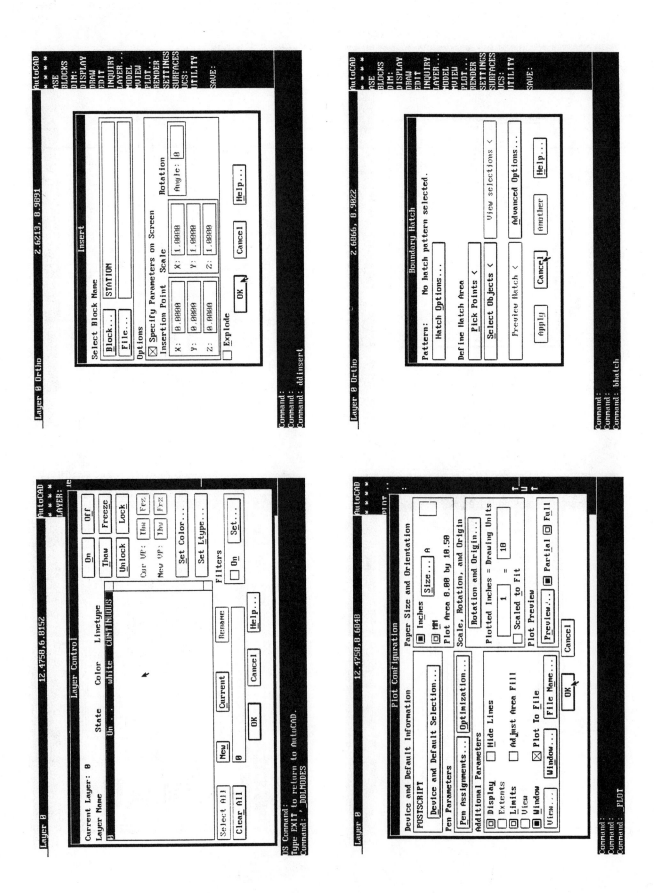

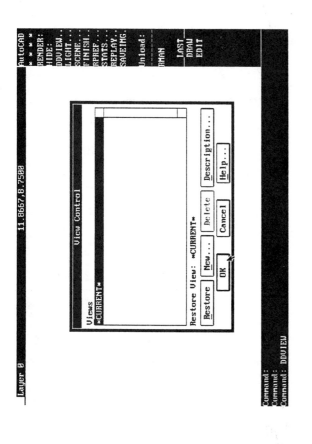

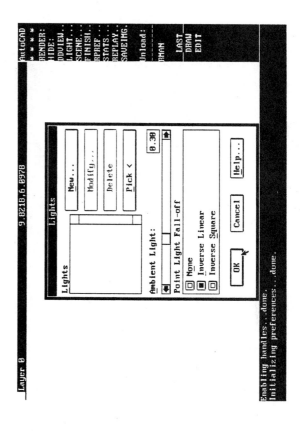

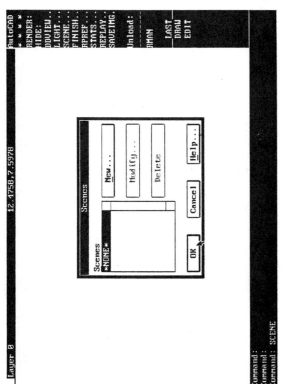

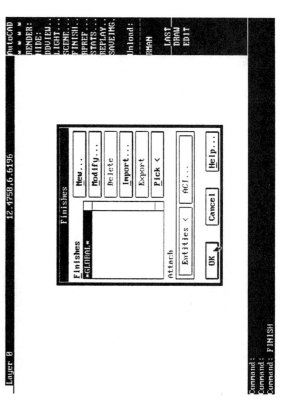

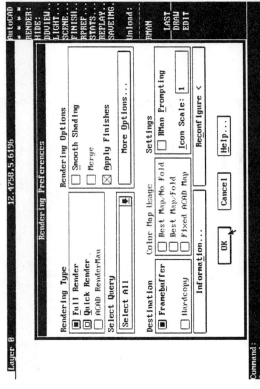

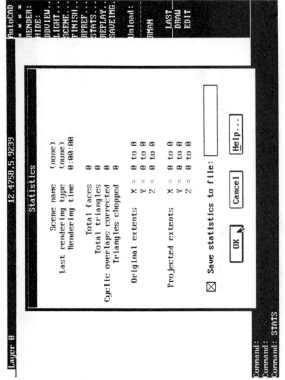

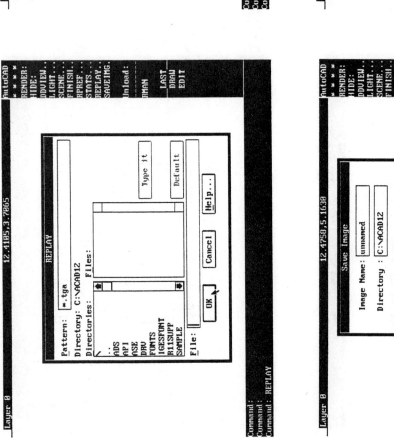

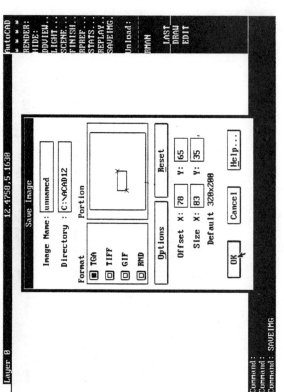

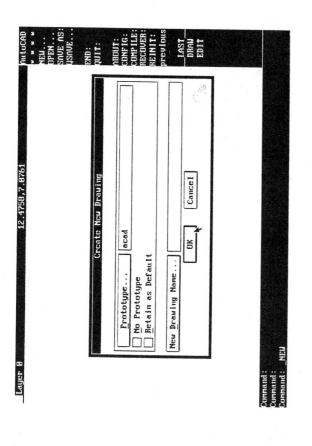

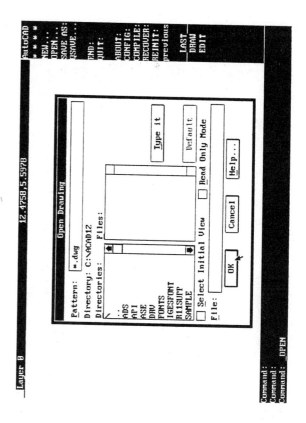

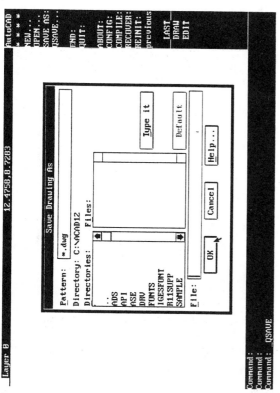

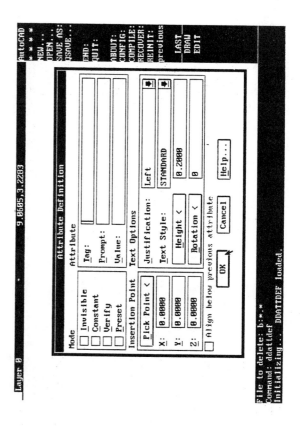

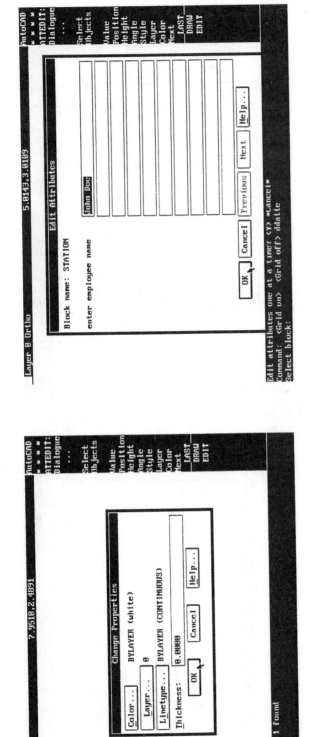

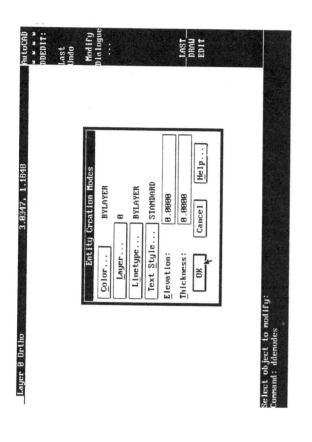

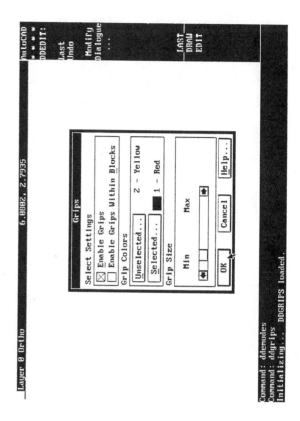

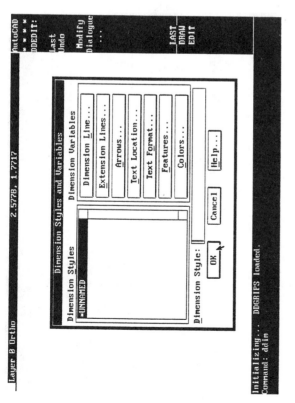

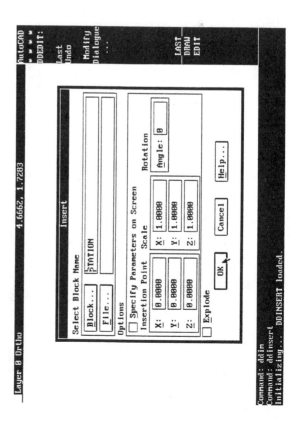

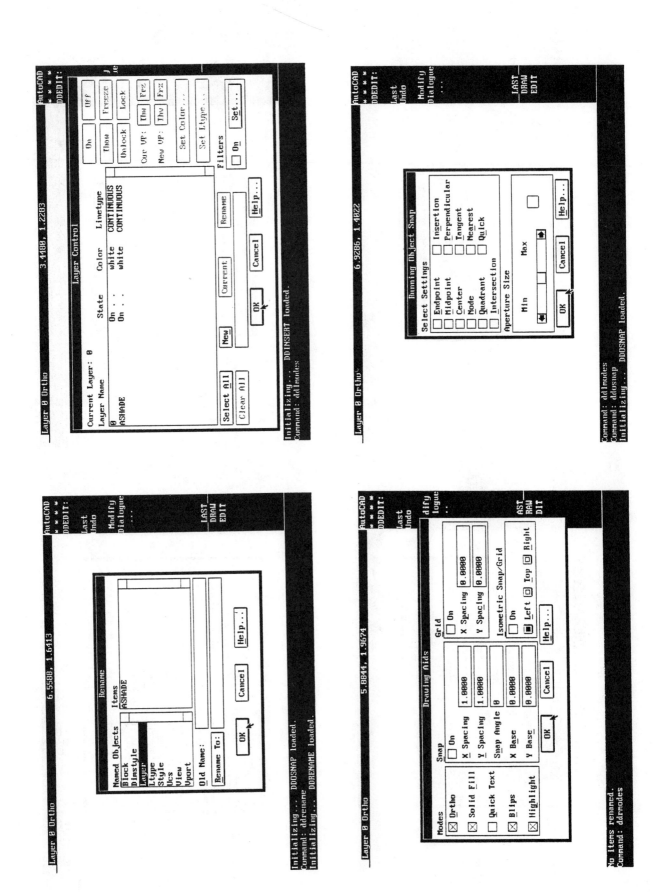

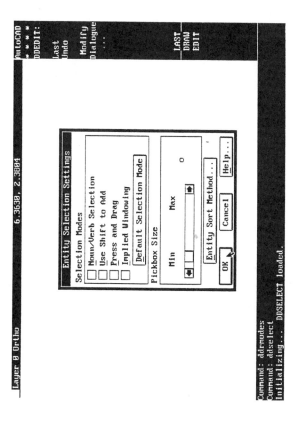

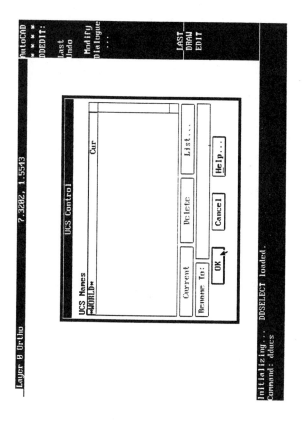

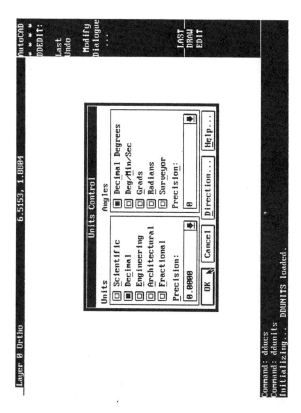

APPENDIX J—AUTOCAD LINETYPES

Border	—— — — · ——
Border2	—·—·—·—·—·— —
BorderX2	—— — · ——
Center	—— – —— – ——
Center2	—·—·—·—·—
CenterX2	—— — — ——
Dashdot	– · — · — · — · — · —
Dashdot2	·–·–·–·–·–·–·–·
DashdotX2	—— · —— · ——
Dashed	— — — — — —
Dashed2	–·–·–·–·–·–·–
DashedX2	—— —— —— —
Divide	– · · — · — · · —
Divide2	·–··–·–·–··–·–··
DivideX2	— · · —— · · —
Dot	· · · · · · · · · · · · · · · · · · · ·
Dot2	· ·
DotX2	· · · · · · · · · ·
Hidden	– – – – – – – – – – – – –
Hidden2	-------------------------
HiddenX2	— — — — — —
Phantom	—— – – —— – – ——
Phantom2	–·–·–·–··–·—·–·
PhantonX2	—— — — ——

Courtesy of Autodesk

APPENDIX K—TABLES

ARCHITECTURAL

FINAL PLOT SCALE	SHEET SIZE				
	A 11 x 8½	B 17 x 11	C 24 x 18	D 36 x 24	E 48 x 36
1/16	176', 136'	272', 176'	384', 288'	576', 384'	768', 576'
3/32	132', 102'	204', 132'	288', 216'	432', 288'	576', 432'
1/8	88', 68'	136', 88'	192', 144'	288', 192'	384', 288'
3/16	66', 51'	102', 66'	144', 108'	216', 144'	288', 216'
1/4	44', 34'	68', 44'	96', 72'	144', 96'	192', 144'
3/8	29'-4", 22'-8"	45'-4", 29'-4"	64', 48'	96', 64'	128', 96'
1/2	22', 17'	34', 22'	48', 36'	72', 48'	96', 72'
3/4	14'-8", 11'-4"	22'-8", 14'-8"	32', 24'	48', 32'	64', 48'
1	11', 8'-6"	17', 11'	24', 18'	36', 24'	48', 36'
1½	7'-4", 5'-8"	11'-4", 7'-4"	16', 12'	24', 16'	32', 24'
3	3'-8", 2'-10"	5'-8", 3'-8"	8', 6"	12', 8'	16,' 12'

ENGINEERING

FINAL PLOT SCALE	SHEET SIZE				
	A 11 x 8½	B 17 x 11	C 24 x 18	D 36 x 24	E 48 x 36
10	110, 85	170, 110	240, 180	360, 240	480, 360
20	220, 170	340, 220	480, 360	720, 480	960, 720
30	330, 255	510, 330	720, 540	1080, 720	1440, 1080
40	440, 340	680, 440	960, 720	1440, 960	1920, 1440
50	550, 425	850, 550	1200, 900	1800, 1200	2400, 1800
60	660, 510	1020, 660	1440, 1080	2160, 1440	2880, 2160
100	1100, 850	1700, 1100	2400, 1800	3600, 2400	4800, 3600
Full Size	11, 8.5	17, 11	24, 18	36, 24	48, 36

INCHES TO MILLIMETRES

in.	mm	in.	mm	in.	mm	in.	mm
1	25.4	26	660.4	51	1295.4	76	1930.4
2	50.8	27	685.8	52	1320.8	77	1955.8
3	76.2	28	711.2	53	1346.2	78	1981.2
4	101.6	29	736.6	54	1371.6	79	2006.6
5	127.0	30	762.0	55	1397.0	80	2032.0
6	152.4	31	787.4	56	1422.4	81	2057.4
7	177.8	32	812.8	57	1447.8	82	2082.8
8	203.2	33	838.2	58	1473.2	83	2108.2
9	228.6	34	863.6	59	1498.6	84	2133.6
10	254.0	35	889.0	60	1524.0	85	2159.0
11	279.4	36	914.4	61	1549.4	86	2184.4
12	304.8	37	939.8	62	1574.8	87	2209.8
13	330.2	38	965.2	63	1600.2	88	2235.2
14	355.6	39	990.6	64	1625.6	89	2260.6
15	381.0	40	1016.0	65	1651.0	90	2286.0
16	406.4	41	1041.4	66	1676.4	91	2311.4
17	431.8	42	1066.8	67	1701.8	92	2336.8
18	457.2	43	1092.2	68	1727.2	93	2362.2
19	482.6	44	1117.6	69	1752.6	94	2387.6
20	508.0	45	1143.0	70	1778.0	95	2413.0
21	533.4	46	1168.4	71	1803.4	96	2438.4
22	558.8	47	1193.8	72	1828.8	97	2463.8
23	584.2	48	1219.2	73	1854.2	98	2489.2
24	609.6	49	1244.6	74	1879.6	99	2514.6
25	635.0	50	1270.0	75	1905.0	100	2540.0

The above table is exact on the basis: 1 in. = 25.4 mm

MILLIMETRES TO INCHES

mm	in.	mm	in.	mm	in.	mm	in.
1	0.039370	26	1.023622	51	2.007874	76	2.992126
2	0.078740	27	1.062992	52	2.047244	77	3.031496
3	0.118110	28	1.102362	53	2.086614	78	3.070866
4	0.157480	29	1.141732	54	2 125984	79	3.110236
5	0.196850	30	1.181102	55	2.165354	80	3.149606
6	0.236220	31	1.220472	56	2.204724	81	3.188976
7	0.275591	32	1.259843	57	2.244094	82	3.228346
8	0.314961	33	1.299213	58	2.283465	83	3.267717
9	0.354331	34	1.338583	59	2.322835	84	3.307087
10	0.393701	35	1.377953	60	2.362205	85	3.346457
11	0.433071	36	1.417323	61	2.401575	86	3.385827
12	0.472441	37	1.456693	62	2.440945	87	3.425197
13	0.511811	38	1.496063	63	2.480315	88	3.464567
14	0.551181	39	1.535433	64	2.519685	89	3.503937
15	0.590551	40	1.574803	65	2.559055	90	3.543307
16	0.629921	41	1.614173	66	2.598425	91	3.582677
17	0.669291	42	1.653543	67	2.637795	92	3.622047
18	0.708661	43	1.692913	68	2.677165	93	3.661417
19	0.748031	44	1.732283	69	2.716535	94	3.700787
20	0.787402	45	1.771654	70	2.755906	95	3.740157
21	0.826772	46	1.811024	71	2.795276	96	3.779528
22	0.866142	47	1.850394	72	2.834646	97	3.818898
23	0.905512	48	1.889764	73	2.874016	98	3.858268
24	0.944882	49	1.929134	74	2.913386	99	3.897638
25	0.984252	50	1.968504	75	2.952756	100	3.937008

The above table is approximate on the basis: 1 in. = 25.4 mm, 1/25.4 = 0.039370078740+

From Goetsch, Nelson, and Chalk, *Technical Drawing*, 2nd edition, copyright 1989 by Delmar Publishers Inc.

INCH/METRIC – EQUIVALENTS					
Fraction	**Decimal Equivalent**		**Fraction**	**Decimal Equivalent**	
	Customary (in.)	**Metric (mm)**		**Customary (in.)**	**Metric (mm)**
1/64 — .015625	.015625	0.3969	33/64 — .515625	.515625	13.0969
1/32 — .03125	.03125	0.7938	17/32 — .53125	.53125	13.4938
3/64 — .046875	.046875	1.1906	35/64 — .546875	.546875	13.8906
1/16 — .0625	.0625	1.5875	9/16 — .5625	.5625	14.2875
5/64 — .078125	.078125	1.9844	37/64 — .578125	.578125	14.6844
3/32 — .09375	.09375	2.3813	19/32 — .59375	.59375	15.0813
7/64 — .109375	.109375	2.7781	39/64 — .609375	.609375	15.4781
1/8 — .1250	.1250	3.1750	5/8 — .6250	.6250	15.8750
9/64 — .140625	.140625	3.5719	41/64 — .640625	.640625	16.2719
5/32 — .15625	.15625	3.9688	21/32 — .65625	.65625	16.6688
11/64 — .171875	.171875	4.3656	43/64 — .671875	.671875	17.0656
3/16 — .1875	.1875	4.7625	11/16 — .6875	.6875	17.4625
13/64 — .203125	.203125	5.1594	45/64 — .703125	.703125	17.8594
7/32 — .21875	.21875	5.5563	23/32 — .71875	.71875	18.2563
15/64 — .234375	.234375	5.9531	47/64 — .734375	.734375	18.6531
1/4 — .250	.250	6.3500	3/4 — .750	.750	19.0500
17/64 — .265625	.265625	6.7469	49/64 — .765625	.765625	19.4469
9/32 — .28125	.28125	7.1438	25/32 — .78125	.78125	19.8438
19/64 — .296875	.296875	7.5406	51/64 — .796875	.796875	20.2406
5/16 — .3125	.3125	7.9375	13/16 — .8125	.8125	20.6375
21/64 — .328125	.328125	8.3384	53/64 — .828125	.828125	21.0344
11/32 — .34375	.34375	8.7313	27/32 — .84375	.84375	21.4313
23/64 — .359375	.359375	9.1281	55/64 — .859375	.859375	21.8281
3/8 — .3750	.3750	9.5250	7/8 — .8750	.8750	22.2250
25/64 — .390625	.390625	9.9219	57/64 — .890625	.890625	22.6219
13/32 — .40625	.40625	10.3188	29/32 — .90625	.90625	23.0198
27/64 — .421875	.421875	10.7156	59/64 — .921875	.921875	23.4156
7/16 — .4375	.4375	11.1125	15/16 — .9375	.9375	23.8125
29/64 — .453125	.453125	11.5094	61/64 — .953125	.953125	24.2094
15/32 — .46875	.46875	11.9063	31/32 — .96875	.96875	24.6063
31/64 — .484375	.484375	12.3031	63/64 — .984375	.984375	25.0031
1/2 — .500	.500	12.7000	1 — 1.000	1.000	25.4000

From Nelson, *Drafting for Trades and Industry—Basic Skills*, copyright 1979 by Delmar Publishers Inc.

MULTIPLIERS FOR DRAFTERS

Multiply	By	To Obtain	Multiply	By	To Obtain
Acres	43,560	Square feet	Degrees/sec.	0.002778	Revolutions/sec.
Acres	4047	Square metres	Fathoms	6	Feet
Acres	$1.562 \cdot 10^3$	Square miles	Feet	30.48	Centimetres
Acres	4840	Square yards	Feet	12	Inches
Acre–feet	43,560	Cubic feet	Feet	0.3048	Metres
Atmospheres	76.0	Cms. of mercury	Foot–pounds	$1.286 \cdot 10^3$	British Thermal Units
Atmospheres	29.92	Inches of mercury	Foot–pounds	$5.050 \cdot 10^7$	Horsepower–hrs.
Atmospheres	33.90	Feet of water	Foot–pounds	$3.241 \cdot 10^4$	Kilogram–calories
Atmospheres	10,333	Kgs./sq. metre	Foot–pounds	0.1383	Kilogram–metres
Atmospheres	14.70	Lbs./sq. inch	Foot–pounds	$3.766 \cdot 10^7$	Kilowatt–hrs.
Atmospheres	1.058	Tons/sq. ft.	Foot–pounds/min.	$1.286 \cdot 10^3$	B.T.U./min.
Board feet	144 sq. in. · 1 in.	Cubic inches	Foot–pounds/min.	0.01667	Foot–pounds/sec.
British Thermal Units	0.2520	Kilogram–calories	Foot–pounds/min.	$3.030 \cdot 10^5$	Horsepower
British Thermal Units	777.5	Foot–lbs.	Foot–pounds/min.	$3.241 \cdot 10^4$	Kg.–calories/min.
British Thermal Units	$3.927 \cdot 10^4$	Horsepower–hrs.	Foot–pounds/min.	$2.260 \cdot 10^5$	Kilowatts
British Thermal Units	107.5	Kilogram–metres	Foot–pounds/sec.	$7.717 \cdot 10^2$	B.T.U./min.
British Thermal Units	$2.928 \cdot 10^4$	Kilowatt–hrs.	Foot–pounds/sec.	$1.818 \cdot 10^3$	Horsepower
B.T.U./min	12.96	Foot–lbs./sec.	Foot–pounds/sec.	$1.945 \cdot 10^2$	Kg.–calories/min.
B.T.U./min	0.02356	Horsepower	Foot–pounds/sec.	$1.356 \cdot 10^3$	Kilowatts
B.T.U./min	0.01757	Kilowatts	Gallons	3785	Cubic centimetres
B.T.U./min	17.57	Watts	Gallons	0.1337	Cubic feet
Cubic centimetres	$3.531 \cdot 10^5$	Cubic feet	Gallons	231	Cubic inches
Cubic centimetres	$6.102 \cdot 10^2$	Cubic inches	Gallons	$3.785 \cdot 10^3$	Cubic metres
Cubic centimetres	10^6	Cubic metres	Gallons	$4.951 \cdot 10^3$	Cubic yards
Cubic centimetres	$1.308 \cdot 10^6$	Cubic yards	Gallons	3.785	Litres
Cubic centimetres	$2.642 \cdot 10^4$	Gallons	Gallons	8	Pints (liq.)
Cubic centimetres	10^3	Litres	Gallons	4	Quarts (liq.)
Cubic centimetres	$2.113 \cdot 10^3$	Pints (liq.)	Gallons–Imperial	1.20095	U.S. gallons
Cubic centimetres	$1.057 \cdot 10^3$	Quarts (liq.)	Gallons–U.S.	0.83267	Imperial gallons
Cubic feet	$2.832 \cdot 10^4$	Cubic cms.	Gallons water	8.3453	Pounds of water
Cubic feet	1728	Cubic inches	Horsepower	42.44	B.T.U./min.
Cubic feet	0.02832	Cubic metres	Horsepower	33,000	Foot–lbs./min.
Cubic feet	0.03704	Cubic yards	Horsepower	550	Foot–lbs./sec.
Cubic feet	7.48052	Gallons	Horsepower	1.014	Horsepower (metric)
Cubic feet	28.32	Litres	Horsepower	10.70	Kg.–calories/min.
Cubic feet	59.84	Pints (liq.)	Horsepower	0.7457	Kilowatts
Cubic feet	29.92	Quarts (liq.)	Horsepower	745.7	Watts
Cubic feet/min.	472.0	Cubic cms./sec.	Horsepower–hours	2547	B.T.U.
Cubic feet/min.	0.1247	Gallons/sec.	Horsepower–hours	$1.98 \cdot 10^6$	Foot–lbs.
Cubic feet/min.	0.4720	Litres/sec.	Horsepower–hours	641.7	Kilogram–calories
Cubic feet/min.	62.43	Pounds of water/min.	Horsepower–hours	$2.737 \cdot 10^5$	Kilogram–metres
Cubic feet/sec.	0.646317	Millions gals./day	Horsepower–hours	0.7457	Kilowatt–hours
Cubic feet/sec.	448.831	Gallons/min.	Kilometres	10^5	Centimetres
Cubic inches	16.39	Cubic centimetres	Kilometres	3281	Feet
Cubic inches	$5.787 \cdot 10^4$	Cubic feet	Kilometres	10^3	Metres
Cubic inches	$1.639 \cdot 10^5$	Cubic metres	Kilometres	0.6214	Miles
Cubic inches	$2.143 \cdot 10^5$	Cubic yards	Kilometres	1094	Yards
Cubic inches	$4.329 \cdot 10^3$	Gallons	Kilowatts	56.92	B.T.U./min.
Cubic inches	$1.639 \cdot 10^2$	Litres	Kilowatts	$4.425 \cdot 10^4$	Foot–lbs./min.
Cubic inches	0.03463	Pints (liq.)	Kilowatts	737.6	Foot–lbs./sec.
Cubic inches	0.01732	Quarts (liq.)	Kilowatts	1.341	Horsepower
Cubic metres	10^6	Cubic centimetres	Kilowatts	14.34	Kg.–calories/min.
Cubic metres	35.31	Cubic feet	Kilowatts	10^3	Watts
Cubic metres	61.023	Cubic inches	Kilowatt–hours	3415	B.T.U.
Cubic metres	1.308	Cubic yards	Kilowatt–hours	$2.655 \cdot 10^6$	Foot–lbs.
Cubic metres	264.2	Gallons	Kilowatt–hours	1.341	Horsepower–hrs.
Cubic metres	10^3	Litres	Kilowatt–hours	860.5	Kilogram–calories
Cubic metres	2113	Pints (liq.)	Kilowatt–hours	$3.671 \cdot 10^5$	Kilogram–metres
Cubic metres	1057	Quarts (liq.)	Lumber Width (in.) Thickness (in.) ÷ 12	Length (ft.)	Board feet
Degrees (angle)	60	Minutes			
Degrees (angle)	0.01745	Radians	Metres	100	Centimetres
Degrees (angle)	3600	Seconds	Metres	3.281	Feet
Degrees/sec.	0.01745	Radians/sec.	Metres	39.37	Inches
Degrees/sec.	0.1667	Revolutions/min.			

From Goetsch, Nelson, and Chalk, *Technical Drawing*, 2nd edition, copyright 1989 by Delmar Publishers Inc.

MULTIPLIERS FOR DRAFTERS (cont'd)

Multiply	By	To Obtain	Multiply	By	To Obtain
Metres	10^{-3}	Kilometres	Pounds (troy)	373.24177	Grams
Metres	10^3	Millimetres	Pounds (troy)	0.822857	Pounds (avoir.)
Metres	1.094	Yards	Pounds (troy)	13.1657	Ounces (avoir.)
Metres/min.	1.667	Centimetres/sec.	Pounds (troy)	$3.6735 \cdot 10^{-4}$	Tons (long)
Metres/min.	3.281	Feet/min.	Pounds (troy)	$4.1143 \cdot 10^{-4}$	Tons (short)
Metres/min.	0.05468	Feet/sec.	Pounds (troy)	$3.7324 \cdot 10^{-4}$	Tons (metric)
Metres/min.	0.06	Kilometres/hr.	Quadrants (angle)	90	Degrees
Metres/min.	0.03728	Miles/hr.	Quadrants (angle)	5400	Minutes
Metres/sec.	196.8	Feet/min.	Quadrants (angle)	1.571	Radians
Metres/sec.	3.281	Feet/sec.	Radians	57.30	Degrees
Metres/sec.	3.6	Kilometres/hr.	Radians	3438	Minutes
Metres/sec.	0.06	Kilometres/min.	Radians	0.637	Quadrants
Metres/sec.	2.237	Miles/hr.	Radians/sec.	57.30	Degrees/sec.
Metres/sec.	0.03728	Miles/min.	Radians/sec.	0.1592	Revolutions/sec.
Microns	10^{-6}	Metres	Radians/sec.	9.549	Revolutions/min.
Miles	5280	Feet	Radians/sec./sec.	573.0	Revs./min./min.
Miles	1.609	Kilometres	Radians/sec./sec.	0.1592	Revs./sec./sec.
Miles	1760	Yards	Reams	500	Sheets
Miles/hr.	1.609	Kilometres/hr.	Revolutions	360	Degrees
Miles/hr.	0.8684	Knots	Revolutions	4	Quadrants
Minutes (angle)	$2.909 \cdot 10^{-4}$	Radians	Revolutions	6.283	Radians
Ounces	16	Drams	Revolutions/min.	6	Degrees/sec.
Ounces	437.5	Grains	Square yards	$2.066 \cdot 10^{-4}$	Acres
Ounces	0.0625	Pounds	Square yards	9	Square feet
Ounces	28.349527	Grams	Square yards	0.8361	Square metres
Ounces	0.9115	Ounces (troy)	Square yards	$3.228 \cdot 10^{-7}$	Square miles
Ounces	$2.790 \cdot 10^{-5}$	Tons (long)	Temp. (°C.) + 273	1	Abs. temp. (°C.)
Ounces	$2.835 \cdot 10^{-5}$	Tons (metric)	Temp. (°C.) + 17.78	1.8	Temp. (°F.)
Ounces (troy)	480	Grains	Temp. (°F.) + 460	1	Abs. temp. (°F.)
Ounces (troy)	20	Pennyweights (troy)	Temp. (°F.) - 32	5/9	Temp. (°C.)
Ounces (troy)	0.08333	Pounds (troy)	Watts	0.05692	B.T.U./min.
Ounces (troy)	31.103481	Grams	Watts	44.26	Foot-pounds/min.
Ounces (troy)	1.09714	Ounces (avoir.)	Watts	0.7376	Foot-pounds/sec.
Ounces (fluid)	1.805	Cubic inches	Watts	$1.341 \cdot 10^{-3}$	Horsepower
Ounces (fluid)	0.02957	Litres	Watts	0.01434	Kg.-calories/min.
Ounces/sq. inch	0.0625	Lbs./sq. inch	Watts	10^{-3}	Kilowatts
Pounds	16	Ounces	Watt-hours	3.415	B.T.U.
Pounds	256	Drams	Watt-hours	2655	Foot-pounds
Pounds	7000	Grains	Watt-hours	$1.341 \cdot 10^{-3}$	Horsepower-hrs.
Pounds	0.0005	Tons (short)	Watt-hours	0.8605	Kilogram-calories
Pounds	453.5924	Grams	Watt-hours	367.1	Kilogram-metres
Pounds	1.21528	Pounds (troy)	Watt-hours	10^{-3}	Kilowatt-hours
Pounds	14.5833	Ounces (troy)	Yards	91.44	Centimetres
Pounds (troy)	5760	Grains	Yards	3	Feet
Pounds (troy)	240	Pennyweights (troy)	Yards	36	Inches
Pounds (troy)	12	Ounces (troy)	Yards	0.9144	Metres

CIRCUMFERENCES AND AREAS OF CIRCLES
From 1/64 to 50, Diameter

Dia.	Circum.	Area	Dia.	Circum.	Area	Dia.	Circum.	Area	Dia.	Circum.	Area
1/64	.04909	.00019	8	25.1327	50.2655	17	53.4071	226.980	26	81.6814	530.929
1/32	.09818	.00077	8⅛	25.5254	51.8485	17⅛	53.7998	230.330	26⅛	82.0741	536.047
1/16	.19635	.00307	8¼	25.9181	53.4562	17¼	54.1925	233.705	26¼	82.4668	541.188
⅛	.39270	.01227	8⅜	26.3108	55.0883	17⅜	54.5852	237.104	26⅜	82.8595	546.355
3/16	.58905	.02761	8½	26.7035	56.7450	17½	54.9779	240.528	26½	83.2522	551.546
¼	.78540	.04909	8⅝	27.0962	58.4262	17⅝	55.3706	243.977	26⅝	83.6449	556.761
5/16	.98175	.07670	8¾	27.4889	60.1321	17¾	55.7633	247.450	26¾	84.0376	562.002
⅜	1.1781	.11045	8⅞	27.8816	61.8624	17⅞	56.1560	250.947	26⅞	84.4303	567.266
7/16	1.3744	.15033	9	28.2743	63.6173	18	56.5487	254.469	27	84.8230	572.555
½	1.5708	.19635	9⅛	28.6670	65.3967	18⅛	56.9414	258.016	27⅛	85.2157	577.869
9/16	1.7671	.24850	9¼	29.0597	67.2007	18¼	57.3341	261.587	27¼	85.6084	583.207
⅝	1.9635	.30680	9⅜	29.4524	69.0292	18⅜	57.7268	265.182	27⅜	86.0011	588.570
11/16	2.1598	.37122	9½	29.8451	70.8822	18½	58.1195	268.803	27½	86.3938	593.957
¾	2.3562	.44179	9⅝	30.2378	72.7597	18⅝	58.5122	272.447	27⅝	86.7865	599.369
13/16	2.5525	.51849	9¾	30.6305	74.6619	18¾	58.9049	276.117	27¾	87.1792	604.806
⅞	2.7489	.60132	9⅞	31.0232	76.5886	18⅞	59.2976	279.810	27⅞	87.5719	610.267
15/16	2.9452	.69029				19	59.6903	283.529	28	87.9646	615.752
1	3.1416	.78540	10	31.4159	78.5398	19⅛	60.0830	287.272	28⅛	88.3573	621.262
1⅛	3.5343	.99402	10⅛	31.8086	80.5156	19¼	60.4757	291.039	28¼	88.7500	626.797
1¼	3.9270	1.2272	10¼	32.2013	82.5159	19⅜	60.8684	294.831	28⅜	89.1427	632.356
1⅜	4.3197	1.4849	10⅜	32.5940	84.5408	19½	61.2611	298.648	28½	89.5354	637.940
1½	4.7124	1.7671	10½	32.9867	86.5902	19⅝	61.6538	302.489	28⅝	89.9281	643.548
1⅝	5.1051	2.0739	10⅝	33.3794	88.6641	19¾	62.0465	306.354	28¾	90.3208	649.181
1¾	5.4978	2.4053	10¾	33.7721	90.7626	19⅞	62.4392	310.245	28⅞	90.7135	654.838
1⅞	5.8905	2.7612	10⅞	34.1648	92.8856	20	62.8319	314.159	29	91.1062	660.520
2	6.2832	3.1416	11	34.5575	95.0332	20⅛	63.2246	318.099	29⅛	91.4989	666.226
2⅛	6.6759	3.5466	11⅛	34.9502	97.2053	20¼	63.6173	322.062	29¼	91.8916	671.957
2¼	7.0686	3.9761	11¼	35.3429	99.4020	20⅜	64.0100	326.051	29⅜	92.2843	677.713
2⅜	7.4613	4.4301	11⅜	35.7356	101.623	20½	64.4027	330.064	29½	92.6770	683.493
2½	7.8540	4.9087	11½	36.1283	103.869	20⅝	64.7954	334.101	29⅝	93.0697	689.297
2⅝	8.2467	5.4119	11⅝	36.5210	106.139	20¾	65.1881	338.163	29¾	93.4624	695.127
2¾	8.6394	5.9396	11¾	36.9137	108.434	20⅞	65.5808	342.250	29⅞	93.8551	700.980
2⅞	9.0321	6.4918	11⅞	37.3064	110.753				30	94.2478	706.858
3	9.4248	7.0686	12	37.6991	113.097	21	65.9735	346.361	30⅛	94.6405	712.761
3⅛	9.8175	7.6699	12⅛	38.0918	115.466	21⅛	66.3662	350.496	30¼	95.0332	718.689
3¼	10.2102	8.2958	12¼	38.4845	117.859	21¼	66.7589	354.656	30⅜	95.4259	724.640
3⅜	10.6029	8.9462	12⅜	38.8772	120.276	21⅜	67.1516	358.841	30½	95.8186	730.617
3½	10.9956	9.6211	12½	39.2699	122.718	21½	67.5442	363.050	30⅝	96.2113	736.618
3⅝	11.3883	10.3206	12⅝	39.6626	125.185	21⅝	67.9369	367.284	30¾	96.6040	742.643
3¾	11.7810	11.0447	12¾	40.0553	127.676	21¾	68.3296	371.542	30⅞	96.9967	748.693
3⅞	12.1737	11.7932	12⅞	40.4480	130.191	21⅞	68.7223	375.825	31	97.3894	754.768
4	12.5664	12.5664	13	40.8407	132.732	22	69.1150	380.133	31⅛	97.7821	760.867
4⅛	12.9591	13.3640	13⅛	41.2334	135.297	22⅛	69.5077	384.465	31¼	98.1748	766.990
4¼	13.3518	14.1863	13¼	41.6261	137.886	22¼	69.9004	388.821	31⅜	98.5675	773.139
4⅜	13.7445	15.0330	13⅜	42.0188	140.500	22⅜	70.2931	393.203	31½	98.9602	779.311
4½	14.1372	15.9043	13½	42.4115	143.139	22½	70.6858	397.608	31⅝	99.3529	785.509
4⅝	14.5299	16.8002	13⅝	42.8042	145.802	22⅝	71.0785	402.038	31¾	99.7456	791.731
4¾	14.9226	17.7206	13¾	43.1969	148.489	22¾	71.4712	406.493	31⅞	100.1383	797.977
4⅞	15.3153	18.6655	13⅞	43.5896	151.201	22⅞	71.8639	410.972			
5	15.7080	19.6350	14	43.9823	153.938	23	72.2566	415.476	32	100.5310	804.248
5⅛	16.1007	20.6290	14⅛	44.3750	156.699	23⅛	72.6493	420.004	32⅛	100.9237	810.543
5¼	16.4934	21.6476	14¼	44.7677	159.485	23¼	73.0420	424.557	32¼	101.3164	816.863
5⅜	16.8861	22.6906	14⅜	45.1604	162.295	23⅜	73.4347	429.134	32⅜	101.7091	823.208
5½	17.2788	23.7583	14½	45.5531	165.130	23½	73.8274	433.736	32½	102.1018	829.577
5⅝	17.6715	24.8505	14⅝	45.9458	167.989	23⅝	74.2201	438.363	32⅝	102.4945	835.971
5¾	18.0642	25.9672	14¾	46.3385	170.873	23¾	74.6128	443.014	32¾	102.8872	842.389
5⅞	18.4569	27.1085	14⅞	46.7312	173.782	23⅞	75.0055	447.689	32⅞	103.2799	848.831
6	18.8496	28.2743	15	47.1239	176.715	24	75.3982	452.389	33	103.6726	855.299
6⅛	19.2423	29.4647	15⅛	47.5166	179.672	24⅛	75.7909	457.114	33⅛	104.0653	861.791
6¼	19.6350	30.6796	15¼	47.9094	182.654	24¼	76.1836	461.863	33¼	104.4580	868.307
6⅜	20.0277	31.9191	15⅜	48.3020	185.661	24⅜	76.5763	466.637	33⅜	104.8507	874.848
6½	20.4204	33.1831	15½	48.6947	188.692	24½	76.9690	471.435	33½	105.2434	881.413
6⅝	20.8131	34.4716	15⅝	49.0874	191.748	24⅝	77.3617	476.258	33⅝	105.6361	888.003
6¾	21.2058	35.7847	15¾	49.4801	194.828	24¾	77.7544	481.106	33¾	106.0288	894.618
6⅞	21.5985	37.1223	15⅞	49.8728	197.933	24⅞	78.1471	485.977	33⅞	106.4215	901.257
7	21.9912	38.4845	16	50.2655	201.062	25	78.5398	490.874	34	106.8142	907.920
7⅛	22.3839	39.8712	16⅛	50.6582	204.216	25⅛	78.9325	495.795	34⅛	107.2069	914.609
7¼	22.7765	41.2825	16¼	51.0509	207.394	25¼	79.3252	500.740	34¼	107.5996	921.321
7⅜	23.1692	42.7183	16⅜	51.4436	210.597	25⅜	79.7179	505.711	34⅜	107.9923	928.058
7½	23.5619	44.1787	16½	51.8363	213.825	25½	80.1106	510.705	34½	108.3850	934.820
7⅝	23.9546	45.6636	16⅝	52.2290	217.077	25⅝	80.5033	515.724	34⅝	108.7777	941.607
7¾	24.3473	47.1730	16¾	52.6217	220.353	25¾	80.8960	520.768	34¾	109.1704	948.417
7⅞	24.7400	48.7069	16⅞	53.0144	223.654	25⅞	81.2887	525.836	34⅞	109.5631	955.253

From Goetsch, Nelson, and Chalk, *Technical Drawing*, 2nd edition, copyright 1989 by Delmar Publishers Inc.

APPENDIX L—GLOSSARY

Absolute coordinates Points designated by a specific X, Y, and Z distance from a fixed origin.

Alphanumeric Numbers, letters, and special characters.

ANSI American National Standards Institute. ANSI is a professional organization which sets standards.

ASCII American Standard Code for Information Interchange. ASCII is a standard computer data communications code.

Aspect ratio The height to width ratio of an image on an output device.

Attribute Information associated with a graphic object.

Baud Data transmission rate of a computer. The baud rate is the number of bits sent per second.

Bill of materials A listing of the parts required to assemble an object. Bills of materials may be extracted from a database.

Bit The smallest unit of information of a binary system.

Buffer Memory reserved for temporary storage of data.

Bug A malfunction or design error in computer hardware or software.

Byte Collection of eight bits which represent one letter.

CAD Computer aided design or drafting.

CAM Computer aided manufacturing.

Command A specific word or other entry to provide an instruction.

Configuration Providing setup for peripheral hardware by installing proper software drivers in a program.

Coordinate A point located by X, Y, and Z directions and represented by real numbers.

CPU Central processing unit. The part of a computer where the arithmetic and logic functions are performed.

Crosshatching Filling in of an area with a design.

Crosshair Horizontal and vertical crossed lines on the display screen which designate the current working point of the drawing.

CRT	Cathode ray tube. The display screen on which the computer display is shown. A CRT is similar to a television screen.
Cursor	Display device, such as a flashing bar or box, that represents the current working point on the display.
Database	The collection of information that is used to form a drawing or used to perform program functions.
Data extraction	Retrieval of data from the database.
Default	A predetermined value for a computer function.
Digitize	Electronically tracing a drawing.
Digitizer	An electronically sensitive pad used to translate movement of a hand-held device to cursor movement on a screen. May also be used to trace drawings.
Directory	A file listing of specific files or other data.
Disk	A circular piece of plastic with a magnetic coating used to store computer data.
Display	Area on a CRT where graphic or text images are displayed.
Dot matrix	A dot grid that is used to display images by displaying specific patterns.
Dragging	Moving of an entity or entities relative to the displacement of an input device.
Drum plotter	A pen plotter that moves both the paper and pen to achieve a plot.
Dual display	Use of two display devices simultaneously.
Entity	A single drawing element such as a line, circle, or arc.
Extension	The last three letters that follow a period in a file name, e.g., .DWG or .EXE .
Fillet	The corner fit or radius between two nonparallel lines.
Flatbed plotter	A pen plotter in which the paper remains stationary and the pen moves in both directions to create the plot.
Floppy disk	A thin plastic disk with a magnetic coating used to store computer data.
Fonts	The design of an alphabet.
Function key	Programmable keyboard key used for a specific purpose by a software program.

Grid   A series of dots arranged in a designated X and Y spacing used for reference purposes when drawing.

Hard copy   The printed or plotted copy of a drawing or data.

Hardware   The physical computer equipment such as the computer, printers, mice, etc.

Hatching   Filling an area with a pattern.

Input device Any device used to enter data into a computer. Examples of input devices are the keyboard, mice, and digitizing pads.

Kilobyte (K) A unit of 1024 bytes.

Layer   An overlay used to store specific data on. A drawing may contain several overlays or layers with data on each.

Light pen   An input device that enters points directly onto the display screen by emitting a light beam that is detected by the CRT.

Macro   Several keystroke operations executed by a single entry.

Mainframe computer The largest and most powerful computer. Mainframes are used where large amounts of data are stored, such as by government and insurance companies.

Megabyte (MB) Unit of storage equal to 1,048,576 bytes (1KB $\times$ 1KB).

Menu   A screen listing of options in a computer program.

Microcomputer A small desktop computer. Usually referred to as a personal computer.

Minicomputer A mid-sized computer of a size and capability between those of a microcomputer and a mainframe.

Mirroring   Reversal of a graphic image around a specified axis.

Modem   Modulator-demodulator. A modem is used to send computer data over telephone lines.

Mouse   A small, handheld input device which is moved around on a surface. This movement is sensed by the computer and a relative displacement of the cursor or crosshair is made.

Network   The linking together of several computer systems.

Operating system Computer program that acts as a translator between the computer and applications programs.

Pan   Movement around a drawing while in a specified magnification.

Pen plotter Output device used to record a CAD drawing by moving a pen over a drawing surface to obtain a hard copy drawing.

Peripheral Any device used in conjunction with a computer, e.g., a printer, light pen, etc.

Pixel Dots that make up the display. The arrangement of displayed pixels determines the image displayed.

Plotter Device used to obtain a hard copy of a graphic display. Plotters may be pen, electrostatic, or dot matrix.

Polar Coordinate system used to specify distance and angle, defined in reference to a specified starting origin.

Program The set of instructions that the computer uses to perform tasks. The program is also referred to as software.

Prompt A message or symbol displayed by the computer which tells the operator that the computer is ready for input.

Puck The handheld input device used with a digitizing tablet to move the crosshairs on the display.

RAM Random access memory. Temporary memory storage area in a computer.

Relative coordinates Points that are located relative to a specified point.

Resolution The measure of precision and clarity of a display.

ROM Read only memory. Permanent memory storage area in a computer.

Rubberbanding "Stretching" a line from a fixed point to the current location of the crosshairs.

Scrolling Vertical movement of text lines.

Snap Drawing aid that allows entered points to "snap" to the closest point of an imaginary grid.

Software Set of instructions used by the computer to perform a task. Software is also referred to as the program.

Stylus A pen-like input device used with a digitizing pad in the same manner as a puck.

Windowing Enlargement or reduction of graphic screen images.

INDEX

T385 I474
DON INMAN

SCREEN PRINTING PROCESS — McKnight Pub Co.
Robert A. BANZHAF

Bregeleisen, J. I.
Dover Publication
TT 273 .B49

Mathilda Schwalbach
TT 273 S3

TT 273 T47   MARIA Termini
                    SILkscreening

$ Weisz. Decal Inc
   TRAINING MANUAL; Decal printing